BLOOMSBURY GUIDES TO ENGLISH LITERATURE

Augustan Literature

DELETED

BLOOMSBURY GUIDES TO ENGLISH LITERATURE

Augustan Literature

A Guide to Restoration and Eighteenth Century Literature: 1660–1789

Edited by Eva Simmons

BLOOMSBURY

The Bloomsbury Guides to English Literature

General Editor: Marion Wynne-Davies

Guide to English Renaissance Literature
  Marion Wynne-Davies

Guide to Romantic Literature
  Geoff Ward

Guide to Victorian Literature
  Jane Thomas

Guide to Twentieth-Century Literature
  Linda R. Williams

Guide to the Novel
  Andrew Michael Roberts

First published in 1994 by
Bloomsbury Publishing Ltd
2 Soho Square
London WIV 5DE

Copyright © Bloomsbury Publishing Plc 1994

The moral right of the author has been asserted

A copy of the CIP entry for this book is available from the British Library.

ISBN 0 7475 1296 5

10 9 8 7 6 5 4 3 2 1

Typeset by Hewer Text Composition Services, Edinburgh
Printed in Britain by Cox & Wyman, Reading, Berks

Contents

Acknowledgements

General Editor
Marion Wynne-Davies

Editor
Eva Simmons

Originator
Christopher Gillie

Contributors
Janet Barron (18th-century prose)
Jennifer Birkett (French literature), University of Birmingham
James Booth (Augustan and Romantic poetry), University of Hull
Clare Brant (Restoration and 18th-century poetry), King's College, London University
Catherine Byron (Irish literature), Loughborough College of Art and Design
Christopher GIllie (Historical and political background), Homerton College, Cambridge
Richard Hawley (Greek and Roman antiquity), Royal Holloway and Bedford New College
Alex Hughes (Britain in the 17th and 18th centuries), University of Birmingham
Theresa Kemp (Britain in the 17th and 18th centuries), Indiana University
David Nokes (18th-century prose), King's College, London University
John O'Brien (French literature), University of Liverpool
Louise Robbins (French literature), King's College, London University
Jonathan Sawday (Renaissance poetry), University of Southampton
Eva Simmons (17th and 18th century literature)
Jim Simpson (German literature), University of Liverpool
Mercer Simpson (Welsh literature)
Geoff Ward (Romantic literature), University of Liverpool
René Weis (Renaissance drama), University College, London
Sue Wiseman (Britain in the 17th and 18th centuries), University of Kent
Marion Wynne-Davies (Renaissance literature), Keele University

Advisor
Angela Smallwood

Editorial
Editorial Director Kathy Rooney
Project Editor Tracey Smith

General Editor's Preface

The Bloomsbury guides to English literature derive directly from the *Bloomsbury Guide to English Literature* (1989), and are intended for those readers who wish to look at a specific period or genre, rather than at the wide-ranging material offered in the original text. As such, the guides include material from the larger and earlier work, but they have been updated and supplemented in order to answer the requirements of their particular fields. Each individual editor has selected, edited and authored as the need arose. The acknowledgements appropriate for the individual volumes have been made in the respective editors' prefaces. As general editor I should like to thank all those who have been involved in the project, from its initial conception through to the innovative and scholarly volumes presented in this series.

Marion Wynne-Davies

Editor's Note

Cross References

A liberal use of cross references has been made. In both the essays and the reference entries, names, titles and topics are frequently marked with an arrow ($\triangleright$) to guide the reader to the appropriate entry in the reference section for a more detailed explanation. Cross-reference arrows appear both in the text and at the end of entries.

Dates

Dates after the names of people indicate their life spans, except when they follow the names of monarchs when they show the length of the reign.

Editor's Preface

The period covered by this book is from the Restoration of Charles II, after the Civil War and Commonwealth periods, to the start of the French Revolution. In those 130 years or so were written some of the great classics of English literature, but also innumerable other texts from the most arcane to the most 'popular' (the latter especially in the later part of the period), read by thousands, or perhaps tens of thousands of people. Many reference books have tended to dwell on so-called 'great books', and some lesser ones, while ignoring or glossing over the vast majority of the rest. Today, the question 'what is literature?' is being asked again, and answers are being given afresh.

The dictionary definitions of literature are extremely broad – much broader than one might think. *Chambers* has 'the art of composition in prose and verse: the whole body of literary composition universally, or in any language, or on a given subject'. *The Shorter Oxford* has 'literary work or production; the activity or profession of a man of letters; the realm of letters', etc. The definitions of 'literary' are similarly diffuse. Therefore the potential list of works which could be included under the heading of 'literature' would seem to be limitless, and the actual list made up according to custom and practice, taste and the culture of any given period.

Numerous factors have contributed to the raising of questions about what constitutes literature today. The work of social historians has provided new evidence about taste and the reading habits of former generations, as well as statistics for such factors as literacy, sales distribution, and readership for given works in former periods. The historians also look to literature for evidence to support some of their arguments, while literary historians and critics are using the social historians' work in the course of theirs. In addition, the work of feminists and others has in its turn brought interest in authors hitherto neglected, including many women, writers of working-class origin, and so forth. Increasingly, the boundaries are becoming blurred between formerly disparate or non-existent intellectual domains. Thus the literary map is being redrawn to include new authors, and to alter the emphases of studies.

This, though, raises new questions about where to draw the line: should non-fictional items of interest and merit be included that formerly would not have been: newspapers, for example, or ballads and broadsheets? In the past the definition of literature was restricted to what we might call high cultural achievements, with some critics tending to focus on authors of fictional or fantasy writing, including novels, poetry and plays, but excluding, say, purely philosophical works, except as they shed light on 'literature'. However, now the list may encompass scientific and philosophical writings, newspapers and pamphlets, 'minor' drama or poetry, novels and stories appealing to the new mass readership of the 18th century, and other forms. This potential for diversity raises other questions, as does my use of the word 'minor': for example, should all literature be accorded equal amounts of attention, without any attempt to create a hierarchy of quality? How valid is the idea of quality in itself? Should we abandon judgemental words like 'minor' and 'major' altogether?

My inclination is to essay a middle ground. On the one hand, I believe that widening the parameters of critical study has revitalized the field, and made it accessible and interesting to students who might not otherwise have become involved. On the other hand, we all have notions of subtlety, skill, artistry, and inividuality, in communicating thoughts, ideas, feelings, even if no uniform ideal concept exists. I believe there is value in discernment, but that the subjective nature of such judgments should be recognized, and orthodoxy abhorred. Thus there are still more, or less, important authors and works, but the list is substantially revised, and variations among critics are legitimate. The point is to be flexible without becoming vapid. I believe, too, that many works are worth considering for reasons other than purely literary quality: historic interest, for example, or rarity on some ground. I also stand with critics such as Raymond Williams and, more recently, Brean Hammond, who believe that it is important to know and understand something of the time, place, and circumstances in which a work was written in order to appreciate it fully and authentically, rather than with those who believe the text itself is all.

This book, then, attempts to marry together types of criticism which have often been kept separate, noting varieties of forms and the importance of genres other than those previously held exclusively to represent and exalt their period, while at the same time giving due consideration to those authors traditionally defined as giants of the time, such as Dryden, Pope, and Swift. Of course this approach has its own pitfalls, not least the potential for agonizing over what to include and what to leave out. But criticism inevitably involves choices, depending partly at least on the critic's, or literary historian's, tastes, and in the end we all apply value judgments to our selections. I have also had to make some painful decisions regarding chronological boundaries. For example, Shakespeare and Spenser are included, because of their influence on subsequent periods, but Chaucer is not, even though he, too, influenced later generations. It is a matter of dating and of degree. Finally, this volume, like the others in the series, is not purely a reference book for literature, even under the broad definition to which I have referred. It also includes references for cultural and historic influences in the period. Here again, difficult choices have had to be made. I hope, however, that this work's particular synthesis will prove useful to many.

The book is in two sections. The first part consists of essays. Those on political history and social context, and on drama are almost exactly as they were written by Christopher Gillie and myself for the *Bloomsbury Guide to English Literature* which preceded this volume. The one on non-dramatic prose is substantially as written by Janet Barron and David Nokes but as, in its original form, it only covered the period from 1700 onwards, I have added some paragraphs to take account of the first part of the Augustan period. The essay on poetry by Clare Brant was specially commissioned for this book. The second part of the book consists of entries on authors, works, genres, etc. These were contributed by Janet Barron, Jennifer Birkett, James Booth, Clare Brant, Catherine Byron, Christopher Gillie, Richard Hawley, Alex Hughes, Theresa Kemp, David Nokes, John O'Brien, Louise Robbins, Jonathan Sawday, Jim Simpson, Mercer Simpson, Geoff Ward, René Weis, Sue Wiseman, and Marion Wynne-Davies, as well as myself. My thanks are due to all of these authors. In addition, I would like to thank Angela Smallwood for her thoughtful, intelligent and friendly assistance with several aspects of the book, including her advice as reader; Marilyn Butler for helpful advice on a number of problems; and Marion Wynne-Davies and Tracey Smith for their careful editing and encouragement throughout. The BBC gave me a leave of absence from my job in order for me to complete this task. My mother, Ilse Meyer, and my aunt, Susan Jacobs, both helped me materially and spiritually. Finally, Paul Crossley provided me with generous support – moral, intellectual, practical, and culinary, especially in the final stages of editing this book. To him I give most special thanks.

Eva Simmons
Cambridge, 1994

Essay section

Introduction: The Augustan Age in perspective

Eva Simmons

The term ▷ 'Augustan' (followed by 'England', 'age', 'era', and so on) has been applied variously, to the entire period 1660–1789 or to only parts of that time, sometimes very loosely indeed, and often without explanation. Historically, there have been repeated debates about when exactly the Augustan age occurred, what it was, or indeed whether such an age existed at all.

Lately new attention has been focused on changes in attitudes and styles of writing in the latter part of the supposed period, and on its relation to the previous and subsequent periods. Many elements more commonly associated with the Romantic (▷ Romanticism) period are already evident in numerous works from roughly the mid-18th century onwards. Some critics, such as René Wellek (*Comparative Literature*, I, 1949) and more recently Marilyn Butler (*Romantics, Rebels, and Reactionaries: English Literature and its Background 1760–1830*, 1981), have suggested that particular emphasis should be placed on these proto-romantic features, although others, such as Cleanth Brooks (*Modern Poetry and the Tradition*, 1939) and James Sambrook (*The Eighteenth Century: The Intellectual and Cultural Context of English Literature 1700–1789*, 1986), treat them simply as new directions in literature, rather than as ruptures of the past (and Sambrook dismisses the notion of 'Augustanism' entirely). One view places these works in a category of their own, labelled ▷ 'Sentiment' or ▷ 'Sensibility', while another fails to see any substantial change (see, for example, Norman Callan's 'Augustan Reflective Poetry', in Boris Ford (ed.), *The New Pelican Guide to English Literature: From Dryden to Johnson*, Vol. 4). But before these issues are discussed, it may be helpful to go back to the origins of the term 'Augustan', to understand how it came about, and what light it throws upon the times it purports to identify, as well as to consider its usefulness today.

The meaning of Augustanism

Broadly speaking, 'Augustan' has been used to signify times in which literature or, more accurately, literature in its relation to politics, supposedly resembled the literature and politics of ancient Rome under Augustan rule. Various English monarchs have been compared, in their own day and subsequently, with the Emperor ▷ Caesar Augustus, while authors of their reigns have been compared with the classical writers of Augustus' time. According to one commonly expressed formula, English monarchs from Charles II onwards have been admired as bringers of peace after periods of war, and as sponsors of the arts, just as Augustus himself was supposed to have been – encouraging the arts to flourish in a new harmonious atmosphere. But even in Augustus' own reign, this view of him, which he encouraged, was questioned, and after his death it became even more controversial. Similarly, in the 18th century, questioning and disillusionment followed the earlier idealization of Augustus, initiating a reappraisal of contemporary rulers.

Dispute arose partly due to the ambiguous character of Augustus, who became sole ruler after the defeat of Antony and Cleopatra at Actium. Even before his accession, he had shared responsibility for killing thousands of citizens thought to threaten the power of the state, under a policy known as the 'proscription'. Yet he claimed afterwards to have restored the ancient freedom of the Republic (in the name of which Julius Caesar had been murdered) and his 41-year rule was peaceful; it was a period in which Rome expanded its colonial boundaries, while the city itself was remodelled, and literature flourished. For example ▷ Virgil and ▷ Horace (▷ Latin literature), both of whom were patronized by Augustus, represented the triumphs of the age and, not surprisingly, they both praised the ruler for his bounty.

However Rome's steep decline began immediately after Augustus' death in AD 14, with a series of corrupt, cruel and incompetent rulers including Tiberius, Nero, Caligula, and Domitian. Some classical historians, especially ▷ Tacitus, presented a deeply critical vision of Augustus as a tyrant who deceived his people into thinking they were free while bringing in autocracy and paving the way for an even worse form of tyranny. Subsequent writers became fascinated with trying to interpret what had happened in this critical period of Roman history: what was the 'meaning', so to speak, of Augustus' rule, and how did his deeds compare with those of their own rulers? He could be seen either as a model for emulation, or as the embodiment of a warning; the last of the 'good' rulers, and a bulwark against chaos, or among the first of the worst: behind him the Republic, after him decay. The process of enquiry had one overriding aim, namely, to improve understanding of the writers' own times, in order to draw moral conclusions and provide moral instruction. This might make it possible to imitate Augustus' triumphs, or avoid his mistakes, depending on the outcome of the investigation.

Augustus and Augustanism in the 17th and 18th centuries

The ▷ Renaissance renewed interest in Italy and its history throughout Europe and, during the 17th and 18th centuries, concern with Augustus' era was widespread. Because European culture was seen to derive substantially from the Roman (Latin still played an important part in literature), and Augustus' reign was so pivotal in the history of Rome, and because writers of Augustus' time were so much admired, the Emperor's life and actions were carefully studied. In England his era held a special fascination, because of the country's own recent turbulent experiences, which included two major revolutions, a period of Republican rule (under ▷ Cromwell), and repeated foreign wars. English translations of ▷ Tacitus at the end of the 16th century, and again at the end of the 17th, helped to stimulate debate.

Much early writing in England, as well as in other parts of Europe, considered Augustus as a model for just and peaceful rule. At the begining of the 17th century ▷ James I encouraged comparisons of himself with the Roman, assisted by authors such as Ben Jonson, who praised him as a successor of Augustus. But at the ▷ Restoration the image of Augustus as healer and patron of the arts acquired a deeper resonance, at least in aristocratic circles. ▷ Charles II set the agenda himself, even more than his grandfather had done, in order to present himself as a symbol of Augustinian rule, almost Augustus re-incarnate. A series of triumphal arches recalling antique victories was built in what is now the ▷ City of ▷ London, and lavish entertainments were designed to celebrate his accession. Poets including ▷ Dryden rose to the occasion: his *Astraea Redux* (1660) (▷ Astraea) greeted Charles' return, 'Oh Happy Age! Oh times like those alone / By Fate reserv'd for Great *Augustus* Throne! / When the joint growth of Armes and Arts foreshew / The World a Monarch, and that Monarch *You*'. And a poem by Alexander Huish actually reworks an Horatian Ode welcoming Augustus back after long wars:

> *Restore thy Country her lost light, good King;*
> *Thine own sweet face, which since like lovely Spring*
> *W'have hop't to see, the day hath merrier gone,*
> *The Sun hath brighter, better shone . . .*
>
> *Long mayst thou live, and make long holy-day,*
> *Good King, unto thy Country . . .*

Such towering hopes were not likely to be fulfilled, on earth at any rate, and disillusion soon set in, as was expressed in such poems as ▷ *Absalom and Achitophel* (1681) and ▷ *Macflecknoe* (1682). In Dryden's own version of the story of Antony and Cleopatra, ▷ *All for Love* (1678), it has been argued, Charles is implicitly identified with Augustus' enemy Mark Antony, neglecting affairs of state in order to gratify his lusts, rather than with Augustus himself. *Macflecknoe* documents Dryden's ostensible despair at the lamentable state of letters in his time, just as ▷ Pope's ▷ *The Dunciad* (1728) was to do in the next generation. Each of these poems sets up mock monarchs of dullness to represent the supposed 'spirit of the Age', against which the poet rails, and which contrasts strongly with the heroic spirit heralded in the earlier poems. The demise of ▷ heroic drama, noted in my essay 'Restoration and 18th-century drama' (see pp. 49–50) also charts the decline from confident admiration of the monarch, and the heroic values ostensibly associated with him, to disillusionment and scepticism. At the same time, the view of Augustus deteriorated.

The critic Howard Weinbrot (*Augustus Caesar in 'Augustan' England*, 1978) suggests this process went hand in hand with the rejection of absolutism and he argues that the term 'Augustan', as a description of the period, is therefore misleading. Augustus' name, increasingly synonymous with tyranny, became a weapon in contemporary debates about artistic, social and political conditions. For example, to Whigs, ▷ James II was an Augustan tyrant, legitimately deposed by ▷ William III, while James's descendants, the ▷ Jacobite Pretenders, were seen as Augustan usurpers. But for some Tories the Augustan usurper was William himself, or else George I or George II, and the Hanoverians were represented as the destroyers of liberty (▷ Whig and Tory). The comparison with Augustus was not confined to monarchs. In the years 1726 to 1742, the Whig Prime Minister ▷ Sir Robert Walpole was portrayed as an Augustan in the worst sense, and ▷ Chesterfield, for example, likened the imposition of the ▷ Licensing Act of 1737 to the oppressions of Augustus. But Walpole's supporters used the same epithets against their political opponents.

There is a distinction, however, between the widespread negative, Tacitean view in the 18th century of Augustus as tyrant, and the literary or cultural idea of an 'Augustan age'. For those who condemned the reign of Augustus the problem remained, how to reconcile the dark view of the ruler himself with the unquestionably sublime capabilities of the Augustan poets, who had so willingly accepted his patronage? One argument held that their artistry alleviated the pains of dictatorship, making it more bearable, as well as more palatable. ▷ Shaftesbury wrote in 1710 that although Augustus was 'a Prince naturally cruel and barbarous', his poets 'were more to him than his Arms or military Virtue; and, more than *Fortune* herself, assisted him in his Greatness, and made his usurp'd Dominions so inchanting to the World, that it cou'd see without regret its Chains of Bondage firmly riveted'. Another ingenious solution was to see the Latin poets as intellectual and moral products of the Republic, since their minds had been formed under it, even though their highest achievements took place under a later tyranny. ▷ Blackwell, in his *Memoirs of the Court of Augustus* (1753 onwards) argues that 'what we loosely term the Stile of the *Augustan Age* was not *formed* under *Augustus*. It was formed under the Common-wealth, during the high struggles for Liberty'. In just such a way, he intimated, the celebrated poets ▷ Milton, ▷ Waller and ▷ Cowley, who published after the Restoration, were in fact shaped by the Commonwealth era in Britain. Blackwell suggested, moreover, that the Augustan poets may even have succeeded in modifying the tyrant's behaviour. Finally, even among those who abhorred the historic Augustus, there were those who, like Coleridge in the 19th century, saw the Republic itself as far from perfect, ruled by an oligarchy of senators, remote from ordinary people.

Thus the idea of Augustus and interest in his period survived despite political scepticism: somehow it was possible to hold in suspension two supposedly inimical ideas: of, on the one hand, Rome fallen under the sway of a despot and, on the other, a flowering of independent literature. In a similar vein, contrasts have been drawn between the high accomplishments of Renaissance Italy and the autocratic nature of many of her rulers; and, in modern times, between the literary achievements of Soviet Russians ('official' as well as dissident writers), and Stalinist oppression. Weinbrot gives some of Dryden's works as examples of his own anti-Augustanism, as well as generally representative of that attitude in the period. Yet the evidence regarding Dryden's and others' views, as Howard Erskine-Hill points out (*The Augustan Idea in English Literature*, 1983), is in fact very mixed. Some of the supposedly anti-Augustan writings cited by Weinbrot, such as Dryden's *Discourse Concerning the Original and Progress of Satire* (1693) and Pope's *Epistle to Augustus* (1737), display ambiguous attitudes towards Augustus which have been variously interpreted by critics, as Weinbrot himself acknowledges. Paradoxically, these works, written in classical traditions of learning and ▷ satire, with their displays of wit, elegance and erudition, are precisely those which may best be said to embody the essence of 'Augustanism' in its literary sense.

As indicated above, several other countries, notably France and Italy, whose classicism antedated that of Britain, also assigned to themselves an 'Augustan' age. Moreover, the term 'Augustan' as an expression of hope for the coming reign, was actually applied in Britain from the 16th century, and revived repeatedly thereafter. But custom has determinedly related it to a period of English literature after the Restoration. As early as 1690 the Jacobite cleric Francis Atterbury questioned, rhetorically, whether 'in Charles II's reign English did not come to its full perfection; and whether it has not had its Augustan age as well as the Latin'. ▷ Anne Finch, in *A Tale of the Miser and the Poet. Written about the Year 1709*, implied a similar view. Her poem refers nostalgically to Charles II's time, when the arts and learning were valued in their own right, and not for the money they could bring, and it ends with a plea for the revival of 'Augustean days . . . when wit shall please, and poets thrive'.

▷ Oliver Goldsmith, in *An Account of the Augustan Age in England* (1759) published in his briefly-lived periodical *The Bee*, identified a different time span for his 'Augustan Age':

> *Some have looked upon the writers in the times of Queen Elizabeth as the true standard for future imitation; others have descended to the reign of James I.; and others still lower, to that of Charles II. Were I to be permitted to offer an opinion upon this subject, I should readily give my vote for the reign of Queen Anne, or some years before that period. It was then that taste was united to genius . . . In that period of British glory, though no writer attracts our attention singly, yet, like stars lost in each other's [sic] brightness, they have cast such a lustre upon the age in which they lived that their minutest transactions will be attended to by posterity with a greater eagerness than the most important occurrences of even empires which have been transacted in greater obscurity . . .*

Hopes for a new Augustan age were invoked repeatedly thereafter, notably in 1727 with the accession of George II, who conveniently carried 'Augustus' as one of his names, and again in 1760, when ▷ Hume questioned, somewhat whimsically, whether the accession of George III could also herald a new Augustan age. And Goldsmith who, writing in the third quarter of the century, as we have seen, thought the Augustan Age had coincided with the reign of Queen ▷ Anne, was himself designated an Augustan by ▷ Vicessimus Knox in 1778 and again by the Scottish essayist John Pinkerton in 1785.

However, the term 'Augustan' suggests not just a relationship between a monarch and the arts, but a standard and type of writing, or indeed a specific cultural identity. This involves ideas of ▷ taste and ▷ wit, aspired to by essayists, dramatists and poets. For example, Pope thought of himself as an Augustan, and Goldsmith sought to revive what he considered to be the flagging spirit of Augustanism. Didacticism is another recurring theme associated with the period, in secular as well as in religious writing. There is also an emphasis upon the powers of reason and scepticism, which may be seen in political and moral philosophy of the period, from ▷ Hobbes and ▷ Locke (▷ Social Contract) through to ▷ Berkeley and Hume. This was echoed by the growing involvement with science: ▷ Newton, for example, seemed to his contemporaries to represent a supreme example of what scientific reason could achieve; as Pope wrote, 'Nature and Nature's laws lay hid in night: / God said, "Let Newton be!" and all was light'.

To these qualities may be added many others widely accepted over the years, although of course not all are present in any one author, or even at any one time. They include: order, strength, dignity, propriety, symmetry, balance, erudition, classical allusion (▷ classic, classics, classical; ▷ classical education and English literature; ▷ classical mythology), refinement, harmony, grace, polite manners, and ▷ spleen. Indeed, many of the most characteristic, as well as the most famous, post-Restoration works are infused by that quintessentially Augustan quality, a compound of invective and gloom. Essays, passages in plays, and poems in the prototype Augustan form, the ▷ heroic couplet; often draw upon Horatian (▷ Horace) or Juvenalian (▷ Juvenal) satiric models, to rail against life, the universe or anything.

Gender proved one particularly fertile area for such vituperation. ▷ Rochester, for example, vilified women and marriage in heroic couplets, while women poets such as ▷ Lady Mary Chudleigh and ▷ Sarah Fyge Egerton used the form to similar purposes, but from a woman's standpoint, condemning men and marriage. Dryden and Pope also used the splenetic, satiric form to discourse on the supposedly lamentable state of literature, to condemn contemporary religion, society and the state, and for personal verbal assaults on their enemies. A bitter battle, largely conducted through verse written in classical forms, broke out between Pope and his allies on the one hand, and a group including the influential ▷ Lord John Hervey and his friend ▷ Lady Mary Wortley Montagu on the other. Pope attacked these two in a series of satiric poems, including ▷ *The Dunciad*. An anonymous author or authors, usually taken to include Lady Mary (though she herself denied responsibility), then hoisted him with his own petard. *Verses Addressed to the Imitator of the First Satire of the Second Book of Horace* (1733) retaliates against Pope in his kind of language:

> Horace *can laugh, is delicate, is clear;*
> *You, only rail, or darkly sneer:*
> *His Style is elegant, his Diction pure,*
> *Whilst none thy crabbed Numbers can endure;*
> *Hard as thy Heart, and as thy Birth obscure . . .*
>
> *If none do yet return th'intended Blow,*
> *You all your Safety to your Dullness owe;*
> *But whilst that Armour thy poor Corps defends,*
> *'Twill make thy Readers few, as are thy Friends . . .*
> (From *The Works of Lady Mary Wortley Montagu*, 5 vols., (1803))

Classical forms other than satire, such as ▷ epics, ▷ pastorals, ▷ epigrams, ▷ odes and panegyrics, were widely used throughout the period, as documented in Clare Brant's essay, 'Restoration and 18th century poetry' (see pp 13–26). Classical allusion is not, though, confined to poetry, it is also seen in drama (especially in the early part of the period) and non-dramatic prose, as well as in painting, sculpture, architecture, furniture design, landscape gardening, music and other fields of cultural endeavour.

Education, commercial writing, and the early novel

Classical practice in literature, as in the works mentioned earlier, was naturally accompanied by classical education in grammar schools (▷ schools in England) and in ▷ universities. The knowledge of Latin, and some Greek, was considered fundamental to a good education. Writers in Augustan England looked to authors in both languages for models and inspiration. ▷ Abraham Cowley, outlining *A Proposition for the Advancement of Learning* in 1661, prescribed a curriculum dominated by Latin authors including Varro, Cato, ▷ Pliny, ▷ Seneca, ▷ Cicero, ▷ Virgil, ▷ Terence and ▷ Plautus, and supplemented by the Greeks ▷ Homer and ▷ Aristotle. He also suggested that the study of classical poetry assisted other areas of study, making the process of enquiry more palatable: 'we conceive that one book ought to be compiled of all the scattered little parcels among the ancient poets that might serve for the advancement of natural science, and which would make no small or unuseful or unpleasant volume'.

Women were usually denied a formal education in the classics, but sometimes managed to obtain it for themselves. There are various accounts of intellectual women studying Latin and Greek on their own, sometimes in secret, or perhaps aided by a sympathetic male relative or friend. Lady Mary Wortley Montagu, for example, taught herself Latin, encouraged by an uncle and by ▷ Bishop Burnet, while the Anglo-Saxon scholar ▷ Elizabeth Elstob was helped to learn her many languages by her brother. ▷ Lucy Hutchinson, who translated Virgil and ▷ Lucretius, was unusual in being highly educated at her father's expense.

But what one might call the 'high' literary tradition to which they belonged formed only one part, indeed perhaps the smaller part in numerical terms, of the writing of the Augustan age. For the 18th century was the first period in which literacy became really widespread, fuelling and feeding off the growing array of written material. In the mid-16th century only 20 per cent of men and 5 per cent of women could sign their names; these figures had increased by the mid-17th century to 30 per cent and 10 per cent respectively; by 1715 they were 45 per cent and 25 per cent; but by 1760, 60 per cent of men and 40 per cent of women were considered 'literate'. Even allowing for the possibility that some of those signing their names may have been able to do only that, for legal purposes for example, a steep rise in literacy is certainly indicated: J. A. Sharpe (*Early Modern England: A Social History*, 1987) draws on contemporary accounts to point out that reading was taught before writing, and so name-signing is probably quite a reasonable indicator of literacy.

These literacy figures point to an expansion in education for women, as well as for men. Although, as Sharpe has also noted, while the standard of education rose in general, the number in higher education and grammar schools declined. The latter, partly to combat this decrease, gradually leavened their classical diet with increasingly 'modern' and utilitarian fare. This aspect of the struggle betweeen classicism and claims for the value of contemporary learning was satirized by ▷ Swift in ▷ *The Battle of the Books* (published 1704). The growing number of charity schools, and boarding schools for girls, also emphasized the useful and moral aspects of learning (rather than the classical), as well as the study of polite manners, although a few women, including ▷ Bathsua Makin and ▷ Mary Astell, set up schools offering more serious studies to members of their sex. There were also local and informal methods that had for long existed to enable some of the poor as well as their betters to learn to read, such as teaching in village schools, or in the home. Thus while the numbers of literate people accelerated, the proportion of those with a classical education declined.

Along with the new literacy went a new demand for reading matter, both 'high' and 'low'; this included philosophical treatises and essays; ▷ periodicals and journals such as the early 18th-century ▷ *Examiner*, ▷ *Tatler*, ▷ *Spectator* and ▷ *Female Spectator*, which offered a mixed fare of gossip, news, and opinion, in the way that ▷ newspapers were increasingly to do; books; popular stories and tales; editions of popular and classic plays; and of course poetry of all kinds. The idea of the literary market-place, as product and concomitant of the century's rapid rise in trade and commercial values, is explored in 'Market, morality and sentiment; non-dramatic prose 1660–1789', by Janet Barron and David Nokes (see pp. 27–38).

Working- and middle-class authors now achieved fame writing for readers from their own classes, as well as from the traditional upper-class readership. ▷ Defoe, subsequently recognized as one of the earliest and most important contributors to what became the novel form, was from a poor tradesman's family, and changed his name to hide his humble origins. ▷ Richardson, whose ▷ *Pamela* (1740) was so successful that it went through four editions in the course of its first year, was the son of a joiner, and had received little education, certainly none of a classical kind. Even Pope, upholder of so many upper-class values, was the son of a linen-merchant, a fact which he took great pains to conceal. Insecurity about his social identity helps to explain his savage attacks on other authors forced to write for money, after he himself had risen from their ranks. Indeed, as Brean Hammond has shown (*Pope*, 1986), the continuing fight of the 'ancients' against the 'moderns', in the late 17th and early 18th centuries, was underpinned by class antagonism and class anxiety. Conservative aristocrats and their circle, many of them gentlemen-amateur authors and scholars, felt threatened by the rival new breed of professionals, whom they viewed contemptuously as low-born *arrivistes*.

Several poets of working-class origin were in fact taken up by aristocratic patrons; some examples are given by Clare Brant in her essay. On the whole, however, literary patronage declined, from the top downwards; the Stuart monarchs, notably Charles II, had encouraged the literary arts, but their Hanoverian successors, though not without aesthetic taste, had little interest in English literature. For this reason, writers had to attract a wider readership in order to get their work published, necessitating and encouraging the development of the more popular styles already discussed. The loss of patronage was deplored by Goldsmith (▷ *The Present State of Polite Learning*, 1759), but Pope prided himself, somewhat disingenuously, on his own literary independence:

> . . . *Verse, alas! your Majesty disdains;*
> *And I'm not used to Panegyric strains;*
> *The Zeal of Fools offends at any time.*
> *But most of all, the Zeal of Fools in rhyme.*
> *Besides a Fate attends on all I write,*
> *That when I aim at praise, they say I bite . . .*
>
> *And when I flatter, let my dirty leaves*
> *(Like Journals, Odes and such forgotten things*
> *As Eusden, Philips, Settle, writ of Kings)*
> *Clothe spice, line trunks, or fluttering in a row.*
> *Befringe the rails of Bedlam and Soho.*
> *(The First Epistle of the Second Book of Horace to Augustus*, 1737)

This new appeal to a popular audience was noticeable in printed texts, as it was in the theatre, and gave rise to the terms ▷ 'hack' as a derogatory word for a popular writer, and ▷ 'Grub Street', as a term for the area in which such writers met, either literally or figuratively. Indeed, taste in entertainment in general, and literature in particular, appears to have been spread across a wider social spectrum at this time, than at any other time in English history.

The 18th century has been referred to as the period which saw the birth of the consumer society, in the modern sense of the term. Books and periodicals helped to create and to satisfy the urge towards consumption, as market products in themselves, and by advertising and conveying news about the latest fashions and trends. As a result, the number of books published each year quadrupled during the course of the 18th century, even though their cost was high – a novel was priced between six and ten shillings. This, for much of the period, was roughly equivalent to a day's wages for a skilled craftsman, or a week's wages for a labourer. The prohibitive pricing was, however, circumvented by both the serialization of longer works and the establishment of ▷ circulating libraries (operating in ▷ Bath from 1725, and in London from 1739). ▷ Richard Brinsley Sheridan's romantic heroine Lydia Languish, in ▷ *The Rivals* (1775), famously 'devours' books from a library in Bath (by now a fashionable city, rivalling London), with titles including *The Tears of Sensibility* (translated from the French *Les Epreuves du sentiment* in 1773), ▷ Sterne's ▷ *A Sentimental Journey* (1768), and ▷ Smollett's ▷ *Peregrine Pickle* (1751) and ▷ *Humphrey Clinker* (1771). Moreover, she is devastated to find novels including *The Reward of Constancy* (1771, author unknown), *The Fatal Connexion* (by Mrs Fogerty, 1773), *Mistakes of the Heart* (translated from French in 1769) and *The Delicate Distress* (by ▷ Elizabeth Griffith, 1769) already lent out, and therefore unavailable to her. In the same play, however, the forthright and old-fashioned Sir Anthony Absolute condemns the libraries and their effects. He declares that 'a circulating library in a town is as an evergreen tree of diabolical knowledge! It blossoms throughout the year! – and depend on it, Mrs Malaprop, that they who are so fond of handling the leaves, will long for the fruit at last!'

As this episode suggests, during the course of our period women became increasingly involved with literature as readers and as theatre-goers. But they also increased their activities as authors in their own right. It is no accident, moreover, that women pioneered or helped to inaugurate new literary forms. Most of them being deprived of classical education, apart from a handful like Hutchinson and Montagu, they had perforce to welcome innovative techniques. Nevertheless, since many kinds of experience – notably sexual and political – were denied to most of them, women usually wrote in forms acceptable to polite society, under the weight of social pressure and moral convention. Those like ▷ Aphra Behn, who wrote about sex in an almost 'masculine' (her word) voice were vilified, and eventually bowdlerized (▷ Thomas Bowdler) into oblivion. Women had therefore to find forms of expression which evaded conventional masculine ones in order to partake fully of literary life. For example, women from Behn and ▷ Delarivière Manley onwards are largely credited with the development of sentimental and romantic themes in literature (and indeed of the novel form itself) – even though men such as Defoe, ▷ Fielding and Richardson obviously made major contributions. Even in poetry, some of the characteristics we consider quintessentially romantic are already present in the poetry of ▷ Anne Finch, who died in 1720.

The growth of the novel in the period has, however, been explained in other ways. Several commentators have shown how the reading and writing of romantic literature, and associated pursuits, such as the following of fashion, and the cultivation of courtship skills, helped to occupy the leisure time now increasingly available to the middle and even lower classes. On the other hand, Janet Todd (*The Sign of Angellica*, 1989) has noted that a number of women, such as ▷ Laetitia Pilkington, wrote to support their children, or else used writing to supplement the living they earned in some other calling. This represented a considerable change, since some of the major women writers of the beginning of the period, among them ▷ Philips, Behn, and Astell, had no children, and concentrated solely upon their writing. In this sense the novel developed partly out of the relationship between social circumstance and literary impulse.

As the period developed, the novel came to perform a complex and paradoxical role in people's lives. On the one hand, romantic plot-lines and sentimental expressions of emotion afforded endless opportunities for narrative variations of suspense and intrigue; on the other, they challenged and partly ameliorated the evaluation of woman as marriage commodity and drudge, as well as offering close studies of social nuance in contemporary settings. Paradoxically, such writing may also be seen as part of the continuing effort to socialize young people of both sexes, and to overcome any resistance to marriage. For young women particularly these works served constantly to inform, or to remind them of their proper roles as maidenly objects of affection, and then as wives and mothers, and to discourage them from having ambitions outside the marital realm. The softening of parental authority, which took place during the 17th and 18th centuries, was accompanied by a new sort of propaganda campaign – to romanticize and therefore to sweeten the pill of having to assume adult responsibilities. Themes of conflict with parents, as in Richardson's ▷ *Clarissa* (1747–8), for example, map the struggles of young people to free themselves, and of their elders to retain control.

Young women also looked to novels for clues as to how to end their celibate state. Virtuous and happy heroines, as well as those seduced and abandoned, offered models of behaviour to imitate or avoid. Novels became 'how to' and/or 'how not to' guides to comportment (in affairs of the heart and other matters), which dramatized and humanized the advice offered in many ▷ conduct books. Numerous plays of the period performed a similar function. In the last part of the century this advice acquired a fresh exigency, since women substantially outnumbered men; many would not marry at all, and others would marry only relatively late in life. By this time, however, a reaction against popular novels was well established; they were increasingly being attacked for their supposed impropriety or frivolity and absurdity and, in some quarters, blamed for creating dissatisfaction with life. They misled young women, it was suggested, into expecting life to be like a sentimental novel. For example, ▷ Hester Chapone said that the reading of sentimental novels 'corrupts more female hearts than any other cause whatever', and another reviewer wrote that 'the youth of both sexes ... fondly imagine ... that everything must yield to the irresistible influence of all-conquering love: but upon mixing with the world, ... they find to their cost, that they have been miserably deceived ...'. Some of the opposition was overtly class-based, part of a wider view that the education of working women would give them ideas above their station. But the social and literary historian Colin Campbell, in *The Romantic Ethic and the Spirit of Modern Consumerism* (1987), argues that the suffering and isolated heroine of so many novels in the 18th century anticipates the outcast hero of the 19th and he considers it likely that the reading of novels was a major factor in the break with traditionalism which occurred in the second half of the century.

New Directions

This brings us back to the question of how to define 'Augustan' and 'Romantic', and the shift from one to the other. This volume has followed a long-accepted practice in placing the demarcation line between the two periods, at the year of the ▷ French Revolution. Some critics have opted for an even later division, at the turn of century (see, for example, the many books with '18th-century literature' in their titles); others for an earlier one, such as 1760 (for example, Marilyn Butler, in *Romantics, Rebels and Reactionaries*), or even 1740 (Arthur O. Lovejoy, 'On the Discrimination of Romanticisms', *PMLA* XXXIX, 1924). The question of where and how to separate periods of literature has always been problematic. One convention is to separate the 'romantic' from the 'classical' in the way of H. J. C. Grierson (*Classical and Romantic*, 1923), or T. E. Hulme (*Speculations*, 1924). But one needs only to think of the many classical influences on the revolutionaries, as well as on the Romantic writers (as in Keats' *Ode on a Grecian Urn*, 1819), or to look for the roots of Byron's satiric poetry in the verses of ▷ Samuel Butler, Dryden and Pope, to see the flaws in any simplistic separation. Another practice, as discussed earlier, has been to stress the continuity of ideas throughout the periods, and to argue against any sort of sharp break between one element and another.

There is a persistent view, however, shared by some of the Romantics themselves, that some kinds of change in literary taste and fashion did develop, or gathered pace, starting roughly in the middle of the 18th century, although they are not sufficient to place a clear division at that point. The mood is characterized partly by a new restlessness and searching, by a fascination with feelings, and by a sympathy with the disadvantaged in society, a general ▷ humanitarianism. The long campaign for the abolition of slavery (▷ William Wilberforce), assisted by a famous legal judgment freeing slaves in England in 1772 (▷ slavery), is an expression of the latter. These phenomena are often referred to collectively as 'sentiment' and 'sensibility'.

Other developments include a taste for the 'primitive' (▷ primitive, primitivism) including the ▷ medieval or ▷ Gothic and Celtic, and in a delight with wildness in general, from natural landscapes (▷ nature) – especially inspiring or terrifying scenes such as high mountains or deep precipices – to the idea of the 'noble savage' or 'natural' man. Images of the noble savage had existed from at least the beginning of the period well before ▷ Rousseau's famous celebration of the type. For example, Behn's ▷ *Oroonoko* describes primitive people in glowing terms, while numerous ▷ Inkle and Yarico narratives and stage plays celebrate the natural man's counterpart, the natural woman. But the idea of the natural man caught hold of the public imagination on a much larger scale in the second half of the 18th century. A succession of visitors to England from far-off countries, such as a South Sea islander called ▷ Omai, seemed to bring the symbol to life. His stay in London is described by a number of writers including ▷ Cowper, ▷ Johnson and ▷ Burney.

Finally, the transition towards Romanticism may be seen in the use of simple forms and styles, rather than the elaborate ones often admired in the earlier Augustan period; in a revival of a simpler notion of religion, including the development of ▷ Methodism from about 1739; in a love of the exotic, including the ▷ oriental, which went along with a scepticism about the superiority of one's own society in relation to the societies of others (as in Johnson's ▷ *Rasselas*,

1759, and Goldsmith's ▷ *The Citizen of the World*, 1762); in a leaning toward morbidity and pessimism, including a fascination with darkness and death; and lastly, in soaring flights of fancy. Indeed although the period saw a classical revival, as Marilyn Butler points out (*Romantics, Rebels and Reactionaries*), this time the models were primitive Greece and Rome, rather than Periclean Athens or Augustan Rome. It was at this time also that the criticism of the Roman ruler Augustus gained a new impetus, as in the eloquent castigation by ▷ Gibbon. Of course there were multiple overlaps among these categories: for example, in Omai and the characters of *Oroonoko* were represented the exotic as well as the primitive, the Gothic novel offered both primitive and gloomy elements; and Gibbon's work, while being part of the classical revival, also incorporated religious scepticism, a questioning of received ideas and a pessimistic spirit.

One of the most characteristic aspects of Romanticism was the new feeling for the wild and awesome aspects of nature. This is quite different from the cultivated and domestic kind hymned by ▷ Marvell, Dryden or Pope. It takes place in the context of a greater freedom to travel, enabling dramatic foreign scenes to become familiar to many more English people, but it also emanates from a gradual shift of the population from country-side to town. As people were driven off the land (▷ enclosures) and separated from their roots in nature and agriculture, and as agriculture itself became more mechanized, there arose a nostalgic and sentimental regard for cultivated nature, together with a new view of human existence in a natural setting. Realistic and sympathetic portraits of villagers and farm-labourers replaced the Virgilian pastoral figures that were commonplace in earlier Augustan writing. These trends are seen in the poetry of Goldsmith, ▷ Crabbe, ▷ Collins, ▷ Thomas Warton, ▷ Akenside and ▷ Gray. Mid-18th century poems, such as ▷ Young's ▷ *Night Thoughts* (1746), may be seen to have inspired Romantic writers like ▷ Wordsworth. The change is also seen in themes chosen for plays, and in stage design, as I have elaborated in 'Restoration and 18th century drama' (see pp. 42, 55–7). It is further evident in non-dramatic prose, such as in the rapturous description of the Alps written by ▷ Horace Walpole in a letter to Richard West in 1739 (▷ letter-writing), which prefigured descriptions of those mountains by Mary Shelley; just as his ▷ *The Castle of Otranto* (1764) was to form a basis for her *Frankenstein* (1817).

Walpole's phenomenally popular 'Gothic story' represents a landmark, not only in its ▷ supernaturalism, and dwelling on the elements of horror and fear (in this it is to some extent a child of ▷ Jacobean drama), but in other aspects, including its medievalism – which leads toward the Romantic and later pre-Raphaelite preoccupation with that period. Its descriptions of dark, subterranean vaults and passages are counterparts to the romantic vistas of craggy heights and vaulting skies. But its clinging atmosphere of elemental gloom and imminent disaster set a pattern for Gothic novels in general, a new form of the Augustan age which rode the transitions in political and intellectual history to survive well into the next century with its key elements intact. Compare for example this passage from *The Castle of Otranto* :

> *A clap of thunder at that instant shook the castle to its foundations; the earth rocked, and the clank of more than mortal armour was heard behind. Frederic and Jerome thought the last day was at hand . . . (then) the walls of the castle behind Manfred were thrown down with a mighty force . . .*

with the following from Mary Shelley's *Frankenstein* (1818):

> *As the night advanced, a fierce wind arose from the woods, and quickly dispersed the clouds that had loitered in the heavens: the blast tore along like a mighty avalanche, and produced a kind of insanity in my spirits that burst all bounds of reason and reflection . . .*

There are important differences between the two, not least the shift to first-person narrative and introspection in the later piece, and the ghostly apparition, which subsequently appears heralded by nature's effects in the former. But they share a sense of nature as something wild, threatening and primitive, even as a participant in the action, influencing and commenting banefully upon it, like a Greek chorus. Once again, this is at a far remove from the early Augustan pastoral view of nature, as a carefully wrought ▷ Golden Age setting for shepherds and shepherdesses to sport and court in. Jerome at another point in Walpole's story seeks out 'the gloomiest shades, as best suited to the pleasing melancholy that reigned in his mind', anticipating the darkly mournful hero-outcasts of Byron.

In ghostly scenes such as this one, Walpole purposefully invokes Shakespeare. This is not merely a backward look, or an attempt to elevate his own material by dressing it in clothing of the Bard, but an announcement of a shift from a certain kind of ▷ neo-classic critical theory to an alternative vision of nature and of art. Since the Restoration Shakespeare had often been condemned for mixing crude comic elements with exalted ones, as well as for failing to observe the ▷ Classical Unities; it was not until the transition from the Augustan to the Romantic periods that Shakespeare was revalued in a manner that would be familiar today. The impulse which in 1823 inspired Edmund Kean to stage *King Lear* with the tragic ending written by Shakespeare, for the first time since ▷ Nahum Tate altered it to a happy ending in 1681, was not entirely the same as that which motivated Walpole's reference to Shakespeare. Both efforts, however, were part of the same wave of so-called 'Bardolatry' which arose in the second half of the 18th century, was highlighted by a Shakespeare Jubilee in 1767, and continued into the next century. Shakespeare's works were revalued, and became appreciated, precisely because of their alleged 'wildness' and irregularity, which earlier generations had rejected. Now they seemed in keeping with, or even to embody, the newly defined spirit of nature.

Walpole, in a letter to Mme du Deffand, informed her in language extraordinarily like that of the Romantics later, that he had written *The Castle of Otranto*, to give 'reign to my imagination; visions and passions choked me. I wrote it in spite of rules, critics, and philosophers . . .'. He continued by informing her that he had composed the work 'for the future, when taste will be restored to the place now occupied by philosophy', and not for the present, 'which wants only *cold reason*'. In an epigraph attached to the second edition, he refers to the work as if to a new form. Yet the epigraph is itself a paraphrase of a passage from the Augustan 'Bible', Horace's *De Arte Poetica* ('On the Art of Poetry'), and his preface to the first edition draws attention to his use of pity and terror, those Aristotelian essentials so favoured by early Augustan dramatists, while the work itself mostly observes the rules of classical drama. A modern editor, W. S. Lewis, in his introduction to *The Castle of Otranto* (1964), describes Walpole's mission as 'to innovate', but he also adds that he wished 'to instruct, and to entertain'. These last two precepts encompass Horatian prescriptions which stand as twin Augustan ideals. Walpole himself refers to his Gothic tale as 'an attempt to blend . . . two kinds of romance, the ancient and the modern'. We might add that it links, inextricably, elements of both Augustanism and Romanticism.

Augustanism did not give way easily to the new Romantic sensibility; it survived late into the 18th century in, for example, the work of Goldsmith, who consciously and deliberately referred back to the Restoration period; in the work of Samuel Johnson, whose preoccupation with reason, 'reasonable' tone, orthodox classical standards of literature, and use of Augustan forms, allies him with writers of an earlier era (although his ▷ *The Vanity of Human Wishes* (1749), which was inspired by Juvenal's tenth satire, has a Romantic concern with futility and death); and Augustanism is even manifest, as we have seen, in some of the comic poetry of Byron – *Don Juan* (1819–24) and *The Vision of Judgment* (1821). Interestingly, the influence of the 18th century has been recognized even beyond Byron's time, for example in the poetry of ▷ Samuel Rogers, who outlived not only Byron but Wordsworth as well, and who continued to write in the Augustan style (J. R. Watson, 'Samuel Rogers: The Last Augustan', in *Augustan Worlds*, ed. Hilson, Jones, and Watson, 1978).

Conclusion

As we have seen, the idea of an Augustan age, in the sense of an era of high achievement informed by classicism and incorporating many classical models, has refused to die, and is still a convenient label for the period 1660–1789, even if incomplete as a definition and summation of all its accomplishments. Critics as careful and diverse as Pat Rogers (*The Augustan Vision*, 1974), Howard Erskine-Hill (*The Augustan Idea in English Literature*) and Margaret Doody (*The Daring Muse: Augustan Poetry Reconsidered*, 1985) insist on the continuing usefulness of the term 'Augustan'; as Doody says, it is 'the term we have . . . the one that inspires recognition'. The French Revolution, with its cataclysmic impact on English thought, marked a break with the past, inspiring fresh radicalism, and then reaction. But the intellectual seeds for those developments, as well as the development of Romanticism itself, lie further back. Thus our idea of 'Augustan' perhaps needs modifying once and for all, to allow that there is no hard line between that period and the one that follows it. We should use the term as a convenient way of marking a time-block and of implying certain ideas, but not to suggest a rigidly enclosed phenomenon.

Restoration and 18th-century poetry 2

Clare Brant

Literary history, culture, theory

The term 'Augustan' (▷ Augustanism) properly refers to those Roman poets who celebrated, sometimes ironically, the ideals and shortcomings of civic life under the emperor ▷ Caesar Augustus. Though useful to suggest some public aspects of late ▷ 17th- and early ▷ 18th-century verse, it misrepresents the poetic diversity of the period as a whole. Nonetheless, it and other labels such as 'the Age of Reason' (▷ Rationalism) continue to be used to create an impression of poetry ruled by ideas of ▷ classical correctness. 'Reason' is often compared unfavourably with 17th-century ▷ metaphysical inventiveness or 19th-century romantic imagination: as Matthew Arnold famously remarked, 'Dryden and Pope are not classics of our poetry, they are classics of our prose'. In fact the poetry of the ▷ Enlightenment is full of ideas and experiments: from early ▷ wit to late ▷ sensibility, poets tested the limits of learning and experience with passion and humour.

Poetic variety was assisted by the expansion of print culture. New outlets for poetry, such as ▷ periodicals and ▷ magazines, appeared alongside an increased number of printed books of poetry. Though poetry still circulated in aristocratic circles in manuscript and on the street in ▷ pamphlets, ▷ ballads and songs, it was this middle ground which came to support most poetry. Its early concentration in London – represented by ▷ Grub Street, the symbolic locale of ▷ hack writers – gave way to provincial centres and networks. ▷ Thomas Gray in ▷ Cambridge, ▷ Anna Seward, 'the Swan of Lichfield', and ▷ William Cowper in rural Buckinghamshire, lived out poetry's move away from metropolitan concerns after the mid-century. It is important to remember that poetry appeared not only in books but also on buildings, tombstones and statuary, on fans and picture frames, in satirical prints and engravings. It was sung, acted and posted with presents. It was a recognized form of argument: ▷ Lady Mary Chudleigh's *The Lady's Defence* (1710) was one of many dialogues in verse. Poems turned up in novels: readers of ▷ Samuel Richardson's ▷ *Clarissa* in 1749, for instance, came across ▷ Elizabeth Carter's much-admired *Ode to Wisdom*; and ▷ Tobias Smollett included a poem by himself on Loch Lomond in *The Expedition of* ▷ *Humphry Clinker* (1771). ▷ Laetitia Pilkington published her poems in her memoirs in 1747. Mary Jones published her verse epistles with her prose correspondence in 1750. ▷ Joseph Addison and ▷ Sir Richard Steele used quotations from classical poets at the head of their periodical essays; and ▷ Ann Radcliffe's epigraphs used English poets to set moods to chapters in her novels. ▷ Samuel Johnson's ▷ *Dictionary* (1755) used quotations from English poets up to his own time to illustrate the meaning of words in contexts. Poetry was used in education to teach rhetoric, grammar and languages. This did not necessarily produce more talented poets, complained ▷ Charles Gildon in 1721, for though schoolboys were made familiar with the poetry of ▷ Homer, ▷ Virgil and ▷ Horace, this taught them only prosody or 'how to frame several sorts of verses in the *Greek* and *Latin* tongue, without giving them the least insight into the art of poetry it self, and therefore only qualifies them for meer versifiers'. Poetry was also connected to oratory: verse prologues and epilogues appealed to spectators to judge plays favourably. It was read aloud in small groups as well as silently by solitary readers. The look of poetry on the page, however, took on special importance in this period. It uses apostrophes to indicate precise rhythms: 'But with the odious smell and sight annoy'd / In haste she does th' offensive herd avoid' ('she' being the Muse, in ▷ Swift's *To Mr Congreve*, 1693). Poems became typographically elaborate, though always elegantly laid out, with italics, capitals and underlinings. As Swift put it,

> *To Statesmen wou'd you give a Wipe,*
> *You print it in* Italick Type.
> *When Letters are in vulgar Shapes,*
> *'Tis Ten to one the Wit escapes;*
> *But when in Capitals exprest,*
> *The dullest Reader smokes the Jest.*
> (*On Poetry: A Rhapsody,* 1734.)

The increasing presence of poetry enlarged people's ideas about the genre. In 1712, when asked to describe 'the chief Qualifications of a good Poet', Sir Richard Steele replied 'a very well-bred Man', but barriers of class and gender varied across the period. The 1730s, for instance, saw working-class poets in vogue, with the success of ▷ Stephen Duck's *The Thresher's Labour* (1735), which earned him a royal pension and a riposte from ▷ Mary Collier in *The Woman's Labour* (1739), pointing out that working-class woman's life was exhausting in specific ways to which she, as a washer-woman, could testify. Duck's exchange of agricultural work for city patronage was not, however, happy, and he committed suicide. Later working-class writers such as ▷ Ann Yearsley also struggled to survive patronage. To participate in high culture could require imitation of its forms: ▷ as Mary Leapor put it, 'You see I'm learned, and I show't the more, / That none may wonder when they find me poor' (*An Epistle to a Lady,* 1748). Though working-class writers used ▷ couplets ably enough, it was hard for them to challenge 'the Mob of Gentlemen who wrote with Ease', in ▷ Pope's phrase. A beggar's daughter in Smollett's ▷ *Peregrine Pickle* (1751) is passed off as a fine lady once she has learnt to recite 'choice sentences from Shakespeare, Otway and Pope'. Knowledge of poetry and the ability to join in games of allusion were marks of ▷ taste which self-educated poets struggled to develop.

For women, class could offset some of the disadvantages of gender. ▷ Katherine Philips and ▷ Anne Finch were recognized talents. Though John Wilmot, Second Earl of ▷ Rochester, asserted that '*Whore* is scarce a more reproachful name / Than *poetess*', women wrote continuously. Most were, however, careful to frame their productions with modest disclaimers. Anna Williams' are typical: 'Censure may be content to spare the compositions of a woman, written for amusement, and published for necessity' (*Miscellanies,* 1766). Two factors helped women. One was recognition of poetry as diverse, connected to specific, plural, various occasions: titles such as 'Miscellanies' and 'Poems on Several Occasions' were widely used by men and women, and this hint towards poetry as miscellaneous allowed for mixed abilities or mixed success. Secondly, women compensated increasingly for a lack of classical forbears as more women published. During the 18th century women cited as illustrious models first ▷ Aphra Behn and then, as a decorous private life became as much a requirement for women writers as talent, her more respectable predecessor ▷ Katherine Philips, the 'matchless Orinda'. In the later 18th century, women also increasingly looked to ▷ Shakespeare as an instance of how a poet with little ▷ Latin and less ▷ Greek could still have merit.

The dubious social status of some poetry meant that many 18th-century poems were published anonymously. But this was also a form of insurance against politically or personally motivated attack. As one anonymous writer lamented in 1779,

> *Poets and Thieves the same attention meet,*
> *Their deaths are hawk'd about from Street to Street;*
> *And the same fate attends the wretches still,*
> *Who go up Helicon or Holborn-Hill.*

Poetic stealing, or plagiarism, was one of the few forms of theft not to carry a capital charge in the 18th century, but poets policed each other vituperatively. Like Johnson's scholar, poets faced 'toil, envy, want, the patron and the jail'. John Philips' *The Splendid Shilling* (1701) was popular for its clever Miltonic ▷ burlesque, but also for its play with cliches concerning poetic penury. Poets' prospects did change: where ▷ Milton was paid £10 for ▷ *Paradise Lost*, ▷ Dryden earned a comfortable £1250 for his translation of ▷ Virgil, and Pope's translation of ▷ Homer made him financially independent. But such sums were exceptional. Swift, with his usual complicated irony, advised poets 'to hire out your Pen, to a Party, which will afford you both *Pay* and *Protection*'. Politically commissioned work mostly concealed its hired origins, but the value of public poetry was officially recognized in 1668 when John Dryden was appointed the first ▷ Poet Laureate. For all that the public bought more poetry, poets still looked to patrons for support. As the Fourth Earl of Abingdon observed about a well-placed dedication, 'it sometimes happens, that the Name of the Patron supplies the want of every other merit, and preserves the work from oblivion.' But there were a number of scandals about poets who suffered destitution or rejection; in 1782 William Hayley hoped the nation would never again see 'A future CHATTERTON by poison dead, / An OTWAY fainting for a little bread.'

Poetry was agreed to be an important proof of national greatness. Poets earned their countries peacetime laurels, and artistic alliances and rivalries evolved across Europe, though not necessarily mirroring relationships between nation-states – English and ▷ French writers, for instance, continued to read and appreciate each others' work even when their countries were at war. Writers, both English and French, attributed French regimentation to a lack of political liberty, while English social freedoms were supposed to be reflected in a less circumscribed literature. But poetic nationalism often involved informed comparisons with other countries' literature, of which travellers sought out specimens. Samples of foreign poetry were analysed both to reveal what themes if any were universal to poetry, and how particular national cultures treated them. ▷ Lady Mary Wortley Montagu, for instance, in 1717 sent Alexander Pope a specimen of Turkish poetry, first in a literal translation and then in English style. She commented on both social and linguistic determinants of poetry: 'Neither do I think our English proper to express such violence of passion, which is very seldom felt amongst us; and we want those compound words which are very frequent and strong in the Turkish Language.' Readers were particularly informed about epic poems from Spain, Portugal, France and ▷ Italy which, together with their knowledge of English ▷ epic poems, created a European inheritance to the classics. Paradoxically, epic was prized both as the most nationalistic (▷ Nationalism) genre, promoting the poet's tribe, and also as the least nationalistic, in that epic heroes usually travelled and created new countries. So Hildebrand Jacob attempted a British epic, *Brutus*, in which the Roman founds an English colony. On a smaller scale, Pope's ▷ *Windsor Forest* (1713), a Tory celebration of the Peace of Utrecht, (▷ Spanish Succession, War of) turns local landscape into international scenery: 'The Time shall come, when free as Seas or Wind / Unbounded *Thames* shall flow for all Mankind'.

Like monarchs in this period, poets had to be secured against pretenders: versifiers, poetasters, scribblers, hacks and dunces. Correct technique was not enough in itself: Charles Gildon lamented that 'this is a Quality that gives the glorious Name of Poets to Fellows without Warmth, without Judgement, without Imagination' (1713). Literary theory used this aesthetic vocabulary consistently in the period. William Duff sums it up in a 1763 essay: 'If, on the one hand, Imagination bestows SENSIBILITY and REFINEMENT on Taste, so on the other, Taste imparts JUSTNESS and PRECISION to Imagination; while Genius is consummated by the proper union of both these faculties with that of Judgment'. Reason alone could not animate the process: 'a certain vital spirit must be infused; and in Poetry, this vital Spirit is INVENTION.' This term, from the Latin *inventio*, implies not just discovering existing forms and relations but, increasingly throughout the 18th century, thinking up new ones as well.

This distinctive combination of conservatism and passion helps to explain some parts of late 17th- and 18th-century poetic theory which are alien to a modern mind: deference to classical writers, insistence on imitating ▷ nature, and adherence to rules in doing so. In fact, not all writers were fans of the classics. Pope declared his support for the ancients: 'the highest character for sense and learning has been obtained by those who have been most indebted to *them*. For to say truth, whatever is very good sense, must have been very good sense in all times.' But Percival Stockdale, despite being in all other respects Pope's warmest admirer, took the opposite view, complaining of 'dictators [who] pay no regard to what passes in life.' ▷ Voltaire temperately suggested that 'The best modern Writers have mix'd the Taste of their Country, with that of the Ancients', but he also complicated moderate positions by upholding neo-classic systems in which French critics rather than classical poets provided guidance about rules.

Rules, according to Pope, were simply 'Nature methodiz'd'. Poetic theory constantly invoked nature, meaning not simply the visible world, but that principle which gives shape and structure to material and conceptual forms of life. Like the idea of 'human nature', it could cover a variety of behaviours, but this variety was not infinite. Nature as represented in texts was defined by the plausible. Poetry was like painting in that both arts represented something by copying it: for example, a portrait copied a person. But if the subject was an invented person, such as Hercules, then what was copied or imitated was the 'type' of a strong man. Poetry described things as they *may* be: 'whenever we speak of poetry as an imitation, we constantly call it an imitation of Nature', explained Alexander Gerard in 1780. Critics urged writers to follow nature, not to encourage slavish conformity, but to assist readers' recognition of subjects, and to make poetry as effective as other kinds of literature in offering instruction and entertainment.

Comparisons between the sister arts of 'voice and verse', as Milton called them, were common in this period. Archetypal musicians such as St Cecilia and King David interested poets from John Dryden to ▷ Christopher Smart. Besides odes and lyrics which were originally sung forms, hymns and libretti linked poetry to music. Critics used musical ideas of harmony and painterly ideas of depiction to try to represent what poetry did, though as Samuel Johnson observed, 'criticism has not yet attained the certainty, and stability of science.' It was a common jibe in the late 17th and 18th centuries that critics were failed poets, though boundaries between criticism and poetry were considered to be legitimately blurred, as when poets, usually imitating Horace's ▷ *De Arte Poetica*, wrote verse criticism of the art of poetry. Abuse of critics was colourful: James Miller, for instance, described critics as 'Those Rats, which tear Books to Pieces, only to come at the Paste they are glewed with'. But Dryden's prefaces and essays, Addison's sympathetic papers on Milton in ▷ *The Spectator* and Johnson's ▷ *Lives of the Poets* successfully developed critical theory and biography as tools for reading poetry. Various factors helped to make the critic a more prestigious figure in the second half of the 18th century: the establishment and spread of respectable magazines which had consistent policies of reviewing; London highbrow society's new interest in serious public conversation about literature, along the lines of French salons; and the necessity of agreeing critical standards as literary production expanded in the provinces.

With criticism more securely established, the formation of a native poetic canon began: Shakespeare was established as the national genius, and Milton, ▷ Spenser and Chaucer were promoted. The ▷ metaphysical poet Donne was regarded by some as uncouth, but still sufficiently interesting to be 'rectified' in Pope's re-versification. Antiquarian interests became mainstream: in 1765 ▷ Thomas Percy published his ▷ *Reliques*, a large collection of old English ballads, and ▷ Thomas Warton published his long *History of English Poetry from the Close of the Eleventh to the Commencement of the Eighteenth Century* (1779–81). Thus, throughout the 18th century, English poetry increasingly defined itself in relation to its own native history, as well as to classical inheritance.

The genres of poetry

Restoration and 18-century poetry used certain distinct genres. An ▷ epigram was a short, witty poem, often involving censure or applause. It manifested brevity, beauty or sharpness, with Martial's epigrams providing a classical model. An ▷ epitaph, a concise memorial poem, usually showed gravity, but could be jocular, like the pair of epitaphs by Pope and Lady Mary Wortley Montagu about two lovers struck by lightning. The form was challenging, since it required specific consideration of the dead person, something general on death, and all in a space short enough to be fitted onto a tombstone if need be. ▷ Elegy was a broad genre, generally about death or the coyness or cruelty of a lover. Commiseration, reproach, sympathy or tenderness predominated, but it could also show passion and restraints on passion. Pope's *An Elegy to the Memory of an Unfortunate Lady* (1717) illustrates sympathy with the griefs of people unknown to the poet, an attitude perfected in ▷ Gray's ▷ *Elegy in a Country Churchyard* (1751). Katherine Philips' *On the death of my first and dearest childe* (published 1667) is a moving example, and Elizabeth Boyd's *On the Death of an Infant of five Days old* (1733) is a powerful description of maternal grief: 'Oh! could the stern-souled sex but know the pain, / Or the soft mother's agonies sustain, / With tenderest love the obdurate heart would burn, / And the shocked father tear for tear return'. Particularly in the late 17th century, poets wrote elegies memorializing fellow poets – for example, ▷ Anne Wharton's elegy on Rochester. ▷ Pastoral, drawing on ▷ Theocritus, Virgil and sometimes Spenser, represented the doings of shepherds or rural ▷ nymphs and swains. It strained for simplicity, a contradiction which often led it into artifice. Pope's *Pastorals*, written when he was 14, were thought to be formally perfect, though by 1776 one poet, writing anonymously, complained of 'the shoals of nonsense that has been eternally written of Delias and Damons, Chloes, Strephons, &c . . . who can read such trash without disgust?' Related forms included ▷ eclogues, uninterrupted by dialogue, and ▷ georgics, poems of agricultural instruction. All these expressed interest in land which could covertly address issues of ownership and occupation through fantasy.

Poetic epistles like prose letters were able to address almost any person or subject and, again like prose letters, they were one of the most widely written forms of the late 17th and 18th centuries. Unfolding in the manner of conversation, smooth, easy and polite, they could be serious or ludicrous, satirical, heroic, descriptive, friendly or hostile. Many poets used ▷ Ovid's *Epistles* as a starting point; others, such as Pope, favoured the Horatian epistle. Descriptive poetry usually involved meditative neo-classical forms rather than the more talkative Augustan modes listed above. Following Milton's *L'Allegro* and *Il Penseroso*, poets played on tactile and aural senses as well as the visual, as in ▷ Anne Finch's study of nightfall, *A Nocturnal Reverie*. Prospect poetry organized hilltop views into narratives which used conventions comparable to those employed by landscape painters such as Claude, where the eye tracked between foreground and horizon in distinct patterns. Detail alternates with broader strokes in ▷ John Dyer's *Grongar Hill* (1726), for example: 'How close and small the hedges lie! / What streaks of meadows cross the eye!' ▷ Didactic writing made instruction palatable by concealing it in lively writing. Compendium poems, ranging over multiple aspects of a topic; were also popular, such as ▷ William Somervile's *The Chase* (1735), a poetical history of hunting. Philosophical enquiries and aesthetic analyses were often attempted: both were combined in ▷ Mark Akenside's blank-verse celebration of *The Pleasures of the Imagination* (1744). Tales and ▷ fables provided self-contained narratives, often with a disturbing twist, and allegorical discussions often involving animals or inanimates. Dryden's religious dialogue ▷ *The Hind and the Panther* (1687) and ▷ Gay's *Fables* (1727–38) brought out the form's playfulness. Extended ▷ allegories were less common: one such was ▷ James Thomson's dreamily sensual Spenserian imitation ▷ *The Castle of Indolence* (1748), in which the Knight of Arts and Industry rescues Britain from indolence with the help of a bard. But allegorical devices such as personification (▷ figures of speech) were ubiquitous.

The large category of lyric covers ▷ odes and songs. Songs were widely written in the late 17th century, since their usual subjects of love and drinking suited much Restoration self-imaging. The French critic ▷ Boileau decreed that 'Even in a Song there must be Art and Sense'; whether bawdy or sacred, songs expressed pleasure in sweetness and easy versification. Odes were ranked high in the generic hierarchy. As Boileau's *The Art of Poetry* (1683) put it, 'The Heart in Elegies forms the Discourse, / The Ode is bolder, and has greater force'. Commentators agreed that odes used disorder creatively; they were, as ▷ George Villiers, the Duke of Buckingham, put it, 'the Muse's most unruly horse'. But in odes the imagination, often depicted as Pegasus, need not be reined in. The ▷ Pindaric ode (▷ Pindar) was particularly celebrated for 'its beautiful wanderings, and its happy returns to the subject' as Charles Gildon put it. Yet the mid- to late-18th century preference for the sublime ode – bold, irregular, elevated – drew attention to its challenges. As one practitioner, Thomas Cooke, put it in 1749, 'of all Sorts of Poetry, none has been so often attempted as the *Ode*, nor with less Success'. Odes were thought to have been sung and danced in ancient times, and it was this patterning of energy which gave them appeal. The ode's importance after the mid-18th century, when many poets preferred it to couplets, is because it expressed order differently, rather than allowing a triumph of passion over reason.

▷ Epic was more discussed than practised, at least until ▷ James Macpherson's poetical prose fragments published in the 1760s, purporting to be by a third-century poet ▷ Ossian. Epic's partly real, partly fictitious stories of illustrious actions performed by heroes was turned creatively into ▷ mock heroic (Dryden's ▷ *Mac Flecknoe*, 1682) and ▷ mock epic (Pope's ▷ *The Rape of the Lock*, 1712 and ▷ *The Dunciad*, 1728). Satirical reversals of scale – in Coleridge's phrase, making the great little and the little great – pointed to communal or ideal scales of value from which the protagonists had departed. The workings of ▷ satire were much discussed in this period. The ancients provided two models, Horace and ▷ Juvenal, loosely equated with smiling and savage satire respectively. Dryden declared that 'The true end of Satyre is the amendment of Vices by Correction'. But was this end best achieved by mocking, deriding and bullying, or by teasing and humorously shaming? Poets tried out different methods of raillery and rage to discover how best for their ends 'sharpest thoughts in smoothest words' (Buckingham) might be conveyed. Not all satire was high-minded: much involved political feuding or personal abuse. Polite literature became acrimonious in satire, but the art of abuse highlighted the art of the poetry which couched it.

Poetry in context: 1660–1700

The Restoration of the monarchy in 1660 put ▷ Charles II on the throne but restored few other institutions. Besides the religious and political upheavals of the ▷ Civil War, commercial and technological innovations were changing English social life. The apparent revival of aristocratic court culture, until the ▷ 'Glorious Revolution' of 1688, distracted from the insecurities and self-inventions of poems as variously theatrical as the verse plays which many poets were also writing for the newly re-opened theatres.

Civil War poetry had been necessarily populist, taking sides, marching down the street, arguing its case, abusing its opponents. Ballads and songs continued to structure much satire, most notably in the roughly rhymed tetrameter couplets of ▷ Samuel Butler's ▷ *Hudibras*, written in four parts between 1662 and 1684. This was immensely popular: the first part ran through nine editions in its first year. Mocking everything from epic to science, it was indiscriminately caustic about faction, whether religious or political:

> *Both Parties joyn'd to do their best,*
> *To Damn the Publick Interest.*
> *And Hearded only in consults,*
> *To put by one anothers Bolts;*
> *T'outcant the Babylonian Labourers*
> *At all their Dialects of Jabberers,*
> *And tug at both ends of the Saw,*
> *To tear down Government and Law.*

As in Swift's satire later, this is not high-minded but knowing. You cannot guess where it will turn next, though many of its tropes are recognizable from earlier traditions. For example, classical satirists attacked opponents for being misers or gluttons. Culpability was illustrated by deviance from a mean: thus hospitality could degenerate into prodigality or contract into parsimony, like Butler's Puritans who 'Quarrel with *minc'd Pies* and disparage / Their best and dearest friend, *Plum-porridge*'. (Pope's miser and glutton in his *Epistle to Bathurst* continue this game.) Nor could you tell for how long such poems would go on: the ramble or survey continues until the poet has had enough. Similarly, Dryden's ▷ *Annus Mirabilis* (1666) packs into its year of wonders the naval war with Holland and the ▷ Great Fire of London, but its pace is set by the compelling nature of the various spectacles it describes rather than by strict calendar time.

This sense of 'uncovering' is common to satire, epistles, tales and fables, popular genres of this period. Dryden's ▷ *The Medall* (1682) uses the coin as an emblem of two-facedness as well as the medal struck by the Whigs to celebrate the acquittal of ▷ Shaftesbury: 'So like the Man; so golden in the Sight / So base within, so counterfeit and light'. Dryden plays with conceits established by earlier ballads about heads stamped on crowns, crowned heads and coinage as an emblem of political fortunes. In ▷ *Absalom and Achitophel* (1681–2) he goes on to use the known Biblical story of a plot against David to represent political treachery as the sinister Shaftesbury masterminds the ▷ Duke of Monmouth in a plot against Charles II. Forms of proper government are debated:

> *What shall we think! Can People give away*
> *Both for themselves and Sons, their Native sway?*
> *Then are they left Defensless, to the Sword*
> *Of each unbounded Arbitrary Lord;*

On the other hand

> *Nor is the Peoples Judgment always true:*
> *The most may err as grossly as the few,*
> *And faultless Kings run down, by Common Cry*
> *For Vice, Oppression and for Tyranny.*

This competitive play of voices carries more instability than the syntactically more complicated antitheses favoured by 18th-century couplets. Though they look smoother in Dryden's verse, both sides are open to surprise, change and disruption.

Social and political restlessness are reflected in Restoration reinvention of genres as mock genres. Parody, irony and ▷ burlesque were popular (▷ figures of speech), though recognition of the matter being reformulated also ensured that orthodoxies lingered. Burlesque distinctively dissolved grand matters into bathetic (▷ figures of speech) effects, in for instance Charles Cotton's translation of the very popular French travesty of Virgil by Paul Scarron: '*Aeneas and his Wand'ring Mates, Were at that time, Angling for Sprats*'. Banality was not wholly the enemy of wit, since it provided occasions for it, as in Dryden's satire of the poetic aspirations of ▷ Elkanah Settle and ▷ Thomas Shadwell in *Mac Flecknoe*. Poets who claimed merit – incessantly troped as 'laurel' or 'bays' – used surprise to guard against boredom, even in mock genres where reversals could be predicted. Rochester was particularly deft at this game, as for example in his song 'Fair Chloris in a pigsty lay', where the nymph's location burlesques pastoral. Yet the poem turns out to be an account of Chloris masturbating: a surprise not just in its frankness but in the way that its image of female self-sufficiency reverses pastoral's obsessive articulation of abandoned lovers' complaints. The incompleteness of heterosexual love is burlesqued by autoeroticism, but it ends with a further surprise by restoring Chloris to pastoral purity, though with an ironic note – ironic about both pastoral and antipastoral – 'She's innocent and pleased'.

Pastoral was especially suited to rewriting since its conventions were static. Even where lovers leave one another, order is reimposed through formulaic laments about departure. But Restoration pastoral is peculiarly dynamic, partly because women used the genre to write about desire. In the 17th century, states of semi-undress were considered more exciting than nudity; the longings and couplings of nymphs and swains thinly veil those of men and women. Love is shown as arousal, exhaustion, rearousal; where bodies mingle, moods dissolve and evolve. For example, in Aphra Behn's *On a Juniper-Tree, cut down to make Busks* (1680), after a couple make love three times,

> ... *Chloris reassum'd her fear,*
> *And chid the Swain, for having prest,*
> *What she alas wou'd not resist:*
> *Whilst he in whom Loves sacred flame*
> *Before and after was the same,*
> *Fondly implor'd she wou'd forget*
> *A fault, which he wou'd yet repeat.*

The shifts between past and future, memory and desire, dizzily mimic the erotic exchange. Yet the lovers are constant: change is displaced onto the tree telling the story which (surprise) is no longer a tree but a pile of sticks for corsets and (surprise again) that transformation was anticipated at the start by the title.

Constant metamorphosis is the mark of late 17th-century poetry, as of Restoration drama, where women so often disguise themselves, as other women, even as men, usually in order to further some sexual aim. The reopening of theatres, and women's new cultural presence, created a new sense of the pleasures and threats of acting. Rochester's phrase, 'Love's theatre, the bed', points to a fascination in poetry with how sex expressed conscious performance (in every sense) rather than authenticity. This was, of course, convenient for libertines who could up and leave at any time on the grounds that no feeling was real, or if real, lasting. It is not, however, ennui which underlies Rochester's moving lyrics about transience – 'All my past life is mine noe more' – though some of his violent verse is hardly philosophical. One such poem, in which the speaker wishes to fuck out his mistress's eyes, is a mock-song, and hence could be seen to expose libertine excess by exaggerating or parodying it. But much male libertine poetry is straightforwardly anxious and violent: women are endlessly figured as towns to be attacked, besieged and conquered. In this troping of love as war, women fought back with strong mythological warriors such as Amazons or planetary deities, such as Diana, who looked down on men from a great height. Men might use the same myths as evidence of unfemininity or frigidity, but female heroism had the longer literary heritage. The popularity of poems by women about female friendship reflected not just actual supportive relations between women, but also a model of emotional constancy and trustworthiness, which misogynist poets consistently denied women showed in matters of love. Platonic love, sensual but apparently asexual, offered women an alternative to faithless heterosexual lovers, and furthermore showed women capable of reasoning philosophically. As 'Philophilippa' wrote in tribute to Katherine Philips' poems about female friendship, 'For there's requir'd (to do that Virtue right) / Courage, as much in Friendship as in Fight'..

Katherine Philips proved herself not only in contemporary, innovative, writing, but also through her display of more traditional skills. In fact she was one of many poets whose success was founded on translation – in her case, of ▷ Corneille. Translation, another form of textual metamorphosis, gave proof of skill based on intellect. Hence it was especially helpful to women, since it allowed them to show intellectual skill which was then modestly diffused through their original's pre-existing reputation. As the ▷ Earl of Roscommon put it, 'And by improving what was writ before, *Invention* labours less, but *Judgment* more'. Before Dryden translated Virgil, according to Elizabeth Thomas, translators had 'his lofty Epick Rhymes / By murd'ring Pens debas'd, to doggerel Chimes'. Rewriting Ovid, ▷ Boccaccio and Chaucer in *Fables Ancient and Modern* (1700), Dryden showed how English verse could revitalize old texts. The linguistic edge to his poetic talents was underlined by his admirers. Comparing Dryden (sprightly, energetic, various) to Pope (regular, harmonious, elevated), ▷ James Beattie in 1776 stressed how Dryden's example transformed English:

> *In Dryden's more correct pieces, we meet with no affection of words of Latin or Greek etymology, no cumbersome pomp of epithets, no drawling circumlocutions, no idle glare of images, no blunderings round about a meaning: his English is pure and simple, nervous and clear, to a degree which Pope has never exceeded and not always equalled.*

Dryden, in his use of English, showed how a poetry of restlessness could also be durable and elegant; he is said to have found it brick and left it marble.

Poetry in context: 1700–1740

Early 18th-century poetry has been most closely associated with the term 'Augustan': civilized, rational, decorous – except where wit allows it to be naughty – and with Alexander Pope as its chief exponent. There was a characteristic urbanity, not only the stability of civic architecture, but the rowdy flow of life on the streets, in for instance John Gay's *Trivia; or, the Art of Walking the Streets of London* (1716), which you might share with a Covent Garden prostitute.

> *'Tis she who nightly strolls with saunt'ring pace,*
> *No stubborn stays her yielding shape embrace;*
> *Beneath the lamp her tawdry ribbons glare,*
> *The new-scowered manteau, and the slattern air,*
> *High-draggled petticoats her travels show,*
> *And hollow cheeks with artful blushes glow;*
> *With flatt'ring sounds she sooths the cred'lous ear,*
> *'My noble captain! charmer! love! my dear!*

This interest in portraiture and types of speech was widespread in early 18th-century poetry. Material detail and social nuance created the illusion of spectatorship, in which the poet's observation appears easy. This stylistic representation of the ordinary made 18th-century poetry self-consciously literary in its appearance, even when its substance extended to low-life concerns. As Pope put it in his ▷ *Essay on Criticism* (1711), 'True Wit is Nature to advantage dressed / What oft was thought, but ne'er so well expressed'. This familiarity of poetic material and ideas also meant that poetry could become much less the prerogative of one class or gender.

Two poets from a slightly older generation showed how the commonplace could be used to reveal multiple meanings. John Philips' Georgic *Cyder* (1706) described the cultivation, manufacture and virtues of cider. It also investigated the apple's role in 'fallen states' from the theological to the drunken, as well as its political symbolism (through toasts) and association with art (through horticulture). *The Art of Cooking* (1708) by ▷ William King did for food what *Cyder* did for drink, using a Horatian ideal of temperance to investigate questions of appetite and the nationalism of gastronomy.

This conjunction of material and mythological worlds is present in Pope's *Windsor Forest*, a Tory panegyric in which the Berkshire countryside becomes the heroic birthplace of national glory, and *The Rape of the Lock*, which was ostensibly written to reconcile the families of a young woman and of a man who had cut off one of her ringlets. This sparkling mock epic has a Miltonic machinery of sylphs, but these spirits fail to protect the heroine Belinda:

> *Transparent forms, too fine for mortal sight,*
> *Their fluid bodies half-dissolved in light,*
> *Loose to the wind their airy garments flew,*
> *Thin glittering textures of the filmy dew.*

Pope's mock heroic is conventionally read as a critique of a society which confuses moral and material values, embodied in the heroine who may equally 'stain her honour or her new brocade'. Pope blames female sexuality for this confusion in his sumptuous celebration of the period's double standard over sexual behaviour. This not only excluded women from desires allowed to men, but expected them to be simultaneously innocent of sexuality, and on guard against it. Though Pope celebrates as well as condemns conspicuous consumption, he is also drawn to the shape-changing instabilities of materiality, as in the sylphs, for example. Interested in optics, Pope went to astronomy lectures: the science of seeing which exposed that what the eye could *not* see was kin to poetry, since poetry both discovered the appearances of the material world and fancifully depicted *un*real worlds. Where the metaphysical poet Donne was interested in comparative miniaturization of tears and globes, and Byron was later poignantly to compare stars and drops of ink as differently durable, Pope was fascinated by the evanescence of cultural forms in an era of innovation, corruption and change: 'And now a Bubble bursts, and now a World'. It makes his poetry surprisingly anxious and elegiac below the surface of order. For Rochester, 'a nothingness the ancients knew' was at least comforting in its continuity; for Pope, the evolution of modernity threatened irreparable rupture from the past.

The transitions between great and little in mock heroic show up physical differences of scale which raise the question of scales by which to measure moral values. Satire involved some agreement between writer and reader as to which scales were best and how to establish them. Pope conservatively evokes terms such as 'good nature', 'good humour' or 'good sense' (often rhymed with contrasting 'offence' or 'pretence'), as if they were self-evident. This approach becomes facile in his ▷ *Essay on Man* (1733–4) – 'Whatever is, is Right' – as arguments for an ordered universe and the limits of reason are sustained largely by smooth versification. Optimism drains away in his later satires: the four ▷ *Moral Essays* (1731–5) are addressed to exemplary figures whose virtues contrast with the follies and vices of contemporary individuals, historical figures and traditional types. In the ▷ *Imitations of Horace* (1733–8), Pope updates Horace but despairs of a society at best anarchic and at worst vicious. Hope is slenderly located in the community of poet and reader, provided the latter is capable of 'good taste', an alliance tested again in Pope's 1743 expanded version of *The Dunciad*, a mock epic about Grub Street's alleged threat to culture. 'Satire's my Weapon, but I'm too discreet / To run a Muck, and tilt at all I meet': Pope appears to oppose mediocrity fearlessly. However, as ▷ Colley Ciber, chief dunce in *The Dunciad*, pointed out with some dignity in his memoirs, not everyone shared Pope's definition of mediocrity. Moreover, although some writers mocked Pope for his small size, his spinal curvature and his ▷ Catholisism, in order to attack his Tory politics, not all the opposition to him was ill-founded. Pope had a talent for countering insult with feud' the effects of which made his anxieties about popular culture even harder to allay. He could be peevish and misogynist as well as an exceptionally elegant writer.

Pope's prominence tends to eclipse other poets, even Tory satirists, such as the densely topical Jonathan Swift, or Samuel Johnson, whose ▷ *London* (1738) and ▷ *The Vanity of Human Wishes* (1749) looked to Juvenal rather than Horace. Swift's *Verses on the Death of Dr Swift* (1739) were a Restoration-style joke, a mock elegy, but their mimicry of chat over cards expressed the 18th-century's interest in idiom, as well as its preoccupation with transcience. Swift's quatrains shaped irony more drily than couplets, but were used less. The couplet's compressions, comparisons and parallels suggested life as a process whose symmetries could only be provisionally stabilized. Like the ubiquitous use of irony, it suggested multiple meanings. The couplet's assurance was also useful for female and working-class poets. ▷ Mary Collier, a gardener's daughter and admirer of Pope, used it to take issue with Pope's negative views on women: 'Yet, with ten thousand follies to her charge, / Unhappy woman's but a slave at large' (*Essay on Woman*, 1746).

A number of critics pointed to the contribution of women in extending culture, but women repeatedly used tropes of ▷ slavery to describe their situation. As ▷ Sarah Egerton put it in 1703, 'Say, tyrant Custom, why we must obey / The impositions of thy haughty sway?' As Stuarts were replaced by Hanoverian dynasts, women reflected on how they were unable to change their rulers. However, many more women were writing. One particularly popular form was the epistle, where the mutual status of correspondents offered women temporary equality, with men as well as with each other. Where 17th-century epistles foregrounded friendship, 18th-century ones highlight writing as part of domestic activities. Johnson's gruff praise of Elizabeth Carter, that she could translate Epictetus and make a pudding, is acted out in women's poetry as they describe themselves 'scribbling' and running households. 'Often, from thoughts sublime as these, / I sink at once – and make a cheese', as Frances Seymour, Countess of Hertford, joked to her friend the Countess of Pomfret.

Some women achieved fame almost in spite of themselves. Lady Mary Wortley Montagu, though aristocratically reluctant to publish, was known as a wit. Her satires, some in collaboration with ▷ Lord John Hervey, prize subtlety: satire should 'like a polish'd Razor keen / Wound with a touch that's scarcely felt or seen'. Her *Town Eclogues* (1716) are thoughtful city pastorals, one of many generic mutations which followed from a quarrel between Pope and ▷ Ambrose Philips about the proper scope of pastoral. Philips' argument that life-like rural speech or activities could modernize pastoral was playfully taken up by Gay in his Spenserian cycle *The Shepherd's Week* (1714). It also became a game in which pastoral was given oxymoronic (▷ figures of speech) locations such as the city or seaside.

High-cultural figurations of landscape were often consciously literary, but open to intellectual enquiries of all sorts. In his Miltonic ▷ *The Seasons* (1726–30), ▷ James Thomson drew together science, geography, history, philosophy and theology to celebrate and explore the natural world. Like Pope an admirer of ▷ Newton, Thomson represents both science and poetry as tracing causes, describing effects and yielding beauty. Frost illustrates the process:

> *The nightly Sky*
> *And all her glowing Constellations, pour*
> *Their rigid Influence down: It freezes on*
> *Till Morn, late-rising, o'er the drooping World*
> *Lifts her pale Eye, unjoyous: then appears*
> *The various Labour of the silent Night,*
> *The pendant Isicle, the Frost-Work fair*
> *Where thousand Figures rise, the crusted Snow,*
> *Tho' white, made whiter by the fining North.*
>
> (*Winter*, 1726)

For all this poem's enthusiastic natural richness, the personifications which crowd it show how early 18th-century poetry is continuously *sociable*.

Poetry in context: 1740–1790

The 1740s have been described as a decade of literary loneliness, though women writers, likely to have isolation imposed on them for writing, continued to quest for community. Poetry is still peopled, but with the deceased, including Pope, to whom many tributes were written after his death in 1744. Fashionable poems – ▷ Edward Young's ▷ *Night Thoughts* (1742–5), ▷ Robert Blair's *The Grave* (1743), Lord Lyttleton's *Monody* on the death of his wife (1747) – all involved mortality, a trend neatly parodied in William Whitehead's *New Night Thoughts on Death* (1747): 'Stop, insatiate worm! / I feel thy summons: – to my fellow-worms / Thou bidd'st me hasten!

– I obey thy call, / For wherefore should I live?' Poems such as ▷ Thomas Parnell's *Night Piece on Death* (1721) had earlier considered how death levelled the already low:

> Those Graves, with bending osier bound,
> That nameless heave the crumbled ground,
> Quick to the glancing thought disclose
> Where Toil and Poverty repose.

In Thomas Gray's *Elegy Written in a Country Churchyard* thought lingered on the same nameless people's resting place:

> Far from the madding crowd's ignoble strife,
> Their sober wishes never learn'd to stray;
> Along the cool sequester'd vale of life
> They kept the noiseless tenor of their way.

Where previously poets picked out figures in crowds or sketched types, now they explored anonymity and rural community. As roads and canals improved, as ▷ travel and ▷ travel writing increased, and as publishing moved out of London, poetry became provincial, regional, exotic – almost anything but metropolitan, though town life still provided poetry with bustle.

This remoteness could be geographical or historical: for instance, in the *Persian Eclogues* (1742) and odes of ▷ William Collins, or Gray's odes *The Progress of Poesy* and ▷ *The Bard* (1757), which follow Thomson's interest in Druids, and commemorate imagination in native archetypes (▷ Welsh literature in English). The idea of the bard appealed as an image of a community poet with power: as John Brown explained in 1763, 'the Poet, though no longer a Legislator, may still occasionally exert his salutory Power, by his Influence on the Passions of the Soul'. Edward I's massacre of Welsh bards was represented almost nostalgically, since his persecution proved that poetry could have power. The bards' Celtic domains also meant a move to the margins, where Englishness was contested – literally, in the ▷ Jacobite Rebellion of 1745 and its aftermath. Northern material remained attractive in ballads, such as Jane Elliot's *The Flowers of the Forest* (1769), and Lady Anne Lindsay's *Auld Robin Gray* (1776). The distancing power of imagination itself was evoked by the controversy surrounding James MacPherson's epic fragments published under the name of ▷ Ossian, and allegedly discovered centuries after they were written. If truly discovered, the fragments would acquire historical lustre; if invented, then what they revealed would be inauthentic. This view does not express a simple suspicion of the imagination, but it supports antiquarian effort against flashy inspiration.

The commodification of poetry, partly represented by Ossian, reflected ambiguities about poetry's commercial possibilities: for instance, the footnotes which Gray strewed round his bardic poems can be seen as making his material both more and less accessible to a general readership. Controversy raged as to whether Ossian was genuine: Johnson and some others were sceptical; yet some like John Brown argued that no modern poet could come up with 'the grand Simplicity of Imagery and Diction, the strong Draughts of rude Manners and uncultivated Scenes of Nature, which abound in all these Poems'. Similar controversy surrounded the poems of ▷ Thomas Chatterton which he briefly passed off as the productions of a 15th-century monk, Thomas Rowley.

Bardic preoccupations gave way to more diverse regional interests, leading to experiments with dialect, best known in ▷ Robert Burns' poems, as in the address to a mouse whose nest had been turned up by the plough: 'Wee, sleeket, cowran, tim'rous beastie, / O, what a panic's in thy breastie!' (1785). Dialect also featured in some of the poems of Susannah Blamire, 'the Muse of Cumberland', and in the unusual poem by 'Ophelia', *Snaith Marsh. A Yorkshire Pastoral* (1754). ▷ Mary Leapor's *Crumble Hall* (1751) plays inventively with pastoral conventions; ▷ Oliver Goldsmith's ▷ *The Deserted Village* (1768) upholds them, despite addressing the effects of rural depopulation on 'Sweet Auburn! loveliest village of the plain'. Many poets attempted to reconcile pieties with social problems, but with variable success, leading ▷ George Crabbe to declare in *The Village* (1783) 'I paint the Cot, / As Truth will paint it, and as Bards will not'.

Much religious poetry of this period was not simply or sentimentally pious, but powerful, even violent. ▷ Christopher Smart's poems about the sacred bard, David, were admired for their elevated formality. His extraordinary *Jubilate Agno* (written 1759–61, but not published until 1939) brings together Biblical references and contemporary life in an idiolectic litany: 'Let Achsah rejoice with the Pigeon who is an antidote to malignity and will carry a letter. / For I bless God for the Postmaster General and all Conveyancers of letters under his care especially Allen and Sherlock.' More conventional liturgical pronouncements appeared in many hymns, which followed those of ▷ Isaac Watts a little earlier in the period: for instance, 'Christians, awake, salute the happy morn' ▷ (John Byrom), 'Rock of Ages, cleft for me' (Augustus Toplady), and 'God moves in a mysterious way' (William Cowper).

Where faith energized reason, reason also composed faith (visibly, in the quatrains of hymns.) Both were affected by the mid- to late- century's movement of ▷ sensibility, though since poetry had always been assumed to involve feeling, sensibility affected it less than prose. William Cowper's ▷ *The Task* (1785), written as therapy for periodic religious depression, brought the feeling mind and thinking heart together to form a poetic subjectivity which reflects on its world and narrates how that world relates to wider ones. Starting with a sofa, the poem turns expansively to books, people and the natural world, each of which contributes to poetic communication.

Fellow-feeling was promoted in a number of anti-slavery poems and in sympathy for various political struggles against tyranny. Such was *Corsica* by Anna Laetitia Aikin (later ▷ Barbauld) in 1773:

> There yet remains a freedom, nobler far
> Than kings or senates can destroy or give;
> Beyond the proud oppressor's cruel grasp
> Seated secure; uninjured; undestroyed;
> Worthy of gods: the freedom of the mind.

The ▷ American War of Independence attracted some interest – Anna Seward's *Monody on the Unfortunate Major André* (1781), lamenting the officer shot as a spy, was one of the poems which made its author prominent. The politics of ▷ William Blake's poems *The French Revolution* (1791) and *America* (1793) were overtly radical, despite their prophetic modes, since this was less ambiguous and dialectical than his symbolism in ▷ *Songs of Innocence and Experience* (1789; 1794).

With ideological tension increasing, moralist poets criticized mistaken sensibility: 'Tis not to mourn because a sparrow dies; To rave in artificial ecstasies', wrote ▷ Hannah More in 1782. But frivolous poetry prospered as well as the sublime: as Richard Tickell complained in 1778, 'The reigning fashion in modern poesy is *Sentimental Panegyric on Married Beauties*. This appears in a thousand various Shapes; from *Bouts Rhimées* on the *wou'd-be Sappho* of Bath, up to Doggerel Epistles to the lovely Amoret'. Provincial centres and spas, such as ▷ Bath, Tunbridge Wells, Brighthelmstone (as ▷ Brighton was then called), Cheltenham and Scarborough, provided renewable audiences. One such collection declared 'The subject of the verses written at these places of public and polite resort is generally Love and the Charms of the Fair.' There were exceptions: Christopher Anstey's constantly reprinted *New Bath Guide* (1766) mixed satire and sentiment in its epistles: thus one admirer asked, 'How came you by such an extraordinary gift / Thus to blend in one poem both YORICK and SWIFT?'

After 1740, then, some poets turned satiric and lyric energies into provincial forms. Politeness concerned cultural community rather than manners. Other poets tested the limits of nature-based genres, such as pastoral or descriptive poetry, to pursue sublime quests, escapist ideals or a more representative, gritty relation between social practices and poetry. But urbanity did not disappear: even as poets explored new areas, they continued to believe in poetry as communicative.

Modern criticism has invested heavily in the idea of ▷ Romanticism as a distinct literary era, and one whose aims and ideals are particularly associated with poetry. Late 20th-century criticism has taken a more flexible attitude perhaps to debates about dividing lines, arguing that there are multiple and sometimes competing ways of representing literary history. The map of women's poetry does not fit neatly onto that of men's. Likewise, categories of race and class, which are not necessarily the same across history, lead us to different views of literature. Historians are comfortable with the idea of a 'long 18th century', from 1660 to 1832, and the publication of ▷ Wordsworth and ▷ Coleridge's *Lyrical Ballads* in 1798 has at times been taken as the literary equivalent of the Great Reform Act in providing a convenient staging-post. But critical interest in cultural differences within periods has complicated literary history, and its relation to historical and cultural interpretation. There are many histories and many cultures involved. War, for example, was not central to the experience of all writers, but continuous conflict formed part of the public domain, and hence the public domain of poetry, from the wars against the Dutch in the 1660s and 1670s to the Napoleonic wars of the 1800s. So too imperial expeditions (▷ imperialism), colonial ventures (▷ colonialism), Grand Tours and voyages of exploration widened the horizons of some and brought oppression to others. Both war and travel stimulated literature's reflections upon national identity and modernity. Poetry's ready identification with conventions made it hospitable to conservative thought, but its association with imagination also made it the vehicle of challenging and progressive ideas.

In place of an old, reductive story of a simple opposition between reason and imagination, where Romanticism heralds the victory of the latter, recent criticism suggests that Romanticism involves responses to ideological developments precipitated particularly by the French Revolution. Similarly significant changes, particularly in the arenas of politics, religion and the economy, can be seen to be taking place from the late 17th century on. Poetry was actively engaged in these cultural transformations throughout the 18th century. In helping to engineer a dynamic cooperation between reason and passion, as well as a recognition of how they could at times contradict one another, poetry expressed one of the chief characteristics of the Enlightenment.

3

Market, morality and sentiment: non-dramatic prose 1660–1789

Janet Barron and David Nokes

No man but a blockhead ever wrote except for money
Samuel Johnson

Early prose and the origins of the novel

Secular, non-dramatic, writing in English dates back to the late 15th century and was already flourishing by the 16th. But its publication proliferated during the ▷ Civil War, when polemicists on both sides recognized the usefulness of widely distributed printed propaganda. Printing presses became cheap and relatively portable, and political ▷ pamphlets, ancestors of today's ▷ newspapers, multiplied. After the ▷ Restoration the presses continued to be used for religious and political propaganda, but also for a wide range of other secular writing, including ▷ broadsides, ▷ ballads, ▷ conduct books, books on cookery, and housewifery in general, and pamphlets on a vast range of topics, both serious and frivolous.

In addition, numerous fictional works were published, some of which look forward to the novel of the 18th century. Much ink has been spilled to determine the question of exactly where and how the novel began. As yet, no answer has emerged which seems universally acceptable. Some literary historians have looked back as far as Elizabethan writers of prose romance, such as Sidney, Nashe, Deloney, and Greene, for ancestors of the novel, or even referred to their stories as early novels. But more serious attention has been given to several post-Restoration works, including ▷ Aphra Behn's ▷ *Love Letters Between a Nobleman and his Sister* (1684–7), whose epistolary form (▷ epistolary novel) was widely taken up in the 18th century, by novelists including ▷ Richardson; and her ▷ *Oroonoko* (1688), whose first-person narrative, involving detailed accounts of the narrator-persona's own feelings in reaction to events, again anticipates many later works. Another important composition is ▷ Congreve's *Incognita: Or, Love and Duty Reconcil'd* (1691) which, in its playful irony, resembles the novels of ▷ Fielding. Congreve defined his own work as a novel, and in its Preface distinguished it from the earlier romance, arguing that novels, including his, 'are of a more familiar nature' than romances, and that 'Romances give more of wonder, novels more of delight'.

Most of the works described above were written for considerations other than financial gain. Some authors were inspired by passionate conviction, others by the desire to exert their influence through argument, others wrote for the sheer pleasure of the task, while others still were motivated by the simple authorial vanity of seeing the offsprings of their imagination bound up in folio or octavo volumes. A very few 17th-century writers, such as Behn, lived on the income from their writing. But it was the 18th century which really saw the emergence of the professional writer on a wide scale; the man or woman who wrote not as a genteel pastime, nor to flatter the self-esteem of a generous patron, but directly for money. For the first time, the spread of literacy, together with the emergence of commercial bookseller-publishers eager to feed the imaginations of an expanding reading public, made the trade of letters a viable, if not always lucrative, profession.

The literary market place

In the early years of the century most of the leading writers still relied more on institutional sinecures, or on a combination of public and private patronage, than on the literary market place for their support. ▷ Richard Steele was a Commissioner for stamps; William Congreve was nominally in charge of licensing hackney carriages; ▷ Daniel Defoe was a government spy; ▷ Jonathan Swift held the livings of two country parishes in Ireland; ▷ Joseph Addison was a career civil servant, finally achieving the position of Secretary of State.

Yet the qualifications required for entry to the professions excluded some authors who had to rely solely on the income from their writing. As a Catholic (▷ Catholicism), ▷ Alexander Pope was unable to hold public office, though he made a virtue of his social exclusion by celebrating his Twickenham retreat as a symbol of independence. His accomplished marketing of the subscription editions of his translations of ▷ Homer netted him an astonishing £10,000 (something in excess of £500,000 in today's terms). It was a commercial coup that other writers could only envy. By contrast, Swift was paid £200 for ▷ *Gulliver's Travels* (1726), and ▷ Oliver Goldsmith £60 for ▷ *The Vicar of Wakefield* (1761–2).

In recent years critical interpretations of 18th-century literature have increasingly questioned the traditional image of the period as an 'age of reason' (▷ rationalism), a peaceful haven of political stability and classical values. Recent studies have revealed the commercial realities that lay behind the ▷ classical façade of the 18th-century literary pantheon. By exploring the subculture of ▷ Grub Street, and by focusing attention on the many previously neglected women writers of the period, modern scholarship has provided a new perspective on this fascinating era in literary history, reminding us of the valuable contributions made by those excluded from the clubs and ▷ coffee-houses of the Augustan establishment.

Aphra Behn, debarred from the professions as a woman, attempted to attract state patronage by her political writings. The *Ode on the Coronation* would, she hoped, secure her a pension or a grace-and-favour house. But no money was forthcoming, and she turned instead to more lucrative markets for her talents in romantic fiction and theatrical comedies.

The career of ▷ Samuel Johnson demonstrates the precariousness of the literary life. Forced by poverty to abandon his studies at Oxford University, he thereby relinquished all hopes of a career in the law or the Church. After an unsuccessful attempt at school-teaching, he arrived in London, virtually penniless, and began to support himself by his writings. Regular contributions to ▷ *The Gentleman's Magazine* provided part of his income, yet his independent projects were also undertaken for commercial reasons. According to legend, ▷ *Rasselas* (1759) was written rapidly to pay the expenses of his mother's funeral; Johnson encouraged such stories as proof of his independence.

In 1755, at the culmination of his labours on the ▷ *Dictionary of the English Language*, Johnson delivered a celebrated epistolary snub to his self-styled patron, the ▷ Earl of Chesterfield: 'Is not a patron, my lord, one who looks with unconcern on a man struggling for life in the water and when he has reached ground encumbers him with help?' His letter is a declaration of literary independence that signals the end of the era of the private patron. Ironically, it was the commercial project of the *Dictionary* which brought Johnson academic recognition, as ▷ Oxford awarded him the degree he had been unable to obtain by more conventional means. In 1762, the award of a Crown pension of £300 a year relieved Johnson of some of the drudgery of ▷ hack work, though he was careful to insist that this was not a reward for political services, but a recognition of literary achievements.

Just before the start of the century, the lapsing of the Licensing Act in 1695 provided the opportunity for a massive expansion of the printing trade. Entrepreneurial publishers ranging from society figures like Jacob Tonson to Grub Street pirates like Edmund Curll played a vital, though sometimes unrecognized, part in shaping the literary culture of the 18th century. The 'Augustan Age' (▷ Augustanism)is often, and rightly, portrayed as a period when classical models and formal rules were of paramount literary importance; yet the commercial judgements of men like these were equally influential in promoting and developing the variety of 18th-century literature, with works ranging from translations of the classics to lurid ▷ Newgate yarns.

It was a time when, according to Martin Scriblerus (▷ Scriblerus Club) (alias Pope), 'paper became so cheap and printers so numerous that a deluge of authors cover'd the land'. What is remarkable about the prose writings of the 18th century, when compared with those of earlier centuries, is their sheer diversity. The rise of the novel and the development of ▷ periodical journalism are only the two most obvious features of this expansion of the literary market. Fabulous adventures (▷ fable), travellers' tales (▷ travel literature), secret histories, spiritual lives, satires, ▷ sermons, ▷ pastorals and panegyrics and works of every conceivable style and tone, calculated to appeal to all ▷ tastes and pockets, rolled from the presses. The pages of Pope's ▷ *Dunciad* are filled with the names of forgotten Grub Street authors, such as Ned Ward, ▷ Eliza Haywood and ▷ Charles Gildon, many of whom eked out a precarious living in the kind of literary sweat-shops hilariously described by Henry Fielding in his play *The Author's Farce* (1730).

Establishment authors, like Pope and Swift, frequently deplored the promiscuous vitality of this new literary world, forseeing the death of civilized values in publishers' lists as the works of classical authors were outnumbered by the ephemeral products of those whom they dubbed the 'moderns' or 'dunces' (▷ The Battle of the Books). The novelists themselves often appeared embarrassed at their own imaginative freedom, prefacing their works with statements which sought to legitimize the seductive appeal of fiction by appealing to some external authority. In referring to his early novels as 'comic epics in prose' Fielding endeavoured to claim a niche for them in the traditional classical pantheon. ▷ Defoe preferred to describe his tales as 'true histories', faking his fictions to read like facts, and filling in the broad sweeps of his adventure stories with minute circumstantial details. To Samuel Richardson, the only justification for fiction was its clear commitment to moral reform, and he presented his novels as exemplary parables in which vice is routed and virtue rewarded. Yet even the sternest critics of literary self-indulgence found the lure of fictional licence irresistible. Swift's ▷ *A Tale of a Tub* (1704) is among other things a satire on the ephemerality of modern culture. 'I have remarked,' says the *Tale*'s narrator, 'that nothing is so very tender as a modern piece of wit'. But, while affecting to deplore this cultural perishability, Swift revels in the world of literary ephemera, turning topical tit-bits into enduring metaphors (▷ figures of speech) for human vanity.

Thus to speak of 'the rise of the novel' in the early 18th century, as if assuming that by then the novel had attained a clear, recognizable identity, is somewhat misleading. There was no single literary genre which sprang fully formed to life with the publication of ▷ *Robinson Crusoe* in 1719. Instead, a variety of contrasting fictional forms competed for attention, ranging from the vivid Grub Street pseudo-biographies (▷ biography) published in the down-market *Applebee's Journal* (1715–36), to witty anecdotal sketches of the ▷ Coverley family presented in ▷ *The Spectator* (1712); or from salacious secret histories, such as ▷ Delariviè Manley's *The New Atalantis* (1709) to satiric fantasies, such as Swift's *Gulliver's Travels*. As late as 1711 ▷ *The Tatler* was still using the word 'novelist' to mean a newspaperman. In much the same way Johnson's *Dictionary* continued to define 'journal' as 'any paper published daily', whereas most of the periodicals so described were not in fact daily publications. In both cases it is clear that the regulatory constraints of etymology had little inhibiting influence on the dynamic growth of the genres themselves. For, despite the Augustan predilection for ▷ neo-classical rules and critical categories, the novel, like ▷ journalism, grew up happily innocent of prescriptive theories. Indeed, the emergence of the novel form in the early 18th century, which often appears an inevitable consequence of changing social conditions, can equally well be presented as the result of a series of felicitous accidents. Defoe was almost 60, and nearing the end of an indefatigably varied career during which he had tried his hand at innumerable forms of business enterprise (all failures) as well as journalism and espionage, when he published *Robinson Crusoe*. Fielding was a celebrated young playwright until ▷ Sir Robert Walpole's introduction of stage censorship with the new Licensing Act of 1737 (▷ theatres) forced him to find an alternative outlet for his literary talents. Richardson was a successful printer, whose decision to turn author was partly inspired by a prudent desire to utilize the spare capacity of his press. This process of 'serendipity', a word coined by ▷ Horace Walpole, continued throughout the century, and it was Walpole's own fortuitous success with his fantasy ▷ *The Castle of Otranto* (1764) which inspired the later vogue for ▷ Gothic fiction.

The career and reputation of Daniel Defoe offers some useful insights into one type of literary enterprise. The son of a Dissenting tallow-chandler, he was a lifelong bankrupt, a tireless entrepreneur and a prolific journalist whose collected works would fill several hundred volumes. For nine years, from 1704 to 1713 he wrote single-handedly his thrice-weekly journal ▷ *The Review*; for much of the same period he was also one of the government's leading spies, sending back secret reports from Edinburgh on the political manoeuvring surrounding the negotiations for the Act of ▷ Union between England and Scotland in 1707. Simultaneously, he was also striving to extricate himself from massive debts, and contriving to stay out of the hands of his many creditors. In both his business ventures and his journalism one finds the same spirit of brinkmanship, the same flirting with disaster. The energy and excitement of his writings co-exist with a kind of literary carelessness and an apparent impatience with more studied effects which led on occasions to disaster. His ironic pamphlet *The Shortest Way with Dissenters* (1702), which counterfeited the violent language of a High ▷ Church zealot, backfired badly when its irony was mistaken for incitement, and Defoe was sentenced to punishment at the pillory. More recently, critics have reassessed the apparent carelessness of Defoe's writing, finding in it the poker-face of a more accomplished literary gamesmanship. The 'failure' of *The Shortest Way* succeeded in exposing the covert menace of High Church policies in a way that more conventional irony (▷ figure of speech) could not have achieved. Similar subtleties may be detected in the 'mistakes' and contradictions which abound in Defoe's novels. Generations of readers have noted the glaring contradictions between what characters say in one part of a novel, and how they behave elsewhere. Well on in her narrative ▷ Moll Flanders is seized by a sudden maternal instinct and delivers a sober lecture on the depravity of mothers who neglect or abandon their offspring. Yet by this stage she herself has happily abandoned innumerable children of her own without a word or a qualm. Her flair for criminality is accompanied by a constant moral patter as she alternately presents herself as a victim of circumstances and an agent of social education. The unconvincingness of her final 'repentance', which conveniently allows her to retire in comfort on her ill-gotten gains, has often appeared to undermine the novel's moral seriousness. Contradictions like these – and there are many other celebrated examples in all the novels – have often been taken as evidence of a slap-dash journeyman approach to the business of authorship. Yet the pattern of these contradictions, in which characters preach like ▷ Puritan moralists yet act like ruthless opportunists, goes to the heart of Defoe's fiction. For all their concentration on mundane details, his novels are fantasies of survival, heroic adventures of social mobility in which individuals single-handedly confront and conquer a host of adverse circumstances. Despite the apparent crudity of their episodic narratives, Defoe's novels are animated by a quality more usually identified with a more self-consciously sophisticated form of fiction, in the characters of his unreliable narrators.

Likewise the unravelling of Jonathan Swift's ironies has been the key to the 20th-century reappraisal of his status as a writer. Earlier critics such as Thackeray viewed his writings as misanthropic and malign: 'A monster gibbering shrieks, and gnashing imprecations against mankind – tearing down all shreds of modesty, past all sense of manliness and shame; filthy in word, filthy in thought, furious, raging, obscene.'

Judgements like these derive from the tendency to identify Swift with the narrators of his satires, seeing in Gulliver's hysterical reaction to the ▷ Yahoos a representation of Swift's supposed alienation from humanity. But Swift is the master of literary disguises, and his chosen narrators are utopians or fanatics, projectors or madmen whose plausible rhetoric of half-truths lead inexorably to such savage conclusions as the eating of babies or the abandonment of human society in favour of life in a stable. As a satirist, Swift aims primarily at the irrational ▷ utopianism which founds its hopes of progress on a refusal to acknowledge the perversities and flaws of human nature itself. From ▷ *A Tale of a Tub* (1704), with its ironic epigraph 'Written for the Universal Improvement of Mankind', to the

Academy of Lagado in *Gulliver's Travels*, whose scientists are engaged in projects to produce sunbeams out of cucumbers, Swift ridicules the visionary enthusiasm which finds inspiration in the belchings of a fanatical preacher, and sublime wisdom in the neighing of a horse.

Born and educated in ▷ Ireland, Swift took holy orders and became a clergyman in the Church of Ireland. Yet he spent most of Queen ▷ Anne's reign in London, pursuing an alternative career as a political journalist. His ▷ *Examiner* articles and his pamphlet *The Conduct of the Allies* (1711) provided a magisterial defence of the Tory government's policy for ending the war with France, and even today offer excellent models of the art of political journalism. Forced to return to his native land on the death of Queen Anne, Swift felt like a virtual exile, and it was several years before he could bring himself to relaunch his journalistic career with a series of powerful pamphlets deploring the miserable economic plight of Ireland. His most celebrated pamphlet, ▷ *A Modest Proposal* (1729), ironically recommends that the people of Ireland should rear their children as food for the tables of their English landlords. The scheme has a savage logic; it is methodically costed, and the arguments are financially flawless. With its plausible phrases and deadpan tone, this satire is a brilliant indictment of a society in which economic exploitation has abnegated the natural ties of humanity and love.

While it is undoubtedly true that Swift's satires dwell on the darker side of human nature, his love of jokes, riddles and *jeux d'esprit* should not be forgotten. From his *Bickerstaff Papers* (1708–9) to his *Directions to Servants* (published posthumously in 1745), a spirit of mischievous and subversive anarchy runs through all his writings. In his most famous poem *Verses on the Death of Dr Swift* (1731), he provided his own obituary, declaring, among other things, that 'fair liberty was all his cry'. The liberty that Swift cherished was less political than intellectual and his satires offer a consistent challenge to our own reasoning powers to find a way through the maze of utopian delusions and political lies.

'The female wits'

At one point in her career, Delarivière Manley worked as Swift's assistant on *The Examiner*, taking over from him as editor in 1711. Manley was already notorious for salacious society scandals: *The Secret History of Queen Zarah* (1705), using the device of a fictional history to avoid prosecution, was an instant success, with its separately published key revealing the code names. In 1709 a further *roman à clef*, *The New Atalantis*, continued this combination of transparent allegory and sexual innuendo. The Whig ministry, worried by her revelations, issued a warrant for the arrest of printer, publisher and author, and Manley was required to name her informers. Exploiting the ambiguities of fictions-as-facts, she declared her only source was divine inspiration. Her reputation as an erotic scandalmonger contributed to the stereotype of the immoral female author. Pope's image of the Grub Street hacks and booksellers as literary whores and pimps takes on further implications in the light of Manley's own life; supplementing her income by a series of affairs, she eventually became the mistress of Alderman Barber, her publisher.

Women writers anxious to avoid such notoriety often published their works anonymously, or prefaced them with humble pleas that they were written in distress. And, though scandalous works sold well, novels which conformed to social mores were more widely acceptable as serious literary efforts. The decline of the patronge system made a clear distinction between the aristocratic lady writing as a graceful accomplishment, and the woman who went against the nature of her sex and engaged in disreputable trade.

Even writers with no literary ambitions tailored their products to the changing literary tastes. Eliza Haywood's early works were titillating confections, and *Love in Excess* (1719) was, with *Robinson Crusoe* and *Gulliver's Travels*, one of the three best-selling works before Samuel Richardson's ▷ *Pamela* (1740–41). But by the 1740s and 1750s, Haywood took on a new tone of conventional conformity, and the 'women's novel' became increasingly associated with the values of hearth and home. It was a compromise which allowed the critic both to praise women for their delicate understanding, and to confine them to 'feminine' gentility which could be disparaged as frivolous.

Similar arguments were often advanced in condescending appraisal of some of the more chatty periodicals. Swift was in no doubt as to the main audience for ▷ Addison's ▷ *Spectator* when he remarked, 'let them fair-sex it to the world's end', and Eliza Haywood exploited this market with the launch of ▷ *The Female Spectator* (1744–6). If anything, Addison seems rather to have relished than repudiated his paper's reputation as providing a genteel education of ladies. When he boasted of taking philosophy out of the schools and colleges, and into 'clubs and assemblies, tea tables and coffee-houses', he made explicit the intention to mingle morality and manners, philosophy and fashion, in an urbane and witty miscellany. And despite a tinge of polite condescension in the tone of its more lightweight contributions, *The Spectator* was remarkably successful in maintaining a style of well-mannered wit. There was, however, a serious side to this endeavour to promote the refined tone and rational debate of coffee-house society to a wider reading public. In the previous century, the Puritan moralist and the fashionable ▷ Cavalier had stood on opposite sides in the ▷ Civil War. Addison and Steele endeavoured to heal this breach, by putting a smile on the face of morality, and restraining the more licentious habits of town rakes and courtly roués. In the genial atmosphere of a fictitious Spectator club, the Whig merchant Sir Andrew Freeport and the Tory squire Sir Roger de Coverley could discuss their differences over a glass of port rather than settling them on the battlefield. One form of anti-social behaviour that Addison particularly deplored was the writing of satires, which he described as 'poisoned darts' that gave 'secret stabs to a man's reputation'. In *The Spectator* he promised he would never 'draw a faulty character which does not fit at least a thousand people, or publish a single paper that is not written in the spirit of benevolence, with love to mankind'.

However, it was the growing popularity of the novel rather than Addison's benevolent pieties which gradually killed off the vogue for satire in the middle years of the century. In broad terms, one might say that satire deals essentially with types, whereas the novel presents us with individuals. 18th-century satire is concerned less with the redemption of individual sinners than with the regulation of general standards of conduct. But the novel, particularly under the influence of Richardson, was more interested in questions of moral identity and the expression of individual consciousness. The distinction between the two genres is not always as clear-cut as this might imply. When in ▷ *Joseph Andrews* (1742) Henry Fielding declares 'once for all, I describe not men but manners; not an individual, but a species', he writes as both satirist and novelist. In the preface to that book, he draws a distinction between comic fiction and satire, and like ▷ *Shamela* (1741), the first ten chapters comprise a burlesque satire on Samuel Richardson's *Pamela*. It is only after this point in the novel that Fielding attempts to transform Joseph's chastity from an absurd parody of Pamela's much vaunted virtue into a mark of fidelity for his beloved Fanny. Similarly, ▷ *Jonathan Wild* (1743), with its consistent ironic attacks on 'greatness', might be regarded more as an extended lampoon than as a novel. It is not until ▷ *Tom Jones* (1749) that Fielding finally achieved his own distinctive form of comic fiction though that novel too contains many incidental satiric and parodic moments.

In Johnson's view there was as great a difference between the literary talents of Richardson and Fielding 'as between a man who knew how a watch was made, and a man who could tell the hour by looking on the dial plate'. Although the terms of the relative judgements have sometimes altered, the temptation to draw comparisons between the literary achievements of these two men has persisted ever since. As authors, they embody two rival traditions of the English novel, appearing as contending 'fathers' of the novel, each disputing the legitimacy of the other's offspring. From Fielding we derive the tradition of comic fiction, a style of writing that revels in its own vivacity and wit, offering its readers a rich and varied diet of social comedy, urbane irony and literary sophistication. From Richardson we derive the novel of moral introspection and psychological insight; his epistolary style offers a kind of fictional confessional dramatizing the dilemmas of individual moral choice.

The morality of *Tom Jones* is based on a simple antithetical contrast: natural instinct versus social hypocrisy, goodness of heart versus cunning of head. Part of the satisfaction of the book comes from the combination of the formal symmetry of its structure (▷ Coleridge referred to it as one of the three best plots ever written) with the apparent freedom and randomness of its ▷ picaresque episodes. In the same way, Tom's artless and impulsive vitality is made acceptable by the artful manipulations of the narrator's tone.

Pamela, Richardson's inspired first-person narrative of a young servant girl's triumph over repeated attempts at seduction by her employer, was an immediate commercial success. 'If all the books in England were to be burnt, this book, next the Bible, ought to be preserved', enthused one reader. Nowadays its reputation is less secure. Modern readers are apt to side with Fielding in regarding its notorious subtitle, 'Virtue Rewarded', as evidence that Pamela is a model of policy rather than purity.

Richardson's next novel, ▷ *Clarissa* (1747–8), is an undisputed literary masterpiece. Again using the epistolary form, Richardson interweaves four narrative voices to construct a novel of great psychological complexity. In its treatment of the contradictions between 'virtue' as reputation and virginity as an extension of moral integrity, Richardson highlights the social hypocrisies where the marriage market puts a high price on maidenhood. Anne Howe, Clarissa's friend, urges the conventional solution of marrying the seducer, but Clarissa follows the path of self-imposed martyrdom. The novel escapes any simplistic morality, reverberating beyond a reductive summary.

The distinction which Johnson drew between the novels of Fielding and those of Richardson, was reapplied by Richardson himself to the novels of ▷ Sarah Fielding, Henry Fielding's sister. Johnson and Richardson both encouraged Sarah Fielding to publish her work. Her best-known novel, *The Adventures of David Simple* (1744), provides a notable contrast to the male novelists' treatment of female characters. Where Pamela and Clarissa struggle with threatening seducers, Sarah Fielding's heroines wryly recognize sexual harassment as a part of the social structure.

It was the development of the ▷ circulating libraries in the later decades of the century which provided the largest market for the mass of novelistic fiction. Many critics were alarmed by the proliferation of light romantic fiction which resulted from these cheaper sources of entertainment. 'This branch of the literary trade', one reviewer remarked, 'appears, now, to be almost entirely engrossed by women.' The naive country girl who has her head turned by these frothy fantasies became a stock figure of fictional stereotypes. From ▷ Richard Brinsley Sheridan's Lydia Languish to ▷ Jane Austen's Catherine Morland, the harmful effects on the uneducated *ingenue* were a favourite topic for literary parody. In ▷ Charlotte Lennox's *The Female Quixote* (1752), the heroine, Arabella, turns from the sterner labours of her father's study to while away her hours with her mother's library, a collection of lengthy French romances which she mistakes for historical accounts. By creating an ironic distance between the heroine and the narrator, Lennox uses this familiar theme to make a social comment on women's education. ▷ Fanny Burney's major novels also focus on the entry of the *ingenue* into a potentially corrupting society. ▷ *Evelina* (1778) uses the epistolary narrative of a woman asking her male mentor for advice. *Cecilia* (1782), her most successful novel, shows an intelligent but naive girl tricked out of her inheritance by an exploitative friend's husband. In drawing attention to the dangers faced by the good-natured but ill-advised heroine Burney contributes to the social debate on the status of women, using the novel as an entertaining medium of discussion.

Sentiment and sensation

In the second half of the century two new styles of writing became suddenly fashionable and all but dominated the fiction market. The first of these was the ▷ sentimental novel. 'What, in your opinion, is the meaning of the word *sentimental*, so much in vogue among the polite?' Lady Bradshaigh asked Richardson. 'I am frequently astonished to hear such a one is a sentimental man; we were a sentimental party; I have been taking a sentimental walk.' Some twenty years later the ▷ Methodist ▷ John Wesley continued to protest against the word as a meaningless foreign neologism. 'Sentimental? What is that? It is not English; he might as well say Continental. It is not sense. It conveys no determinate idea.' Probably the most celebrated of sentimental novels was Henry Mackenzie's *The Man of Feeling* (1771) in which the tears of the hero, Harley, flow freely throughout the narrative. As a benevolent innocent with the most delicate ▷ sensibility, Harley is constantly cheated, deceived and hurt by the more worldly figures he encounters; yet his sufferings carry with them a *tendresse* of pleasure; his humiliations discover the exquisite sensations of injured integrity. Towards the end of the novel his apparently unrequited love for Miss Watson results in his physical decline until, on his deathbed, she reveals her love for him and he dies of sheer happiness. A similar pattern of innocent suffering can be found in Goldsmith's *The Vicar of Wakefield* (published 1766) which presents a parallel confrontation between naive benevolence and unscrupulous power. Goldsmith's vicar, Primrose, is a man who takes his 'consummate benevolence' to 'a romantic extreme'. With an authentically sentimental relish for the moral authority of suffering, Goldsmith dwells on the vicar's 'pleasing distress' at the repeated trials and tragedies heaped upon him by Thornhill, the malicious libertine squire.

Mackenzie's novel was an immediate best-seller. ▷ Burns wore out two copies of the work, calling it 'a book I prize next to the Bible'. Johnson was less impressed, commenting scornfully on 'the fashionable whine of sensibility'. In 1773 ▷ Mrs Barbauld offered a psychological justification for this type of fiction in her *Inquiry into the kind of distress which exerts agreeable sensations*, emphasizing the evocation of a sympathetic tenderness on the part of the reader. 'Tenderness,' she wrote, 'is, much more properly than sorrow, the spring of tears.'

For modern readers the best-known fictional example of the cult of sensibility is in fact a partial parody of the genre. ▷ Laurence Sterne's ▷ *A Sentimental Journey through France and Italy* (1768) exploits many features of the sentimental style, yet does so with a tone of ironic self-consciousness that constantly trembles on the brink of satire. Like Mackenzie's Man of Feeling whose face is bathed in tears while listening to another's tale of woe, Sterne's ▷ Yorick, hearing of the death of a monk to whom he had behaved uncharitably, 'bursts into a flood of tears'. But whereas Harley's tears are the sign of his refined sensibility, Yorick's tears are produced with a sudden and comic exaggeration. Yorick is a virtuoso of the nervous system, conjuring up both tears and blushes with a facility which testifies less to his goodness of heart than to his incorrigible instinct for self-dramatization. Sterne's masterpiece, ▷ *Tristram Shandy* (1760–7), is another teasing work whose success transformed Sterne from an obscure Yorkshire clergyman into a leading literary celebrity, but whose eccentricities have divided critical opinion ever since. Johnson declared 'nothing odd will do long; *Tristram Shandy* did not last', but a formalist critic in our own century has asserted that '*Tristram Shandy* is the most typical novel of world literature'.

'In a word, my work is digressive, and it is progressive too, – and at the same time', announces Tristram in the book's first volume. It is significant that he puts the word 'digressive' first. With its black and marbled pages, its flash-backs and interpolations, its asterisks, blanks and dashes, *Tristram Shandy* is a novel which denies any conventional notions of narrative development. The first four volumes take place while Tristram, the hero/narrator, is still in the womb, and the book ends before it begins. Yet this work, which seems to break all the rules, and which consistently demonstrates the inability of rules, plans, theories and systems to cope with the accidents and vagaries of human life, is nevertheless held together by a curious pseudo-logic of its own. This is the absurd determinism of the association of ideas, as expressed in ▷ Locke's ▷ *Essay Concerning Human Understanding* (1690), which Tristram describes as 'a history-book of what passes in a man's own mind'. Each of Sterne's characters, Walter, Toby and Trim, is locked in his own private world of associations; their conversations present the collisions of words rather than the communication of thoughts; their actions are all bounded by accident.

Beside the inventiveness of Sterne, the more conventional comic skills of ▷ Tobias Smollett may seem stolid and predictable. Trained as a surgeon, Smollett published his first and some would say his best novel, ▷ *Roderick Random*, in 1748, when he was still only 26. Like all Smollett's novels, this work is a robust picaresque, episodic in form, slapstick in humour and brisk in pace. Some of its best moments are autobiographical, drawing on Smollett's own experience as a ship's surgeon. His next novel, ▷ *Peregrine Pickle* (1751), also has a nautical flavour, with its collection of old sea-dog characters such as Commodore Hawser Trunnion and the peglegged Lieutenant Hatchway. His final novel, ▷ *Humphry Clinker* (1771), is epistolary in form though the tone owes more to Fielding than to Richardson. In it a group of assorted characters including the irascible old valetudinarian Matthew Bramble and a Methodist coachman Humphry Clinker (who turns out to be Bramble's son) make a grand tour of ▷ Britain from Bristol, ▷ Bath and ▷ London, to ▷ Edinburgh and the ▷ Highlands, presenting us with a broad panorama of 18th-century society. The idiomatic clashes of the different ▷ letter-writing styles provide a constant ▷ humorous tone, and the book is rich in comic misadventures, though the plot itself is highly derivative. As one recent critic has written, 'it is as though Tom Jones has given way to Baedeker.'

The other fictional form which enjoyed considerable popularity in the later decades of the century was the Gothic novel. In terms of the market place, the date at which the Richardsonian novel of moral instruction began to give way to the Gothic novel of crepuscular phantoms can be pinpointed with some accuracy. In 1777 ▷ Clara Reeve published a novel called *The Champion of Virtue*, a title which clearly suggests a continuation of Richardsonian preoccupations. The following year, however, she reissued the same novel in a revised form and with a new title, *The Old English Baron, A Gothic Story*, evidently attempting to exploit the new trend in public tastes. However, the origins of the Gothic novel are usually traced back to Horace Walpole's *The Castle of Otranto*, a self-indulgent fantasy of fake ▷ medievalism which deliberately revels in its extravagant use of supernatural and 'marvellous' elements. One recent critic (Pat Rogers) has written: '*The Castle of Otranto* is preposterous; its setting is Hollywood-medieval, a Ruritanian version of chivalric times. Its plot is frankly incredible, jumpily constructed and flatly recounted.' Yet much of the novel's overt implausibility is a calculated device to move away from the classical symmetries and rational morality of Augustan literature. Walpole was a fashionable dilettante whose spirit of whimsicality led him to create his 'little Gothic castle' at ▷ Strawberry Hill, and also inspired this little Gothic tale. Like the young ill-fated poet ▷ Thomas Chatterton, who passed off his 'Rowley' poems as genuine medieval manuscripts, and the fraudulent ▷ James Macpherson who claimed to be 'translating' his pastiche ▷ Celtic epic ▷ *Ossian*, Walpole at first maintained a pretence that *The Castle of Otranto* was an authentic medieval story. For all of these writers, medievalism was a kind of fancy-dress, enabling them to evade the sober responsibilities of neo-classical literary forms and indulge their imaginations in a world of supernatural fantasy. For the Gothic novel entailed a reversal or rejection of many classical values. Instead of Pope's cherished landscape of 'Nature methodiz'd' with its well-proportioned country houses and Palladian villas, the Gothic landscape consists of dark forests and ruined castles, with gloomy dungeons and secret labyrinthine passageways. In place of the daylight world of rational debate and urbane ironies, Gothic fiction presents a nightmare world of torture and fantasies, irrational fears, ancient curses and nameless threats.

Gothic fiction can be divided into two broad categories, the novel of terror and the novel of horror. Practitioners of the novel of terror, from Clara Reeve to ▷ Ann Radcliffe, were interested in using the Gothic form as a means of exploring the psychology of fear. In her most famous novel, ▷ *The Mysteries of Udolpho* (1794), Radcliffe described the effect of terror on the mind: 'A terror of this nature, as it occupies and expands the mind, and elevates it to a high expectation, is purely sublime, and leads us, by a kind of fascination, to seek even the object from which we appear to shrink.' Echoing here some of the sentiments in ▷ Burke's treatise *On the Sublime and the Beautiful* (1759), Radcliffe also demonstrates an affinity with ▷ Wordsworth who, in *The Prelude* (1799–1805), describes how he 'grew up /

Fostered alike by beauty and by fear'. In fact all of the apparently supernatural phenomena in Radcliffe's novels turn out to have perfectly rational, if somewhat contrived, explanations; the ghostly, diabolic presences that haunt her heroines are invariably products of illusionist trickery working on terrified imaginations. Unlike some other Gothic writers, Radcliffe has a perfect control of her plots, and part of the appeal of her novels lies in the ingenuity with which she supplies psychologically convincing explanations for the most apparently mysterious events. Nor is this merely a thriller-writer's gimmick. Radcliffe is interested in the gradations of intimidation and characteristically explores two related levels of fear. The abbeys, castles, dungeons and convents where her heroines find themselves are always reputedly cursed or haunted. Consequently when nocturnal apparitions occur, her heroines are thrown into the kind of superstitious dread satirized by Jane Austen in *Northanger Abbey* (published 1818). But typically, in the morning these imaginary terrors are replaced by a yet more insidious fear, as the heroines gradually realize that they are at the mercy not of ghosts and goblins, but of malevolent human beings. It is some indication of the popularity of Gothic fiction that Radcliffe earned £500 for *The Mysteries of Udolpho*, whereas Jane Austen was paid only £10 for her parody of the genre in *Northanger Abbey*.

A good example of the novel of horror is Matthew 'Monk' Lewis's *The Monk* (1796), which Byron described as representing 'the philtered ideas of a jaded voluptuary'. In this extravagant sadistic fantasy Lewis exploits all the charnel-house images that have since become the cliches of Hammer horror films. His heroine, Agnes, having been separated from her lover, is condemned to perpetual incarceration among rotting corpses in the vaults beneath her convent. With undisguised relish Lewis pictures bloated toads and slimy lizards crawling across her flesh and describes how, on waking, Agnes would often find 'my fingers ringed with the long worms which bred in the corrupted flesh of my infant'. The monk Ambrosio, the villain of the novel, crowns a career of vice by raping and killing Antonia, a 15-year-old girl, among these rotting bodies in the vault, having already murdered her mother Elvira. In order to escape the soldiers of the Inquisition, Ambrosio sells his soul to the Devil, who transports him to a mountain peak. There, before being hurled to his death, he is told that Elvira was in fact his mother, and Antonia his sister. Yet this conclusion is less a form of moral retribution, than a final gloating irony in this lurid sensationalist tale.

Loosely based on Arabian sources, ▷ William Beckford's *Vathek* (French edition 1782, English edition 1787) is another orgiastic tale of hedonism, sorcery and murder, that culminates in damnation. Although Beckford's work, like Lewis's, is filled with a self-indulgent horror, this aspect of Gothic fiction also has its serious side. Throughout the Gothic literature of the late 18th and early 19th centuries, writers as diverse as Beckford, James Hogg (*The Private Memoirs and Confessions of a Justified Sinner*, 1824) and Mary Shelley (*Frankenstein*, 1817) explored Faustian themes and Satanic images that represented the dark side of ▷ Enlightenment thought.

Non-fictional prose

Modern critical tastes have tended to value fiction above other kinds of prose writing, but in the 18th century this was not always the case. Many of the century's most gifted prose stylists wrote not novels but ▷ histories and ▷ biographies, essays, travel books and letters. Apart from the fact that many novels were written in epistolary form and that several of Pope's satires were couched in the form of epistles, the familiar letter was itself a well-respected literary genre. Pope felt no more compunction about altering and polishing his personal correspondence for publication than he did about revising and changing his different versions of ▷ *The Rape of the Lock* or ▷ *The Dunciad*. For him, these letters were less autobiographical documents than parts of his literary *oeuvre*, to be edited and revised in the same way as any other work. Among the more notable letter-writers of the period were ▷ Lady Mary Wortley Montagu, Horace Walpole and the ▷ Earl of Chesterfield. Montagu's letters are witty, jaunty and civilized, with just an edge of malicious satire to give them bite. They reflect a life of rich variety; at the age of seven, Montagu was the infant favourite of the ▷ Kit-Cat Club; during her marriage she travelled throughout Europe and Turkey, finally retiring to live in Italy. Her letters are full of perceptive comments on the customs of the countries she visits, always animated by a tone of self-deprecating irony. Thus to one correspondent she comments, 'this letter is as long and as dull as any of Richardson's!'.

Horace Walpole was a prolific and assiduous letter writer, of whom it has been said that he organized his life to suit the needs of his correspondence. Self-consciously arranging both the occasions and the recipients of each letter, Walpole constructed a correspondence which suggests a life devoted to the delivery of *bon mots* and an experience translated into a seamless sequence of anecdotes. The Earl of Chesterfield's letters have fared least well with later readers. Their complacent tone of worldly wisdom seems designed to recommend a life of superficial elegance at the expense of more serious or humane concerns. Yet Chesterfield's notions of civilized life derive from a tradition initiated by *The Spectator* and his constant stress upon politeness and the social graces offers a useful insight into a significant strand of 18th-century thought.

Among biographers, ▷ James Boswell still holds pride of place. Although later scholars have revealed his ▷ *Life of Samuel Johnson* (1791) to be full of distortions and omissions, its quality of animation, dramatizing Johnson's oracular wit and sober sentiments in a lively series of encounters and anecdotes, captures much of his relish for conversation, for disputation and for life. Boswell's own journals, though full of the vanity of self-display, stand alongside ▷ Samuel Pepys' *Diary* and Swift's *Journal to Stella* as fascinating portraits of the day-to-day excitement of social life; all of these works weave together intimate private dramas with vivid representations of social and public issues.

Perhaps least often read now are the great works of Augustan scholarship: ▷ Edward Gibbon's ▷ *The Decline and Fall of the Roman Empire* (1776–88), the philosophical writings of Locke and ▷ Hume, Burke and ▷ Adam Smith. All of these in their different ways share certain humanist assumptions that are common to the literature of the period. Although each pursued a separate discipline of study, these authors thought of their works not as specialist treatises for students, but as philosophical essays designed for the educated general reader. While never amateurish or condescending, they are works which, in both style and tone, assume the centrality of their concerns to be human culture as a whole. As such they are expressions of that Enlightenment spirit which sought to promote the pursuit of knowledge not in the sheltered confines of universities and colleges, but in the coffee-houses, clubs and country houses of a civilized society. Johnson gave memorable expression to such sentiments. At the conclusion of the preface to his *Dictionary of the English Language* he writes: 'It may gratify curiosity to inform it that the *English Dictionary* was written with little assistance of the learned, and without any patronage of the great; not in the soft obscurities of retirement, or under the shelter of academic bowers, but amidst inconvenience and distraction, in sickness and in sorrow.' The name of Johnson has recurred several times throughout this essay, and that is hardly surprising. No one better exemplifies the achievements and anxieties, the triumphs and tribulations of the professional writer of his day. Johnson turned the life of writing into a kind of moral struggle against bigotry and ignorance, against poverty, prejudice and pretensions. Some of his more celebrated utterances may appear dogmatic or prescriptive, but this is a false impression resulting in part from Boswell's creation of him as a man of maxims. In fact, the most enduring characteristic of Johnson's writing is its tolerance in the patient exploration of the complexities and fallibilities of human nature. In his ▷ *Lives of the Poets* (1779–81) he combines balanced judgements with personal pronouncements, in assessing the writers of his own and the previous age. In *Rasselas* (1759) and in the ▷ *Vanity of Human Wishes* (1749), he explores that 'hunger of the imagination' which both fuels the creative impulse, and leads to the inevitable insufficiency of human desires. In his *Preface to Shakespeare* (1765) (▷ Shakespeare criticism) he articulates literary axioms which lie at the heart of Augustan ▷ humanism (and which, incidentally, help to explain his disparagement of *Tristram Shandy*): 'nothing can please many and please long, but just representations of general nature.'

Having begun this essay with Johnson's defence of writing for personal gain, it seems appropriate to end it with his definition of literature's public responsibilities. 'The only end of writing,' he declared, 'is to enable the readers better to enjoy life, or better to endure it.'

Restoration and 18th-century drama

4

Eva Simmons

Introduction

The period begins with the re-opening of the theatres in 1660, after an interval of eighteen years, and in very different circumstances from before. Recent criticism has suggested that the Commonwealth Proclamation in the crisis year 1642, ordering the playhouses to be shut down, was not due merely to any ▷ Puritan objections to the theatre as such, but because numerous plays in the preceding years had been openly critical of parliamentary as well as royal policies. Thus closing them was partly what we would now call an act of political repression. The intervening period saw some productions, mostly clandestine – although from time to time the companies attempted open performances, sometimes with severe repercussions.

In the 1650s ▷ Sir William D'Avenant found a legal loophole which permitted the staging of musical performances, and he mounted, openly and successfully, four operas (▷ opera in England), including ▷ *The Siege of Rhodes* (1656) and *The Cruelty of the Spaniards in Peru* (1658). These were effectively the first entertainments of their kind in England, although they drew on earlier ▷ masques for some techniques. Despite the dearth of public performances, the taste for plays survived throughout the ▷ Interregnum, which saw the publication of large numbers of plays, including dozens of new ones. Some of the readers of these were readily assimilated into the new audiences of the 1660s, and from then on playreading as well as theatre going became an increasingly popular pastime.

The period 1660–1800 is marked by innovation from its outset. The advent of women, both as actresses and as dramatists, had a profound impact on the staging of plays and the responses to them. The shape and layout of the theatres changed, together with the style of acting, and the nature of the audiences. New themes came into prominence in the plays, partly as a reaction to new social and political conditions and partly in response to the technical changes just mentioned. Within the period also, there were discernible shifts of topic, theme and style of acting. Nevertheless, the theatres continued to operate under varying degrees of ▷ censorship. This encouraged the staging of plays expressing attitudes of loyalty to the reigning monarch and prevailing ethics, and meant that some plays considered politically or socially dangerous were suppressed. Censorship was applied most rigorously during periods of political tension, such as the Popish Plot (▷ Titus Oates) resulting in large-scale persecutions of ▷ Catholics and the Exclusion crises of the 1680s when unsuccessful attempts were made in ▷ Parliament to exclude the Duke of York (later ▷ James II) from the succession, and again in the 1730s, when satirical attacks on the Government contributed to the passing of the Licensing Act of 1737 (▷ theatres).

In the past, histories of the theatre and drama have tended to focus on so-called 'canonical' texts: those identified by generations of commentators as representing the best in their periods. In the 20th century the reinforcement of this pattern became known as the 'Leavisite' tradition, after the literary critic F. R. Leavis, who isolated certain 'great books' which he considered central to civilization. The implication has been that these and only these are worthy of serious study. But the approach has been challenged repeatedly. The Reverend Montague Summers issued new editions of plays by 'lesser' ▷ Restoration dramatists, including ▷ Aphra Behn and ▷ Thomas Shadwell, in the first decades of this century, and Leslie Hotson's *The Commonwealth and Restoration Stage* (1928) broke new ground in research on the theatre of the ▷ 17th century. More recently, writers including Robert D. Hume, Judith Milhous, Margot Heinemann, Martin Butler, Fidelis Morgan, Dale Spender and Janet Todd have contributed to a re-evaluation of many 'forgotten' dramatists and works, including many by women.

The theatres

▷ Charles II loved the theatre, and was from the beginning of his reign an enthusiastic patron of it, but when he officially re-opened the theatres, he sought to ensure political loyalty from that quarter by confirming existing monopolies to two trusted courtiers: Sir William d'Avenant and ▷ Sir Thomas Killigrew, as well as by re-establishing a system of censorship. The pattern of monopolies lasted, with interruptions, for most of the 18th century.

On confirmation of their patents, D'Avenant and Killigrew formed two companies, the ▷ Duke's and ▷ King's companies, respectively, and set about finding venues for their performances. For a brief period they used existing theatres which were re-opened for the purpose, including a few dating back to Elizabethan times. In March 1660 D'Avenant began converting Lisle's Tennis Court at ▷ Lincoln's Inn Fields. This introduced the proscenium, or framed stage, to the English theatre for the first time. But although he had extended the property, it was felt that it was still too small, and needed a substitute. D'Avenant died in 1668, and it fell to his widow, ▷ Lady Mary D'Avenant, who had inherited the patent, to carry out the work. The new theatre, designed by ▷ Christopher Wren, stood on the river front in Dorset Garden (▷ Dorset Garden Theatre), where it had access both by road and from the water by boat. The Duke's company moved here in 1671, still under Lady Mary's control, until she transferred it to her son Charles in 1673.

Killigrew meanwhile had moved his company to an old riding school in Bridges Street, Drury Lane, which he converted to a theatre – the first Theatre Royal (▷ Drury Lane Theatres). This opened in May 1663, and survived until 1672, when it was destroyed by fire. He then commissioned a new theatre, possibly also by Wren, on a site close by.

The acting area on the ▷ Restoration stage included a deep forestage or apron stage, which projected beyond the proscenium into the pit, past the side boxes. Proscenium doors admitted the actors directly onto the forestage. Here the prologue and much of the dialogue were spoken, clearly audible, and the speakers clearly visible, to the surrounding audience, some of whom might even be seated on the stage itself. The proscenium arch contained a curtain or painted cloth that could be lowered or raised to reveal the interior stage, which had receding rows of painted flats and shutters in grooves on either side. These in turn could be closed or opened, adding further depths to the set or action. Numerous Restoration plays contain 'discovery scenes', indicating that the shutters are opened to reveal behind them other settings or actors, who might then perhaps move forward to join in action nearer the audience. The result was considerable versatility, including the option to change settings in full view of the audience, and with them mood and pace during scenes. Balconies above the stage were also used for some of the action. However there was no naturalistic illusion of landscapes or interiors in the modern sense, but rather a decking of the stage with images and objects to suggest various locations.

A characteristic feature of Restoration drama was its use of elaborate effects – such as cupids or other figures floating on 'clouds' above the stage – aided by mechanical devices. Lighting, for performances were staged mainly in the afternoon, was largely daylight, admitted through the windows, as well as candelabra hung from the centre of the proscenium, and footlights or 'floats' – literally candles, or wicks threaded through corks, floating on troughs of water or oil at the front. Rows of candles and oil lamps, placed in brackets and coloured by strips of stained glass or tinted silk, as well as hand-held candles, lanterns and torches, added light to acting areas further back. Snuffers stood by because of the constant threat of fire.

In addition to the patent theatres were Court theatres, including the Cockpit at ▷ Whitehall, and the Hall Theatre, built in 1665. Two ▷ Inns of Court – the Inner Temple and the Middle Temple – put on plays, sometimes involving Duke's and King's Theatre actors, as part of their festivities. Musical performances took place in private homes and at Court. Several ▷ 'nurseries', training grounds for younger performers, also existed briefly, and mounted their own productions. Killigrew set up one of them in 1667, at Hatton Garden; another was established by Lady D'Avenant after her husband's death, in the Barbican; she was involved in the running of a third at Bun Hill in Finsbury Fields, but this lasted only nine weeks. The nurseries were the butt of opposition from several quarters, but actors sometimes succeeded in 'graduating' from them into the patent companies. Finally, strolling players performed at fairs and other venues from time to time.

Playhouses also proliferated throughout the provinces, as well as in Scotland and Ireland. Today there are only three playhouses surviving from the 18th century (the earliest still remaining): the Theatres Royal in Richmond (Yorkshire), Bristol and Margate. Another Georgian theatre, the Theatre Royal at Bury St Edmunds (opened 1819), has the distinction of preserving its original proscenium to this day.

The most important theatres in this context were the two patent houses, and these carried on a fierce rivalry. From the first the Dorset Garden specialized in staging very elaborate performances, including many operas, while the Theatre Royal concentrated on plays. In 1682 matters came to a head with the failure of the King's Company, which was effectively absorbed into the Duke's to form the ▷ United Company. The United Company continued performances of spectacles at Dorset Garden and plays at Drury Lane.

Corruption and mismanagement led three of the principal actors, headed by ▷ Thomas Betterton, to secede in 1695, returning to Lincoln's Inn Fields, which they named the 'New Theatre'. In 1705 Betterton left for Her Majesty's Theatre, also known as the Queen's Theatre, Haymarket, or simply, the ▷ Haymarket, a newly opened playhouse designed by the dramatist and architect ▷ John Vanbrugh. The company was managed in turn by Vanbrugh and ▷ William Congreve. But the theatre suffered financial problems; it proved too large for spoken drama, and in due course became the first English opera house, staging many of ▷ Handel's operas. It was burnt down in 1789, and in 1791 a new theatre was built, known first as the King's and later the Queen's.

Theatre construction and alteration continued over the next two decades. In 1714, Lincoln's Inn Fields was refurbished in grand style by the architect and designer Edward Shepherd (1670–1747), with mirrors lining the interior walls, and then run by the actor-manager ▷ John Rich – son of the late ▷ Christopher Rich whose dishonesty and incompetence had contributed to the secession of the actors mentioned above. The theatre became known by different names: sometimes the New Theatre and sometimes the Little Theatre.

In 1720 a new theatre was erected by ▷ John Potter in the Haymarket, almost opposite the Opera House. Confusingly, this was also known variously as the New Theatre, or Little Theatre in the Hay; or even as the French Theatre in the Haymarket. Scenery was still painted onto flats, and lighting was by overhead chandeliers with wax or tallow candles. As in the Restoration period, the curtain rose and fell only at the beginning and end of the play. The Licensing Act forced it to close down and it stood empty for ten years, whereupon it was taken over by the actor and dramatist ▷ Samuel Foote. In 1766 it became a 'Theatre Royal'; it stood until 1820 when the present Theatre Royal, Haymarket, was erected nearby.

In 1732 Shepherd planned the first ▷ Covent Garden Theatre, or Theatre Royal, on the site of the present Royal Opera House, to which John Rich transferred. A contemporary print shows a proscenium with two doors surmounted by balconies, and behind it an inner frame. Another device apparently surviving from the Restoration period is the 'transparent scene': a translucent surface which could be lit from behind to produce special effects. On Rich's death in 1761, the theatre was taken over by his son-in-law, John Beard (?1716–91), who passed the patent to the dramatist ▷ George Colman the Elder, and three partners, in 1767. The theatre was substantially altered in 1784 and rebuilt in 1792, mainly to allow it to hold many more spectators. It was destroyed in a great fire in 1808. A new theatre was built on the same site the following year.

The 1730s saw increasing tensions between the government and the stage. Some in high places were concerned about the rapid and apparently unchecked rise in the number of playhouses, and disputes about who should exercise control were fuelled by a number of satirical performances openly criticizing the government. Notable among these were several by ▷ Henry Fielding, who eventually sided with ▷ Sir Robert Walpole's opposition. In 1737 Walpole, precariously clinging to dwindling power, succeeded in bringing in a Licensing Act which re-established a monopoly of theatrical entertainment. This was assigned to two playhouses: Covent Garden and Drury Lane, the latter managed by ▷ David Garrick from 1747. Not surprisingly, the Act was not entirely successful in limiting theatrical activity. For example, the actor-manager James Lacy (1696-1774) defied the law at intervals after its enactment. And the ▷ Goodman's Fields Theatre in Ayliffe Street, despite being ordered like the Haymarket to close in 1737, resumed performances using subterfuges to evade the law until 1742. Here it was that Garrick made his first appearance before London audiences.

Garrick's impact on the theatre was immense not only on methods of acting, but also on the physical conditions of performance. One innovation during his tenure as manager at Drury Lane was precipitated by a number of incidents in which audience rowdiness erupted literally onto the stage, seriously interfering with the performance. In 1763 Garrick announced an increase in the capacity of the auditorium, while prohibiting seating from the area around the stage whose presence had been allowed since the Restoration. The manager of Covent Garden, John Beard, quickly followed suit.

Further, in 1765 Garrick introduced stage lighting concealed from the audience, an effect used in ▷ Richard Brinsley Sheridan's ▷ *The School for Scandal*. He also used naturalistic cut-out scenery designed by ▷ De Loutherbourg, an Alsatian who had already made his name in Paris. In the later years of the century, the ▷ Gothic revival seen in other areas of literature and culture of the period was also reflected on stage in scenes displaying dark and rugged mountains, misty and mysterious lakes, or gloomy ruined castles in the Gothic style. Some of Garrick's changes were ultimately to contribute to an effect of added unreality, as well as a loss of contact between actors and audience.

The efforts to enlarge Drury Lane continued during and after Garrick's tenure. The theatre was extensively altered and expanded by the Adam brothers (▷ Robert Adam) in 1775. In the following year, upon Garrick's retirement, it was taken over by Sheridan, who rebuilt and extended it yet again in 1794, and remained in charge until its destruction by fire in 1809. The removal of spectators from the stage effectively widened the gulf between actors and audience. The last decades of the century saw an increase in the use of the curtain to separate scenes from one another, and doors were added to the side scenes for entrances and exits, ostensibly to aid naturalism. In due course they came to replace the proscenium doors altogether, and eventually the box set, and the limiting of acting to the area behind the proscenium completed the rift between actors and audience. Plays were performed in increasingly large theatres, entirely behind the proscenium frame, and the intimacy and immediacy of drama in earlier eras was lost.

The performers, their companies and their audiences

The period is highlighted by some of the great names of theatre tradition, including some individuals of extraordinary versatility, Thomas Betterton, ▷ Charles Macklin, Samuel Foote, David Garrick and ▷ John Philip Kemble, for example, not only acted in but also wrote plays (although some were merely adaptations of older plays), as well as managing their companies. ▷ Richard Steele, in addition to contributing to and editing or co-editing at various times ▷ *The Tatler*, ▷ *The Spectator*, *The Guardian*, *The Theatre* (the first English theatrical journal) and other publications, was a theatre manager and also wrote several influential plays. ▷ Colley Cibber was a manager as well as actor and dramatist, and in his memoirs made a serious contribution to theatre history. Sir John Vanbrugh designed theatres in addition to writing successful plays. Henry Fielding managed the Haymarket during the 1730s until its closure in 1737, after which he became a celebrated novelist; another dramatist, ▷ George Colman the Elder, managed Covent Garden when the plays of ▷ Oliver Goldsmith were first produced there, and took over the Haymarket later. Sheridan, as we have seen, became a manager as well as a dramatist of lasting reputation; ▷ Susannah Centlivre started as an actress, before becoming one of the most successful dramatists of her generation. The actress ▷ Kitty Clive also wrote several plays, including some that were quite successful, and ▷ Charlotte Charke not only acted in dozens of roles, but wrote plays and managed companies as well. However, women dramatists, like other women writers, were subject to attack by men, as in the satire, *The Female Wits* (1696), and ▷ *Three Hours After Marriage* (1717) by ▷ Pope, ▷ Gay and ▷ Arbuthnot, which mocks the Countess of Winchilsea (▷ Anne Finch) through the character of Phoebe Clinket. One character says of her that 'the poor girl has a procidence [prolapse] of the pineal gland, which has occasioned a rupture in her understanding . . . instead of puddings, she makes pastorals, or when she should be raising paste [pastry], is raising some ghost in a new tragedy'.

Other important figures on the Restoration stage include ▷ Michael Mohun, ▷ Edward Kynaston and ▷ Charles Hart, all of whom had begun their careers as boy actors playing largely female roles, as well as ▷ William Smith, William Mountfort (1664–92), ▷ Elizabeth Barry, ▷ Anne Bracegirdle, for whom several of Congreve's parts were written, and of course Ellen or ▷ Nell Gwyn. She retired from the stage after she became Charles II's mistress, but remained its ardent patron and admirer. ▷ Susanna Cibber, ▷ Anne Oldfield, ▷ James Quin, ▷ Spranger Barry, ▷ Peg Woffington and ▷ Sarah Siddons are among major actors and actresses in the 18th century. Each era also had its noted comedians, including ▷ James Nokes and Thomas Jevon (or Jevorn, d1688) during the early Restoration period, and ▷ John Lacy, Thomas Doggett (1670–1721) and ▷ William Penkethman (or Pinkethman) later on.

The most important innovation at the beginning of the period is the introduction of actresses to the stage. Before the Restoration, women had acted occasionally: the casts of court masques included some female members of royalty, and a woman had acted in D'Avenant's ▷ *The Siege of Rhodes* in 1656. But the general rule in England had been for men and boys to act the women's parts. However, on the Continent, actresses had already become commonplace, and Charles II during his years of exile had become accustomed to seeing them. In August 1660 he ordered D'Avenant and Killigrew to place women in all female roles, and his subsequent patent suggested that it was indeed improper to do otherwise.

From a modern standpoint, the insistence on having women play women's parts may be considered as a feminist act. However, there is ample evidence that many male contemporaries saw it chiefly as adding a prurient element to their enjoyment of the theatre, Charles's ostensible views notwithstanding. The diarist ▷ John Evelyn (1620–1706) complained bitterly that 'Foul and undecent women now (and never till now) were permitted to appear and act . . . inflaming several young noblemen and gallants . . .' More than 40 years later, ▷ Sir Richard Steele, in quite a different frame of mind, remarked that a woman's presence was a great help to a dull production, so that 'When a poet flags in writing lusciously, a pretty girl can move lasciviously, and have the same good consequences for the author'. The dramatic motif of woman disguised as man, in order to further some – usually romantic – end, had in ▷ Shakespeare's time relieved the burden on young actors struggling with womanish movements and vocal patterns. After the Restoration it became a means whereby actresses could put on breeches, and show off shapely ankles and calves. ▷ Pepys commented that a woman acting in a man's role 'had the best legs that ever I saw, and I was very well pleased with it'. Many stage directions and lines in the plays, as well as the revealing dresses of the period, also contributed to an emphasis on the women's sexuality. On the other hand, wearing breeches made it possible, at least by the early 18th century, for a woman to experience briefly and without censure, freedom from cumbersome skirts in the manner of a man. ▷ Bernard de Mandeville, in *The Fable of the Bees* (1714), wrote that when a woman wore breeches 'Upon the Stage it is done without Reproach, and the most Vertuous Ladies will dispense with it in an Actress, tho' everybody has a full view of her Legs and Thighs; but if the same Woman, as soon as she has Petticoats on again, should show her Leg to a Man as high as her Knee, it would be a very immodest Action, and every Body will call her impudent for it'.

The position of the actress was ambiguous. That many actresses were kept by wealthy lovers, or performed individual sexual favours in return for gain, is undeniable. The acting profession was then, as later, a precarious one, and the temptation to reinforce their incomes in this way must have proved irresistible to many actresses. However, some dramatic historians, such as John Harold Wilson, have exaggerated the extent to which their function was synonymous with that of courtesan or even prostitute. Many actresses, including those known to be 'unchaste', also gained lasting reputations as artists; ▷ Elizabeth Barry, for example, was said to be ruthlessly promiscuous, and was frequently condemned on this account. Yet she was much admired as both a comic and tragic actress, and as a tragedienne is reported to have performed with great dignity and pathos. It is important to note that male actors also occupied a paradoxical position during much of the period. They were considered to be relatively low down on the social scale (an Act of ▷ James I had made them technically vagabonds). Pepys, visiting the actors at one theatre backstage, remarked that 'the clothes are very poore, and the actors but common fellows'. On the other hand, actors frequently enjoyed close associations with courtiers (including several dramatists), and, in many cases, the respect of other critical theatre-goers as well. Gradually during the 18th century the status of actors and actresses rose, boosted by Garrick's success and enjoyment of public esteem, as well as the growing popularity of the theatre and interest in the performers generally. But it is clear that for a long time there were conflicts in the attitudes towards all performers, and towards actresses particularly.

The actress ▷ Katherine Corey claimed to be the first woman in her profession: she played the part of Desdemona in a production of *Othello* in December 1660. Occasionally, as with Thomas Killigrew's *The Parson's Wedding* in 1664 and again for a time during the early 18th century, plays were performed by casts made up entirely of women. Some individual women became celebrated for playing particular male roles, notably Peg Woffington as Sir Harry Wildair in ▷ Farquhar's ▷ *The Constant Couple* (1699) and, less famously, Susanna Cibber as Macheath in Gay's ▷ *The Beggar's Opera*. Colley Cibber's talented, versatile and quirky daughter Charlotte Charke, given from childhood to dressing in male attire, became as famous in her performances of men's roles as of women's. She acted the two in rapid succession, sometimes playing a man's part on one night and a woman's on the next, and occasionally, a man's and a woman's in different performances of the same play: for example she was both ▷ Macheath and ▷ Polly Peachum in *The Beggar's Opera*. During a month and a half of a single season in 1734 she acted about a dozen men's roles, including Macheath in Roman dress, George Barnwell in ▷ Lillo's ▷ *The London Merchant*, Townly in Vanbrugh's and Cibber's *The Provok'd Husband*, and gay Lothario in ▷ Nicholas Rowe's *The Fair Penitent*. And once she played Sir Fopling Flutter, the part made famous by her father in ▷ Sir George Etherege's ▷ *The Man of Mode*.

Early in the 18th century the ratio of men to women in the acting profession was almost two to one. One company listed 20 men and 11 women in the first decade. At Lincoln's Inn Fields account books for the years 1724–25 bear the names 28 men and 16 women. Gradually the proportion of women rose, together with the total number of performers employed in the profession, as the number of theatres multiplied. The average for the years 1729 to 1747 was 74, and in a single season, 1729–30, over 250 named performers are listed in the bills.

As for the management structure, during the first years after the Restoration the acting profession was dominated, as already noted, by the two patent companies, which merged into the United Company in 1682. Each company had a core group of performers which shared what was left of the profits after running costs had been paid from general receipts. This group was headed by the largest shareholder, in effect the manager, and augmented by salaried 'hirelings' who might eventually become shareholders, as well as musicians, scene keepers and other non-acting personnel. In the 1690s control of the United Company passed to the unscrupulous Christopher Rich, a profiteer with little or no interest in performers or acting standards, precipitating the secession of Betterton, Barry and Bracegirdle already mentioned, to form another sharing company in 1695.

The double system of management, actor-manager on the one hand and proprietor-manager on the other, persisted into the 18th century: Rich in charge of Drury Lane, and Betterton of Lincoln's Inn Fields. After 1705 when Vanbrugh opened the Queen's Theatre in the Haymarket, companies and varieties of organization proliferated until the Licensing Act of 1737 restored the system of two patents. Meanwhile from 1705 opera, developing as an increasingly separate form of entertainment, had its own management structure.

The dominant figure on the stage during the Restoration and early 18th-century years was undoubtedly Thomas Betterton, both because of his reputation, and his ability. He was equally acclaimed in tragedies and comedies and played mostly leading roles with the Duke's Company, the United Company, and finally his own at Lincoln's Inn Fields. A contemporary portrait shows him as a stout man, quite unlike today's ideal of a romantic actor, but dignified and imposing in a silk robe wrapped and folded round his large body, a cravat loosely tied and the locks of a shiny wig flowing down his back. He excelled in Shakespearean parts, including Hamlet, Macbeth, Lear, Othello, Mercutio (*Romeo and Juliet*) and Sir Toby Belch (*Twelfth Night*), but also in contemporary ones such as Heartwell in Congreve's ▷ *The Old Bachelor*. He married Mary Sanderson (or Saunderson), one of the first English actresses and the first to play a succession of Shakespeare's great female characters, including Lady Macbeth, Ophelia and Juliet. They often appeared opposite one another on the stage, setting a precedent to be followed by other couples, from the Mountforts, Cibbers and Bullocks onwards into the 20th century. Other family members also became involved, and the 18th century saw many great acting families and dynasties, including the Bullocks, Mills, Thurmonds, Penkethmans, Kembles and Booths. Early on children also began to feature prominently in stage productions: a Miss Willis, aged five, danced at Lincoln's Inn Fields in 1704, and a ten-year-old girl played Cupid in a masque at Drury Lane later in the same year. In the third quarter of the century it became fashionable to have plays entirely acted by children. Acting became, and remained into the 20th century, a family business.

Acting styles during the Restoration era can be deduced from contemporary portraits, some written accounts, and largely from the manner of the plays themselves. For comedies it appears to have been more or less an extension of the comportment of gentlemen and women in society, that is, formal and deliberate, involving a large number of elaborate gestures and facial expressions in a curious mixture of flamboyance and decorum. The close links between the theatre and the court must have been reflected on stage, with actors and actresses modelling their performances in many plays on those of well-bred courtiers. The extremes of this style are frequently mocked, as in the characters of Monsieur de Paris, in ▷ William Wycherley's ▷ *The Gentleman Dancing Master* (1672), and Lord Foppington in Vanbrugh's ▷ *The Relapse* (1697). For tragedies the style remained solemn and declamatory, or 'theatrical ... stiff and affected', according to a contemporary, possibly even involving chanting, until Macklin pioneered and Garrick perfected a more 'natural' approach. Betterton's method has been described as 'dignified, graceful, yet somewhat heavy and florid ... interpreting admirably those interminable heroic generals who abound in that period of Restoration melodrama'.

Commentators on the period, such as John Harrington Smith, J. H. Wilson, Peter Holland and J. L. Styan, stress the intimate relationship between actors on stage and the audience, as shown in the many asides and direct addresses to the audience in the plays, delivered from the projecting apron. During the 18th century acting methods underwent a considerable alteration. In the first decades of the century ▷ Quin, and others in his generation, continued in the style of Betterton and his contemporaries, but Macklin and then Garrick reacted to Quin's heavy formality, introducing what seemed to theatre goers to be greater naturalism and simplicity, accompanied by a subtle expression of voice, face and gesture. Quin was eventually forced to retire from what had been an outstanding career, including the roles of Othello, Lear and Falstaff. But alongside this change came an increasing emphasis on performing skills other than acting: dancing, singing, juggling and acrobatics.

The tendency toward greater naturalism, fuelled by the rise of ▷ Romanticism, encompassed a reappraisal of some traditional roles, particularly those of Shakespeare. The part of Shylock in *The Merchant of Venice* had long been played in a low, buffoonish style. In 1741 Macklin, later to become Garrick's great rival, appeared as a tragic and dignified, though still villainous, Shylock: 'the Jew that Shakespeare drew', in ▷ Alexander Pope's words. The impact was instant; the audience applauded so much that he had to pause after each speech to allow for the interruptions, and he became famous overnight. Changes in the depiction of Hamlet happened more gradually. From Shakespeare's time he had been portrayed as an heroic 'man of action'. But in the second or third quarter of the 18th century, actors including Richard Brinsley Sheridan's father ▷ Thomas and David Ross (1728–90) are believed to have begun the trend toward playing him as the irresolute, thoughtful, melancholy personality familiar to audiences in the 20th century.

Towards the end of the 18th century came another change, moving toward the florid acting styles of the 19th century, accompanied by a tendency to rant and shout. The enlargement of the theatres and shrinking of the apron now demanded that actors and actresses raise their voices and expand their gestures if they were to be heard and seen from the top gallery. The celebrated tragic actress ▷ Sarah Siddons refused to comply, causing some criticism that she was no longer always audible. But the practice was consistent with her concept of dramatic integrity; she disdained to 'play to the gallery'. She was enormously respected as well as admired for her dignity and grace, the deep beauty of her voice, her consistent professionalism and her capacity to move audiences.

Along with changes in acting methods, came changes in the approach to dress. In 1759 ▷ John Wilkes had pleaded for a return to the Roman tradition whereby actors always dressed 'according to the fashion of the country where their scene was laid'. In 1773 Macklin dressed his *Macbeth* in tartan costumes, and played the title role with a Scottish accent. Garrick responded with a *King Lear* in old English clothing. A famous portrait shows Peg Woffington in quasi-Elizabethan costume as Mistress Ford in *The Merry Wives of Windsor*. And Siddons attempted to marry authenticity with dramatic propriety, wearing costumes not only true to their historical context but also to the genre employed: thus tragedy demanded heavy garments and simple, natural hairstyles and headgear, in contrast to some of the elaborate creations of her predecessors.

Yet at the same time as Garrick and others were attempting to instil verisimilitude into the trappings and substance of their performances of Shakespeare, they were busy rewriting many of the plays, including some scenes which had escaped onslaught from Restoration revisers. A famous example is Garrick's alteration of *Hamlet* in 1772, omitting 'scenes of low humour' (including the Grave Diggers' scene), 'improving' the character of Laertes, and altering the circumstances of the Queen's death. *King Lear*, given a happy ending by ▷ Nahum Tate in 1681, had been changed again by ▷ George Colman the Elder, although he retained much of Tate's action, including the happy ending, as did Garrick in his version. Audiences in the 18th century, like their predecessors in the 17th, could not bear to see such injustice as was done to Cordelia. ▷ Samuel Johnson wrote that Shakespeare's ending was intolerable. The philosopher ▷ David Hume said that 'An action, represented in tragedy, may be too bloody and atrocious ... The mere suffering of plaintive virtue, under the triumphant tyranny and oppression of vice, forms a disagreeable spectacle, and is carefully avoided by all masters of the drama.' Most plays were rewritten in one form or another, and several were used as sources for short pieces focusing on just a few characters, in the manner of the time. Garrick's *Florizel and Perdita* (1756) is derived from *The Winter's Tale*, for example; his *The Fairies* (1755) from *A Midsummer Night's Dream*; and *Catherine and Petruchio* (1756) from *The Taming of the Shrew*.

Throughout the period acting was a strenuous and demanding profession, not least because of the size of a company's repertory, with programmes sometimes changing from day to day. During the season of 1721–2 John Mills (d1736) probably performed in 60 of the 70 plays put on at Drury Lane, including major roles in Marlowe, Shakespeare, Ben Jonson, Vanbrugh, Congreve and Farquhar. ▷ Robert Wilks acted at least 170 times, and Barton Booth in at least 35 roles, in addition to sharing in the company's management. Mary Porter (d1765) acted in 28 and Anne Oldfield in 26 roles in one season. Rehearsals in such circumstances were almost continuous, and inevitably scanty for any particular play. Furthermore, actors often had to double up, performing several roles in a single play and less frequently, during the 18th century, in plays in different theatres on a single night. Kitty Clive, for example, acted in Colley Cibber's *The Lady's Last Stake* at Drury Lane and ▷ Henry Fielding's *The Virgin Unmask'd* at the New Theatre on the Bowling Green on the same evening in January 1747. These factors meant that the actors had to remember huge numbers of lines, which could sometimes lead to complaints about distortions of the text and inappropriate ad-libbing. But some actors took pride in their retentive abilities: Garrick had up to 96 varied roles in his personal repertory and ▷ William Smith boasted that he could perform in any of 52 at a moment's notice.

Training facilities existed throughout the period. The Restoration nurseries have already been mentioned. In addition, senior actors and managers undertook to train the more junior recruits. In 1744 Macklin founded his own school to train actors according to his style of disciplined naturalism. Some performers in the period underwent long apprenticeships, but this did not guarantee that their careers would endure. Charlotte Charke is a prime example of an actress and dramatist who began with the best connections and hopes for her future, but ended up acting mostly in provincial theatres, or managing puppet shows, and living in terrible poverty. Income from acting was often uncertain as it depended largely on receipts. Salaried performers could not always be certain of being paid at all, and indeed payment was not made on days when there were no performances.

However, from the Restoration era onwards, leading performers could earn well: in 1694, Betterton received five pounds a week, plus a present of 50 guineas a year, and Barry received 50 shillings a week. In addition such actors, and later also some other theatre staff, were able to augment their incomes with the proceeds of 'benefits' staged on their behalf. (The profits from the third night of every production – if it survived that long – automatically belonged to the author.) The so-called 'Theatrical Fund', was established in 1765 as a form of insurance whereby a performer could claim from 30 to 65 pounds a year from retirement, or to provide a stipend for an actor's widow and surviving children on his death.

As to the audience, for many years after the Restoration it was far less heterogeneous than it had been in Shakespeare's time, containing a large number of upper-class men and women. Relatively high admission prices, ranging from one to four shillings, kept the poorest members of society away (in 1684 the average labourer's wage was only eight pence a day). But earlier views of the audience as almost exclusively aristocratic, by commentators such as Allardyce Nicoll, John Wain and A. S. Bear, have now been discounted: at present it is thought that it included a cross-section of middle- and upper-class society, including some merchants and 'citizens'. During the Restoration period, these were frequently ridiculed and actually insulted in the plays, and theories vary as to how much they joined in laughing at themselves, refused to identify with the absurd characters on stage and laughed at 'other' citizens shown as bigoted and stupid, suffered in silence, fought back or simply stayed away from plays known or presumed to be particularly offensive. A softening in dramatists' attitudes towards these classes beginning late in the 17th century, as well as the campaign to 'clean up' the stage, may represent an increasingly successful rearguard action of such individuals and/or changing social conditions. The economic strengthening and social 'legitimizing' of the bourgeois classes during the 18th century encouraged them to exercise their influence on the stage as on other cultural and social ventures. The expansion of the theatres, with the audiences gradually becoming more heterogeneous, coincided with a change in the manner of depicting the middle classes. Merchants and their families ceased to be mere objects of ridicule and were humanized into heroes and heroines, to be admired, criticized, pitied, laughed at or laughed with, according to the text.

Life in the theatre was marked by outbursts of violence during much of the period, to an extent that would seem incredible today. In 1669 Edward Kynaston was beaten up by ruffians hired by a rival, and in 1692 William Mountfort was murdered by Lord Mohun and his agents. Elizabeth Barry and ▷ Elizabeth Bowtell, required to struggle in their roles of Roxana and Statira during a revival of ▷ Nathaniel Lee's *The Rival Queens* (1677), came literally to blows, and the stabbing prescribed by the text became a real assault, with the dagger penetrating flesh. In 1735 Macklin killed a fellow-actor, Thomas Hallam, during a brawl in a green-room – the scene of frequent altercations among members of the acting profession.

Audiences were also often the source of strife. The disturbances caused by Restoration audiences are well known, but riots often took place in and outside theatres during the 18th century. These could cause substantial damage to theatres, and force closures and cancellations of runs by indigenous or visiting performers. In 1744 raised ticket prices at Drury Lane precipitated a riot there. Violent scenes occurred again in 1749, 1755, 1759, 1763, and 1789 over ticket prices and other matters. Competition to gain entry to particularly popular performances often degenerated into bloody fights, and political, religious and personal factions among the spectators also caused many outbursts, including clashes between supporters of rival performers. The riots of 1755, during performances of a ballet called *The Chinese Festival*, spread over several days. They ended with the theatre being torn apart and forced to close. The cause was 'patriotic' hostility to the French performers during a period of high tension with France, which erupted despite Garrick's efforts to pass many of the dancers off as Swiss. In the last years of the century, sentiments ran high over events associated with the ▷ French Revolution; ▷ Thomas Holcroft had to bring out some of his works anonymously, for fear of reaction because of his known links with ▷ William Blake and ▷ Tom Paine.

Apart from the complaints about violence, dramatists were frequently frustrated by their audiences' apparent indifference to their efforts. Some authors ensured applause by packing the audience with friends and even hired 'clapper-men', who would react with suitable enthusiasm to the play. But many plays and players attracted major followings, and some theatre goers were willing to pay large sums to attend particular performances of their choice. The actress ▷ George Anne Bellamy reported that several individuals, including members of the nobility, were willing to pay 100 pounds each to see her perform on a single night, whose proceeds were for her benefit.

The dramatists and the plays

The earliest plays to be performed after the Restoration were, not surprisingly, revivals of plays from earlier periods including many written shortly before the ▷ Civil War and many by Shakespeare. The latter were frequently revised to fit new notions of decorum, poetic justice, and/or French and other concepts of propriety, unity and symmetry, fostered by the ▷ neo-classical revival. For example, an early revision of *The Tempest* invents a character called Hippolytus, a man who has never seen a woman, to balance the character of Miranda, the woman who has never seen a man, other than her father. Just as, after the chaos of the preceding period, Restoration architects looked back to Greece and Rome for ideal models of order, symmetry, harmony and grace, so many Restoration dramatists looked to the ▷ classics, either directly, or via French theorists and practitioners such as ▷ Corneille and ▷ Racine, for models, precepts and subject matter, in composing their plays, rapidly expanding a process begun earlier in the century. A complex body of neo-classical dramatic theory developed, much indebted to ▷ Aristotle and ▷ Horace. This stressed the importance of preserving unities of time, place and action (▷ Classical unities). Theorists also focused on Aristotle's views that ▷ tragedy's chief task was to arouse pity (for the suffering protagonists) and fear, which the drama was to purge through a process called catharsis; and that dramatic action should imitate life, this process being defined as ▷ mimesis.

From Horace dramatists borrowed the view that drama has twin functions: to instruct, and to give pleasure (entertain). They also adopted notions of decorum, that is, a dramatic construction which is appropriate to its subject and to a genteel audience, that excludes obscenity, or anything too distasteful or revolting ('Medea must not butcher her children in front of the audience') and that avoids an awkward mixing of genres. From these theories the neo-classicists derived their own notions of poetic justice; what could be more instructive, they argued, than to reward virtue and punish vice? Shakespeare was censured for his failure to administer poetic justice, as well as his supposed rough-hewn mingling of tragic and comic elements. One of ▷ Dryden's chief criticisms of *Troilus and Cressida* was that 'Cressida is false, and is not punished'. Shakespeare was seen as a flawed genius, who could only benefit from having his works 'improved' by the present generation. Many earlier plays, by Shakespeare and others, were re-written to sanitize or even excise some of the most salacious lines, by authors conscious of post-Puritan and bourgeois criticism of the drama, and concerned in this as in other matters to observe at least some trappings of decorum (▷ Thomas Bowdler).

It is important to note, however, that theory and practice often diverged, and English drama was never as strict in preserving the 'unities', for example, as was the French. Furthermore, tragedies frequently introduced scenes of the most ghastly horror onto the stage: a famous engraving of Elkanah Settle's *The Empress of Morocco* (1673), staged at Dorset Garden, shows a backdrop with the bodies of several mutilated victims of torture, stripped and hanging on spikes and hooks upside down, while bones and dismembered bits of human remains litter the floor. ▷ Delarivière Manley (1663–1724), in *The Royal Mischief* (1696), shows a character shot from a cannon, his lover collecting his 'smoking Relicks' and covering them with burning kisses. ▷ Aphra Behn, one of the foremost adaptors of older comedy, repeatedly defended herself against charges of immorality in her plays. Dryden himself accused of impropriety; in words which look forward to much of later drama, he wrote, "Tis charg'd upon me that I make debauch'd persons . . . my Protagonists, or the chief persons of the *Drama*; and that I make them happy in the conclusion of my Play; against the Law of Comedy, which is to reward virtue and punish vice . . . But, lest any man should think that I write this to make libertinism amiable . . . I must farther declare . . . that we make not vicious persons happy, but only as heaven makes sinners so: that is by reclaiming them first.'

Other elements admitted by neo-classicists to the drama included love and the idea of 'Admiration', that is, that a character or action should be admirable. Dryden argued that love itself was admirable. A natural consequence was the writing of plays about love and honour, and about conflicts between the two, in which the period abounded. The workings of neo-classicism, though it influenced some comedy of the period, are seen most clearly in the so-called heroic plays, as well as non-dramatic poetry, exemplified in Dryden's verses. Indeed Dryden explained that he 'modelled [his] heroic plays by the rules of an heroic poem'. Plays, such as Dryden's *Tyrannic Love; or, the Royal Martyr* (1669), *The Conquest of Granada* (1670) and ▷ *Aureng-Zebe* (1675), employed the rhymed heroic ▷ couplet as their medium, with what to modern tastes often seems a ridiculous effect. D'Avenant, with *The Siege of Rhodes* and other plays, Sir Robert Howard (1626–98), ▷ John Crowne, Elkanah Settle (1648–1724), ▷ Thomas Otway, Nathaniel Lee and ▷ John Banks all contributed to the repertoire of heroic plays as well.

A feature of such plays was their exotic settings. Elizabethan and ▷ Jacobean tragedy was frequently set in Italy (partly because of its ▷ Italian antecedents in the theatre) and to a lesser extent in Greece. After the Restoration the growing influence of foreign novels and plays placed in distant venues, as well as the growth of trading and other links with hitherto unknown places, contributed to a taste for plays set among Christians and Moors in Spain, Morocco and several countries of the Middle East, and even among the Chinese and the Indians of North and South America. Such settings became the norm for plays of this kind: the popular understanding of the term ▷ 'oriental' (vague and undefined as that was), being almost synonymous with concepts of despotism, cruelty and luxury, made such settings ideal for plays involving spectacle, horror and scenes of high passion and intrigue, until writers such as ▷ Dr. Johnson and ▷ Goldsmith adopted more cosmopolitan attitudes to their distant fellow-beings.

The altered values and concerns of later generations have meant that today most Restoration tragedies are forgotten, and heroic dramas were mocked even in their own time, notably in Buckingham's (▷ George Villiers) ▷ *The Rehearsal* (1671), which singles out D'Avenant and Dryden for satiric attack, with devastating wit. Dryden himself recognized the potential for ridicule when he had Nell Gwyn berate an actor who would have carried her 'dead' body off the stage at the end of *Tyrannic Love*, 'hold, are you mad? you damn'd confounded Dog,/I am to rise and speak the Epilogue', thus undercutting the seriousness of his own preceding action. The modern critic Anne Righter has suggested that Restoration tragedy is 'less serious' than contemporary comedy, even 'essentially frivolous' in its penchant for easy solutions and its intellectual emptiness. A few tragedies, however, would be worthy of more attention than they have been given in recent years, especially some of the political and history plays, such as Nathaniel Lee's ▷ *Lucius Junius Brutus* (1680), and one or two tragedies of ▷ Thomas Southerne. A fine, half-forgotten, blank-verse tragedy which focuses strongly on conflicts between love and honour is Thomas Otway's ▷ *Venice Preserv'd* (1682). The play's urgent intensity, emphasis on character, chronicle of betrayals and mounting atmosphere of despair, link it with Jacobean tragedy. Tracing the failure of a rebellion against the Venetian senate, it has sometimes been viewed as predominantly Tory propaganda. But the manifest corruption of the authorities which Otway displays, and measure of (however qualified) sympathy which he allows the reluctant plotter Jaffeir, make it a more complex political statement. The play shows the moral turmoil which is produced when rulers are unjust, and that to preserve honour, let alone happiness, under them is impossible. But violent plots require violent plotters whose behaviour even toward their ostensible friends and allies is unpredictable, and whose success could presage a new era of chaos. The play may perhaps be read as ▷ Hobbesian, in that it appears ultimately to discourage rebellion, but it offers no easy solutions, and its strongest message is that the onus is on rulers to do justice by their people. Performed during a time of unrest after the so-called 'Popish Plot', the play had topical relevance.

Not only tragedies have been forgotten. Amongst the hundreds of comedies written during the period, only a handful survive today, in the sense of being widely known and regularly performed. They are the work of no more than half a dozen dramatists, including Etherege, Wycherley, Congreve, Vanbrugh, Farquhar, Dryden, and to a lesser extent Behn, although Dryden is chiefly remembered now for his poetry and non-dramatic prose. From the 18th century, the comedies of Goldsmith and ▷ Sheridan are still well known; otherwise most drama, from the Jacobeans to the late 19th century, is virtually unknown today, even though the period encompasses literally hundreds of plays of immense diversity, including many that were highly successful and acclaimed in their own time. A strange paradox has arisen: many people today have heard of Betterton, Garrick and Sarah Siddons, but few ask what – apart from the handful of Restoration comedies and plays by Shakespeare – they performed.

The reasons for this are manifold: apart from the changes in taste already mentioned, some plays fell victim to circumstances outside their authors' control: for example ▷ Thomas Shadwell, author of many fine comedies and ▷ Poet Laureate after the ▷ 'Glorious Revolution' of 1688, was pilloried by his arch-enemy Dryden who, unfortunately for Shadwell, gained the more lasting reputation. Shadwell's alleged ineptitude and dullness have been proclaimed over the years via the poem ▷ *MacFlecknoe* and kept most people from investigating his work further. Colley Cibber, a tolerable and in his way innovative, if not brilliant, dramatist, experienced the same fate at the hands of Alexander Pope and ▷ *The Dunciad*. Most so-called Restoration dramatists, and not a few that followed, suffered from the Victorian obsession with virtue and propriety. It was not deemed seemly to read, let alone perform, many of the plays from preceding generations; Restoration comedies were vilified most of all. Aphra Behn was subjected to a violently anti-feminist backlash that took hold during her lifetime, mounted in the years following her death, and eventually developed into a concerted campaign to obliterate her memory altogether. Sir Walter Scott, in a well-known anecdote, related that his grand-aunt returned some of Behn's novels which he had sent her at her own request, saying that she now felt ashamed to read a book which, 60 years before, she had heard read aloud in the best circles in London. Scott attributed the change to the gradual improvement of taste and sense of delicacy in the time leading up to his own. The publisher John Pearson was exconated when, in 1872, he published a collection of Behn's works, along with others by Restoration and early 18th-century dramatists including ▷ Susannah Centlivre.

This represented the end of a long process of decline in the attitude toward women dramatists: Behn's first play *The Forc'd Marriage*, put on at the end of 1670, has a prologue celebrating its authorship by a woman, as a sort of novelty – though Behn was not the first English woman to have a play performed (that distinction may belong to the woman better known as a poet, ▷ Katherine Philips. But opposition gathered during the 1670s, such that Behn soon felt obliged to defend herself in print, not only for the alleged bawdiness of her work, but for the mere fact that she as a woman dared to write at all. In an epilogue she asked rhetorically, 'What has poor Woman done, that she must be / Debar'd [*sic*] from Sense and sacred Poetry? . . . pray tell me then, / why Women should not write as well as Men.' She and many of her successors survived the mockery of male contemporaries, only to have their work eclipsed altogether by more narrow-minded subsequent generations. The number of women writing for the stage dwindled from about 1720, although a few prospered in each decade of the 18th century.

Behn, the first professional woman dramatist, was also among the most versatile dramatists of the era: she attempted, with varying degrees of success, virtually every genre for the stage, and portrayed almost every comic and perhaps tragic type known in her period. In many ways her plays paralleled those of the significant male dramatists of her time: she excelled at comedy, portraying the intricacies of courtship and marriage with wit and finesse. She was at her best with farcical intrigue comedy, handling multiple and complex plots without ever losing the thread of any individual one. Underlying the humour, however, was a serious vein: unlike many of her male contemporaries, she appears to have sustained a faith in the powers of true romantic love, foreshadowing many dramatists of the next century. Moreover, again unlike many male writers, she viewed the problems of love and marriage from a woman's point of view, idealizing and at the same time satirizing the typical rake character of the period, but also showing the harm which his machinations could inflict on women who took him at face value. Several plays show a sympathetic understanding of the unchaste woman, including the courtesan, or the 'wronged woman' who has rashly forfeited her chastity in the pursuit of love. Ismena in Behn's *The Amorous Prince* (1671) reproaches a suitor, 'as most gallants are, / You're but pleased with what you have not; / And love a Mistress with great Passion, 'till you find / Yourself belov'd again, and then you hate her'. In plays including this one, Behn re-examines the concept of feminine 'virtue', defining it not as virginity like most of her contemporaries, but as something we would now call integrity. Her most sustained theme is the evils of the so-called 'forced marriage': the marriage imposed on unwilling young people by greedy and ambitious relatives. Virtue consists in remaining true to one's own desires, even if that means defying the older generation and, in the case of women, giving up one's virginity to a man truly loved.

Probably the most successful and able of Behn's immediate successors was Susannah Centlivre, two of whose 19 comedies, ▷ *The Busie Bodie* (1709) and ▷ *The Wonder: A Woman Keeps a Secret* (1714), remained among the four most frequently re-printed and performed of any, except for those of Shakespeare, until late in the 19th century. Like Behn she excelled at comedy with complex intrigue plots, displaying with vitality and style young people, in pursuit of their own romantic ends, outwitting others functioning as pillars of established authority. But unlike Behn, who was a high Tory (▷ Whig and Tory), she championed Whigs and Whig interests in several plays and, again unlike Behn, she fervently opposed Catholicism, which she referred to as 'the Romish Yoke'. Furthermore, in keeping with her more fastidious times, the overt sexual element is omitted from her plays. Two of these, *The Gamester* (1705) and *The Basset Table* (1705), follow a contemporary convention in exposing current vice – in this case the fashionable one of gambling. She was also a fine craftswoman, creating superb acting roles, including five intended for the same actor in various disguises ($\triangleright$ *A Bold Strike for a Wife*), which rendered several of her plays favourites of Garrick and Kitty Clive. Garrick chose her play *The Wonder* for the last performance of his career.

From the Restoration onwards, plays were heavily preoccupied with themes of courtship and marriage, treated in ways varying from high comedy including farce, to tragedy. Indeed the term 'Restoration Comedy' conjures up in people's minds scenes of witty courtship and flirtation, underpinned by conflict: the 'battle of the sexes'. Many plays contain debates, implicit or explicit, about the value or otherwise of marriage as an institution, and discussions concerning the bases on which marriages should be contracted: whether for love or money; according to the choices of parents or lovers; between old and young ('January-May' matches); or lovers of similar age, and so forth. But these themes are not in any sense unique to the drama of the period. They permeate literature of many kinds, including a vast body of $\triangleright$ pamphlet material which was digested by increasing numbers of middle-class readers.

The genre has roots in some misogynistic writing of the $\triangleright$ Middle Ages, in which marriage was denigrated precisely because it bound men closely to women – the descendants of the flawed Eve. However it was strongly fuelled by the $\triangleright$ Reformation, with the protagonists dividing along religious lines. Increasingly, the institution of marriage was defended by $\triangleright$ Protestant Reformers, who accused Catholics of attacking marriage and sanctioning immorality ('whoring') as an alternative, so men could satisfy their sexual needs without having to resort to wedlock. A Reformist priest, Thomas Becon, in his *Boke of Matrimony* (1563), attacks 'Masse and Monckery' and its alleged opposition to matrimony, which is, he says, a state 'holy blessed ... although counted of the Papistes neuer so Seraphicall ...'. Catholics did not on the whole attack marriage as such, but continued to value celibacy as the highest state for those who could attain it, stimulating further attacks from Protestants for their supposed hypocrisy.

In the 17th century the debate over marriage intensified, and at the same time became secularized, erupting through the hundreds of pamphlets also written by, and largely appealing to, members of the middle-classes. Marriage was contrasted to whoring as a way of life; many pamphlets also focused on characters of courtesans or prostitutes, drawing moral conclusions from tales of their prosperity or downfall. Religious attitudes continued to inform many of the pamphlets but, increasingly, pamphlets by women responded to those by men, especially to the satiric ones attacking women. Later, women such as the polemicist poet $\triangleright$ Sarah Fyge, $\triangleright$ Mary Astell and poet and essayist $\triangleright$ Lady Mary Chudleigh attacked marriage for its patriarchal enslavement of their sex.

Images of slavery pervade both the pamphlets and the drama, with human and especially sexual relations seen in terms of the enslavement of one partner to another, or the enslavement of both to the oppressive conditions of marriage. The Civil War had heightened public concern with personal freedom, but growing censorship limited the parameters for discussion about the exercise of freedom in the political sphere. After the Restoration, the loosening of the strictures on individual sexual morality permitted a new outlet for debates about freedom, which took the form of a revived focus on the battle of the sexes. The growth of slavery in the New World also contributed to a widespread preoccupation with the metaphoric as well as literal manifestations of this institution.

Together, plays and pamphlets illustrate the debate about marriage and sexual relations in the 17th and 18th centuries. Indeed on one level, many plays may be seen as dramatized versions of a debate which constitutes a social correlative to the religio-political clash continuing in society, and exploding periodically into overt conflict. Examples are the 'Popish Plot' debacle beginning in 1678, the $\triangleright$ 'Rye House Plot' a few years later, to assassinate Charles II, and Monmouth's Rebellion (Duke of $\triangleright$ Monmouth), culminating with the so-called 'Glorious Revolution'– although the latter phenomena had distinct and various ends in view. Several late 17th-century pamphlets express concern that, because of Catholic influence on society in general and the gentry in particular, marriage as an institution was declining. But the drama shows, on the whole, no such concern. In keeping with dramatic tradition, and the reality of most people's lives, dramatists assumed that most of their characters would marry. But the plays are increasingly preoccupied with the concept of love and/or marriage as slavery, for the man or the woman, depending on the point of view. The metaphoric treatment of these themes in comedies was paralleled by more literal uses in the serious plays, of situations in which individuals are enslaved to one another via imprisonment, although they are also sometimes 'slaves of love'. So-called 'proviso scenes' in which men and women spell out the terms on which they are prepared to submit to the restrictions of marriage, and make bargains to this effect, form the climaxes to some Restoration comedies, the most famous example being the scene between Millamant and Mirabell in Act IV of Congreve's ▷ *The Way of the World* (1700). From 1670 onwards, after the first effective civil divorce, this too became a topic in some plays – seen as the only escape from an impossible union.

In the 1690s came a series of so-called 'marital discord plays', which followed more soberly in the footsteps of Behn. A major figure in this regard is the neglected dramatist, Thomas Southerne, who borrowed heavily from Behn. In several of his plays he shows the appalling situation of the wife, tied to a philandering and cruel husband, 'this hard condition of a woman's fate', in the words of one of his women characters. Vanbrugh takes up the theme in ▷ *The Relapse* (1697), written as a satiric sequel to Cibber's ▷ *Love's Last Shift* (1696), which showed the husband repenting of his unkindness to his wife, and undergoing a reform.

Today the best-known plays of the Restoration and early 18th century periods are some of the so-called wit comedies or Comedies of ▷ Manners by Etherege, Wycherley, Congreve, Vanbrugh and Farquhar. The form has an antecedent in the wooing of ▷ Beatrice and Benedick in Shakespeare's *Much Ado About Nothing*. But after the Restoration, Dryden helped develop it with what some consider the first true 'Restoration Comedy', ▷ *The Wild Gallant* (1663), in which an impoverished gallant, Loveby, is secretly supplied with money by his mistress, Constance. She articulates the plight of the woman in the period, 'tied to hard unequal laws: The passion is the same in us, and yet we are debarred the freedom to express it'.

Some plays of Etherege and Wycherley illustrate more clearly the inequalities of men and women: in Etherege's ▷ *The Man of Mode* (1676) women mistrust and betray one another. The heroine Harriet wins the appalling Dorimant away from the weak and stupid Bellinda and unscrupulous Loveit, but it is clear that her money forms a large part of her attraction in the match, making up for the ruin of his estate, and thus implicitly rescuing him from the slavery of poverty, although this is not stated in these terms. Margery Pinchwife, the title character in Wycherley's ▷ *The Country Wife* (1675), is pathetic and misguided; her denigration comes because she has not learned to guard her true interests in the harsh world of the city. The pursuit of 'interest', both financial and general, is a frequent theme in plays from a period heavily influenced not only by commercial changes in society, but also the writings of the contemporary social commentators Hobbes and François de la Rochefoucauld (1613–80), and the Greek philosopher ▷ Epicurus as adumbrated by the Roman ▷ Lucretius. Lucretius's works, translated and published during these years, contributed to a flirtation with 'atheism' by some Restoration writers and others. Denying the existence of an after-life implied, so it was thought, making the most of this one – even if that meant ignoring or downgrading the interests of others.

Many critics, such as Nicoll, J. H. Wilson, Bonamy Dobree and Clifford Leech, have attempted to organize Restoration comedies into categories, but this is a thankless task as there are so many overlaps between genres. For example, one frequently mentioned category is the Spanish Romance, such as Sir Samuel Tuke's *The Adventures of Five Hours*, commissioned by Charles II (1663), but in the prologue and preface to *The Wild Gallant* Dryden also acknowledges a Spanish origin. The so-called 'split-plot tragi-comedy', exemplified by Dryden's ▷ *Marriage à la Mode* and Behn's *The Widow Ranter*, is another, but here the comic plots have elements from various of the supposed categories. In *Marriage à la Mode*, for example, the lovers Palamede and Doralice exchange banter normally thought of as belonging to the 'comedy of wit', as they arrange a liaison. In another scene Leonidas is identified as the son to the usurper of Sicily, Polydamas, in lines that look forward to a great deal of 'exemplary' and 'sentimental' comedy. In yet another scene illicit meetings and mistaken identities parallel those of comedy of intrigue. Congreve's ▷ *The Double Dealer* (1694), considered among the great comedies of wit because of its sparkling language, also contains many intrigue elements, as shown in its enormously complex and brilliantly managed plot. Shadwell wrote several comedies influenced by Ben Jonson's theory of 'humours' (Comedy of ▷ Humours), as suggested in the *Dramatis Personae* to *The Sullen Lovers* (1668), which lists characters including 'a morose melancholy man', 'a conceited poet' and 'a familiar loving coxcomb', and in Shadwell's own dedication to the play. But the work has 'witty' and intrigue elements as well. In fact there are often overlaps among intrigue comedy, wit comedy and farce.

Similar problems arise in discussing tragedies, which are sometimes divided into categories including heroic tragedy, horror tragedy – glorying in scenes of torture, such as *The Empress of Morocco* – and pathetic tragedies, including some of Lee and John Banks. But again, there are many overlaps between and among categories; for example, Behn's *Abdelazar* (1676) has both horror and 'heroic' elements. And there have been numerous debates about whether some of Lee's plays really were 'pathetic', and how, in any case, this term should be defined. Happier compromises than those referred to above have been achieved by such authors as Robert D. Hume in *The Development of English Drama in the late Seventeenth Century* and A. H. Scouten in *The Revels History of Drama*. Hume discusses plays according to period, although this too leaves something to be desired, because of the inevitable exceptions and overlaps. But he also discusses some individual plays according to the categories into which they supposedly fit, such as the 'French' Farce, ▷ 'Reform Comedy', 'Wit Comedy', 'Sex Comedy', 'City Intrigue Comedy', 'Augustan Intrigue Comedy' and so on. Scouten's categories are much broader ('New Drama', 'Political Plays against the Puritans', and 'Social Comedy', for example), and much of his discussion is according to author.

Behn was one of the earliest to exhibit tendencies toward what has been variously described as 'sentimental', 'exemplary', or 'reform' comedy, the 'comedy of sensibility', and more recently, 'humane comedy'. These are critics' sometimes crude attempts to define a transition between plays dominated by hard wit comic elements of the high Restoration period and the genres that followed. The terms have often been accompanied by a blanket condemnation of the new modes, as representing a loss of wit and humour without any compensatory gain. But as Shirley Strum Kenny (coiner of the term 'humane comedy') has suggested, some of the older drama had much in the way of cynicism and callousness to discredit it, and there were mitigating features of the new.

The change is attended by attacks on the stage – most famously by the Reverend ▷ Jeremy Collier in a piece entitled *A Short View of the Immorality and Profaneness of the English Stage*, written in 1698. His tirade on the alleged loose morality and profane language of the plays was the more effective, if perhaps also more puzzling, because of his evident knowledge of the texts from reading, if not seeing them performed. But the movement toward reform had been started well before: a long vituperative poem by Robert Gould, *Satyr Against the Playhouse*, written in 1685 and published four years later, is said to have heralded the controversy. Finally, the change is linked with political developments: for example, the ascendancy of the Whigs after the Revolution of 1688, bringing with them a backlash against the supposed immorality and irreligion of the Tory dramatists. Writers such as ▷ John Locke, whose works were widely distributed after the Revolution, had far more positive views of human nature than those of his predecessors Thomas Hobbes and Sir Robert Filmer (c1590–1653), whose ideas had strongly influenced many Tories. The loss of patronage by the Royal family was also an important factor: as stated above, Charles II was a keen patron of the theatre, and his cultured but wry, satiric personality had a substantial influence on its development during his reign. His brother James II, while less involved in the minutiae of play composition and performance, had also continued the tradition of patronage for the brief period of his reign.

In the 1690s and early 1700s plays began to emerge that were less overtly bawdy and had a more sympathetic and 'moral' attitude toward some of their leading characters and human nature in general. Vanbrugh and Farquhar, although often classed among, and sharing characteristics with, Restoration dramatists, also belong in many ways to this later era. For example, in Farquhar's ▷ *The Beaux' Stratagem* (1707), Aimwell, under the guise of his wealthy brother, spends most of the play courting Dorinda for the sake of her fortune. But at the crucial moment he confesses his poverty, and releases her from her vows. At this she decides to marry him anyway, moved by his 'Matchless Honesty'. This is a far cry from Etherege or Wycherley.

A feature of these plays is their softened attitude to the country, which had been seen as a wasteland of ignorance and dullness by many satiric dramatists, though not by poets, of the Restoration. Many Restoration dramatists associated the country with settled property-based marriages, contrasting them to the 'freedom' of the town. But later dramatists and audiences came increasingly to accept the conventional forms of match-making, and with them, the country seat and its environment where so many wealthy and genteel families made their home. A stock motif of Restoration comedy is young lovers refusing to accept the partners of their parents' choice, and insisting instead upon making their own choices. In the 18th century, this is replaced typically by situations in which lovers think they are choosing for themselves, but unwittingly become attracted to partners who have in fact been intended for them by their elders all along. Thus at the end conflict is avoided, and the parents are vindicated, indeed revealed as sensible and far-sighted. The effect is an affirmation of the wisdom of the older generation, and by extension, of settled social forms and values. Rebellion against such parents is unjustified, since they have the true interests of the younger generation at heart. The forced marriage motif survives, however, in some plays, including Eliza Haywood's *A Wife to be Lett* (1723), and several plays by Centlivre.

Another common feature of plays of the period is the reform of a major protagonist. This is in keeping with the more optimistic view of human nature and aspirations espoused not only by Locke, but also by ▷ Shaftesbury and later ▷ David Hume, ▷ David Hartley, Pope and others. For many decades, plays exhibited gamblers, wife-beaters and others deemed guilty of wrongdoing repenting of their ways – though usually not until the last act. Colley Cibber's *Love's Last Shift*, in which the abandoned wife succeeds in reforming her errant and impoverished husband, is generally agreed to have been a key transitional play in this regard. The husband Loveless, struck by remorse, ends by celebrating the 'chast Rapture of a Vertuous Love'. Meanwhile in a secondary plot, an older man admonishes and successfully disciplines the coquette Hillaria.

Women are also shown repenting, notably by women dramatists including Susannah Centlivre and ▷ Mary Pix. The latter, whose *The Spanish Wives* (1696) had championed women's freedom somewhat in the style of Behn, though less racily, reforms the heroine of *The Deceiver Deceived* (1697) after one bout of adultery. The genre overlaps with the so-called 'exemplary drama' or 'drama of sensibility', epitomized by Steele's ▷ *The Conscious Lovers* (1722), in which the lovers of the title agonize over the propriety of all their actions. In the second half of the century, parallel with theories about the natural 'benevolence' of human nature, the so-called 'sentimental comedy', epitomized by Hugh Kelly's (1739–77) *The False Delicacy* (1768), developed. Also ▷ Richard Cumberland's ▷ *The West Indian* (1771) contains a number of elements typical of the genre, including the reform of a rake, vice exposed and outwitted, virtue rescued from distress and honourable simplicity triumphant.

Sheridan and Goldsmith reacted against what they saw as a surfeit of pathos and morality: they consciously attempted to revive the spirit of Restoration comedy with plays such as ▷ *She Stoops to Conquer* (1773), ▷ *The Rivals* (1775) and ▷ *The School for Scandal* (1777). So successful were their efforts that many people not too well acquainted with the stage today believe them to belong to the earlier era. And yet in its more 'benign' atmosphere and softened attitude to country life, for example, as well as certain elements of the plot, *She Stoops to Conquer*, at least, belongs to a later period than true Restoration comedy, and has much more in common with Farquhar, let us say, than with dramatists like Etherege, Wycherley, Behn or Congreve.

Along with the changes in comedy came new types of serious drama, although heroic plays remained popular into the 18th century. New approaches to Shakespeare have already been referred to, providing in some cases greater authenticity and in others fresh distortions, until Edmund Kean mounted full-scale restorations of Shakespeare's own texts in the 19th century. The later 18th century may be considered as a transitional period in this regard. ▷ John Banks and others developed a variety of tragedy focusing on the sufferings of women, at a time when the numbers of women dramatists were growing, and pamphlets presenting the views and concerns of women were proliferating. Such plays of John Banks include *Vertue Betray'd: or, Anna Bullen* (1682), on Anne Boleyn; *The Island Queens* (1684), on Mary Queen of Scots; and *The Innocent Usurper* (1694), on the execution of Lady Jane Grey. Congreve experimented with the form in the ▷ *The Mourning Bride* (1697), and ▷ Nicholas Rowe took it further with *The Fair Penitent* (1703), *The Tragedy of* ▷ *Jane Shore* (1714) and *The Tragedy of Lady Jane Grey* (1715). There is a link between such plays and some of the comedies of Southerne, Cibber, Vanbrugh and Centlivre, which also focus on the sufferings of women, albeit in less sombre contexts.

Today Banks is usually considered a practitioner of so-called 'pathetic tragedy', encompassing elements of pathos, designed to move rather than thrill or shock the spectator, while Rowe's plays are known as ▷ 'she-tragedies'. But the two may be seen to overlap. Again negotiating with these, and developing gradually in the period, was the domestic or bourgeois tragedy, characterized by a focus on the lives of ordinary citizens, rather than the kings and queens of the heroic variety. A landmark of this genre is ▷ George Lillo's ▷ *The London Merchant: or the History of George Barnwell* (1730), which ends with Barnwell repenting of his crimes before being executed. However, as Allardyce Nicoll points out in *A History of English Drama 1660–1900*, the roots of bourgeois tragedy, like those of so many other 'new' forms, lie in the Restoration period – particularly with Otway.

Burlesque plays and satires, fathered by George Villiers' *The Rehearsal*, became increasingly popular during the first decades of the 18th century. Among the most famous of these were Pope, Gay and Arbuthnot's resentful satire on contemporary women dramatists, *Three Hours After Marriage* (1717), and Fielding's ▷ *Tom Thumb* (1730), reworked as *The Tragedy of Tragedies* (1731), again mocking heroic plays. Gay's *The Beggar's Opera* (1728), technically a ballad-opera, is known to many today mainly as the source for Brecht's *The Threepenny Opera*. This comedy of low-life has antecedents in the 'rogue literature' of the 16th and 17th centuries, including some masques by Jonson. But its success was instantaneous: staged by ▷ John Rich, himself a dramatist as well as actor-manager, it is said to have made 'Gay rich and Rich gay'. This and later plays, notably by Fielding, mounted a sustained satiric attack on Sir Robert Walpole, eventually leading, as we have seen, to the Licensing Act of 1737, whereby the latter was able to subdue his critics and control the stage with a much firmer hand. It resulted in Fielding and others abandoning the stage and contributed, indirectly, to the development of the novel in the 18th century, as Fielding and others now concentrated their efforts on this less rigorously controlled, and therefore less risky, form of endeavour.

A dramatic form that developed in the 17th century, but became much more popular in the 18th is the 'after-piece', a short pantomime or farce intended to be performed after a more serious play, so the audience would be sent home laughing. Increasingly, these entertainments were considered essential to attract audiences to the theatre and, as the demand grew, many earlier plays were re-written in lighter and much abbreviated form. Just as pamphlets on marriage, written in serious or bitingly satiric vein in the 17th century were increasingly reworked into light, frivolous pieces in the 18th, so full-length, skilfully made comedies and tragi-comedies were later turned into little afterpieces. Garrick altered Wycherley's ▷ *The Country Wife* to *The Country Girl* (1766); a play by Betterton, *The Amorous Widow* (performed c1670) became a two-act farce, *Barnaby Brittle* (1782); Behn's *The Revenge* (1680), itself a sombre tragi-comic alteration of a savage satire by John Marston (?1575–1634), eventually became – via a comic and farcical adaptation by Christopher Bullock (1690–1722) called *A Woman's Revenge* (1715) – a droll, *The Stroler's Pacquet* (1742). 17th- and 18th-century dramatists were not on the whole concerned with problems of plagiarism, let alone copyright. In addition, dancing, singing, acrobatics, juggling and other forms of non-dramatic entertainment – including performances by many visiting companies from the continent – frequently functioned as entr'actes or after-pieces, as well as being staged in their own right, or integrated into plays.

Late in the century the influence of German (▷ German Influence on English Literature) and, once again, French dramatists became important to the English stage (▷ French Literature in England), at a time when the work of German poets and philosophers, in particular, was having a growing impact on the English Romantic poets. Plays of ▷ Kotzebue and René-Charles Guilber Pixérécourt (1773–1844), for example, translated and reworked by ▷ Thomas Holcroft and ▷ Elizabeth Inchbald, became immensely popular. The translations were to include works known to us now as melodramas, at first literally containing music, from the turn of the century.

In the final years of the century, reaction against the supposed bawdiness of many plays, alluded to above, began to bite in earnest. Readers of ▷ Jane Austen may recall the horrified response of the older generation upon finding the young people in *Mansfield Park* engaged in an amateur performance of Inchbald's *Lover's Vows*. Restoration comedy, which had remained part of the repertory throughout most of the century, was attacked once again, in a period marked by the rise of the ▷ Evangelical Movement. Even ▷ Hannah Cowley's *A School for Greybeards* (1786), itself a 'refined' and 'cleaned-up' version of Behn's genuinely outspoken *The Lucky Chance* (1686), was considered shocking. The stage was set for Thomas Bowdler's edition of Shakespeare (1818), new plays in the 19th century that were even more overtly moral and religiously inspired than their predecessors of the 18th, and the disappearance of Restoration plays altogether, until the revivals of this century.

Reference section

Abelard, Peter (1079–1142)

A philosopher in the University of Paris early in the 12th century. At the height of his fame he fell in love with a young girl, Heloise (Eloise), and became her tutor. She bore him a child and to appease the anger of her uncle, Abelard proposed that they should be secretly married; open marriage was out of the question as it would obstruct Abelard's career in the Church. The marriage took place against Heloise's wishes, for she did not want her lover to risk his future prospects for her sake, and she refused to admit to it when challenged to do so. She took refuge in a convent, and her uncle avenged himself on Abelard by causing him to be castrated. Thereafter a correspondence took place between them. Abelard was eventually condemned for heresy (1141). The trial broke his health, and he died; his remains were secretly conveyed to Heloise, who died in 1164 and was buried in the same grave. Their love affair became legendary and the subject of imaginative literature. Alexander Pope's ▷ *Eloisa to Abelard* (1717) is a poem on the subject.

Absalom and Achitophel (1681)

A ▷ satire in heroic couplets by ▷ John Dryden, allegorizing the political crisis of the last years of ▷ Charles II in terms of the Old Testament story of King David and his rebellious son Absalom (2 *Samuel* 13–19) (▷ Bible). Charles had no legitimate son and his heir was his brother James, Duke of York, a Catholic (▷ Catholicism in Britain), whose succession was feared by many as a menace to the ▷ Church of England and the liberty of Parliament. The ▷ Whigs, led by Anthony Ashley Cooper, the ▷ Earl of Shaftesbury, introduced a Bill excluding James from the throne and substituting Charles's illegitimate son, the ▷ Duke of Monmouth. Dryden wrote his poem at the king's suggestion, in order to influence the public against the Whigs. His handling of the biblical story glamorized the king, by paralleling his licentiousness with that of the patriarch David, and represented the Whigs as anarchic enemies of God's anointed. Monmouth becomes Absalom, Shaftesbury becomes the evil tempter Achitophel, the Duke of Buckingham appears as Zimri, and ▷ Titus Oates as Corah. Part II, which was published in 1682, is mainly by ▷ Nahum Tate, but includes a vivid passage by Dryden (ll 412–509) satirizing the poets Settle and ▷ Shadwell under the names Doeg and Og.

Act

In politics, a law which has been passed through both Houses of ▷ Parliament and accepted by the monarch. Until this process is completed, it is called a Bill.

In drama, a division of a play; acts are sometimes subdivided into scenes. The ancient Greeks did not use divisions into acts; the practice was started by the Romans, and the poet-critic ▷ Horace (1st century BC), in his *Ars Poetica*, laid down the principle that the number of acts should be five. In the 17th century, plays were still commonly divided into five acts; later the convention favoured three.

Act of Settlement (1701)

An ▷ Act of Parliament excluding the heirs of the deposed Catholic monarch ▷ James II, and all other Catholics (▷ Catholicism in Britain), from the throne. The Act supplemented the ▷ Bill of Rights of 1689, which in turn confirmed in law events of the ▷ Glorious Revolution of 1688. The Act of Settlement conveyed the succession to the ▷ Protestant German House of Hanover (▷ George). It was passed following the death of ▷ Queen Anne's only surviving child, the Duke of Gloucester, in 1701, and in anticipation that she would die childless, as in fact she did. In this case the throne would revert to James I's granddaughter Sophia, the Electress of Hanover and nearest Protestant relation to the ▷ Stuarts, and to her heirs, rather than to James II's Catholic son. Thus, the Act confirmed the concept of a constitutional monarchy, overriding the superior hereditary rights of James's son, who became known as the ▷ Old Pretender. In addition, the Act stipulated that the monarch must belong to the ▷ Church of England, that he or she must not leave the country without the permission of Parliament, nor involve the country in wars to defend the territories of foreign monarchs, nor appoint foreigners to Government posts. Furthermore, it provided for judges to receive fixed salaries, and prohibited their removal without the action of Parliament, except in the case of an offence proved in a court of law. These provisions assisted the separation of powers between the monarchy, Parliament and the judiciary, which ▷ Locke had thought essential to liberty.

Acting, the profession of

Acting began to achieve recognition as a profession in the reign of Elizabeth I. The important date is the building of The Theatre – the first theatre in England – by James Burbage in 1576. It was followed by many others in London, and theatres soon became big business. Previously, actors had performed where they could, especially in inn yards and the halls of palaces, mansions and colleges. They continued to do so, but the existence of theatres gave them a base and (though they still required an official licence) independence such as they badly needed in order to win social recognition.

Until the mid-16th century acting was practised by many kinds of people: ordinary townsmen at festivals, wandering entertainers, boys and men from the choirs of the great churches, and members of the staffs of royal or aristocratic households. It was from these last that the professional actors emerged. They still wore the liveries – uniforms and badges – of the great households, but the connection was now loose (good performers could transfer from one household to another) and was chiefly a means of procuring a licence to perform. This licence was essential because the City of London, around which dramatic activity concentrated, feared that the theatres were centres of infection for the recurrent ▷ plague epidemics (which from time to time sent the companies away on tour), and disliked acting as a morally harmful and anomalous way of life. Moreover, the royal court, which favoured the stage, was nonetheless on guard against it as a potential source of sedition. Censorship and licensing, however, had the advantage of helping to distinguish the serious performers from the vulgar entertainers.

By the time of Elizabeth's death two great companies were dominant: the Lord Chamberlain's Men, for whom ▷ Shakespeare wrote, and the Lord Admiral's Men, headed by the leading actor of the day, Edward Alleyn. Women did not perform; their parts were taken by boys who enlisted as apprentices. Companies of boy actors from the choirs of St Paul's and the Chapels Royal also had prestige (see *Hamlet* II.2), especially in the 1570s. The establishment of the profession owed most to the dramatists, but much to the energy of actor-managers and theatre proprietors such as Philip Henslowe, Edward Alleyn, James Burbage and his son Richard.

Actresses were allowed to perform after the ▷ Restoration of the monarchy (1660). The status of the profession continued to rise, aided by the theatre's ceasing to be the entertainment of all classes and becoming a fashionable pleasure of the London West End. In the 18th century the genius and culture of ▷ David Garrick greatly enhanced the prestige of the profession. From his time on, there is a long roll of great acting names; the drama, however, declined until the end of the 19th century, partly because the intrinsic value of plays came to be considered secondary to the merit of their performance.

▷ Puritanism; Theatres.

Adam, Robert (1728–92)

Architect. His work is representative of the middle period of ▷ Augustan taste, as the earlier period of it is expressed in the buildings of ▷ Christopher Wren and ▷ John Vanbrugh. The earlier period was bold and dramatic in its display of shapes and ornaments; the Adam period was graceful and delicate. He was a particularly fine interior designer and is famous for the designs of his ceilings and mantelpieces. His taste was much influenced by ancient Roman architecture in Italy, for instance the ruins of the town of Pompeii and the palace of the Emperor Diocletian (AD 245–313) at Spalato (Split). The last he used as the pattern for a fine urban development (demolished in 1936) overlooking the Thames in London; he carried it out with the help of his brother James, and thus called it the Adelphi from the Greek for 'brothers'. His work in London, like most good 18th-century architecture there, has been ruined or destroyed, but Edinburgh has preserved some of his best street architecture and a number of country houses survive, either designed throughout by him or ornamented in part. These include Harewood House (Yorkshire), Mersham-le-Hatch (Kent), Syon House (near London) and Kenwood (Hampstead, London).

Addison, Joseph (1672–1719)

Poet, politician and essayist, Addison is now best known for his contributions to two periodicals, ▷ *The Tatler* (founded by ▷ Richard Steele) and ▷ *The Spectator* (which he co-edited with Steele). *The Tatler* appeared three times a week in 1709–11, and *The Spectator* was issued daily, 1711–12 and 1714. *The Tatler* and *The Spectator* were designed as coffee-house periodicals, aiming to elevate the level of conversation by discussion of manners, morals, literature and philosophy. Addison claimed that they were enormously influential, as each printed copy could be passed around at least 20 people. The character of ▷ Sir Roger de Coverley, a country gentleman, was largely created by Addison.

Addison's first literary success was a poem, *The Campaign* (1705), celebrating the victory of ▷ Blenheim the previous year. His classical tragedy *Cato* (1713) was also a contemporary success. In his political career, Addison was a ▷ Whig Member of Parliament, and, briefly, a Secretary of State.
Bib: Samuel Johnson's life of Addison, in *Lives of the Poets*; Smithers, D., *The Life of Joseph Addison*; Otten, Robert M., *Joseph Addison*.

Adonis

A supremely beautiful youth in Greek myth. Beloved by ▷ Aphrodite, he was cured of a mortal wound by Persephone on condition that he spent half the year with the latter in the underworld and half with the former on the earth. The myth thus symbolized the change from winter to summer.

Advancement of Learning, The (1605)

A philosophical treatise by ▷ Francis Bacon published in 1605 in English, and expanded in a Latin version entitled *De Augmentis Scientiarium* published in 1623.

The purpose of the book is to suggest ways in which the pursuit of knowledge can be encouraged, and the methods of observation and recording of both natural and human phenomena improved. To this end, Bacon's work proposes nothing less than a taxonomy of all knowledge, a proposition strikingly similiar to that advanced by the French Encyclopaedists of the 18th century (▷ *L'Encyclopédie*).

Perhaps the most influential aspect of *The Advancement* is the methodology which Bacon employs. In surveying all fields of knowledge Bacon offers a form of catalogue of existing fields of enquiry. This attempt at classification, whereby branches of knowledge are grouped together under common headings, relies on a system of particularization. In each subject which is considered, Bacon argues that the first step is the fresh observation of the detail of the phenomena. Once the detail, or particularities, had been assimilated it would become possible, through the process of induction, to assert the general propositions under which groups of phenomena could be considered. This method signalled a break from what Bacon considered to be the traditional methods of enquiry (which involved deduction from generalized propositions) and demanded the re-examination of observable phenomena through the process of experimentation.

As a theorist of scientific method (rather than as an experimenter in his own right) Bacon was to have considerable influence on the early founders of ▷ The Royal Society, particularly in the area of language reform. On the question of language, and

the idea of an appropriate language for scientific discourse, *The Advancement of Learning* is a key text. At the same time, the importance of language to Bacon's project necessitated an exploration of poetic language which was to be influential for poets of the later 17th century, in particular ▷ Abraham Cowley.
▷ Dissociation of Sensibility.

Adventures of Captain Singleton
▷ *Captain Singleton, The Adventures of*

Adventures of Roderick Random, The
▷ *Roderick Random, The Adventures of.*

Advice literature

Debates about the status and nature of women altered advice literature in the 18th century. Women were still addressed as maids, wives or widows, but the debate about friendship in ▷ marriage inevitably brought up the question of the education of women (▷ education; ▷ women, education of); and this fed into debates on conduct (▷ conduct literature). The changes in advice on conduct are subtle, and the literature continued to advise the woman to adapt herself to circumstances, and particularly to her husband. For example, a relatively conservative advice book, *The Lady's New-Year's Gift: or, Advice to a Daughter* by George Savile, Marquis of Halifax, concentrates on the need for a woman to adapt her feelings. He recommends 'wise use of everything [one] may dislike in a husband' to transform that which might breed 'aversion' to be 'very supportable'. But he hopes that his daughter gets 'a Wise Husband, one that by knowing how to be Master ... will not let you feel the weight of it'. In *Letters Moral and Entertaining* (1729–33), ▷ Elizabeth (Singer) Rowe has a character note the relationship between feelings and conduct when she says, 'I was sensible of the delusion and how easily vice betrays an unguarded mind.' ▷ Mary Wollstonecraft's (early) ▷ *Thoughts on the Education of Daughters* (1787) adds the perception that feelings and conduct are linked to the argument for education. She writes, 'in a comfortable situation a cultivated mind is necessary to render a woman contented; and in a miserable one it is her only consolation.'
▷ Feminism; Feminism, Augustan, in England; Women, status of; Women's movement, The.
Bib: Jones, Vivian, *Women in the Eighteenth Century*.

Aeneas

Hero of the Latin epic ▷ *Aeneid* by ▷ Virgil. Traditions about him had existed long before Virgil's poem. He was the son of Anchises and the goddess ▷ Aphrodite, and the son-in-law of Priam; king of Troy. In Homer's ▷ *Iliad* (v) he is represented as the chief of the Trojans and one of the most formidable defenders of Troy against the Greeks. Other records stated that after the fall of Troy, he set out to seek a new kingdom with some of the surviving Trojans, and eventually settled in central Italy. By Virgil's time, the Romans were already worshipping Aeneas as the father of their race.
▷ Golden Age.

Aeneid

An ▷ epic poem by the Roman poet ▷ Virgil (70–19 BC). The poem tells the story of ▷ Aeneas, from his flight from Troy during the confusion of its destruction by the Greeks to his establishment as king of the Latins in central Italy and his death in battle with the Etruscans. The poem thus begins at a point near where Homer left off in the ▷ *Iliad*, and its description of the wanderings of Aeneas is parallel to the description of the wanderings of Odysseus in Homer's ▷ *Odyssey*. It is divided into 12 books, of which the second, fourth and sixth are the most famous: the second describes the destruction of Troy; the fourth gives the tragedy of Queen Dido of Carthage, who dies for love of Aeneas; the sixth shows Aeneas' descent to the underworld and the prophetic visions of those who are to build the greatness of Rome.

Virgil wished to relate the Rome he knew, a settled and luxurious civilization which threatened to degenerate into complacent mediocrity, to her heroic past, and to inspire her with a sense of her great destiny in world history. The *Aeneid* is thus a central document for Roman culture, and inasmuch as Roman culture is the basis of the culture of Western Europe, it has remained a central document for European culture too. Among several notable translations of the *Aeneid* is one by ▷ John Dryden (1697).

Aeolists

In ▷ Swift's satire ▷ *A Tale of a Tub* (1704), a fictional sect of believers in direct inspiration: 'The learned Aeolists maintain the original cause of all things to be wind...'. Swift's satire is an attack on all pretensions to truth not in accord with right reason or properly constituted authority, and the Aeolists, in Section VIII, are a kind of climax to the work. He associates them particularly with the ▷ Dissenters, who based their religious faith on belief in direct intimations from the Holy Spirit to the individual soul; Jack, who represents ▷ Presbyterianism in the *Tale*, is a leader of the sect.

Aeschylus (525–456 BC)

With ▷ Sophocles and ▷ Euripides, one of the three great tragic poets of ancient Greece. Only seven of his 70 plays survive; of these the best known are *Agamemnon*, *Choephori* and *Eumenides*, making up the *Oresteia* trilogy. Aeschylus is the great starting point of all European tragedy, but it was the derivative tragedy of the Latin poet ▷ Seneca which influenced the great period of English tragedy between 1590 and 1630. Reacting against this, ▷ Milton deliberately based his tragedy ▷ *Samson Agonistes* (1671) on the Greek pattern.

Ages, Golden, Silver, etc.

The Greek poet Hesiod (8th century BC), in *Works and Days*, writes of an ideal golden age in the past, comparable to the Garden of ▷ Eden; from this period, he considered that there had been a progressive decline through the silver, bronze, and heroic ages until his own time. ▷ Virgil, in his fourth *Eclogue*, writes of a child who is to restore the golden age. This has sometimes been interpreted as a prophecy of the birth of Christ. ▷ Milton, in *On the Morning of Christ's Nativity* (1629), hopes that following Christ's birth, 'Time will run back and fetch the age of gold' (XIV. 135). The ▷ Restoration of ▷ Charles II led to suggestions that the golden age had been restored with his accession. But the image of the golden age remained a potent one, for poets, dramatists, historians, philosophers and others, among them ▷ Aphra Behn, whose ▷ pastoral poem *The Golden Age* (1684), is adapted from a translation of lines by the Italian poet Torquato Tasso (1544–95); and ▷ Pope, who laments the loss of the golden age in ▷ *Essays on Criticism* (line 478). The idea of a golden age is important in ▷ Utopian literature.

Akenside, Mark (1721–70)

Poet. Son of a butcher in Newcastle-upon-Tyne, and a physician by profession. He wrote the influential *The Pleasures of Imagination* (1744), a philosophical poem in Miltonic blank verse. The assured reflective modulations of the poem influenced William Wordsworth's style in *The Prelude*, the subject matter of which – childhood impressions, the moral influence of landscape – is often the same. Akenside also wrote lyric poems and odes.
Bib: Houpt, C. H., *Mark Akenside: A Biographical and Critical Study*.

Albion

The most ancient name for Britain, used in Greek by Ptolemy and in Latin by Pliny. The word possibly derived from Celtic, but it was associated by the Romans with the Latin *albus* = white, referring to the white cliffs of Dover. From the Middle Ages on it has often been used poetically to stand for Britain, notably by ▷ William Blake. ▷ Dryden refers to it in his patriotic play *Albion and Albanius* (1685).

Alexander the Great (356–323 BC)

He succeeded to the throne of Macedon in 336 BC after the assassination of his father Philip II. Alexander began by consolidating his father's hegemony. Then he embarked on a rapid career of conquest which took his armies as far as the valley of the Indus in north-west India.

Alexander became a prominent figure in European literature, especially in France; a long 12th-century French poem entitled *Li Romans d'Alexandre* was written in lines of 12 syllables, hence originating the term 'alexandrine' for a line of that length. Diverse accounts of Alexander's life, much overlaid by legend, resulted in medieval versions of comparable diversity, depending on whether the writer was secular in his inspiration, using Alexander as a type of chivalric ideal, or morally inspired, seeing him (in contrast to Diogenes) as a man governed by his will and appetites, or theologically influenced by Orosius as a diabolic type bedevilled by satanic pride. Another line of interest derived from the fact that he had had ▷ Aristotle as a tutor and was supposed to have corresponded with philosophers, so that he could be seen as a type of Platonic

'philosopher-king' (▷ Platonism). This diversity was further embroidered by the legend that Alexander was not in fact the son of Philip but of the magician Nectanebus, the last independent king of Egypt, who visited Alexander's mother Olympias, in the shape of a dragon.

In the 17th century ▷ Restoration dramatist, ▷ Nathaniel Lee, wrote a tragedy called *The Rival Queens* on the theme of Alexander's fatal love for two women, Statira and Roxana. In the ▷ Renaissance, Alexander always figures among 'the Nine Worthies'.

All for Love, Or the World Well Lost (1678)

Tragedy in blank verse by ▷ John Dryden, based on ▷ Shakespeare's *Antony and Cleopatra*, but modified in accordance with Dryden's concern for the principles of neo-classicism. Dryden concentrates on the last stage of Antony's career, after the Battle of Actium. Antony's general Ventidius, his wife Octavia, and his friend Dolabella, all plead with him to leave Cleopatra, and make peace with Caesar. Antony is on the point of complying, but then he is led to believe that Dolabella is his rival for Cleopatra's affections, and he rejects both Octavia and Cleopatra. The desertion of the Egyptian fleet, followed by a false report of Cleopatra's death, lead Antony to take his own life. He falls on his sword and dies in Cleopatra's arms, after which she kills herself with an asp. Dryden stages a meeting between Cleopatra and Octavia which does not take place in Shakespeare's version, and he softens some of Shakespeare's language. His play achieves economy, elegance, and fluency, but lacks the range of Shakespeare's. Nevertheless *All for Love* is a masterpiece of its kind, and generally considered to be Dryden's best play.

Allegory

From the Greek, meaning 'speaking in other terms'. A way of representing thought and experience through images, by means of which (1) complex ideas may be simplified, or (2) abstract, spiritual, or mysterious ideas and experiences may be made immediate (but not necessarily simpler) by dramatization in fiction. In England, allegory was most used during the ▷ Middle Ages, less so during the ▷ Renaissance.

Since the 17th century deliberate and consistent allegory has continued to decline; yet the greatest of all English allegories, ▷ *The Pilgrim's Progress* by John Bunyan, is a 17th-century work. The paradox is explained by Bunyan's contact with the literature of the village sermon, which apparently continued to be conducted by a simple allegorial method with very little influence from the ▷ Reformation.
▷ Fable.

Amaryllis

A name used for a shepherdess in Greek and Latin ▷ pastoral poetry, *eg* by ▷ Theocritus, ▷ Virgil, and ▷ Ovid, and borrowed by English pastoralists such as Spenser.

Amazons

A race of female warriors occurring in ancient Greek legend, and said by the historian ▷ Herodotus to live in Scythia, north of the Black Sea. The word is often used pejoratively to describe aggressive women, women hostile to men, or women in power instead of men.

Amelia (1751)

A novel by ▷ Henry Fielding. Unlike ▷ *Joseph Andrews* and ▷ *Tom Jones*, *Amelia* deals with married love, and was Fielding's own favourite, although it was fiercely attacked by ▷ Johnson and ▷ Richardson, among others.

Set against a background of squalor and poverty, the novel opens with the imprisonment of the innocent but careless husband Captain Booth. In prison Booth meets the courtesan Miss Matthews, an old admirer who invites him to share the clean cell she has been able to afford. Booth accepts, though feeling guilty about his virtuous wife Amelia, and the two characters exchange stories about their past lives.

An old friend Colonel Bath pays Booth's bail and takes Miss Matthews as his mistress. Once out of jail, Booth turns to a life of gambling while trying to curry favour with the great. An aristocratic acquaintance assures Amelia that Booth will get his commission and invites her to accompany him to a masquerade. But 'My Lord' is a rake plotting to seduce Amelia, with the connivance of Colonel Bath and the Booths' landlady, Mrs Ellison.

Just as Amelia is about to set out to the masquerade, a fellow lodger, Mrs Bennet warns her that 'My Lord' had ruined her own life and is now threatening to destroy Amelia's 'virtue'. After several complications the plot ends happily; the Booths are rescued by their good friend Dr Harrison, and Amelia discovers that her virtue is rewarded as she will inherit her mother's fortune.

American colonies

The original thirteen colonies settled by the English which formed the first states of the United States of America (▷ American Independence, The War of), were Massachusetts, New Jersey, New York, Rhode Island, Connecticut, New Hampshire, Pennsylvania, Delaware, Virginia, Maryland, North Carolina, South Carolina, Georgia. Their population grew from 340,000 in 1700 to 1,200,000 by 1760, and to 3,000,000 by 1776.

The early colonies are now represented on the American flag by the thirteen stripes, while states established afterwards are symbolized by the stars.

American Independence, The War of (1775–83)

Also known as the American Revolution. Tensions between American settlers and their rulers in England had been building up since the 17th century: a major outbreak of hostilities, Bacon's Rebellion, had already taken place in Virginia in 1676. The intractability of ▷ George III in the later 18th century added more fuel to the fire, and conflict was precipitated by legislation favouring the London East India Company, at the expense of American shippers. Three cargoes of tea imported under the new regulations were thrown into Boston harbour by men disguised as Indians in 1773, an event described jocularly as the 'Boston Tea Party'. Fighting did not erupt until 1775, however, when the British Government attempted to arrest two American leaders at Lexington near Boston: the first shots were fired there by the British, and actual fighting broke out at Concord. On the 4th July 1776 the Congress of insurgent states issued 'The Declaration of Independence', partly inspired by the writings of ▷ Thomas Paine, and which in turn contributed to the thinking behind the ▷ French Revolution. ▷ George Washington became commander-in-chief of the insurgents. The Americans' cause was greatly helped when the French and Spanish declared war on Britain in 1777, and key defeats of the British took place along the Delaware at Trenton and Princeton (1776), Saratoga (1777) and Yorktown (1781), when the British surrendered. In 1783 peace was made in Paris and the 13 colonies (▷ American colonies) became a union of independent states, the United States of America. George Washington became the first US president, and a constitution was drawn up and ratified in 1788.

American Revolution

▷ American Independence, The War of

Amphibology, amphiboly

A sentence having two possible meanings owing to the ambiguity of its construction.

Amphibrach

A verse foot composed of a long syllable between two short ones, or an accented foot between two unaccented ones. It is rarely used in English verse.

Ana, -ana

A collection of memorable quotations from a writer, or sayings by a famous person, or anecdotes about him, *eg* Shakespeariana, Johnsoniana. Usually a suffix at the end of a name, as in these examples.

Anacoluthon

▷ Figures of speech.

Anacreontics

Any kind of melodious verse, lyrical, and concerned with love and wine. From the Greek poet Anacreon (6th–5th centuries BC). ▷ Byron called his friend Thomas Moore 'Anacreon Moore', because he translated the Odes of Anacreon into English.

Anacrusis

The use at the beginning of a line of verse of a syllable additional to the number required by the given metrical pattern.

Anagram

A literary game in which a word is disguised by changing the order of its letters so as to make a different word.

Anapaest

A metrical foot having two short or unaccented syllables followed by a long or accented one. It is usually mixed with ▷ iambics.

Ancien Régime

A French phrase, commonly taken over in English, to signify the political and social order in France before the Revolution of 1789, and more loosely to indicate a former state of order.

▷ French Revolution.

Angel

From the Greek 'messenger' (of God). The best known example of this function of messenger is the annunciation by the Angel Gabriel to the Virgin Mary of the birth of Christ. Biblical information on angels comes especially from *Revelation*, but there is further detail in the *Book of Enoch* (not included in the Bible or Apocrypha).

In general, angels are conceived as a range of beings extending between man and God. The medieval view was that they have a hierarchy in this descending order: seraphim, cherubim, thrones; dominions, virtues, powers; principalities, archangels, angels – the nine orders being grouped into three choirs, of three orders each. A more widespread notion was that angels have as leaders seven Archangels; Uriel, Raphael, Raguel, Michael, Sariel, Gabriel, Jerahmeel. These names derive from the *Book of Enoch*, but only three of them are well known: Michael the Warrior, Gabriel of the Annunciation and Raphael, who is sent to warn Adam in Eden in Book V of ▷ John Milton's ▷ *Paradise Lost*.

Earlier, their representation had something in common with the mystical winged warriors of non-Christian traditions, but as in the last three centuries Christian belief has become increasingly rationalized, so angels have been increasingly sentimentalized. Thus cherubs and seraphs are represented in 18th- and 19th-century art as the winged heads of children, and 'cherub' is a common designation for a pretty child; so also we speak of 'a seraphic smile' – often a baby's.

The name 'angel' was also given to a coin (Noble).
▷ Angels, Fallen.

Angels, Fallen

The myth of the Fall of the Angels derives from *Isaiah* 14:12 'How art thou fallen from Heaven, O Lucifer, son of the morning!' where ▷ Lucifer was the morning star (planet ▷ Venus) but became identified with ▷ Satan in his unfallen condition. ▷ John Milton in ▷ *Paradise Lost* uses the Lucifer myth and also gives to the angels that fell with him the names of pagan gods.

Anne (1665–1714)

Queen of England from 1702 until her death. Anne was the younger daughter of ▷ James II by his first wife, Anne Hyde, and was educated in the ▷ Protestant faith. When in 1672 her father became a ▷ Catholic, she remained loyal to the ▷ Church of England. She joined the party of his enemy, the Protestant William of Orange (later ▷ William III) when he landed in England in 1688, although she was later drawn into some of the intrigues on her father's behalf, and toward the end of her life favoured the succession of her Catholic half-brother.

In 1683 she was married to Prince George of Denmark, to whom she remained devoted. Her reign was dominated by the War of the ▷ Spanish Succession, which she inherited from William III and continued with encouragement from her confidante, the Duchess of ▷ Marlborough. She also presided over the ▷ Act of Union with Scotland in 1707. During much of her reign the Whig party was in the ascendancy, but from 1710 the Tories took over (▷ Whig and Tory parties), supported by the Queen. Between 1684 and 1700 she had 17 pregnancies, but several ended with miscarriages, and none of her children survived her. This precipitated a constitutional crisis, before the ▷ Act of Settlement was confirmed, and the monarchy reverted to the House of Hanover upon her death.

Annus Mirabilis (1667)

A poem by ▷ John Dryden dealing with the 'wonderful year' between the summer of 1665 and that of 1666, especially the sea battles against the Dutch, the ▷ Plague and the ▷ Great Fire of London. It is written in 'heroique stanzas', pentameter quatrains rhyming *abab*, which were felt at the time to possess an epic breadth and dignity lacking in the shorter-lined lyric metres of much 17th-century poetry. Its style is public and declamatory, the emphasis being on rapid narrative and imaginative gusto, and its epic hero is a collective one: the English people or London.

Anspach, Elizabeth, Princess of (1750–1828)

Dramatist, poet and letter-writer. Elizabeth Berkeley's first marriage was to Lord Craven, during which period she challenged convention by publishing her own poetry and allowing her play *The Miniature Picture* (1780) to be staged at ▷ Drury Lane Theatre. Although ostracized by polite society, she was accepted by other writers, and her work was admired by ▷ Horace Walpole who printed one of her early dramatic pieces, *The Sleep-Walker* (1778), and to whom she dedicated *Modern Anecdote* (1779). She was widowed in 1791 and embarked upon her second marriage, to Ansbach, in the same year; after this, the remainder of her plays were acted privately. She is also known for a series of letters discussing her journeys to Russia and Constantinople (1785–6), which rival those of Lady Mary Wortley Montagu (▷ Orientalism). Her *Memoirs* offer a lively account of the age, but hardly display the proto-feminism (▷ Feminism) with which she is credited; for example, she writes that, 'whenever women are indulged with any freedom, they polish sooner than man'.

Bib: Rodgers, K. M., *Feminism in Eighteenth-century England*.

Anstey, Christopher (1724–1805)

Minor poet and author of *New Bath Guide* (1766), an extremely successful book containing letters in verse form supposedly sent by people in ▷ Bath. The letters describe in a humorous fashion the exploits of the fictitious Blunderbuss family.

Bib: Powell, W. C., *Anstey: Bath Laureate*.

Anthology

A collection of short works in verse or prose, or selected passages from longer works, by various authors. Some anthologies lay claim to authority as representing the best written in a given period, *eg* the Oxford Books (of Seventeenth-Century Verse, etc.) and others are standard examples of taste at the time of compiling, *eg* Palgrave's *The Golden Treasury of the Best Songs and Lyrical Poems in the English Language* (1861). Others have had an important influence on taste, or on later literary development, ▷ *Percy's Reliques*, for example.

Anti-climax

▷ Figures of speech.

Antony and Cleopatra (1606–7)

A tragedy by ▷ Shakespeare, probably written in 1606–7, and first printed in the First Folio edition of his collected plays in 1623. The source is Sir Thomas North's translation (1587 edition) of ▷ Plutarch's *Lives*.

Mark Antony, with Octavius Caesar and Lepidus, is one of the 'triumvirate' (43–31 BC) which rules Rome and its empire, and he is Rome's most famous living soldier. At the opening of the play, he is the lover of ▷ Cleopatra, Queen of Egypt, and, to the disgust of his officers, he is neglecting Rome and his political and military duties. All the same, he cannot ignore Rome, and from time to time he reacts strongly against Cleopatra when he remembers his public position and his reputation. His strained relations with Octavius Caesar are temporarily mended when he marries Caesar's sister, Octavia, but he soon abandons her and returns to Cleopatra. Caesar is enraged, and is in any case anxious to secure sole power over the empire for himself. Open war breaks out between them, and Antony is defeated at the sea battle of Actium, largely owing to Cleopatra's attempt to participate personally in the campaign. After Antony's final defeat on land, he attempts to kill himself, and eventually dies of his wounds in the arms of Cleopatra, who has taken refuge in her 'monument'. This is a mausoleum which she had built so that she and Antony could lie together in death; it serves as a kind of miniature fortress. After Antony's death, she makes a bid for survival by pitting her wits against Caesar's. When she sees that she has failed, she takes her own life. The two death scenes, her own and Antony's, are amongst the most famous scenes in Shakespeare's work.

One of the ironies of the tragedy is that Cleopatra loves Antony just because he is a great Roman hero, and yet, in order to get full possession of him, she has to destroy this part of him. At a deeper level, Rome and Egypt are set in dramatic contrast: Rome stands for the political world, with its ruthless and calculating manoeuvring for power; Egypt stands for the heat and colour of passion, tending always to dissolution and corruption.

▷ John Dryden's ▷ *All for Love* is also a tragedy about Antony and Cleopatra; a comparison of the two plays is instructive in showing the changes that had come about in English verse in the intervening period.

Aphorism, apophthegm

A terse sentence, weighted with sense; with more weight of wisdom than an ▷ epigram need have, but less elegance.

Aphrodite

In Greek myth, goddess of physical beauty and sexual love. Her cult was widespread; in Rome she was known as Venus; in Syria, and the Middle East as Astarte, Ashtaroth, Ishtar. She was also called Anadyomene ('sprung from the foam'); and because this occurred near the island of Cythera, she was Cytherean. Zeus married her to Hephaestus (Lat. Vulcan) but owing to his ugliness she was unfaithful to him with Ares. She was the mother of Eros. (Lat. Cupidos) the boy–god of desire and the rival of Persephone for the love of ▷ Adonis. She competed with Hera and Athene for the prize of a golden apple for the greatest beauty, to be awarded by Paris, and won the contest.

Apollyon

In the Bible, *Revelation* 9:11, Apollyon is 'the angel of the bottomless pit'. He is chiefly famous in English literature for his appearance in ▷ Bunyan's D ▷ *Pilgrim's Progress*, where he is identifiable with Satan. Apollyon means 'destroying'.

Apologue

A little story, very often a ▷ fable, with a moral.

Apophthegm

▷ Aphorism, apophthegm

Apostrophe

▷ Figures of speech.

Apprenticeship

A system of training undergone by youths entering on a trade or craft. The apprentice was indentured to a master in the craft, *ie* entered into a contract with him, to serve him in return for maintenance and instruction for seven years, usually between the ages of 16 and 23. The apprentice was a member of the master's household and the master was responsible for his behaviour before the law. Thus apprenticeship provided social control, as well as a form of education, and tended to maintain standards in manufacture and professional conduct. It also had the social advantage of mixing the classes and ensuring that the landed classes retained interest in trade, for the smaller landed gentry commonly indentured their younger sons, who had no land to inherit, to master craftsmen, especially in London. Until the 18th century (when the gentry, grown richer, tended to despise trade) this mixture of classes, as well as large numbers, made the London apprentices a formidable body of public opinion both politically and, for instance, in the Elizabethan theatre. Apprenticeship was systematized by law under the Statute of Artificers, 1563. It had its beginnings in the ▷ Middle Ages. Usually women were not permitted to be apprenticed: in this way they were excluded from skilled paid work, although wives, daughters and sisters often helped in the work of their male relatives. Until the 17th century, apprenticeship was the only way to enter most trades and professions.

Arabian Nights Entertainments

Also known as *The Thousand and One Nights*, this collection of stories supposed to be told by Scheherazade was probably put together by an Egyptian story-teller around the 15th century. The stories became well-known and popular in Europe early in the 18th century. English translations have been made by Edward Lane in 1840 and, with greater literary merit, by Sir Richard Burton in 1885–88.

▷ Children's books.

Arbuthnot, Dr John (1667–1735)

Close friend of ▷ Alexander Pope, ▷ Jonathan Swift and ▷ John Gay, with whom he collaborated in the satiric sallies of the ▷ Scriblerus Club. Arbuthnot was physician in ordinary to Queen Anne and a Fellow of the ▷ Royal Society; he was widely admired for his medical science and for his genial wit. His most famous satire is 'The History of John Bull' (1712), a series of pamphlets advocating an end to the war with France which turned the arguments of Swift's *Conduct of the Allies* into a comic allegory. He also had a hand in such collaborative Scriblerian satires as *The Memoirs of Martin Scriblerus* (1741), *The Art of Sinking in Poetry* (1727) and ▷ *Three Hours after Marriage* (1717). Among his more important scientific writings are his *Essay on the Usefulness of Mathematical Learning* (1701) and his *Essay concerning the nature of Aliments* (1731).
Bib: Aitken, G. A. (ed.), *The Life and Works of Dr John Arbuthnot*; Beattie, L. M., *John Arbuthnot, mathematician and satirist*.

Areopagitica (1644)

Title of a ▷ pamphlet, published on 28 November 1644, by ▷ John Milton. In June 1643 ▷ Parliament had passed an ordinance which attempted to licence the press – in effect it was designed as a form of covert political ▷ censorship, which allowed officers of Parliament to search for, and confiscate, unlicenced books. Milton's *Areopagitica* was offered as a powerful statement on behalf of liberty of the press. In arguing for such liberty, Milton was aligning himself with radicals such as William Walwyn and Richard Overton, and entering a forceful plea for the free dissemination of information and ideas without which, in his opinion, it was impossible for individuals to make genuine political choices. In discussing this question of choice, *Areopagitica* can be thought of being a precursor of one of the major themes of Milton's ▷ *Paradise Lost*. The title itself implicitly compares the Parliament of England, to whom Milton was addressing his comments, to the Supreme Court of ancient Athens which met on the hill Areopagos, situated to the west of the Acropolis.

▷ Levellers, The.

Aristotle (384–322 BC)

A Greek philosopher, born at Stageira, and so sometimes called the Stagirite. He was first a pupil of ▷ Plato, later developing his thought on principles opposed to those of his master. He was tutor to the young ▷ Alexander the Great. His thought covered varied fields of knowledge, in most of which he has been influential. His best known works are his *Ethics*, *Politics* and ▷ *Poetics*.

The difference between Aristotle and Plato has been described as follows: Plato makes us think in the first place of an ideal and supernatural world by turning our minds to ideal forms which are the truth in terms of which imperfect earthly things can be known and judged; Aristotle turns us towards the natural world where things are what they are, perfect or imperfect, so that knowledge comes through study and classification of them in the actual world. It can thus be seen that whilst Plato leads in the direction of mysticism, Aristotle leads towards science. Until the 13th century, Christian thought tended to be dominated by Plato, but medieval Christian thought, owing to the work of ▷ Thomas Aquinas, found Aristotelianism more acceptable.

The *Poetics* is based on the study of imaginative literature in Greek from which Italian critics of the 16th century, and French dramatists and critics of the 17th century such as Corneille, ▷ Racine and ▷ Boileau constructed a system of rules. Sidney knew Aristotle chiefly through the Italians, who had derived from Aristotle some rules not to be found in him – notably the unities of time and place (▷ Classical Unities). ▷ Dryden and ▷ Samuel Johnson, were respectful of and deeply influenced by French neo-Aristotelianism, but they refused to be bound by it, unlike some second-rank critics such as ▷ Thomas Rymer. The 19th century reacted strongly against the attitude, but in this century the elimination of the neo-Aristotelian superimpositions of the ▷ Renaissance has revived interest in the discernment displayed in the *Poetics*.

Armstrong, John (1709–1779)

Medical doctor, friend of ▷ James Thomson, and author of didactic poems in blank verse, including the mildly erotic *Economy of Love* (1736), and *The Art of Preserving Health* (1744).

Ars Poetica (Art of Poetry)

▷ Horace.

Arthur, King

If there is a historical figure behind King Arthur, it may be that of a British chieftain, active some time in the 5th or 6th century, who resisted Saxon invaders after the Roman garrisons had abandoned Britain. Documentary evidence and archaeological data provide us with only a vague picture of the historical events of these centuries, and so the historical location of an Arthur figure continues to be a subject of great debate.

The writer responsible for putting King Arthur firmly on the map of British history was Geoffrey of Monmouth who, in his *Historia Regum Britanniae*

(*History of the Kings of Britain*), c 1138, provided a continuous account of the British kings from Brutus onwards and made the reign of King Arthur the high spot of this sequence. Under Arthur's rule, Britain regains its status as a unified Christian nation, and gains international power and prestige too. This version of British history, though challenged by some late-medieval historians, appears to have been generally accepted and became a standard feature of accounts of insular history.

King Arthur became an important feature of the English literary and historical landscape, and Arthurian narrative was constantly open in the course of its development for appropriation as a means of expressing and exploring different kinds of political and cultural ideals. ▷ Spenser's epic, ▷ *The Faerie Queene*, has the figure of Prince Arthur as its central protagonist, and later writers such as ▷ Ben Jonson, ▷ Milton and ▷ Dryden all planned major works on Arthurian topics (although only Dryden actually produced an Arthurian text, his dramatic opera *King Arthur*). The history of Arthurian narrative has periods of decline and revival, though the subject of Arthur always seems to have been available as a cultural reference point.
Bib: Lacy, N. et al. (eds.), *The Arthurian Encyclopedia*,

Artifice, The (1722)

Play by ▷ Susannah Centlivre, her last, recently revived in London. The action actually incorporates several 'artifices' spread across four linked but separate plot lines: 1 Sir John Freeman, in love with Olivia, has been disinherited in favour of his younger brother Ned, who is also courting Olivia, and has been promised her hand in marriage by her father, Sir Philip Moneylove. 2 Ned has seduced an apparently poor Dutchwoman, Louisa, who has borne him a son. She comes to England to obtain justice, and tricks Ned into marrying her. Sir John is reunited with his fortune and with Olivia, and Louisa reveals herself as an heiress. 3 Old Mr Watchit is jealous of his young wife and locks her up when he goes out. But Ned contrives to gain access to her apartments, and to court her. By another trick she humiliates her husband, and he is forced to grant her more liberty. 4 The Widow Heedless, set upon marrying a lord, is wooed by the unscrupulous gambler, Tally, and is also by the Ensign Fainwell, both in disguise. Fainwell exposes Tally, wins the Widow, and reveals his true identity. The play was originally criticized as designed 'to encourage adultery, to ridicule the clergy and to set women above the arbitrary power of their husbands. . .'.

Astell, Mary (1666–1731)

Sometimes claimed as 'the first English feminist', Mary Astell was a writer and intellectual, who published influential tracts on the duties and injustices of marriage, the most famous being ▷ *A Serious Proposal to the Ladies for the Advancement of Their True and Greatest Interest* (1694), which appeared anonymously as the work of 'a Lover of Her Sex'. With the help of several patrons, most notably William Sancroft, the archbishop of Canterbury, Astell was able to live independently in London and make a career of writing. Her views on the equality of the sexes were, however, modified by her conservative politics and her religious commitment to the Anglican Church. A wife's status in relation to her husband was, she argued, in the nature of a voluntary contract, but: 'It may be any Man's Business and Duty to keep Hogs; he was not Made for this, but if he hires himself out to such an Employment, he ought conscientiously to perform it'.
Bib: Perry, Ruth, *The Celebrated Mary Astell*.

Astraea

In Greek myth, 'the star maiden', usually considered to be the daughter of Zeus and Themis. During the Golden Age she lived on earth as the benefactress of humanity (▷ Ages, Golden, Silver, etc.). The name was adopted by the playwright, ▷ Aphra Behn.

Astraea Redux ('Astraea Returning', 1660) is a poem by ▷ John Dryden about the restoration of ▷ Charles II.

Atheism

Disbelief in God. In the ▷ Middle Ages and the 16th and 17th centuries, atheism was abhorrent; it was equivalent to a denial of conscience – an attitude shown in the play *The Atheist's Tragedy* (1611) by Cyril Tourneur. There were some who adopted this position and effectively challenged the power of organized religion. Christopher Marlowe was charged with it in 1593. Nevertheless atheism at this period was different from the systematic belief that man's reason suffices for his welfare. This belief grew in the 18th century and emerged in the ▷ French Revolution, influencing such English intellectuals as ▷ William Godwin and through him Shelley, whose atheism caused him to be expelled from Oxford, and for whom ▷ Platonism sufficed. Different, but still 18th-century in its sources, was the atheism of ▷ Utilitarians such as James Mill (1773–1836) and John Stuart Mill, who were less naïve about reason than Godwin but, as practical men, saw religion as unnecessary in their scheme for human betterment.

Atheist, The: or The Second Part of the Soldier's Fortune (1684)

Play by ▷ Thomas Otway; his last. A comedy, with many intrigue elements. Porcia (played by ▷ Elizabeth Barry in the original version) is pursued by an unwanted suitor, her late husband's brother, who tries to force her to marry him. She approaches Beaugard (first played by ▷ Thomas Betterton) in masquerade, to take up her cause and, in effect, marry her instead, although she claims at first to hate him. Beaugard is also pursued by Lucretia, but he remains loyal to Porcia, whereupon Lucretia plots her revenge, disguising herself as a man in the process of attempting to mismate various characters. Meanwhile Courtine and Sylvia, lovers in ▷ *The Soldier's Fortune*, have now married, but the union is unhappy, and he abandons her. Various complications are resolved after an improbable last scene, where numerous characters mistake one another's identities in the dark. It is interesting that the men in the play are largely passive, while most of the action is initiated by women.

Atticus, T. Pomponius (109–32 BC)
Atticus was a correspondent of Cicero and learned
in Greek literature. ▷ Alexander Pope refers to
▷ Joseph Addison under this name in lines which
he originally sent as a reproach to the older man in
a letter in about 1715. They were first published in
1722 after Addison's death, and appear in revised
form in the *Epistle to Dr Arbuthnot* (1735).

Aubrey, John (1626–97)
Biographer and antiquary. Aubrey was a man of
endlessly fascinated speculation on every aspect of
the world. In an unmethodical way he produced
(though never published) an invaluable record of
people, events and happenings of the period in which
he lived. The record of personalities preserved by
Aubrey is often factually untrustworthy, and yet
his *Brief Lives* is still an important document not
least because of its penetrating assessment of his
subjects' lives and works. If nothing else, Aubrey has
preserved a running critical commentary on many of
the figures from the 17th century whose works are
read in the 20th century.
▷ Biography.
Bib: Dick, O. L. (ed.), *Aubrey's Brief Lives*.

Augustanism
There are two aspects to 'Augustanism', one political,
the other more strictly literary.
1 *Political Augustanism* In the decades following the
Restoration a more or less fanciful parallel between
recent English history and that of early imperial
Rome was developed, following similar gestures
by ▷ Ben Jonson earlier in the century. Both the
Emperor ▷ Augustus (27 BC–AD 14) and ▷ King
Charles II could be felt to have restored order to the
state as legitimate successors to rulers who had been
assassinated by Republicans (Julius Caesar, Charles
I). Both preserved the forms of constitutionality, and
kept at least the appearance of a balance of power
between Senate or Parliament and the head of state.
Both rulers, and their successors, presided over an
expansion of imperial power which extended their
own civilization over more 'barbarous' peoples, by
means of military power – the army in the case of
Rome, the navy in the case of Britain. Where there
had previously been the *Pax Romana* there would
now be a *Pax Britannica*. Both ▷ Whigs and Tories
could feel reassured by this parallel, though naturally
a Whig would tend to stress the constitutionality of
the new order, while a Tory such as ▷ Alexander
Pope stresses its Stuart legitimacy: 'And Peace
and Plenty tell, a *Stuart* reigns' (*Windsor Forest*).
Political Augustanism is concerned essentially with
society and with public issues, and is optimistic
about British civilization and its role in the world as
imperial power. It is detectable in such diverse works
as▷ Daniel Defoe's ▷ *Robinson Crusoe* and ▷ James
Thomson's *Castle of Indolence*.
2 *Literary Augustanism* The reign of Augustus
coincided with the golden age of Roman culture
and literature, and the major writers of the time, such
as ▷ Horace and ▷ Virgil, explicitly celebrated
the Roman imperial destiny. During the period
of stability and growing prosperity following the

▷ Restoration the somewhat naïve adulation of
the classics found in such Tudor writers as George
Chapman and Ben Jonson was replaced by a growing
understanding of, and sense of equality with, the
great Latin writers. At last English literature was
coming of age in terms of self-conscious theoretical
confidence, technical sophistication and diversity
of genre and metrical form. The foundation of the
▷ Poet Laureateship as a regular court office was
a sign of this new confidence. In his essays ▷ John
Dryden constantly parallels the achievements of
modern English writers with their classical ancestors.
The young Alexander Pope picked up the spirit
of the age very young and was promoted by his
friends as an English Virgil. The true poet, it was
vaguely felt, would follow Virgil in writing first
▷ pastorals (which require only technical skill and
little experience of life), then would move on to
▷ Georgics, or longer discursive compositions, and
would crown his life's work with an ▷ epic. With
a little licence this pattern could be read into the
careers of the earlier English writers, ▷ Edmund
Spenser and ▷ John Milton, who were achieving
classic status at this time. Ornamental, courtly forms,
such as the ▷ sonnet and Spenserian stanza, were
now despised as childishly 'gothic', or employed with
a conscious sense of their quaint primitiveness. The
'heroic' ▷ couplet emerged as the most dignified
▷ metre of which English verse was felt to be
capable. Since the English language, lacking the
sounding mellifluousness of classical Latin, could not
support lines the length of the Latin hexameter, nor
dispense with the 'barbarous' ornament of rhyme,
then the best recourse, it was felt, was to regularize
and dignify the pentameter couplet. (Blank verse is
of course a much more natural English parallel to
the Latin hexameter, but the best poets were wisely
unwilling for the time being to risk comparison
with the recent example of Milton.) Alongside
the cultivation of the couplet a doctrine of 'kinds'
grew up which prescribed specific 'high' or noble
vocabulary for epic writing, and different vocabularies
for the other genres. This notion, which reflects
the class consciousness of the new bourgeoisie as
much as any purely literary doctrine, is seen at its
most rigid in ▷ Thomas Parnell's *Essay on the
Different Stiles of Poetry* (1713). The neo-classical style
which resulted from this regulation of metre and
language could hope to appeal both to the traditional
Aristotelian classicist of the time, who required an
'imitation' of permanent nature, and the Lockean
rationalist, who could see ▷ Sir Isaac Newton's
'laws' of nature reflected in the couplet's combination
of formal exactitude and infinite variety.
It is important to stress that such Augustanism is,
like ▷ Romanticism, the artificial construction of
literary historians, and never constituted a systematic
programme or manifesto for poetry. The summary
above lends it a coherence and exactitude which it
never achieved in the work of any poet. Like most
literary movements Augustanism was only defined
after it was virtually over. The noun 'Augustanism'
seems not to have come into use until the early
20th century. In 1904 ▷ Theodore Watts-Dunton
accused ▷ Thomas Gray of being 'a slave to

Augustanism', a judgement that Gray himself would have found quite bewildering. In the later 19th and early 20th century all 18th-century poetry tended to be characterized as overformal and emotionless, and the terms 'Augustan', 'Augustanism' and 'The Augustan Age' frequently served to obscure rather than illuminate the poetry of the period.

Bib: Ford, B. (ed.), *New Pelican Guide to English Literature, Vol. 4: From Dryden to Johnson*; Rogers, P., *The Augustan Vision*; Rogers, P., *Hacks and Dunces: Pope, Swift and Grub Street*; Novak, M., *Eighteenth Century English Literature*; Sambrook, J., *The Eighteenth Century*; Doody, M. A., *The Daring Muse: Augustan Poetry Reconsidered*.

Augustus
▷ Caesar, Augustus

Aureng-Zebe (1675)
Heroic play by ▷ John Dryden, based on a contemporary account of the struggle between the four sons of Shah Jahan, the fifth Mogul emperor, for the succession to the throne. Dryden made several crucial changes to his source, notably to the character of Aureng-Zebe, who in Dryden's version remains loyal to his father, even though he is betrayed by him. This morality pays off in that at the end of the play he receives the crown legitimately. The character of Indamora, a captive queen whom Aureng-Zebe loves, was invented by Dryden. At the end they are united, with the blessings of the emperor who had pursued Indamora for himself.

Austen, Jane (1775-1817)
Novelist. Her novels in order of publication are as follows: *Sense and Sensibility* (1811), *Pride and Prejudice* (1813), ▷ *Mansfield Park* (1814), *Emma* (1816), *Northanger Abbey* and *Persuasion* (1818). The last two, published posthumously, are her first and last work respectively in order of composition. Fragments and early drafts include: *Lady Susan* (pub 1871), *The Watsons* (1871) and *Sanditon*, on which she was working when she died, published in 1925.

She restricted her material to a narrow range of society and events: a prosperous, middle-class circle in provincial surroundings. However, she treated this material with such subtlety of observation and depth of penetration that she is ranked among the best of English novelists. A French critic, Louis Cazamian, writes of her method that it is 'so classical, so delicately shaded ... that we are strongly reminded of the great French analysts'. Her classicism arose from respect for the sane, clear-sighted judgement of the ▷ Augustan age that had preceded her, but its vitality is enhanced by the ▷ romanticism of her own period, so that her heroines acquire wisdom by a counter-balancing of the two. She brought the English novel, as an art form, to its maturity, and the wide range which that form covered later in the 19th century owed much to the imaginative assurance which she had given it.

Her life as a clergyman's daughter was outwardly uneventful but it is probably not true that this accounts for the absence of sensationalism in her novels; her circle of relatives and friends was such as could have given her a wide experience of contemporary society. The restriction of the subject matter of her fiction seems to have been dictated by artistic considerations. D. W. Harding's essay 'Regulated Hatred: An Aspect of the Work of Jane Austen' (*Scrutiny*, 1940) credits her with being a caustic satirist and critic of society.

Bib: Austen-Leigh, J. E., *A Memoir of Jane Austen*; Lascelles, M., *Jane Austen and her Art*; Mudrick, M., *Jane Austen: Irony as Defence and Discovery*; Trilling, L., 'Mansfield Park' in *The Opposing Self*; Leavis, Q. D., *A Critical Theory of Jane Austen's Writings* (*Scrutiny*); Southam, B. C. (ed.), *Jane Austen: The Critical Heritage*; Cecil, D., *A Portrait of Jane Austen*.

Authorized Version of the Bible
▷ Bible in England.

Autobiography
The word came into English at the very end of the 18th century. In the 19th and 20th centuries writing the story of one's own life has become a common literary activity. However, the practice already had an ancient history, and English autobiography may be divided into two overlapping segments in this period: 1 the spiritual confession and 2 the memoir.

1 The spiritual confession has as its basic type the *Confessions* of St Augustine of Hippo (345–430) written in Latin who described his conversion to Christianity. Such records of the inner life existed in the English Middle Ages, *eg* the *Book of Margery Kempe* (15th century), but the great age for them was the 17th century, when the ▷ Puritans, depending on the Word of God in the Bible and the inner light of their own consciences, made a practice of intensive self-examination. By far the best known of these records is ▷ Bunyan's ▷ *Grace Abounding to the Chief of Sinners* (1666). It is characteristic of such works that they contain detailed accounts of the emotional life, but little factual description of events.

2 The memoir, on the other hand, of French derivation, originates largely in the 17th century and owes much to the practice of extensive letter-writing which then developed, *eg* the letters of Madame de Sévigné (1626–96). An example of this type is ▷ Margaret Cavendish's 'A True Relation of My Birth Breeding and Life' appended to *Nature's Pictures* (1656). An example from 18th-century England is the fragmentary *Memoirs* (pub 1796) by the historian ▷ Edward Gibbon. But the objective memoir and the subjective confessions came together in the *Confessions* of the French-Swiss ▷ Jean-Jacques Rousseau, and this is the most prevalent form of the outstanding English autobiographies of the 19th century. A number of fictional works in the 18th century purport to be memoirs, or are in fact memoirs disguised as fiction, for example, ▷ Delarivière Manley's *The Adventures of Rivella* (1714).

B

Bacon, Francis, 1st Baron Verulam and Viscount St Albans (1561–1626)

Politician, philosopher and essayist, Francis Bacon rose to the rank of Lord Chancellor, before being dismissed from that office in the same year in which he attained it – 1621. Bacon's offence was, technically, his conviction for accepting bribes whilst a judge in chancery suits. The cause of his conviction, however, was the ascendency of political enemies he had made in the course of his ambitious career.

It is, however, as an essayist and, more importantly, as one of the earliest theoreticians of scientific methodology, for which Bacon has become famous. A series of works – including *The Advancement of Learning* (1605 expanded into *De Augmentis Scientiarum* in 1623), *De sapientia veterum* (1609, translated as *The Wisdom of the Ancients* in 1619) and the incomplete *Novum Organum* (1620) – established his claims to philosophical and methodological pre-eminence amongst his contemporaries. The *De Augmentis* and the *Novum Organum* formed the first two parts of his enormous project, gathered under the title *Instauratio Magna*, which remained unfinished but which proposed nothing less than a re-ordering of all fields of human enquiry. In addition Bacon wrote a history of the reign of Henry VIII (published in 1622), a collection of anecdotal stories (1625) and a ▷ utopian work based on the new scientific endeavours of the age, *The New Atlantis* (1626). His major philosophical works were written in addition to his contribution to the law and his *Essays*, which were first published in 1597 and issued in a final form (much expanded) in 1625.

Until recently, Bacon's reputation tended to rest on his *Essays* which represent a series of terse observations in the style of ▷ Seneca rather than the more fluid meditations to be found in the writings of ▷ Montaigne, who is credited with originating the essay as a distinctly modern form. More and more attention is, however, now being paid to his theoretical work in the area of scientific methodology and taxonomy. It was Bacon who, in the later 17th century, was to be celebrated as the true progenitor of the ▷ New Science, not least because of his intense interest in the language of science, and in the forms of discourse appropriate to different rhetorical and methodological projects. As a scientist, in the modern sense, his contribution to knowledge was negligible. But as the author of a series of 'manifestos' which set out to establish the basis for inductive or experimental philosophy, his influence on later generations of English philosophers was incalculable. The 'Baconian' method was the legacy of his work – that is, an adherence to the importance of observation and definition of the particular, rather than a delight in deduction from the general – and the basis for his reputation in later periods.

Bib: Spedding, J., Ellis, R. L., and Heath, D. D. (eds.), *Works of Francis Bacon* (7 vols.); Rossi, P. *Francis Bacon. From Magic to Science* (trans. S. Rabinovitch; Vickers, B. (ed.), *Essential Articles for the Study of Francis Bacon*.

Baconian
▷ Bacon, Francis.

Badman, The Life and Death of Mr (1680)

A moral ▷ allegory by ▷ John Bunyan, author of ▷ *The Pilgrim's Progress*, and, apart from the more famous work, the only one of Bunyan's fictions to remain widely known. It is the biography of a wicked man told by Mr Wiseman, and contains vivid and dramatic detail. Its realism and its psychology make it one of the forerunners of the novel.

Baillie, Joanna (1762–1851)

Friend of ▷ Sir Walter Scott and prolific author of plays based on the ▷ Shakespearean model (*Plays of the Passions*; 1798, 1802, 1812), five of which were acted. She also wrote poems in couplets, and lyrics on sentimental and patriotic themes (*Fugitive Verses*, 1790; *Metrical Legends*, 1821; *Poetic Miscellanies*, 1823).

Ballad

Traditionally the ballad has been considered a folkloric verse narrative which has strong associations with communal dancing, and support for that link has been found in the derivation of the word 'ballad' itself (from the late Latin verb *ballare* – to dance). More recently scholars have viewed the association between ballads and dance forms rather more sceptically. Generally, the term is used of a narrative poem which uses an elliptical and highly stylized mode of narration, in which the technique of repetition with variation may play an important part. Often ballads contain repeated choral refrains but this is not a universal feature.

Ballad forms can be identified in early English texts: the brief narrative about *Fudas* in the ▷ Harley manuscript has been hailed as the earliest English example of the form. The so-called ▷ Broadside ballads, sold in Elizabethan times, were narrative poems on a wide range of subjects printed on a single side of a broadsheet. From the 18th century onwards, collections of folk popular ballads began to be made and the form was taken up by some of the most influential poets of the late 18th century as a folkloric form of expression. ▷ Wordsworth's and ▷ Coleridge's collection of poems ▷ *Lyrical Ballads* (1798) does not contain many poems in ballad form (apart from the brilliant balladic composition ▷ *The Ancient Mariner*) but the function of the title seems to be to arouse associations of oral, non-literary poetic forms. In this collection, art is used to conceal art.
Bib: Bold, A., *The Ballad*.

Ballard, George (1706–55)

Writer, antiquarian, and historian, born at Campden in Gloucestershire. His mother was a midwife, and he was apprenticed to a women's clothing maker. Early in life he developed a reputation for learning, leading Lord Chedworth to provide him with a pension for life. Ballard collected books and documents, and drew up histories and genealogies of individuals, families and monuments. He was part of a circle of antiquaries, who collected and classified

artifacts, books and manuscripts. He had a sister with literary interests, and this may have influenced composition of his best-known work, the *Memoirs of Several Ladies of Great Britain* (1752), which contains biographies of 64 learned and literary women from the ▷ Middle Ages to his own day. He wrote it, as he said in the preface, in order to remove 'the vulgar prejudice of the supposed incapacity of the female sex'. His work is considered a major source of information about educated women of the past, and has been extensively used by biographers and anthologists since the 18th century.
Bib: Perry, R. (ed.), *Memoirs of Several Ladies of Great Britain*.

Bank of England, The
The Bank of England was founded in 1694, based on suggestions by William Patterson. It first existed as a corporation with a special charter to raise loans for the government of ▷ William III to pay for the wars against France. By degrees, in the 18th and 19th centuries it became the keeper of the government's funds, as well as of the funds of other banks. Thus it grew into the first 'Central Bank' in the world. Although it was a private corporation until 1946, when it was nationalized, it had long worked so closely with the Treasury that its independence of the government had been only nominal.

Banks, John (b c 1650)
Dramatist. He trained as a lawyer, but turned to the stage in 1677, when the success of Nathaniel Lee's *The Rival Queens* led him to write *The Rival Kings*. Banks specialized in writing pathetic tragedies, featuring injured heroines. He was ahead of his time as the vogue for such plays, sometimes known as ▷ She-Tragedies, did not really develop until the last decade of the century. He could not find a publisher for his *The Innocent Usurper*, or a theatre to perform it in, until 1693, ten years after it was written; it was then banned for political reasons. *The Island Queens*, concerning the execution of Mary, Queen of Scots (1684), also met with indifference until 1704, when it achieved success under the title, *Albion's Queen*. Other plays include *The Unhappy Favourite* (1681), about Elizabeth I and Essex; *Virtue Betrayed* (1682), on Anne Boleyn; and *Cyrus the Great* (1696), which had considerable success in performance at ▷ Lincoln's Inn Fields, although its run was curtailed by the death of one its leading actors.

Baptists
An important sect of Nonconformist ▷ Protestants; originally one of the three principal branches of English ▷ Puritanism, the other two being the Independents (▷ Congregationalism), and the ▷Presbyterians (Calvinists). Their especial doctrine is that the rite of baptism must be administered to adults, and not to infants. They began as an offshoot of the Independents in the first decade of the 17th century, and made rapid progress between 1640 and 1660 – the period of the ▷ Civil War and the ▷ Interregnum, when the Puritans usurped the position of the ▷ Church of England. One of the foremost exponents of the Baptist Church in the second half of the 17th century was ▷ John Bunyan.

Barbauld, Anna Laetitia (Aikin) (1743–1825)
English poet, essayist and writer for children. Her father ran a Dissenting academy in Warrington (of which she wrote 'Here callow chiefs and embryo statesmen lie'), and he taught her Latin and Greek. Her brother, John (a doctor), was proud that some of her first poems were written at his house. They published some pieces together (in *Miscellanous Pieces in Prose* 1773) but the first of her poems to be published was the 'Ode on Corsica' (1768). She was already a known poet when her *Poems* (1773) were published: they went through four editions in twelve months. When she married M. Rochemont Barbauld her father wrote that she was under 'the baleful influence of [▷ Rousseau's] *nouvelle Heloise*'. She and her husband ran a boys' school together before travelling in France and coming to London, where the marriage broke down. Rochemont Barbauld eventually committed suicide. Barbauld spent much of the rest of her life in Stoke Newington, London, writing for ▷ periodicals, including *The Spectator, The Guardian* and the *Freeholder*. Her *Lessons for Children* (1778) and *Hymns in Prose for Children* (1781) were in the new genre of educational publications. She published the long narrative poem *Eighteen Hundred and Eleven* (1812), and edited the work of other writers including ▷ Mark Akenside, ▷ William Collins and the correspondence of ▷ Samuel Richardson. She knew ▷ Hester Chapone, and met ▷ Maria Edgeworth in 1799.
Other publications: *Epistle to William Wilberforce* (1791).
Bib: Aikin, Lucy (ed.), *Works* (1825); Rogers, Betsy, *Georgian Chronicle: Mrs Barbauld and Her Family*; Scott, W.S., *Letters of ... Barbauld and Maria Edgeworth*.

Bard
A member of the privileged caste of poets among the ancient Celtic peoples, driven by the Romans and then the Anglo-Saxons into ▷ Wales and ▷ Ireland and, legend has it, exterminated in Wales by Edward I. The term became known to later English writers from references in Latin literature. Poets such as ▷ Shakespeare, ▷ John Milton and ▷ Alexander Pope refer to any serious poet as a 'bard'. In the 18th century, partly as a result of the growing antiquarian interest in druidism, the term came to designate a mysteriously or sacredly inspired poet, as in ▷ Thomas Gray's famous ▷ ode ▷ 'The Bard' (1757).

'Bard, The' (1757)
One of ▷ Thomas Gray's two famous 'Pindaric Odes' (▷ ode; the other being 'The Progress of Poesy'). The last surviving Celtic ▷ bard stands on a mountain-top and calls down curses upon King Edward I and the English army as they march below. He prophesies the end of Edward's royal house and its ultimate replacement by the (Welsh) house of Tudor. He concludes by throwing himself into the River Conway beneath. There is a stagey wildness

about the work which irritated ▷ Samuel Johnson, though its failure to 'promote any truth, moral or political' did not prevent it from being very popular at the time.

Barker, Jane (fl 1688–1726)

Poet and novelist. She came from a ▷ Catholic Royalist family which remained loyal to the ▷ Stuart monarchs during the ▷ Civil War and to ▷ James II after the accession of ▷ William (III) and ▷ Mary. She spent most of her life in Lincolnshire. Her poetry is both political and personal, including themes such as friendship and love; it includes *Poetical Recreations* (1688), and *A Collection of Poems Referring to the Times* published in 1700. Her novels include *Love Intrigues* (1713) and *Exilius* (1715). A collection, *Entertaining Novels*, was also published in 1715. Barker remained unmarried, a fact which she discussed in *A Patchwork Screen for the Ladies* (1723). She became popular, and some of her works ran to several editions.

Baroque

A term mainly applied to the visual arts, particularly architecture, and (with a somewhat different meaning) to music, but now increasingly used in literary contexts also. It derives from the Italian word *barocco* meaning rough and unpolished, and was originally used to denote extravagance or excessiveness in the visual arts. Thence it came to designate the exuberant, florid architecture and painting characteristic of Europe during the period of absolute monarchies in the 17th and 18th centuries. The more restrained, constitutionalist climate of Britain prevented baroque architecture from taking firm hold, and the few examples (*eg* Castle Howard and Blenheim Palace, both by ▷ Sir John Vanbrugh) date from shortly after the ▷ Restoration, when French taste was in the ascendant. English ▷ neo-classicism, when it aimed at large-scale grandeur, tended to be more sober and austere, like ▷ Sir Christopher Wren's St Paul's. In domestic contexts the greater economic and political power of the lesser aristocracy and the rising merchant class in England, meant that the modest convenience of the Palladian style (▷ Andrea Palladio) was preferred to full-blown baroque. ▷ Alexander Pope's patron Lord Burlington was the most prominent advocate of the Palladian style and Pope wrote his fourth ▷ *Moral Essay*, on the discomforts of baroque magnificence, under Burlington's influence.

In music the term denotes the new, more public, expressive and dramatic style, characterized by free recitative, and most typically seen in the new genre of opera, originating in the Italy of Monteverdi in the late 16th century. It is closely associated with the introduction of new, more expressive and louder instruments, ideal for public performance, such as the transverse flute, the violin and the harpsichord, which at this time began to supplant the softer recorder, viol and virginals, suitable to the intimate, often amateur, music-making of the ▷ Renaissance. The term is now applied to all music between this time and the onset of the classicism of Haydn and Mozart in the later 18th century. The baroque style

in music came to England late, and its first great English exponent is ▷ Henry Purcell (1659–95), who wrote the first English opera, *Dido and Aeneas* (1689; libretto by ▷ Nahum Tate).

The epithet 'baroque' has recently come to be used in literary contexts by analogy with its use in the other arts. Thus the extravagant Italianate conceits of the Catholic poet Richard Crashaw who ended his life in Rome, can be called 'baroque'. The florid, public quality of ▷ John Dryden's ▷ *Annus Mirabilis*, may also be termed 'baroque', with its innocent celebration of national pride and adulation of the monarch, the literary equivalent of the mural paintings of the Italian baroque artist Verrio, who worked in England, and whose English pupil, James Thornhill, decorated the Painted Hall at Greenwich early in the 18th century. Like ▷ Classical and ▷ Romantic the word has also developed a wider application beyond its strict historical period.

Barry, Elizabeth (1658–1713)

The first well-known English actress, said to have been trained by the ▷ Earl of Rochester, who boasted he could make an actress of her in six months; she became his mistress and later had a daughter by him.

She began by acting at the ▷ Dorset Garden Theatre, probably in 1675, but her career blossomed in 1679–80, with a series of tragic roles which earned her 'the Name of Famous Mrs Barry, both at Court and City'.

Throughout her career she was adored for her acting talents – being admired equally in comic and tragic roles – and sharply satirized for her alleged promiscuity: a contemporary commentary describes her as 'the finest Woman in the World upon the Stage, and the Ugliest Woman off't'. She played Lady Brute in the first production of ▷ *The Provok'd Wife* (1697), Mrs Marwood in the original ▷ *The Way of the World* (1700), and dozens of important roles in plays by contemporary and earlier authors, including many of ▷ Shakespeare's. Succeeding generations of actresses viewed her as an ideal to which they aspired.
Bib: Highfill, P.H. Jr., Burnim, K.A. and Langhans, E.A. (eds.), *A Biographical Dictionary of Actors, Actresses, Musicians, Dancers, Managers, and Other Stage Personnel in London 1660–1800*.

Barry, Spranger (?1717–77)

Actor, manager. He was over six feet tall and noted for his striking good looks which, added to his natural acting ability, made him one of the leading actors in his generation and a great rival of ▷ David Garrick.

Born in Dublin, he made his early reputation in the Irish theatre, acting with Garrick. Barry came to London in 1746, where he performed indifferently, first as Othello and then as Macbeth. However his next role, as Castalio in ▷ Thomas Otway's *The Orphan*, was highly acclaimed, and it became one of his most popular successes.

In 1747 ▷ Drury Lane, where he was acting, came under Garrick's management, and in the following season he and Garrick alternated as

Hamlet and Macbeth, drawing large crowds. However, the growing rivalry between them caused Barry to leave for ▷ Covent Garden in 1750, after which a famous 'Romeo and Juliet War' ensued, with the two actors playing Romeo simultaneously at separate performances in the respective houses.

In 1756 Barry began ambitious plans for a theatre of his own in Crow Street, Dublin, which opened in 1758, but the theatre failed and was eventually taken over by a rival.

Barry returned to London and carried on an intermittent association with Garrick until 1774, when he left for Covent Garden, remaining there until his death.

Bastard

A bastard is born out of wedlock, ie has no legal parents; in law, he is *filius nullius* = the son of no one. When land, and with it, status, derived from the legal father, the bastard could inherit nothing by his own right. In early medieval times an exception was sometimes made for bastards in ruling families; thus William I of England (1027–87) took the appellation William the Bastard. But in general a bastard was by law something of a social outcast. However, the idea developed that the bastard is compensated for his lack of rights by unusual natural energies; this is implicit in ▷ Henry Fielding's ▷ *Tom Jones*. Bastards could inherit by the testament, ie legally admitted last wishes of the father. When, by the 18th century, property owning became more varied and flexible, one of the bastard's social problems was relieved.

Bath

A city in the west of England with hot springs with certain mineral properties which afford relief to those with rheumatic diseases. In the 18th century, largely owing to the energies of Richard (▷ Beau) Nash, the city became a brilliant social centre; nearly everyone of eminence in politics, literature or the arts at some time visited or lived there. Hence its prominence in the literature of the time. Nash, who virtually ruled Bath, was a civilizing influence on fashionable society: by his discipline he improved the manners of the rich but ill-bred country gentry, and by refusing to allow the wearing of swords in public assemblies he helped to reduce the practice of ▷ duelling.

▷ Austen, Jane.

Bathos

▷ Figures of speech.

Battle of the Books, The (1697, published 1704)

(A Full and True Account of the Battel Fought last Friday, Between the Ancient and the Modern Books in St James's Library). A prose satire by ▷ Jonathan Swift, written while he was staying with ▷ Sir William Temple. Temple's essay on 'Ancient and Modern Learning', with its praise of the Epistles of Phalaris, had been attacked by the critics Wotton and ▷ Bentley, the latter proving that the Epistles were false. Swift's *Battle of the Books*, satirizes the whole dispute, parodying the scholars' concern with

minutiae. The ancients (ie the classical writers) are given the stronger claims, but overall the satire leaves the issue undecided.

Baxter, Richard (1615–91)

Theologian, religious writer and autobiographer. Baxter was one of the dominating figures in the period of the English ▷ Civil War. A chaplain to ▷ Oliver Cromwell's army, Baxter served after the ▷ Restoration as chaplain to ▷ Charles II, but he soon fell out with the king on religio-political grounds. Though an initial supporter of the Parliamentarian cause in the Civil War, Baxter's experiences in the New Model Army, in particular his exposure to the thinking of the ▷ Levellers, Seekers, ▷ Quakers and Behmenists, led him to adopt rather more conservative postures. In the 1650s his position changed once more and he emerged as a strong supporter of the Protectorate, dedicating his *Key for Catholics* (1659) to Richard Cromwell. Baxter's stance on religious issues has been defined as one of the earliest examples of ecumenicism or, as he put it in his *A Third Defence of the Cause of Peace* (1681): 'You could not have truelier called me than an *Episcopal – Presbyterian Independent*.' A prolific writer, Baxter composed over 100 works on religious topics, including *The Saints Everlasting Rest* (1650) and *Call to the Unconverted* (1657). His spiritual autobiography, *Reliquiae Baxterianae* (1696), has come to be recognized as his major work. This 800-page folio volume is one of the most important of 17th-century ▷ autobiographies.
Bib: Schlatter, R. B., *Richard Baxter and Puritan Politics*; Keeble, N. H. (ed.), *The Autobiography of Richard Baxter*; Webber, Joan, *The Eloquent 'I': Style and Self in Seventeenth-century Prose*.

Bayes

The name of a character in *The Rehearsal*, a play by the Duke of Buckingham (▷ Villiers, George) and others, printed in 1672. Bays, or laurels, compose the wreaths with which poets are crowned, and the character was meant as a satire on ▷ Sir William D'Avenant, and also on ▷ John Dryden, who was later created official ▷ Poet Laureate. ▷ Alexander Pope used the same name, in the form Bays, for the Poet Laureate, ▷ Colley Cibber, in *The New Dunciad* (1742), and in the 1743 version of ▷ *The Dunciad*, which has Cibber as hero.

Bear-baiting, bull-baiting

From the ▷ Middle Ages to the 16th century a popular pastime, in which a bull or bear was tied to a stake and then attacked by bulldogs or mastiffs. Bull-baiting continued longer, and these 'sports' were made illegal only in 1835. In Elizabethan times, bear-baiting was an alternative amusement to drama; 'bear gardens' (notably the Paris Garden) were situated in the same region as the theatres – Southwark, on the south bank of the Thames. The theatres themselves were used for the purpose. Earlier in the 16th century, ▷ Erasmus spoke of herds of bears being kept in the country to supply the bear gardens. The ▷ Puritans disliked the meetings as scenes likely to lead to disorder, but humane disapproval did not come before the middle of the 17th century, when the famous diarist, ▷ John Evelyn, spoke of being 'heartily weary of the rude and dirty pastime'; ▷ Sir Richard Steele attacked the cruelty of the sport in ▷ *The Tatler*. In country places, badgers were often used as cheap alternatives to bulls and bears – see the poem *Badger* by ▷ John Clare (1793–1864).

Beatrice and Benedick

Two characters in ▷ Shakespeare's comedy *Much Ado About Nothing*. They hate each other and engage in witty exchanges of repartee. The hatred is only apparent, however, and they are brought together in love by a trick. Quarrelsome lovers are often compared to them and a generation of sparring lovers in many ▷ Restoration comedies is deeply indebted to their example. The most famous of this type are Millamant and Mirabell in ▷ Congreve's ▷ *The Way of The World*.

Beattie, James (1735–1803)

Schoolteacher and later Professor of Philosophy at Aberdeen University. His pseudo-medieval poem in Spenserian stanzas, *The Minstrel: or the Progress of Genius* (1771–4), popularized the mystique of the poet as solitary figure, growing to maturity amid sublime scenery. He also wrote a prose *Essay on Truth*, attacking the scepticism of the philosopher ▷ David Hume from a position of orthodox piety.
  ▷ Bard; Romanticism.

Beau (Brummel, Nash)

'Beau' is a French word which came into use in the 18th century for an elegant young man, especially as suitor to a lady. The word also prefixed the names of certain famous men of fashion and elegance, notably Beau Nash (1674–1762), the famous Master of Ceremonies at ▷ Bath, and Beau Brummel (1778–1840), friend of George IV in his ▷ Regency days (1810–20) and leader of London fashion.

Beau Tibbs

Character in ▷ Oliver Goldsmith's ▷ *A Citizen of the World*. He boasts of familiarity with the rich and famous, but in reality is poor and obscure.

Beaux' Stratagem, The (1707)

Play by ▷ George Farquhar, one of his most successful and popular. Aimwell and Archer, two impoverished gentlemen, come to Lichfield in the guise of master and servant. They go in search of a rich wife for Aimwell, intending to split the proceeds. Aimwell courts Dorinda, daughter of Sir Charles and Lady Bountiful. Archer carries on a flirtation with the landlord's daughter, Cherry, while at the same time, in a separate intrigue, he pursues the unhappily married Mrs Sullen. Aimwell wins Dorinda, but in a fit of honesty, admits his deception. He gives all the money he has gained from the match to Archer, who however remains single. Late in the action, Aimwell finds he has inherited a title and estate, and all ends well for him and his bride to be. The play is vigorous and at times wildly funny, but a partly unconventional ending. Its atmosphere derives largely from ▷ Restoration comedy, but several plot factors link it with the more 'moral' plays of the later 18th century. The play contains a number of incisive comments about women's position in society, particularly in the lines and character of Mrs Sullen.

Beckford, William (1759–1844)

Novelist and travel writer. Chiefly remembered for his ▷ Gothic novel *Vathek*, Beckford also wrote travel books, and was an extravagant collector of Gothic curiosities. Son of a Lord Mayor of London, Beckford's substantial family wealth enabled him to create Fonthill Abbey, where he lived in eccentric and scandalous seclusion.
  ▷ Hervey, Elizabeth.

Bedlam

A famous lunatic asylum. Originally it was a priory, founded in 1247, for members of the religious order of the Star of Bethlehem. Lunatics were admitted to it in the 14th century, and in 1547, after the dissolution of the monasteries, it was handed over to the City of London as a hospital for lunatics. The name became shortened to Bedlam, and a Bedlamite, Tom o'Bedlam, Bess o'Bedlam, became synonyms for lunatics; Bedlam itself, a synonym for lunatic asylum. In modern English, 'bedlam' is a scene of uproar and confusion.
  Bib: Showalter, E., *The Female Malady*.

Beggar's Opera, The (1728)

By the poet ▷ John Gay, a play with numerous songs to the music of folk tunes. It is the earliest and by far the most famous of the 'ballad operas', which were light entertainments as opposed to the serious Italian operas fashionable in England, and which dealt with life in low society. In part it was a political attack on the Prime Minister, Robert Walpole. The daughter of a receiver of stolen goods falls in love with Macheath, a highwayman who is imprisoned in Newgate, where the warder's daughter also falls for him and procures his escape. As a class of literature, *The Beggar's Opera* belongs to the mock heroic; another example from the time is ▷ Fielding's novel ▷ *Jonathan Wild the Great* (1743), which is about a master criminal. The effect of such works was to make their appeal through the lawless zest for life of the characters, coupled with an ironic exposure of their baseness. *The Beggar's Opera* is a classic of the English stage, and its music has been reset by later composers such as Arthur Bliss and Benjamin Britten. It was adapted by the German dramatist Bertolt Brecht in *Die Dreigroschenoper* (*The Threepenny Opera*). *The Beggar's Opera* had an overture by the German musician Pepusch, also arranged from folk tunes.
  ▷ Opera in England.

Behn, Aphra (1640–1689)

English poet, dramatist and writer of fiction, also known as 'Astrea'. Little is known of her early life; the earliest record we have is the anonymous 'The Life and Memoirs of Mrs Behn Written by One of the Fair Sex' which prefaced the first collection of her writings. She may have lived in Surinam, as she presented a feather costume for the play

▷ *The Indian Queen*. She also worked as a royal spy in Holland (at the instigation of ▷ Sir Thomas Killigrew), but was not paid, despite repeated pleas for money on her return in 1667. She may have been imprisoned for debt. She began to write for money, and has been singled out by critics since Virginia Woolf (see *A Room of One's Own*) as the first Englishwoman to earn her living by writing, though the precise meaning of this description is open to dispute. She wrote eighteen plays, of which *The Forc'd Marriage* was the first, produced at the Duke's Theatre in 1670. In the preface to *The Dutch Lover* (1673), she complains that 'the day 'twas acted first, there comes to me in the pit a long, lithe, phlegmatic, white, ill-favored, wretched fop . . . this thing, I tell you, opening that which serves it for a mouth, out issued such a noise as this to those that sat about it, that they were to expect a woeful play, God damn him, for it was a woman's.' Her best-known plays are currently ▷ *The Lucky Chance* (1686) and ▷ *The Rover* (1679). *The Lucky Chance* details the plight of young women married to rich, foolish old city men. In *The Widow Ranter* she dramatizes colonial America. In prose fiction she wrote ▷ *Love Letters Between a Nobleman and His Sister* (1684–7) and ▷ *Oroonoko, or the Royal Slave* (c 1688), set in colonial Surinam. Her poems (famously) include 'The Disappointment', and she also wrote about desire in 'To the Fair Clarinda, Who Made Love to Me, imagin'd more than Woman': 'Fair lovely Maid, or if that Title be/Too weak, too Feminine for Nobler thee,/Permit a Name that more Approaches Truth: And let me call thee, Lovely Charming Youth./This last will justify my soft complaint;/ . . . And without Blushes I the Youth persue,/When so much beauteous Woman is in view.'

As a woman writer Behn was attacked for her lewd language and daring themes, and her own unconventional lifestyle has tended to obscure criticism of her work by moral condemnation.

Her works are collected in: *The Histories and Novels of the Late Ingenious Mrs Behn* (1696).
Bib: Spender, D., *Women of Ideas*; Spender, D., *Mothers of the Novel*; Spencer, J., *The Rise of the Woman Novelist*; Duffy, M., *The Passionate Shepherdess: Aphra Behn, 1640–89*; Goreau, A., *Reconstructing Aphra*.

Belial

In ancient Hebrew means 'worthlessness', but given as a proper name in the ▷ Bible (*Deuteronomy*: 13), it was used by 17th-century ▷ Puritans to describe fashionable and dissipated people – 'sons of Belial'. ▷ Milton makes Belial a fallen angel.

Bellamy, George Anne (?1731–88)

Born at Fingal in Ireland on St George's Day, hence her Christian name, to the actress Mrs Bellamy and her lover, James O'Hara, second Baron of Tyrawley. She made her stage debut at ▷ Covent Garden, where her mother was engaged, in 1741, and in 1743 she played for the first time with ▷ David Garrick. In 1745 Bellamy and her mother performed at ▷ Smock Alley in Dublin, alongside Garrick and ▷ Spranger Barry. She soon quarrelled with

Garrick, and in 1748 was hired at ▷ Covent Garden, where she became one of the leading actresses. In 1749 she eloped with George Montgomery Metham to Yorkshire, giving birth to a son, George, later that year. Metham, however, reneged on a promise of marriage, and she returned to Covent Garden in 1750. Garrick determined to patch up his dispute with her and, in a famous episode, persuaded her to appear again at ▷ Drury Lane, playing Juliet to his Romeo, in competition with the *Romeo and Juliet* of Barry and ▷ Susanna Cibber. The rival performances lasted 12 nights, until Covent Garden ended its run and Drury Lane triumphed with a 13th. In 1767, now in failing health, Bellamy left the stage and moved in with the actor Henry Woodward. He died in 1777, and she afterwards lived largely off loans and gifts, pursued by creditors. During her years on the stage she played some 96 roles, excelling in those demanding pathos and grief, including Cordelia, Juliet, Calista in *The Fair Penitent* (1703), Imoinda in ▷ Thomas Southerne's *Oroonoko* (1696), and Indiana in ▷ *The Conscious Lovers*. Her autobiography, *An Apology for the Life of George Anne Bellamy* was published in 1785.
Bib: Hartmann, C., *Enchanting Bellamy*.

Bentham, Jeremy (1748–1832)

An extremely influential thinker, associated with the theory known as ▷ Utilitarianism. The basis of his thought was: 1 that human motives are governed by the pursuit of pleasure and avoidance of pain; 2 that the guiding rule for society should be the greatest happiness of the greatest number; 3 that the test of value for human laws and institutions should be no other than that of usefulness. These views he expounded in *Fragment on Government* (1776) and *Introduction to Principles of Morals and Legislation* (1780). His principal associates were James Mill (1773–1836) and John Stuart Mill (1806–73); collectively they were known as the Philosophical Radicals, and together they established a practical philosophy of reform of great consequence in 19th-century Britain. But their excessive rationalism frustrated sympathy and imagination in education and the relief of poverty. Bentham's thought derived from the sceptical 18th-century French 'philosophes' such as Helvetius and 18th-century English ▷ rationalists such as ▷ David Hartley and ▷ Joseph Priestley. It was, in fact, the outstanding line of continuity between 18th-century and 19th-century thinking.
Bib: Stephen, L., *The English Utilitarians*; Pringle-Patterson, A. S., *The Philosophical Radicals and other essays*; Atkinson, C. M., *Life*.

Bentley, Richard (1662–1742)

Distinguished as a classical scholar and noted for his despotic personality as Master of Trinity College, Cambridge. He is satirized by ▷ Jonathan Swift in ▷ *The Battle of the Books* and by ▷ Alexander Pope in ▷ *The Dunciad* (Bk. IV, 201–75).

Berkeley, George (1685–1753)

Irish churchman and a philosopher in the tradition of ▷ Descartes and ▷ John Locke but the opponent of the latter. Locke had affirmed the independence of matter and mind; Berkeley held that the reality of anything depended on its being perceived by a conscious mind; thus mind (and spirit) had primacy over matter. Nature is the experience of consciousness, and the evidence of Universal Mind, or God. He considered that Locke's insistence on external matter and physical causes led to ▷ atheism; but his own lucid and precise prose is as much the vehicle of reason as Locke's. While Locke led towards scientific scepticism, Berkeley's faith, combined with reason, maintained the religious vision in an essentially rational century. His philosophy is expressed in *A New Theory of Vision* (1709), and in *Principles of Human Knowledge* (1710). His *Dialogues of Alciphron* (1732) are distinguished for their grace of style.

Bib: Wild, J., *Berkeley: a study of his life and philosophy*; Luce, A. A., *The Life of Berkeley*; Warnock, G. J., *Berkeley*.

Berry, Mary (1763–1852)

Dramatist and philosophical prose writer. Mary Berry and her sister Agnes (1764–1852) were brought up by their grandmother and allowed to educate themselves. They were much admired by ▷ Horace Walpole who dedicated books to them and allowed Mary Berry to edit several of his manuscripts, although she published these editions under her father's name, rather than her own. Mary was also friendly with several contemporary female authors, including Harriet Martineau and ▷ Joanna Baillie; indeed, the latter wrote the epilogue and prologue for Berry's play, *Fashionable Friends* (1801). The sexual freedom condoned by this play, together with Mary's own rejection of marriage, suggests that in terms of gender politics she was somewhat radical (▷ Feminism, Feminism, Augustan). However, her history *A Comparative View of the Social Life of England and France from the Restoration of Charles II* (1828–31) reveals a more conservative attitude.

▷ Women, Status of.

Bib: Moers, E., *Literary Women*.

Betterton, Mary (1637–1712)

Actress, one of those competing for the title of the first professional actress. She joined ▷ Sir William D'Avenant's company, probably in 1660 and her first known appearance was as Ianthe in D'Avenant's revision of ▷ *The Siege of Rhodes* in 1661. In the same year she played Ophelia to ▷ Thomas Betterton's Hamlet, and in 1662 the two were married.

Her talents were varied: she played innocent young girls, coquettes, and forceful characters such as Lady Macbeth and the Duchess of Malfi, apparently with equal skill. In the late 1660s, she and her husband took the young actress ▷ Anne Bracegirdle into their home, virtually adopting her as a daughter. Throughout her career she maintained a reputation for 'virtuous' living: ▷ Cibber described her as leading 'an unblemish'd and sober life'. After her husband's death in 1710, she appears to have suffered some sort of mental breakdown, probably exacerbated by the poverty in which he left her. She was buried in ▷ Westminster Abbey, next to her husband.

Betterton, Thomas (1635–1710)

The greatest English actor of his generation, he probably began acting in the late 1650s. By 1661 he had joined the ▷ Duke's Company, in which he purchased a share and so was involved in theatrical finances as well as acting for most of his career.

As an actor, he succeeded from the beginning, making a particular impression as Hamlet, coached by ▷ Sir William D'Avenant, who had seen it performed earlier by an actor under ▷ Shakespeare's tutelage, and who had himself been taught by a pupil of Shakespeare's.

In 1662 Betterton was sent by ▷ Charles II to France, on the first of several missions to research the latest developments in French drama and, opera, so as to bring new ideas to the English stage. Returning to England, he proceeded to build on his reputation with a succession of great roles, especially in Shakespeare. Betterton continued acting almost to his death, dying in great poverty. He is buried in ▷ Westminster Abbey.

Bib: Milhous, J., *Thomas Betterton and the Management of Lincoln's Inn Fields* 1695–1708; Highfill, P. H. Jr., Burnim, K. A. and Langhans, E. A. (eds.), *A Biographical Dictionary of Actors, Actresses, Musicians, Dancers, Managers, and Other Stage Personnel in London* 1660–1800; Lowe, R., *Thomas Betterton*.

Beulah, The Land of

In the ▷ Bible, *Isaiah* 62:4. A Hebrew word meaning 'married'. In Bunyan's ▷ *Pilgrim's Progress* it lies in sight of the Heavenly City and beyond the reach of Giant Despair. It signifies the state in which the soul is 'married' to God.

Bible, The

The Bible is usually divided into two parts.

1 Old Testament

The Christian term for the first and larger part of the Bible, consisting of the sacred writings of the Jews. It concerns the peculiar, divinely ordained destiny of the Jewish race from earliest times, and it is considered by Christians to expound the divine promise which the New Testament fulfils not merely for the Jews but for the whole of mankind. The Old Testament is divided into books which are grouped by Jews into three main sections, as follows:

1 The Torah ('Law', otherwise called the Pentateuch), consisting of five books *Genesis*, *Exodus*, *Leviticus*, *Numbers*, *Deuteronomy*. They are called 'the five books of Moses'. The first two are narrative and descriptive, and move from the creation of the world to the escape of the Jews from slavery in Egypt. The remainder contain laws and discourses.

2 The Prophets. This section is divided into two in the Hebrew Bible: the 'Former Prophets', consisting of *Joshua*, *Judges*, the two books of *Samuel* and the two books of *Kings*; and the 'Latter Prophets', consisting of *Isaiah*, *Jeremiah*, *Ezekiel*, and the Minor Prophets. The books of the Former Prophets tell the story of the establishment of the Jews in the kingdom

of Israel, and their subsequent history. The Latter Prophets contain history together with prophetic discourses.

3 The Sacred Writings, or Hagiographa, which are divided into three sections: (i) the Poetical books, consisting of *Psalms, Proverbs, Job*; (ii) the five 'Rolls', which are read at special seasons in the Jewish year: *Song of Songs, Ruth, Lamentations, Ecclesiastes, Esther* – of these *Esther* and *Ruth* are narratives; the other three are poetic meditations; (iii) *Daniel, Ezra, Nehemiah* and *Chronicles*, all consisting mainly of historical narrative.

2 New Testament
The second and shorter part of the Bible, containing the sacred books of the Christians. It is divided into books, on the pattern of the Old Testament, and dates as a whole collection from the end of the 2nd century AD. It is customary to divide the books into four groups.

1 The three Synoptic (*ie* 'summary narrative') Gospels of Saints Matthew, Mark and Luke, and the *Acts of the Apostles*. The Gospels are narratives about Jesus Christ, and *Acts* is the narrative of the missionary careers of the apostles (including St Paul) after Christ's death.

2 The Epistles (letters) of St Paul. The four shortest of these are addressed to individuals: two to Timothy, and one each to Titus and to Philemon. The remainder are addressed to various early Christian communities. These are the Epistles to the Romans, Galatians, Ephesians, Philippians, Colossians, two to the Corinthians, and two to the Thessalonians. The Epistle to the Hebrews has been ascribed to Paul, but is nowadays considered to be by a disciple of his.

3 The Catholic Epistles, so called because they were directed to Christians generally. Two of these are ascribed to St Peter, and one each to James and Jude.

4 The Johannine writings, by tradition ascribed to the Apostle John. These are the Gospel of St John – distinguished from the Synoptic Gospels as probably not intended as a historical narrative – the Epistles of John, and the poetic, visionary narrative called the *Apocalypse*, or *Revelation*.

In the Middle Ages the only version of the Bible authorized by the Church was the Vulgate, the translation into Latin by St Jerome, completed in 405. Partial translations were made into Old English before the 11th century. From the 14th century translations were made by reformers, who believed that men without Latin should have the means of seeking guidance from divine scripture without dependence on Church authority. The main translators were Wycliffe (14th century), Tyndale and Coverdale (16th century). The last-named was the producer of the *Great Bible* (also called Cranmer's Bible after the Archbishop of the time), but Henry VIII, concerned for his intermediate position between Catholics and Protestants, ended by restricting its use. Under the Catholic Mary I (1553–8) English reformers produced the *Geneva Bible* abroad, with annotations suited to ▷ Puritan Calvinist opinion; and in 1568 the so-called *Bishops' Bible* was issued

by the restored Anglicans to counteract Puritan influence. Finally, in 1611 the Authorized Version was produced with the approval of ▷ James I. For three centuries it was to be the only one in general use, and it is still the prevailing version. In the 19th century it was revised (Revised Version) and recently a new translation has been authorized and produced (New Testament 1961; Old Testament 1961; Old Testament Apocrypha 1970). A ▷ Catholic translation, the Douai Bible, was issued at about the same time as the Authorized Version.

In spite of various other translations. Catholic and Protestant, in the 19th and 20th centuries the Authorized Version is by far the most important for its literary and social influence. It was based on previous translations, especially that of Tyndale, so that the cast of its prose is characteristically more 16th than early 17th century in style. Nonetheless much of it is of supreme eloquence, *eg* the Book of *Job*, and last 15 chapters of *Isaiah*. It was for many people in the 17th and 18th centuries the only book that was constantly read, and it was familiar to all from its use in church and education. The musical cadence of Authorized Version prose can be often heard in the prose of English writers, whether or not professing Christians.
Bib: Daiches, D., *The King James' Version of the Bible.*

Bill of Rights (1689)
1 An Act passed by ▷ Parliament, according to which the powers of the king were restricted. In particular, he could no longer suspend laws without the consent of Parliament; nor could he dispense with laws in individual cases. The importance of the Act was less the specific ways in which royal power was limited than Parliament's implicit decision to take over the sovereignty of the government from the Crown. This Bill and the events that led up to it, the flight of ▷ James II (1685–8) and his replacement by ▷ William III and Mary II (the ▷ Glorious Revolution), were the real starting-points of 'constitutional monarchy' in England, *ie* a monarchy under which it is accepted by both Crown and people that the representatives of the people are the real sovereigns of the country. Because Britain does not have a written constitution, such historical traces as the Bill of Rights are the major signs of how power has been transferred and located.
2 The first ten Amendments to the Constitution of the United States, all adopted in 1791. Their guarantee of individual rights was an answer ro criticism of the Constitution, which had hindered its ratification.

Billingsgate
The London fish market, situated by one of the gates of the City by the riverside. In the 17th century the market was famous for the coarse language heard there; hence 'billingsgate' has become synonymous with violent and abusive language.

Biography
The chief source of inspiration for English biographers was the Greek ▷ Plutarch whose *Parallel Lives* of Greek and Roman great men was

translated into English by Sir Thomas North in 1579 and was widely read. Biography had been practised before in England; there had been the lives of the saints in the Middle Ages, and in the 16th century Cavendish's life of the statesman Cardinal Wolsey had appeared. The regular practice of biography, however, starts with the 17th century, not merely owing to the influence of North's translation of Plutarch, but as part of the outward-turning, increasingly scientific interest in many kinds of people (not merely saints and rulers) which in the 18th century was to give rise to the novel. Biography is a branch of history, and the art of historical writing advanced with biography: Edward Hyde, ▷ Earl of Clarendon, included fine biographical portraits in his history of the Great Rebellion, written between 1646 and 1670. ▷ Izaak Walton's lives of ▷ John Donne (1640), Sir Henry Wotton (1651), ▷ Richard Hooker (1665), ▷ George Herbert (1670) and Bishop Sanderson (1678) are closer to our modern idea of biography, and they are landmarks, if not originals, in the form inasmuch as the subjects, though eminent men, were humble enough to lead ordinary lives in touch with usual experience. Women writers in that period also excelled at biography. The royalist ▷ Margaret Cavendish wrote a biography of her husband William Cavendish, Duke of Newcastle, and ▷ Lucy Hutchinson wrote a poignant account of the life and death of her parliamentarian husband, Col. John Hutchinson. In the 18th century the writing of biographies became habitual; and also biography, or autobiography, became a way of disguising pure fiction, eg in the novels of ▷ Defoe. ▷ Samuel Johnson was a master of biography in his ▷ Lives of the Poets (1779–81), most notable among which is his Life of Mr Richard Savage, previously published in 1744. The outstanding biography of the century, however, is the life of Johnson himself by ▷ James Boswell, 1791. As an intimate and vivid account of a great man, it was never equalled in the 19th century when so many biographies were written.
Bib: Gittings, R., The Nature of Biography.

Blackmore, Sir Richard (c 1655–1729)
Poet and physician to ▷ Queen Anne. The dullness of his lengthy epic, Prince Arthur (1695) and The Creation: a philosophical poem demonstrating the existence and providence of God (1712) earned the ridicule of ▷ Alexander Pope in ▷ The Dunciad (Bk. II, 370ff). He also wrote a Satyre against Wit (1700).

Blackwell, Elizabeth (?1700–58)
Naturalist, born in Aberdeen. She eloped to London with the Scottish physician and adventurer Alexander Blackwell, who was imprisoned for debt. In order to raise money, she published A Curious Herbal Containing Five Hundred Cuts of the Most Useful Plants Which are Now Used in the Practice of Physick in two volumes, in 1737 and 1739. The books consisted of pictures of plants, drawn, engraved and coloured by herself, with descriptions added in Latin by her husband. The herbal was approved by leading members of the College of Physicians, became immensely popular, and was later expanded into five volumes. Alexander Blackwell was executed in

Sweden in 1747, allegedly for plotting against the government.

Blair, Robert (1699–1746)
Scottish clergyman and author of The Grave (1743), a ▷ blank-verse genre piece blending ▷ Gothic sinisterness, banal piety and a pseudo-Shakespearean sublimity, imitated from Hamlet. Its enjoyable imaginative gusto ensured that it retained its popularity throughout the century, and beyond.

Blake, William (1757–1827)
Poet and artist. The self-educated son of a London hosier, Blake earned his living by engraving illustrations for books. His own poems are engraved rather than printed, and he wove into his text pictures which elaborated the poetic theme. His earliest poems, Poetical Sketches show the influence of earlier lyric writers and ▷ Macpherson's Ossianic writings. His next works, the ▷ Songs of Innocence (1789), and ▷ Songs of Experience (1794) are startlingly original. Intended, on one level, for children, they are simple but symbolically resonant lyrics 'Shewing the Two contrary States of the Human Soul'. In Innocence the world is unthreatening and without morality, and God is trusted implicitly. The Experience poems, which often parallel those of the earlier volume in setting or title, depict with fierce moral indignation, a fallen world of repression and religious hypocrisy. There is no simple relation of progression or superiority between the 'contrary states', and Blake makes no attempt to reconcile their contradictions. They remain in unresolved dialectical opposition to each other.

In later works Blake elaborated his revolutionary interpretation of Christian theology using invented characters representing psychological or spiritual forces. In Thel (etched c 1789), in rhythmical unrhymed lines usually of seven stresses, the protagonist, confronted with the interdependence of life and death, creation and destruction, flees back to the shadowy world of the unborn. Tiriel was written at about the same time. The French Revolution (1791), America (1793) and Visions of the Daughters of Albion (1793) show Blake's reaction to the American and French revolutions, which he saw as releasing the energies of humanity, so long repressed by the forces of absolutism, institutionalized religion and sexual inhibition. In ▷ The Marriage of Heaven and Hell (etched c 1793) Blake expressed in a series of prophetic statements and 'Memorable Fancies', mainly in prose, his contempt for 18th-century rationalism and institutionalized religion.

Because his works remained virtually unknown and he developed no lasting relationship with an audience, his later prophecies became increasingly formless and obscure. He was also unwilling to be too explicit in case he should invite trouble from the authorities. The Book of Urizen (1794) focuses on the tyrannical figure of Urizen, ('your reason' or 'horizon'?) who symbolizes the inhibiting powers of control and restriction. Urizen is in constant war with Orc, a Satanic force of revolutionary energy. The Book of Ahania, The Book of Los (1795) and Vala (1797), subsequently rewritten as The Four

Zoas (1804) develop similar themes with increasing intricacy and elusiveness. His last two prophetic books *Milton* (1804) and *Jerusalem* (1804) are often impenetrable, but include some striking passages. They show a new emphasis on Christian humility and self-sacrifice. In *Milton* he elaborates on his famous observation that ▷ Milton was 'of the Devil's party without knowing it'. Milton is shown returning to earth in the form of Blake himself, in order to correct his earlier mistake. Blake is one of the most intellectually challenging of English poets, with a unique insight into the pieties and ideological deceptions of his time.

Bib: Davis, M., *William Blake: A New Kind of Man*; Bronowski, J., *William Blake and the Age of Revolution*; Glen, H., *Vision and Disenchantment: Blake's Songs and Wordsworth's Lyrical Ballads*; Bottrall, M. (ed.), *William Blake: Songs of Innocence and Experience* (Macmillan Casebook); Paley, M. D., *William Blake*; Erdman, D. V., *Blake: Prophet Against Empire*; Bloom, H., *Blake's Apocalypse*.

Blank verse

Verse which is unrhymed, and composed of lines which normally contain ten syllables and have the stress on every second syllable, as in the classical ▷ iambic pentameter.

The first user of the iambic pentameter in English was Chaucer and he used it in rhyming couplets, *eg* *The Prologue* to The Canterbury Tales. The first user of blank verse was Henry Howard, Earl of Surrey (1517–47), who adopted it for a translation of the second and third books of ▷ Virgil's ▷ *Aeneid* in order to get closer to the effect of the metrically regular but unrhymed Latin ▷ hexameters. The effect in Surrey is that Chaucer's measure is being used but without rhyme:

> *They whisted all, with fixèd face attent,*
> *When prince Aeneas from the royal seal*
> *Thus gan to speak.*

The dramatist Christopher Marlowe (1564–93) first gave blank verse its distinctive quality. In his plays, he combined the rhythm of the verse with the normal rhythm and syntax of the sentence, so that the effect begins to be like natural speech expressed with unusual music:

> *Hell hath no limits, nor is circumscrib'd*
> *In one self place: for where we are is hell,*
> *And where hell is, there must we*
> *ever be . . .*
>
> *(Dr Faustus)*

Blank verse as used by Marlowe was carried on by ▷ Shakespeare, who employed it with steadily increasing flexibility and power. His contemporaries did the same, but in his immediate successors' work great freedoms are taken with the ▷ metre, and the rhythm of the sentence begins to dominate over that of the line, so that the effect is of rhythmic paragraphs of speech.

The next phase is the epic use of blank verse by ▷ Milton in ▷ *Paradise Lost* (1667), who gave the weight of Latin syntax to the long sentences

and accordingly moved away from speech rhythms. ▷ Wordsworth and ▷ Coleridge at the beginning of the 19th century lightened the Miltonic effect back towards colloquialism.

▷ Free verse; Metre.

Blenheim (1704)

An important battle in the War of the ▷ Spanish Succession in which the forces of ▷ John Churchill, Duke of Marlborough, and Prince Eugene of Savoy defeated the French forces of Louis XIV under Marshal Tallard, near the village of Blindheim (anglicized, Blenheim) in Bavaria.

Bloody Assizes

Judicial trials of unusual ferocity held after the failure of ▷ Monmouth's Rebellion against James II. Judge Jeffreys condemned large numbers of the small rebel army to death and sentenced many more to transportation to penal colonies (▷ Botany Bay).

Blower, Elizabeth (b 1763)

Novelist, born in Worcester. She took to writing to help support her family. She wrote four novels, *The Parsonage House* (1780), *Features from Life: or A Summer Visit* (1780), *George Bateman* (1782) and *Maria* (1785). They display humour and satire, as well as vivid characterization. Blower has been described as a direct predecessor of ▷ Jane Austen. Bib: Todd, J (ed.), *A Dictionary of British and American Writers 1660–1800*.

Bluestocking

The 'Blue Stocking Ladies' were a group of intelligent, literary women in the mid 18th century who held evening receptions for serious conversation. As a setting for discussions in which both sexes were included, the evenings were a deliberate attempt to challenge the social stereotypes which confined intellectual debate to male gatherings and relegated the female sex to trivial topics. By bringing men and women together in this atmosphere, it was hoped that the 'polite' codes of gallantry could be disposed of. The chief hostesses included ▷ Elizabeth Montagu, Elizabeth Carter, ▷ Mary Delany and later, ▷ Hannah More.

The name 'bluestocking' is thought to derive from the stockings of Benjamin Stillingfleet, who, too poor to buy evening dress, attended in his daytime blue worsteds. ▷ Hannah More's poem *Bas Bleu* (1786) helped to establish the use of the term as referring to the society women, although Admiral Boscawen is traditionally credited with coining the collective noun.

Boadicea (d AD 61)

A Celtic queen (also Bonduca, Boudicea) who is a national heroine because of her rising against the Roman occupying forces. Her people were the Iceni of what is now the county of Norfolk; she was defeated by Suetonius Paulinus and killed herself. She has been celebrated by a number of poets, including ▷ William Cowper.

Boccaccio, Giovanni (?1313–75)

Italian humanist scholar and writer, born near Florence. His literary studies began in Naples where he wrote his first works but he later returned to Florence and was employed on diplomatic missions for the Florentine state. He publicly lectured on ▷ Dante's *Divine Comedy*, was a friend of Petrarch and the centre of a circle of humanist learning and literary activity. His works included a wide range of courtly narratives, a vernacular imitation of classical epic and a number of important encyclopaedic works in Latin which occupied the last years of his life. Boccaccio's vast narrative compilations in Latin and in the vernacular provided narrative sources for many later English writers, including ▷ Dryden, Keats and Tennyson.

Boileau, Nicolas (1636–1711)
French critic and poet. The ▷ Earl of Rochester's *Satyre Against Reason and Mankind* broadly follows his Eighth Satire. Through his *Art Poetique* (*The Poetic Art*) (1674), based on ▷ Horace's *Ars Poetica*, and his translation of the Greek treatise *On the Sublime*, attributed to ▷ Longinus, he fostered in ▷ French literature the ideals of classical urbanity and regularity of form. He influenced ▷ John Dryden, who revised a translation of his *Art Poetique*, and ▷ Alexander Pope, whose ▷ *Essay on Criticism* was partly based on it, and whose ▷ *Rape of the Lock* owes something to the French poet's mock-epic, *Le Lutrin*. In the Romantic and Victorian periods Boileau's name became synonymous with stifling (and foreign) neo-classical decadence.

Bold Stroke for a Wife, A (1718)
Play by ▷ Susannah Centlivre, the only one for which she claims to have used no sources but her own invention. Anne Lovely has four guardians, all of whom must give their consent before she can marry: Sir Philip Modelove, an 'old Beau', who cares only for French fashions, and loves operas, balls and masques; Periwinkle, a 'silly half-witted Fellow . . . fond of everything antique and foreign', who dresses in the fashions of the previous century; Tradelove, a broker and cheat; and Obadiah Prim, a 'very rigid Quaker'. Colonel Fainwell is in love with Lovely, and sets out to win her by approaching each of the guardians in various disguises, and with various feigned schemes. One of his characters, Simon Pure, has given the phrase 'the real simon pure' to the English language. The means by which Fainwell succeeds in his plan forms the chief interest of the action. The play provides a wonderful vehicle for a versatile actor: three members of the Bullock family were in the original production, and many other renowned actors, including ▷ John Philip Kemble and Charles Kemble (1775–1854), have played the part of Fainwell. *A Bold Stroke for a Wife* achieved great popularity and became a stock item in the English repertory, surviving until the last quarter of the 19th century. It was acted in command performances before George II and George III.

Bolingbroke, Henry St John (1678–1751)
Tory politician, and writer chiefly on political matters. He favoured the ▷ Stuart (Jacobite) succession on the death of ▷ Queen Anne in 1714, and when the Whigs took power and the Hanoverian

George I was declared king, he was impeached. He fled to the court of the Pretender in France, but in 1723 was pardoned and returned to England. He became a friend of ▷ Alexander Pope and his rationalist, Deist views strongly influenced the ▷ *Essay on Man* which is addressed to him. In 1749 he published *The Idea of a Patriot King*, which argued that the king's role should be as a national leader, above the corruption of politics.
▷ Deism.

Booth, Barton (?1679–1733)
Actor, manager, poet: the leading tragic actor of his generation. Booth became interested in the theatre while performing in a play at Westminster School, and afterwards joined the profession. In 1709 he became the leading tragic actor at ▷ Drury Lane, but in the following year, after a quarrel about the distribution of management duties in the company, he helped lead a break-in to the premises which turned into a violent affray. The dispute was revived in a different form in 1713, with Booth insisting on sharing in the company's management, a position he won only after action in court. In his new position of power he was able to take on major new roles including King Lear, Jaffeir in ▷ Thomas Otway's ▷ *Venice Preserv'd* and Timon of Athens.

An admirer of ▷ Thomas Betterton, Booth is said to have imitated him – lapsing, at worst, into a monotonous intoning style of delivery; he is reported to have lacked the capacity for humour in his performances. At his best he acted with great dignity and grace, while also possessing fiery qualities enabling him to perform such roles as Othello and Hotspur with passion.

Bib: Highfill, P. H. Jr., Burnim, K. A. and Langhans, E. A. (eds.), *A Biographical Dictionary of Actors, Actresses, Musicians, Dancers, Managers, and Other Stage Personnel in London 1660–1800.*

Booth, Hester (?1690–1773)
Actress and dancer. Hester Booth (née Santlow) began her career as a dancer at ▷ Drury Lane in 1706, moving to the ▷ Queen's Theatre, Haymarket, in 1708. She began acting in the following year, with the role of Prue in ▷ Congreve's ▷ *Love for Love*. Thereafter she played a variety of comic and serious roles, major and lesser. She married ▷ Barton Booth in 1719 and left the stage around 1733, the year of her husband's death. Theatre goers admired her more for her dancing than for her acting, commenting on its smoothness, and her interpretative abilities as a dancer.

Boothby, Frances (fl 1669)
English Restoration dramatist, whose tragicomedy *Marcelia: or the Treacherous Friend* (1670) was performed before ▷ Alpha Behn's plays – at the ▷ Theatre Royal, in 1669. It is her only known work. The plot concerns misapprehensions and deceits in love, initiated by the king's desire for a new lover, Opening, 'I'm hither come, but what d'ye think to say? / A Womans Pen presents you with a Play,' it goes on to make great play of leaving the stage, returning only to express great surprise that

the audience is still there despite female authorship. The tragicomic denouement restores stability to the original relationships.

▷ Polwhele, Elizabeth

Borough

One of the synonyms of 'town', used specifically for a town which has been incorporated and given privileges of limited self-government; also used until the 20th century for a town with the right to elect a Member of Parliament.

Most constituencies had remained unchanged since the ▷ Middle Ages; in consequence, some towns had grown to great size with inadequate representation in Parliament, or none at all, while others were represented by more than one Member although they had sunk into insignificance or even, in a few cases, had ceased to exist. This meant great power for the landed aristocracy, and great deprivation of power for the large and growing middle class. Some boroughs ('towns' – but often mere villages) were called 'pocket boroughs' because they were virtually owned by one landlord, who had them 'in his pocket', ie caused them to elect the Members of his choice; others were called 'rotten boroughs' because few inhabitants possessed the right to vote, and they were easily and habitually bribed. The law of 1832 redistributed Members of Parliament so as to correspond to the great centres of population, but limited the franchise (right to vote) to those who possessed a level of income such as ensured that electors belonged at least to the middle class.

Boswell, James (1740–95)

Best known for his biography of ▷ Samuel Johnson whom he met in 1763, Boswell was also a copious diarist. Eldest son of Alexander Boswell, Lord Auchinleck, Boswell studied law at Edinburgh, Glasgow and Utrecht, and reluctantly entered the legal profession.

From 1760 onwards, Boswell published many pamphlets, often anonymously. After meeting Johnson, he travelled in Europe, where he met ▷ Rousseau and ▷ Voltaire. Rousseau fired him with enthusiasm for the cause of Corsican liberty, and he cultivated a lifelong friendship with General Paoli; in 1768 he published an *Account of Corsica*, which attracted considerable international recognition.

In 1769 Boswell, by now a Scottish advocate, married his cousin Margaret Montgomerie. But Boswell longed to be part of London literary culture, and made journeys to the capital as frequently as he could. Here he was elected a member of ▷ The Club, though his habit of 'scribbling' memoranda of conversations, with the aim of writing Johnson's *Life*, irritated some of its members.

In 1773, Boswell and Johnson made their tour of the Hebrides (see ▷ *The Journal of a Tour to the Hebrides*). From 1777 to 1783 Boswell wrote a series of articles for the *London Magazine* under the pen-name of 'The Hypochondriack'. In 1782 he inherited the Scottish estate on his father's death, and his last meeting with Johnson was in 1784.

Boswell attempted, unsuccessfully, to make a career in politics, while working on the *Life of Samuel Johnson*, which appeared in 1791.
Bib: Pottle, F. A. (ed.), *Boswell's London Journal, 1762–63*; Hill, G. B. (ed.), revised Powell, L. F., *Life of Johnson and Journal of a Tour to the Hebrides*.

Botany Bay

In New South Wales, Australia, near Sydney. Captain Cook landed there in 1770 and took possession of it for the British Crown. From 1787 Australia was used for convict settlements, ie convicted criminals sentenced to transportation were sent there. They were not in fact sent to Botany Bay, but the name was used in common speech to cover convict settlements in Australia generally. The bay received its name from Joseph Banks, a botanist accompanying Cook, because of its rich plant life. The brutality of the system of transportation and the suffering it imposed is only now being traced by scholarship and reflected in public opinion. It involved injury not only to the transportees and their families but also to the native peoples whose lands were invaded and appropriated.

▷ Penal system.
Bib: Hughes, R., *The Fatal Shore*.

Bow Bells

The church of St Mary-le-Bow in ▷ Cheapside, London, has always been famous for its peal of bells. The church is in the middle of the City of London, so that to be born within hearing of the Bow Bells has been the test of being a true Cockney, ie Londoner.

Bow Street

In London; Covent Garden Opera House is in Bow Street. The chief Magistrates' Court in London has been situated there since 1735, when it opened in the house of the first Bow Street ▷ Magistrate. His successor, the novelist ▷ Henry Fielding, was given a house in Bow Street separate from the court-house. Fielding was exceptionally successful as a Magistrate in ridding London of its crime. He and his brother established the Bow Street Runners, the predecessors of the Metropolitan Police.

Bowdler, Thomas (1754–1825)

Famous for *The Family Shakespeare*, 1818; an edition in which 'those words and expressions are omitted which cannot with propriety be read aloud in a family'. He later published an edition of ▷ Gibbon's ▷ *Decline and Fall of the Roman Empire* similarly expurgated. From these we get the word 'bowdlerize', meaning to expurgate.

Bowles, William Lisle (1762–1850)

Poet and clergyman; ultimately chaplain to the Prince Regent. His *Sonnets* (1789), sentimental effusions delivered in the person of 'the wanderer', were extremely popular, and revived interest in the sonnet form. ▷ Samuel Taylor Coleridge and ▷ Robert Southey were impressed by them. The preface to his edition of ▷ Alexander Pope (1806) took its critical stance from his former teacher at Winchester,

▷ Joseph Warton, and prompted Lord Byron's 'Letter on W. L. Bowles's Strictures on Pope' (1821).

Bowtell (Boutell, Bootell), Elizabeth (c 1650–97)

Actress. Born Elizabeth Ridley she joined the ▷ King's Company at ▷ Bridges Street Theatre about 1670, afterwards specializing in the playing of 'breeches' parts, although her most famous role was as Queen Statira in ▷ Nathaniel Lee's *The Rival Queens* (1677). During one performance a quarrel between her and ▷ Elizabeth Barry, who was appearing in the play as Roxana, degenerated into genuine violence on stage. The dispute arose over the possession of a prized prop (a veil). Required to stab Statira on stage, Barry as Roxana lunged at her with such force that she pierced her flesh 'about a Quarter of an Inch', according to a near contemporary. Bowtell retired in 1696.

Bracegirdle, Anne (1663–1748)

Actress, singer. She came into the Bettertons' (▷ Betterton, Thomas; ▷ Betterton, Mary) household as a sort of surrogate daughter in about 1688 and in that year she became a member of the ▷ United Company, playing a succession of roles in contemporary plays, as well as speaking prologues and epilogues for many of them. In 1693 Bracegirdle acted in ▷ William Congreve's first play, ▷ *The Old Bachelor*. By the following year she had become a leading member of the United Company, but in 1695 she joined Betterton and Elizabeth Barry in seceding from the company to form a separate troupe at ▷ Lincoln's Inn Fields. There she played the first Angelica in Congreve's ▷ *Love for Love*, and in 1700 Millamant – a part written for her by Congreve – in ▷ *The Way of the World*. Congreve was among a number of prominent men who courted or admired her from a distance.

Throughout her life Bracegirdle was celebrated for her supposed virtue, some of the comments being possibly ironic. She was lauded for her abilities in both comic and tragic acting modes, her style in the latter tending towards pathos, as well as for her beauty, charm, and generosity toward fellow-performers and those in need. She was buried at ▷ Westminster Abbey.

Bib: Highfill, P. H. Jr., Burnim, K. A. and Langhans, E. A. (eds.), *A Biographical Dictionary of Actors, Actresses, Musicians, Dancers, Managers, and Other Stage Personnel in London 1660–1800*; Howe, E., *The First English Actresses*.

Bradstreet, Anne Dudley (1612–1672)

Bradstreet is 17th-century North America's most renowned woman poet. Born in Northampton, England, to Dorothy Yorke and Thomas Dudley, she arrived in the New World in 1630, two years after her marriage to Simon Bradstreet. When her poetry was taken without her permission by her brother-in-law and published in England under the title of *The Tenth Muse Lately Sprung up in America*, she became the first colonist to have a volume of poetry published. Although she maintained an outer appearance of adhering to Puritan conventions, her poetry (most notably, 'Contemplations') works within English and biblical traditions and extends those traditions in the direction of 19th-century romanticism. Her poems are equally notable for the manner in which she subverts traditional attitudes about women's capabilities and social roles. She also wrote a series of 'Meditations' that convey to her children her own religious struggles and convictions. Renowned in her own time but ever concerned with revising and improving her literary talents, she died on 16 September 1672 in Andover, Massachusetts.

Bridewell

A royal palace until 1555, then a penitentiary. It was largely destroyed in the ▷ Fire of London in 1666. New Bridewell, used for the same purpose, was built in 1829 and pulled down in 1864. The idea of a penitentiary lies behind the more modern idea of the reformatory, *ie* the place to which offenders are sent when they are considered too young to be sent to prison, and in the 19th century 'Bridewell' was used as a synonym for such institutions.

Bridges Street Theatre

▷ Drury Lane Theatres.

Brighton

An English seaside resort on the south coast, one of the first to become fashionable when, in the 18th century, sea-bathing was first held to be good for health. Early in the next century the Prince Regent (▷ Regency) made Brighton his favourite resort and built the oriental-style Pavilion there. Since then, Brighton has remained one of the largest of a line of seaside resorts extending almost the whole length of the south coast.

Britain, British, Briton

Britain (Latin: *Britannia*) was the name given by the Romans to the island that includes modern England, ▷ Wales and ▷ Scotland, though the Roman province of Britain (AD 43–410) only reached the south of Scotland. Speaking of pre-Roman times, we call the island Ancient Britain and we call its mixed people Ancient Britons.

Political, rather than descriptive, the term was revived when King James VI of Scotland became also ▷ James I of England (including Wales) in 1603 and called himself King of Great Britain. It was officially adopted by ▷ Parliament when England and Scotland were united in 1707 (Act of ▷ Union). In 1801 the United Kingdom of Great Britain and Ireland was formed, but most of ▷ Ireland became separate again in 1922. Terms now in use are:

British Isles: Great Britain and all Ireland, geographically.

United Kingdom: Great Britain and Northern Ireland.

Great Britain, or *Britain*: England, Scotland and Wales, geographically.

British: Loosely to UK or to Britain.

Briton: a native of the UK, but the term is rarely used. A native calls himself an Englishman, Scotsman, Welshman or Ulsterman (N. Ireland).

Britisher: American name for a Briton.

England and *English*: These are often loosely and wrongly used for Britain and British, simply because England is the largest partner and English is the common language.

Britannia

The Latin name for Britain. It became a poetic name for Britain in personification. Since 1672 Britannia has been represented as a woman with helmet, shield and trident on certain coins. It is thus a symbol in which a connection between empire, militarism and the economy is established. The poem, 'Rule Britannia' by ▷ James Thomson has been sung to music by Arne as an unofficial national anthem.

British Museum

The British Museum is on the site of the former Montagu House, which held the library and collection of Sir Hans Sloane, a physician and secretary to the ▷ Royal Society. The museum was established in 1759; the present buildings were constructed 1823–47. The British Library, formerly contained in the museum and other buildings, is in the process of being transferred to new premises in Euston Road.

Broadside Ballads

Popular ▷ ballads, printed on folio sheets. They formed a cheap method of publishing songs on topical subjects. The term 'broadside' meant that only one side of the paper was printed. They were a means of issuing news items, political propaganda, religious controversy, travellers' tales, attacks on (or defences of) women, the last words of condemned criminals, and so on. Often decorated with wood-cut prints, they were a major source of information in the 16th and 17th centuries. The British Library possesses a unique collection of broadsides amongst the 'Thomason Tracts'.

Bib: Reay, B., *Popular Culture in Seventeenth-Century England;* Shepard, L., *The History of Street Literature.*

Brobdingnag

Fabulous land of giants where Gulliver is left ashore in ▷ Gulliver's Travels.

Brooke, Charlotte (d 1793)

Irish translator and poet. She nursed her father, a dramatist, until he died in 1783. She contributed an anonymous ▷ translation to *Historical Memoirs of Irish Bards* (1786), and published *Reliques of Irish Poetry* (1788) by subscription. She also wrote a tragedy, *Belisaious*, which is lost. In her translation she is concerned with the difficulty of translating not only words and genre but cultural contexts. Introducing her translation of elegies she notes, 'in the original, they are simple and unlearned, but pathetic to a great degree, and this is a species of beauty in composition, extremely difficult to transcribe into any other language'.

▷ Irish Literature in English
Bib: Gantz, K. F., *Studies in English.*

Brooke, Frances (1724–1789)

Important as the author of the first Canadian novel, she was born Francis Moore in Claypole, England, grew up in Lincolnshire and Peterborough, and was educated at home. By 1748, she had moved to London and established herself as a woman of no small literary importance, with friends like ▷ Samuel Johnson, ▷ Anna Seward and ▷ Fanny Burney. She married the Reverend John Brooke in 1755, but enjoyed a measure of freedom to pursue her literary interests. Under the name 'Mary Singleton, Spinster,' she edited *The Old Maid*, a weekly periodical (1775–6). She tried to persuade actor/manager ▷ David Garrick to produce her blank verse tragedy *Virginia*, but he was unwilling to do so, and it was finally published in 1756, with other poems and translations. She also translated, from the French, Marie-Jeanne Riccoboni's *Letters from Juliet, Lady Catesby, to her Friend, Lady Henrietta Campley* in 1760. Meanwhile, her husband had left for Canada. After the appearance of her ▷ epistolary novel, *The History of Lady Julia Mandeville* (1763), she went to join her husband, who was stationed in Quebec as military chaplain. This work, suitably concluding with the deaths of both central characters, enjoyed popular success. Frances Brooke's stay in Quebec (until 1768) informed *The History of Emily Montague*, which is popularly considered the first Canadian novel (1769). The book's major characters and correspondents, Edward Rivers and Arabella Fermor, describe in considerable detail political and social aspects of 18th-century Canada, with notable emphasis on the landscape, and on the relations between the English and the French.

After Frances Brooke's return to England, she translated Framéry's *Memoirs of the Marquis de St Forlaix* (published in 1770), and Millot's *Elements of the History of England, from the Invasion of the Romans to the Reign of George the Second* (published in 1771). There is critical debate about whether Frances Brooke is the author of the anonymous novel *All's Right at Last; or, The History of Miss West* (1774), although Lorraine McMullen's 1983 biography of Brooke supports the attribution. Brook's next novel, *The Excursion* (1777), is about a heroine in London seeking success as a writer; David Garrick comes under direct attack for not supporting new work. From 1773 to 1778, Frances Brooke was involved, with actress Mary Ann Yates, in managing the Haymarket opera house. Three of her dramatic works were staged: *The Siege of Sinope: A Tragedy*, in 1781; *Rosina* and *Marion*, both comic operas, in 1783 and 1788. Her last novel, *The History of Charles Mandeville* (1790), was not published until after her death. She is buried in Sleaford, Lincolnshire, England.

Bib: McMullen, L., *An Odd Attempt in a Woman: The Literary Life of Frances Brooke.*

Browne, Sir Thomas (1605–82)

Physician and author. Sir Thomas Browne studied medicine at Montpellier, Padua and Leiden, and began practising medicine in 1633, before moving in 1637 to Norwich, where he spent the rest of his life. Browne's most influential work was ▷ *Religio*

Medici (1642, re-issued in an authorized edition in 1643), a title which can be translated as *The Religion of a Physician*. The conjunction between religious meditation and an enduring fascination with observation of the most minute details of the physical world informs the *Religio*, which stands as both the determined act of creation of an authorial persona, and as a disquisition which attempts to reconcile scepticism and belief.

In some ways, Browne can be thought of as a ▷ Baconian (▷ Francis Bacon) in his adherence to the principles of observation, and his determination to refute ideas commonly entertained by the credulous. But his Baconianism is tempered with a vein of mysticism. The two tendencies in his thought are displayed in his later works – *Pseudodoxica Epidemica*, or *Vulgar Errors* (1646); *Hydriotaphia*, or ▷ *Urn Burial* (1658); and *The Garden of Cyrus* (1658).
Bib: Keynes, Sir G. (ed.), *Works*, 4 vols.; Bennett, J., *Sir Thomas Browne*.

Brownists

A ▷ Puritan religious sect founded by Robert Browne (1550?–1633?); from about 1640 they were known as Independents, and since the 18th century they have been Congregationalists. Their best-known doctrine is that on the evidence of the New Testament each religious congregation should be self-governing, so that there should be no over-riding Church, *eg* no government through bishops under a central figure such as the Pope or, in the Anglican system, the Crown.
    ▷ Congregationalism.

Buckingham, Duke of
▷ Villiers, George, Duke of

Bunyan, John (1628–88)
Bunyan was the son of a tinsmith. He was born at Elstow, near Bedford, and educated at the village school. Of Baptist sympathies, he fought in the ▷ Civil War, although little is known of his military activities. With the persecution of the ▷ Puritans which followed the ▷ Restoration of Charles II, Bunyan's Non-Conformist beliefs came under severe censure, and in 1660 he was arrested for preaching without a licence.

For most of the next twelve years Bunyan was imprisoned in Bedford jail, where he began to write. His spiritual autobiography, ▷ *Grace Abounding to the Chief of Sinners*, appeared in 1666, and the first part of his major work, ▷ *The Pilgrim's Progress* was published in 1678. *The Pilgrim's Progress* was largely written during this period of imprisonment, though it is probable that Bunyan completed Part I during a second spell in jail in 1676; the full text, with the addition of Part II, was published in 1684. A spiritual allegory strongly in the ▷ Puritan tradition, it tells of the pilgrimage of Christian to reach the state of grace. Bunyan's other major works, *The Life and Death of Mr Badman* (1680) (▷ *Badman, The Life ...*) and ▷ *The Holy War* (1682), are also spiritual allegories.

Burke, Edmund (1729–97)
Statesman and political philosopher; described by Matthew Arnold as 'our greatest English prose-writer'. Born in Dublin, he pursued his political career in England, and was a Member of ▷ Parliament for much of his life. Although never attaining high office, his political status was considerable, due mainly to his formidable powers of oratory and polemical argument. His early work *A Philosophical Inquiry into the Origin of our Ideas of the Sublime and the Beautiful* (1756) marks a transition in aesthetic theory from the neo-classicism of ▷ John Dryden and ▷ Alexander Pope. Influenced by ▷ Longinus and ▷ Milton, it emphasizes the sense of awe inspired by both art and nature. His most celebrated work, ▷ *Reflections on the Revolution in France* (1790), argues for the organic, evolutionary development of society, as opposed to the brutal surgery and doctrinaire theories of the French revolutionaries.

Burke's character reveals a number of paradoxes. His writings combine the cautious, pragmatic instincts of a conservative politician with a passionate rhetorical style. He regarded all forms of political innovation with suspicion, yet defended the cause of the American rebels in *On Conciliation with the Colonies* (1775). He attacked the corrupt practice of court patronage and the exploitative activities of the East India Company, yet retained for himself many benefits of the systems he deplored.
Bib: Cone, C. B., *Burke and the Nature of Politics* (2 vols.); Stanlis, P. J. (ed.), *Edmund Burke: The Enlightenment and the Modern World*; Wilkins, B. T., *The Problem of Burke's Political Philosophy*.

Burlesque
A form of satirical comedy (not necessarily dramatic) which arouses laughter through mockery of a form usually dedicated to high seriousness. The word is from the Italian, *burla* meaning 'ridicule'. Burlesque is similar to ▷ parody, but parody depends on subtler and closer imitation of a particular work.
    ▷ Satire.

Burnet, Gilbert, Bishop (1643–1715)
Whig cleric, who played an important part in the build-up to the ▷ Glorious Revolution of 1688 and the accession of ▷ William III and Mary II. Born at Edinburgh, Burnet entered Marischal College, Aberdeen at the age of 10, studying first law and then divinity. In 1669 he became professor of divinity at Glasgow, but resigned in 1674 because of a dispute with his former patron, the Earl of Lauderdale. He settled in London, where he was made chaplain of the Rolls Chapel and later lecturer at St Clements. Burnet incurred the hostility of ▷ Charles II, who took away his lectureship, and on the accession of ▷ James II he left for the Continent. There he allied himself with William of Orange, whom he accompanied back to England as royal chaplain. He became Bishop of Salisbury in 1689. His *History of the Reformation* was published 1679–81 and 1714; his *History of My Own Time* (1724–34) remains a primary source of information about the period.

Bib: Clarke and Foxcroft, *Life of Bishop Burnet*; Jones, J. R., *The Revolution of 1688 in England*.

Burnet, Thomas (1635–1715)

English cleric, born at Croft in Yorkshire, became a pupil of Tillotson and Clerk of the Closet to ▷ William III, but had to resign in 1692 because of opposition incurred by his unorthodox *Archaeologia Philosophica*, which treats the Fall of Adam and Eve as an allegory. He influenced ▷ Addison, ▷ Young and ▷ Burke, and his *Telluris Theoria Sacra* (1680–89, translated into English 1684–9), was also an important source for ▷ Thomson's *The Four Seasons*.

Burney, Dr Charles (1726–1814)

Charles Burney was the friend of ▷ Samuel Johnson, ▷ David Garrick and ▷ Sir Joshua Reynolds. An organist and musical historian, he also wrote travelogues of France, Italy, Germany and the Low Countries of the journeys he made to collect material for his *History of Music* (published 1776–89). He was the father of ▷ Fanny Burney.

Burney, Fanny (Frances, Madame D'Arblay) (1752–1840)

Daughter of ▷ Dr Charles Burney, Fanny grew up in the distinguished company of ▷ Johnson, ▷ Sir Joshua Reynolds, ▷ Garrick and the ▷ Bluestockings. In 1786 she was appointed as an attendant upon Queen Charlotte, wife of George III, and in 1793 she married a French exile, General D'Arblay. From 1802–12, interned by Napoleon, she and her husband lived in France.

Burney's major novels are ▷ *Evelina* (1778), *Cecilia* (1782) and *Camilla* (1796). Their common theme is the entry into society of a young girl, beautiful and intelligent but lacking experience of the world; during subsequent adventures the girl's character is moulded. Burney was a great admirer of ▷ Richardson, and his influence is apparent in her use, in her first novel, of the epistolary (*ie* letter-writing) form.

Burney was also well known for her diaries and letters. Her *Early Diary* (1889) covers the years 1768–78, and contains many sketches of Johnson and Garrick; her *Diary and Letters . . . 1778–1840* (published 1842–6) is a lively account of life at court. Amongst her admirers, ▷ Jane Austen shows Burney's influence.

Bib: Simons, J., *Fanny Burney*.

Burns, Robert (1759–96)

Scottish poet. He was born in poverty, the son of a peasant or 'cottar', but he nevertheless became well-read in the Bible, Shakespeare, 18th-century English poetry, and also learnt some French. His best work, in the Lowland Scots dialect, was precipitated by his reading of ▷ Robert Fergusson, and was written between 1785 and 1790, during most of which time he was working as a farmer, an occupation which undermined his health. In 1786 his *Poems Chiefly in the Scots Dialect* were published in Kilmarnock, and made him famous. He moved to ▷ Edinburgh where a new edition of the volume appeared in

the following year, and where he was lionized as a 'natural' genius. He intended to emigrate to Jamaica with Mary Campbell but she died in childbirth in 1787. He was a hard drinker and womanizer, and two years after Mary Campbell's death he took as his wife Jean Armour, who had already borne children by him. He leased a farm and secured preferment in the excise service in Dumfries, despite his earlier sympathies for the ▷ French Revolution and the war of ▷ American Independence. He devoted himself to reworking Scottish songs, which appeared in James Johnson's *The Scots Musical Museum* (1793–1803) and George Thomson's *Select Scottish Airs with Poetry*. But he became further impoverished, and succumbed to persistent ill health.

Perhaps Burns's best-known poems are sentimental lyrics, such as *Auld Lang Syne*, or love songs like *Ae fond Kiss*, *Highland Mary*, and 'O my love's like a red, red rose'. His *Cotter's Saturday Night* celebrates Scottish peasant life in Spenserian stanzas, and other poems express a keen sympathy with the downtrodden and oppressed. But it is his comic satires which are now considered his best work: *To a Mouse*; *The Twa Dogs*; *Tam O'Shanter*; *The Folly Beggars*. It is significant that those poems which attack Calvinism and the hypocrisy of kirk elders, such as *The Twa Herds* and *Holy Willie's Prayer*, were omitted from the Kilmarnock *Poems* of 1786. Even during his lifetime Burns was beginning to be viewed as a kind of Scottish ▷ Poet Laureate, with all the distortions which this inevitably involved. Over the past two centuries, this status, together with the patriotism of Burns Night, have served to promote a glamorized myth, at the expense of a true appreciation of Burns's poetry.

▷ Scottish literature in English.

Bib: Daiches, D., *Robert Burns*; Jack, R. D. S., and Noble, A. (eds.), *The Art of Robert Burns*; Spiers, J., *The Scots Literary Tradition*.

Busie Body, The (1709)

Play by ▷ Susannah Centlivre. Sir George Airy, a wealthy young man, is in love with Miranda, but her old guardian Sir Francis Gripe, intends her for himself. Sir Francis' son, also George's friend, Charles, is in love with Isabinda, whose father Sir Jealous Traffick wants her to marry a Spaniard. Charles's suit is additionally hindered by his impoverishment: his father has tricked him out of his inheritance, while Miranda is being denied her inheritance by Gripe. Another of Gripe's wards, Marplot, does his best to help the lovers, but invariably adds complications because of his bungling naïveté. The action proceeds by means of a series of scenes of deception and intrigue, often frustrated by Marplot. Eventually, Charles disguises himself as the Spanish suitor and marries Isabinda under her father's nose; his fortune is restored by means of writings stolen from Sir Francis by Miranda, while Miranda herself is also united with her lover. The appeal of the well-meaning but witless Marplot helped to make the play so popular that in 1710 it was played simultaneously at both ▷ Covent Garden and ▷ Drury Lane, and it survived well into the 19th century. A sequel, *Marplot in Lisbon, or, The*

Second Part of the Busie Body (1710), achieved less success.

Butler, Charlotte (fl 1673–95)

Popular ▷ Restoration actress and singer, from a well-to-do family that had fallen on hard times. She specialized in playing young girls, as well as acting in breeches parts (women disguised as men and wearing men's clothes). She was alleged to be highly promiscuous, and was as famous for her supposed list of lovers as for her comic talent and beautiful voice. Between 1675 and 1692 she played at least 19 roles.
Bib: Howe, E., *The First English Actresses: Women and Drama 1660–1700.*

Butler, Samuel (1612–80)

Poet. The son of a Worcestershire farmer, he became the friend of ▷ Thomas Hobbes and ▷ Sir William D'Avenant. His ▷ mock-heroic satire on Puritanism, ▷ *Hudibras*, employs deliberately rough and ready tetrameter couplets which were frequently imitated by later poets and became known as 'hudibrastics'. Butler's other works were neglected, and most of them, including the Theophrasilan of *Characters*, and the satire on the ▷ Royal Society, *The Elephant in the Moon* (it is actually a mouse trapped in the telescope), were not published until 1759, when his *Genuine Remains* appeared.
Bib: Johnson, S., in *Lives of the Poets;* Jack, I., *Augustan Satire.*

Button's Coffee-house

Button's was set up in Russell Street, Covent Garden, in 1712 as a rival to ▷ Will's Coffee-house. It was named after its proprietor Daniel Button, a retired servant of ▷ Joseph Addison, who helped him with the venture.

Byrom, John (1692–1763)

Poet. Inventor of a system of shorthand, Fellow of the ▷ Royal Society and student of religious mysticism. His posthumous *Miscellaneous Poems* (1773) are notable for their colloquial ease and moderate eloquence of tone.

Caesar

The name of an aristocratic ('patrician') family in ancient Rome; the family claimed descent from the legendary ▷ Aeneas, supposed founder of Rome. The name was made famous by the general and statesman Gaius Julius Caesar (▷ Caesar, Gaius Julius), whose adopted son, Octavianus, also called himself Caesar. Octavianus became Augustus Caesar (▷ Caesar, Augustus), the first Roman Emperor, and thereafter Caesar became the adopted name of all the Roman Emperors, until the fall of Constantinople in 1453. The German Holy Roman Emperors, claiming to be the heirs of the Roman Emperors of the West, adopted the title Caesar as 'Kaiser'; similarly the Russian Emperors, claiming to be heirs of the Roman Empire of the East, adopted it as 'Czar'. Thus from the first century the family name of Caesar virtually became a title, 'Emperor'. As Julius Caesar became dictator of Rome, 'Caesarism' has come to mean belief in autocracy.

Caesar, Augustus (Gaius Julius Caesar Octavianus) (63 BC–AD 14)

Great-nephew of Julius Caesar, and his adopted son. He adopted the surname Caesar and was awarded the title of Augustus by the Roman Senate. He overcame the political enemies and assassins of his uncle, Julius, and after defeating his other rivals (notably Mark Antony), he achieved complete power and became first Emperor of Rome. ▷ Horace, ▷ Virgil, ▷ Ovid, Propertius, Tibullus and ▷ Livy were his contemporaries; in consequence, 'an ▷ Augustan age' has become a term to describe a high peak of literary achievement in any culture, whenever such achievement shows similar qualities of elegance, restraint and eloquence. In these qualities, France in the 17th century and England in the 18th century consciously emulated the Augustan age of Rome.

▷ French literature in England.

Caesar, Gaius Julius (?102–44 BC)

Roman general, statesman and writer. He conquered Gaul (ie modern France) and in 55 and 54 BC undertook two expeditions to Britain. He described these wars in *De Bello Gallico*, a work long and widely used in English education for instruction in Latin. His victories led to civil war against his chief political rival, Gneius Pompeius, generally known in English as Pompey, whom he defeated. He then became dictator in Rome, but he was assassinated by other patricians, led by Marcus Brutus, for overthrowing Roman republican institutions. For the Middle Ages, Julius Caesar represented all that was great in Rome. His life was described by the Greek biographer ▷ Plutarch and this with Plutarch's other biographies was translated into English by Sir Thomas North. ▷ Shakespeare used it as the basis of his play *Julius Caesar*.

Callisto

In Greek myth, a ▷ nymph, and companion of the hunting goddess Artemis. ▷ Zeus loved her, and his jealous queen, Hera, transformed her into a bear, in which shape she was killed by Artemis.

Calvin, John (1509–1604)

French religious reformer and author of the *Institutes of the Christian Religion* (1535). He settled in Geneva, which was to become, under Calvin's influence, an important centre of one of the most disciplined and militant branches of ▷ Protestantism.

Calvin's teachings were widely influential in England, Scotland, France and Switzerland in the 17th century and later. Out of the *Institutes* and his book on ▷ predestination (published in 1552) emerged the five chief points of 'Calvinism', namely its belief in: (1) 'predestination', which holds that God determined in advance who shall be 'elected' to 'eternal life' and who shall be condemned to everlasting damnation; (2) 'particular redemption', or the choosing of a certain predetermined number of souls redeemed by Christ's death; (3) 'original sin', which holds that the infant enters the world in a state of sinfulness, carrying with it the burden of Adam's fall; (4) 'irresistible grace', which argues that those chosen to be of the 'elect' have no means of resisting that choice; and (5) the final perseverance or triumph of the 'elect'.

Taken with Calvin's views on Church government and the relation between state and ecclesiastical power, 'Calvinism' was to be of enormous influence on the ▷ Church of England in the 16th and 17th centuries. From the early 17th century onwards his doctrines became those of the established church. Calvin's *Institutes* became a recognized textbook in the universities, and it was not until the rise of Arminianism under Archbishop William Laud in the pre-Civil War (▷ Civil Wars) years that an effective opposition to Calvin's influence was mounted.
Bib: Dickens, A. G., *The English Reformation*.

Cambridge Platonists

A group of thinkers at Cambridge University in the mid-17th century. Their aim was to combine reason with revealed religion, and to counteract the religiously destructive tendencies of the thought of ▷ René Descartes and ▷ Thomas Hobbes. Their concern with true religion was combined with a care for clarity of thought and for religious tolerance. Their chief representatives were Henry More (1614–87), Ralph Cudworth (1617–88), Benjamin Whichcote (1609–83) and John Smith (1618–52).

▷ Platonism and neo-Platonism.
Bib: Patrides, C. A. (ed.), *The Cambridge Platonists*.

Cambridge University

One of the two oldest English universities. Its origins are obscure, but it was in existence early in the 13th century, and was probably founded by students emigrating from Oxford. Like Oxford, it is famous for the organization of its students and scholars into colleges, these being independent self-governing bodies whose governing members usually, though not necessarily, hold office in the university as well. It achieved importance equal to Oxford only in the 15th century. From then onwards the two universities have liked to think of themselves as rival leaders of English intellectual life, a habit they retain in spite of the founding of many other universities in the 19th and 20th centuries. In literature, Cambridge has been noted for the number of outstanding English poets educated there, including ▷ Donne, ▷ Milton and ▷ Dryden. ▷ Universities.

Campbell, The Clan

A Scottish clan, headed by the Duke of Argyll, which in the 17th and 18th centuries was one of the most powerful clans in the ▷ Highlands. The heads of the clan became dukes in the 18th century; their ancient Gaelic title is Macallum Mhor – the 'Great Campbell'. It was steadfast under its chiefs in its support of the ▷ Presbyterian Church and the ▷ Protestant succession, and in this it was opposed to other leading Highland clans who tended to support the ▷ Catholic House of ▷ Stuart.

Capitalism

The system by which the means of production is owned privately. Production is for private profit and productive enterprise is made possible by large-scale loans of money rewarded by the payment of interest.

Before about 1350, in England as in much of the rest of Europe, there was little opportunity for capitalism. On the land, the economic unit was the manor (corresponding approximately to a village) which consumed its own produce and had little left over for sale. The economic relations were feudal, ie the landlords provided protection to the peasants in return for economic services; the peasants were mostly serfs, ie they were bound to the land they worked on and were unable to sell their labour freely. The towns were small and manufacture was by master craftsmen, who worked with their own hands, and employed ▷ apprentices and journeymen only in small numbers. The masters combined in craft guilds which regulated trade and limited profits to a communally arranged 'just price'. Moreover, commerce, except for the export of wool, was mainly limited to the districts round the towns. Finally, it was difficult to borrow money for capital investment, partly because the Church disapproved of the taking of interest on money loans, since it regarded this as the sin of usury. The economic bond was not, in fact, a money relationship but a personal one, bound up with an elaborate system of rights and duties. These divided society into something more like castes than the modern social classes, which are differentiated chiefly by wealth.

But by the lifetime of Chaucer capitalism was making beginnings. Towns were growing, and they now contained a substantial middle class, as the *Prologue* to *The Canterbury Tales* illustrates. Master craftsmen were gradually becoming employers of labour rather than workers themselves; this was particularly true in the manufacture of cloth, which required a variety of processes impossible for one man, or even one guild, to undertake alone. The craft guilds were becoming supplemented by the merchant companies, such as the Merchants of the Staple, who had a monopoly of the export of wool to the cloth manufacturers of Flanders. In the 15th and 16th centuries the export of cloth by Merchant Adventurers became even more important than this older commerce of the export of wool. The economic cause of the Hundred Years' War was Edward III's

determination to protect the English wool staple towns – ie those through which the export of wool was channelled into Flanders – from the threat of France. To sustain the war, Edward III and Henry V had to borrow extensively from foreign bankers, who were finding methods of escaping the Church's prohibition of usury. On the land the serfs were becoming independent wage-earners, able to sell their labour freely and where they pleased, because of the shortage of labour that resulted from the Black Death epidemics (about 1350). Lack of labour caused many landowners to turn their arable land into pasture and to enclose open land with hedges. This process continued in Tudor times for economic reasons, despite a labour surplus. It weakened the landowners' ties with the peasantry and encouraged the 'drift to the towns' which drained the countryside in the 18th and 19th centuries.

The rapid growth of capitalism in the 17th and 18th centuries was aided by the ▷ Reformation, since certain of the ▷ Puritan sects – notably the Calvinist Presbyterians (▷ Calvin, John) – found that religious individualism gave support to and was supported by economic individualism. Between 1580 and 1640 the Puritans opposed the English dramatists (eg Ben Jonson, Thomas Middleton, Philip Massinger) who satirized the money-loving, socially ambitious middle classes, among whom the Puritans had their main strength. By the end of the 17th century, however, Puritanism was losing its ferocity; the traditional non-economic bonds of community were by then gravely weakened, and the novels of ▷ Daniel Defoe depict the loneliness of men guided predominantly by economically individualistic motives.

The full triumph of capitalism came only with the fulfilment of the ▷ Industrial Revolution in the 19th century. Workers were, for the first time on a large scale, employed in the mass, in factories. The employers (backed by a number of gifted theorists, such as ▷ Adam Smith, ▷ Jeremy Bentham, ▷ Thomas Malthus and David Ricardo) developed a ruthless philosophy, according to which their relationship with their workers should be governed entirely by the economic laws of supply and demand, with which the state interfered, in their opinion, only at the cost of wrecking national prosperity, even if the interference were dictated by the need to save the workers from intolerable misery. This stream of opinion among the industrialist employers was, however, progressively opposed by Evangelical Christians among the politicians (eg Lord Shaftesbury), by socialists of the school of Robert Owen and by the very popular novelists between 1830 and 1860, such as Elizabeth Gaskell, Benjamin Disraeli and Charles Dickens. The most cogent and revolutionary opposition, however, was formulated in the work of Friedrich Engels, *The Condition of the Working Class* (1845) and of Karl Marx, *Das Kapital* (1867).

Captain Singleton, Adventures of (1720)

A novel by ▷ Daniel Defoe. Like the heroes and heroines of Defoe's other novels, Singleton has at first no morality and takes to a life of wandering adventure; some of this takes place in Africa (which Defoe knew only from reading and hearsay). Later he becomes a pirate in the Indian Ocean and further east; finally he settles down in England, a respectable married man, converted to a religious life. The story is told in the first person.

Carleton, Mary (?1633–1673)
English writer, born in Canterbury. She adapted the codes and conventions of scandalous chronicle to her own case. She was already married when she moved to London, claiming to be a German lady or princess. She soon married John Carleton, but when each discovered the other did not have the estate they pretended, he accused her of bigamy. A corpus of writings grew up around the case. Apart from the defences each made of their own case there was *The Case of Madam Mary Carleton* and *A True Account* (both 1663), and *An Historical Narrative of the German Princess*.

Mary Carleton acted in a satire about her own story, called *The German Princess*. She was later convicted of theft and transported to Jamaica. She escaped, but was eventually caught and hanged.
Bib: Bernbaum, E., *The Mary Carleton Narratives*.

Carter, Elizabeth (1717–1806)
English correspondent, poet, linguist and ▷ Bluestocking. She lived with her father (who was a preacher at Canterbury cathedral) in Deal, Kent. He taught her Latin, Greek and Hebrew; she also learned French, Italian, Spanish, German and some Arabic. Skilled also in music, mathematics and geography, she spent her life studying. She translated Epictetus, published a volume of poetry, made ▷ translations from French and Italian, wrote for ▷ Samuel Johnson's ▷ *The Rambler* (March 1750–March 1752) and ▷ *The Gentleman's Magazine* (to which Johnson also contributed). Her correspondence with ▷ Catherine Talbot and ▷ Elizabeth Montagu display a sharp critical intellect. She regarded ▷ Katherine Philips's poetry about friendship between women as 'very moral and sentimental'.

Publications: *Poems on Particular Occasions* (1738); *Poems* (1762); *Letters from Mrs Elizabeth Carter, to Mrs Montagu, between the Years 1755 and 1800* (3 vols) (1817); *Memoirs of the Life of Mrs Elizabeth Carter*, edited by Montagu Pennington (1807); *A Series of Letters between Mrs Elizabeth Carter and Miss Catherine Talbot from the year 1741 to 1770, to which are added, letters from Mrs Elizabeth Carter to Mrs Vessey, between the years 1763 and 1787* (4 vols) (1809).
▷ Fielding, Sarah

Cartesianism
The philosophy of ▷ Descartes.

Casanova De Seingalt, Giacomo (1725–98)
An Italian adventurer, author of scandalous Memoirs. His name has become synonymous in English with a 'man who prides himself on his sexual attractiveness'.

Castalia, Castalian Spring
▷ Muses.

Castle of Indolence, The (1748)
A poem in ▷ Spenserian stanzas by ▷ James Thomson. Its first canto deals with the 'pleasing land of drowsyhed' governed by the wizard Indolence. The poet himself ('a bard . . . more fat than bard beseems'), his friends ▷ James Quin the actor, ▷ Lord Lyttelton, and others live a life of sensuous ease in Indolence's castle, until they become bloated and are thrown into a foul dungeon. The second canto depicts the progress of the Knight of Industry from the ancient world to Britain, where he creates the new order of 'social commerce' and imperial expansion, and ends by conquering Indolence and freeing his victims. The poem presents a fascinating mixture of whimsical irony and serious ▷ 'Augustan' didacticism. Lord Lyttelton wrote the stanza describing Thomson himself (I, stanza 68) and the last four stanzas of Canto I were written by Thomson's friend ▷ John Armstrong.
▷ Augustanism; Bard.

Castle of Otranto, The (1764)
One of the first so-called ▷ Gothic novels, by ▷ Horace Walpole. The fantastic events are set in the Middle Ages, and the story is full of supernatural sensationalism. The story concerns an evil usurper, a fateful prophecy about his downfall, a mysterious prince disguised as a peasant, and his eventual marriage to the beautiful heroine whom the usurper had intended as his own bride.

Catholic Emancipation, The Act of (1829)
A law by which Roman Catholics in England were awarded full political rights, *eg* to be elected as Members of ▷ Parliament. They had been deprived of these rights by legislation of various kinds since the time of the ▷ Reformation. The Act was of particular importance for the rights of Irish Roman Catholics, who, after they lost the Irish Parliament in 1800, bitterly resented their exclusion from Westminster.
▷ Catholicism (Roman) in Britain; Catholicism (Roman) in English literature.

Catholicism (Roman) in Britain
After the ▷ Reformation in Britain in the 16th century, many people remained loyal to the Catholic faith, precipitating repeated periods of discord with ▷ Protestants. Early in the 17th century these culminated in the ▷ Gunpowder Plot of 1605. Later, ▷ Charles II converted to Catholicism, but was able to keep it secret and avoid openly antagonizing the Protestant forces. The first Test Act of 1673 imposed various penalties on Catholics, including prohibiting them from voting and from holding any public office. During Charles's reign, Catholics were periodically persecuted, especially during the time of the Popish Plot in 1678 (▷ Titus Oates). Religious conflicts also underlay the ▷ Rye House plot of 1683. Charles's brother, ▷ James II, was openly Catholic, and within months of his accession in 1685, Charles's illegitimate son, the Protestant ▷ Duke of Monmouth, attempted to claim the throne. A battle fought at ▷ Sedgemoor ended in defeat for

Monmouth's forces, and was followed by brutal reprisals at the so-called ▷ Bloody Assizes. Religious conflict erupted once more with James's passage of the Edict of Toleration, suspending the first Test Act, persecution of Protestant ▷ Dissenters, and other moves to further the Catholic cause, culminating in his announcement of his intention to restore Catholicism as the established faith. The birth of his son in 1688, which would have ensured continuation of the Catholic line, brought matters to a head, precipitating the ▷ Glorious Revolution of that year, the removal of James, and the accession of ▷ William III and ▷ Mary II. The ▷ Act of Settlement of 1701 excluded Catholics from the throne. The impending death of Queen ▷ Anne brought the religious question once more to the fore, before the Protestant succession was confirmed in 1714. This precipitated a ▷ Jacobite rebellion in 1715, on behalf of James's son, also called James, known as the ▷ Old Pretender, who remained a Catholic. Jacobite agitation continued over the next few decades, but the question of the succession was finally resolved when the forces of James's grandson, Charles Edward Stuart, were defeated at Battle of ▷ Culloden in 1746. Catholics were eventually granted equal rights with Protestants in the Catholic Emancipation Act of 1829. Some major literary figures in England have been Catholics, including ▷ Wycherley, ▷ Dryden, who converted from Protestantism with the accession of James II in 1685, and ▷ Pope.

▷ Catholicism (Roman) in English literature; Recusancy.

Catholicism (Roman) in English literature

Until the Act of Supremacy (1534) by which King Henry VIII separated the English Church from Roman authority, and the more violent revolution in Scotland a little later, both countries had belonged to the European community of Catholic Christendom. This community was a genuine culture, allowing great unity of belief and feeling together with great variety of attitude. In the 16th century this community of cultures broke up, owing not only to the ▷ Protestant rebellions but also to the increase of national self-consciousness, the influence of non-Christian currents (especially ▷ Platonism), and the gradual release of various fields of activity – political, commercial, philosophical – from religious doctrine. The Counter-Reformation after the Catholic Council of Trent (1545–63), even more than the ▷ Reformation, tended to define Roman Catholicism in contrast to Protestantism. Thus, although the dramatists and lyric poets in England from 1560 to 1640 showed a plentiful survival of medieval assumptions about the nature of man and his place in the universe, in conflict with newer tendencies of thought and feeling, the Roman Catholic writers in the same period began to distinguish themselves from their non-Catholic colleagues. The clearest example in the 17th century is the poet Richard Crashaw. ▷ Milton's epic of the creation of the world, ▷ *Paradise Lost*, is in many ways highly traditional, but the feeling that inspires it is entirely post-Reformation. By the 18th century,

however, religion of all kinds was becoming a mere department of life, no longer dictating ideas and emotions in all fields, even when sincerely believed; it is thus seldom easy to remember that the poet ▷ Alexander Pope was a Roman Catholic. By the 19th century, writers of strong religious conviction were increasingly feeling themselves in a minority in an indifferent and even sceptical world. They therefore tended to impress their work once more with their faith, and this was especially true of the few Catholic writers, since Catholic faith was dogmatically so strongly defined, eg the poet Gerard Manley Hopkins. The century also saw a revival of Anglo-Catholicism. From the time of the Reformation there had been a school of opinion which sought to remain as close to Roman Catholicism as ▷ Anglican independence allowed. This wing of the Church was important under ▷ Charles I, but lost prestige until it was revived by the Oxford Movement.

Catullus, Gaius Valerius (?84–54 BC)

A Roman lyrical poet, famous especially for a cycle of poems addressed to his beloved Lesbia. He was one of the Latin poets who had an extensive influence over English ▷ lyric poetry in the 16th and 17th centuries. For instance Ben Jonson's *Song to Celia* is modelled on Catullus, and so is ▷ Andrew Marvell's *To his Coy Mistress*. Jonson, with his sensitive and profound Latin scholarship, was the most important English follower of Catullus and he transmitted the strength and delicacy of the Latin poet to the 'Cavalier' lyricists and to Marvell. The most important period for Catullus's influence on English poetry was therefore 1600–50.

Cavalier

A word, meaning 'horseman', which was used for the supporters of ▷ Charles I in the ▷ Civil War. It was first used as a term of reproach against them by their opponents, the supporters of ▷ Parliament, the ▷ Roundheads; in this sense it meant an arrogant and frivolous man of the court. Soon, however, it was accepted with pride by the Royalists themselves. It is a mistake to think of the Cavaliers as merely members of the court and the aristocracy; many of the aristocracy supported Parliament and many of the Cavaliers were fairly modest country gentlemen who never came near the court. The Cavalier Parliament sat from 1661 to 1678 after the restoration of ▷ Charles II and was so called because the king's supporters won most of the seats.

Cave, Jane (1757–1813)

Poet. A devout Anglican with ▷ Methodist inclinations, Cave constantly battled against the sense of duty which called her away from her poetry. She published her witty and fast-moving collection *Poems on Various Subjects* (including an ▷ elegy on her maiden name) in 1783 and revised it in 1786 when she married Thomas Winscom, in an attempt to expunge any material in danger of being considered impious. While the 1786 version contains interesting material in relation to gender, as she focuses on the importance of marriage and motherhood, its tone is heavier and less spirited than the 1783 edition. In later editions she added some abolitionist writing.

Cavendish, Margaret, Duchess of Newcastle (?1624–74)

The life and writings of Margaret Cavendish perfectly illustrate the fate of a woman who endeavoured to compete on equal intellectual terms with men. ▷ Samuel Pepys described her as a 'mad, conceited, and ridiculous woman' and yet she was much admired for her erudition. Her chief publications include scientific and philosophical works such as *Observations upon Experimental Philosophy* (1666) and *Grounds of Natural Philosophy* (1668), together with poems, plays, and letters. Her ▷ autobiography is contained in *Nature's Pictures* (1656) and it was followed in 1667 by a ▷ biography of her husband that was a considerable success. Though she was lavishly entertained by the ▷ Royal Society in 1667, it was never suggested that she be elected to a Fellowship.

Bib: Meyer, G. D., *The Scientific Lady in England 1650–1760*; Jones, K., *A Glorious Fame*.

Cecilia, St

Patron saint of music and the blind; martyred for her faith, in Rome, AD 230, or possibly in Sicily rather earlier. Her association with music depends on a passing reference in the medieval account of her life. Her legend is told by Chaucer in the *Canterbury Tales*, and she is further commemorated by ▷ John Dryden in one of his most famous poems, *Song for St Cecilia's Day*, and by ▷ Alexander Pope in his *Ode for Music on Saint Cecilia's Day*. ▷ Handel set both these poems to music.

Celestial City

The name by which Heaven is denoted in ▷ John Bunyan's ▷ *Pilgrim's Progress*. It is contrasted with the ▷ City of Destruction.

Celtic Literature

▷ Irish Literature; Scottish Literature; Welsh Literature.

Censorship and English literature

Systematic censorship has never been an important restriction on English writing except in times of war; but English writers have certainly not always been entirely free.

Until 1640 the monarch exercised undefined powers by the Royal Prerogative. Early in her reign, Elizabeth I ordered dramatists not to meddle with politics, though this did not prevent Norton and, Sackville's *Gorboduc* with its warnings on national disorder; but Ben Jonson, Chapman and Marston found themselves in prison for *Eastward Hoe* (1605) because it offended the Scots friends of ▷ James I of England. In the reign of ▷ Charles I the term 'Crop-ears' was used for opponents of the king who lost their ears as a penalty for criticizing the political or religious authorities. Moreover, printing was monopolized by the Stationers' Company, whose charter might be withdrawn by the Crown, so that the monopoly would cease.

In the ▷ Civil War, Parliament was in control of London, and issued an edict that the publication of any book had to be licensed. The edict provoked ▷ John Milton's ▷ *Areopagitica*, an appeal for freedom of expression. Its influence was not immediate; after the ▷ Restoration of the Monarchy, Parliament issued a similar edict in the Licensing Act of 1663 Theatres. The Act was only for a period, however, and in 1696 it was not renewed. The lapsing of the Licensing Act was the starting point of British freedom of the press except for emergency edicts in times of war in the 20th century, although in the early 19th century the government attempted a form of indirect censorship by imposing a tax on periodicals which restricted their sale among the poor. Nonetheless there are still laws extant which restrict freedom of political expression beyond certain limits.

Censorship in the theatre has been a special case since the 18th century. ▷ Henry Fielding's comedies attacking the Prime Minister, ▷ Robert Walpole, led in 1737 to the restriction of London theatres to two 'patented' ones – ▷ Covent Garden and ▷ Drury Lane – and the Court official, the Lord Chamberlain, had to license plays. In 1843 the Theatres Act removed the restriction on the theatres and defined the Lord Chamberlain's powers to the restraint of indecency. The Lord Chamberlain's censorship came to an end in 1968.

Centlivre, Susannah (d 1723)

Actress, dramatist, essayist and poet, known in her time as 'the celebrated Mrs Centlivre'. She survived anti-feminist criticism to become the most prolific dramatist, and one of the most successful of either sex, of her day. Two of her comedies, ▷ *The Busie Body* (1709), and ▷ *The Wonder: A Woman Keeps a Secret* (1714), were among the four most frequently performed, apart from those of Shakespeare, in the late 19th century, and her ▷ *A Bold Stroke for a Wife* was popular for most of the 18th century. She excelled in writing intrigue comedy, somewhat in the style of ▷ Aphra Behn, but less sexually explicit, and in a softened tone.

Centlivre's origins are obscure, and her birth date has been placed variously between 1667 and 1680. Her plays suggest a knowledge of French acquired, according to contemporaries, from a tutor. One account has her masquerading as a youth and studying at Cambridge University, before coming to London as a strolling actress.

Still in her teens, Susannah married an army officer, Mr Carroll, who died soon afterwards, apparently in a duel. She began publishing poetry, as well as copies of her letters, genuine or otherwise, to ▷ George Farquhar and others. Her first play, a cross between a tragedy and a tragi-comedy, called *The Perjur'd Husband*, appeared at ▷ Drury Lane in 1700. In 1707 she married Joseph Centlivre, the 'yeoman of the mouth' to Queen Anne, ie the Queen's master cook, but continued to write for most of her remaining life; her total output was 19 plays. The farcical *The Busie Body* immediately became part of the stock repertory, succeeding largely because of the engaging nature of the well-meaning but foolish character, Marplot. A sequel, *Marplot in Lisbon* (1710), was less well received. In other plays, such as *The Gamester* (1705) and *The Basset Table* (1705), Centlivre attacked the fashionable vices of gambling and card-playing. She was closely associated with many of the literary figures of the period, in addition to Farquhar, including ▷ Richard Steele, William Burnaby, ▷ Eliza Haywood, ▷ Delarivière Manley, Catherine Trotter, ▷ Nicholas Rowe ▷ Mary Pix, ▷ Colley Cibber, and the actress ▷ Anne Oldfield, who played leading roles in several of her plays. Her death came after a prolonged period of ill-health, and she was buried at St Paul's church, in Covent Garden.

Bib: Bowyer, J., *The Celebrated Mrs Centlivre*; Morgan, F. (ed.), *The Female Wits*.

Chapbooks

The name for a kind of cheap literature which flourished from the 16th to the 18th century, after which they were replaced by other forms. They were so called because they were sold by 'chapmen' or travelling dealers. Their contents consisted commonly of traditional romances retold, often from the French, in crude form: *Bevis of Hampton*, *Guy of Warwick*, *Till Eulenspiegel*, *Doctor Faustus*, are examples. Some of them, such as *Dick Whittington*, about the poor boy who ended up as Lord Mayor of London, have survived as children's stories to the present day, and are often the theme of Christmas ▷ pantomimes.

Bib: Shepard, L., *The History of Street Literature*.

Chapone, Hester (Mulso) (1727–1801)

English poet, letter-writer and ▷ Bluestocking. She learned languages, music and later, French and Latin. In 1745 she published the poem 'To Peace. Written during the late Rebellion, 1745'. For ▷ Samuel Johnson's periodical ▷ *The Rambler* (March 1750–March 1752) she wrote fictional epistles, and she also contributed to *The Adventurer* (1753). She had influence on and opinions about her contemporaries among them ▷ Samuel Richardson – whom she admired, and Samuel Johnson, as well as ▷ Elizabeth Carter, ▷ Mary Wollstonecraft and ▷ Elizabeth Montagu. She married John Chapone in 1760 but he died within a year. She continued to write, producing *Letters on the Improvement of the Mind* (1773) dedicated to Montagu, *Miscellanies in Verse and Prose* (1775) and *A Letter to a New-Married Lady* (1777). Her works were published in six volumes in 1807.

Characters, Theophrastian

In the early 17th century a form of ▷ essay devoted to the description of human and social types grew up, and collections of such essays were known as 'Characters'. The origin of the fashion is in the brief sketches by one character of another in the comedies of the time – *eg* those of Dekker and Jonson – and in the verse satires of such poets as Donne and Hall. The tone was always light and often satirical; as a literary form Characters displaced the satirical ▷ pamphlet popular in the last decade of the 16th century, written by such men as Greene and Nashe.

The basic pattern of the form was the *Characters* of the ancient Greek writer Theophrarus (3rd century BC) hence the designation 'Theophrastian'.

The two most famous collections were those of Sir Thomas Overbury – partly by other hands – published in 1614, and *Microcosmographie* by John Earle, published in 1628. The fashion continued, though it became less popular, throughout the 17th century and into the 18th. It was eventually superseded by the more elaborate and individualized studies by ▷ Addison and ▷ Steele in the *Spectator*, especially the ▷ De Coverley papers, and by the growth of the 18th-century novel.

Charity Schools

▷ Schools in England.

Charke, Charlotte (1713–60)

Actress, manager, puppeteer, dramatist, novelist. Youngest child of the actor, manager, and dramatist ▷ Colley Cibber and his wife, the former actress Katherine Shore (▷ Katherine Cibber). By the time she was four, Charlotte was expressing a preference for masculine clothing, which continued intermittently throughout her later career. In 1730 she married Richard Charke, a musician and actor employed at ▷ Drury Lane. She worked as an actress and dancer at Drury Lane and joined her brother ▷ Theophilus Cibber and other performers in deserting to the Haymarket Theatre in 1733. There she added more than a dozen male roles to her repertory of female ones, including in ▷ Macheath in ▷ *The Beggar's Opera*, George Barnwell in ▷ *The London Merchant*, and Lothario in ▷ *The Fair Penitent*. Later she acted Polly in *The Beggar's Opera*, and Millwood in *The London Merchant*. In 1736 Charke joined ▷ Henry Giffard's company at ▷ Lincoln's Inn Fields. From 1737 she managed a succession of businesses, including a puppet theatre. In 1745 she was married again, clandestinely, to John Sacheverell. He died soon afterwards, leaving her penniless, and her subsequent series of odd jobs in London and the provinces did nothing to alleviate her distresses. Estranged from her father for many years, she attempted unsuccessfully to heal the rift in 1755. Her memoirs, *A Narrative of the Life of Mrs Charlotte Charke*, were published in eight instalments, in 1755, and again posthumously, in 1775. Her published works also include a play, *The Art of Management* (1735), the novel *The History of Henry Dumont, Esq., and Miss Charlotte Evelyn* (1756), and two short novels, *The Mercer; Or Fatal Extravagance* (1755) and *The Lover's Treat; Or Unnatural Hatred* (1758).

Bib: Highfill, P. H. Jr., Burnim, K. A. and Langhans, E. A., (eds.) *A Biographical Dictionary of Actors, Actresses, Musicians, Dancers, Managers, and Other Stage Personnel in London 1660–1800*; Todd, J. (ed.), *A Dictionary of British and American Women Writers*.

Charles I

King of Great Britain and Ireland (1625–49). The causes of religious and economic conflict were so strong during his reign that it ended in civil war

(▷ Civil Wars), his defeat and execution. He had limited intellectual abilities, but created around him a court of taste, refinement and distinction. His own connoisseurship led to a fine collection of pictures, later dispersed by ▷ Oliver Cromwell, who sold them to obtain international currency. Charles's patronage of the Flemish artist Van Dyck resulted in some highly flattering portraits which have done the king much good with posterity. His personal qualities, his tragic end and his nobility in its endurance were the basis of a strong sentimental, sometimes even a religious, devotion to his memory. For example, there are churches dedicated to 'Charles the Martyr' in a few places (eg Tunbridge Wells) in Britain.

Charles II

King of Great Britain and Ireland (1660–85). The ▷ Restoration of the monarchy brought him back from exile after the ▷ Interregnum since the execution of his father, ▷ Charles I, in 1649. Politically unscrupulous, he was nonetheless one of the most intelligent kings in English history. His court was a centre of culture and wit as well as of moral licentiousness. His lack of scruple enabled him to raise the monarchy to a new pitch of popularity, in spite of the growing strength of Parliament and its increasing independence of royal authority. His was the last royal court in England to be a centre of cultural vitality.

Charter companies

These were joint-stock companies authorized by the Crown to make treaties, to set up trading colonies and to employ armed forces for their protection. The British Empire in India, the Far East and Africa was developed almost entirely by them. The British government took over their responsibilities only when forced to do so by political pressure, eg in India (1858), in Nigeria (1900), in Rhodesia (1923). ▷ Joint-stock companies; East India Company.

Chatterton, Thomas (1752–70)

Poet. Chatterton's father, a schoolmaster in Bristol, died before he was born, and he was educated at a charity school, then apprenticed to an attorney. He wrote precociously in all the genres of the day: mock-heroic couplets, hudibrastics (▷ Hudibras), political satire imitative of ▷ Charles Churchill, African eclogues in the manner of ▷ William Collins and elegiac poetry in the manner of ▷ Thomas Gray. But his most original compositions were pseudo-medieval concoctions concerned with 15th-century Bristol. Influenced by the fashionable medievalism of ▷ James Macpherson, ▷ Thomas Percy, and ▷ Horace Walpole, Chatterton claimed to have discovered lyric poems and a 'tragycal enterlude' by a 15th-century monk, Thomas Rowley, among the documents of the church of St Mary Redcliffe, where his uncle was sexton. The publisher Dodsley rejected the pieces, but they deceived Walpole for a time, and the poet was encouraged to move from Bristol to London. He published some non-medieval poems in journals under his own name, and a burletta (comic opera) by him was accepted

for performance at Drury Lane. Then, at the age of 17, in a fit of despondency, he poisoned himself with arsenic.

It was not until seven years later that the Rowley poems were definitively unmasked by the Chaucerian scholar, Thomas Tyrrwhitt. Their language is an artificial amalgam of medieval, Elizabethan and contemporary elements, typical of the omnivorous eclecticism of the period. But occasionally, as in 'An Excelente Balade of Charitie', Chatterton succeeds in evoking a unique exotic world of his own. During the Romantic period Chatterton's reputation lost all associations with hackwork and ▷ Grub Street, and only the 'medieval' lyrics were remembered. His early death took on a mythical quality, making him a symbol, even a stereotype, of youthful poetic genius neglected by a prosaic world. ▷ William Wordsworth referred to Chatterton as a 'marvellous Boy' in Resolution and Independence. ▷ Samuel Taylor Coleridge wrote A Monody on the Death of Chatterton. ▷ Keats dedicated his Endymion to his memory, and Shelley compared him with Keats in Adonais.
Bib: Kelly, L., The Marvellous Boy: The Life and Myth of Thomas Chatterton.

Cheapside

A street in the City of London. In the ▷ Middle Ages it was the site of a busy market and owed its name to the Old English word céap, 'to buy and sell'.

Chelsea

A district in the West End of London, bordering the north side of the Thames, and well known for its literary and artistic associations. Sir Thomas More, author of Utopia, lived there, and so did Thomas Carlyle, the 'Sage of Chelsea'. In the 19th century it became, and has remained, a centre for painters. Its most famous architectural monument is the Chelsea Hospital, designed by ▷ Christopher Wren and founded as a home for disabled solders by ▷ Charles II.

Cherub (pl. cherubim(s))

In the Old Testament of the Bible angelic beings who in Genesis 3:24 guard Paradise; in Ezekiel I attend the divine chariot; in I Kings I:6 and 8 are pictured in Solomon's Temple. They are depicted with the wings of birds and with human or animal faces. In medieval Christian tradition they were held to be the second of the nine orders of ▷ angels. When classical influence widely affected Christian art in the 16th and 17th centuries, cherubim came to be represented as winged (bodiless heads of) children. They lost all grandeur of mystical and religious symbolism and were chiefly used as decorative motifs. They even become closely associated with the classical image of the child god of love, ▷ Cupid, used in a similar way as a decorative motif on furniture, walls, etc.

Cheshire Cheese, The

A tavern off ▷ Fleet Street in London, and a favourite resort of Ben Jonson, and, after it was rebuilt, of ▷ Samuel Johnson and of Yeats, who liked to claim it as a haunt. It still exists.

Chesterfield, Philip Dormer Stanhope, 4th Earl of (1694–1773)

Statesman, diplomat and man of letters. In his youth he made 'a grand tour' of Europe, and on his return was made a gentleman of the bedchamber to the Prince of Wales, later George II. He became a Whig member of parliament for St Germains in Cornwall in 1715, and for Lostwithiel in 1722. But in 1726 his father's death brought him his title, and he moved to the House of Lords. He also served as ambassador to The Hague, 1728–32, and as Lord Lieutenant of Ireland, 1745–6. He became an opponent of ▷ Sir Robert Walpole, and changed from a Whig to a Tory in consequence. Chesterfield moved in literary circles, as a friend of ▷ Addison, ▷ Pope, ▷ Swift, ▷ Gay, ▷ Voltaire, ▷ Montesquieu and others. But he antagonized ▷ Samuel Johnson, who had vainly appealed to him for help in publishing his ▷ *Dictionary*. When Chesterfield later praised the work, Johnson revenged himself with a disdainful letter, saying Chesterfield's support had been delayed so long, 'till I am indifferent, and cannot enjoy it . . . till I am known, and do not want it'. But Chesterfield is known chiefly through his copious correspondence, and particularly the letters which he wrote to his son and his godson, both named after him. In them he offered advice based on his own worldly experience: how to dress, how to behave, and how to succeed in society. The emphasis was on acquiring a wide range of accomplishments without becoming too learned in any particular thing and, above all, to demonstrate good breeding. His son was also advised to make good connections in order to prosper. Chesterfield's letters have been criticized for passages which appeared to defend superficiality, or even to display a less than perfect concern with morality. But he was also considered a man of great wit, who wrote with agreeable style.

Bib: Dobrée, B. (ed.), *Letters of Chesterfield*, 6 vols.

Chevalier of St George

'Chevalier' is French for 'horseman' and in medieval France was equivalent to knight. After the ▷ Glorious Revolution of 1688 and the ▷ Act of Settlement of 1701 excluding the ▷ Catholic members of the House of ▷ Stuart from the English throne, James Stuart, the son of ▷ James II, was known as the Chevalier of St George as a courtesy title; he was otherwise known as the ▷ Old Pretender (*ie* claimant to the throne) in distinction from his son, Charles Stuart, known both as the 'Young Pretender' and the 'Young Chevalier'.

Chevy Chase, The Ballad of

A famous English ▷ ballad, probably dating from the 15th century. It issues from the border wars which were intermittent between England and Scotland from the 14th to 16th centuries. Lord Douglas, head of the principal Scottish border family, attacks Percy, Earl of Northumberland, who has defied him by coming for a three days' hunt on the Scottish side of the border. Both Percy and Douglas are killed in the ensuing battle. The ballad has been well known since Bishop ▷ Percy published it in his *Reliques* in 1765, but, earlier, ▷ Joseph Addison had praised the poem in the *Spectator* as had ▷ Sir Philip Sidney in his *Apologie*.

Children's books

Until the 19th century, children were not regarded as beings with their own kind of experience and values, and therefore did not have books written specifically for their entertainment. The literature available to them included popular versions of old romances, such as *Bevis of Hampton*, and magical folk-tales, such as *Jack the Giant-Killer*, which appeared in ▷ chapbooks. Children also read such works as ▷ John Bunyan's ▷ *Pilgrim's Progress*, ▷ Daniel Defoe's ▷ *Robinson Crusoe* and ▷ Jonathan Swift's ▷ *Gulliver's Travels*; ▷ Perrault's collection of French fairy-tales appeared in English as *Mother Goose's Fairy Tales* in 1729.

During the ▷ Romantic period it was recognized that childhood experience was a world of its own and, influenced in many cases by Rousseau's ideas on education, books began to be written specially to appeal to children. Such works as Thomas Day's *Merton and Sandford* (1783–9), ▷ Maria Edgeworth's *Moral Tales* (1801) and Mrs Sherwood's *The Fairchild Family* (1818) usually had a serious moral tone, but showed an understanding of a child's mind that was lacking from Anne and Jane Taylor's cautionary tales in verse.

It was not until the Victorian period that writers began extensively to try to please children, without attempting to improve them at the same time.

Chippendale, Thomas (1718–79)

A famous furniture designer, noted for the combination of elegance and solidity in his designs. His work was very much imitated so that 'Chippendale style' is the most familiar pattern of 18th-century furniture in England.
▷ Furnishings and furniture.

Chloë

In ancient Greek pastoral, a name for a shepherdess, *eg Daphnis and Chloë* (2nd century AD). In 17th- and 18th-century mock-pastoral, the name was sometimes given to disguise actual ladies when they were referred to in poetry or prose. ▷ Pope used the name for Lady Suffolk in his *Moral Essays*.

Chudleigh, Lady Mary (1656–1710)

English poet and polemicist. She replied to John Sprint's misogynist sermon *The Bride–Woman's Counsellor*. Although some modern critics think such extreme cases as Sprint's of the insistence on male superiority were read as a joke, Chudleigh replied seriously with *The Ladies Defence*, a verse defence of women, published in the second edition of her *Poems on Several Occassions* (1703). She also published a collection of *Essays Upon Several Occassions* (1710). She wrote *The Ladies Defence* for women, she says, 'out of the tender Regard I have for your Honour, joyn'd with a just Indignation to see you so unworthily us'd'. The poem borrows the character of Sir John Brute from ▷ Vanbrugh's ▷ *The Provok'd Wife*, a play dealing in the misfortunes

of mismarriage. Sir John is suitably brutal, but the Parson more legalistically insidious, asserting that for women, 'Love and Respect, are, I must own, your due; / But not'till there's Obedience paid by you.'
Bib: Ferguson, Moira, (ed.), *First Feminists*; Browne, Alice, *The Eighteenth Century Feminist Mind*.

Church of England

The history of the Church of England is closely bound up with the political and social history of England. In the ▷ Middle Ages the Church of England was a division of the Catholic Church of Western Europe. Ultimate authority over it, as over the rest of the Catholic Church, was vested in the Pope in Rome. The clergy consisted of an order of priests who, at the humblest level, had in their charge the village churches and the parishes (each more or less coincident with a village) that surrounded them. The parishes were grouped into regions known as 'sees', each of which was governed by a bishop, and the sees (bishoprics) were grouped into two provinces under two archbishops, those of Canterbury and York, the Archbishop of Canterbury being the senior. The bishops and the archbishops attended Parliament, and the Church had its own assemblies or convocations, attended by the senior clergy and representatives of the lower clergy, *ie* the parish priests. This organization of the Church has survived to the present day, with the important difference that since the 16th century the Pope has ceased to be the Church's supreme authority.

The Church of England became independent in 1534, when Henry VIII caused Parliament to pass the Act of Supremacy which declared him to be the 'Supreme Head of the English Church and Clergy'. The Roman Catholics were at that time and remained a small minority, but during the first half of the 17th century the extreme Protestants (the ▷ Puritans) grew in strength, especially in London and in the south and east. Their hostility to the monarchy and their dislike of religious direction by bishops led in the end to the ▷ Civil War and the overthrow of ▷ Charles I. Under the Protectorship of the Puritan ▷ Oliver Cromwell, the Church of England ceased to exist as a state religious organization, but in 1660 the monarchy and the Church of England were restored, and Puritans were excluded from the Church, from political rights and from attendance at the universities of ▷ Oxford and ▷ Cambridge. From this time, the Puritans (then called ▷ Dissenters or Nonconformists) set up their own Churches. Within the Church, religious differences remained and were the basis of the newly emerging political parties, the Whigs being more in sympathy with the Puritans and the Tories being closer to, though never identified with, the Roman Catholics (▷ Whigs and Tories).

During the 18th century the apathy into which the Church of England had fallen was shaken by the religious revival led by ▷ John Wesley, who worked mainly among the poorer classes. Although Wesley was forced to form a separate Methodist Church, his example inspired the Evangelical Movement within the Church of England, which by the 19th century was an important force towards social reform.

Churchill, Charles (1731–64)

Poet and political writer. A secret marriage, contracted at the age of 17, brought an end to his academic career at ▷ Cambridge. He entered the ministry, but after several years as a curate he separated from his wife and embarked on a literary and political career, associating himself with the political aspirations of ▷ John Wilkes. In 1763 he eloped with the 15-year-old daughter of a Westminster tradesman, but died suddenly in the following year at the age of 33.

There is a distinctive vigour to Churchill's use of the ▷ heroic couplet, though he lacks refinement or nuance. His subject matter in such poems as *The Rosciad* (1761) (by which he made his reputation), *The Prophecy of Famine* (1763), *An Epistle to William Hogarth* (1763) and *The Author* (1763) remains consistently public and Augustan, at a time when other writers were turning to more intimate themes. He lacks the restraint and poise of ▷ Dryden and ▷ Pope, however, and his spontaneity anticipates in tone the couplet satires of Byron. *The Rosciad* parades the theatrical figures of the day before a judgment panel consisting of Shakespeare and Ben Jonson, and they award the laurel, predictably, to ▷ David Garrick. In other poems Churchill discusses contemporary politics and the nature of satire. He also wrote less successful works in hudibrastic tetrameters (▷ metre; ▷ *Hudibras*), such as *The Ghost* (1762–63), in which he attacked ▷ Samuel Johnson.
Bib: Smith, R. J., *Charles Churchill*.

Cibber, Colley (1671–1757)

Actor, manager, dramatist. His first known role was as a servant in *Sir Anthony Love* in 1690, while his first opportunity at a substantial role came in 1694 in ▷ William Congreve's ▷ *The Double Dealer*. In 1696 he wrote his first play, ▷ *Love's Last Shift*, often seen as a landmark in the transition from 'hard wit' Restoration comedy to the 'comedy of sensibility'. He himself played the first of many fop parts, Sir Novelty Fashion, which he had created for himself; he afterwards played Lord Foppington in ▷ Sir John Vanbrugh's satiric sequel to the play, ▷ *The Relapse* (1696).

In 1730 Cibber was chosen, amid great controversy, as ▷ Poet Laureate. He retired from ▷ Drury Lane in 1733, afterwards writing an opera libretto, poems, essays, more plays, and his ▷ autobiography, *An Apology for the Life of Colley Cibber* (1740), still considered a primary source of information about the theatre in his time.

Throughout his life, Cibber excited controversy, involving himself in quarrels with several prominent men, notably the authors John Dennis and ▷ Henry Fielding and, most damagingly, ▷ Alexander Pope, with whom he kept up a running battle of insults for many years. His ironic misfortune was that Pope, as the better writer, gained a more lasting reputation, so that many students today know of Cibber only through Pope's harsh satires, and his real merit is forgotten.

On the other hand, he made many loyal friends, who praised his wit and good company, and remained loyal to him in extremity. His acting was celebrated and vilified by turns; he was said to be a marvellous comic, but often execrable in tragedy, which he refused to abandon.

Bib: Hayley, R. (ed.), *The Plays of Colley Cibber*; Koon, H., *Colley Cibber: A Biography*.

Cibber, Katherine (1669–1734)

Singer, actress. Born Katherine Shore into a musical family, she studied voice and harpsichord with ▷ Henry Purcell. She married the actor ▷ Colley Cibber in 1693, much against her father's wishes, and with him had seven children, including the actress ▷ Charlotte Charke and actor-manager, ▷ Theophilus.

Katherine Cibber began acting at the ▷ Dorset Garden Theatre in the season of 1693–4, and appeared with the same company (the ▷ United Company) at ▷ Drury Lane in the following year. She specialized in romantic roles, often involving singing.

Cibber, Susanna Maria (1714–66)

Actress, singer, dramatist. Susanna Cibber was the daughter of Thomas Arne, an upholsterer. In 1732 she sang the title role in Carey and Lampe's *Amelia* at the ▷ Haymarket Theatre, and two months later, she performed Galatea in ▷ George Handel's *Acis and Galatea*. In 1734 she married the recently widowed ▷ Theophilus Cibber, with whom she had two children, although both of these died in infancy.

The marriage was a bitter failure: her husband's taste for frequenting brothels, and his general profligacy, meant that he was perpetually in debt, and he soon began to seize his wife's assets, including portions of her salary, as well as her wardrobe and personal effects, in order to satisfy his creditors.

In 1737 she began an affair with a family friend, William Sloper, egged on by her husband, who eventually forced her at gunpoint to spend the night with Sloper. This was part of Cibber's scheme to extract money from the wealthy Sloper, and in 1738 Cibber sued Sloper, but succeeded in winning only ten pounds in damages that year, and only five hundred of the ten thousand he was claiming at the end of another lawsuit in the following year.

In 1741, after a discreet absence, and the birth of her first child by Sloper, Susanna Cibber returned to the stage, both acting and singing with great success. She sang in Handel's *Messiah*, first in Dublin, and then at its London debut in ▷ Covent Garden.

Susanna Cibber seems to have been supremely gifted both as a singer and as an actress: she is said to have been Handel's favourite, and he wrote some of his best music expressly for her to perform; as an actress she played mostly in tragedy, eliciting conflicting reports as to the variety of her gestures and tones, but the general agreement was that she could wring tears out of the most hard-hearted audience. Her Juliet and Ophelia were particularly celebrated for their pathos. At her death ▷ Drury Lane stayed closed in honour of its greatest actress. She is also known to have co-authored at least one play, *The Oracle* (1752). She was buried in ▷ Westminster Abbey.

Bib: Mann, D. (ed.), *The Plays of Theophilus and Susannah Cibber*; Highfill, P. H. Jr., Burnim, K. A. and Langhans, E. A. (eds.), *A Biographical Dictionary of Actors, Actresses, Musicians, Dancers, Managers, and Other Stage Personnel in London 1660–1800*.

Cibber, Theophilus (1703–58)

Actor, dancer, dramatist, manager, the fourth child of the actor-manager ▷ Colley Cibber, and the singer and dancer ▷ Katherine Cibber. Cibber was educated at Winchester College, but left at the age of 16 to join the ▷ Drury Lane Theatre, where his father was co-manager. Still in his teens, in addition to acting in a range of established plays, he was already writing or adapting other plays and appearing in them, including *Henry VI* (1723) and *Apollo and Daphne* (1723).

Despite his unscrupulousness as an individual (▷ Susanna Cibber), Cibber maintained his reputation as an actor during most of his life: he excelled as a comedian, specializing in the playing of fops, but was also compelling in broader roles, including that of Pistol, whose name he acquired as a nickname. Less successfully, he played some serious parts, largely Shakespeare, including Iago, Othello, Hamlet, and even (at the embarrassingly advanced age of 40) Romeo. As a manager he at times showed considerable common sense and expertise, but his career was blighted by his truculence which involved him in personal conflicts throughout his life. As an author he was undistinguished, his works showing that tendency, exhibited in other areas of his life, to prey upon the efforts of others.

Bib: Mann, D. (ed.), *The Plays of Theophilus and Susannah Cibber*.

Cicero, Marcus Tullius (106–43 BC)

Roman statesman, and writer on rhetoric, politics and philosophy. Politically he is famous for his vigorous resistance to the conspiracy of Catiline against the government of the Republic. This is the theme of Ben Jonson's tragedy *Catiline*, of which Cicero is the hero. Cicero's mastery of eloquence in his various writings, and his prestige in ancient Rome, caused him to be much admired in the ▷ Middle Ages and afterwards. ▷ Locke considered Cicero to be an important exponent of the concept of natural law. In the 18th century Cicero, whose murder was condoned by ▷ Augustus, came to be seen as a martyr in the cause of liberty and the Roman Republic. A *Life of Cicero* by Conyers Middleton (1741) assisted this interpretation. ▷ Bolingbroke and ▷ Thomson praised Cicero, and ▷ Cumberland wrote a play about him in 1761.

Cinderella

A widespread fairy tale, known in English from its version by the French collector of fairy tales, ▷ Charles Perrault, whose work was translated into English in about 1729. Cinderella means the 'little cinder girl', because in the story she is made to do all the hard work of the house by her cruel elder step-sisters, and is dirty with the ashes of the fire. Aided by her fairy godmother, she wins a prince in marriage. Recent interpretations of this story focus on the sexual jealousies and competition it implies.

Circulating libraries
A library from which books may be borrowed. Such libraries were in private hands in the 18th century and subsisted on subscriptions from clients. The first circulating library started in 1740 and as the institution spread so the reading habit greatly increased. It was the more important since, apart from ▷ chapbooks, books were very expensive in the 18th century.
Bib: Leavis, Q. D., *Fiction and the Reading Public.*

Citizen of the World, A (1760–62)
A collection of letters about life in London by ▷ Oliver Goldsmith, ostensibly the correspondence of a Chinese man living in the city, Lien Chi Altangi. It first appeared as *Chinese Letters* in John Newbery's *The Public Ledger* (1760–61). The letters were published under its present title in 1762. The letters comment on English customs and practices, the moral and ethical characteristics of English people, and on literature. Their fresh and naïve view of commonplace matters provides rich satire. The work's ironic view of the author's own culture links it with other sceptical works of the period, such as ▷ Voltaire's *Candide* and ▷ Johnson's ▷ *Rasselas.* It also displays the late 18th-century fascination with matters oriental (▷ Orientalism).

City, The
The customary way of referring to the oldest and most central part of ▷ London, occupied now chiefly by commercial offices and with only a small resident population. The term is also used to designate collectively the chief financial institutions of the country, situated there, such as the ▷ Bank of England and the ▷ Stock Exchange. Despite its smallness – it is commonly referred to as the 'square mile' – the Lord Mayor of the City of London has outstanding importance as a ceremonial representative in the nation for business and commercial interests.

City Heiress, The; Or, Sir Timothy Treatall (1682)
Play by ▷ Aphra Behn. Tom Wilding, a charming Tory (▷ Whig and Tory) rake, is pursuing the rich and beautiful widow, Lady Galliard. She is attracted to him but does not trust him. He is also conducting an intrigue with the young heiress, Charlot Get-all, as well as keeping a mistress, Diana. Wilding's friend, Sir Charles Merriwill, is also interested in Lady Galliard, and becomes Wilding's rival for her affections. Meanwhile Wilding has been disinherited by his uncle, the 'old seditious Knight' Sir Timothy Treatall. Wilding schemes with Diana to pass her off to his uncle as Charlot, and Sir Timothy marries the mistress, mistaking her for the heiress. In a tempestuous scene Lady Galliard agrees to sleep with Wilding, but regrets it immediately afterwards and rejects him, opting instead for Sir Charles. Wilding turns to the faithful Charlot for solace. Writings stolen from Sir Timothy by Wilding and

friends prove the old man to have been involved in treasonable activities, and he is forced to desist from them, and even to make peace with his nephew. The play is one of several with a political bent by Behn, a lifelong staunch Tory herself. A large part of its interest derives from the psychological interplay between Wilding and Lady Galliard, but it contains some hugely farcical scenes, and keeps up an entertainingly rapid pace.

City of Destruction
In ▷ Bunyan's ▷ *Pilgrim's Progress* the town from which the pilgrim, Christian, flees to the ▷ Celestial City, *ie* Heaven. The City of Destruction stands for the world divorced from spiritual values, doomed to the destruction that is to overcome all the merely material creation.

Civil War
England has had two recognized periods of civil war:
1 The more important, in the 17th century, is also called the Great Rebellion. It was fought between the King (▷ Charles I) and ▷ Parliament, and divided into the First Civil War (1642–6), ending with the parliamentary victory at Naseby (1645) and the capitulation of Oxford (1646), the royalist capital, and the Second Civil War (1648–51), which also ended with parliamentary victory, this time over the Scots. They had been the allies of Parliament in the First Civil War, but took the king's side in the Second. The issues were complicated; the economic interests of the urban middle classes coincided with their religious (▷ Puritan) ideology and conflicted with the traditional economic interests of the Crown, correspondingly allied with ▷ Anglican religious belief.
2 The other occurred in the 15th century and is usually known as the Wars of the Roses.

Clandestine Marriage, The (1766)
Comedy by ▷ George Colman the Elder, and ▷ David Garrick, inspired by the first plate in ▷ Hogarth's ▷ *Marriage à la Mode* series. The play concerns the secret marriage of Fanny Sterling to her father's clerk, Lovewell. Sir John Melvil, who had proposed to marry Fanny's affected older sister, instead falls in love with her, as does his uncle, the foppish Lord Ogleby. Eventually the complications are resolved, with the help of Lord Ogleby, who becomes an ally to the couple, and Fanny and Lovewell are able to disclose their marriage and find happiness. The play was a great success and it was revived frequently throughout the 19th century, and into the 20th.

Clarendon, Edward Hyde, Earl of (1609–74)
Statesman and historian; author of *The True Historical Narrative of the Rebellion and Civil Wars in England* about the ▷ Civil War, during which he had supported ▷ King Charles I. The published history combines two separate manuscripts: a history written 1646–8 while the events were fresh in the author's mind, and an ▷ autobiography written between 1668 and 1670, in exile and without the aid of documents. In consequence, Books I–VII are superior in accuracy to Books VIII–XV, with the exception of Book IX, which

contain material written in 1646. Clarendon's history is a literary classic because of its series of portraits of the participants in the war. His book is a notable contribution to the rise of the arts of biography and autobiography in England in the 17th century and contributed to the development which in the 18th century produced the first English novels.

As a statesman, Hyde was at first a leading opponent of Charles I, but his strongly Anglican (▷ Church of England) faith led him to take the Royalist side shortly before the war. He became one of the king's chief advisers. He followed the royal court into exile, and was ▷ Lord Chancellor and ▷ Charles II's chief minister at the ▷ Restoration (1660). The king's brother, the future ▷ James II, married his daughter, so that he became grandfather of Queen Mary II and Queen Anne. He was made the scapegoat for the unpopularity of Charles II's government in its early years, however, and was driven into exile in 1667. He lived the remainder of his life in France.

▷ Histories and Chronicles.
Bib: Huehns, G., *Selections from the History of the Rebellion and the Life*; Wormald, B. H. G., *Clarendon, Politics, History and Rebellion*; Firth, C., *Essays, Historical and Literary*.

Clarissa (1747–8)

An ▷ epistolary novel by ▷ Samuel Richardson. The central characters are Clarissa Harlowe, Anna Howe, Lovelace and John Belford. Clarissa's family wishes her to marry the odious suitor, Solmes, a wealthy man whom she abhors. The marriage is proposed to elevate the Harlowes socially, yet in the motives of Clarissa's brother and sister there is also a disturbing undertone of sadistic sexuality. As she refuses to accept Solmes the family ostracizes her within their home.

Lovelace, a handsome rake, is initially the suitor of the elder sister Arabella, but his real interest is in Clarissa. When the family ill-treats her he poses as her deliverer and persuades her to escape with him to London, promising that he will restore her in the esteem of her relatives. But the apparently respectable house where they stay is in reality a brothel.

Lovelace's attempts at seducing Clarissa are unsuccessful, and he eventually resorts to drugging her and then rapes her. Through this theme Richardson explores the hypocrisy of a society which equates 'honour' with virginity. Clarissa dies after the rape, not from shame but from a spiritual integrity which cannot be corrupted. In the self-martyrdom of the heroine, Richardson achieves a psychological complexity which transcends the limitations of purported morality.
Bib: Flynn, C., *Samuel Richardson*; *A Man of Letters*.

Classic, classics, classical

These words are apt to cause confusion. The term 'classic' has been used to denote a work about whose value it is assumed there can be no argument, *eg David Copperfield*. The word particularly implies a changeless and immutable quality; it has sometimes been used to deny the need for reassessment,

reinterpretation and change. Because only a few works can be classics, it may be argued that the term is synonymous with the best. This is not necessarily the case, especially with regard to changes in literary taste and a constantly changing canon of texts.

'Classics' is the study of ancient Greek and Latin literature. 'Classic' is used as an adjective as well as a noun, *eg* Dickens wrote many classic novels. 'Classical' is mainly used as the adjective for 'classics', *eg* classical scholarship.

Classical education and English literature

Classical education is based on the study of the 'classics', *ie* the literature of ancient Greece and Rome, principally from ▷ Homer to the great Latin poets and prose writers (*eg* ▷ Virgil, ▷ Ovid, ▷ Cicero) from the 1st century BC to the 1st century AD. Latin is more closely bound up with western history and culture, and is the easier language for English speakers to study; consequently it has been more widely used in schools than Greek, and it has been studied at earlier stages of education. Roman literary culture was, however, based on that of the Greeks.

Medieval Europe (Christendom) grew out of the ruins of the western Roman Empire; the Church, like the Empire, was still ruled from Rome; its philosophy was deeply influenced by the Greek philosophers and its language continued to be Latin. The Church controlled the universities and the classics were the basis of medieval university education, especially that part of it known as the 'Trivium' – grammar, rhetoric and logic. Nonetheless, many of the Greek and Roman writers were known principally through inferior versions of their texts and they were valued chiefly in so far as the Church could use them for its own purposes.

The movement known as the ▷ Renaissance started in Italy in the 14th century; it was, first of all, the enthusiastic rediscovery and collection by scholars of ancient classical texts, and the development of new and more accurate methods of studying them. It did not long remain merely a scholarly movement; the scholars influenced the writers and artists, and these in turn, in the 15th and 16th centuries, aroused enthusiasm in the upper classes of all western Europe. The Renaissance practice of studying the classics for their own sake and not under the direction of the Church, brought the discovery of a new principle of growth in literature and the other arts. Knowledge of the classics became a principle of discrimination: those who did not have it were by implication more primitive in their development and often from a lower social class.

The Renaissance first seriously affected England early in the 16th century. The pattern for classical education in the national public schools and the more local grammar schools was formed by such men as John Colet (?1467–1519), High Master of St Paul's School. Sir Thomas More, author of *Utopia* and Chancellor to Henry VIII, gave prestige to humanist values in the royal court. Erasmus visited England from Holland and made friends among these and other English humanists.

But ancient Greece and Rome, in its greatest days, were pagan; their values were social rather than religious. Thus there was the possibility of divided loyalty between the Rome that was the starting-point of so much European art, thought and politics, and the latter Rome that was the centre of the originally Hebrew and very unclassical religion of Christianity. The Roman Catholic Church in the 15th and early 16th centuries at first responded favourably to the humanists of even when they were critical of its traditions and practices. The thought and outlook of pagan Greece and Rome nevertheless did not agree well with the ancient Hebrew roots of Christianity as shown in the Old and New Testaments of the Bible. The 16th-century Protestant ▷ Reformation was partly the outcome of humanist criticism of the Church, but it was also a return to the Word of God as the Bible displayed it. Thus, from 1560 to 1660, much English imaginative writing has two aspects: the poets ▷ Edmund Spenser and ▷ John Milton, for example, have a Protestant aspect, which is biblical and Hebraic; and a classical aspect, strongly inspired by the classical Renaissance. The poet Ben Jonson is much more classical than Protestant, while ▷ George Herbert is strongly religious in the moderately Protestant, Anglican tradition, and despises the kind of subject matter (eg 'classical pastoral') which Jonson accepted. Both, however, had a classical education.

Another division arose from the difference between native literary traditions, which continued in their non-classical character, and the classical qualities and standards which many writers felt should permeate and regulate the native tradition. This division did not correspond to religious differences: the most Latin of all English poets is the ▷ Puritan, John Milton. ▷ Shakespeare is well-known for his indifference to the classical 'rules' which critics like Sir Philip Sidney thought necessary to good drama, while his contemporary, Ben Jonson, favoured them, though not slavishly.

Classical and native traditions of literature rivalled and nourished each other until the middle of the 17th century, and so did Protestant biblical and secular classical philosophies of life. But after the ▷ Restoration in 1660, religious passions declined and sceptical rationalism began to take their place. Thus began the most classical period of English art and literature, the so-called ▷ Augustan age of the 18th century. Yet within their neo-classical horizon, the best English writers even of this period retained strong elements of native idiom; this is true of the poets, ▷ John Dryden and ▷ Alexander Pope, and of the prose writers ▷ Jonathan Swift and ▷ Samuel Johnson.

The ▷ French Revolution of 1789 was, at one level, the outcome of 18th-century reason, criticism and scepticism, but it challenged the 18th-century classical qualities of order, intellectual proportion and balance, and the view of man as fulfilled only in a civilized structure of society.

Classical mythology

Ancient Greek mythology can be divided between the 'Divine Myths' and the 'Heroic Myths'.

The divine myths are known in differing versions from the works of various Greek poets, of whom the most notable are ▷ Homer and Hesiod. Hesiod explained the origin of the world in terms of a marriage between Earth (Ge or Gaea) and Sky (Uranus). Their children were the 12 Titans: Oceanus, Crius, Iapetus, Theia, Rhea, Mnemosyne, Phoebe, Tethys, Themis, Coeus, Hyperion, and Cronos. Cronos overthrew his father, and he and Rhea (or Cybele) became the parents of the 'Olympian gods', so called from their association with the sacred mountain Olympus. The Olympians, in their turn, overthrew Cronos and the other Titans.

The chief Olympians were Zeus and his queen Hera. The other gods and goddesses were the offspring of either, but usually not both, as Zeus was usually at war with Hera. They seem to have been seen as male and female aspects of the sky; their quarrels were the causes of bad weather and cosmic disturbances. The principal offspring of Zeus were Apollo, Artemis, Athene, ▷ Aphrodite (sometimes represented as a daughter of Uranus out of the sea), Dionysus, Hermes, and Ares. Zeus had three sisters, Hestia, Demeter (the corn goddess) and Hera (also his wife), and two brothers, Poseidon who ruled the sea, and Hades who ruled the underworld. From the 3rd century BC the Romans adopted the Olympian gods, denoting them by the Latin names more commonly known to later European writers. Uranus, Apollo, and some others remained the same. Gaea became Tellus; Cronos = Saturn; Zeus = Jupiter (or Jove); Hera = Juno; Athene = Minerva; Artemis = Diana; Hermes = Mercury; Ares = Mars; Hephaestus = Vulcan; Aphrodite = Venus (and her son Eros = Cupid); Demeter = Ceres; Poseidon = Neptune. There were numerous minor deities such as nymphs and satyrs in both Greek and Roman pantheons.

The Olympian deities mingled with men, and rivalled one another in deciding human destinies. They concerned themselves particularly with the destinies of the heroes, ie those men, sometimes partly divine by parentage, who were remarkable for the kinds of excellence which are especially valued in early societies, such as strength (Heracles) or cunning (Odysseus). Each region of Greece had its native heroes, though the greatest heroes were famous in legend all over Greece. The most famous of all was Heracles (in Latin, Hercules) who originated in Thebes. Other leading examples of the hero are: Theseus (Athens), Sisyphus and Bellerophon (Corinth), Perseus (Argolis), the Dioscuri, or Twins, ie Castor and Pollux (Laconia), Oedipus (Thebes), Achilles (Thessaly), Jason (Thessaly), Orpheus (Thrace). Like the Greek gods and goddesses, the Greek heroes were adopted by Roman legend, sometimes with a change of name. The minor hero of Greek legend, ▷ Aeneas, was raised to be the great ancestral hero of the Romans, and they had other heroes of their own, such as Romulus, the founder of Rome, and his brother Remus.

After the downfall of the Roman Empire of the West, classical deities and heroes achieved a kind of popular reality through the planets and zodiacal signs which are named after them, and which, according to astrologers, influence human fates. Thus in Chaucer's *The Knight's Tale*, Mars, Venus, Diana and Saturn occur, and owe their force in the poem as much to medieval astrology as to classical legend. Otherwise their survival has depended chiefly on their importance in the works of the classical poets, such as Homer, Hesiod, ▷ Virgil and ▷ Ovid, who have meant so much to European culture. In Britain, important poets translated and thus helped to 'naturalize' the Greek and Latin poems; *eg* both Gavin Douglas in the 16th century and ▷ Dryden in the 17th century translated Virgil's ▷ *Aeneid*; Chapman in the 16th century and ▷ Pope in the 18th century translated Homer's epics. In the 16th and 17th centuries, poets used major and minor classical deities to adorn and elevate poems intended chiefly as gracious entertainment, and occasionally they added deities of their own invention.

While European culture was understood as a more or less distinct system of values, the poets used classical deities and heroes deliberately and objectively. In the 19th century, however, the deep disturbance of European beliefs and values caused European writers to use classical myth more subjectively, as symbols through which they tried to express their personal doubts, struggles, and beliefs ▷ *Odyssey; Iliad*.

Classical unities

Criteria for drama based on those of ▷ Aristotle in his *Poetics*. He argued that dramatic action should be plausible, and therefore should take place in a single location, or locations close to one another, in the space of 24 hours, and should focus on a single storyline, rather than leaping from plot to plot. Many classical Greek tragedies observe these rules. In the 17th century they were revived by ▷ neo-classicists, and French dramatists such as ▷ Corneille and ▷ Racine were much affected by them. In England, ▷ Thomas Rymer and ▷ John Dennis articulated neo-classical theories of tragedy which included homage to the classical unities. But most practising dramatists in England barely observed these rules. ▷ Dryden's views on the subject were complex. In his congratulatory poem, *To My Friend, the Author*, addressed to the English dramatist Peter Motteux, he praised Motteux's tragi-comedy *Beauty in Distress* (1698) for its model adherence to the unities. However, in his *Essay of Dramatic Poesy* (1668) and *Heads of an Answer to Rymer* (1677), he defended contemporary departures from neo-classical theory, including his own, on the grounds that the later plays had greater variety and interest than those of ancient times. He argued that 'although the Plays of the Ancients are more correctly Plotted, ours are more beautifully written'.

▷ Classic, classics, classical; Classical education and English literature; Nicolas Boileau; French literature in England.

Cleland, John (1709–89)

Novelist and journalist, most famous for his novel *Fanny Hill: Memoirs of a Woman of Pleasure*, published in two volumes in 1748 and 1749 and immediately suppressed as pornography. An unexpurgated edition of the book published in England in 1963 was seized by police and became the subject of a trial. Cleland also wrote *Memoirs of a Coxcomb* (1751) and several other novels and dramatic pieces.

Cleopatra of Egypt (51–30 BC)

The last in the dynasty of the Ptolemies. The chief authority for the facts of her life is the Greek historian ▷ Plutarch (1st century AD) in his life of Mark Antony. She was joint sovereign of Egypt with her younger brother Ptolemy Dionysus. Driven out of Egypt, she withdrew to Syria, where she met the Roman general ▷ Julius Caesar while she was preparing to counter-attack. Caesar took her side, re-established her on the throne, and made her his mistress. When Caesar was assassinated, she became the mistress of Caesar's ally Mark Antony, until they were jointly defeated by Caesar's nephew and adopted son, Octavianus. She then committed suicide. Her love affair with Antony is the subject of ▷ Shakespeare's ▷ *Antony and Cleopatra* and ▷ Dryden's ▷ *All for Love*.

Climax

▷ Figures of speech

Clio

▷ Muses.

Clive, Catherine (Kitty) (1711–85)

Actress, singer, dramatist, and pamphlet-writer. Kitty Clive (née Raftor) joined the ▷ Drury Lane Theatre in 1728 where she spent most of her career, and quickly became one of its leading comic actresses, as well as singing in operas, entr'actes, and afterpieces. Her first major success was as ▷ Polly in ▷ *The Beggar's Opera* (1728), followed by roles in *The Old Debauchees* (1732) and *The Covent Garden Tragedy* (1732), written specially for her by ▷ Henry Fielding.

She herself wrote afterpieces, farces and a pamphlet, *The Case of Mrs Clive* (1743), which attacked the managements of Drury Lane and ▷ Covent Garden theatres. She was for many years a close friend of ▷ Horace Walpole. In 1769, she retired, and died 16 years later, after frequent bouts of illness. Her admirers praised her for her wit, intelligence, expressive features, and comic sense of timing. She was buried in Twickenham churchyard.
Bib: Highfill, P. H. Jr., Burnim, K. A. and Langhans, E. A. (eds.), *A Biographical Dictionary of Actors, Actresses, Musicians, Dancers, Managers, and Other Stage Personnel in London 1660–1800*.

Cloth manufacture

The export of wool was the foundation of English commercial prosperity, but in the 14th century cloth-making began to overtake it in importance. It was carried on in villages and small towns in East Anglia, in the Cotswold hills and other regions of the west, and in the hill country in the north. Since it required the combination of several crafts – carding, spinning, weaving, fulling, dyeing and finishing – it gave rise to the first great capitalist industrialists, the clothiers, who gave out the work to the various craftsmen often in scattered villages, and then marketed the finished product.

▷ Capitalism.

Club, The

Later known as the 'Literary Club', an informal group founded in the winter of 1763-4 and meeting at this time in the Turk's Head Tavern, Soho. Original members included ▷ Samuel Johnson, ▷ Sir Joshua Reynolds, ▷ Oliver Goldsmith and ▷ Edmund Burke, ▷ Thomas Percy, ▷ David Garrick and ▷ James Boswell were among those of later elected.

Clubs

Private associations, organized for a common recreational purpose; sometimes recruited from men of common beliefs or opinions, eg the political clubs, sometimes from a particular profession, such as the authors' and actors' clubs, sometimes from the casual gatherings of friends. They have been important in English life since the mid-17th century, when they first appeared by name in association with particular ▷ coffee houses – as important in English social life then as the café in France later. But the principle may be said to go back to the later years of the 16th century, when (according at least to tradition) poets met in taverns. The Mermaid in London, for example, was attended by ▷ Shakespeare, Ben Jonson, Sir Walter Ralegh, John Donne and others. Francis Beaumont's lines, *Master Francis Beaumont to Ben Jonson*, describe meetings at this tavern. In the early years of the 18th century there is frequent mention of clubs in the periodical essays of ▷ Joseph Addison and ▷ Sir Richard Steele; ▷ Jonathan Swift was a leader of the Brothers' Club and founded the ▷ Scriblerus; ▷ Dr Johnson founded the Literary Club in 1763-4 (▷ T Club), which met at the Turk's Head Tavern. In the later 18th and early 19th centuries clubs began to leave the taverns and use their own buildings.

Cobbold, Elizabeth (c 1764-1824)

Cobbold was a northern poet, spending most of her life in Liverpool and Manchester. She began publishing when she was 19 with *Poems on Various Subjects* (1783), and followed this with *Six Narrative Poems* (1787). The poetry is bold and energetic, but the subject matter simply repeats the conventional interest in the mysterious and exotic. Her fascination with the sensational continued in her novel *The Sword, or Father Bertrand's History of His Own Times* (1791), a medieval romance which was published under her married name, Clarke. This first marriage lasted only six months, but she soon met John Cobbold, a wealthy Liverpool brewer, and married him in 1792. Her writing continued and she published several pieces of poetry including an ode on the Battle of Waterloo. Perhaps her most interesting work is *The Mince Pye* (1800), a satire of contemporary nationalistic feeling (▷ nationalism). In this later work the energies of her youthful poetry remain, but are directed with a sharp and intelligent wit.

▷ Gothic novels.

Cockpit

A small arena where the sport of cockfighting took place. The sport was widely popular in England from the ▷ Middle Ages until the 19th century. The term was extended to describe any region where war often takes place (eg Belgium, the 'cockpit of Europe').

Coffee and coffee-houses

Coffee was introduced into England from the east in the mid-17th century, and from the ▷ Restoration until the mid-18th century coffee-houses were fashionable public resorts in London. Certain coffee-houses became meeting places for supporters of particular political parties (▷ Whig and Tory), or for the members of particular professions. ▷ Will's Coffee-house became the centre for men of letters; the Cocoa Tree Chocolate-house became the home of Tory politicians, while the Whigs went to St James's Coffee-house; ▷ Lloyd's became popular with merchants; and so forth. In the later 18th century more tea was imported, and as such luxuries were now distributed more widely, ordinary people took to drinking it in their homes. So the century of the flourishing coffee-house was succeeded by that of the domestic tea-party as the typically English social occasion. Some of the coffee-houses survived in other forms; thus Lloyd's became the central office in London for marine insurance, and White's became one of London's most fashionable ▷ clubs.

▷ Button's Coffee-house.

Coleridge, Samuel Taylor (1772-1834)

Poet and critic. Son of a Devon clergyman, he was educated in London and at Jesus College, Cambridge. He left Cambridge to enlist in the Dragoons under the pseudonym Silas Tomkyn Comberbache, and although he returned after a matter of months he never completed his degree. His early religious leanings were towards ▷ Unitarianism. In 1794 he made the acquaintance of ▷ Robert Southey, with whom, under the influence of the ▷ French Revolution, he evolved a communistic scheme which they called ▷ Pantisocracy. Together they wrote the tragedy *The Fall of Robespierre*. In 1795 Coleridge married Sara Fricker, Southey marrying her sister. His *Poems on Various Subjects* were published in 1796, at about the time he met ▷ Wordsworth. The two poets became friends, and lived close to each other for a time in Somerset. *Kubla Khan* and the first part of *Christabel* were written at this period, though they were not published until later. The joint publication, *Lyrical Ballads*, which included Coleridge's *The Rime of the Ancient Mariner*, appeared in 1798. Coleridge expressed his loss of faith in the French Revolution in *France, An Ode* (1798).

In 1798-9 he travelled in Germany and came under the influence of the transcendental philosophy of Schlegel and Kant, which dominates his later theoretical writing. During 1800-4 he moved near to Wordsworth in Keswick, and fell unhappily in love with Wordsworth's sister-in-law, Sarah Hutchinson, a relationship referred to in *Dejection: An Ode* (1802).

He began to give public lectures and became famous for his table talk. In 1809 he founded a periodical, *The Friend*, which was later published as a book (1818). Early in his life he had become reliant on opium and never succeeded in fully controlling the addiction.

He quarrelled with Wordsworth in 1810, and in later life he lived in the homes of various benefactors, including the surgeon, James Gillman, who helped him to cope with his addiction. He became increasingly Tory in politics and Anglican in religion, developing an emotionalist conservatism in the tradition of Burke. In 1817 appeared *Biographia Literaria*, his autobiographical and cristicism.

Coleridge's poetic output is small, diverse, but of great importance. His 'conversation poems', such as *Frost at Midnight* (1798) *This Lime-Tree Bower and My Prison* (1800), continue and deepen the reflective tradition of Gray and Cowper, culminating in the poignant *Dejection: An Ode* (1802). On the other hand his major symbolic works, such as *The Rime of the Ancient Mariner* (1798), *Kubla Khan* (1816) and *Christabel* (1816), plumb new psychological and emotional depths, and can be seen to develop along similar lines as his famous theoretical definition of imagination in *Biographia Literaria*, Chapter 13. His perspectives are consistently more intellectually alert than those of his friend Wordsworth, though the expression of his philosophical ideas is sometimes confused. His sympathetic but discriminating analysis of Wordsworth's work in *Biographia Literaria* is a model of unfussy analytical method. As both practitioner and theorist, Coleridge is central to ▷ Romanticism.

Bib: House, H., *Coleridge*; Lowes, J. L., *The Road to Xanadu*; Coburn, K., *In Pursuit of Coleridge*; Holmes, R., *Coleridge*; Jackson, J. R. de J. (ed.), *Coleridge: The Critical Heritage*, Jones, A. R., and Tydeman, W., *Coleridge: The Ancient Mariner and Other Poems* (Macmillan Casebook); Fruman, N., *Coleridge: The Damaged Archangel*; Cooke, K., *Coleridge*; Hamilton, P., *Coleridge's Poetics*; Wheeler, K. M., *The Creative Mind in Coleridge's Poetry*; Sultana, D. (ed.), *New Approaches to Coleridge*; Magnuson, P., *Coleridge's Nightmare Poetry*.

Collier, Jane (1710–1754/5)

English writer and social critic. She knew Latin and Greek, and numbered ▷ Sarah Fielding among her friends, as well as ▷ Samuel Richardson, whose ▷ *Clarissa* she criticized. Anonymously, she published *Essay on the Art of Ingeniously Tormenting* (1753) – 'general instructions for plaguing all your acquaintence'. This demonstrates the power of satire and burlesque in pointing to the need for social change. For instance, she advises the tormenting of female servants; 'Always scold her, if she is the least undressed or dirty; and say you cannot bear such beasts about you. If she is clean and welldressed, tell her that you suppose she dresses out for the fellows.' In the next chapter she advises on the patroness's treatment of her humble female companion, noting, 'there is some difficulty in giving rules for tormenting a dependant, that shall differ from those laid down for plaging and teazing your servants, as

the two stations differ so little in themselves.' With Sarah Fielding she wrote *The Cry: a New Dramatic Fable* (1754).

Collier, Jeremy (1650–1726)

Cleric and writer. Born at Stow-cum-Quy in Cambridgeshire, Collier was educated at Ipswich and Cambridge, and became rector of Ampton near Bury St Edmunds, and a lecturer at Gray's Inn. His life subsequently involved repeated conflicts with the authorities because of his unorthodox religious and political views and behaviour: he was imprisoned for his reply to ▷ Bishop Burnet's *Inquiry into the State of Affairs* (1688), arrested on suspicion of Jacobitism in 1692, and outlawed for giving absolution to two condemned political criminals in 1696. However, it was his *A Short View of the Immorality and Profaneness of the English Stage* (1698) which caused the most lasting furore, this time among dramatists against whom the attack was directed. A war of words ensued, with ▷ Congreve, ▷ Dryden and ▷ Vanbrugh among those responding to Collier, and he replying in turn. Although his stance was by no means unique in its day, he is credited with influencing the development of ▷ sentimental drama. His onslaught was the more effective for the knowledge he displayed of dramatic texts, if not performances. He became a bishop in 1713. His works also include the *Great Historical, Geographical, Genealogical, and Poetical Dictionary* (1701–1721) and *An Ecclesiastical History of Great Britain* from (1708–1714).

Collier, Mary (1679–after 1762)

English poet who worked as a rural labourer, washerwoman, brewer and later, housekeeper. She paid for the publication of *The Woman's Labour* (1739), and in the reprinted version of 1762 argued that she wrote it in reply to the labourer-poet ▷ Stephen Duck's *The Thresher's Labour*. Her poem testifies to the drudgery of women's field labour: 'When night comes on, unto our home we go, / Our Corn we carry, and our Infant too; / Weary indeed! but 'tis not worth our while / Once to complain, or rest at every Stile; / We must make haste, for when we home are come, / We find again our Work but just begun.' Her poetry is a determined self-conscious articulation of the particular interlocking circumstances of gender and status. She later published, by subscription, *Poems on Several Occasions* (1762).

▷ Leapor, Mary; Little, Janet; Yearsley, Ann.
Bib: Landry, Donna, *The Muses of Resistance*; Lonsdale (ed.), *Eighteenth Century Women's Poetry*.

Collins, William (1721–59)

Poet. The son of a hatter in Chichester, he published his *Persian Eclogues* in 1742 while he was still an undergraduate at Oxford. Their elegant exoticism and musical use of the pentameter couplet (▷ metre) made them popular, and they were reissued in 1757 as *Oriental Eclogues*. However his *Odes on Several Descriptive and Allegorical Subjects* (1746), which includes much of his best work, achieved little success at the time. The ▷ romantic

Ode on the Popular Superstitions of the Highlands of Scotland Considered as a Subject of Poetry was written about 1749 but not published until 1788. In 1750 he suffered a mental breakdown and wrote no more verse before his death nine years later in Chichester. Collins's small output shows a fragile combination of exquisite classical control and intense lyricism. In such poems as *Ode* ('How sleep the Brave'). *To Evening* and *The Passions* he develops his own distinctive rococo idiom, involving the constant use of pretty personifications and classical abstraction, reminiscent of the friezes on Wedgwood pottery. His rhythms and tone are peculiarly original, and often quite haunting, though the influence of ▷ Thomas Gray, ▷ James Thomson and ▷ John Milton is often evident.

Bib: Johnson, S., *Lives of the Poets;* Garrod, H. W., *Collins;* Carver, P. L., *The Life of a Poet: A Biographical Sketch of William Collins.*

Colman, George, the Elder (1732–94)
Dramatist, essayist, theatre manager. He controlled first ▷ Covent Garden, and then the ▷ Haymarket Theatre, and was responsible for staging the earliest productions of ▷ Oliver Goldsmith's plays, as well as writing dozens of plays, masques and operas himself. He began writing poetry while still a pupil at Westminster School, and after receiving a degree at Oxford University and being called to the bar, he still retained his literary interests. Through his friendship with ▷ David Garrick, he became involved in the theatre, and eventually abandoned law as a career. In 1760 his first play, the farcical *Polly Honeycombe*, billed as a 'dramatic novel', was produced at ▷ Drury Lane. Six years later he collaborated with Garrick on ▷ *The Clandestine Marriage*, his most successful work.

After inheriting a fortune from his mother, Colman purchased a major interest in the ▷ Covent Garden Theatre, which came under his joint management in 1767. Among his ventures there were productions of Goldsmith's *The Good-Natur'd Man*, and ▷ *She Stoops to Conquer*. In 1776 Colman acquired the Little Theatre in the Haymarket, where in 1781 he successfully staged ▷ John Gay's ▷ *The Beggar's Opera*, with women cast as the men, and vice versa.

▷ Colman, George, the Younger.
Bib: Burnim, K. A., *The Plays of George Colman the Elder;* Wood, E. R. (ed.), *The Plays of David Garrick and George Colman the Elder.*

Colman, George, the Younger (1762–1836)
Dramatist, miscellany writer, and theatre manager. Son of ▷ George Colman the Elder. He was educated at Westminster School and Oxford, like his father. Again like his father, he was intended for the law, but preferred the stage, and had a musical farce, *The Female Dramatist*, produced at the ▷ Haymarket Theatre in 1782. In 1784 he secretly married the actress Clara Morris, of whom his father disapproved, and re-married her in open ceremony in 1788. In 1789, his father having been stricken with paralysis and suffering from mental deterioration, he took over management of the Little Theatre in the

Haymarket. He proved an effective manager, despite a penchant for personal extravagance which, among other factors, involved him in a series of quarrels and lawsuits. As a dramatist he was prolific, contributing more than 20 plays and musical entertainments, including several which became firm favourites, such as the comic opera ▷ *Inkle and Yarico* (1787). In 1824 he was appointed Examiner of Plays, a title he retained to his death. He proved a fastidious censor, excising all supposedly blasphemous and indecent references, even though some of his own productions skirted close to the margins of propriety.

▷ Censorship; Colman, George, the Elder.
Bib: Tasch, P. A. (ed.), *The Plays of George Colman the Younger;* Sutcliffe, B. (ed.), *Plays by George Colman the Younger and Thomas Morton.*

Colonel Jack (1722)
The History and Remarkable Life of Colonel Jacque, a novel by ▷ Daniel Defoe. Jack is abandoned by his parents, becomes a thief, a soldier, a slave on an American plantation, a planter, and eventually a rich and repentant man back in England. The sequence through crime, suffering and repentance, and from poverty to prosperity, is typical of Defoe's novels.

Colonialism
Although it is known that colonies were established in early history, the term is now taken to refer to nationalistic appropriation of land dating from the ▷ Renaissance period in the west, and is usually understood as perpetrated on the black or coloured peoples in Asia, Africa, Australasia, the Americas or the Caribbean by the white western European powers. Colonialism does not have to imply formal annexation, however. Colonial status involves the imposition of decisions by one people upon another, where the economy or political structure has been brought under the overwhelming influence of another country. Western colonialism had its heyday from 1450 to 1900. It began in the Renaissance with the voyages of discovery; the new territories were annexed for their material resources and for the scope they offered to missionary efforts to extend the power of the Church. By the 18th century, Britain had acquired control of India, Canada and other territories, and ranked as the greatest European colonial power. The loss of the colonies of North America in the ▷ American War of Independence was a blow, but not a devastating one. Concern about the conditions of slaves in some of the colonies fuelled the anti-slavery movement (▷ William Wilberforce). One consequence of this movement was the renewed popularity of ▷ Thomas Southerne's play ▷ *Oroonoko* (1696), based on ▷ Aphra Behn's novel of the same name, which featured a black slave as its hero.

Comedy
▷ Humours, comedy of; Manners, comedy of.

Comical Revenge, The: or, Love in a Tub (1664)
Play by ▷ Sir George Etherege, his first, with a complex and partly tedious series of plots in four different modes: 1 heroic, or mock-heroic,

concerning love and honour, and including a duel, in rhymed couplets; 2 witty sparring courtship between Sir Frederick Frollick and the Widow; 3 gulling or trickery, of Sir Nicholas Cully, who is deceived into marrying a whore; 4 farce involving outright clowning, mainly by the absurd Dufoy and his associates. The title derives from the predicament of Dufoy, who has contracted venereal disease, and must sweat in a tub as part of the 'cure'.

Commedia dell'arte

A kind of Italian comedy, developed in the 16th century, in which the plot was written but the dialogue was improvised by the actors. Certain characters regularly recurred in these plays, and in the 18th century they were adopted in England (by way of France) and became part of the English puppet shows (eg ▷ Punch and Judy) and of the ▷ pantomime tradition. Such characters, anglicized, include Harlequin, his mistress Columbine, Pantaloon, Punch.

Common land

Land held in common by the peasantry of a village, and used for the pasturage of their cattle. By the 19th century farms were grouped into fairly large holdings all over the country, and such commons as had not been enclosed were used chiefly for recreation, eg cricket and various field sports.
  ▷ Enclosures, Enclosure Acts.

Common Law

A system of law in use in Great Britain (excluding Scotland), some parts of the Commonwealth and the United States, which retained the system after renouncing English political authority. The term arose in the Middle Ages and meant the law common to the whole people as distinct from law governing only sections of it, such as the Law Merchant or local customary law. It is also distinguished from Statute Law, made by Act of Parliament, and from Equity, a system supplementary to Common Law beginning in the 15th century. Common Law is 'case made', ie based on precedent judgments, and originally derived from acknowledged custom. The Common Law system differs from the law in most other European countries (including Scotland) in that the English legal system did not undergo the influence of the study of Roman Law in the 16th century. The difference is important politically, since Roman law emphasizes the power of the state, and by its avoidance the English lawyers of the 17th century were better able to defend the liberties of the subject against the claims of the ▷ Stuart kings.

Common metre

A four-line stanza alternating four and three stresses and alternating rhymes. It is especially common in ▷ hymns, carols and ▷ ballads.

Common Prayer, The Book of

The first Book of Common Prayer was prepared under the supervision of Archbishop Cranmer and issued in 1549 to meet the needs of the Church of England for services and prayers in the vernacular. It is of great importance as a work of literature, for Cranmer succeeded in combining the plainness and directness of English with the dignity and sonority of Latin. Prayer Book language became a familiar and formative influence in speech and writing second only in importance to the Bible itself. There were revisions in 1552 and 1559. The Prayer Book authorized in 1662 was substantially the 1559 revision. A fairly extensive revision was blocked by Parliament in 1928. There are now alternative forms of the various services in use.

Communism

Communism may be interpreted in two ways: 1 the older, imprecise sense covering various philosophies of the common ownership of property; 2 the relatively precise interpretation understood by the Marxist-Leninist Communist Parties throughout the world.

  1 The older philosophies derive especially from the Greek philosopher ▷ Plato. His Republic proposes that society should be divided into classes according to differences of ability instead of differences of wealth and birth; the state is to provide for the needs of all, and thus to abolish rivalries and inequalities between rich and poor; children are to be educated by the state, and women are to have equal rights, opportunities and training with men. In England, one of the most famous works based on these ideas of Plato is Sir Thomas More's Utopia (1516) (▷ Utopian literature). More's prescriptions are similar to Plato's in many respects, but though he also requires equal opportunity and training for men, he goes against Plato in keeping the monogamous family intact, whereas Plato wanted a community of wives and children to be brought up by the state. Both Plato and More require for their schemes an all-powerful state in the charge of an intellectual aristocracy; what we should call 'enlightened totalitarianism'.

  In practical experiment, the vows of poverty taken by members of orders of monks and friars and the communal ownership of property in such communities may have kept alight for people in general the ideal of the freedom of the spirit attainable by the renunciation of selfish material ambitions and competition. Protestant sectarian beliefs emphasizing the equality of souls led to such an abortive communistic enterprise as that of the ▷ Levellers in the ▷ Interregnum. In America, a number of experiments were undertaken by immigrant sects such as the Amana community, and under the influence of the English socialist Robert Owen and the French socialists Fourier and Cabet, but few of them lasted long.

  2 Modern so-called 'scientific' communism, based mainly on Karl Marx and Lenin, differs from certain forms of modern socialism by affirming the necessity for revolutionary, as distinct from evolutionary, methods to be followed by a period of dictatorship.

Companies, joint-stock

Companies whose profits are distributed among the shareholders. They began in the 16th century and largely superseded the older 'regulated company' whose members traded each on his own account and combined only for common protection. The greatest of the regulated companies was the Merchant Adventurers, founded in the 15th century; the greatest of the joint-stock companies was the ▷ East India Company founded in 1600: in the latter half of the 18th century the status of this changed from being a purely commercial concern to being an organ of imperial power, the effective sovereign power in Bengal.

▷ Capitalism; Charter companies; Colonialism.

Compleat Angler, The, or the Contemplative Man's Recreation (1653)

A discourse on the sport of fishing by ▷ Isaak Walton. Its fifth edition has a continuation by Charles Cotton (1630-87) and came out in 1676. The book has been described as perhaps the only handbook of art and craft to rank as literature. This is because Walton combines his practical instruction with digressions about his personal tastes and opinions, and sets it in direct, fresh description of the English countryside which may be contrasted with the artificial pastoralism which had hitherto been characteristic of natural description. The book has the form of a dialogue mainly between Piscator (Fisherman) and Venator (Hunter), which takes place the banks of the river Lea near London. Cotton's continuation is transferred to the banks of the river Dove between Derbyshire and Staffordshire.

Conduct literature (Britain)

During the 16th and 17th centuries there was a proliferation of books on conduct for women, such as William Gouge's of *Domesticall Duties*. These prescribed the way in which a woman should behave in all circumstances and often gave very detailed guides to personal conduct, from sexual behaviour to appropriate reading.

▷ Advice literature; Epistolary novel

Congregationalism

Congregationalists differ from other Christians not so much on credal beliefs as on their ordering of church life. For them, Christ rules primarily through the local congregation rather than through the Pope or bishops. In the 16th century, followers of this belief were called Brownists, after their founder, Robert Browne; by the mid-17th century they were known as Independents. It was in this period that the movement had special importance; it became widely influential amongst the Parliamentary opponents of ▷ Charles I and numbered ▷ Oliver Cromwell among its supporters. With other ▷ Dissenters they went through hard times after the ▷ Restoration but survived to be part of the Evangelical Revival. During the 19th century the independent congregations formed county and national unions.

Congreve, William (1670–1729)

Dramatist and poet, born at Bardsey near Leeds, into a military family. He was educated at Kilkenny, and at Trinity College in Dublin, where he was a fellow-student of ▷ Jonathan Swift. In 1690 he entered the Middle Temple, but did not practise as a lawyer. Instead he began writing: his first published work was a novel, *Incognita* (1692), followed by three stage comedies: ▷ *The Old Bachelor* (1693), ▷ *The Double Dealer* (1694), ▷ *Love for Love* (1695). Congreve's one tragedy, ▷ *The Mourning Bride*, was written in 1697. Congreve was a particular target of the ▷ Rev. Jeremy Collier's attack on the theatre, *A Short View of the Immorality and Profaneness of the English Stage*, in 1698, and he responded vehemently in his *Amendments of Mr Collier's False and Imperfect Citations* (1698). But the assault may have helped to discourage him from writing: his interest in the stage declined after the performance of his comedy, ▷ *The Way of the World*, in 1700. This, despite its subsequent fame and lasting popularity, into our own time, was not at first a success. Congreve did not depend on the stage for his livelihood, although he retained his involvement in the management of ▷ Lincoln's Inn Fields Theatre until 1705, and managed the new Queen's Theatre in the ▷ Haymarket together with ▷ Vanbrugh after that date. He accepted some government posts, and continued to write intermittently, composing a masque, *The Judgment of Paris* (1701); an operatic piece, *Semele* (1710), which provided part of the libretto for an oratorio by ▷ Handel; a prose narrative, *An Impossible Thing* (1720); and several poems. He brought out an edition of Dryden's works in 1717. Congreve was an admirer of the actress ▷ Anne Bracegirdle, for whom he wrote several of his best roles. His friends included ▷ Steele, ▷ Pope and ▷ Swift. He went almost blind in his last years, and died following a coach accident at Bath. He is buried in Westminster Abbey. Congreve's comedies are distinguished by their verbal play and wit, in the ▷ Restoration ▷ comedy of manners mode. His art is satiric, and he created a number of memorable characters.

Bib: Johnson, S., *Lives of the Poets*; Love, H., *Congreve*; Morris, B. (ed.), *William Congreve*.

Conscious Lovers, The (1722)

Play by ▷ Sir Richard Steele, his last, adapted from ▷ Terence's *Andria*, and sometimes considered as an archetype of Augustan 'exemplary comedy', in contrast to ▷ Restoration 'wit comedy', and a landmark in the development of the later 'sentimental comedy'. It is also seen as a vehicle for the expression of Whig attitudes and values, again in contrast to the Tory values espoused in much of Restoration comedy (▷ Whig and Tory). Young Bevil thinks of himself as consistently virtuous, but this conflicts with his desires. He secretly supports the beautiful but impoverished Indiana, whom he also loves. However, in accordance with his father's wishes, he proposes marriage to Lucinda, while concealing the fact from Indiana. Lucinda is in turn loved by Bevil's friend Myrtle. On the wedding day Bevil regrets his commitment to Lucinda, and offers to help Myrtle to a match with her, describing it as an humanitarian act. In Act V Indiana is revealed as Lucinda's elder half-sister, and therefore heiress to half their father's fortune. She is united with

Young Bevil, and Lucinda with Myrtle. The play's title derives from the thought and attention that Bevil Junior and Indiana give to their own emotions. Steele intended them to be admired, and the play as a whole to give moral guidance. But it generated a great controversy, with critics variously pointing to its supposed hypocrisy, its didacticism, and the seriousness of its tone.

Consciousness

In its most general sense consciousness is synonymous with 'awareness'. In a more specifically Freudian context it is associated with the individual's perception of reality. For Freud, of course, the impression which an individual has of his or her experience is partial, since awareness is controlled by the processes of the unconscious, which are never recognized in their true form. More recently 'consciousness' has been associated with the ▷ Enlightenment view of individualism, in which the individual is conceived of as being distinct from society, and is also held to be the centre and origin of meaning. Following from this, what distinguishes humanity is its alleged capacity for autonomy, and hence freedom of action. The ▷ Romantic equivalent of this philosophical position is that literature is the expression of the pre-existent 'self' of the writer, and that the greatest literature is that which manifests the writer's consciousness most fully. These views of consciousness should be distinguished from the Marxist version, in which the self is 'produced' through 'material practices', by means of which social relations are generated. Theories of consciousness affect notions of the relationship between writer and reader, and it is in working out such relationships that the concept of 'consciousness' is important in current literary critical debate.

Constant Couple, The: Or, A Trip to the Jubilee (1699)

Comedy by ▷ George Farquhar. Angelica is in love with the rake, Sir Harry Wildair, who takes her for a whore. He finds himself in a position where he must marry her or fight; he decides matrimony is the bolder course, and marries her. In the secondary plot, Lurewell has become a coquette after being apparently abandoned by Colonel Standard. The situation is found to have been based on a misunderstanding, and the couple are reunited. The play was so well received that Farquhar followed it up with a sequel, *Sir Harry Wildair* (1701), which proved far less successful.

Cophetua, King

A legendary king of North Africa who was indifferent to women until he fell in love with a beggar-maid whom he married. The legend occurs in a traditional ▷ ballad published in ▷ Thomas Percy's *Reliques* and there are several allusions to it in Elizabethan plays and elsewhere.

Copyright, law of

The right of writers, artists and musicians to control reproduction of their works. The right is now established law in most countries. The first copyright law in England was passed under Queen Anne in 1709. Before this, it was possible for publishers to publish books without the author's permission, and without allowing him or her any profits from sale, a practice very common during the lifetime of ▷ Shakespeare. Until 1909, the laws of the United States did not adequately safeguard British authors against having their works published there without their permission and without giving them suitable financial return.

▷ Shakespeare's plays; Stationers' Register.

Corey, Katherine (?1635–?)

Actress, Katherine Corey (née Mitchell) claimed to be the first professional English actress; she may have played Dol Common in a production of Ben Jonson's *The Alchemist* in December 1660, and certainly played the part in 1664.

Corneille, Pierre (1606–84)

One of the great French classical dramatists whose work exiled English writers have encountered during the ▷ Interregnum. His dramas, *Le Cid* (1636–7), *Horace*, *Polyeucte* and *Cinna* (between 1640 and 1643), debate the conflict between duty and love, passion and honour, and highlight the difficulties posed by the heroic ethos. They show the influence also of the neo-classical conception of the unities (▷ classical unities), Corneille's critical essays (the *Examens* and the *Discours*) were pioneers in serious drama criticism. ▷ Dryden was an admirer, but his heroic dramas did not match Corneille's attainments.

Country Wife, The (1675)

Comedy by ▷ William Wycherley. The irrational jealousy of Pinchwife, instead of keeping his naïve country wife faithful to him, puts ideas into her head which are encouraged by the libertine Horner. Horner has convinced the men of the town that he is impotent, but secretly seduces several of their wives. Most treat him merely as a means for their sexual satisfaction, and in one of the play's most famous scenes (IV, 3) Horner, pretending as a cover for his activities that he is offering china for sale, tells the women that he has sold out of china, a code meaning that he has exhausted his energy for sexual congress. Margery, the country wife of the title, cares for him more than the others, and is hurt when he rejects her and forces her to return to her husband. Meanwhile Pinchwife's sister, Alithea, is to be married to Sparkish. The latter pretends to affection but is interested only in the money which Alithea will bring as dowry, and takes her for granted. She is attracted to Harcourt, who really loves her, but resists his attentions out of duty to Sparkish. Eventually Sparkish is revealed in his true colours, and she marries Harcourt. The play's chief assets are the comedy of its scenes, heavy with dramatic irony, and the author's caustic wit. Its free treatment of sexuality drew condemnation even in its own time, and there has been critical debate about whether Horner was intended as a hero, to be admired for his cleverness, or a vicious object of Wycherley's satire. It was adapted by ▷ Garrick as *The Country Girl* (1766).

Couplet

A pair of rhymed lines of verse of equal length. The commonest form is the so-called ▷ heroic couplet of 10 syllables and five stresses in each line. It was first used in Chaucer's ▷ *Legend of Good Women*.

> *A thousand times have I herd men telle*
> *That ther is joye in heven, and peyne in helle . . .*

The heroic couplet had its most prolific period between 1660 and 1790 when many poets from ▷ Dryden to ▷ Crabbe used it; its master was ▷ Pope:

> *Most souls, 'tis true, but peep out once an age,*
> *Dull sullen pris'ners in the body's cage.*
> (*Elegy to an Unfortunate Lady*)

▷ Blank verse was a derivative of the couplet.

The eight-syllable (octosyllabic) couplet gives a lighter, less dignified rhythm. It was also used by Chaucer (*The Romaunt of the Rose, The Book of the Duchess, The House of Fame*) in his earlier work. It is less common after 1600 than before, but a notable later user of it is ▷ Jonathan Swift (*eg On the Death of Dr Swift*).

Court of Chancery

A Court of law under the ▷ Lord Chancellor, head of the English judicial system. The Court grew up in the 15th century to deal with cases which for any reason could not be dealt with efficiently by the established law courts administering ▷ Common Law. The practice developed a system of law supplementary to Common Law, known as Equity. Few things so neatly demonstrate the disadvantage of women in English law as the fact that they are treated as the legal equivalents of orphans and lunatics, through one of the special fields of jurisdiction Equity was created to cover. By the 19th century Chancery procedure became excessively complex, its relationship with other courts of law was ill-defined, and judgments were often delayed for years – hence Charles Dickens' satire of the Court in his novel *Bleak House*. The system was reformed by the Judicature Act, 1873. (The idiom 'in chancery' means 'remaining undecided indefinitely'; a 'ward in Chancery' is an orphan whose interests are in the care of Chancery.)

Covent Garden Theatres

In 1732 Edward Shepherd (1670–1747) planned the first Covent Garden Theatre, or Theatre Royal, on the site of the present Royal Opera House, to which the actor-manager ▷ John Rich transferred from Lincoln's Inn Fields. The name derives from a convent which had stood on the site previously. Following the Licensing Act of 1737 the Covent Garden Theatre was one of only three theatres in London to be granted a licence. In 1773 Oliver Goldsmith's ▷ *She Stoops to Conquer* was staged here for the first time, and ▷ Charles Macklin mounted his innovative production of *Macbeth*, dressed for the first time in 'Scottish' costume. The present theatre opened in 1858.

Coverley, Sir Roger de

A fictional character invented by the essayist ▷ Sir Richard Steele for the pages of ▷ *The Spectator*, and developed by his colleague ▷ Joseph Addison. The name was taken from a north country dance, Roger of Coverley. Sir Roger was at first a member of an imaginary club, the Spectator Club, where Steele in his journalist guise of the 'Spectator' purported to be studying human nature. In the hands of Addison, Sir Roger came to take up much more space than the other members; the papers devoted to describing his life (20 by Addison, eight by Steele, and two by Budgell) are much the best known parts of *The Spectator*. In his conservatism, his devotion to the Church of England, and his kindly but despotic control of his tenants, he is a typical squire of the time, but in his civilized manners he is deliberately made superior to the general run of country squires (compare Squire Western in ▷ Fielding's ▷ *Tom Jones*). In his simplicity and idiosyncrasies he was individual, with a literary relationship to Don Quixote. Though the 'Coverley Papers' are not a novel, the envisioning of the character is distinctly novelistic, so that they rank among the precursors of the English novel. Addison's especial aim, beyond entertainment, was to civilize the country squire; a secondary aim was the political one of making fun of the Tory English gentry.

Cowley, Abraham (1618–67)

Poet and essayist. Ever since ▷ Samuel Johnson's disparaging comments on Cowley in his ▷ *Lives of the Poets* (1779–81), Cowley's reputation has suffered, and yet Cowley is one of the most important and influential of the mid-17th-century poets. A Royalist in politics, he accompanied Queen Henrietta Maria into exile in Paris in 1644–6, returned to England in 1654, was imprisoned in 1655 and later released.

His chief works include: *Poeticall Blossoms* (written 1633), a collection of poetry published in 1656 which contained Pindaric odes (▷ Pindar) and ▷ elegies on William Harvey among others, and an essay on the advancement of science: *A Proposition for the Advancement of Experimental Philosophy* (1661). Cowley's attachment, after the Civil War, to the figures associated with the early ▷ Royal Society is evidenced both in his important ▷ ode, celebrating the Royal Society (first published in Thomas Sprat's *History of the Royal Society*) and his celebration of scientific figures and their works in his poetry.

As well as celebrating the advance of science, Cowley also composed an unfinished ▷ epic, *A Poem on the Late Civil War* (1679), which he abandoned at the point when the war began to turn against the Royalist forces. He also anticipated ▷ John Milton's ▷ *Paradise Lost* in attempting a biblical epic, *Davideis* ('A sacred poem of the Troubles of David', published in the *Poems* of 1656). In the 19th century and through much of the 20th, Cowley was read as a species of inferior John Donne or Thomas Carew, yet the range of his writing (which embraced science, ▷ translation and experiments in form and ▷ metre as well as critical statements on the nature of poetic discourse) make him an important figure in his own right.

Bib: Hinman, R., *Abraham Cowley's World of Order*; Trotter, D., *The Poetry of Abraham Cowley*.

Cowley, Hannah (1743–1809)

Dramatist and poet. In 1772 she married Thomas Cowley, a clerk and newspaper writer, and together they moved to London, where she began writing for the theatre. In 1783 her husband went to India with the ▷ East India Company, while she remained in London looking after their three children and continuing to write, a total of 11 comedies and two tragedies, as well as several long narrative romances. She also carried on a poetic correspondence with the poet Robert Merry, which was satirized by ▷ William Gifford. Cowley's comedies have a self-conscious morality which stresses the importance of marriage and proper relations between spouses. Her most successful plays include *The Belle's Stratagem* (1780) and *A Bold Stroke for a Husband* (1783). Cowley's *A School for Greybeards* (1786) is a revised and 'sanitized' version of ▷ Aphra Behn's ▷ *The Lucky Chance* (1686), which did not prevent it being attacked for supposed immorality.

Cowper, William (1731–1800)

Poet and letter-writer. Son of the rector of Great Berkhamsted in Hertfordshire, he was called to the bar in 1754, and through family connections was offered the post of Clerk of the Journals in the House of Lords. However, the early death of his mother, his experiences of bullying at public school and a thwarted love affair had caused severe neurosis which led him to contemplate suicide at the prospect of the clerkship examination. He spent a year in an asylum and thereafter led a retired life on his own private income, first in the home of Morley and Mary Unwin in Huntingdonshire and then after Morley's death with Mary Unwin in Olney. They planned to marry in 1773, but Cowper's conviction of his own personal damnation prevented this.

In Olney he came under the influence of the evangelical Rev. John Newton with whom he published *Olney Hymns* (1779), including 'Hark my soul! it is the Lord', and 'God moves in a mysterious way'. In 1780 Newton left Olney for London and Cowper's life became less spiritually strenuous. Mary Unwin encouraged him to write, in order to counteract his religious melancholia. His *Poems* (1782) contain *Table Talk*, and eight moral satires in heroic ▷ couplets which, though uneven in quality, display a distinctive unforced sententiousness which is one of his most attractive poetic characteristics. The volume also includes *Boadicea: an Ode* and *Verses supposed to be written by Alexander Selkirk* ('I am monarch of all I survey'). In the same year Cowper's published his famous comic ballad *John Gilpin*. He made the acquaintance of Lady Austen, who suggested the scheme of the ▷ mock-heroic, discursive poem ▷ *The Task: A Poem in Six Books*, which appeared in 1785, and is in the more 'natural' medium of ▷ blank verse, rather than couplets. He followed this with an undistinguished translation of ▷ Homer (1791). In 1794 Mary Unwin died, and Cowper's only subsequent work is the introspective and despairing *Castaway*, published after his death,

as were his *Letters* (1803), which are among the most famous in the language.

Cowper's work illustrates the movement away from the public themes of Augustanism towards a more domestic and personal poetry of ▷ sensibility. His work eschews brilliance or technical virtuosity, and can be banal. But at their best his ▷ lyrics are delicately moving, and his ▷ couplet and ▷ blank-verse writing achieves an unassuming lucidity of tone, which evokes profound resonances.

▷ Romanticism; Selkirk, Alexander.
Bib: Cecil, D., *The Stricken Deer*; King, J., *William Cowper: A Biography*; Hutchins, B., *The Poetry of William Cowper*; Priestman, M., *Cowper's Task: Structure and Influence*; Newey, V., *Cowper's Poetry: A Critical Study and Reassessment*.

Crabbe, George (1754–1832)

Poet. Crabbe was born at Aldeburgh in Suffolk and his work is intimately associated with the region. He practised medicine before taking orders in 1781. Crabbe's earliest works, *The Library* (1781) and the anti-pastoral *The Village* (1783), have an heroic ▷ couplet metre and a public, discursive tone already distinctly old-fashioned at the time. ▷ Samuel Johnson gave advice on the composition of the second poem, and in his grimly stoical vision of life and his distrust of pretension and excess, Crabbe resembles Johnson in temperament. *The Village* is relentless in its rejection of the conventions of literary pastoralism, showing nature with bitter realism as it was known to the poor. In his later works: *The Parish Register*, 1807; *The Borough*, 1810; *Tales in Verse*, 1812; *Tales of the Hall*, 1819, he depicts the diverse lives of his parishioners in a series of highly original short stories in couplets, a form which he made peculiarly his own. His best work treats social outcasts and extreme psychological states, as do a number of poems by ▷ William Wordsworth. But where Wordsworth's approach is transcendental and contemplative, Crabbe's involvement with his characters is compassionate in a more down-to-earth and intimate way. In *Peter Grimes* (Letter XXII of *The Borough*) the landscape of coastal East Anglia becomes an evocative symbol for the protagonist's breakdown and despair. Crabbe's narrative artistry, and uncompromising realism were admired by ▷ Jane Austen who remarked half-seriously that he was the only man she could ever think of marrying.
Bib: Crabbe, G. (Junior), *Life*; Pollard, A. (ed.), *Crabbe: The Critical Heritage*; Bareham, T., *George Crabbe*; New, P., *George Crabbe's Poetry*.

Critic, The: Or, a Tragedy Rehearsed (1779)

Satiric comedy by ▷ Richard Brinsley Sheridan, using the 'play within a play' technique employed in ▷ *The Rehearsal* in order to mock contemporary dramatic technique. In the first act Dangle discusses with his wife, a fellow theatregoer called Sneer, and the author, Sir Fretful Plagiary, the fact that a new tragedy, *The Spanish Armada*, is being prepared at ▷ Drury Lane. In the second and third acts, Puff invites the three men to observe a rehearsal of his play, which concerns the approach of the Armada. Tilburnia, daughter of the governor of Tilbury Fort, expresses her love for one of the Spanish prisoners, Don Ferolo Whiskerandos. As in *The Rehearsal*, the acting of the absurd play is accompanied by the fatuous explanations and instructions of the author, and scathing comments of his guests. The play ends with the destruction of the Spanish fleet, and strains of 'Rule Britannia', ▷ Handel's 'Water Music', and the march from *Judas Maccabaeus*. The tragedy was intended to satirize the works of dramatists such as ▷ Colman and ▷ Cumberland, of whom Sir Fretful Plagiary is a caricature. The play was acted 131 times before 1800.

Critique

A term used in critical theory. Traditional conceptions of 'criticism' have privileged the acts of judgement and comparison but have often anchored them in the unspecified sensitivity of the reader. Criticism presupposes a direct relationship between reader and literary text; the reader responds to the stimulus of particular verbal forms which are evaluated according to their appeal to a universal human condition. The practice of 'critique' in a literary context, however, concerns itself not just with producing readings of primary texts and accounting for those social, cultural, or psychological motivations which are responsible for its appearance in a particular form, but also with appraising critical readings of those texts. Critique addresses itself to questions of why individual texts should be accorded importance at particular historical moments, and implicates 'criticism' in its more traditional guise as a process whereby meanings are constructed, as opposed to being passively discovered.

Cromwell, Oliver (1599–1658)

Chief commander of the Parliamentarian forces in the ▷ Civil War against ▷ Charles I and Lord Protector of the Realm (1653–8) in place of a king. He belonged to the land-owning class in the east of England and supported the Independents among the ▷ Puritans. It was his generalship that defeated the forces of Charles I and the Scottish supporters of ▷ Charles II after the execution of Charles I. After his death, his son, Richard Cromwell, succeeded as Lord Protector for some months, after which Charles II was restored by the action of one of Oliver's generals, General Monk, in 1660. After 1660 his reputation suffered the censure of his political opponents and it was not until Thomas Carlyle published *Oliver Cromwell's Letters and Speeches* (1845) that his stature was generally appreciated.

Crowne, John (?1640–?1703)

Dramatist. Crowne published a ▷ romance in 1665, and his first play, *Juliana, or the Princess of Poland*, a tragi-comedy, in 1671. Thereafter, he experimented with various genres: a court masque, *Calisto*; a tragedy, *Andromache*; and a comedy based on a play by Molière (*Le Sicilien ou L'amour peintre*), *The Country Wit*, all appeared in 1675. The heroic verse tragedy, *The Destruction of Jerusalem*, was performed

in two parts in 1677. Several political plays followed. Crowne became a favourite of ▷ Charles II, and later Queen Mary (▷ Mary II). His greatest success, *Sir Courtly Nice; Or, It Cannot Be* (1685), modelled on a Spanish play (▷ Spanish influence on English literature), remained popular for over a century.
Bib: McMullin, B. J., *The Comedies of John Crowne: A Critical Edition*.

Culloden, Battle of (1746)

A battle in the north of Scotland in the 1745 ▷ Jacobite Rebellion on behalf of the House of ▷ Stuart in the attempt to recover the British throne from the House of Hanover, which had been installed by Parliament in 1714. The Jacobites, consisting mainly of Scottish Highland clans commanded by Prince Charles Edward Stuart ('Bonnie Prince Charlie'), were decisively defeated by the Duke of Cumberland – Butcher Cumberland to his enemies. Not only did Culloden end the rebellion but it practically put an end to the Highland clan system, which remains chiefly in name by force of romantic nostalgia.

▷ Scotland; Scottish literature in English.

Cumberland, Richard (1732–1811)

Dramatist, poet, novelist, translator, essayist, associated with the rise of sentimental domestic comedy on the English stage. He began writing poetry while still a pupil at school in Bury St Edmunds. After further education at Westminster School and ▷ Cambridge University he published his first play, *The Banishment of Cicero*, in 1761. Disappointed in his career aspirations in government, he turned in earnest to writing for the stage. He continued this activity even after his political fortunes improved, eventually completing over 50 plays, operas and adaptations of plays. His first success of any consequence was with the comedy, *The Brothers*, in 1769. In 1770 he wrote his most famous play, generally considered his best, ▷ *The West Indian*, and ▷ Garrick staged it in the following year. Even so his work was often under attack for its supposed sentimentality, and ▷ Sheridan satirized him as the vain and defensive Sir Fretful Plagiary in ▷ *The Critic* (1779). However, Cumberland was sympathetic to the causes of others, especially outcast and vilified groups. He defended the Jews in *The Jew* (1794), which was translated into several languages including Yiddish and Hebrew, and remained popular well into the 19th century. *The Jew of Mogadore* (1808) again portrays a Jew in a kindly light, and Cumberland also defended Jews in articles in *The Observer*, written under a Jewish pseudonym. His efforts did much to rescue Jews from the villainous antisemitic image hitherto afforded them on the stage. In addition to plays, he wrote two novels, translations of Greek plays, ▷ epic poetry, and pamphlets expressing his views on controversial topics of the day.
Bib: Borkat, R. F. S. (ed.), *The Plays of Richard Cumberland*.

D

Dactyl
A verse foot consisting of an accented syllable followed by two unaccented ones. It thus gives a light falling rhythm, and is commonly used with ▷ trochees in lines which end in an accented syllable or an iambus.
▷ Metre.

Dame schools
Schools for poor children in the 18th and 19th centuries, especially in country towns and villages. Unlike the charity schools, they were run by private initiative, especially by single women supplementing their income by teaching reading and writing.
▷ Schools in England.

Damon
A shepherd poet in ▷ Virgil's eighth ▷ eclogue. Hence the name is sometimes used in English ▷ pastoral poetry for a shepherd and sometimes as a pseudonym for a real person.

Dante Aligheri (1265–1321)
Poet and philosopher. Very little is known about the early life of Dante. He was born in Florence and married Gemma Donati in 1285. His involvement in Florentine politics from 1295 led in 1300 to his exile from Florence. He never returned, and died at Ravenna in 1321. According to his own report, he was inspired throughout his life by his love for Beatrice, a woman who has been identified as Beatrice Portinari (d 1290).

It is difficult to date Dante's work with any precision. The *Vita Nuova* (1290–4) is a lyric sequence celebrating his inspirational love for Beatrice, linked by prose narrative and commentary sections. His Latin treatise *De Vulgari Eloquentia*, perhaps begun in 1303–4 but left unfinished, is a pioneering work of literacy and linguistic commentary. Here Dante considers the state and status of Italian as a literary language, and assesses the achievements of earlier French and Provençal poets in elevating the status of their vernacular tongues. The *Convivio* (1304–7) is an unfinished philosophical work, a 'banquet of knowledge', composed of prose commentaries on allegorical poetic sequences. Dante's political ideas, specifically the relationship between the Pope, Emperor, and the universal Empire, are explored in *De Monarchia* (c 1310). Dante may not have begun his principal work, the *Divina Commedia*, until as late as 1314. This supremely encyclopaedic work, which encompasses a discussion of every aspect of human experience, knowledge and belief, recounts the poet's imagined journey, with ▷ Virgil as his guide, through Hell and Purgatory and finally through the agency of Beatrice herself, to paradise.

Dante was read and admired by English poets in the 16th and 17th centuries, including ▷ Milton, and one of the earliest translations (of part of the *Inferno*) appeared in 1719.
Bib: Holmes, G., *Dante*.

Daphne
In Greek myth, the daughter of a river god and beloved by Apollo. When he pursued her, she was changed by her mother, the earth-goddess Ge, into a laurel tree. Hence the laurel (or bay tree) became the favourite tree of Apollo, god of the arts, and triumphant poets were crowned with its leaves on his feast-days.

D'Arblay, Madame
▷ Burney, Fanny.

Darwin, Erasmus (1731–1802)
Poet and physician; grandfather of the zoologist Charles Darwin. He wrote a lengthy poem, *The Botanic Garden* in grotesquely elaborate ▷ couplets, on the subject of the scientific classification of plants (Part II: *The Loves of the Plants*, 1789; Part I: *The Economy of Vegetation*, 1791).

D'Avenant, Lady Henrietta Maria (d 1691)
Theatre proprietress; wife of ▷ Sir William D'Avenant. She took over management of the ▷ Duke's Company after his death in 1668, and saw his plans for a new theatre at ▷ Dorset Garden to completion. Lady D'Avenant was born in France, and met William during his stay there, probably in 1646. He visited France again about ten years later and brought her back to England as his wife in 1655. She had at least nine children by him, and also cared for some of his children by his earlier marriages. As theatre manager she operated effectively, delegating many artistic and technical problems, ensuring the publication of her husband's works and founding ▷ nurseries for the training of young actors and actresses. She defended the interests of the actor-manager George Jolly after a campaign by her husband and ▷ Thomas Killigrew to cheat him and squeeze him out of the profession. In 1673 she ceded control of the company to her son Charles, but held on to her shares in the company and various rights, including income from a fruit concession at the playhouse.
Bib: Hotson, L., *The Commonwealth and Restoration Stage*.

D'Avenant (Davenant), Sir William (1606–68)
Theatrical innovator, impresario, dramatist and poet, D'Avenant's career spanned the reign of ▷ Charles I, the ▷ Interregnum and the ▷ Restoration. A pivotal figure in the history of the English theatre, he was involved in most of the developments of this transitional period, including the dissemination of theatrical techniques associated with the aristocratic cultural form of the ▷ masque to the public stage, the creation of new genres (he is credited with the first English ▷ opera), and the introduction of actresses to the professional English stage. He adapted some of ▷ Shakespeare's plays to the new theatrical conditions, including ▷ *The Tempest* with ▷ Dryden (1667) in a version which was the basis of English productions until 1838. During the 1650s, as official Interregnum disapproval of stage plays waned, he openly mounted several musical performances, including ▷ *The Siege of Rhodes* (1656) which is often considered to be the first English opera. When the theatres reopened in 1660 D'Avenant and

▷ Killigrew obtained the only two patents granted
by ▷ Charles II allowing them to stage theatrical
performances in London. D'Avenant formed the
▷ Duke's Company and began converting Lisle's
Tennis Court at ▷ Lincoln's Inn Fields as a
theatre. After his death D'Avenant's widow, ▷ Lady
Henrietta Mary D'Avenant, inherited his patent.

Davys, Mary (1674–1732)

Dramatist and novelist, originally from Dublin. Her
husband was the Reverend Peter Davys, and through
him she knew English satirist ▷ Jonathan Swift. Her
husband died in 1698, and she came to England,
where she lived by writing. Her first fiction was
Amours of Alcippus and Lucippe (1704, republished
1725), and she wrote about Ireland in *The Fugitive*
(1705, rewritten 1725). Life in York, in the north of
England, is worked into her comedy *The Northern
Heiress, or the Humours of York*, which was staged
in 1716. She set up a coffee-house in Cambridge,
and published later works by subscription, *The
Reform'd Coquet, or Memoirs of Amoranda* (1724) and
Works (1725), which includes revisions of earlier
writings. She also wrote the poem 'The Modern
Poet' and other fictions and comedies, including *The
Accomplish'd Rake, or Modern Fine Gentleman* (1727).
Bib: Lonsdale, Roger (ed.), *Eighteenth-Century
Women Poets*.

De Loutherbourg, Philip James (Philippe Jacques) (1740–1812)

Painter, set designer, of noble Polish descent.
In 1771 after a successful exhibition in Paris
De Loutherbourg moved to London, where he
met ▷ David Garrick, and presented him with
proposals for co-ordinated improvements to the
lighting, scenes, costumes and mechanical effects at
▷ Drury Lane.

Engaged at the theatre, De Loutherbourg
'astonished the audience', according to one
observer, by his skilful and innovative use of various
translucent coloured silks, lit from behind and
mobile, to give changing effects of richness, subtlety,
and depth to the sets. His detailed and naturalistic
cut-out scenery was likened to fine paintings of
contemporary and fantastic views. In 1781 he became
a member of the ▷ Royal Academy.

Admired in his day by Thomas Gainsborough
(1727–88), De Loutherbourg is now considered
one of the most influential designers for the English
stage, bringing both imagination and technical
abilities to bear, so as to create scenes and spectacles
of unprecedented realism and magnificence. Much
of his work can be seen as an important early
contribution to the ▷ Romantic movement in
literature and art.

Declaration of Independence (1776)

The assertion of independence by the American
colonists, starting-point of the United States. It was
signed by 13 states. Although the Committee that
ordered the drafting of the Declaration included such
hard-headed, 18th-century rationalists as Benjamin
Franklin, their document (and the Constitution

of 1787) may be seen as essentially ▷ Romantic
in its idealization of freedom for the individual.
▷ American Indepence, War of

Decline and Fall of the Roman Empire, The (1776–88)

By ▷ Edward Gibbon; the most eloquent and
imposing historical work in the English language.
It begins at the height of the Roman Empire in
the 1st and 2nd centuries AD – an age with which
Gibbon's own era, so deeply imbued with Latin
scholarship, felt strong kinship. It then proceeds
to record the successive stage of Roman decline,
the rise of Christianity, the struggle with the
Eastern Roman Empire (the Byzantine) centred
on Constantinople (Byzantium), and that empire's
eventual extinction by the capture of Constantinople
in 1453. As an account, it has of course become
somewhat outdated, but as an imaginative epic (still
regarded as substantially true) and an expression of
the background to modern Europe as understood
in the 18th century, it remains a much-read and
very important work. Its structure is as spacious
as the subject, and is sustained by the energy of
Gibbon's style. The attitude is one of 18th-century
truth-seeking, and of urbane irony towards the
Christian religion, whose growth Gibbon sees
as one of the agents of destruction of classical
civilization. Gibbon's sceptical mind is at the same
time constantly critical of human pretensions to self-
sufficiency, the attainment of wisdom, and integrity
of motive; in such respects he is in the tradition of
the great satirists of his century, ▷ Alexander Pope
and ▷ Jonathan Swift.

Defoe, Daniel (1660–1731)

Son of a London tallow-chandler, James Foe, Defoe
changed his name in about 1695 to suggest a higher
social status. His writings reflect his ▷ Puritan
background: Defoe was educated at Morton's
academy for ▷ Dissenters at Newington Green,
and his pamphlet of 1702, *The Shortest Way with
Dissenters*, landed him in the pillory when its ironic
attack on Dissenters was taken seriously.

Defoe's attempts to make a living form a
colourful picture. Various business enterprises
failed dramatically, including the scheme of marine
insurance, unfortunately timed during a war, and
a disastrous project to breed civet cats. Between
1703 and 1714 he worked as a secret agent for the
▷ Tory government of Robert Harley, writing many
political (and anti- ▷ Jacobite) pamphlets.

Defoe produced some 560 journals, tracts and
books, many of them published anonymously or
pseudonymously. His reputation today rests on his
novels, a genre to which he turned with great success
late in his life.

*The Life and strange surprising Adventures of Robinson
Crusoe* (▷ *Robinson Crusoe*) appeared in 1719 and
its sequel, *The Farther Adventures of Robinson Crusoe*,
was published some months later. 1720 saw the
publication of the *Life and Adventures of Mr Duncan
Campbell*, and *Captain Singleton*; 1722, ▷ *Moll
Flanders*, ▷ *A Journal of the Plague Year*, *The History
of Peter the Great*, and *Colonel Jack*; 1724, ▷ *Roxana*,

the *Memoirs of a Cavalier*, and *A New Voyage round the World*; and 1726, *The Four Voyages of Capt. George Roberts*. His guide-book, *A Tour through the Whole Island of Great Britain*, appeared in three volumes, 1724–6.

Among Defoe's later works are *The Complete English Tradesman* (1726), *A Plan of the English Commerce* and *Augusta Triumphans* (1728), and *The Complete English Gentleman*, not published until 1890. Defoe died in Moorfields, and was buried in the area now called Bunhill Fields.

Bib: Moore, J. R., *Daniel Defoe: Citizen of the Modern World*; Richetti, J., *Defoe's Narratives: Situations and Structures*; Bell, Ian A., *Defoe's Fiction*.

Deism

A form of religious belief which developed in the 17th century as an outcome of the ▷ Reformation. ▷ Edward Herbert evolved the idea that, while the religion revealed in the Gospels was true, it was preceded by ▷ 'natural' religion, according to which by his own inner light a man could perceive all the essentials of religious truth. Herbert's deism was further expounded in the 18th century by others (often in such a way as to suggest that the Christian revelation as presented in the Gospels was redundant), and it suited the 18th-century cool and rational habit of mind which tended to see God as abstract and remote. ▷ Bishop Butler among the theologians and ▷ Hume and ▷ Kant among the philosophers, exposed the unsoundness of deistic arguments in the 18th century, and in the 19th century the growth of the genetic sciences demolished the basic assumptions of deism, that human nature and human reason have always been constant, in a constant environment.

Delany, Mrs Mary (1700–88)

One of the famous letter writers of the 18th century. She had a wide circle of friends among the famous people of her day.

Delilah

In the ▷ Bible (*Judges* 16) a woman beloved by the Jewish hero Samson. She betrayed him to the Philistines by cutting off his hair in which lay his divinely given supernatural strength. In Milton's ▷ *Samson Agonistes* she is called Dalila, and she is Samson's wife.

Denham, Sir John (1615–69)

Poet and playwright. He took the Royalist side in the ▷ Civil War, translated Book II of the ▷ *Aeneid* into pentameter ▷ couplets (*The Destruction of Troy, 1656*) and published a play in blank verse, *The Sophy* (1642). His *Cooper's Hill* (1642; enlarged version, 1655), a topographical poem describing the scenery around Windsor, was much admired and imitated. In it he abandons the ▷ enjambments of his Virgil translation, preferring a balanced end-stopped couplet. The passage on the Thames was cited and imitated by poets from ▷ Dryden onwards as the perfection of heroic couplet writing:

> O could I flow like thee, and make thy stream
> My great example, as it is my theme!
> Though deep, yet clear, though gentle, yet not dull,
> Strong without rage, without o'er-flowing full.

The lines are comically parodied in ▷ Pope's ▷ *Dunciad* (Bk. III, II. 163–6). ▷ Samuel Johnson, in his *Lives of the Poets* (1781), called Denham 'one of the fathers of English poetry'.
▷ Augustanism.

Dennis, John (1657–1734)

Although Dennis's efforts as a poet and playwright are undistinguished, he was one of the foremost literary critics of the ▷ Augustan era. His feud with ▷ Pope for which he is best remembered, was angry and ill-tempered on both sides, but Dennis's critical views, favouring ▷ blank-verse ▷ epics on Christian themes, are worthy of more serious attention. Among his most notable works are *The Advancement of Reformation of Modern Poetry* (1701), *The Grounds of Criticism in Poetry* (1704) and *An Essay on the Genius and Writings of Shakespeare* (1712).
Bib: Paul, H. G., *John Dennis, his Life and Criticism*; Hooker, E. N. (ed.), *The Critical Works of John Dennis*.

Descartes, René (1596–1650)

French philosopher and mathematician. In ethics and religious doctrine he was traditional, but in method of thought he was the starting point of the total reliance on reason – ▷ rationalism – that was pre-eminent in the later 17th and 18th centuries. In his *Discours de la Méthode* (1637) he reduced knowledge to the basic principle of *Cogito, ergo sum* (I think, therefore I am), from which intuition he deduced the existence of God and thence the reality of the external world. He also distinguished mind and matter, finding their source of combination again in God. It was Descartes's writings that drew ▷ John Locke, the dominant figure in English rationalism, to the study of philosophy.

Deserted Village, The (1770)

A poem in heroic ▷ couplets by ▷ Oliver Goldsmith, written in protest against the enclosure of common land by powerful landowners. The poet recalls his youth in Auburn in the traditional terms of idyllic ▷ pastoral, and laments the present desolation and depopulation. Goldsmith's conventional literary opposition between rural innocence and commercial corruption, prompted ▷ George Crabbe's realistic portrayal of the grimness of peasant life in *The Village* (1783).

Diaries

As a form of literature in English, diaries began to be significant in the 17th century. The spirit of criticism from the ▷ Renaissance and the stress on the individual conscience from the ▷ Reformation combined with the political and social turbulence of the 17th century to awaken people to a new awareness of personal experience and its possible interest for general readers. The private nature of the diary form made it attractive to women writers. Thus the art of the diary arose with the art of ▷ biography and ▷ autobiography. Diaries may first be divided into the two classes of those clearly meant to be strictly private and those written more or less with an eye to eventual publication. A further division may be made between those which are interesting chiefly as a record of the time in which the writer lived and those which are mainly a record of his personality.

The best known of the English diaries is that of ▷ Samuel Pepys (1633–1703), which was both purely private (written in code) and entirely unselfconscious, as well as an excellent record of the time. His contemporary ▷ John Evelyn (1620–1706) is less esteemed partly because his diary is a more studied, self-conscious work. ▷ Jonathan Swift's *Journal to Stella* (covering the years 1710–13) is a personal revelation but unusual in that it was addressed to the woman Swift loved. The diary of the ▷ Quaker ▷ George Fox (1624–91) is a record of his spiritual experience for the education of his followers. In the 18th and early 19th centuries the most famous diary is that of the novelist ▷ Fanny Burney (Madame D'Arblay, 1752–1840), considered as a record of the time ingenuously imbued with her own personality. The diary of the great religious reformer ▷ John Wesley (1703–91) is comparable to that of Fox as a spiritual record, with a wider outlook on his time.

Dictionary of the English Language (1755)

Usually known as 'Johnson's Dictionary', it was compiled by ▷ Samuel Johnson and published in 1755. It was accepted as authoritative for about a hundred years. The excellence of the work is not so much its scholarship as its literary intelligence. It is weak in etymology, as this was still an undeveloped science, but it is strong in understanding of language, and in particular the English language. In the Preface, Johnson writes a short grammar, but he points out that English simplicity of forms and freedom from inflexions make an elaborate one (as grammar was then understood) unnecessary. He makes clear that the spirit of the English language had been unduly influenced by the spirit of French, and he rejects the idea that correctness should be fixed by the authority of an Academy, since the inherent mutability of language will always cause it to follow its own laws. Johnson thus began the English habit of relying upon current English dictionaries and manuals of usage to discover the best existent expression: Fowler's *Modern English Usage* and the Oxford *New English Dictionary* are 20th-century descendants of 'Johnson's Dictionary'.

Didactic literature

Literature designed to teach, or to propound in direct terms a doctrine or system of ideas. In practice, it is not always easy to identify; so much literature is didactic in intention but not in form; sometimes writers renounce didactic intentions but in practice use didactic forms. Thus ▷ Spenser declared that *The Faerie Queene* was meant to 'fashion a gentleman . . . in vertuous and gentle discipline', but the poem may be enjoyed for its imaginative

vision without much regard to its didacticism, and the same is true of ▷ Bunyan's ▷ *Pilgrim's Progress*. In the 18th century much poetry had at least didactic leanings, such as ▷ Pope's ▷ *Essay on Criticism* and his ▷ *Essay on Man*; minor work by other poets is more unmistakably didactic. The prevalence of didactic poetry in the 18th century arose from the especially high regard this century had for ancient Greek and Latin literature: Hesiod's *Works and Days* (Greek, 8th century BC) and ▷ Lucretius' *De Rerum Natura* (Latin, 1st century BC) being the major examples of didactic verse. The Romantic poets of the early 19th century (▷ Wordsworth, ▷ Coleridge, Shelley, Keats) reacted against the 18th-century ▷ Augustans, and since then there has been a persistent prejudice against explicit didacticism.

▷ Conduct literature.

Diderot, Denis (1713–84)

French philosopher, novelist, dramatist and critic, and major figure of the French ▷ Enlightenment; born at Langres in Champagne. He was educated by Jesuits and was employed as a tutor, and by a bookseller. Diderot became an ▷ atheist, and his arguments for the equality of all mankind anticipate those of the ▷ French Revolution. His was a period of ferocious censorship in France, and Diderot was persecuted by the authorities, and was for a time imprisoned because of his *Lettre sur les aveugles* ('Letter on the blind' 1749), which set out his materialistic and anti-clerical views. He was known in England particularly for his work on ▷ *L'Encyclopédie*, translated and expanded from Ephraim Chambers' *Cyclopaedia* (1728). At first, Diderot worked together with the mathematician D'Alembert, later he headed it alone. The work was published in 17 volumes between 1751 and 1765, with a further 11 volumes of plates completed in 1772. It was an anthology of 'enlightened' views on politics, philosophy and religion, and included contributions by ▷ Voltaire, ▷ Montesquieu, and ▷ Rousseau. It sought to harness all available knowledge, and to show the order and interdependence of its various branches, in a manner embodying the humanistic and rational ideals of the *philosophes*, including Diderot's own iconoclasm. The *Encyclopédie* was repeatedly banned because of its perceived challenge to the established order. Later Diderot became a favourite of Catherine II of Russia, whom he visited in 1773, and who gave him financial support. His fiction includes *La Religieuse*, a study of convent life, and *Jacques le fataliste et son maitre* (c 1774). His *Supplement aux voyages de Bougainville* (published posthumously, 1796) contrasts morals and customs of the natural inhabitants of Tahiti with those of civilized Europeans, to the detriment of the latter. *Le Neveu de Rameau* (date uncertain, probably between 1761 and 1774, published posthumously) is a satiric study of society, in the form of a dialogue between the author, in the role of a philosopher idealist, and a disillusioned beggar. The work was translated by ▷ Goethe and it influenced the philosopher Hegel, who saw in it a portrait of the 'alienated man'. Diderot's views

about literature and life were also expressed in his vast correspondence with society figures and other writers. He admired ▷ Samuel Richardson, whom he described him as a 'painter of nature', to the point of adulation, and greatly helped to popularize his books on the Continent. Much in Diderot's work anticipates views of some later ▷ Romanticists: he has been described as a ▷ pantheist, as well as an atheist. His plays were mostly short melodramas.
Bib: Crocker, L. G., *Diderot, the Embattled Philosopher*.

Dido (Elissa)
In Roman legend, the daughter of a king of Tyre, and the reputed founder of the city of Carthage. ▷ Virgil brings her into his epic of the founding of Rome, the ▷ *Aeneid*; she falls in love with ▷ Aeneas when he is shipwrecked on the North African coast, and when he forsakes her to fulfil his destiny, she kills herself. The Romans identified her with the guardian goddess of Carthage.

She is the subject of a tragedy, *Dido* (1594) by Christopher Marlowe and Thomas Nashe, and of the opera *Dido and Aeneas* by ▷ Nahum Tate to music by ▷ Henry Purcell, produced in 1689–90.

Dillon, Wentworth
▷ Roscommon, Fourth Earl of.

Dismal science, The
Political economy; so called by Thomas Carlyle because the social thought of such writers as ▷ Adam Smith, ▷ Jeremy Bentham, ▷ Thomas Malthus and David Ricardo tended to be pessimistic about the alleviation of poverty and inhumanly indifferent to the consequences of economic laws as they saw them.

Dissenters
A term used for those ▷ Puritans who, owing to their 'dissent' from the established ▷ Church of England, were refused certain political, educational and (at first) religious rights from the second half of the 17th Century. They were not permitted to enter Parliament, they could not enter a university, and, until 1688, they could not join together in worship. Puritans were not formally restricted in this way before 1660. They were released from their political restraints in 1828. In the 19th century it became more usual to call them ▷ Nonconformists or Free Churchmen. The term does not apply to Scotland, where the established Church is ▷ Presbyterian not the episcopalian Church of England.

Dissociation of Sensibility
A critical expression made famous by T. S. Eliot and used in his essay *The Map Poets* (1921, included in his *Selected Essays*). He states: 'In the seventeenth century a dissociation of sensibility set in, from which we have never recovered; and this dissociation . . . was aggravated by the influence of the two most powerful poets of the century, ▷ Milton and Dryden.' Eliot's argument is that before 1660 poets, in particular the ▷ Metaphysical poets, were 'engaged in the task of trying to find the verbal

equivalent for states of mind and feeling', and that after that date 'while the language became more refined, the feeling became more crude'. Poetry, henceforward, is put to more specialised purposes: 'Tennyson and Browning are poets, and they think; but they do not feel their thought as immediately as the odour of a rose. A thought to Donne was an experience; it modified his sensibility.' The implication behind the argument is that poets (with exceptions) ceased to bring all their faculties to bear upon their art '▷ Racine or Donne looked into a good deal more than the heart. One must look into the cerebral cortex the nervous system, and the digestive tracts.'

The theory has had great influence. Those who uphold it support it with the evidence provided by the rise of modern prose after 1660, and the gradual displacement of poetry from its centrality in literature thereafter; poetry either subjected itself to the rational discipline of prose (*eg* ▷ Pope), or, in the 19th century, it tended to cultivate areas of feeling to which this rational discipline was not relevant (*eg* Swinburne). However, the theory has been attacked for various reasons. Eliot himself felt that he had used the expression too simplified a way (*Milton*, in *Poets and Poetry*) and that the cause of the process were more complicated than his earlier essay had implied. Other writers have suggested that such a dissociation did not happen; or that it happened in different ways at different periods; or that, if it did happen, no deterioration in imaginative writing can be attributed to it. See Frank Kermode, *Romantic Image* and F. W. Bateson in *Essays in Criticism, vol. I*

Divorce
Until 1857 divorce was possible only through Church courts which had kept their authority over matrimonial relations since before the ▷ Reformation, while losing it in nearly all other private affairs of laymen. Even after a marriage had been dissolved by a Church court, a special ('private') act of Parliament was necessary before the divorce was legalized. In consequence, divorces were rare and only occurred among the rich and influential. Adultery and cruelty were the accepted grounds, and the wife was commonly in an unfavourable position, so that no divorce was granted on account of a husband's adultery until 1801. The law of 1857 added desertion as a ground for divorce, and proceedings were taken out of the hands of the Church courts and put under the courts of the realm. ▷ Marriage; Women, Status of.

Docwra, Anne (1624–1710)
Quaker author of numerous pamphlets in which she argued for the supremacy of God's word over human laws, and the importance of the 'inner light' as a revelation of God's love. She supported women's active involvement in the Church, and also pleaded for religious tolerance, although she was forceful in attacking those whom she felt were enemies of the Quaker cause. Among these was an apostate Quaker, Francis Brigg, with whom she engaged in a vigorous and colourful pamphlet war. Docwra defended ▷ George Fox against accusations of indulgence.

Dogberry and Verges
Comic constables in ▷ Shakespeare's play, *Much Ado About Nothing*. Dogberry is famous for his misuse of words – compare ▷ Mrs Malaprop in ▷ Sheridan's *The Rivals*.

Don Juan
The hero of legends from various European countries. His exploits were the subject of the Spanish play *El Burlador de Sevilla* by Tirso de Molina (1571–1641), who gave him his distinctive character of sensual adventurer. Plays and stories were woven round him in French and Italian, and he is the protagonist of an opera by Mozart (*Don Giovanni*). In English literature by far the most important work about him is the satirical epic *Don Juan* (1819–24) by Byron; he was also the subject of a forgotten play *The Libertine* (1676) by ▷ Thomas Shadwell.

Dorset, Sixth Earl of (1638–1706)
Poet and patron. Charles Sackville, Lord Buckhurst, and later Earl of Dorset, was a ▷ Restoration courtier and author of ▷ satires and ▷ lyric poems (*Works*, 1714). ▷ John Dryden's *Discourse concerning the Original and Progress of Satire* is addressed to him, and contains high praise for his poetry.

Dorset Garden Theatre
The Dorset Garden Theatre, also known as the Duke's Theatre because of its patronage by the Duke of York, later ▷ James II, was designed by ▷ Sir Christopher Wren for ▷ Sir William D'Avenant, and was considered the most magnificent public theatre when it opened in 1671.

The stage had four doors, two on each side, admitting the performers to a deep forestage or apron stage which projected into the pit, past the side-boxes. On this the prologue was spoken, and much of the acting took place, allowing great intimacy between actors and audience. Scene changes were carried out in full view of the audience, the curtain or front 'scene' being moved only at the beginnings and ends of performances; actors could step forward or backward into different, perhaps newly revealed, 'sets' as they were speaking. This made possible fast-paced, fluid action, particularly in comedy. From the first the Dorset Garden specialized in staging the very elaborate performances, including many operas, as distinct from the Theatre Royal Drury Lane (▷ Drury Lane Theatres), which concentrated on plays. After the ▷ King's Company and ▷ Duke's Company were merged in 1682, Dorset Garden continued for a time to be the main venue for spectacles. In 1689 it was re-named the Queen's Theatre, in deference to Queen ▷ Mary II. It gradually fell out of use, and was demolished in 1709.

Double-Dealer, The (1694)
Busy and rather bitter play by ▷ William Congreve. At its heart is the Machiavellian character of Maskwell, an arch dissembler and schemer. Setting himself up as everyone's friend and ally, he contrives to deceive and entrap each character in his single-minded plot to indulge his own lust and greed. His aim is to displace his supposed friend Mellefont, both in the fortune Mellefont is due to inherit from his uncle and aunt, Lord and Lady Touchwood, and in the hand of Cynthia as his wife. The means by which he almost succeeds are shown with infinite skill, as he manipulates other gullible and fallible characters, and situations, with breathtaking credibility. He seduces and then uses Lady Touchwood, and exploits the unhappiness of two other couples. A recurring feature is the ease with which the wives manage to allay their husbands' suspicions of their cuckoldry. Only two characters emerge from this comparatively unstained: Cynthia, and Mellefont – but even he is tainted (as Congreve points out in the preface) by his blind and stubborn adherence to Maskwell. The play's seamy and unpleasant atmosphere is mitigated by scenes of high comedy. It recalls, to some extent, ▷ William Wycherley's ▷ *The Plain Dealer*, and looks forward to ▷ Oliver Goldsmith's *The Good-Natur'd Man*.

Doubting Castle
In Part I of ▷ John Bunyan's ▷ *Pilgrim's Progress*, the castle belonging to the Giant Despair, where Christian and Hopeful lie prisoners. In Part II the castle is destroyed by the champion Greatheart.

Drapier's Letters (1724)
A series of pamphlets by ▷ Jonathan Swift against a monopoly to issue copper coins in Ireland, granted by the English Government to the Duchess of Kendal (George I's mistress) and sold by her to William Wood ('Wood's halfpence'). The Irish considered that the monopoly would be economically harmful to them. Swift wrote in their support in the semblance of a Dublin 'drapier' (= draper), *ie* an ordinary shopman. The pamphlets are an example of his apparently moderate, plain style carrying an immense force of irony; they were so effective that the Government had to withdraw the monopoly.

Drinks
Ale was a universal drink in the Middle Ages, until in the 16th century beer (like ale, brewed from malt) became more popular; a thin brew called 'small beer' was drunk by children and servants and by the poor. The reason for this general use was the poor availability of fresh drinking water. A 16th-century traveller was surprised to be offered, in some parts of the country, milk instead of beer. ▷ Wine was drunk freely by the richer classes from the early ▷ Middle Ages; most of it was imported from France, Germany or the Mediterranean countries, but the grape vine was cultivated in Britain to some extent until the 18th century. In the countryside, wines were made out of local plants and fruits (elderberry, cowslip, dandelion) extensively until the 19th century; cider and perry, from fermented apples and pears respectively, were rivals to ale and beer in some parts. Another very common country drink was the ancient mead, brewed from fermented honey, now seldom found. In the 17th

century tea and coffee were introduced, and for a hundred years (approximately 1650–1750) London enjoyed a flourishing 'café' life with its coffee-houses (▷ coffee and coffee-houses). Chocolate, as a drink, was also fashionable by the mid-18th century. Tea had become a national drink by the 19th century; the English habit of adding milk was not until then usual. It replaced beer as a normal drink for women, especially in the middle classes. For a short time in the 18th century the working classes, especially in London, took to gin in preference to beer, with great injury to their health. Even after the imposition of taxes on this spirit (distilled from malt) in 1751, drunkenness, from excessive drinking of comparatively cheap spirits in so-called 'gin-palaces', remained a national problem until the 20th century. This accounts for the extent of teetotalism, ie temperance movements, appealing for total abstinence from alcoholic drinks, in working-class religious and political circles in the 19th century

Drury Lane Theatres

The first was an old riding school in Bridges Street, converted by ▷ Thomas Killigrew to form the original Theatre Royal, Drury Lane, also known as the King's Theatre.

In 1682 the ▷ King's Company was absorbed by the ▷ Duke's, and the resulting ▷ United Company continued to stage plays at Drury Lane, and the larger spectacles and operas at ▷ Dorset Garden. After a difficult period under ▷ Christopher Rich, the theatre prospered with ▷ Colley Cibber, ▷ Robert Wilks, Thomas Doggett (c1670–1721), and various other managers jointly in charge, and then again under ▷ David Garrick, who took over in 1747.

In 1776 upon Garrick's retirement, Drury Lane was taken over by ▷ Richard Brinsley Sheridan, who continued to run it until its destruction by fire in 1809. The present theatre opened in 1812.

Dryden, John (1631–1700)

Poet, critic, dramatist. By family background and personal sympathies he was on the ▷ Puritan, anti-monarchical side during the Protectorate, and in an early poem, *Heroique Stanzas* (1659) he eulogized ▷ Oliver Cromwell, who had died in 1658. However, like many others, he welcomed the ▷ Restoration, composing *Astræa Redux* (1660) and *Panegyric* (1661) to welcome the king's return. With the ▷ Earl of Rochester he dominated English letters in the reign of Charles II, being appointed ▷ Poet Laureate in 1668 and Historiographer Royal in 1670. On the accession of James II in 1685 Dryden became a Catholic, and refusing to abandon his new faith after 1688, he was stripped of the Laureateship and other royal appointments.

It was in the theatre that Dryden enjoyed the greatest financial success, and between 1663 and 1681 he wrote almost a play a year. His best dramatic work, ▷ *All for Love* (1677), is an entirely new version of ▷ Shakespeare's *Antony and Cleopatra*. *The Indian Empress* (1667), *The Conquest of Granada* (1669–70), and ▷ *Aureng-Zebe* (1675) are heroic dramas on the grand model of the French dramatist

▷ Corneille. He also wrote comedies such as ▷ *Marriage à la Mode* (1673).

Dryden's first poetic works, such as his brilliant *Upon the death of the Lord Hastings* (1649), belong to the overblown decadence of 'metaphysical' wit. ▷ *Annus Mirabilis* (1667) looks at the events of 1666, including sea engagements with the Dutch and the ▷ Great Fire. It maintains a ▷ baroque elaboration of imagery, but presented in a new public, Augustan manner. His greatest works are political ▷ satires in ▷ heroic ▷ couplets, a form which his example secured in pre-eminence for several decades after his death. ▷ *Absalom and Achitophel* (1681–2) shows an ironic assurance of tone, a novelist's eye for telling characterization, a complex layering of imagery, and a virtuoso flair for fast-running narrative. Occasionally his satire is biting and cruel, as in the passage on ▷ Shaftesbury (Achitophel). Elsewhere there is good-humoured 'raillery' in the portrait of the ▷ Duke of Buckingham (Zimri) ('A man so various, that he seem'd to be / Not one, but all Mankind's Epitome'), and broad farce in the passage on Settle and ▷ Thomas Shadwell in Part II.

▷ *The Medall* (1682) continued the attack on the first Earl of Shaftesbury, while ▷ *MacFlecknoe* (1682) shows Dryden in a more relaxed, uninhibited mood, again attacking Shadwell (the man who was to succeed him as laureate) in a burlesque lampoon which is purely, even at times surrealistically, comic. The two long didactic poems ▷ *Religio Laici* (1682) and ▷ *The Hind and the Panther* (1687), on the religious question which at the time divided his sympathy, contain fine passages, but their didactic mode makes them difficult to admire today. Similarly the rhetoric of his Pindaric odes (*eg Alexander's Feast*, 1697) tends to be regarded now as artificial. Despite its public and impersonal cast, Dryden's poetry can on occasion be deeply moving, as in the elegy on his friend ▷ John Oldham. His last poetic work, *Fables Ancient and Modern* (1699), is a series of translations from ▷ Homer, ▷ Ovid, ▷ Boccaccio and Chaucer.

Dryden has been called 'the Father of English prose'. He set his own stamp on the new informal, persuasive style, which under the new constitutional system, replaced the ornamental court prose of the absolutist Tudors and early Stuarts. He also produced the first extended works of literary theory in the language. *A Discourse concerning the Original and Progress of Satire* relates the different classical styles of satire found in ▷ Juvenal and ▷ Horace to modern English writing, including his own. His celebrated essay *Of Dramatic Poesy* discusses the principles of drama and judiciously compares the qualities of Ben Jonson and ▷ Shakespeare. The *Preface to the Fables* (1700) brings a very modern sense of historical perspective to the question of the development and enrichment of literary language.
Bib: Johnson, S., in *Lives of the Poets*; Ward, C. E., *Life*; Eliot, T. S., in *Selected Essays*; Leavis, F. R., in *Revaluation*; van Doren, M., *The Poetry of Dryden*; Bredvold, L. I., *John Dryden's Intellectual Milieu*; Nichol Smith, D., *John Dryden*; Kinsley, J. and H., *Dryden: the Critical Heritage*; Wykes, D., *A Preface to Dryden*; Rogers, P., *The Augustan Vision*.

Duck, Stephen (1705–56)

Known as the 'Thresher Poet', and often described as 'the first proletarian author'. He was discovered working as a thresher and writing in the Wiltshire countryside, brought to London, and given a salary and accommodation near Richmond by Queen Caroline; he was also assisted by ▷ Pope. He subsequently studied and became a clergyman. His *The Thresher's Labour* is one of the early poems showing the hardships of country life and labour, in contrast to the idealized pictures painted by ▷ pastoral tradition. It was included in *Poems on Several Occasions* (1738). Later, in poems such as *On Richmond Park, and Royal Gardens*, Duck succumbed to the same idealizing tendencies as his forbears. He ended by drowning himself.

Duelling

Two kinds have existed: the judicial combat and the duel of honour.

Judicial combat was practised from the 12th century until the 16th century in England, though never so freely as in France. By this practice, a dispute which would now be settled by court of law was decided by combat before a judge or the king, on the assumption that God would defend the right. In *Richard II*, Shakespeare introduces a duel of this kind, between Mowbray and Bolingbroke.

The more familiar 'duel of honour', by which an alleged injury by one gentleman to another was settled by combat privately arranged between them, was never legal and did not become common until the 17th century. Before this, such an injury would more probably be settled by the hiring of assassins. The social code regulated the duel of honour strictly and so long as the regulations were kept, the survivor was likely to escape legal penalty. These duels were fought with either pistols or swords; by degrees, especially when towards the end of the 18th century the wearing of swords by gentleman went out of fashion, pistols became the more usual weapon. The frequency of duels can be judged by their apperance in 17th- and 18th- century plays and novels. In the early 19th century the law was used much more severely against duellists, and the religious ('evangelical') revival of the time condemned duels as immoral.

Duenna, The (1775)

Comic opera by ▷ Richard Brinsley Sheridan. Don Jerome is attempting to force his daughter Louisa to marry the rich but unpleasant converted Jew, Isaac, and locks her up to await the marriage. However, she loves Don Antonio, and uses her duenna as a go-between, to carry messages. Jerome discovers the duenna's role in their affair, and dismisses her, but Louisa escapes disguised as the duenna, while the latter impersonates her mistress and receives Isaac. Meanwhile, Louisa's brother and Antonio's friend, Don Ferdinand, has fallen in love with Donna Clara, who is to be forced into a convent. She too escapes from her father, and the two young women join forces. The duenna tricks Isaac into marrying her, and into helping Louisa and Antonio to marry. Ferdinand and Clara are also united, and

Jerome is reconciled to both situations. The play was successfully performed at ▷ Covent Garden.

Duke's Company, The

Acting company formed by ▷ Sir William D'Avenant after the Restoration of Charles II. It performed from June 1661 at the former Lisle's Tennis Court in ▷ Lincoln's Inn Fields, which had been converted to a theatre. In November 1671 the company moved to a new playhouse at ▷ Dorset Garden, also known as the Duke's Theatre, where it remained until its union with the ▷ King's Company to form the ▷ United Company in 1682.

Duke's Theatre, The

▷ Dorset Garden Theatre.

Dunciad, The (1728–43)

A ▷ mock-heroic ▷ satire in pentameter ▷ couplets by ▷ Alexander Pope, satirizing his literary enemies. In the earlier three-book version, published anonymously in 1728, the hero is the scholar Lewis Theobald (spelled 'Tibbald' in the poem), whose *Shakespeare Restored* (1726) had offended Pope by pointing out mistakes and oversights in his edition of Shakespeare's works (1725). In a brilliantly appropriate stroke, which two centuries later would have been considered daringly modernist, *The Dunciad* itself is presented in a scholarly edition, complete with learned footnotes, as though it were a classic. In the notes Pope and his friends (under the pseudonym ▷ Scriblerus) discuss the knotty textual cruxes of the work, draw attention to its various poetic excellences, and heap straight-faced praise upon the solecisms of other critics and poets. In 1742 Pope issued a fourth book under the title *The New Dunciad*, and in 1743 the whole four-book version reappeared with a new hero, the popular playwright, ▷ Colley Cibber, who to much derision had been made ▷ Poet Laureate in 1730, and thus appears as ▷ Bayes.

In Book I Cibber is snatched from his benighted labours by the goddess Dulness and is crowned Laureate in succession to Laurence Eusden, who now 'sleeps among the dull of ancient days'. In Book II the new King of the Dunces presides over a modern ▷ Grub Street version of the ancient classical games, including a pissing match (to determine 'Who best can send on high/ The salient spout, far-streaming to the sky'), a patron-tickling contest, and a competition to see who can dive deepest into the open sewer of Fleet-ditch. The book ends with the company being read to sleep by the works of John Henley and ▷ Sir Richard Blackmore: 'Soft creeping words on words, the sense compose,/ At ev'ry line they stretch, they yawn, they doze.' In Book III Cibber sleeps in the lap of Dulness and has visions, in true classical style, of the future triumph of the goddess and the destruction of civilization. Book IV traces the pantomimic progress of Dulness through the realms of science and letters ('*Art* after *art* goes out, and all is Night'), and ends in biblical solemnity with a description of the restoration of the ancient Empire of Chaos. Despite its sometimes irritating plethora of topical references, the poem is a unique masterpiece. Its nervous, ironic tone merges raucous vulgarity, exquisite sensuousness, surreal fantasy, euphoric farce and sombre despair in strange and original evocative effects.

D'Urfey (Durfey), Thomas (1653–1723)

Dramatist and song-writer, born in Devon, he probably trained originally for the law. He became a close friend of ▷ Charles II, who liked to hum his songs. He often stayed with the Earl of Dorset at Knowle, where there is a portrait of him painted in his sleep, according to one anecdote, for he hated the idea of being portrayed. He wrote 33 plays, including tragedies, comedies and opera, but is best remembered for his comedies, including *Madam Fickle* (1676), and *A Fond Husband* (1677), both comedies of intrigue, and political satires such as *The Royalist* (1682), and *Sir Barnaby Whigg* (1682). *Love for Money* (1691), and *The Richmond Heiress* (1693) both show tendencies toward ▷ Reform comedy. He also adapted a number of earlier works, including Shakespeare's *Cymbeline*, renamed *The Island Princess* (1682). Some of his plays' perceived bawdiness made him a target for attack by ▷ Jeremy Collier. His own and other ballads were published together in six volumes, under the title of *Wit and Mirth, or Pills to Purge Melancholy* (1720–21).

Dyer, John (?1700–58)

Poet and painter. Born in Carmarthenshire, Dyer studied painting under Jonathan Richardson and visited Italy in 1724–5. In 1741 he entered the Church. His most important work, *Grongar Hill* (1727), is a topographical landscape poem in the tradition of ▷ Sir John Denham's *Cooper's Hill* and ▷ Alexander Pope's ▷ *Windsor-Forest*, but its fluent use of tetrameter rather than pentameter (▷ metre) couplets gives it a lyrical *élan* all of its own. Moreover, Dyer's painterly eye leads him to focus, in a most original way, on the transient visual effects which succeed each other as he climbs up from the valley of the Towy. Dyer's feeling for the ▷ picturesque, rooted in his study of the paintings of Claude and Poussin, was influential on later poetry until well into the Romantic period. In 1740 appeared *The Ruins of Rome*, and in 1757, *The Fleece*, long discursive and didactic poems in Miltonic ▷ blank verse. The second emulates the example of ▷ John Philips' *Cyder*, in its celebration of British scenery and British industry. It attempts to encompass all aspects of the wool trade, from the techniques of sheep-farming, modern and ancient, to the growing prosperity of Leeds and Sheffield and the growth of trade which promises to distribute British woollen manufactures 'over the whole globe'.

Bib: Humphrey, B., *John Dyer*.

East India Company
The best known of the ▷ Charter Companies, given a monopoly of eastern trade by Queen Elizabeth in 1600. Competition with the Dutch in the East Indian islands turned its attention to the Indian mainland, where in the 18th century its extensive commercial influence developed into political power. To protect its Chinese trade, it gained control of the Burmese and Malayan coasts down to Singapore, which it founded in 1819. After the Indian Mutiny of 1857 it was taken over by the British government, which had shared its rule in India since ▷ Pitt (the Younger)'s Indian Act of 1784. It was familiarly known as John Company and its ships as East Indiamen.

▷ Companies, joint-stock.

Eclogue
A short ▷ pastoral dialogue, usually in verse. The most famous example is the *Bucolics* of the Latin poet, ▷ Virgil. The word is often used as equivalent for ▷ idyll, a pastoral poem without dialogue.

Eden, Garden of
In the ▷ Bible (*Genesis* 2 and 3), the dwelling place of the first man and woman, Adam and Eve. Eden is thought of as a place of perfect bliss where there was no conflict, sickness or suffering, and human needs were satisfied by the fruit of the garden. But it also contained the trees of life and of knowledge; eating the fruit of the latter would give Man the knowledge of good and evil, and so God forbade it to him. Eve, however, succumbed to temptation by the serpent, and Adam followed her example. In consequence, God drove them from the garden. Their disobedience is the symbol of the myth of 'the Fall of Man'. The most famous paraphrase of the story is Milton's ▷ *Paradise Lost* which also includes an account of the fall of the ▷ angels.

Edgeworth, Maria (1767–1849)
Novelist. Her tales are commonly set in Ireland. Her work is minor but still read for its vivacity, good sense and realism. *Castle Rackrent* (1800) and *The Absentee* (1812) are two of her works still in print. She was also an excellent writer for children (see *Tales*, ed. Austin Dobson). She collaborated with her father, a noted educationist, in *Practical Education* (1798), influenced by the French-Swiss thinker ▷ Rousseau. She was admired by ▷ Jane Austen, ▷ William Thackeray, ▷ John Ruskin, Turgenev and Walter Scott, whom she influenced. She has recently been re-evaluated by ▷ feminist critics as a liberal contributor to women's social history.
Bid: Clarke, I. C., *Life*; Newby, P. H., *Maria Edgeworth*; M. S., Butler *Maria Edgeworth*.

Edinburgh
Since the middle of the 15th century the capital of Scotland. The union of the crowns in 1603, when James VI of Scotland became also ▷ James I of England, left Edinburgh still with its same political status, since the governments of the two countries remained separate. In 1707, however, the union of the parliaments removed the political capital to London and for half a century greatly reduced Edinburgh's prestige: it was now only the centre of the Scottish legal and Church systems. In the second half of the century, however, Edinburgh had a notable revival. Intellectuals such as the philosopher ▷ David Hume, the historian Robertson and the economist ▷ Adam Smith, challenged the intellectual domination of London. In the early 19th century the poet-novelist Walter Scott and the very influential ▷ *Edinburgh Review* made it possible to say that, culturally, Britain contained two metropolises. However, this was at the expense of an independent Scottish culture, since before the Scottish Renaissance Scottish writers tended to adopt English styles and standards.

▷ Scotland; Scottish literature in English.

Education
The Reformation was not altogether helpful to the spread of education. Henry VIII dissolved the monasteries and friaries in 1536 and 1539, and since these made important contributions to the universities ▷ Oxford and ▷ Cambridge suffered at least financially. A minor ill-effect of Henry's action – minor only because the numbers affected were small – was the closure of the nunnery schools, the only institutions for the education of girls. Much worse was the closing down of many grammar schools under Edward VI. Many of these, established by town guilds and by chantries, had religious affiliations, and Edward VI's Protestant politicians gladly made this the excuse for seizing the funds with which they had been endowed. Some, indeed, were refounded with the title 'King Edward VI Grammar School', with the result that for three centuries this boy king enjoyed the reputation of being a great patron of education, but in fact far more schools were lost than refounded.

These setbacks were, however, temporary. Gradually, from 1560, new schools were opened, including some (for instance, Rugby) which later became famous as public schools. The universities also recovered from their difficulties, and it was in the reign of Elizabeth I (1558–1603) that they were first attended by large numbers of the great men of the age, including the poets Ralegh, ▷ Spenser, Sidney and Marlowe, and the philosopher statesman, ▷ Francis Bacon. The college system was now strongly established; it imposed effective discipline and established the relationship between tutor and student as the principal method of instruction, which it is to the present day, at least in Oxford and Cambridge. Young men of the upper classes began to be sent to the universities as a regular practice to complete their education, unless they completed it in the London Inns of Court.

It was not until the 17th century that the well-known public schools – especially Winchester and Eton – became predominantly aristocratic. The young nobleman had been more often educated, until he went to the university, by tutors in his home. Gentlemen, however, commonly went to grammar schools. At Repton, then a grammar school, the first 20 names on the list of pupils in 1564 include the sons of 5 gentlemen, 13 small farmers and 4 tradesmen. There were often entrance fees into the grammar schools, graduated according to the rank of the pupil, but some of the town schools, such as the one probably attended by ▷ Shakespeare in Stratford, were free to the sons of burgesses, *ie* established citizens.

Boys received a predominantly ▷ classical education – chiefly in Latin literature – as they were to continue to do until late in the 19th century, though at the universities they might in addition acquire some knowledge of mathematics and the sciences and Aristotelian philosophy (▷ Aristotle). The universities still followed the medieval pattern of the trivium and the quadrivium, though thinking was much freer and more varied, and no longer included theology. Teaching continued to ignore what were known as the 'mechanical arts'. It was beginning to be a practical age, however and in 1597 Sir Thomas Gresham founded Gresham College in London, for lectures which included physic (*ie* medicine), law and navigation, as well as the more 'liberal' subjects. Gresham College lasted until 1768, by which time other institutions of a similar kind existed. The Inns of Court were attended especially by young men who, like the poet John Donne, were ambitious but not wealthy, for a legal training was the most useful practical one for a public career in politics and administration as well as the law itself.

Until the later 19th century, upper-class education was commonly pursued for the general cultivation of the mind and manners; it included knowledge of the ancient cultures and the arts; increasingly, it required travel. The lower a boy (or a girl) stood in the social scale, the more practical and vocational his training had to be. It was not, however, until the reign of Queen ▷ Anne (1702–14) that much was done, apart from the increasingly expensive apprenticeship system, for the really poor. In that reign, the Church of England began the establishment of large numbers of ▷ Charity Schools which, by the end of the reign, were giving free or nearly free elementary education to about 25,000 children throughout England. The education included religious instruction. At the end of the 18th century, children in industrial areas were employed so extensively in factories that even charity schools were not available to them. For such children, after 1780, there were the Sunday Schools, which again were partly religious and partly concerned to inculcate the elements of literacy and numeracy.

The Dissenting Academies were started by the large minority of the English ▷ Puritans, who came to be called ▷ Dissenters or Nonconformists in the 18th century, because they 'dissented from', or refused to conform with, the Articles of Anglican belief, and were thus excluded both from the universities and from most of the grammar and public schools. The Academies were often of high quality, since it was natural to the earnestness of the Dissenting mind to take education with deep seriousness. Since the Dissenters were particularly strong among the commercial classes, the tendency of their education was more scientific and technical than that of the public schools and the universities, and capable of developing major scientists such as

the chemist ▷ Joseph Priestley, who attended the Daventry Academy.

The distinction of the Dissenting Academies was the more noticeable because the universities were in a state of decadence. The historian ▷ Gibbon describes in his autobiography the complete indifference of the Oxford authorities to whether he was present or absent as a student, although they awoke into indignation and expelled him when he underwent his temporary conversion to Catholicism. Both universities developed fine schools of mathematics in the 17th century, and Cambridge produced the most distinguished scientist of the age in ▷ Isaac Newton (1642–1727), but the intellectual complacency which was characteristic of the weaker side of 18th-century civilization reduced them to apathy as teaching centres. The young men of fashion who attended them often learned more from the Grand Tour of Europe which they made after, or sometimes instead of, their university careers, in the company of a tutor.

Egerton, Sarah Fyge
▷ Sarah Fyge.

18th-century literature
In the 18th-century many of the seeds planted in the 17th century (▷ 17th-century literature) by writers such as ▷ Dryden and ▷ Locke came to fruition. It is often referred to as the Age of ▷ Enlightenment or of Reason (▷ Rationalism), because of the philosophical preoccupation with the rational faculties. Religious faith was no longer enough, it had to be buttressed, and could indeed be undermined, by the workings of the intellect. ▷ Berkeley, building on the arguments of Locke and ▷ Descartes, argued that the mind actually defined reality. In science ▷ Newton explained the state of ▷ nature by means of mathematical models, not Biblical exegesis, although God was not excluded from his universe, and his work was seen as providing a rational ground for belief. In addition, the brilliance of his own mind seemed to contemporaries to symbolize the capabilities of the human intellect. Poets and prose writers, including ▷ Mandeville, ▷ Pope and later, ▷ Johnson, implied the supremacy of ▷ reason, as much in their measured tones and ordered lines as in the views they expressed, although all three were men of strong personal passions. Mandeville delighted in the offence given by his iconoclastic theories of human nature and society, while Pope's verse, when directed against his enemies, used the balanced ▷ couplet form to disguise potent and sometimes vicious animosity. Johnson's emotional swings are faithfully documented by ▷ Boswell. However, ▷ Hutcheson and ▷ Hume moved away from the theoretical preoccupation with reason, being more concerned with innate perception and feelings, as part of the century's growing concern with ▷ sensibility. Hume indeed argued famously that 'reason is, and ought only to be, the slave of the passions'. In the drama, ▷ Farquhar and ▷ Centlivre continued the tradition of the ▷ Restoration period, but with a less harsh perspective, which softened further as it was

influenced by ▷ sentiment or sensibility. ▷ Colley Cibber, ▷ Steele, ▷ Garrick, ▷ Cumberland and ▷ Inchbald are important dramatists in this tradition, and themes of virtue and repentance are common in their plays.

The 18th century saw a vast increase in Britain's overseas trade, fostering rapid growth of the middle classes. Political conflict between the Tories, representing the traditional landed gentry, and the Whigs (▷ Whig and Tory), more often associated with mercantile interests, played as growing apart in literature as in public life. The Whigs, politically dominant for much of the century, were supported by leading literary figures such as ▷ Addison, Steele and Centlivre, while others, including ▷ Bolingbroke, Pope, ▷ Swift and ▷ Manley, remained Tory. The century saw the development of the periodical and periodical essay (▷ reviews and periodicals) as vehicles for political polemic, but also for observations about contemporary life, morals and fashions. Addison and Steele began ▷ *The Tatler* in 1709, followed by ▷ *The Spectator* (1711–12), and *The Guardian* (1713). Swift published the rival ▷ *The Examiner*, later taken over by Manley. ▷ Haywood's ▷ *The Female Spectator*, in imitation of *The Spectator*, is an early example of the growing wave of women's periodicals and magazines.

Other forms of popular literature also flourished. The novel is one of the most important developments of the 18th century. ▷ Behn ▷ Congreve and Manley had led the way, ▷ Defoe, Haywood, ▷ Fielding, and ▷ Richardson followed, succeeded in turn by ▷ Smollett, ▷ Sterne, ▷ Burney and ▷ Edgeworth right up to ▷ o ▷ Austen; these are only the best remembered of hundreds of novelists, men and women. The novel was a genre particularly favoured by women writers, as a vehicle to express freely their own experience. Women delighted especially in the new form of the ▷ Gothic novel, although the first work of this type, ▷ *The Castle of Otranto*, is by a man, ▷ Horace Walpole. ▷ Anne Radcliffe, ▷ Clara Reeve and ▷ Mary Wollstonecraft were among numerous others at this time who experimented with the genre, though it was Mary Shelley, a generation later, who made it most famous.

Poetry underwent changes parallel with those in other literary genres. Early in the period a few poets. particularly women, such as ▷ Lady Mary Chudleigh and ▷ Anne Finch, had expressed personal passions in their work. During the course of the century, such subjective expressions of feeling or emotion became natural and integral, rather than incidental or suppressed, to a much wider range of poetry. Moreover the emotion itself was of a different variety. The dominant emotion in ▷ satire, favoured by ▷ Gay, ▷ Swift and Pope, for example, is anger. But now emotions such as sympathy and nostalgia became important, together with changing attitudes to ▷ nature, foreshadowing those of the ▷ Romantic period. This meant not only the physical environment, but human nature as well. Both were sentimentalized (▷ sentimental), as in the novel and the drama. An important theme, assisted by the spread of ▷ enclosures, is a eulogy

for traditional forms of agriculture, and the labourers and scenery associated with it, as in some of the ▷ pastoral poetry of ▷ Thomson, ▷ Goldsmith and ▷ Crabbe. The feeling for unfettered nature also resulted in a cult of admiration of nature's wild and ▷ picturesque aspects, together with a certain philosophical gloom, as in Thomson's ▷ *The Seasons* and Gray's ▷ *Elegy in a Country Churchyard*

Toward the end of the century the ▷ American War of Independence and the ▷ French Revolution made a tremendous impact on writers in England. ▷ Thomas Paine anticipated and sustained the former, with his influential pamphlets, and he celebrated the latter. Even ▷ Burke had sympathy with the American Revolution The poets ▷ Coleridge, ▷ Blake and, at first, ▷ Wordsworth supported Paine, and rejoiced in the humanistic ideals implied by the French Revolution in particular. But its growing savagery alarmed Coleridge and alienated Wordsworth, leading him towards orthodoxy in later life, while Burke's later writings crystallised his reaction. The next generation of poets, including ▷ Byron, Keats, and Shelley found other causes to support, in the growing restlessness of subject nations in Europe, while Wordsworth turned his attentions to the marginalized poor of his own nation. But the Romantic movement is also, to a degree, a retreat into even further subjectivity. At the end of the century, the cause of ▷ feminism, fostered by the Revolutions, was revitalized by the cogent arguments of ▷ Mary Wollstonecraft. At the same time her husband, the philosopher William Godwin (1756–1836), offered a fresh appeal to reason.

Elegy

An elegy is usually taken to be a poetic lament for one who has died, or at least a grave and reflective poem. In ancient Greek and Latin literature, however, an elegy was a poem written in a particular ▷ metre (line of six dactylic feet alternating with lines of five feet) and it had no necessary connection with death or gravity; the Latin poet ▷ Ovid used it for love poetry. Following his example, John Donne wrote a series of elegies with amorous or satirical themes. Most of the famous elegies in English, however, follow the narrower and more widely accepted definition: ▷ Milton's *Lycidas* was inspired by the death of his friend Edward King; Shelley's *Adonais* laments that of the poet Keats; ▷ Gray's ▷ *Elegy Written in a Country Churchyard* is a meditation on life and death. All of these are in the ▷ pastoral convention; the first two imitate *The Lament for Bion* by Moschus, a Greek poet of the 3rd century BC, while the third is a variant of it.

Elegy Written in a Country Churchyard (1751)

A poem by ▷ Thomas Gray, in iambic pentameter quatrains, rhyming *abab* (▷ metre). Its quiet subtlety of tone raises the platitudes of conventional graveyard musing to a unique intensity, and several of its eloquent generalizations and phrases have become proverbial: 'Some mute inglorious Milton', 'the madding crowd's ignoble strife', 'Melancholy mark'd him for her own', 'Full many a flower is born to blush unseen, And waste its sweetness on the desert air.'

▷ Samuel Johnson, though contemptuous of Gray's more inspirational experiments such as the Pindaric odes, had high praise for this poem: 'The *Churchyard* abounds with images which find a mirror in every mind and with sentiments to which every bosom returns an echo.'

▷ Elegy; Sensibility.

Elements, The (Four)

The 'four elements' are the ancient Greek and medieval conception of the basic components of matter; they are air, fire, earth and water. It was a division made by Empedocles of Sicily and adopted by ▷ Aristotle. Aristotle was writing before the beginnings of chemical analysis and considered matter in regard to the 'properties' or qualities that he believed all things to possess; these he found to be 'hotness', 'coldness', 'wetness' and 'dryness'. His four elements contained these properties in different combinations: air = hot and wet; fire = hot and dry; earth = cold and dry; water = cold and wet. These, therefore, were the basic constituents of nature. Aristotle's great prestige in the ▷ Middle Ages caused his theory to dominate the thought of the time. The medieval alchemists, forbears of the modern analytical chemist, noticed that the properties of various kinds of matter change, *eg* iron becomes rust, and they deduced from Aristotle's theory that materials could be changed, provided that they retained the same basic properties, *eg* lead could be changed into gold. The theory dominated European thought until the 17th century, when the English 'natural philosopher' and chemist Robert Boyle (1627-91) taught that an element is to be regarded as a substance in itself and not as a substance with certain basic properties. Since Boyle, chemists have discovered that elements are very much more numerous than the original four, and that air, fire, earth and water are not in fact elements at all. Nonetheless, the pervasiveness of these so-called 'four elements' in our environment has caused them to keep their hold on the modern imagination when it is not engaged in scientific thinking, so that they are still employed as symbols for the basic constituents of our experience of the world in some imaginative literature.

The theory of the 'four elements' was connected in classical and medieval times with the medical and psychological theory of the 'humours', or four basic liquid constituents of the body. The blood humour ('hot and wet') is linked to air; choler ('hot and dry') associated with fire; phlegm ('cold and wet') corresponds to water and melancholy ('cold and dry') to earth. The preponderance of one or other of these humours in the make-up of a person's character was supposed to determine the temperament.

▷ Humour.

Eloisa to Abelard (1717)

An Ovidian monologue in heroic couplets by ▷ Alexander Pope, based on the tragic love affair between the medieval philosopher ▷ Abelard (1079-1142) and Heloise (Eloisa) the daughter of a canon at Notre Dame Cathedral. Eloisa's family, disapproving of the affair, had Abelard castrated, and she became a nun. Their later correspondence on theological and philosophical issues is famous. In Pope's poem Eloisa writes from her convent, expressing her unabated longing, with a mixture of 'romantick' melancholy and theatrical rhetoric. The poem's combination of spirituality and eroticism illustrates the emotional, ▷ Catholic side of Pope's temperament.

Elstob, Elizabeth (1683-1756)

Anglo-Saxon scholar and translator, Elstob was born in Newcastle-upon-Tyne, and by 1691 both her parents were dead. Although her guardian opposed women's education, Elstob published *An English Anglo-Saxon Homily, on the birth-day of St Gregory* (1709), having gone to Oxford with her brother. She may have established a day school. She regarded herself as the first woman to study Anglo-Saxon, and in the preface to the *Homily* she justified women's learning: 'it will be said, What has a Woman to do with Learning? This I have known urged by some Men, with an Envy unbecoming that greatness of Soul, which is said to dignify their Sex. For if Women may be said to have Souls, and their Souls are their better part and that what is best deserves our greatest Care for its Improvement. We must retort the Question. Where is the fault in Womens seeking after Learning?' She also published *The Rudiments of Grammar for the Anglo-Saxon Tongue, first given in English with an apology for the study of northern antiquities* (1715).

Bib: Ferguson, M., *First Feminists*.

Enclosures, Enclosure Acts

The term 'enclosure' describes the partitioning and appropriation by individuals of land that was previously either open (▷ open field system) and farmed by communities, or uncultivated and available to anyone for gathering wood or fruit, or grazing animals. Enclosure entailed erecting physical barriers – hedges or fences – to separate land from its surroundings and transferring the responsibility for drainage and other matters onto individual caretakers. It could be done by mutual 'agreement' among owners of private land – 'sensibly dividing the country among opulent men,' as ▷ Adam Smith wrote – or by Act of Parliament, the latter especially when large tracts of land were involved. However, sometimes wealthy people simply enclosed or sold off common land, without any negotiation or legislation at all. The process resulted in a concentration of ownership in far fewer hands than before. It led to increased crop yields, healthier and fatter livestock, and greater wealth for large-scale owners. But it also increased poverty among the dispossessed who were unable to afford the new arrangements, such as the smaller landowners, tenant farmers and agricultural labourers. They had always led a precarious existence, exercising their ancient cultivation, grazing and gathering rights on what had been common land. Many were deprived of their rights and all their property, often being driven off the land altogether. Their plight contributed to rural poverty

(▷ Poor Laws), and also to the rapid growth of towns, especially London, as people flocked to them in search of work. Although enclosure is usually associated with the middle and late 18th century, it began as early as the 15th, though not on the same scale. The first part of Thomas More's *Utopia* (1516) is a stinging attack on enclosures, and their effects on poorer farmers and farmworkers. Some of his descriptions of people unable to find employment, falling into crime and ending up in prison or even hanged for theft, could as well apply to the 17th and 18th centuries.

After the ▷ Civil War, and especially after the ▷ Glorious Revolution of 1688, estates began to grow larger, aided by careful purchases of land and strategic marriages. The practice of marrying oneself or one's children for money, or to add a title and perhaps an estate to a fortune, forms the stuff of much ▷ Restoration and 18th-century comic drama and novel writing. ▷ Wycherley's ▷ *The Country Wife* (1675), ▷ Etherege's ▷ *The Man of Mode* (1676), ▷ Behn's ▷ *The City Heiress* (1682) and ▷ *The Lucky Chance* (1687), and ▷ Richardson's ▷ *Clarissa* are just some of the numerous works that deal with these subjects, with variations and sometimes ambiguities as to the precise social classes and backgrounds of the protagonists. Some families acquired enormous wealth and huge estates: a new class of ultra-rich landowners emerge whose main concern was to increase their farm yields and profits even further. Enclosures offered a way. By 1700 about half the cultivatable land had been enclosed, but there still remained a broad stretch of unenclosed land, including parts of East Anglia and much of the Midlands. A series of Acts was passed, accelerating the process of enclosure especially in the second half of the 18th century. From 1760 to 1799 enclosures brought between two and three million acres of land into cultivation.

The resulting increase in surplus wealth created a leisure class and the development of aesthetic ▷ taste, as a stimulus to consumption. But escalating rural poverty encouraged a new kind of poetry, such as ▷ Goldsmith's ▷ *The Deserted Village* and ▷ Crabbe's *The Village* (▷ village, English), protesting against the sufferings of the rural poor and recalling happier times. This social change was a factor in the growth of ▷ Radicalism and the ▷ Romantic movement.

Bib: Plumb, J. H., *England in the Eighteenth Century*; Williams, R., *The Country and the City*; Porter, R., *English Society in the Eighteenth Century*; Sharpe, J. A., *Early Modern England 1550–1760*.

Encyclopédie, L'

An encyclopaedia published in 28 volumes between 1751 and 1772, under the editorship of ▷ Diderot (1713–84) and (until 1758) the mathematician D'Alembert (1717–83). Its contributors included ▷ Voltaire, ▷ Rousseau, ▷ Montesquieu, Buffon (1707–88) and Turgot (1727–81). The work originated in a translation of the English *Cyclopaedia, or the Universal Dictionary of Arts and Sciences* (1728) of Ephraim Chambers (d 1740), but the French version was intellectually more ambitious and more

impressive. It was guided by a trust in reason and rationalistic explanation, and the desire to destroy superstition and the beliefs thought to arise from it. The works fierce attacks on Church and State proved potent criticism of the ▷ Ancien Regime (it was suppressed at various stages of its composition) and heralded the overthrow of the monarchy in the ▷ French Revolution. It reinforced European rationalism and in England influenced ▷ Jeremy Bentham and through him the 19th-century Utilitarians (▷ Utilitarianism).

End-rhyme

Rhyme occurring in the usual position, *ie* at the end of a line; internal rhymes occur in the middle of a line, and head-rhymes are the correspondence of the beginnings of words, *ie* alliteration.

End-stopped lines

Lines of verse, especially ▷ blank verse, which end at the end of a sentence or at strongly marked pauses within the sentence. The opposite effect is produced by run-on lines, when the syntax makes the voice go on to the next line without pause.
▷ Enjambment.

English language

Historically, the language is categorized into three periods: ▷ Old English, extending to the 12th century; Middle English, from the 12th to the 16th centuries; and Modern English.

Old English consisted of Anglo-Saxon and Jutish dialects, and was called English because the language of the Angles was the earliest discoverable in writing. Old English was strongly modified by Scandinavian elements in consequence of the Danish invasions, and Middle English by an extensive infusion of French vocabulary.

Middle English was divided into a variety of dialects; Langland, for instance, the author of *Piers Plowman*, wrote in the West Midland dialect; the author or authors of *Sir Gawain and the Green Knight* and *Pearl* wrote in a dialect from farther north, and Chaucer in the East Midland dialect. Because London was the chief city of England and the seat of the royal court, and because Caxton established his printing press there in the 15th century, East Midland became the forebear of Modern English. Since the 15th century English has not undergone important structural changes; social differences of speech as between the classes have been of greater importance, at least for literary purposes, than regional ones.

Exceptions to this statement have to be made, however, for the form of English spoken and written in southern Scotland, and for those regions of the British Isles where until comparatively recent times Celtic languages were predominant: north-west Scotland, Wales and Ireland. In Ireland especially, a variety of spoken language known as Hiberno-English tends to follow the substratum of Irish Gaelic (▷ Irish literature in English). In different ways Southern Scots is also important; it is a highly codified variety of non-standard English and has been unusual in that it has enjoyed a long-established written form (▷ Scottish literature). The literature in Scots (known in the Middle Ages as Inglis and today sometimes as Lallans, *ie* Lowlands) is considerable, whether one thinks of the late medieval poets, such as Dunbar, Douglas and Henryson, an 18th-century poet such as ▷ Burns, or a 20th-century one like Hugh MacDiarmid. However, from the 17th century eminent Scottish writers took to writing in standard English, and this became universal amongst prose writers of the 18th century (▷ Hume, Robertson, ▷ Adam Smith).

'The Queen's English' is the term used for the language spoken by the educated classes in England; linguists, however, prefer the term 'Standard English'. The pronunciation most in use among educated people is known as 'Received Pronunciation'.

English vocabulary is basically Germanic, but it also contains a very large number of Latin words: French, of course, developed from Latin, and many of these Latin words entered English in their French form after the Norman Conquest in the 11th century. For about two and a half centuries the upper classes were French-speaking. Vestiges of this social difference survive in such distinctions as the word 'sheep' used for the live animal, and 'mutton' for the same animal when it is eaten at table; the English shepherds who cared for the sheep ate very little meat, whereas their Norman-French masters were chiefly concerned with the animal when it had been transformed into food. Even after the aristocracy became English-speaking in the 14th century, the adoption of French words continued to be frequent owing to the strong influence of French culture and ways of life on the English educated classes. Latin words, however, have also entered English independently of their French forms; the 'clerks', *ie* the literate class of the earlier Middle Ages, used Latin as a living language in their writings; they were churchmen, and Latin was the language of the Church all over Western Europe. In the 16th century, there was a new and different kind of influx from Latin owing to the fresh interest taken by scholars in ancient Latin culture.

The Latin contribution to the basically Germanic English vocabulary has resulted in a large number of Latin and Germanic synonyms, with important consequences for subtleties of English expression. The associations of Latin with the medieval Church and with ancient Roman literature cause the words of Latin origin to have suggestions of grandeur which the words of Germanic origin do not possess; thus we use 'serpent' in connection with religious and mythological ideas, *eg* the story of the Garden of Eden, but 'snake' will do in reference to the ordinary reptile. On the other hand, the Latinate word is emotionally less intimate than its Germanic synonym; when we wish to lessen the painfulness of death, we say that a man is 'deceased', instead of saying that he has 'died'. This kind of differentiation clearly carries important pragmatic consequences, yielding differences in tone and register. Thus, socially, it is often considered vulgar to use the synonym of French or Latin construction, as suggesting a disposition to speak stylishly rather than truly; many

people consider it vulgar to use the French 'serviette' instead of the older 'napkin', the latter is also of French origin, but is more fully anglicized.

Some English writers, *eg* ▷ Milton and ▷ Samuel Johnson, and some periods of literature, especially the 18th century, are often singled out for their preference for the Latin part of the vocabulary, and in the 19th century the preference was sometimes regarded as a fault. Correspondingly, some literature is admired for its reliance on mainly Germanic vocabulary, *eg* the ▷ ballads, and the poems of John Clare, and Christina Rossetti, but in this kind of judgement Latin and French words adopted long ago and grown fully familiar are allowed to have the same merit as words of Germanic descent. Language which shows sensitiveness to the value of contrasting Latinate and Germanic vocabulary is always allowed peculiar merit; such is the case with ▷ Shakespeare.

English has borrowed words from many other languages; the chief of these is ancient Greek which contributed extensively during the 16th century ▷ Renaissance, and coloured the language similarly to the Latin contribution at the same time. Borrowings from other languages are more miscellaneous and less distinctive; the most distinctive are the modern borrowings from colloquial American diction.

Bib: Baugh, A. C., *A History of the English Language*; Carter, R. (ed.), *Language and Literature: An Introductory Reader in Stylistics*; Fowler, R., *Linguistic Criticism*; Carter, R. and Simpson, D. (eds.), *Language, Discourse and Literature: An Introductory Reader in Discourse Stylistics*.

Enjambment

A term describing the continuing of the sense from line to line in a poem, to the extent that it is unnatural in speaking the verse to make a pause at the line ending. The effect is that of 'run-on' lines.
▷ End-stopped lines.

Enlightenment

The term was originally borrowed into English in the 1860s from German (*Aufklärung*), to designate the spirit and aims of the French philosophers of the 18th century, such as ▷ Diderot and ▷ Voltaire. But as historical perspectives have changed the word has come to be used in a much wider sense, to denote the whole period following the ▷ Renaissance, during which scepticism and scientific rationalism came to dominate European thinking. Enlightenment grew out of Renaissance at different times in different countries. In Britain, the empiricism of ▷ Francis Bacon (1561–1626) and the secular pragmatism of ▷ Thomas Hobbes (1588–1679) mark its early stages. Its golden age began however with ▷ John Locke (1632–1704) in philosophy, and ▷ Sir Isaac Newton (1642–1727) in science, and it reached its height in the first half of the 18th century. Locke argued that 'Reason must be our last judge and guide in everything', and rejected medieval philosophy as superstition. Newton's theory of gravitation seemed to explain the mysteries of the solar system. The fact that Newton had also worked on optics was ingeniously alluded to in ▷ Alexander

Pope's couplet: 'Nature, and Nature's Laws lay hid in Night. God said, *Let Newton be*! and All was *Light*'.

The onset of Enlightenment in Britain coincided with the bourgeois revolution and many of its values reflect the optimistic temper of the newly dominant class, as much as any abstract philosophical system. In contrast to the previous ideology of static hierarchy, appropriate to a landowning aristocracy and its peasant underclass, the new ideology of merchants and professional men placed its emphasis on understanding and dominating the environment. God lost his numinousness, becoming a kind of divine mathematician, and the ▷ Deist thinkers of the time rejected the dogmas of the scriptures in favour of 'natural religion' based on an understanding of God's laws through science. Pope expresses this idea in classic form in his ▷ *Essay on Man* (1733–4), cleverly blending it with the older hierarchical idea of the Great Chain of Being. Pope's *Essay* stands as a compendium of popular Enlightenment ideas, expressing the expansive confidence of the middle class that 'Whatever *is*, is *right*.' It was easy for the middle-class reader of the day to feel that British philosophy, science, trade and imperialism were all working together to advance civilization throughout the world. It is a myth projected in many of the works of Pope, ▷ James Thomson and other writers of the time.

As the 18th century developed, the bourgeoisie's confidence in its progressive destiny faltered, reaching a crisis after the ▷ French Revolution in what we now call the ▷ Romantic movement. ▷ William Blake attempted to restore the pre-Enlightenment numinousness of God and nature, rejecting Newton's 'particles of light', and the idea of inert matter or empty space. Imagination, not science, was for him the key to nature: 'Every thing possible to be believ'd is an image of truth.' Percy Bysshe Shelley, using politically resonant imagery, asserted that 'man, having enslaved the elements, remains himself a slave' and warned of the dangers of 'an unmitigated exercise of the calculating faculty' (one of the characteristic institutions of the Enlightenment period was, of course, the slave trade). Even the fundamentally materialist John Keats complained about the prosaic nature of Enlightenment philosophy:

> There was an awful rainbow once in heaven:
> We know her woof, her texture; she is given
> In the dull catalogue of common things.
> Philosophy will clip an Angel's wings.
>
> (*Lamia*, 231–4)

More recently 'Enlightenment' has been given a yet wider historical application by the German philosophers Theodor Adorno and Max Horkheimer, whose book, *Dialectic of Enlightenment* (1944) sees the manipulative, calculating spirit of Enlightenment as the identifying characteristic of western civilization. They trace its manifestations from Odysseus's tricking of the primitive bumpkin Polyphemus, to the treatment of people as means rather than ends which characterizes both modern totalitarian politics and consumer capitalism. Recent ecological movements, which advocate a respect for nature, rather than an exploitation of it, continue the same dialectic.
▷ Augustanism.

Bib: Willey, B., *The Eighteenth-Century Background*; Redwood, J., *Reason, Ridicule and Religion: The Age of Enlightenment in England*.

Ephelia

The name used by a late 17th-century poet writing in English, whose identification is made all the more difficult by the fact that it is a name frequently used by other writers, or as the name of the recipient of a poem. How much weight we give to the internal evidence of poems – such as the poems to 'Strephon' – depends on how literally we imagine these poems can be related to a 'life'. The guesses at the identity of this author have included ▷ Katherine Philips's daughter, Elizabeth Mordaunt.

Publications attributed to this name include: *Panegyric to the King* (1678); *Female Poems on Several Occasions* (1679), and *Advice to His Grace* (1681/2).
Bib: Greer, G. *et al.*, *Kissing the Rod*.

Epic

1 A narrative of heroic actions, often with a principal hero, usually mythical in its content, offering inspiration and ennoblement within a particular cultural or national tradition.

2 The word denotes qualities of heroism and grandeur, appropriate to epic but present in other literary or even non-literary forms.

Epics occur in almost all national cultures, and commonly give an account of national origins, or enshrine ancient, heroic myths central to the culture. For European culture at large, much the most influential epics are the ▷ *Iliad* and the ▷ *Odyssey* of ▷ Homer and the ▷ *Aeneid* by ▷ Virgil. C. S. Lewis in *Preface to Paradise Lost* makes a helpful distinction between primary and secondary epics: primary ones, such as Homer's, are composed for a society which is still fairly close to the conditions of society described in the narrative; secondary epics are based on the pattern of primary epics but written for a materially developed society more or less remote from the conditions described, *eg* Virgil's *Aeneid*. In English literature the Old English *Beowulf* may be counted as a primary epic. A number of attempts at secondary epic have been made since the 16th century, but ▷ John Milton's ▷ *Paradise Lost* is unique in its acknowledged greatness and its closeness to the Virgilian structure. ▷ Spenser's *The Faerie Queene* has many epic characteristics, but, in spite of the important classical influences upon it, the poem's structure is derived from the 'romantic epic' of the 16th-century Italian poets, Ariosto and Tasso; moreover, though allegory often plays a part in epics, the allegorical elements in *The Faerie Queene* are so pervasive as to present a different kind of imaginative vision from that normally found in them.

Many other works in English literature have epic qualities without being definable as epics. For example, ▷ Fielding described ▷ *Tom Jones* as a comic epic, and it is this as much as it is a novel: a series of adventures of which Tom is the hero, but of which the consequences are loss of dignity rather than enhancement of dignity.

Epic simile

Prolonged similes, commonly used in ▷ epic or ▷ heroic poetry, giving the subject described a spaciousness suited to its grandeur. Thus in ▷ *Paradise Lost* Bk. I, ▷ Milton wants to say that the fallen Satan is as big as a whale; this would be to use an ordinary simile. He expands it to an epic simile thus:

> *As huge as ...*
> *... that Sea-beast*
> *Leviathan, which God of all his works*
> *Created hugest that swim th'Ocean stream:*
> *Him haply slumbring on the Norway foam*
> *The Pilot of some small night-founder'd Skiff,*
> *Deeming some Island, oft, as Sea-men tell,*
> *With fixed Anchor in his skaly rind*
> *Moors by his side under the Lee, while Night*
> *Invests the Sea, and wished Morn delays:*
>
> *So stretcht out huge in length the Arch-fiend*
> *lay ...*

Epicurus (342–270 BC)

Greek philosopher and founder of the Epicurean school of philosophers. He is best known for his principle that pleasure is the beginning and end of the blessed life. This has commonly been misunderstood to mean that the purpose of life is to seek pleasure; in fact Epicurus meant by pleasure the acquisition of a mind at peace, and this implied for him the pursuit of virtue and hence a life of asceticism rather than excess. His best-known disciple is the Latin poet ▷ Lucretius, who expounded the philosophy in his poem *De Rerum Natura (Concerning the Nature of Things)*. The Epicureans were rivals of the Stoics, who taught that the end of life was fortitude and liberation from the passions.

Epigram

For the ancient Greeks the word meant 'inscription'. From this, the meaning extended to include very short poems notable for the terseness and elegance of their expression and the weight and wit of their meaning. The richest of the ancient Greek collections is the *Greek Anthology*; the greatest Latin masters were ▷ Catullus and Martial. Ben Jonson's *Underwoods* contains epigrams in that tradition. After him, epigrams became shorter and most commonly had satirical content; ▷ Pope was the greatest master of this style, and his poems include many epigrams.
▷ Aphorism.

Epistolary novel

A novel in which the story is told through letters written by the characters: thus the action is seen from multiple points of view, rather than through the eyes of an omnipotent narrator or narrator/*persona*. The tradition of narratives structured in letters has both sacred and secular antecedents, in the biblical Epistles of St Paul and the medieval cycle of letters between Heloise and ▷ Abelard.

An early example of the epistolary novel in English in ▷ Aphra Behn's *Love Letters Between a Nobleman and His Sister* (1684–7); ▷ Richardson further popularized the form in ▷ *Clarissa* and ▷ *Pamela*, as did ▷ Smollett in ▷ *Humphrey Clinker*, and Harriet Lee in *Errors of Innocence* (1786). ▷ Rousseau's *La Nouvelle Helöise* (1761) and Laclos' *Les Liaisons Dangereuses* (1782), French versions of the epistolary novel, were also well known in Britain. The genre, though supplanted by narrative novels during the 18th century, survived as a minority form well into the 19th century, and there are occasional examples of it even in recent times.

Epitaph

An inscription on a tomb, or a short verse or prose inscription that might serve such a purpose. As literary compositions, epitaphs became popular in the ▷ Renaissance, and the requirement of brevity gives epitaphs a resemblance to ▷ epigrams. The 18th century, the great age of the epigram, was also that in which the epitaph was most cultivated.

Essay

'Essay' derives from the French *essai*, meaning 'experiment', 'attempt'. As a literary term it is used to cover an enormous range of composition, from schoolboy exercises to thorough scientific and philosophical works, the only quality in common being the implied desire of the writer to reserve to himself some freedom of treatment. But the essay is also a recognized literary form in a more defined sense: it is understood to be a fairly short prose composition, in style often familiarly conversational and in subject either selfrevelatory or illustrative (more or less humorously) of social manners and types. The originator of the form was the great French writer ▷ Montaigne.

Montaigne's essays were published in completed form in 1595, and translated into English by John Florio (1603). His starting-point is '*Que sais-je?*' ('What do I know?') and it leads him into a serious inquiry into his own nature as he feels it, and into investigations of facts, ideas and experiences as he responds to them. In 1597 the first great English essayist, ▷ Francis Bacon, published his first collection of essays, of a very different kind: they are impersonal and aphoristic, weightily sententious. The character writers ▷ Sir Thomas Overbury and John Earle (?1601–65) use the classical model of the Greek writer Theophrastus, reminding one that with so indefinite a form it is impossible to be too precise about the dating of starting-points. ▷ Abraham Cowley published the first essays in English closely corresponding to what is now understood by the form, and perhaps shows the first sign of its degeneracy: easiness of tone, which in Montaigne is a graciousness of manner introducing a serious and interesting personality, but which in less interesting writers may be an agreeable cover for saying nothing in particular.

In the early years of the 18th century ▷ Addison and ▷ Steele firmly established what is now known as the 'periodical essay' – a kind of higher journalism, intended often to please rather than instruct, but in their case to instruct through pleasure. In creations such as ▷ Sir Roger de Coverley, they developed the Theophrastian character into a personal, idiosyncratic portrait anticipating the characterization of the novelists a little later in the century. Their graciousness and lightness of tone take point and interest from their serious and conscious social purpose. ▷ Dr Johnson in *The Rambler* and in his essays as ▷ 'The Idler' used the weighty, impressive style soon to be regarded as unsuitable for the medium. ▷ Oliver Goldsmith in *The Citizen of the World* (1762) perfected the graceful, witty manner which came to be considered ideal for it.

▷ Characters, Theophrastian.

Essay Concerning Human Understanding (1690)

A philosophical treatise by ▷ John Locke. Locke emphasizes reason as the dominant faculty of man. All knowledge is acquired through experience based on sense impressions; there are no 'innate ideas', *ie* no knowledge arises in the mind independently of impressions received from the outside world. These impressions divide into primary qualities, *ie* those that are measurable such as size, number, form, etc., and secondary ones, such as colour, sound and scent, which are not demonstrably part of the object, but dependent on the observer. Knowledge begins with perception of agreement or disagreement in the qualities observed in the objects or, as Locke calls them, 'ideas'. He distinguishes between rational judgement, which identifies and analyses ideas, and 'wit', which relates them by their resemblances; the distinction is practically one between reason and imagination and gives advantage to reason. Faith, *eg* in religious doctrine, is not distinct from reason, but the assent of the mind to a belief that accords with reason. Thus Locke appeals to clear definition in language and expression; he depreciates the intuitive and imaginative faculties of the mind and elevates the rational ones. His thesis accords with the reaction at the end of the 17th century against the intolerance and fanaticism of the religious conflicts which had prevailed during the first half of it. The influence of his philosophy is impressed on the imaginative prose literature of the first 30 years of the 18th century, for instance in the realism of ▷ Daniel Defoe. Later in the century, the novelist ▷ Laurence Sterne made ingenious use of Locke's theory of the association of ideas in ▷ *Tristram Shandy*.

Essay on Criticism (1711)

Written when he was only 21 and published when he was 23, ▷ Alexander Pope's compendium of neo-classical poetic theory in ▷ heroic couplets was highly praised by ▷ Joseph Addison, and helped to make his reputation. Pope defends the poetic art by arguing, in the tradition of ▷ Aristotle, ▷ Horace, and more recently ▷ Boileau, that 'true wit' is merely an 'imitation' of nature, and is not startling and original like the 'false wit' of the discredited 17th-century ▷ Metaphysical Poets. '*True wit is Nature* to Advantage drest, What oft was *Thought*, but ne'er so well *Exprest*'. Moreover nature has already been perfectly understood by the revered ancient Greek and Latin poets, and the modern poet need not go to the trouble of copying direct from it since: 'To copy *Nature* is to copy *Them*'. Exception is however made for those of great genius who '*rise to Faults* true Criticks *dare not mend*; . . . And *snatch a Grace* beyond the Reach of Art'.

The aphoristic quality of some lines in the poem seems to bear out Pope's ideas on true wit: 'To Err is *Human*; to Forgive, *Divine*'; 'For *Fools* rush in where *Angels* fear to tread'. However, the best poetry in the *Essay* is as idiosyncratic and figuratively adventurous as anything in the Metaphysical Poets of the previous century, as for example the description of the blockheads, too dull to perceive that they are being satirized: 'Still humming on, their drowzy Course they keep, And *lash'd* so long, like *Tops*, are lash'd *asleep*' (600–1) or the deliberately bad lines, imitating various vices of versification: 'And ten low Words oft creep in one dull Line' (347). Despite its parade of sober respectability Pope's *Essay* is best seen as the protective camouflage of a brilliant poet adapting to the prosaic temper of the times, rather than a seriously pondered theoretical system. It is however important as a summary of neo-classical and Augustan maxims.

▷ Augustanism.

Essay on Man (1733–4)

After the scurrilities of ▷ *The Dunciad* (1728) ▷ Alexander Pope turned to the philosophical poem which he hoped would crown his poetic career. The *Essay* was published anonymously so as to wrong-foot his enemies, who were not sure whether to damn it as Pope's, or to praise it as superior to anything Pope could have achieved. In four heroic-couplet epistles, addressed to the Tory politician ▷ Lord Bolingbroke, the poet attempts with cheerful optimism to 'vindicate the ways of God to Man', arguing that 'Whatever *is*, is *right*'. Pope expounds the medieval and ▷ Renaissance concept of a 'chain of being', with its primitive blend of theology and natural philosophy, and reconciles it uneasily with the modern empirical science of ▷ Sir Isaac Newton. The work became a kind of handbook of popular ▷ Enlightenment notions throughout Europe and was extensively translated.

It expresses the ▷ Deist view that God can be apprehended through nature, and not only through 'revealed' scriptures. 'Lo! the poor Indian, whose untutor'd mind/Sees God in clouds, or hears him in the wind'. The 'natural religion' of the poem, influenced by Bolingbroke, and by the Whig philosopher, the third ▷ Earl of Shaftesbury, incurred a magisterial rebuke from the Swiss professor of divinity Jean Paul de Crousaz, and Pope, a Catholic, was embarrassed to discover that his work was potentially heretical. Today Pope's facile blend of science and religion appears spiritually trivial in comparison with both the consistent 'atheist' Deism of ▷ Rochester, and the sense of original sin of an orthodox Christian such as ▷ Jonathan Swift. The poem does however give brilliant poetic expression to a mood of enlightened confidence and *élan* which characterizes the period, even when what is being said is quite unremarkable: 'Know then thyself, presume not God to scan;/ The proper study of Mankind is Man.' And it contains some fine passages and isolated ▷ couplets: 'The spider's touch, how exquisitely fine!/ Feels at each thread, and lives along the line.'

▷ Enlightenment.

Essay to Revive the Ancient Education of Gentlewomen, An (1673)

A prospectus for a school at Tottenham, just north of London, by ▷ Bathsua Pell Makin. This prospectus is also an argument for women's education, and is an early part of the debate about the education of women in literacy, numeracy and languages (see also ▷ Catharine Macaulay, ▷ Mary Wollstonecraft, ▷ Sarah Fielding). The tract confines itself to the education of gentlewomen, never suggesting that education should spread throughout society, but it does make a significant argument for broadening the accepted curriculum for girls to place more emphasis on languages and literacy. Makin also situates her argument historically (note the word 'revive' in the title) and this serves to remind readers of a tradition of women's education before the English Civil War.

▷ Education; Women, Education of.

Essentialism

Philosophically, 'essences' are those aspects of an object that are innate to it or constitute its identity. In ▷ Aristotle they are distinguished from 'accidents', those characteristics that belong to objects, but are not definitive of them. So traditionally, 'essence', an 'ideal' or a defining concept, was said to precede 'existence', the particular physical properties that all objects have. In Christianity the division was between the pre-existent soul and the body, as it exists in time. ▷ Descartes distinguished mind and matter (the body). Mind could be inferred from intuition, but the body could be only suspected. Proof of its existence depended on a God who would not deceive us in our experience of the world. ▷ Locke, by contrast, did not subscribe to notions of innate ideas and categories. His equivalent for the notion of an essence was closer to a physicist's understanding of molecular or atomic structures, that is, composed of smaller, physical bodies. The ideas that men have of totality or similarity, causality or power derive from imaginative interpretations deriving from our sense-data, rather than from some extra-human, pre-ordained categories. The term 'essentialism', therefore, contains opposing views that have in common that they are concerned with discovering or inferring the underlying, hidden and defining structure of the world.

In ▷ materialist accounts essentialism has come to be associated with attempts to deny the primacy of history as a formative influence on human affairs and human personality. Essentialism challenges the emphasis on the autonomy of the individual as a theoretically 'free' agent who is the centre and creator of meaning. If the divisions and categories of the world are always already there where is left room for human action and decisions? To question the notion of an essence, though, was thought by some, including ▷ Berkeley, to put at risk a coherent human identity. The replacement of an essentialist view by one that emphasizes consciousness as the bearer of categories, as in the work of ▷ Kant, influenced the ▷ Romantic movement.

Etherege, Sir George (?1634–92)

Dramatist, one of those who set the style of ▷ Restoration comedy after the return to the throne of ▷ Charles II. Etherege may have studied at ▷ Cambridge University, and is believed to have spent some of his early adulthood in France. He read law at the Inns of Court. His first play, ▷ *Love in a Tub; Or, The Comical Revenge* (1664), composed partly in rhymed couplets, established him in court circles, but his next play, ▷ *She Wou'd if She Cou'd* (1668) was a relative failure. Both these plays show the influence of ▷ Molière. In 1668 Etherege was appointed secretary to the English ambassador to Constantinople. Returning to England in 1671, Etherege continued to write and his last, most famous play, ▷ *The Man of Mode* came in 1676. Some time after 1677 Etherege married a widow, Mary Arnold, it is said for her fortune. In 1685 he was appointed Ambassador at Ratisbon (Regensburg), and abandoned his wife. He had an affair with the actress ▷ Elizabeth Barry, among his many intrigues with women; Barry bore him a daughter. In 1689 he joined the deposed King ▷ James II in Paris, where he died. Known as 'Gentleman George', Etherege epitomized to many of his contemporaries the sort of hell-raising rake depicted in his plays. The part of Bellair in *The Man of Mode* is thought to be a self-portrait, while the flamboyant Dorimant is said to have been modelled on his friend, the Earl of Rochester. His comedy depends primarily on his witty and often cynical dialogue among characters in fashionable society. Several of his comic types were used by later dramatists, such as ▷ Wycherley, ▷ Behn, and ▷ Congreve, and his fluent, easy style set a precedent for many of their plays.

Bib: Rosenfeld, S., *The Letterbook of Sir George Etherege*; Underwood, D., *Etherege and the Seventeenth Century Comedy of Manners*.

Eton College

Probably the best-known of the ▷ public schools. It was founded by King Henry VI in 1440 and was associated with Henry's other foundation of King's College, ▷ Cambridge, to which the Eton boys could pass, usually between the ages of 14 and 18. The fall of Henry VI, and the Wars of the Roses that brought about his fall, caused Eton College to begin taking fee-paying boys to make up for loss of income by royal patronage; hence the majority of boys were soon not the 'poor scholars' for whom it was founded, but sons of nobility and other wealthy families. In this way Eton became associated with privilege.

Eugenia

Name used by a writer who attacked John Sprints *The Bride-Woman's Counsellor* (1699) in *The Female Advocate* (1700), arguing that, although the woman

is bound to passive obedience, yet 'I defy the meekest woman in the world, if she meets with an unreasonable, domineering, insolent creature . . . to forbear wishing it otherwise.'
▷ Chudleigh, Lady Mary
Bid: Browne, A. *The Eighteenth Century Feminist Mind.*

Euphemism
▷ Figures of speech.

Euripides (480–406 BC)
The last of the three great Athenian writers of tragedy, the other two being ▷ Aeschylus and ▷ Sophocles. Like them, Euripedes was admired by ▷ Milton, who emulated the Greeks in ▷ *Samson Agonistes.* Among Euripides's surviving plays are *Alcestis, Medea, Hippolytus, Andromache, Hecuba, Bacchae, Electra, The Trojan Women, Orestes, Heracles, Iphigenia at Aulis, Iphigenia among the Tauri, Ion.*

Evangelical Movement
A movement for ▷ Protestant revival in the Church of England in the late 18th and early 19th century. It was stimulated partly by ▷ John Wesley's ▷ Methodist revival and the activities of other sects (especially among the lower classes) outside the ▷ Church of England; it was also a reaction against the ▷ rationalism and scepticism of the 18th century aristocracy, and against the ▷ atheism of the ▷ French Revolution. Politically, the movement tended to be conservative and was therefore strong among the Tories, whereas the Whigs (especially their aristocratic leaders such as ▷ Charles James Fox) retained more of the 18th-century worldliness and scepticism (▷ Whig and Tony). In doctrine the Evangelicals were inclined to be austere, to attach importance to strength of faith and biblical guidance, and to oppose ceremony and ritual. Socially they developed a strong sense of responsibility to their fellow human beings, so that one of their leaders, ▷ William Wilberforce, devoted his life to the cause of abolishing slavery and the slave trade in British dominions, and later Lord Shaftesbury (1801–85) made it his life-work to alleviate the social and working conditions of the working classes. The leaders of the movement were laymen rather than clergy, and upper class rather than lower class, amongst whom the Nonconformist sects were more actively influential.

Eve
▷ Eden, Garden of.

Evelina (1778)
A novel in letters by ▷ Fanny Burney. Evelina has been abandoned by her aristocratic father, and her socially much humbler mother is dead. She has been brought up by her guardian, a solitary clergyman. As a beautiful, well-bred, and intelligent young girl, she pays a visit to a friend in London, where she falls in love with a handsome aristocrat, Lord Orville, is pursued by an unscrupulous rake, Sir Clement Willoughby, and is much embarrassed by vulgar relatives, especially her grandmother, Madame Duval. The convincing and delightful part of the novel consists in its acute and lively social observation, in many ways superior to anything of the sort yet accomplished in the 18th-century novel, and anticipating the maturer art of ▷ Jane Austen in the early 19th century.
▷ Epistolary novel.

Evelyn, John (1620–1706)
Chiefly remembered as a diarist. His diary, published in 1818, covers the years 1641–97, and includes impressions of distinguished contemporaries, customs and manners, and accounts of his travels. He published ▷ translations from Greek, Latin and French, as well as essays on the practical arts (gardening, the cultivation of trees, engraving, architecture). He also wrote an interesting ▷ biography of a court lady (*The Life of Mrs Godolphin*, unpublished until 1847).
▷ Diaries.
Bib: *Diary*, ed. E. S. de Beer; Ponsonby, A., *Life*; Hiscock, W. G., *John Evelyn and his Family Circle*; Marburg, C., *Mr Pepys and Mr Evelyn.*

Examiner, The
1. A right-wing (Tory) journal, started by ▷ Lord Bolingbroke and continued by ▷ Jonathan Swift. Engaged in controversy with the left-wing (Whig) writers, ▷ Joseph Addison and ▷ Sir Richard Steele (▷ Whig and Tory).
2. A weekly periodical founded by John and Leigh Hunt in 1808, famous for its radical politics.

Expedition of Humphrey Clinker, The (1771)
▷ *Humphrey Clinker, The Expedition of.*

F

Fable

In its narrower, conventional definition, a fable is a short story, often but not necessarily about animals, illustrating a piece of popular wisdom, or explaining unscientifically a fact of nature. Animals are commonly used as characters because they are readily identified with simplified human qualities, as the fox with cunning, the lamb with meekness, the wolf with greed, the ass with stupidity. In primitive folklore, fables are worldwide. Sophisticated literatures favour the moral fable, the leading European tradition for which was established by the Greek fabulist Aesop. However, though fables are plentiful in English as in every literature, used illustratively and ornamentally amongst other matter, English literature is comparatively poor in strict fabulists. ▷ John Gay's *Fables* are usually regarded as pleasant minor works; ▷ John Dryden's *Fables Ancient and Modern* (1699) are mostly not fables.

A broader interpretation of the term 'fable' allows a wider range of depiction: a tale which is a comment in metaphor on human nature, less directly figurative than allegory, and less roundabout in reaching its point than parable. In this broader meaning, English literature perhaps produced the greatest of all fables, Swift's ▷ *Gulliver's Travels*. But this broader interpretation admits an aspect of fable into almost any serious fiction; thus critics sometimes speak of a novelist's 'fable' in trying to express the underlying intention implicit in a novel.

▷ Allegory.

Factories

In the sense of industrial buildings in which large numbers of men were at work under one roof, as opposed to domestic industry with the workers in their own homes, factories existed to some extent in the 16th century. It was in the 18th century, however, with the invention of labour-saving machines and then of steam power to drive them, that the factory system became general. Pockets of domestic industry continued well into the 19th century, but it became increasingly the exception. Large industrial towns grew up haphazardly to accommodate the new factories.

Another use of the word 'factory' is to denote a centre for 'factors', *ie* men of commerce who transact trade on behalf of their employers. In the 18th century the ▷ East India Company established such factories in India, *eg* at Madras.

▷ Industrial Revolution.

Fairs

The early fairs were large markets held at particular times of the year in or near country towns; they attracted buyers and sellers from a distance. Until this century, every country town held its weekly market day on which the farmers of the district brought their cattle and vegetable produce for sale; a fair was a grand market, attracting trade from a wider region, and lasting for a week or more. They became established institutions after the Norman Conquest, and the largest, such as the Stourbridge Fair at Cambridge, were of national and even international importance. Towns found them profitable, not merely because they profited local craftsmen, but because the town corporations were able to collect special payments or 'dues' from the visiting merchants. Apart from commerce, fairs afforded entertainment of many sorts; today their commercial importance is slight and a fair is thought of as merely a travelling collection of roundabouts, swings, peepshows, etc. attractive mainly to children. These would formerly have been regarded as mere 'sideshows'; however they always had prominence and particularly popular were the exhibitions of 'monsters' such as 'the fattest woman in the world', animals with two heads, and other abnormalities.

Falconer, William (1732–69)

Author of a popular poem, *The Shipwreck* (1762; revised 1769), describing the sinking of a ship off the coast of Greece. Falconer himself drowned at sea.

Family

Family has been in most societies the route by which property, wealth and status or their lack have been transmitted. ▷ Marriage in any formalized sense, according to some authorities did not become established in England until after the 11th century, before which polygamy was practised. The household, which included others beside members related by ties of kin, was the domestic unit of significance and the economically productive unit. Only at the ▷ Reformation did a new ideology of marriage and of the parental role develop, which gave dignity to the wife as her husband's helpmeet and emphasis to the duty of father and mother to raise their children in the fear and knowledge of God. In the 18th century this ideal grew, with an emphasis on the importance of maternal intimacy: suckling her own children, instead of sending them out to nurse, playing with them and instructing them were construed as the proper activities of the mother. The male role throughout was defined in relation to positions held outside the home with which his greater authority inside it was associated.
Bib: Stone, L., *The Family, Sex and Marriage in England 1500–1800*; Davidoff, L. and Hall, C., *Family Fortunes*.

Fanshawe, Catherine (1765–1834)

Poet and letter-writer. Fanshawe came from a genteel background, which encouraged the education and cultural activity of women. In some ways perceptions of Fanshawe resemble those of ▷ Jane Austen, for during the 19th century she was considered a feminine, refined and respectable author, whose poetry was suitable for young women. However, on reading her work now it seems impossible that anyone could miss the sharp and incisive irony. Fanshawe parodies different ▷ discourses, satirizes political conventions and displays a worldly and somewhat cynical view about women's position in polite society. She and her sisters are also accredited with editing the memoirs of Lady Ann Fanshawe, who was an important ▷ Renaissance woman.

Farce

A term used for comedy in which ▷ realism is sacrificed for the sake of extravagant humour. Its derivation is from stuffing used in cookery, and as a literary term it was applied to light and frivolous material introduced by actors into the medieval mystery plays. Normally it is now applied to lightweight comedies only.

Farquhar, George (1678–1707)

Dramatist, whose topics and style straddle those of the ▷ Restoration period and of the 18th century, showing some elements of ▷ Reform comedy. The son of a Church of England clergyman, Farquhar was born in Londonderry, and entered Trinity College, Dublin. Lacking funds, and the ambition to study, however, he left and turned to acting, at the ▷ Smock Alley Theatre in Dublin. There he met ▷ Robert Wilks, who became his friend and acted in several of his subsequent plays. The accidental wounding of another actor during a performance of Dryden's *The Indian Emperor* shocked him profoundly, and he left the stage and turned to writing for the theatre instead. In 1697 Farquhar went to London, where his first play, *Love and a Bottle*, was performed successfully at the Theatre Royal in 1698. With ▷ *The Constant Couple; Or, A Trip to the Jubilee* (1699) he became fully established as a popular dramatist, Wilks acting the role of Sir Harry Wildair, and ▷ Susanna Verbruggen the part of Lady Lurewell. Sir Harry later became a favourite breeches part for actresses, including ▷ Peg Woffington. The play's sequel, *Sir Harry Wildair* (1701) was less successful. Farquhar obtained a commission in the army, but failed to obtain advancement. He did however travel through various parts of England, recruiting for the military, and used his experiences of army life to satiric effect in ▷ *The Recruiting Officer* (1706). The influence of changing theories about drama which took hold toward the turn of the century is evident in several of Farquhar's plays, especially *The Twin Rivals* (1702) and his last play, ▷ *The Beaux' Stratagem* (1707), which show a more humane and spontaneous attitude to life than the works of some authors of the high Restoration period. The contemporary dramatist ▷ Susannah Centlivre praised him for avoiding the risqué elements which so offended the ▷ Rev. Jeremy Collier, prompting him to write his *A Short View of the Immorality and Profaneness of the English Stage*. Centlivre's fulsome appreciation of Farquhar led to a correspondence between them, later published. In 1703 Farquhar married a woman who is said to have deceived him into believing her an heiress. He died in poverty after a lengthy illness.
Bib: Farmer, A. J., *Farquhar*.

Faust

The Faust myth is much older than those legends which crystallize round the historical figure of Faust and form a part of it. The myth of men seeking great earthly power from demons at the cost of their immortal souls goes back to the ancient Jews at about the time of Christ, and centres on several figures of medieval European Christendom. In the 16th century the myth received new vitality through the influence upon it of various bodies of ideas: ▷ Renaissance humanism, in its sceptical and critical

spirit; ▷ neo-Platonic mysticism, in its conception of the potentially immense reach of the human mind; and the Protestant ▷ Reformation, in its adherence to the pure Word of God as opposed to ▷ humanist claims for reason and ▷ Catholic claims for authority. The historical Faust was an early 16th-century German philosopher who was ridiculed by other intellectuals for his extravagant pretensions to magical powers. Nonetheless, pamphlets and plays built up a widespread, partly comic and partly serious image of him as the pattern of human arrogance eternally damned for his preference of human learning over the Holy Word. Mephistopheles, the devil with whom Faust makes his bargain in the fictional accounts, was himself condemned to eternal suffering and regarded himself in this light. Christopher Marlowe's *Doctor Faustus* is much the most interesting product of this tradition.
▷ German influence on English literature.

Female Spectator, The (1744–46)

A monthly ▷ essay paper, launched by ▷ Eliza Haywood, and loosely modelled on ▷ *The Spectator*. Haywood's paper, under the guide of a crusade against the sins of society, carried salacious gossip and scandalous accounts of individuals' indiscretions. More seriously, the editor attacked profligacy and gambling, and warned against reckless romance, while at the same time opposing arranged marriages, and arguing in favour of divorce. The paper developed a correspondence column, in which topical concerns were raised by readers, with replies by Haywood herself. After its demise, Haywood briefly ran a weekly paper with a similar format called *The Parrot*.
Bib: Adburgham, A., *Women in Print*.

Female Tatler, The

Title given to two separate journals whose names were intended to invoke ▷ *The Tatler*.
1 Publication launched in 1709 by ▷ Delarivière Manley, under the pseudonym of 'Mrs Crackenthorpe, a Lady that knows Everything'. The journal was a vehicle for her Tory views, but also contained anecdotes of contemporary life, as well as gossip and sometimes scandalous accounts of the activities of real people, whose names were often thinly disguised. After threats of legal proceedings from some of them, Manley resigned her editorship in November 1709, and *The Female Tatler* passed into more discreet hands. It then devoted itself to accounts of women noted for their achievements, stories, and some ▷ sentimental verses, and survived to March 1710.
2 A rival paper, also started in 1709, by the dramatist Thomas Baker, who is also thought to have produced a spurious number of Steele's ▷ *The Tatler* in 1711. His *The Female Tatler* resembled Manley's creation, and the two hurled abuse at one another for a time, before Baker's publication closed down.
Bib: Adburgham, Al., *Women in Print*.

Feminism

In literary criticism this term is used to describe a range of critical positions which argue that the distinction between 'masculine' and 'feminine' is formative in the generation of all discursive practices. In its concern to bring to the fore the particular situation of women in society, 'feminism' has a long history, and can be taken to embrace an interest in all forms of women's writing throughout history. In its ▷ essentialist guise, feminism proposes a range of experiences peculiar to women, which are, by definition, denied to men, and which it seeks to emphasize in order to compensate for the oppressive nature of a society rooted in what it takes to be patriarchal authority. A more ▷ materialist account would emphasize the extent to which gender difference is a cultural construction, and therefore amenable to change by concerted political action. Traditional materialist accounts, especially those of Marx, have placed the issue of 'class' above that of 'gender', but contemporary feminism regards the issue of 'gender' as frequently cutting across 'class' divisions, and raising fundamental questions about the social role of women in relations of production and exchange. Insofar as all literature is 'gendered', then feminist literary criticism is concerned with the analysis of the social construction of 'femininity' and 'masculinity' in particular texts. One of its major objectives is to expose how hitherto 'masculine' criticism has sought to represent itself as a universal experience. Similarly, the focus is adjusted in order to enable literary works themselves to disclose the ways in which the experiences they communicate are determined by wider social assumptions about gender difference, which move beyond the formal boundaries of the text. To this extent feminism is necessarily the focus of an interdisciplinary approach to literature, psychology, sociology and philosophy.

Psychoanalytic feminism, for example, often overlaps with socialist feminism. It approaches the concept of gender as a problem rather than a given, and draws on Freud's emphasis on the instability of sexual identities. The fact that femininity – and masculinity – are never fully acquired, once and for all, suggests a relative openness allowing for changes in the ways they are distributed. Literature's disturbance and exploration of ways of thinking about sexual difference have proved a rich source for feminist critics.

▷ Women's movement.

Bib: de Beauvoir, S., *The Second Sex;* Greene, G. and Kahn, C. (eds.), *Making a Difference: Feminist Literary Criticism;* Millett, K., *Sexual Politics;* Spender. D., *Feminist Theorists;* Wollstonecraft, M., *Vindication of the Rights of Women.*

Feminism in Augustan literature in England

Feminist consciousness in English writing was expressed from at least the early 17th century, as evidenced by a series of pamphlets, and a play, in which women were in turn attacked, and defended themselves – the so-called *Swetnam the Woman-Hater* controversy. During and after the ▷ Civil War period, the Duchess of Newcastle (▷ Cavendish, Margaret) wrote a number of plays in which she championed women's causes, including one in which she suggests an institution of learning for women. In 1663 ▷ Mary Carleton arrived in

England, fraudulently describing herself as a German princess: the story of her supposed escape from an unwanted marriage and flight to England is narrated in a pamphlet possibly written by her. The poet ▷ Katherine Philips is sometimes held up as an example of early feminism, because of her intense friendships with women, which she celebrated in her poetry, and the fact that she wrote at all in a period when merely to write was discouraged, disparaged, and often ridiculed by men as an unfeminine act. However, she at first refused to publish her works, on the grounds that she thought it unfit for her sex, until some appear to have been published without her permission.

Women's advent in the theatre as actresses and dramatists marked a new phase in literary and social history in general, as well as in the history of women's endeavours. Their presence on the stage was ambiguous. Some of the finest roles for women, and toughest characterizations, come out of the drama of this period, but actresses were often sexually exploited as well as savagely criticized. The dramatist, poet and novelist ▷ Aphra Behn is justly celebrated as the first professional woman writer in England, and possibly the first feminist, although not the first English woman dramatist: that title is disputed, because of disagreements about what constitutes original work, in an era of frequent translation and plagiarism. Candidates appear from the 16th century. But Behn's work, and her image as an independent and successful writer, influenced generations of women, including many of the amateur and professional poets, novelists, dramatists, and editors who followed her, such as ▷ Sarah Fyge Egerton, ▷ Elizabeth Singer Rowe, ▷ Lady Mary Chudleigh, the ▷ Countess of Winchilsea, and ▷ Sophia, as well as ▷ Mary Pix, ▷ Catherine Trotter-Cockburn, ▷ Eliza Haywood, ▷ Delarivière Manley, ▷ Susannah Centlivre, and ▷ Lady Mary Wortley Montagu. As a dramatist Behn also influenced men such as ▷ Southerne whose plays, along with some by ▷ Vanbrugh, ▷ Farquhar, and ▷ Nicholas Rowe, express a new consciousness of women's oppression. As a novelist, she is a forerunner of ▷ Congreve and ▷ Defoe.

In the 1660s and 70s the literary and pedagogic activities of ▷ Bathsua Pell Makin, who built on the work of the continental reformer ▷ Anna Maria von Schuurman, helped to revive interest in women's education. ▷ Hannah Woolley was in turn influenced by Makin, at first teaching, and then writing for women, although most of her work focuses on domestic rather than intellectual concerns. A more sustained campaign was mounted, beginning in the 1690s, by ▷ Mary Astell. Her polemical prose treatises demanding better education for women and better treatment for women in marriage, as well as her own determined celibacy, have made her a contender for the title of first English feminist, in something resembling the modern sense of the term. Some of her ideas were revived by ▷ Elizabeth Montagu, and her influence was felt for many years.

By the early 18th century, the activities of religious and other reformers had wrought their effect on writers of both sexes: the works of Centlivre,

Manley and Haywood are much less sexually outspoken than Behn's, for example. At the same time women's causes were more frequently taken up by men including ▷ Steele, Rowe, Defoe and ▷ Richardson. Steele attacked accepted attitudes towards women's education and women's subjugation in marriage, in early editions of ▷ *The Tatler* and ▷ *The Spectator*, and ▷ Jonathan Swift helped a number of literary women to publish their work. But Swift was in other respects deeply misogynistic, and could as easily attack female writers as assist them, and even Steele's attitudes to women veered increasingly towards orthodoxy. And if suffering heroines like those in Rowe's so-called ▷ she-tragedies, or Richardson's ▷ *Clarissa*, drew attention to women's plight, they also mark a shift to portraying a more passive type of woman, whose presence increasingly dominated drama and novel as the century progressed. By the mid-18th century women's position in some traditional areas of power, such as politics, was also declining. But women continued to have their defenders among men, and to hold their own in public life. A serious celebration of women's intellectual achievements was offered by ▷ George Ballard, in his *Memoirs of Several Ladies of Great Britain* (1752), a biographical dictionary of learned women from the 16th century to his own day. And actresses such as ▷ Charlotte Charke and ▷ Margaret (Peg) Woffington became famous partly through their portrayals of male characters in so-called 'breeches' roles. (This is different from the Restoration dramatic device of women characters disguising themselves as men, usually in pursuit of some lover, and returning to their female dress at a later point in the play.) In addition, the growth of ▷ Methodism gave new opportunities to women as preachers and writers of ▷ sermons and religious tracts, as the ▷ Puritan sects had done for women of an earlier generation.

Throughout the period men and women wrote for the improvement of both sexes, but often specifically of women. These essays, tracts and books form much of the ▷ advice and ▷ conduct literature which proliferated. They range from the most sternly religious to cosy advice on romantic matters, forerunners of our 'agony aunt' columns. Some of this was offered, along with tips on fashion and beauty, by the publisher and bookseller John Dunton in his periodicals, including *The Ladies Dictionary* and *Athenian Mercury*, brought out in the 1690s. In his memoirs Dunton claimed to have wanted to restore the knowledge of truth and happiness among 'the Fair Sex', although much of the guidance which he offers to women is of a very conventional nature. There was also a fund of domestic advice, such as that provided later by ▷ Hannah Glasse. And in lighter vein were periodicals such as Manley's ▷ *The Female Tatler*, and Haywood's ▷ *The Female Spectator*, modelled on *The Tatler* and *The Spectator*. Critics have disagreed as to how one should view such endeavours. Some have seen these ancestors of women's magazines as limiting to women, reinforcing frivolous and domestic stereotypes. But they had at least the virtue of providing practical information to women hungry for such material, and of helping to legitimize entertainment for women at a time when they were being deluged with reminders of their duty.

But parallel with these activities in the middle of the century were the intellectual gatherings and literary productions, of the ▷ Bluestockings, women such as ▷ Elizabeth Carter, Elizabeth Montagu and ▷ Hannah More. ▷ Frances Brooke revived ideals of celibacy for women in her weekly, *The Old Maid* (1755–6), and in 1770 *The Lady's Magazine* was launched, which defended women's equality in intelligence. Women found it easier than ever before to publish their poetry: between the beginning and the end of the century the number of those publishing collections of their verse had risen from two to thirty. Even a few working-class women, such as ▷ Mary Leapor, and ▷ Ann Yearsley found publishers. Women whose lives had led them into unconventional channels, such as ▷ Lady Sarah Pennington, ▷ Laetitia Pilkington and ▷ Hester Thrale Piozzi, also resisted social pressures on their sex, and passed on their often painful experiences through their writing. A new generation emerged of serious women authors, including ▷ Frances Sheridan, ▷ Anna Laetitia Barbauld, Hannah More, ▷ Hannah Cowley, ▷ Ann Radcliffe, ▷ Maria Edgworth, ▷ Elizabeth Inchbald and ▷ Mary Wollstonecraft, challenging the achievements of men in almost every field of literature, and building a basis for the important male and female authors, especially the novelists, of the 19th and 20th centuries.

Bib: Adburgham, A., *Women in Print*; Mahl, M. R., and Koon, H. (eds.), *The Female Spectator: English Women Writers Before 1800*; Figes, E., *Sex and Subterfuge: Women Writers to 1850*; Goreau, A., *The Whole Duty of a Woman: Female Writers in Seventeenth Century England*; Doody, M., *The Daring Muse: Augustan Poetry Reconsidered*; Hobby, E., *Virtue of Necessity: English Women's Writing 1649–88*; Rodgers, K., *Feminism in Eighteenth-century England*; Todd, J., *The Sign of Angellica: Women, Writing and Fiction, 1660–1800*; Howe, E., *The First English Actresses: Women and Drama 1660–1700*.

Ferguson, Adam (1723–1816)
Scottish philosopher and historian, often thought of as the founder of modern sociology. Born at Logierait in Perthshire, Ferguson became chaplain to the Black Watch regiment, and later succeeded his friend ▷ David Hume as keeper of the Advocates' Library in Edinburgh. He was made a professor at Edinburgh University, first of Natural Philosophy, then of Moral Philosophy and finally of Mathematics. His *Essay on the History of Civil Society* (1767) analyses human existence in terms of man's social nature and tendency to form groups; it represents a landmark in the development of sociology as an academic discipline. In it he also argued that the growing division of labour encouraged individualistic pursuit of gain, and worked against the interests of the social group. Other writings include *Institutes of Moral Philosophy* (1769) and *The History of the Progress and Termination of the Roman Republic* (1782) which became a standard work.

Bib: Kettler, D., *The Social and Political Thought of Adam Ferguson.*

Fergusson, Robert (1750–74)
Poet. A clerk in the Commissary Office in Edinburgh, he died in the local Bedlam after falling ill and becoming prey to religious melancholy. He wrote extensively in English in the usual genres of the day: ▷ lyrics imitative of ▷ William Shenstone, tetrameter (▷ metre) fables and Miltonic ▷ blank verse. But his most important poetry is in the Scots vernacular and builds on the tradition begun by Allan Ramsay, often employing Ramsay's distinctive stanza forms. His *Auld Reekie* and *Hallow-Fair* depict the urban scene with pungent particularity. He intended to translate ▷ Virgil's ▷ *Georgics* and ▷ *Aeneid* into Scots, but the project was never realized because of his early death. The 1782 edition of Fergusson's works helped inspire some of ▷ Robert Burns's best poetry.

Field sports
Sport taking place in the open countryside, consisting of some sort of hunting or racing. The main kinds have been:
Coursing. The pursuit of animals' (usually hares) with hounds using sight and not scent; a combination of hunting and racing.
Falconry. ▷ Hawking.
▷ *Fowling.* The hunting of birds, by hawking, trapping, shooting.
▷ *Hawking.* The hunting of birds with hawks specially trained for the purpose. Shooting drove this sport out of fashion in the later 17th century.
Horse-racing. This originally took place across country. It became extremely fashionable in the reign of ▷ Charles II and has remained so ever since.
▷ *Hunting.* Usually implies hunting on horseback with hounds.
Shooting. Usually at birds. Until the 17th century the usual weapon was the long bow or the crossbow, but guns called fowling-pieces or bird-pieces came in during the 16th century and in the second half of the 17th century became general. 'Huntin', shootin' and fishin'' were the stereotypical pastimes of the country gentleman and aristocracy.

Fielding, Henry (1707–54)
Born at Sharpham Park in Somerset, the son of a lieutenant. After the death of his mother when he was II, Fielding was sent to Eton. At the age of 19, after an unsuccessful attempt to elope with an heiress, Fielding tried to make a living in London as a dramatist.
In 1728 his play *Love in Several Masques* was successfully performed at ▷ Drury Lane, and Fielding departed for university at Leyden, where he studied classical literature for about 18 months. On his return to London he continued his career as a dramatist, writing some 25 plays in the period 1729–37. His dramatic works are largely satirical, the most successful being ▷ *Tom Thumb* (performed in 1730). Fielding also edited four periodicals, *The Champion* (1739–41), *The Covent Garden Journal*

(under the pseudonym Sir Alexander Drawcansir, 1752), *The True Patriot* (1745–6) and *Jacobite's Journal* (1747–8), but his major achievement is as a novelist.
▷ *Shamela*, a parody of ▷ Richardson's ▷ *Pamela*, published in 1741, was developed into the theme of ▷ Joseph Andrews (1742), an original and comic creation. In 1743 Fielding published ▷ *The Life of Jonathan Wild the Great*, a satire on the criminal class comparable in its inversion of values to ▷ John Gay's ▷ *Beggar's Opera*. In the same year his lesser-known satire, *A Journey From This World to the Next*, also appeared. ▷ *Tom Jones*, his greatest work, was published in 1749, and ▷ *Amelia* in 1751.
In 1748 Fielding was made Justice of the Peace for Westminster, and pursued a successful career of social reform. In 1754, his health failing, he embarked on a journey to Lisbon in search of a better climate, but died on the way. *A Journal of a Voyage to Lisbon*, his final achievement, was published posthumously the following year.
▷ Fielding, Sarah.
Bib: Alter, R., *Fielding and the Nature of the Novel*; Rogers, P., *Henry Fielding*; Rawson, C. J. *Henry Fielding and the Augustan Ideal under Stress.*

Fielding, Sarah (1710–68)
Sarah Fielding, sister of the novelist ▷ Henry Fielding, was highly praised by ▷ Samuel Richardson, who rated her achievements more highly than her brother's: 'his was but a knowledge of the outside of a clockwork machine, while yours was that of the finer springs and movements of the inside'. Her first appearance in print consisted of contributions to her brother's works.
Sarah Fielding's first novel, *The Adventures of David Simple*, began to appear in 1744, and proved a great success. In its interpretation of social conventions from a female point of view, it provides a revealing contrast with the attitudes expressed by male writers; the heroine, Cynthia, is subjected to constant sexual harassment condoned as socially acceptable behaviour. The second volume of *David Simple* appeared in 1747, and the final volume in 1753.
Sarah Fielding's concern for female education is evident in *The Governess or The Little Female Academy* (1749). Its success as a (somewhat pious) moral novel for young people ensured that it stayed in print for over 150 years.
In 1754, Sarah Fielding published *The Cry*, a dramatic fable co-written with her friend ▷ Jane Collier. In this allegorical framework the heroine tells her story to representatives of truth and justice, malice and exploitation.
Samuel Richardson was the publisher of Sarah Fielding's next work, *The Lives of Cleopatra and Octavia*, in which the two characters give different versions of their lives. In 1759 Richardson again helped with the printing of *The History of The Countess of Dellwyn*, a further critique of male-dominated society. Her later works include *The History of Ophelia* (1760) and a translation of Xenophon's *Memoirs of Socrates* (1762).
Bib: Grey, J., 'Introduction' to *The Governess.*

Fiennes, Celia (1662–1741)

English Protestant travel writer, and daughter of a regicide. She travelled around the English counties alone and accompanied, riding and using a coach. Her 'Book' was first published in part in 1888. Its descriptions combine the interests of a traveller with details which make the familiar social territory strange – for example, her vivid story of the recovery of a human relic in the abandoned monastery at York.

Fifth Monarchy Men

A sect of ▷ Puritans who believed, on the basis of a prophecy in the Bible (*Daniel 2*), that ▷ Oliver Cromwell's rise to power was a preparation for the Second Coming of Christ, and the establishment of the great fifth and last monarchy; the previous four had been the Assyrian, the Persian, the Greek and the Roman. In disillusionment, they began to turn against Cromwell and after the ▷ Restoration of the monarchy in 1660 they tried to raise a rebellion in London. It was easily suppressed and the leaders were executed.

Figures of speech

Alliteration The beginning of accented syllables near to each other with the same consonantal sound, as in many idiomatic phrases: 'safe and sound': 'thick and thin'; 'right as rain'. Alliteration is thus the opposite of ▷ rhyme, by which the similar sounds occur at the ends of the syllables: 'near and dear'; 'health and wealth'. Alliteration dominated the pattern of Old English poetry; after the Conquest, French influence caused rhyme to predominate. However, in the 14th century there seems to have been an 'alliterative revival', producing such important poems as ▷ *Piers Plowman* and ▷ *Sir Gawain and the Green Knight*. Alliterative verse was accentual, *ie* did not depend on the regular distribution of accented syllables in a line, but on the number of accented syllables in the lines.

After the 14th century, rhyme and the regular count of syllables became the normal pattern for English verse. Alliteration, however, continued to be used unsystematically by every poet.

Anacoluthon From the Greek: 'not following on'. Strictly speaking, this is not a figure of speech, but a grammatical term for a sentence which does not continue the syntactical pattern with which it starts. However, it may be used deliberately with the virtue of intensifying the force of a sentence *eg* by the sudden change from indirect to direct speech.

Anti-climax
    ▷ *Bathos* (below).

Antithesis A method of emphasis by the placing of opposed ideas or characteristics in direct contrast with each other.

Apostrophe A form of direct address often used by a narrator in the middle of his narrative as a means of emphasizing a moral lesson.

Assonance The rhyming of vowel sounds without the rhyming of consonants.

Bathos From the Greek: 'death'. The descent from the sublime to the ridiculous. This may be the result of incompetence in the writer, but ▷ Alexander Pope used it skillfully as a method of ridicule:

Here thou, great ANNA! Whom three realms obey
Dost sometimes counsel take – and sometimes tea.
                    (*The Rape of the Lock*)

Pope wrote an essay *Bathos, the Art of Sinking in Poetry*, as a travesty of the essay by ▷ Longinus, *On the Sublime* (1st century AD). Longinus had great prestige as a critic in Pope's time.

Climax From the Greek: 'a ladder'. The climb from lower matters to higher, with the consequent satisfying of raised expectations.

Euphemism A mild or vague expression used to conceal a painful or disagreeable truth, *eg* 'he passed on' for 'he died'. It is sometimes used ironically.

Euphuism A highly artificial quality of style resembling that of John Lyly's *Euphues*.

Hyperbole Expression in extreme language so as to achieve intensity.

Innuendo A way of expressing dislike or criticism indirectly, or by a hint; an insinuation.

Irony From the Greek: 'dissimulation'. A form of expression by which the writer intends his meaning to be understood differently and less favourably, in contrast to his overt statement:

It is a truth universally acknowledged, that a single man in possession of a good fortune must be in want of a wife.

This opening sentence of ▷ Jane Austen's *Pride and Prejudice* is to be understood as meaning that the appearance of such a young man in a neighbourhood inspires very strong wishes in the hearts of mothers of unmarried daughters, and that these wishes cause the mothers to behave as though the statement were indeed a fact.

Dramatic irony occurs when a character in a play makes a statement in innocent assurance of its truth, while the audience is well aware that he or she is deceived.

Litotes Emphatic expression through an ironical negative, *eg* 'She's no beauty', meaning that the woman is ugly.

Malapropism A comic misuse of language, usually by a person who is both pretentious and ignorant. The term derives from the character Mrs Malaprop in ▷ Richard Brinsley Sheridan's play ▷ *The Rivals* (1775). This comic device had in fact been used by earlier writers, such as ▷ Shakespeare in the portrayal of ▷ Dogberry in *Much Ado About Nothing*.

Meiosis Understatement, used as a deliberate method of emphasis by irony, *eg* 'Would you like to be rich?' – 'I should rather think so!'

Metaphor A figure of speech by which unlike objects are identified with each other for the purpose of emphasizing one or more aspects of resemblance between them. A simple example: 'the camel is the ship of the desert'.

Mixed metaphor is a confused image in which the successive parts are inconsistent, so that (usually) absurdity results: 'I smell a rat, I see it floating in the air, but I will nip it in the bud', *ie* 'I suspect an evil, and I can already see the beginnings of it, but I will take action to suppress it.' However mixed metaphor is sometimes used deliberately to express a state of confusion.

Dead metaphor is one in which the image has become so familiar that it is no longer thought of as figurative, *eg* the phrase 'to take steps', meaning 'to take action'.

Metaphysical conceit
▷ Metaphysical Poets.

Metonymy The naming of a person, institution or human characteristic by some object or attribute with which it is clearly associated, as when a king or queen may be referred to as 'the Crown';

> *Sceptre and Crown*
> *Must tumble down,*
> *And in the dust be equal made*
> *With the poor crooked scythe and spade.*
> ('The Levelling Dust', ▷ James Shirley)

Here 'Sceptre and Crown' refer to kings, and perhaps more broadly to the classes which control government, while 'scythe and spade' stand for the humble peasantry. Metonymy has taken on additional meanings since the advent of Structuralism. One of the originators of Russian Formalism, Roman Jakobson, draws a distinction between 'metaphor' – the linguistic relationship between two different objects on the grounds of their similarity – and 'metonymy' as a means of establishing a relationship between two objects in terms of their contiguity. Where metaphor is regarded as a major rhetorical device in *poetry*, metonymy is more usually associated with *prose*.

Oxymoron A figure of speech formed by the conjunction of contrasting terms; it derives from two Greek words meaning 'sharp and dull'.

Palindrome A word or sentence that reads the same backwards or forwards, *eg*

> *Lewd did I live; evil I did dwel*
> (Phillips, 1706)

Paradox A statement that challenges the mind by appearing to be self-contradictory.

Pathetic fallacy A term invented by the critic John Ruskin (*Modern Painters*, Vol. III, Pt. iv, Ch. 12) to denote the tendency common especially among poets to ascribe human emotions or qualities to inanimate objects, *eg* 'an angry sea'. Ruskin describes it as dividing writers into four classes: those who do not use it merely because they are insensitive; superior writers in whom it is a mark of sensitivity; writers who are better still and do not need it because they 'feel strongly, think strongly, and see truly'; and writers of the best sort who use it because in some instances they 'see in a sort untruly, because what they see is inconceivably above them'. In general, he considers that the pathetic fallacy is justified when the feeling it expresses is a true one.

Personification A kind of metaphor, by which an abstraction or inanimate object is endowed with personality.

Play on words A use of a word with more than one meaning or of two words which sound the same in such a way that both meanings are called to mind. In its simplest form, as the modern pun, this is merely a joke. In the 16th and 17th centuries poets frequently played upon words seriously; this is especially true of ▷ Shakespeare and dramatists contemporary with him, and of the ▷ Metaphysical Poets, such as John Donne and George Herbert.

This very serious use of puns or plays upon words decreased in the 18th century, when ▷ Samuel Johnson censured Shakespeare's fondness for puns (or, as Johnson called them, 'quibbles'). The reason for this disappearance of the serious 'play upon words' was the admiration of educated men for what Bishop Sprat in his *History of the Royal Society* (1667) called 'mathematical plainness of meaning', a criterion emulated by poets as well as by prose writers.

Modern poets and critics have recovered the older, serious use of the play on words. Ambiguity of meaning which in the 18th century was considered a vice of expression, is now seen as a quality of rich texture of expression, though of course 'good' and 'bad' types of ambiguity have to be distinguished.

Rhyme A verbal music made through identity of sound in the final syllables of words. Several varieties of rhyme exist:

End-rhyme When the final syllables of lines of verse are rhymed.

Internal rhyme When one at least of the rhyming words is in mid-line; as in 'fair' and 'air' in the following couplet by Swinburne:
We have seen thee, O Love, thou art
fair; thou art goodly, O Love;
Thy wings make light in the air as wings of a dove.

Masculine rhymes are single stressed syllables as in the examples already given.

Feminine rhymes are on two syllables, the second of which is unaccented. As in the following from Marlowe's *Passionate Shepherd*:

> *And I will make thee beds of roses*
> *And a thousand fragrant posies;*
> *A cap of flowers, and a kirtle*
> *Embroider'd all with leaves of myrtle*

Half-rhymes (pararhymes) are the rhyming of consonants but not of vowels (contrast ▷ *Assonance*). They are sometimes used as an equivalent for full rhymes, since consonants are more noticeable in rhyme music than vowels. Change in pronunciation sometimes has the effect of changing what was intended as full rhyme into half-rhyme, as in the following example from Pope:

> *Tis not enough, taste, judgement, learning, join;*
> *In all you speak, let truth and candour shine.*

In the 18th century, 'join' was pronounced as 'jine'.

Simile Similar to metaphor, but in similes the comparison is made explicit by the use of a word such as 'like' or 'as'.

Syllepsis A figure of speech by which a word is used in a literal and a metaphorical sense at the same time, *eg* 'You have broken my heart and my best china vase'.

Synecdoche A figure of speech by which a part is used to express a whole, or a whole is used to express a part, *eg* 'fifty sail' is used for fifty ships, or the 'smiling year' is used for the spring. In practice, synecdoche is indistinguishable from ▷ metonymy. Like metonymy this figure depends upon a relationship of contiguity, and is regarded as one side of the opposition between 'poetry' and 'non-poetry'. Both metonymy and synecdoche operate by combining attributes of particular objects, therefore they are crucial rhetorical devices for the representation of reality, and are closely related to ▷ realism as a literary style insofar as they function referentially.

Transferred epithet The transference of an adjective from the noun to which it applies grammatically to some other word in the sentence, usually in such a way as to express the quality of an action or of behaviour, *eg* 'My host handed me a hospitable glass of wine', instead of 'My hospitable host handed me . . .'.

Zeugma A figure similar to ▷ syllepsis; one word used with two others, to only one of which it is grammatically or logically applicable.

Finch, Anne, Countess of Winchilsea (1660–1720)

English poet, at present best known for her 'A Nocturnall Reeverie', esteemed by William Wordsworth (1770–1850). With ▷ Anne Killigrew she was a Maid of Honour to Mary of Modena and married Heneage Finch. After James II fled, they moved to Kent and she wrote poetry. A few poems were printed, but she published *Miscellany Poems on Several Occassions* (1713). Finch uses the natural world in a distinctive and subtle way in her poetry, linking landscape and state of mind in a way that blends the features of the inner and outer worlds, politics and place. She also had a vein of sharp satire – in 'Unequal Fetters' she wrote: 'Marriage does but slightly tye men / Whil'st close Pris'ners we remain / They the larger slaves of Hymen / Still are begging Love again / At the full length of all their chain.'

Fire of London, The Great

In 1666 over 13,000 houses, 87 churches and the old St Paul's Cathedral were destroyed. Celebrated accounts of it occur in the contemporary diaries of ▷ John Evelyn and ▷ Samuel Pepys. Owing to disagreements among the citizens, the innovative and independent architect ▷ Christopher Wren was not allowed to carry out his great plan for rebuilding the City, whose streets accordingly now still follow the twisting lines of the old City; but he rebuilt St Paul's and many other churches. A beneficial consequence of the fire was that it ended the terrible epidemic of plague which had devastated London in 1665.
▷ Plague of London, The Great.

Flecknoe, Richard (17th century)

A poet who was the victim of a satire by ▷ Andrew Marvell, *Fleckno, an English Priest at Rome* (1645). Dryden chose the title ▷ *Mac Flecknoe* (son of Flecknoe) for his satire against ▷ Thomas Shadwell.

Fleet Prison

A royal prison in London from the 12th century (Falstaff is sent there at the end of ▷Shakespeare's

Henry IV, Part II), used for debtors after 1641 and demolished in 1848. It is described in Charles Dickens's *The Pickwick Papers*. Clergymen imprisoned in the Fleet sometimes conducted secret marriages, *ie* without the formalities of licence or 'banns'. Such marriages were legal though the clergyman was liable to a fine – a penalty which was no deterrent to one already bankrupt.

Fleet Street

A street in London which used to be the headquarters of most of the national newspapers. 'Fleet Street' is often used as a synonym for ▷ 'journalism' although most of the papers have now moved from the street.

Flodden, Battle of (1513)

The invading Scottish forces under King James IV, fighting in alliance with France which had been invaded by Henry VIII of England, were heavily defeated by the English general, the Earl of Surrey. James himself was killed, as well as large numbers of his nobility. The battle was commemorated by a famous dirge *The Flowers of the Forest*, the best-known version of which is by Jean Elliott (1727–1805).

Fontenelle, Bernard le Bovyer (Bouvier) de (1657–1757)

French author, born at Rouen, a nephew of ▷ Corneille. Educated as a lawyer he followed in his uncle's footsteps by abandoning this profession in favour of literature, at first writing for the theatre. Failing at this, despite the help of his uncle, he turned to other forms of authorship including a history of the French theatre, satires, criticism, and scientific and moral treatises. His *Dialogue des morts* (1683), in imitation of the classical Greek writer Lucian, established his reputation. He became a member of the French Academy in 1691, and of the Academy of Sciences in 1697. He was praised for his clarity and wit, as well as his ability to render complex scientific theories in simple language that could be easily understood even by non-scientists. He was admired by a number of English authors including ▷ Aphra Behn, who in 1688 translated his *Entretiens sur la pluralité des mondes* (*A Discovery of New Worlds*), and *Histoire des oracles* (*The History of Oracles and the Cheats of the Pagan Priests*).

Food

For much of English history meat has been the most valued form of food, and a profusion of meat on a table was regarded as a sign of prosperity. Salads ('sallets') began to come into general use among the middle and upper classes only in the 17th century. The consumption of potatoes, introduced by Sir Walter Raleigh in the 1580s, spread slowly, and it was not until the 19th century that it became really common, and a staple food among the poor. Sugar was another important innovation; cane sugar was cultivated in the West Indies in the 17th century and took the place of honey and other sweeteners that had gone by the name of 'sugar' in earlier times. (Although sugar continues to be consumed in large quantities, it is mostly no longer imported but made from home-grown beet; the effect on the economy of the West Indies has been severe.) By the 18th century vegetables were extensively cultivated by all classes, and were eaten with meat as plentifully as they are today. Overeating of meat continued to be a chief cause of bad health among the richer classes, hence the frequent apoplexies in 18th-century novels and plays. Lavish orchards were a feature of great houses at least as early as the 16th century, and fruits such as dates, figs and oranges were imported.

Diet greatly expanded in the 18th and 19th centuries with the increase in the variety of imports. Fruits, such as bananas and pineapples, originally imported cheaply from the Empire as a fashionable novelty, have remained popular to the present time.

Foote, Samuel (1720–77)

Actor, manager and dramatist, born at Truro to a landowning family. He trained for the law, but moved instead, like many of his contemporaries, to the stage. He studied with ▷ Macklin and played the title role in *Othello* to Macklin's Iago in 1744. He also acted at the ▷ Smock Alley Theatre in Dublin. In 1747 he leased the 'Little Theatre in the Hay' (▷ Haymarket Theatres), opening with a piece of his own called *The Diversions of the Morning*, which proved a great success, and which he followed with more of his own productions. In 1766 a riding accident caused him to lose a leg, but he was acting again only five months later. Out of sympathy, he was given a patent for life at the Haymarket. His plays, mainly social and political satires, include *Taste* (1752) and *The Minor* (1760). He was an excellent mimic, and became the subject of legal action by a number of people whom he had imitated on stage. He also wrote two pamphlets on acting and dramatic theory. ▷ Samuel Johnson praised his broad humour and wit, and he was sometimes nicknamed the 'English Aristophanes'.

Forty-five, The

The rebellion or rising of 1745, *ie* the second of the two main ▷ Jacobite attempts in the 18th century to regain the throne of Great Britain for the Catholic branch of the House of ▷ Stuart. It was led by Charles Stuart ('Bonnie Prince Charlie' to his Scottish supporters, the 'Young Pretender' to his enemies), elder son of the claimant James Stuart (the 'Old Pretender'). Charles succeeded in rousing the ▷ Highlands and occupying ▷ Edinburgh. He then advanced into England and reached Derby. He had by then attracted very few English supporters, and retreated to ▷ Scotland. He was defeated by the Duke of Cumberland in 1746 at the Battle of ▷ Culloden in northern Scotland, but escaped abroad.

Forty Shilling Freeholders

The class, outside the towns, who from the 13th century until the ▷ Reform Bill of 1832 possessed the minimum property qualification to vote for a representative in ▷ Parliament, or to be elected as one. 'Freeholder' implies owning land, not renting it from another landowner; 'forty shillings' is the annual value of the land.
   ▷ Franchise.

Fourteenth of July

The French annual national festival, dating from the storming of the Bastille, a state prison in Paris, on 14 July 1789. This was the first triumph of the ▷ French Revolution, and marked the end of the ▷ Ancien Régime.

Fourth Estate, The

Traditionally, and for political purposes, English society was thought until the 20th century to have three estates: the lords spiritual, the lords temporal, the commons. ▷ Carlyle alludes to a Fourth Estate, *ie* the press, implying that the newspapers have an essential role in the political functions of society. He attributed the phrase to the 18th-century statesman ▷ Edmund Burke.

Fowling

Any form of hunting birds. Since the 17th century shooting with guns has been the only common method but previously shooting with the bow and arrow, trapping or ▷ hawking were used. Guns (called bird-or fowling-pieces) began to make their appearance in the 16th century but the crossbow was still the more efficient weapon. Trapping was either by gins (using some kind of net) or by placing lime along the twigs of trees so that the bird's feet stuck to it on alighting. Hawking was deemed the most aristocratic of these sports, until it gave place to shooting in the 17th century.
   ▷ Hunting.

Fox, Charles James (1749–1806)

Principal leader of the Whig party from 1775 (the beginning of the ▷ American War of Independence) until his death. The crown was not then above politics and the Tories, almost continuously in power during the same period, had the support of George III (▷ Whig and Tory) Fox's fearless opposition in the House of Commons to the policies of the government in America, in Ireland and in regard to the ▷ French Revolution caused the king to refuse his offer of participation in the government in 1804, when he became convinced of the rightness of the war against France. Fox was dissolute in private life but set a high standard of political independence of mind. His principal political opponents were the Prime Ministers Lord North during the American war and ▷ William Pitt the Younger during the French one. Though powerful in opposition, he was less effective in office; but his service as Foreign Secretary in the Whig governments of 1782 and 1806 was too brief to show results.

Fox, George (1624–91)

Religious leader. He founded the Society of Friends (▷ Quakers), and left a journal of his spiritual experience, published in 1694. Apart from its religious importance, Fox's Journal is one of the classics amongst the English ▷ diaries.

Fox-hunting

This sport began to reach its outstanding prestige in 18th-century England. Deer, the chief object of hunts in earlier centuries, were less available as land came increasingly under cultivation, but foxes did not diminish and were just as much an enemy to farmers. Special packs of foxhounds were bred and were given names often taken from the great country houses where they were kept, such as the Quorn, the Pytchley, the Badminton – which became famous far beyond hunting circles. The 18th-century ▷ enclosures of land into hedge-divided fields increased the danger and skill of 'riding to hounds', and this as much as anything steadily enhanced its popularity among the landed aristocracy who hunted for the sport and not merely to protect their poultry, like the farmers. To kill a fox by any method other than the approved one of hunting it with hounds and on horseback came to be regarded as little better than criminal; to be a Master of Hounds was to occupy a great social position; to misuse terminology (*eg* to call the hounds 'dogs') was to betray not merely laughable ignorance but a shameful sign of ill-breeding.

▷ Field sports; Hunting.

Franchise

Normally understood as the right to vote for a representative in Parliament. From the reign of Edward I, when representatives of the Commons were first summoned to Parliament, until 1832, this right was possessed by landowners whose land was worth at least 40 shillings a year and by the citizens of certain towns (parliamentary boroughs) in which the qualifications varied. The first Parliamentary Reform Bill of 1832 arranged a property qualification which enfranchised the middle classes uniformly throughout Britain. The Reform Bill of 1867 enfranchised the working classes of the towns and the third, in 1884, extended the franchise to include men of all classes everywhere. In 1918 women were enfranchised on reaching the age of 30 and in 1928 they were accorded the vote, like men, at 21. Enfranchisement was one of the main demands made by the Suffragette movement. The franchise today is said to be 'universal', *ie* it excludes only minors (*ie* people under 18), certified lunatics, criminals serving a sentence and Peers of the Realm (*ie* holders of titles of nobility and bishops, who are entitled to sit in the House of Lords).

▷ Forty Shilling Freeholders; Parliaments; Women, Status of.

Francis, Anne (1738–1800)

Poet and translator. Anne Francis was a distinguished scholar; she had a ▷ classical education, learning Latin, Greek and Hebrew. After her marriage to Revd Robert Francis, she published a translation of the *Song of Solomon* (1781) which she also edited, and in 1785 she brought out *The Obsequies of Demetrius Poliorcetes*, which reworked some of Plutarch's writing. Francis was also an admirer of ▷ Goethe and wrote *Charlotte to Werther: A Poetical Epistle* (1787) as a vehicle for defending him against what she felt were unjust accusations. Several more personal works remain, for example the elegies and odes to her family published in *Miscellaneous Poems* (1790). In light of this detailed and scholarly activity, it is surprising that Francis should think that such

work was 'an *improper* undertaking for a *woman*' (Preface to the *Song of Solomon*).

Free trade

Nowadays the term is understood to mean trade between nations without restrictions either in the form of the prohibition of certain commodities or in duties (taxes) on their importation. The view that trade should be so conducted was expressed most influentially in ▷ Adam Smith's *Wealth of Nations* (1776).

In the early 17th century the term was used for trade unrestricted by the monopolies granted (for a price) by the Crown to certain individuals. In the 18th century the term was a euphemism for smuggling.

French literature in England

The history of the cross-Channel literary flow from France to England is to no small degree the history of the translations and adaptations undergone by French literature. In the later 17th and early 18th centuries, translations were supplemented by (undistinguished) adaptations, notably those which represent the barest thread of imitation of French classical drama. One such adaptation was ▷ Ambrose Philips' *The Distrest Mother* (1712), behind which stands ▷ Racine's *Andromaque* (1667). Its success is recounted in ▷ Samuel Johnson's *Life* of Philips, a success greater than the original would have had in England at that time. This exemplifies the degree to which the ▷ Restoration was culturally as well as politically out of sympathy with the French classical idiom. It was left to ▷ Dryden to put Corneille back on the literary agenda, while English ▷ comedy of manners was indebted to Molière. ▷ Alexander Pope and Johnson, in the following century, attended to the criteria of taste laid down by ▷ Nicolas Boileau and René Rapin (1621–87); and with rise of the novel, ▷ Sterne can be found looking back to Rabelais rather than to contemporary French influence. But the important French work in the 18th century was the result of a collective enterprise rather than an individual piece: ▷ *L'Encyclopédie*. It provided a focus for the *philosophes*, ▷ Diderot, ▷ Voltaire and Rousseau, and a forum larger than that which Voltaire, for example, enjoyed with ▷ John Locke. More famously, its criticisms of the ▷ Ancien Régime prefigured the French Revolution.

French Revolution (1789–94)

The immediate effect of the French Revolution was to abolish the French monarchy, to reduce forever the rigid class divisions of French society, and to begin wars (lasting till 1815) which for the time being extensively altered the map of Europe. Its lasting effect was to inspire the European mind with the belief that change is historically inevitable and static order unnatural, and to imbue it with modern ideas of democracy, nationalism and equality at least of opportunity.

The immediate effect on England was confusing, for many of the changes being brought about in France had already occurred here in the 17th

century, especially the establishment of the sovereignty of the elected representatives of the people in ▷ Parliament in 1688 (▷ Glorious Revolution). Such changes had occurred here, however, without the same upheavals, partly because English society and politics had always been more fluid than in the other larger states of Europe, and though unjustified privileges and inequalities existed, there were few definable between the Whigs on the left who were neutral or sympathetic to the Revolution, and the Tories on the right who feared it from the start (▷ Whig and Tory). Only when Napoleon took increasing charge of France and became Emperor (▷ Napoleon I) in 1804 did Britain become united in fear of French aggression. However, ▷ Edmund Burke, published in 1790 his ▷ *Reflections on the Revolution in France*, one of the most eloquent documents of English political thinking, foretelling the disasters which the Revolution was to bring, and condemning it as ruthless surgery on the living organism of society. His opponent ▷ Tom Paine answered him with *The Rights of Man* (1791), and the younger intellectuals agreed with Paine. ▷ Wordsworth wrote later in *The Prelude* 'Bliss was it in that dawn to be alive', and ▷ William Blake wore a revolutionary cockade in the streets; ▷ Southey and ▷ Coleridge planned the ideal communist society, ▷ Pantisocracy; the philosophic novelist ▷ William Godwin published *Political Justice* and *Caleb Williams* to prove that reason was the only guide to conduct and society needed by man. Later Wordsworth and Coleridge came round to a view closer to Burke's, and the younger generation, ▷ Byron and ▷ Shelley, saw them as traitors, the more so because the defeat of Napoleon at Waterloo introduced a phase of political and social repression everywhere. But the older generation (except perhaps Southey) did not so much go back on their earlier enthusiasms as think them out more deeply; the philosophical conservatism of the older Coleridge was as radical in its thinking as the ▷ Utilitarianism of the philosophical radicals, ▷ Bentham and John Stuart Mill.
Bib: Everest, K., *Revolution in Writing: British Literary Responses to the French Revolution.*

Funds, The; The Funded Debt; Fund-holders
From the reign of ▷ William III the government sought to finance its wars by borrowing from private investors, issuing 'bonds' ('debentures') in acknowledgement of the loan and paying regular interest. This is the ▷ National Debt. It became the commonest investment for small investors and was the source of many 'private incomes' in the 19th century.
▷ Bank of England.

Furnishings and furniture
The 17th and 18th centuries saw a steady advance towards modern standards of comfort. Carpets, formerly used, if at all, as wall-hangings or table coverings, found their way to the floor; walls were panelled in wood; chairs became plentiful in the second half of the 17th century, and the 18th was the great age of English furniture design: furniture of all kinds became light, graceful, adapted to the comfort of the users. Looking-glasses, still uncommon at the beginning of the 17th century, were usual at the end of it. Wallpapers – known since the 16th century – came into general use in the 18th. Even the poor came by then to have the simplest comforts, including 'cottage' versions of 18th-century furniture designs – ▷ Chippendale, Hepplewhite, ▷ Sheraton.

Fyge, Sarah (1669/72–1722/3)
English author of the verse *The Female Advocate, or an Answere to a late Satyr against the Pride, Lust and Inconstancy etc., of Women* (1686), which she claimed to have written when she was fourteen. This was a reply to an attack on women by Robert Gould (1683), 'written by a lady in vindication of her sex'. The defence begins with a reworking of the much-disputed question of the nature of Eve – 'The Devil's strength weak Woman might deceive, / But Adam only tempted was by Eve, / She had the strongest Tempter, and least Charge; / Man's knowing most, doth make his sin more large.' Fyge claimed in a poem (published in *Poems on Several Occassions, together with a Pastoral*, 1703) that in the 1680s her father banished her to a village far from the comfort of friends. She wrote one of the elegies in *The Nine Muses* (1700) and had two husbands, first Field, and then the Reverend Thomas Egerton, to whom she was unhappily married. In *The Liberty* she wrote 'My daring Pen, will bolder Sallies make, / and like myself, an uncheck'd freedom take.'
▷ Manley, Delarivière
Bib: Medoff, Jeslyn, 'New Light on Sarah Fyge (Field, Egerton)', *Tulsa Studies in Women's Literature*, 1, 2 (1982), pp. 155–75.

Gainsborough, Thomas (1727–88)

English painter, born at Sudbury in Suffolk, he became one of the 36 founders of the English Academy. He lacked formal training as an artist, and taught himself to paint by copying trees, rocks and other objects that he saw in the countryside around him, his style being influenced by Dutch painting. He developed into a successful landscape artist and portrait painter, whose clients included some of England's wealthiest nobility, including members of the royal family. His contemporary ▷ Sir Joshua Reynolds described him as a genius and suggested he had founded an English school of art.

Gambling (Gaming)

A favourite English pastime since the Middle Ages. The use of dice ('hazard') goes back to pre-Christian times. Playing cards were introduced in the 15th century and were early used for gambling by all classes in the towns. In the reign of Elizabeth I gambling-houses (gaming-houses) had to be licensed by the Crown, and such licences were granted to courtiers. By the 18th century, upper-class society gambled extensively, and for high stakes. The London ▷ clubs were gambling rooms for men, and fashionable resorts such as ▷ Bath and Tunbridge Wells used their assembly rooms primarily for gambling and dancing. The 18th-century Lord Sandwich is supposed to have invented 'sandwiches' so that he would not need to get up from the gaming-table for a meal. The dramatist ▷ Richard Brinsley Sheridan ruined his finances by his heavy gambling.

Sport, especially horse-racing, has always had gambling as one of its main attractions; horse-races have appealed to rich and poor gamblers since ▷ Charles II first made them fashionable. Fights of all kinds – between cocks, dogs or men – have always been used as pretexts for gambling. Among team games, cricket was such a pretext in the 18th century, and in the 20th century the most popular of all forms of gambling is conducted through 'football pools'.

But the most serious of all forms of gambling has been the kind known as 'financial speculation' and is a product of the capitalist (▷ Capitalism) economic system. Already early in the 17th century, adventurers known as 'projectors' were raising loans for investment in more or less illusory enterprises by encouraging the gambling spirit in country gentlemen; they and their foolish clients, known as 'gulls', were a common subject of ▷ Jacobean comedies, such as Ben Jonson's *The Alchemist* and *The Devil is an Ass*. Just over a hundred years later gambling speculations caused the major financial crisis known as the ▷ South Sea Bubble, which brought ▷ Robert Walpole to power as the 'first Prime Minister'. Debtors' prisons such as the ▷ Marshalsea (the scene of much of Charles Dickens's novel *Little Dorrit*) were filled with rash speculators until imprisonment for debt was abolished in the mid-19th century.

Game laws

'Game' means animals suitable for hunting and protected in the breeding season to ensure that supplies should not fail. Such animals in England have been hares, foxes and deer. Other animals, such as rats and rabbits, are 'vermin' and may be killed at any time. Certain birds, especially pheasants and partridges, are 'game birds'. Game of all sorts on private estates and in royal forests was protected at all times by severe game laws from depredations by poachers, so that the owner of the land should enjoy the monopoly of hunting the game on his own land. As the ▷ magistrates who enforced the laws were themselves the landowners who had secured their imposition in Parliament, there was until the 19th century a fierce warfare between the landlords with their gamekeepers on the one side, and the poor who needed the game for food on the other; no part of the English penal system was so disproportionately severe.
Bib: Thompson, E. P., *Whigs and Hunters*.

Gardens and literature

The later 17th and the 18th centuries were periods in which comfort and elegance became important civilized values: buildings to provide shelter from the unreliable British weather began to ornament the grander gardens; orangeries, for instance, containing orange trees in tubs and galleries for sauntering out of the rain, were introduced in the reign of ▷ William III. After 1725, gardens became means of escape from the formality of 18th-century civilization and the old formal garden went out of fashion. Large gardens were designed increasingly with eyes that appreciated the wildness of 'picturesque' landscape, a taste formed partly by 17th-century Italian and French painters such as Salvator Rosa and Claude. Thus gardens became to some extent imitations of pictures; if the landscape were not wild enough, dead trees might be planted, *eg* in Kensington Gardens, London. Imitation Greek temples, such as those in Claude's pictures, were erected at suitable viewpoints, for instance on an island in a probably artificially created lake. ▷ Alexander Pope was fond of carefully constructed caves ('grottoes'). Later in the century, the taste for these architectural ornaments called 'follies' became more exotic: Chinese pagodas were built and imitation ruins of medieval Gothic castles were very common.

The 18th-century taste for 'wild' gardens was closely related to the literature of the period; it was indeed stimulated by ▷ James Thompson's landscape poems the ▷ Seasons. Later 18th-century poets, such as ▷ William Collins, ▷ William Cowper, ▷ Thomas Gray and others, wrote landscape poetry; much of it gives the impression of the poet enjoying a landscape from a distance or from a sheltered spot, as the landed gentry enjoyed their landscape gardens from their drawing-room windows. Designers of landscape gardens became artists with great prestige. The poet ▷ William Shenstone (1714–63) devoted his life and his fortune mainly to the landscaping of his property Leasowes. The most famous designer was Lancelot ('Capability') Brown (1715–83), who refused to allow any merely useful building, such as stables, to remain in sight of the house. But comfort, if not convenience, was maintained: 18th and early

19th-century novels frequently mention 'shrubberies' – picturesque, sheltered walks, where the ladies could walk out of the weather. At the very end of the century, the books on landscape gardening and on the picturesque in landscape by Repton were widely read and coincided with the rise of the English school of landscape painters such as Cotman and Crome.

Bib: Hadfield, M., *A History of British Gardening*.

Garrick, David (1717–79)

Actor, theatre manager, dramatist, whose genius as an actor greatly enhanced the theatrical profession in social prestige, and who was also responsible for far-reaching innovations in the theatre.

In 1737 he came to London with ▷ Samuel Johnson who had been his tutor at Lichfield, and entered Lincoln's Inn, but his career there did not last. He had shown a taste for theatricals early in his youth, and in 1740 he put together a burlesque play based on characters of ▷ Henry Fielding, *Lethe: or Aesop in the Shades*, which was performed at a benefit night for ▷ Henry Giffard.

In 1741 Giffard took a small company including Garrick to Ipswich, and here the actor performed regularly for the first time, making his debut as Aboan in ▷ Thomas Southerne's *Oroonoko*, before returning to Giffard's Theatre at ▷ Goodman's Fields. Garrick, still unknown, played Richard III, to a rapturous reception. In 1742 Garrick travelled to Dublin with ▷ Peg Woffington, who became his mistress, and together they joined the ▷ Smock Alley Theatre. They returned to London and in 1742 Garrick opened his first season at ▷ Drury Lane. Denied their salaries by the irresponsible manager Charles Fleetwood, Garrick, ▷ Charles Macklin, and several other actors rebelled in 1743. Eventually, after a series of further disruptions, including several riots at the theatre, and a season at ▷ Covent Garden (1746–47), Garrick became a joint manager at Drury Lane in 1747. Two years later he married the actress Eva Maria Veigel.

Garrick proved a vigorous and creative manager, reviving the fortunes of Drury Lane, and adding to his own status as the leading actor of his generation. His sensitive and naturalistic acting style, inspired by that of Macklin but perfected by Garrick himself, set a standard for the period, making the previous formal and 'stagey' methods of acting seem outmoded. In 1763, after further rioting at the theatre, Garrick abolished the long practice of allowing spectators on the stage. He introduced lighting concealed from the audience which he had observed during a professional visit to Paris, and engaged the brilliant scene designer De Loutherberg, who created a series of sets in naturalistic, romantic style that complemented Garrick's own style of acting. He also wrote a number of plays, and rewrote others to conform with the tastes of his time, including *The Lying Valet* (1741), ▷ *Miss in Her Teens* (1747), in which he himself played the part of the fop, Fribble, ▷ *The Clandestine Marriage* (1766) (in collaboration with ▷ George Colman the Elder), *The Country Girl* (1766) (a revision of ▷ William Wycherley's ▷ *The Country Wife*), *The Irish Widow* (1772), *Bon Ton; Or*

High Life Above Stairs (1775), and reworkings of several plays of Shakespeare.

Garrick retired in 1776 and died at his home in London after a long and painful illness. He was buried at Westminster Abbey, near the monument to Shakespeare who had provided him with many of his finest tragic roles, including Richard III Hamlet (his most popular part) Macbeth, and Lear. Garrick also excelled in comedy, his best parts including Abel Drugger in Ben Jonson's *The Alchemist*, Benedick in *Much Ado About Nothing*, and Bayes in the Duke of Buckingham's ▷ *The Rehearsal* (▷ George Villiers) in which he triumphed when he imitated several well-known contemporary actors.

Bib: Murphy, A., *The Life of Garrick*; Oman, G., *David Garrick*; Kahrl, G. M. and Stone, G. W., *David Garrick, A Critical Biography*; Kendall, A., *David Garrick: A Biography*; Wood, E. R (ed.) *Plays by David Garrick and George Colman the Elder*.

Garth, Sir Samuel (1661–1719)

Doctor and member of the Whig clique known as the ▷ Kit-Cat Club. His ▷ heroic couplet poem *The Dispensary* (1699) is a burlesque attack on the claim of apothecaries to exclusive control over the dispensing of medicines.

Gay, John (1685–1732)

Dramatist and poet, born at Barnstaple in Devon, the youngest son of William Gay. In 1708 he published 'Wine', a poem to celebrate the Act of Union between England and Scotland (▷ Union, Act of) and in 1711 a pamphlet *The Present State of Wit*. The following year he became a 'domestic steward' to the Duchess of Monmouth, and in 1714 secretary to Lord Clarendon, Tory envoy to Hanover. However, the accession to power of the Whigs threw him again upon his own resources. His farce, *The What D'Ye Call It*, a burlesque on what he deemed to be the moral and emotional falsity of heroic tragedy, as well as the growing taste for sentiment in comedy, followed in 1715. The play, which also satirized the idealization of country life, became a target for attack by the enemies of ▷ Pope, whom he had befriended. Gay's *Trivia, or the Art of Walking the Streets of London* (1716), on the conditions of life in the capital, is now considered a minor classic. In 1717 he collaborated with Pope and ▷ Arbuthnot on the satirical ▷ *Three Hours After Marriage* caricaturing a number of contemporary literary figures. This was an initial success, but then lapsed from favour. Gay's *Poems on Several Occasions* (1720) made him some money, which he invested in the South Sea Company. When this failed, he was temporarily ruined (▷ South Sea Bubble).

Gay is best known for his ballad opera, ▷ *The Beggar's Opera* (1728). An instant success, the piece was said to have made 'Gay rich and Rich (the theatre manager) gay'. The so-called Newgate pastoral', with music by the German composer Pepusch, satirized the London underworld, and corruption in general. It was also read as an attack on the ruling party of ▷ Sir Robert Walpole, who retaliated with Licensing Act of 1737, restricting the activities of the theatre. The sequel, *Polly* (1729), was banned by the Lord Chamberlain, although published by subscription. In his last years Gay lived mainly with two of his patrons, the Duke and Duchess of Queensberry in Wiltshire. He wrote the libretto for ▷ Handel's *Acis and Galatea* in 1731. Gay returned to London in 1732, and there died suddenly. He was buried in Westminster Abbey, where his epitaph, written by himself, is 'Life is a jest, and all things show it; I thought so once, and now I know it'.

Bib: Johnson, S., *Lives of the Poets*; Melville L., *The Life and Letters of John Gay*; Irving, W. H., *Gay, Favourite of the Wits; Sutherland, J., Pope and his Contemporaries*.

Genre

In its use in the language of literary criticism the concept of 'genre' proposes that particular groups of texts can be seen as parts of a system of representations agreed between writer and reader. For example, a work such as ▷ Aristotle's ▷ *Poetics* isolates those characteristics which are to be found in a group of dramatic texts which are given the generic label ▷ 'tragedy'. The pleasure which an audience derives from watching a particular tragedy emanates in part from its fulfilling certain requirements stimulated by expectations arising from within the form itself. But each particular tragedy cannot be reduced simply to the sum of its generic parts. It is possible to distinguish between tragedies by ▷ Sophocles, ▷ Shakespeare, or Edward Bond, yet at the same time to acknowledge that they all conform in certain respects to the narrative and dramatic expectations of the category 'tragedy'. Each example, therefore, repeats certain characteristics which have come to be recognized as indispensable features of the genre, but each one also exists in a relationship of difference from the general rule. The same kind of argument may be advanced in relation to particular sorts of poetry, or novel. The concept of genre helps to account for the particular pleasures which readers/spectators experience when confronted with a specific text. It also offers an insight into one of the many determining factors which contribute to the formation of the structure and coherence of any individual text.

Gentleman

The French 'gentile homme' meant 'nobleman', man of aristocratic descent. The tradition of courtly love required, however, that a gentleman's behaviour should correspond to his birth, *eg* in Chaucer's 14th-century translation of the *Roman de la Rose*: 'he is gentil bycause he doth as longeth to a gentylman'. By the 17th century the feeling that a gentleman was known by his behaviour more than by his birth was firmly established and ▷ James II is said to have remarked that he could turn a man into a nobleman but God Almighty could not turn him into a gentleman.

By the 19th century the title was allowed to all men of the educated classes, though being occupied in trade was still regarded as a barrier; in this respect the 19th century was perhaps less liberal than the 16th. Frequent explorations of the term in Anthony Trollope's novels show it as a site of contest: everyone wanted to claim they were a gentleman and its moral connotations were quite unstable. Though in theory it was behaviour that counted, appearances for most people counted still more, as is shown in Magwitch's notions of a gentleman in Dickens's *Great Expectations*. The ▷ public schools, at least since the 17th century had associated the idea of gentleman with education, especially a classical education in Greek and Latin literature; in the 19th century the public schools were greatly increased in numbers and the association of the rank of gentleman with a public school education persists to the present day.

Gentleman Dancing Master, The (1672)

Play by ▷ William Wycherley, inspired partly by Calderón de la Barca's *El Maestro de Danzar*. 14-year-old Hyppolyta is forcibly betrothed to the stupid fop, Monsieur de Paris, but schemes to evade the watch kept on her and her woman Prue, to keep them in the house and away from men. She is attracted to Gerrard, and tricks her suitor into bringing Gerrard to her window. The pair meet secretly, but are interrupted by her father, Don Diego, alias Mr Formal. Hyppolyta passes Gerrard off as her dancing master, employed to teach her the fashionable dance the Corant, and gains permission for him to visit her again. Gerrard is confused but drawn to her beauty, and her fortune. He plans their elopement. After many more farcical episodes, the two are married. Mr Formal reveals that far from being 'of an honourable house', as he has claimed, he is descended from a long line of merchants. He accepts the marriage, while Monsieur de Paris is obliged to return to Mrs Flirt, a 'common woman of the town', with whom he has had an affair. This is one of Wycherley's least appealing plays, and was not successful.

Gentleman's Magazine, The

Founded in 1731, it was the first to call itself a 'magazine'. It included, as later magazines were to do, a wider variety of material than the ▷ Reviews, including political reports which, in 1739–44, were contributed by ▷ Samuel Johnson.

George

The name of six of the kings of England belonging to the Houses of Hanover and Windsor. George I (reigned 1714–27) was great-grandson of ▷ James I (1603–25) and ruler ('Elector') of the German principality of Hanover. He was invited to take the throne of Britain, thereby superseding the ▷ House of Stuart, because the surviving members of this family were ▷ Catholics. George II, 1727–60; George III, 1760–1820; George IV, 1820–30; George V, 1910–36; George VI, 1936–52.

▷ Windsor, House of; Act of settlement.

George Barnwell. The History of
▷ *London Merchant, The*.

Georgian

A term for the architectural style of the period 1714–1810, under ▷ George I, II and III. Georgian architecture was severe but balanced in its proportions. It was influenced partly by the Palladian (▷ Palladio, Andrea) style of ▷ Inigo Jones and partly by the direct experience of English travellers who made the Grand Tour of Italy and admired its classical buildings. The term is not usually applied to 18th-century literature; in other arts its suggestion of elegance and proportion is often modified by a taste for satire and caricature, as in ▷ Hogarth's paintings. It was followed by the ▷ Regency style.

Georgic

Virgil's *Georgics* (from the Greek word for a farmer) comprise four poems, addressed to the Emperor Augustus (▷ Caesar, Augustus), describing the techniques of agriculture. During the 17th and 18th centuries they were extensively imitated in English, in ▷ blank verse or pentameter couplets (▷ metre), examples being ▷ John Philips's *Cyder*, ▷ John Dyer's *The Fleece*, and, in a more general way, ▷ Alexander Pope's ▷ *Windsor Forest* and much of ▷ William Cowper's *The Task*. ▷ John Gay's *Trivia*, set in London, is a humorous 'urban Georgic'.

Georgics

A poem on agricultural life by the Latin poet ▷ Virgil; it describes the peasant's year and contrasts the virtues of life in natural surroundings with the burdensomeness of urban luxury. The poem was of great influence on the tradition of ▷ pastoral poetry from the 16th to 18th centuries.

German influence on English literature

In the cultural interchange between the two literatures Britain has on balance been the dominant partner. German men and women of letters during the 18th century were far more likely to have a lively awareness of current developments in English literature than were their English counterparts in developments in Germany. For example, the status of ▷ *Paradise Lost* as an epic poem was debated, ▷ Alexander Pope's ▷ *Rape of the Lock* was read and discussed, ▷ Oliver Goldsmith, ▷ Edward Young, ▷ Laurence Sterne and ▷ James Thomson all known and admired. In this way English literature was able to play a crucial role in the process by which German writers of the late 18th century succeeded in exerting their independence from the prevailing standards of neo-classical decorum which French models seemed to dictate. The writers of the *Sturm und Drang* ('Storm and Stress'), as later the German romantics, looked to Britain rather than France for support and justification of their revolutionary project. Shakespeare's status as a German classic dates from this time, and the early attempts of ▷ Gothold Ephraim Lessing (1729–81), ▷ Johann Wolfgang von Goethe and Friedrich Schiller (1759–1805), who also translated *Macbeth*, to provide a repertoire for a German national theatre owed a great deal to the English dramatist. So when German theatre first made an impression in Britain, the new stimulus contained many, though unrecognized, indigenous elements. Interest in German theatre seems to have been kindled by the Scot Henry Mackenzie who gave an address on the subject to the Royal Society of Edinburgh in 1788. During the 1790s the English stage experienced a vogue for German plays, but the public's taste was essentially for the ▷ Gothic, and the most performed writer was the justly forgotten ▷ August von Kotzebue (1761–1819). It was not in drama, however, that the first impact of the new German literature was felt but in the novel. Goethe's epistolary novel *Die Leiden des jungen Werthers* (*The Sorrows of Young Werther*) (1774) was a landmark for it was the first work of German literature to achieve European recognition. It was translated into most European languages and reached Britain in 1799, significantly via a French version. The novel's apparent defence of suicide caused a storm of righteous indignation, but the huge popularity of the novel, here as elsewhere, had much to do with the fact that it appealed to a taste for 'sentimental' literature which had already been established in Germany and Britain by, among others, ▷ Samuel Richardson. Other currents made themselves felt also. Bishop ▷ Percy's *Reliques of Ancient English Poetry* (1765) had stimulated Herder and, through him, Goethe to explore their own native oral tradition of 'natural' *Volkspoesie*. This interest is reflected in the novel in Werther's admiration of ▷ *Ossian*, James Macpherson's collection of supposed fragments of lost Celtic epics, which had appeared in 1765.

This discovery of German literature by an English audience unfortunately soon met an insurmountable obstacle in the form of war. In the wake of the ▷ French Revolution a climate of opinion was created which was deeply and indiscriminately suspicious of all mainland European influence as ▷ Jacobin, subversive and unpatriotic.

German Princess, The

▷ Carleton, Mary

Ghosts

'Ghost' in modern English nearly always denotes a spirit of a dead person appearing to the living, though the older sense remains in the religious use of 'Holy Ghost'. For literary purposes ghosts may be divided into five kinds.

1 Earthbound spirits of popular tradition; they are not allowed to rest in the grave until a wrong done to them or by them has been set right, *eg* vengeance taken for murder. ▷ Hamlet's father is such a ghost.

2 Dream apparitions, commonly sent with a message or a warning to the sleeper, *eg* the murdered man appearing to his friend in Chaucer's *Nun's Priest's Tale* and perhaps the ghost of Caesar appearing to Brutus in Shakespeare's *Julius Caesar* IV.3.

3 ▷ Protestant belief in the 16th century was that a ghost might be a disguised emissary of the Devil; this is important in *Hamlet* 'Be thou a spirit of health or goblin damn'd' (*Hamlet* I.4.41) – Hamlet does not know whether the ghost really is his father or a devil with his father's appearance.

4 On the other hand the ghost Banquo (*Macbeth* III. 4) may be regarded as a hallucination both of

Macbeth's guilty conscience; another common form of 'ghost'

5 Finally, there is the comic or melodramatic kind of ghost, a kind of literary caricature of the first type, common in the ▷ Gothic tales of the 18th and early 19th century, and in more light-hearted Victorian tales, *eg* Charles Dicken's *Christmas Carol*.
▷ Supernatural.

Gibbon, Edward (1737–94)

One of the greatest English historians, author of ▷ *The Decline and Fall of the Roman Empire* (1776–88). His reputation rests almost entirely on this work, but his *Memoirs* (1796), put together from fragments after his death, are one of the most interesting biographies of the 18th century. In 1761 he published in French his *Essai sur l'Etude de la Littérature*, translated into English in 1764; it was more successful abroad than at home. He was also a Member of Parliament, 1774–81.
Bib: Low, D. M., *Edward Gibbon*; Young, G. M., *Gibbon*; Sainte-Beuve, C.-A., in *Causeries dy Lundi* vol viii.

Giffard, Anna Marcella

▷ Giffard, Henry.

Giffard, Henry (1694–1772)

Actor, manager. The date and place of his first stage performance are uncertain, but by 1720 at the latest he was acting at the ▷ Smock Alley Theatre in Dublin, where he remained for at least seven years, acting in a variety of young romantic lead roles. He married his second wife, Anna Marcella Lyddall (1707–77), the actress and singer, c1729.

By 1731 Giffard and his wife had appeared at the ▷ Haymarket Theatre, but later that year he took over running ▷ Goodman's Fields Theatre, refurbishing it and engaging a number of new actors. He opened a new theatre, also known as Goodman's Fields, in 1733. In 1737 he took the script of a satiric play to ▷ Sir Robert Walpole, and this was used, in part, by the Government as a pretext for passing the ▷ Licensing Act. Lacking a patent, Giffard was forced out of business, although he subsequently staged some performances at the fringes of the law, including the first performance of *The Winter's Tale* for over a hundred years.

By 1740 Giffard had successfully petitioned for permission to re-open Goodman's Fields, both managing and acting at the theatre. His reputation later rested not so much on his acting talents, which were not always wholeheartedly received, as on his abilities as a manager. He was also remembered for his encouragement of other actors, not least ▷ David Garrick, to whom he gave his first acting opportunity, in 1741.

Giffard, William (1756–1826)

Journalist. He began as a shoemaker's apprentice, and rose to be an influential writer and editor of the right-wing press. He edited *The Anti-Jacobin* (1797–8) to counteract opinion sympathetic to the ▷ French Revolution, and became editor of the famous Conservative *Quarterly Review* in 1809.

Gildon, Charles (1665–1724)

English author and editor, he was an early epitome of a ▷ hack, turning his hand to any literary endeavour that might earn him some money. His productions included pamphlets, a collection of poems, dialogues, and other items entitled *Miscellany* (1692), a *Life* of the actor ▷ Thomas Betterton (1710), and a revision of Langbaine's *An Account of the Dramatic Poets* (1696), as well as editions of works by ▷ Shakespeare and by ▷ Aphra Behn (1696). Numerous plays are attributed to Gildon himself, including *The Roman Bride's Revenge* (1696), *Phaeton* (1698), *Love's Victim* (1701), and *The Patriot* (1703); several of these involve revisions of earlier plays. He also on occasion acted as stage producer.
Bib: Backscheider, P. (ed.), *The Plays of Charles Gildon.*

Gilpin, William (1724–1804)

Aesthetic theorist. Gilpin's work was very important in establishing the cult of the ▷ Picturesque, as well as in heralding certain themes valued by the ▷ Romantic poets. He based his ideas upon journeys he undertook to the most 'picturesque' parts of Britain, including the Lake District and the Scottish Highlands, and published his theories in *Three Essays: On Picturesque Beauty; On Picturesque Travel; and On Sketching Landscapes* (1792). His efforts were not universally praised, and he was satirized in the figure of Dr Syntax by Coombe.

Glasse, Hannah (1708–70)

Writer, especially on housekeeping, she was at one time 'Habit Maker' to the Princess of Wales. Glasse prided herself on the plainness and simplicity of her writing style, so that the most ignorant servant would be able to understand it. Her works include *The Compleat Confectioner* (1742), *The Art of Cookery Made Plain and Easy* (1747), and *The Servant's Directory, or House-keeper's Companion* (1760). All of these were hugely popular. Four children's books are also attributed to her.

Glencoe

A valley in ▷ Scotland, where in 1692 the Campbell clan massacred a branch of the Macdonald clan. The Macdonald chief (out of pride) had delayed taking the oath of allegiance to ▷ William III and this was the pretext for the massacre, the real motive possibly being clan warfare. William III's Scottish administrator shared the guilt because he authorized the action.

Glorious Revolution

A name given to the removal by ▷ Parliament of ▷ King James II (1685–88) and the substitution of his daughter ▷ Mary II and her husband ▷ William III in 1688. The reason for the quarrel between James and Parliament was not so much that James was a ▷ Catholic as that he was using every means in his power to assert the superiority of royal power (in the name of his religion) over the power of Parliament. His policy united the whole nation against him, except for a very small minority of Catholics, and the success of Parliament finally settled the question of whether sovereign power lay with the king or with Parliament; this problem had been left unsolved when the period of republican rule (1649–60) had been succeeded by the ▷ Restoration of the monarchy. In 1688 the Revolution was a bloodless one, though there was subsequently some fighting in Ireland and Scotland. The consequences of the event were that the passionate religious and political disagreements which had so divided the nation since the beginning of the 17th century were greatly lessened, and a new temper of reasonable debate took their place; the change is typified by the *Letters concerning Toleration* (begun 1689) by the philosopher ▷ John Locke.

Glover, Richard (1712–85)
Member of Parliament for Weymouth (1761–8), and author of epics and. His ▷ ballad 'Hosier's Ghost', which attacked the naval policy of the Walpole government, was printed in ▷ Thomas Percy's *Reliques*.

Godwin, William (1756–1836)
Philosopher and novelist. His central belief was that reason was sufficient to guide the conduct, not merely of individuals but also of all society. His principal work was *The Inquiry concerning Political Justice* (1793). Man he believed to be innately good and, under guidance of reason, capable of living without laws or control. Punishments he declared (at a time when the English ▷ penal system was one of the severest in Europe) to be unjust; as were the accumulation of property and the institution of marriage. The Prime Minister, ▷ William Pitt (the Younger), decided that the book was too expensive to be dangerous. Godwin's best-known novel, *Caleb Williams*, came out in 1794: it was written to demonstrate the power for injustice accessible to the privileged classes. Godwin was a brave man, not merely with the pen; but his naïvety as a thinker would have left him without influence if his opinions had not agreed so well with the more extreme currents of feeling provoked by the contemporary ▷ French Revolution. As it was, he influenced a number of better minds, including, for a very short time, the poet ▷ Coleridge and, for a much longer period, Shelley, who became his son-in-law. Godwin's wife was ▷ Mary Wollstonecraft, an early propagandist for the rights of women and authoress of *A Vindication of the Rights of Woman* (1792).

Goethe, Johann Wolfgang von (1749–1832)
German poet; the greatest European man of letters of his time. His fame was due not only to the wide scope of his imaginative creation, but to the many-sidedness and massive independence of his personality. From 1770 to 1788 he was an inaugurator and leader of the passionate outbreak known in German as the *Sturm und Drang* – 'storm and stress' – movement, but from 1788 (after his visit to Italy) he represented to the world a balanced harmony inspired by the ▷ classicism he had found there. But he did not lose his sense that the spirit is free to find its own fulfilment according to its own principle of growth. At the same time, from 1775 he was prominent in the affairs of the German principality of Weimar (whose prince was his friend), concerning himself with practical sciences useful to the state, and thence with a serious study of botany and other natural and physical sciences to the point of making significant contributions to scientific thought. His commanding mind was admired in France, England, and Italy, with whose literatures Goethe was in touch; he corresponded with Byron; Walter Scott translated his *Goetz von Berlichingen*, which dated from the romantic phase of Goethe's career; he encouraged the young Thomas Carlyle.

Goethe is most famous for his double drama of ▷ *Faust*, but other works that became famous in England include the romantic drama already mentioned; the epic *Hermann and Dorothea*; a study in ▷ romantic sensibility *The Sorrows of Young Werther*; the novel *Wilhelm Meister*, an example of the *Bildungsroman*, and a large body of ▷ lyrical verse.

Golden Age
▷ Ages, Golden, Silver, etc.

Goldoni, Carlo (1707–93)
Italian dramatist, much influenced by ▷ Molière and the ▷ *commedia dell'arte*, who in turn influenced the English stage. He wrote some 250 comedies, tragedies, tragi-comedies and opera libretti in French, Italian and his native Venetian dialect. He reformed the Italian theatre, modernizing both the language and the action of the drama, and increasingly reflecting middle and even lower-class values and taste, so as to bring the stage closer to its audience. He adapted the *commedia dell'arte* to make it more socially relevant, and contributed to the emerging *opera buffa*, a form of comic opera without spoken dialogue. Among Goldoni's most famous pieces are *La Locandiera* (*The Mistress of the Inn*), *and* I Due Gemelli Veneziani (*The Venetian Twins*), written between 1748–52, and *Arlecchino. Servitore di Due Patroni* (*Harlequin, the Servant of Two Masters*) (1753). In 1761 he became attached to the French court, where he stayed until the Revolution (▷ French Revolution)
▷ Italian influence on English literature.

Goldsmith, Oliver (1730–74)
Dramatist, novelist, essayist, and poet. Born in Ireland, he studied at Trinity College, Dublin, but ran away to Cork after being disciplined by his tutor. He returned, however, and graduated in 1749. He applied for ordination, but was rejected, then was given 50 pounds to study for the law, but gambled it away. After this, he studied medicine at Edinburgh and at Leyden but it is unclear whether he obtained the medical degree to which he later laid claim. In 1756 he came to London, penniless, and supported himself with a variety of occupations, including messenger, teacher, apothecary's assistant, usher, and ▷ hack writer for a periodical.

In 1758 he translated Marteilhe's *Memoirs of a Protestant, Condemned to the Galleys of France for His Religion* and in 1759 his *Enquiry into the Present State of Polite Learning in Europe.* His 'Chinese Letters', written for John Newbery's *The Public Ledger* (1760–1) were reissued in 1762 as *The Citizen of the World*, a satiric view of England written from the supposed viewpoint of a Chinaman. His first real success as a writer was with the poem 'The Traveller', published in 1764. A number of his works are now highly valued, including ▷ *The Citizen of the World*; his life of Beau Nash (1762); his novel, ▷ *The Vicar of Wakefield*; a poem, ▷ *The Deserted Village*; and the plays *The Good Natur'd Man* (1768), and ▷ *She Stoops to Conquer* (1773) written, like the plays of ▷ Richard Brinsley Sheridan, in reaction to the sentiment of many plays of the period, and with the intention to revive the spirit of ▷ Restoration comedy. He wrote much else, including histories of England, Greece and Rome, and biographies of Voltaire, Bolingbroke and Parnell.

Goldsmith was a friend of ▷ David Garrick and ▷ Samuel Johnson, and figures largely in ▷ James Boswell's *Life of Johnson* (1791). Johnson praised his writing for its 'clarity and elegance', and later generations have repeatedly praised his literary 'charm', a quality made up of humour, modesty, vitality, and graceful lucidity. These he combined with the ▷ Augustan properties of balance and proportion. He died of a fever, deeply in debt, and the Literary Club (▷ Club, The) which he had helped to found in 1764 erected a monument to him in Westminster Abbey. Garrick wrote an epitaph to comment on his greatness as an author and reputed failings in other areas: 'Here lies Nolly Goldsmith, for shortness called Noll, Who wrote like an angel, but talked like poor Poll'.

Bib: Forster, J., and Wardle, R. M. *Lives*; Balderston, K. B. (ed.), *Letters*; Ginger, J., *The Notable Man*; Danziger, M. K., *Oliver Goldsmith and Richard Brinsley Sheridan*; Swarbrick, A. (ed.), *The Art of Oliver Goldsmith*.

Gooch, Elizabeth Sarah (b 1756)
Novelist, poet and autobiographer. Elizabeth Gooch's most fascinating work is her ▷ autobiography, *Life* (1792), partly because of the difficulties she encountered and the sordid world she was forced to live in, but mainly because of the rapid-paced narrative and her penchant for vivid sensationalism. She was the daughter of a Portuguese Jewish father who died when she was three, and her stepfather never fully accepted her into his family. She was sent to school at Fountains Abbey where she entered into a romance, which was thwarted. Following this she was 'married off' to William Gooch who was more interested in her dowry than in showing her any real affection. It was not long before Gooch accused her of adultery and sent her to France, where she became a prostitute. The subsequent years saw a series of escapades in which she acted on stage, fled from debtors, disguised herself as a man so as to follow her lover into battle, and persistently tried to wring money out of her embarrassed family. By 1788 she was in prison, from where she wrote *Appeal to the Public*. Gooch's later life is obscure, but several novels and a biography of Thomas Bellamy, all written between 1795 and 1800, remain.

Good-Natur'd man The (1768)
▷ Oliver Goldsmith's first play, a ▷ satire on genteel or sentimental commedy (▷ sentiment) and contemporary theories of benevolence. Young Mr Honeywood, the eponymous good-natured man, is so afraid of hurting or offending others that he entirely neglects his own interest. He runs himself into debt in order to treat his supposed friends, and even woos Miss Richland, whom he himself loves, on behalf of the vain and scoundrelly Jack Lofty, falsely believing him to be a man of honour. Honeywood's uncle, Sir William Honeywood, whose own good nature is far more discerning, vows to teach him a lesson, and arranges for bailiffs to arrest him. Miss Richland secretly pays his debts, and he is finally shamed into admitting the folly of his behaviour, while his uncle admonishes him to respect himself, for 'He who seeks only for applause from without, has all his happiness in another's keeping'.

In a related plot Miss Richland's guardian, Nicholas Croaker, wishes to force her and his son Leontine to marry. They are equally reluctant: Miss Richland loves Honeywood, while Leontine loves Olivia, whom he has brought to England masquerading as his long-departed sister as she in turn evades another odious guardian. They attempt to elope, but are discovered. Eventually all turns out well, and the various pairs of lovers are united.

The play was originally produced at ▷ Covent Garden, with the part of Sir William being played by ▷ Garrick. But at its first performance the bailiffs' scene was hissed by the audience as too 'low'. The scene was cut for a time, and the play became a success. It has been revived recently at the Orange Tree Theatre in Richmond.

Goodman's Fields Theatres
The first Goodman's Fields Theatre of which any details survive was opened by theatre manager and dramatist Thomas Odell (1691–1749) in Whitechapel in 1729, and lasted intermittently until 1751; another theatre by the same name was opened by ▷ Henry Giffard in Ayliff Street in 1733. Like several other theatres this was ordered to close in 1737 under the terms of the ▷ Licensing Act, but continued performances at the fringe of the law until 1741, the year of ▷ David Garrick's professional debut at this venue as Richard III. The theatre became a warehouse, and burned down in 1802. The present building dates from 1812.

Gordon riots
Riots in London in 1780, led by Lord George Gordon against a law passed in 1778 to relieve the condition of Roman Catholics. The riots form the climax of Charles Dickens's novel *Barnaby Rudge*.

Gothic
A term for the style of architecture which dominated western Europe in the Middle Ages. Its main features were the pointed arch and the ribbed vault. In England, this period is divided into three: Early English (13th century), Decorated (14th) and Perpendicular (15th–16th). A fine example of the last is King's College Chapel, Cambridge.

▷ Gothic revival.

Gothic novels

A genre of novels dealing with tales of the macabre and supernatural, which reached a height of popularity in the 1790s. The term 'Gothic' originally implied 'medieval', or rather a fantasized version of what was seen to be medieval. Later, 'Gothic' came to cover all areas of the fantastic and supernatural, and the characteristics of the genre are graveyards and ghosts.

▷ Walpole's ▷ *The Castle of Otranto* is generally seen as the earliest Gothic novel. ▷ 'Monk' Lewis, ▷ William Beckford and ▷ Mrs Radcliffe are notable exploiters of the genre. The vogue for Gothic novels soon produced parodies; Thomas Love Peacock's *Nightmare Abbey* and ▷ Jane Austen's *Northanger Abbey* are among the best examples.

Gothic revival

An architectural style now chiefly associated with the reign of Victoria (1837–1901). A taste for Gothic had in fact started in the 18th century; its starting point is associated with ▷ Horace Walpole's design of his home, Strawberry Hill (1747). The taste for Gothic spread between 1750 and 1830; as an artistic style it remained a minority cult, but as a sentiment it grew with the popularity of the sensationalism of the ▷ Gothic novels and with the rise of the ▷ romantic cultivation of the sensibility. In the 18th century, the taste for Gothic tended to be fanciful and sensational rather than deeply serious, although it gained seriousness from such a publication as ▷ Thomas Percy's *Reliques*; the 19th-century, Romantic Revival, especially the novels of Walter Scott, produced a deeper and much more genuine feeling for the ▷ Middle Ages.

▷ Furnishings and furniture; gardens.

Grace Abounding to the Chief of Sinners (1666)

The spiritual autobiography of ▷ John Bunyan author of ▷ *The Pilgrim's Progress*. The torments undergone by Christian in the latter book are substantially those of Bunyan in the earlier one. Bunyan had a similar spiritual awakening to Christian's, being aroused by a book; he suffers the terrible conviction of sin, like Christian's; he believes himself to commit the sin of blasphemy as Christian thinks he does in the Valley of the Shadow of Death; at last he achieves confidence in God's mercy. Much of the narrative is an account of painful mental conflict; but Bunyan never lost the sanity of perception into the fanaticism and mental morbidity of others, such as the old man who told him that he had certainly committed the sin against the Holy Ghost (for which there is no forgiveness). The book records how he developed that compassionate understanding of other men's spiritual conflicts which makes *The Pilgrim's Progress* the antecedent of the great English novels.

Graves, Richard (1715–1804)

Novelist. Graves was the rector of Claverton and a well-known figure in ▷ Bath society. He is best remembered for his novel *The Spiritual Quixote, or*

the Summer Rambles of Mr Geoffrey Wildgoose (1773), which recounts the comic journeys of a ▷ Methodist preacher. The figure of Wildgoose satirizes the Methodist George Whitefield (1717–70) whom Graves had met during their student days at Oxford. **Bib:** Hill, C. J., *The Literary Career of Graves*.

Gray, Thomas (1716–71)

Poet and prose-writer. The sole survivor of 12 children, Gray was born in Cornhill, London. His father, a scrivener, was mentally unbalanced and Gray was brought up by his mother, who sent him to Eton, where he made friends with ▷ Horace Walpole. He went on to Peterhouse, ▷ Cambridge, and gained a high reputation for his ▷ Latin poetry, though he failed to take a degree. In 1739 he embarked on a tour of the continent with Walpole, but in 1741 they quarrelled and Gray returned alone. He turned to the study of law, and began a tragedy, *Agrippina*, which remained unfinished. The death of Richard West, a close friend from his Eton days, in 1742, precipitated a period of poetic activity, in which he produced his *Ode on a Distant Prospect of Eton College* (published 1747), *Sonnet on the Death of Richard West* and *Ode to Adversity* (published in Dodsley's *Collections*, 1748). Also in 1742 he began ▷ *Elegy Written in a Country Churchyard*, while staying with his mother and aunt at their retirement home in Stoke Poges. The poem was carefully revised over a long period and eventually appeared in 1751, achieving instant recognition as a masterpiece.

From 1742 Gray lived in Peterhouse and later Pembroke College, Cambridge, except for a period (1759–61) in London where he pursued his studies in the British Museum. Relations with Walpole were soon restored and it was the death of Walpole's cat which inspired Gray's delightful ▷ mock-heroic *Ode on the Death of a Favourite Cat* (1748). The *Odes by Mr Gray* (1757), comprising his two Pindaric Odes, *The Progress of Poesy* and ▷ *The Bard*, was the first book published by Walpole's Strawberry Hill press. In the same year he was offered the laureateship on the death of ▷ Colley Cibber, but refused. In 1761 he wrote a number of poems reflecting a mixture of bookish scholarship and romantic primitivism, very characteristic of the period: *The Fatal Sisters*; *An Ode, The Descent of Odin*; *An Ode (From the Norse-Tongue)*, *The Triumphs of Owen*; *A Fragment* (from the Welsh). They were published in 1768 in Dodsley's collected edition of his works, *Poems by Mr Gray*. In the same year Gray was appointed Professor of Modern History at Cambridge, though he never delivered a lecture. In 1769 he travelled in the Lake District and *his Journal* (1775), relates his reactions to its sublime scenery. His letters reveal a profoundly learned, but witty and entertaining personality.

Gray's reflective works, in particular the *Elegy*, are masterpieces of the hesitant, personal poetry of ▷ sensibility. His odes, although not so successful, reflect the restless experimentalism of his period. It has been too easy to cast Gary either as a half-hearted ▷ Augustan or a timid pre-romantic, both tendencies being encouraged by ▷ William Wordsworth's dogmatic strictures on the language of his *Sonnet on the Death of Mr West*, and ▷ Samuel

Taylor Coleridge's corrective follow-up in *Biographia Literaria*, Chapter XVIII. It is better to see him in his own right. His particular poetic strengths are an ease of personification and abstraction (shared by his contemporaries ▷ William Collins and ▷ Samuel Johnson and emulated by John Keats in his Odes), and a restrained but eloquent felicity of phrasing, which places some of his lines among the best-remembered in the language: 'where ignorance is bliss/ 'Tis folly to be wise'; 'And Melancholy mark'd him for her own.'

▷ Augustanism; Bard; Romanticism.

Bib: Johnson, S., in *Lives of the Poets*; Arnold, M., in *Essays in Criticism* (2nd series); Ketton-Cremer, R. W., *Thomas Gray: A Biography*; Leavis, F. R., in *Revaluation*; Tillotson, G., in *Augustan Studies*; Powell Jones, W., *Thomas Gray, Scholar*; Starr, H. W. (ed.), *Twentieth-Century Interpretations of Gray's Elegy*.

Great Britain
▷ Britain

Great Fire of London
▷ Fire of London, The Great.

Greek literature
Until Greece was conquered by the Romans in 146 BC, it was a country of small states, mixed racial stock and cultural origins from all round the eastern Mediterranean. These states attained a high level of self-conscious political and artistic culture, which later enriched the Roman Empire and was thence transmitted to medieval and modern Europe.

The beginnings of Greek literature cannot be dated but its first period ended about 500 BC. The period contains ▷ Homer's epics, the ▷ *Iliad* and the ▷ *Odyssey*, and the poems of Hesiod. Homer's epics are the real starting point of European imaginative literature; Hesiod's *Theogony* is one of the principal sources of our knowledge of the Greek religious system. In English literature since the 18th century, the term ▷ elegy has implied narrower limits of subject and treatment than it had for the Greeks and the Romans, but the Greek evolution of the elegy and the ▷ lyric in this period has shaped our ideas of the character and resources of the short poem. An important variety of the lyric (whose principal characteristic was originally that it was intended to have musical accompaniment) was the 'Pindaric ode', so called after its most famous practitioner, ▷ Pindar; this was much imitated by English poets from the 17th to 19th centuries.

The second period (500–300 BC) is called the 'Attic Period' because it centred on the greatest of the Greek cities, Athens, capital of the state of Attica. The outstanding imaginative achievement of the Athenians was the creation of dramatic literature. The 'choral lyric', sung by choirs on religious occasions and especially on the festival of the wine-god Dionysus, was developed into a dialogue by Thespis in the 6th century. In the 5th century this was further developed into dramatic tragedy by three writers whose works have a fundamental influence on all our ideas of the theatre: ▷ Aeschylus, ▷ Sophocles and ▷ Euripides. The primitive

religion of the Greeks, based on the worship of the gods as the all-powerful forces of nature, was the origin of Greek ▷ tragedy; it was also the origin of comedy, of which the greatest Greek writer was Aristophanes. Athens, in this period, also developed Greek prose literature, in the works of the first of the historians, ▷ Herodotus, in the immensely influential philosophies of ▷ Plato and ▷ Aristotle, and in political oratory, especially that of Demosthenes.

Demosthenes achieved fame by his efforts to sustain the Greeks in their wars (357–338 BC) against Philip of Macedon, a state to the north of Greece. The war ended with the Macedonians making themselves the dominant power in Greece. They did not actually destroy the independence of the states, but the intensity and many-sidedness of Greek city life diminished. However, Philip's son ▷ Alexander the Great (ruled 336–323 BC) took Greek culture with him in his rapid conquests round the eastern Mediterranean and as far east as north-west India. The result was the 'Hellenistic Period' lasting until the Roman conquest, after which it did not cease but went into a new phase. The culture of Greece now became a climate of civilization shared by many lands; it was no longer even centred in Greece but in the university city of Alexandria in Egypt. The price paid for this expansion was that without the sustenance of the vigorous Greek city life, the literature lost its force, depth and originality, though it retained its secondary qualities such as grace and sophistication. The best-known imaginative works of this period are the '▷ pastoral' poems by ▷ Theocritus and others; they influenced the Roman poet ▷ Virgil, and were extensively used as models by ▷ Renaissance poets in the 16th and 17th centuries.

In the Graeco-Roman period (146 BC–AD 500), the Greeks were the teachers and cultural allies of their conquerors, the Romans. ▷ Latin literature written under Greek influence now excelled what continued to be written in Greek. Yet Renaissance Europe felt so much closer to the Romans than to the Greeks that it was the Greek writers of this period who influenced it more deeply than the earlier Greeks did. The historian and biographer ▷ Plutarch, for instance, was widely read in England in the age of ▷ Shakespeare, who used him as a sourcebook for his plays. The Greek romances, the best known of which is *Daphnis and Chloe* by Longus (2nd century AD), were imitated by 16th-century writers such as Sir Philip Sidney in his *Arcadia*. To this period also belongs one of the most influential pieces of Greek literary criticism, the treatise *On the Sublime* by ▷ Longinus.

In considering the influence of Greek literature on European, and in particular on English, literature, we have to distinguish between the influence of Greek philosophy and that of Greek imaginative writing. Plato and Aristotle had profound effects on Christian thought. Plato was made dominant by St Augustine of Hippo (4th–5th century), until St Thomas Aquinas replaced his influence by that of Aristotle. In the 16th century, Plato again became most important, but now as a source of

▷ humanist as well as of religious ideas. Aristotle remained dominant as the first philosopher of literature for three centuries, and together they are still regarded as the important starting points of European philosophy. Greek imaginative writing, on the other hand, made its impression on European, and especially English, imaginative writing chiefly through its assimilation by Roman writers. It was not, for example, the unexcelled Greek dramatists who impressed themselves on the equally unexcelled English dramatists of the age of Shakespeare, but the comparatively inferior Roman ones, ▷ Plautus in ▷ comedy and ▷ Seneca in tragedy. Only in the 30 years of the ▷ Romantic Revival that followed the ▷ French Revolution did English writers (partly under German influence) really discriminate between Greek and Roman literature, and value the Greeks more highly. It must not be forgotten that Greek culture was based on maintaining slaves and that their women were excluded from public life and restricted to the household (▷ women, status of). Neither class was considered as capable of full humanity as free Greek males. The extraordinary privilege accorded to Greek culture in western thought has often obscured these details.

▷ Classical education; Classical mythology; Latin literature; Pastoral, Classical; Platonism and Neo-Platonism.

Green, Matthew (1696–1737)
Author of *The Spleen* (1737), a tetrameter (▷ metre) couplet poem advocating the simple life as a cure for boredom and 'splenetic' irritableness.

Greenwich Observatory
Erected by the order of ▷ Charles II in 1675 to advance nautical astronomy. Charles also inaugurated the office of Astronomer Royal. The longitudinal meridian passes through the Observatory from Pole to Pole. Greenwich Mean Time is time based on this meridian. In 1946 the observatory was moved to Herstmonceux in Sussex to escape the smoke and bright lights of London; in 1990 it was moved again, to Cambridge.

Griffith, Elizabeth (1727–93)
Dramatist, novelist, editor, and friend of the actresses ▷ Kitty Clive and ▷ Peg Woffington. Griffith was the daughter of the comedian and actor-manager Thomas Griffith, and probably born in Dublin. From 1749 to 1753 she worked as an actress at ▷ Smock Alley in Dublin, and then at ▷ Covent Garden until 1755. In 1757 she published, together with her husband Richard Griffith, *A Series of Genuine Letters Between Henry and Frances* purporting to tell the story of their own courtship. In 1764 the couple effectively separated when she moved to London, having earlier returned to Ireland. However, their correspondence continued and was published in four more volumes between 1767 and 1770. Griffith wrote three ▷ epistolary novels, *The Delicate Distress* (1769), *The History of Lady Barton* (1771) and *The Story of Lady Juliana Harley* (1776), as well as a *Collection of Novels* (1777) and *Novellettes* (1780), originally serialized in the *Westminster Magazine*. Her plays included *The Double Mistake* (1766), *The School for Rakes* (1769), *A Wife in the Right* (1772), and she translated numerous works from the French, notably some volumes of ▷ Voltaire. Many of her works were noted for their politeness and decorum, overlaid with moral comment, but she also attacked women's unequal position in marriage and society.

▷ Feminism in Augustan literature in England.

Griffiths, Isabella (?1713–64)
Editor and probable reviewer for the *Monthly Review*, founded by her husband in 1749. She was a target for attacks by ▷ Goldsmith and ▷ Smollett for presuming to alter their work, when she edited it for the review. Her husband denied that she had written for his journal, but his testimony is thought unreliable.

Bib: Todd, J. (ed.), *A Dictionary of British and American Women Writers 1660–1800*.

Grimm's *Fairy Tales*
German folk-tales collected by the brothers Jacob (1785–1863) and Wilhelm (1786–1859) Grimm, and published 1812–15. They first appeared in English in a volume illustrated by ▷ George Cruickshank and containing such stories as 'Snow White', 'Hansel and Gretel' and 'Rumpelstiltskin'. They were the first collectors to write down the stories just as they heard them, without attempting to improve them.

▷ Children's books.

Grub Street
A street in London frequented in the 18th century by ▷ hack writers. Hence 'Grub-street' (adjective or noun) indicates literature or journalism of a low order. In the 19th century it was renamed Milton Street.

Grub Street Opera, The (1731)
Satiric entertainment by ▷ Henry Fielding, set in Wales and featuring songs using new words to popular melodies by Purcell and Handel, among others. In it the King and Prime Minister, ▷ Robert Walpole, are mocked in the characters of Sir Owen Apshinken (Welsh *Ap* = 'son of'; German *Schinken* = 'ham'), and the butler Robin ('robbing'). At the end the butler and staff all confess to having robbed the master's household over a long period. The play, following hard on the heels of the controversial *Ballad Opera*, was banned and never performed, but has recently been staged by a touring company for the first time. It is an attack on the aristocracy in general as well as the government, and is interesting in that it reverses earlier conventions whereby servants assist (or confuse) their masters' intrigues: here the rakish and foppish young squire Owen Apshinken conspires to frustrate his servants' amours, in hopes of seducing one of them, and the servants' affairs have an importance equalling or greater than that of their masters.

▷ Grub Street.

Grundy, Mrs
A symbol of narrow-minded, intolerant, out-of-date moral censoriousness. Mrs Grundy is a character in

an otherwise forgotten play, *Speed the Plough* (1798) by Thomas Morton. She herself never appears, but her neighbour, Mrs Ashfield, is constantly worried about what Mrs Grundy's opinion will be about this or that incident or piece of behaviour.

Gulliver's Travels (1726)

A satirical fable by ▷ Jonathan Swift. It exploits the contemporary interest in accounts of voyages, *eg* William Dampier's *New Voyage* (1697). ▷ Daniel Defoe's fictional account of Robinson Crusoe's voyages had been published in 1719, and had achieved great popularity; this was partly due to Defoe's strictly factual presentation, such that his book could quite well pass for a true account. Swift has his hero, Lemuel Gulliver, recount his adventures with the same sober precision for the effect of accuracy, following, as does Defoe's Crusoe, the philosopher ▷ John Locke in describing only the primary – *ie* objective, measurable – qualities of his strange environments, and ignoring the secondary qualities of colour, beauty, etc., which are more subjective, less verifiable, and so more likely to arouse a reader's disbelief. Swift's intention in doing this was of course not to deceive his readers into supposing that Gulliver's fantastic adventures were true, but to make them realize the absurdity, and worse, of accepted human characteristics when they are looked at from an unfamiliar point of view. Thus in Part I, ▷ Lilliput, Gulliver is wrecked on an island where human beings are little bigger than insects, and their self-importance is clearly laughable, but in Part II, ▷ Brobdingnag, he is himself an insect in a land of giants, and made to feel his own pettiness. In Part III, contemporary scientists of the ▷ Royal Society are held up for ridicule: science is shown to be futile unless it is applicable to human betterment – the science of Swift's day had not yet reached the stage of technology. Part IV is about the land of the ▷ Houyhnhnms, where horses are endowed with reason but human beings are not; the point here is that the horses recognize that Gulliver has reason, unlike the ▷ Yahoos of the island which he so much resembles, but they succeed in demonstrating to him that human reason is woefully inadequate for the conduct of life because of the mischievousness of the human mind. Swift was, after all, a Christian, and believed that Man would destroy himself without divine aid.

Swift was such a good story-teller that his fable became popular for the sake of the narrative, and though it was in no ordinary sense a novel, his close attention to factual detail (the way in which, especially in Parts I and II, Gulliver is continuously

under the pressure of his environment) takes a long stride in the advance of novelistic art.

▷ Lagado, Luggnagg.

Gunpowder Plot (1605)

A conspiracy by a section of English Roman ▷ Catholics to destroy the Protestant government of ▷ James I by blowing up the ▷ Houses of Parliament at a time when the king and the members of the Houses of Lords and Commons were all in the building. The plot was inspired by the ▷ Jesuits and led by Robert Catesby, but undertaken by Guy Fawkes. The date was fixed for 5 November and the explosives were all laid; but the plot was betrayed and Fawkes was arrested on the threshold of the cellar on 4 November. 5 November has since been celebrated annually with fireworks and bonfires on which Guy Fawkes is burnt in effigy.

Memories of the Gunpowder Plot helped to fan the flames of anti-Catholic feeling in the later 17th century as, for example, in the time of the Popish plot crisis (▷ Titus Oates).

Gwynn (Gwyn, Guinn, Guin), Nell (Eleanor) (Ellen) (?1642–87)

Actress, dancer. One account of Gwynn's early years has her hawking herring in the streets of London, before she became an orange seller at the ▷ Bridges Street Theatre, under 'Orange Moll', in about 1663. By 1665 she had graduated to the stage, aided by the actor ▷ Charles Hart, who became the leading actor in the ▷ King's Company and reputedly Gwynn's lover.

Gwynn quickly gained a reputation as a brilliant comic actress and dancer, 'pretty witty Nell'. By 1667 she had become the mistress of Charles Sackville, Lord Buckhurst, and two years after that, one of the mistresses of King Charles II. She gave birth to a son, later the Duke of St Albans, in 1670. She resumed acting soon afterwards, but left the stage permanently in 1671, living in a house in Pall Mall provided for her by the king. She continued as an avid patron of the stage, bringing large parties to performances. She also gave away substantial sums to the poor, and used her influence to free some prisoners from gaol. Gwynn remained a favourite of the court circle, and of the people, despite many satiric or even venomous attacks on her.

Bib. Howe, E., *The First English Actresses*; Wilson, J. H., *All the King's Ladies: Actresses of the Restoration*; Wilson, J. H., *Nell Gwynn*; Chesterton, C., *Nell Gwynn*; Bevan, B., *Nell Gwynn*.

H

Habeas Corpus

A legal writ which begins with these Latin words (= 'thou shalt have the body') The purpose is to order that an arrested person should be brought before a judge to test the legality of his restraint. The writ was used in the ▷ Middle Ages, as far back as the 12th century, but its use was defined by Parliament in the Habeas Corpus Act of 1679. It has long been considered one of the foundations of liberty.

Hack

Abbreviated from 'hackney', as in hackney-carriage. Since about 1700 it has been a derogatory term for an author, implying that the author can be hired for little money, to go wherever the hirer pleases; hence, a bad writer, one without originality, later often used of a journalist. The term was also a slang word for a prostitute, meaning one who could be 'ridden' for a small sum.

Halkett, Lady Ann (1623–1699)

English memoirist, born Ann Murray. She wrote a memoir of her earlier life in 1677–8. In 1647 she fell in love with Colonel Joseph Bampfield, a Royalist agent. In 1648 she helped with the plan to aid the escape of the Duke of York (the second son of ▷ Charles I), who rewarded her with a pension when he became king (▷ James II). Rumours that Bampfield's wife was still alive disturbed her, but she believed his version of events until 1653, when she discovered conclusively that his wife was still alive. In 1652 she met Sir James Halkett, whom she later married. But before they were married she ran into Bampfield again in London. Her description of their exchange is typical of the engaging way in which the memoir tells the story of her past: 'He [Bampfield] said he desired me only to resolve him one question, which was whether or not I was married to Sir J.H. [Halkett]. I asked why he inquired. He said because if I was not, he would then propose something ... both for his advantage and mine ... I said nothing a little while, for I hated lying, and I saw there might be some inconvenience to tell the truth, and (Lord pardon the equivocation) I said, "I am" (out loud, and secretely said, "not").' She later became a teacher.

▷ Cavendish, Margaret; Fanshawe, Lady Ann; Hutchinson, Lucy.
Bib: Loftis, (ed.), *The Memoirs of Anne, Lady Halkett and Ann, Lady Fanshawe.*

Hamilton, Lady Mary (1739–1816)

Novelist, born in Edinburgh to Alexander Leslie, the fifth Earl of Leven and his wife Elizabeth. She was married twice: to Dr James Walker and, after his death, to Robert Hamilton. She spent most of her life in France, but wrote in English, although one of her works was translated into French. Her five novels are mostly in the ▷ epistolary mode, and have ▷ romantic plots but an earnest moral tone, including appeals for women's right to education. They display considerable erudition, with a number of characters discussing the classics, science, and other serious topics, including architecture and contemporary literature.

▷ Feminism in Augustan literature in England.

Hampton Court

A palace on the Thames built by Cardinal ▷ Wolsey and a principal royal residence in the 16th and 17th centuries. It has an addition designed by ▷ Christopher Wren.

Handel, George Frederick (1685–1759)

Composer. Born in Germany, he was appointed chief musician to George, Elector of Hanover, who became George I of Britain (1714–27). Handel visited England in 1710 and settled there in 1712; he became a naturalized British citizen in 1726. He had studied in Italy and was deeply experienced in French music, but in many respects he was in harmony with the English tradition, whose last great master, ▷ Henry Purcell, had died in 1695. Nonetheless, Handel at first had an uneven career in England. He first attempted to establish ▷ opera in the Italian style; his opera *Rinaldo* was a success in 1711. Yet opera in the end reduced him to bankruptcy and he became the exponent of the art of oratorio, which he transformed from its original religious feeling and setting into a much more theatrical form. His first oratorio, *Esther* (1720), resembled the ▷ masques that had been popular in fashionable circles since early in the previous century. *Semele, Susanna* and *Judas Maccabus*, to mention a few of the 16 oratorios that followed, are choral dramas. His masterpiece was *The Messiah*, first performed in Dublin in 1741. Handel established the oratorio as the most popular English musical form for the next two centuries. Others of his choral works included his choral settings for ▷ John Dryden's poems, *Ode on St Cecilia's Day* and *Alexander's Feast.*
Bib: Deutsch, O. E., *Handel: A Documentary Biography.*

Hands, Elizabeth (fl 1785)

Poet. A neglected writer of great skill and variety, Hands had to contend with contemporary prejudice against her class (she was a servant) as well as her sex. She was sharply aware of both social barriers, writing the ▷ satirical 'Ode on a Dishclout' (▷ ode), and inverting conventional gender roles in her pastorals, where she makes the female nymphs sing in competition describing the beauty of their lovers, the male shepherds. Her most ambitious work, *The Death of Ammon*, was published in 1789 and focuses upon incest and rape.
Bib: Landry, D., *The Muses of Resistance.*

Hanover, House of
▷ George; Windsor, House of.

Harcourt, Mary (c 1750–1833)

Diarist. Mary Harcourt married a commander in the British army, William Harcourt, in 1778, and travelled with him when he was on active duty. Her accounts of what she saw during these periods reflect the horrors of war, show the small, and often neglected, acts of pity and heroism, as well as uncovering the political motivations behind the

objectives. Her work was published by the *Harcourt Papers* in 1792–5.
▷ Diaries; Nationalism.

Hardwicke's Marriage Act (1753)

An Act of Parliament intended to regulate and clarify the forms of marriage. It arose because of a growing number of clandestine marriages, as well as elopements and abductions of heiresses, as well as the ambiguities in what actually constituted a marriage owing to differences between the ▷ Common Law and ecclesiastical law, and contradictions within the laws themselves. The Act made it illegal to marry without a church service, required parental consent for the marriage of anyone under 21, defined times and places in which a marriage could take place in order to be legal, required all marriages to be entered into a church register, and transferred the control of marriage from the ecclesiastical to the secular courts. The Act was criticized by some for inhibiting the free expression of love among the young, and subjecting them to the tyranny of their elders. In fact parental attempts to control their children's choices in marriage were nothing new, and form the basis of the plots of many stage comedies of the ▷ Restoration and 18th century.
Bib: Stone, L., *The Family, Sex and Marriage in England 1500–1800*; Alleman, G. S., *Matrimonial Law and the Materials of Restoration Comedy*.

Harrow School

▷ Public school. It was founded in 1571 for poor children of the neighbourhood. After 1660 the school took children from the whole country, and in the 18th and 19th centuries it became immensely fashionable. In the 19th century the ▷ Eton v. Harrow cricket match became one of the most fashionable social occasions of the London season.

Hart, Charles (?1630–83)

Actor, manager. He began his career as a boy actor, playing women's parts, at the Blackfriars Theatre. After the theatres were closed in 1642, he fought in the service of the king, and is said to have acted clandestinely in the late 1640s. Hart resumed acting openly, at the Red Bull Theatre, about the time of the ▷ Restoration, and in late 1660 he joined the ▷ King's Company under ▷ Thomas Killigrew, now performing primarily or wholly in men's roles. He is reputed to have been, during the 1660s, a lover of ▷ Nell Gwynn.

During his lifetime his reputation rested particularly on his abilities in tragic roles: he is said to have acted with great precision and concentration such that nothing could distract him from his performance; and to have been able to draw full houses. He was for a time the main rival of ▷ Thomas Betterton, who imitated his style on at least one occasion.

Hartley, David (1705–57)

A philosopher best known for his theory of association of ideas, based on the thought of ▷ Sir Isaac Newton and of ▷ John Locke in the 17th century. In his *Observations on Man* (1749) Hartley denied that moral ideas were inborn in man, holding that they derived from associations of pleasure and pain with certain behaviour. The higher pleasures derive from the lower, and culminate in the love of God. This philosophy of mechanistic psychology was very influential in the first half of the 19th century, especially on the ▷ Utilitarian school of thinkers. ▷ Coleridge was at first strongly under Hartley's influence, but later rejected it, asserting that the human personality was active in its growth, not passive as Hartley's theory implied. ▷ Wordsworth, however, based much of his feeling for nature's creative influence on human personality on Hartley.

Hawking (falconry)

The sport of using birds of prey (hawks, falcons, etc.) for the pursuit of other birds and of small mammals such as rabbits and hares. In England as in every other European country it was both a popular and a fashionable sport until in the 17th century it was driven out by the use of the gun. Different species were considered appropriate to the various ranks of society, *eg* the eagle for emperors, gerfalcons for kings, peregrines for earls, goshawks for yeoman, sparrow-hawks for priests, kestrels for servants. The hawk was kept on the wrist of the falconer and released when the prey or 'quarry' came into view. The training of the hawk, *eg* not to fly away with its prey, is a long and complicated process.

Haymarket Theatres

The first major theatre in the Haymarket was built in 1705 according to a design by the dramatist and architect ▷ John Vanbrugh and immediately occupied by ▷ Thomas Betterton and his company. Until Queen Anne's death in 1714 it was known as Her Majesty's Theatre or the Queen's Theatre, and then the King's Theatre, or simply the Haymarket. However, the theatre suffered financial problems since it proved too large for spoken drama, and in due course became the first English opera house, staging many of ▷ Handel's operas. After three theatres were destroyed on that site the present theatre, known as Her Majesty's, was built by Beerbohm Tree (1853–1917) in 1897.

In 1720 another theatre was erected in the Haymarket, which was known variously as the New Theatre, Little Theatre, Little Haymarket, Little Theatre in the Hay or alternatively, the French Theatre in the Haymarket, because of its frequent use by French as well as Italian performers. Eventually, confusingly, it too became known just as the Haymarket. It stood until 1820 when the present Theatre Royal, Haymarket, was erected nearby.

A third theatre in the area was in a converted tennis court built in nearby James Street in 1634.

The name Haymarket derives from an actual hay market which existed from 1664 to 1830.

Haywood, Eliza (?1693–1756)

Haywood's literary career spanned some 30 years, from the publication of *Love in Excess or The Fatal Enquiry (1719)* to *Jemmy and Jenny Jessamy (1753)*. Harwood was a prolific and highly successful writer:

works known to be by her amount to almost 100 and she may also have published anonymously.

Like ▷ Delarivière Manley and ▷ Aphra Behn, Haywood's literary reputation has been obscured by the notoriety of her personal life. ▷ Alexander Pope satirized her in ▷ *The Dunciad*, as a 'Juno of majestic size. With cow-like udders, and with ox-like eyes', her sexual favours offered as the prize in a urinating contest. Yet Pope's vituperative attack, which has been regarded as evidence of misogyny, should be read in the context of the satire on literary hacks; the rival contestants Curll and Chetwood are no less damningly portrayed.

Haywood's novels were widely acclaimed, bringing her something of the status of a 'bestseller'. Their great diversity in tone and scope reflects a period of considerable change in novelistic fashions; the earliest works use romantic names, while the later employ 'character' types such as Trueworth, Saving and Gaylord, and there is an increasing emphasis on the female experience and the heroine as central character.

Haywood was also a prolific journalist, founding, amongst other periodicals, *The Female Spectator*, a women's equivalent to the periodicals of ▷ Addison and ▷ Steele. The articles generally deal with issues of social conduct and moral behaviour, and show an advanced attitude to sexual politics. Haywood also had a brief theatrical career in both writing and acting; her play, *A Wife to Be Let* (1724), was staged at Drury Lane with the author herself as a leading actress, and in the 1730s her frequent stage appearances included roles in *Arden of Faversham* and *The Opera of Operas* (1733), her own operatic version of ▷ *Tom Thumb*.

Her Majesty's Theatre
▷ Haymarket Theatres.

Herbert, Edward, 1st Baron Herbert of Cherbury (1583–1648)
Poet, philosopher and diplomat. Edward Herbert (Lord Herbert of Cherbury) was the elder brother of George Herbert, and a friend of John Donne, Ben Jonson and Thomas Carew, and an ardent Royalist before the ▷ Civil War. Herbert's major works were his autobiographical *The Life of Lord Herbert Written by Himself* (published by ▷ Horace Walpole in 1765); his philosophical *De Veritate* (1624) and his volume of poems *Occasional Verses* (1665).

The *Life*, written when Herbert was in his 60s, recalls his adventures as a younger man, prior to his return from Paris in 1624, where he had been ambassador. The *De Veritate*, which was of considerable influence in the 17th century, attempts to explore rationalist positions in the general field of religious experience. Herbert's own religious position was that of an orthodox Anglican, of a strongly anti-Calvinist persuasion.

Although his poetry was not published until 1665, the major portion of his verses was written before 1631. His poetic contemporaries thus included both his brother and Donne, of whose verses Herbert's poetry is strongly reminiscent.

▷ Calvin, John; Deism.

Bib: Herbert, C. A., 'The Platonic Love Poetry of Lord Herbert of Cherbury', *Ball State University Forum* II; Hill, E. D., *Edward, Lord Herbert of Cherbury*.

Herbert, George (1593–1633)
Poet. Herbert shares with John Donne the distinction among 17th-century poets of still being widely read in modern times. Though he was not ordained as a priest until 1630, and though court connections ensured that the earlier part of his life was spent in cosmopolitan circles, all the extant poems are devotional in nature.

His poetry was first published in 1633, when *The Temple: Sacred Poems and Private Ejaculations* appeared under the auspices of his friend Nicholas Ferrar shortly after Herbert's death. The collection met with enormous approval, and was a considerable influence on Richard Crashaw, amongst others. The poems in *The Temple* are deceptively simple. Yet in his exploitation of the speaking voice, and in the complexity of the complete structure of the volume of poems, Herbert rivals Donne for a fierce logical presence in his verse. Of considerable importance to Herbert's poetic undertaking is his espousal of a direct form of poetic discourse – one that, in many respects, looks forward to the reformist projects of later 17th-century theoreticians of language.

Herbert's other major work was the prose manual *A Priest to the Temple* (1652) which is a form of conduct-guide for the ideal Anglican priest. ▷ Izaac Walton published a *Life* of Herbert in 1651.
Bib: Hutchinson, F. E. (ed.), *The Works of George Herbert*; Vendler, H., *The Poetry of Herbert*; Summers, J. H., *George Herbert: His Religion and Art*; Strier, R., *Love Known: Theology and Experience in George Herbert's Poetry*.

Herodotus (5th century BC)
Greek historian. His main theme is the wars of the Persians against the Greeks and other nations.

Heroic couplet
▷ Augustanism; couplet.

Heroic drama
Type of play popular during the period after the ▷ Restoration in Britain, with central characters of exalted stature, such as kings, queens and military generals, and a florid style of verse, usually rhymed ▷ couplets. The plays were modelled on ▷ French ▷ classical tragedies, especially those of ▷ Corneille and ▷ Racine, and often featured themes of conflict between the forces of love and honour. However, they were less careful of the ▷ classical unities than their French models. ▷ D'Avenant's ▷ *The Siege of Rhodes* was one of the earliest plays to display features of heroic drama, and his dedication to an edition of 1663 discusses 'héroique Plays'. Robert Howard's ▷ *The Indian Queen* (1664) helped to establish the type in Britain, and ▷ Dryden became one of its chief exponents, with plays including *The Indian Emperor* (1665), *The Conquest of Granada* (1665) and ▷ *Aureng-Zebe* (1675). ▷ Buckingham's satire of heroic plays, ▷ *The Rehearsal*, played a large

part in bringing the form into disrepute, although ▷ Congreve's ▷ *The Mourning Bride* still displays some heroic features.

Herrick, Robert (1591–1674)

Poet. Robert Herrick's poetry was published in a collection entitled *Hesperides* (1648) which appeared together with a companion volume, *His Noble Numbers*. Numerous manuscript versions of his poetry circulated in the 17th century, but the vast majority of his verse is represented in the 1648 publication.

He has long been associated with the Cavalier poets, although his writing is of a quite different kind. Herrick's chief stylistic models were the epigrammatic Latin poetic styles to be discovered in the works of ▷ Catullus and ▷ Horace (▷ epigram). His delight in the epigrammatic style contrasts with his other memorable poetic achievement – the creation of fantasies which combine ▷ pastoral motifs with minutely observed details of nature. The poem which opens the 1648 collection ('The Argument of His Book') sets out his poetic manifesto, which is revealed to be one of nostalgic longing for a rural ideal, probably unobtainable.

Bib: Martin, L. C. (ed.), *Robert Herrick's Poetical Works*; Rollin, R. B., & Patrick, J. M. (ed.), *Trust to Good Verses: Herrick Tercentenary Essays*.

Hervey, Elizabeth (c 1748–c1820)

Novelist. Hervey was the half-sister of ▷ William Beckford, who is thought to have had her in mind when he attacked sentimental novels in *Modern Novel Writing*, although his attack could equally well be directed at ▷ Hannah More or ▷ Mary Robinson. Whatever the intention, Hervey appears to have been genuinely upset, partly because the accusation was not particularly just. Her works exhibit some of the plot characteristics of sentimental novels, for example in *Louisa* (1789), where the heroine selflessly devoted to the illegitimate child of her betrothed, but her character sketches and descriptive passages are sharper and more self-consciously witty than Beckford's summation suggests.

Hervey, John, Baron of Ickworth (1696–1743)

Writer and politician. Son of the Earl of Bristol, whose title he inherited in 1723. In 1720 he married the maid of honour to the Princess of Wales, Molly Lepell, who was often mentioned in the letters and verses of ▷ Pope. He became MP for Bury, and supported ▷ Sir Robert Walpole. In 1730 he became Vice Chamberlain to George II. Later he was made Lord Privy Seal, and became a confidant of Queen Caroline. His *Memoirs of the Reign of George the Second*, not published until 1848, describes the events of the period with keen satire. Pope developed a fierce animosity toward Hervey, whom he made a target for his own satire. He resented Hervey's friendship with ▷ Lady Mary Wortley Montagu, whom he himself admired, and despised Hervey's supposed 'feminine' behaviour, including taking extreme care with his diet because of ill-health, and using rouge to disguise his pallor. Pope lampooned

him savagely him in the character of Sporus, in the *Epistle to Dr Arbuthnot*, and in ▷ *The Dunciad*. As with Pope's other target, ▷ Colley Cibber, the attacks were sufficient to damn him in the eyes of posterity, and even in his own time Hervey was ridiculed with another nickname used by Pope, 'Lord Fanny'.

Hexameter

A line of verse having six metrical feet. ▷ Metre.

Hibernia

The Latin name for Ireland; used poetically.

Highlands, The

The name given to the north and west of ▷ Scotland. As a region, it is distinctive not merely because it is more mountainous than the Lowlands of the south and east, but for reasons of race, language and history. The Highlands are predominantly Celtic and the Celtic language of Gaelic used to prevail there, although it is now gradually dying out. Socially, the Highlanders until the 18th century lived under the semi-tribal 'clan' system, which again was never characteristic of most of the Lowlands. Economically, the Highlands have always been poorer than the Lowlands, which possess highly developed industry and agriculture.

Highwaymen

Robbers on the highways, usually on horseback. They became common in the 18th century, when travel greatly increased, owing to improvements in roads and in vehicles, and when policing was still very inadequate.

Mail coaches especially were robbed, the practice being for the masked highwayman to stop the coach by pointing a pistol at the coachman. Highwaymen usually acted individually, not in gangs, but often with the assistance of inn-servants who passed them information about rich travellers. In the 19th century, as the danger of highwaymen decreased, so they tended to be romanticized as 'gentlemen of the road'; this coincided with a fashion for tales about criminals in the 1830s. Thus Harrison Ainsworth in *Rookwood* (1834) popularized ▷ Dick Turpin, an 18th-century highwayman, in consequence of which he has become something of a folk-hero like Robin Hood, though the evidence is that he was a commonplace criminal. Earlier ▷ *The Beggar's Opera* (1728) by ▷ John Gay gives a more challenging and cynical account of the phenomenon.

Hind and the Panther, The (1687)

A didactic poem in heroic ▷ couplets by ▷ John Dryden, written after his conversion to ▷ Catholicism in 1685, and counterbalancing his earlier defence of the Church of England, ▷ *Religio Laici* (1682). It takes the form of a perfunctory allegory, in which the Hind (the Church of Rome) and the Panther (the Church of England) debate at length the merits of their different beliefs.

▷ Prior, Matthew.

Hippocrene

▷ Muses.

Histories and Chronicles

Histories and chronicles are important in the study of literature in two ways: as sources for imaginative material and as literature in their own right. However, with the exception of the Venerable Bede, it was not until the 17th century that English historians began to achieve the status of major writers.

The True Historical Narrative of the Rebellion and Civil Wars in England by Edward Hyde, Earl of Clarendon (▷ Clarendon), is the first major historical work to rank as distinguished literature in English. Clarendon began it in 1646 but it was not published until 1702–4. It is told from the point of view of an important participator in the events and is notable especially for its portraits of other participators. Clarendon was a royalist; his younger contemporary ▷ Gilbert Burnet (1643–1715), told the story of the second half of the century from the opposing political viewpoint in his most important work, *The History of My Own Time*. Burnet was more of a professional historian than Clarendon (who was primarily a statesman who took to history partly in self-justification) and he initiated historical writing as a major branch of literary activity and scholarship. The distinguished historical writing of William Robertson (*History of Scotland during the Reigns of Queen Mary and James VI*, 1759, and *Charles V*, 1769), of the philosopher ▷ David Hume (*History of Great Britain*, pub 1754–61) and the lighter histories of England by the novelist ▷ Tobias Smollett (1756) and by ▷ Oliver Goldsmith (1764) have been superseded by later work, but ▷ Edward Gibbon's ▷ *Decline and Fall of the Roman Empire* (1776–88) is a work not only of history but of English literature and, in the quality of its outlook on civilization, an 18th-century monument. The 18th century was the one in which antiquarian scholarship became thoroughly established; the antiquarians were interested by the nature of their studies in the detailed life of the past.

History of England from the Accession of James II

The history by ▷ Thomas Macaulay (Vols. 1 & 2, 1848; 3 & 4, 1855; 5, 1861) is a thorough, detailed account of two reigns: ▷ James II and ▷ William III. It is unfinished and was originally intended to extend to the time of ▷ George I (1714–27) and further. The period covered is perhaps the most crucial for English political development. James II, a ▷ Catholic, tried to enforce his will in the Catholic interest against Parliament, which frustrated him and expelled him from the throne in the ▷ Revolution of 1688. Parliament then summoned William from Holland to reign jointly with his wife, who was also James's daughter ▷ Mary II (1689–94). William was the champion of the ▷ Protestant cause in Europe, and Mary was also Protestant.

Macaulay's politics were strongly in the ▷ Whig parliamentary tradition and his history is an epic of the triumph of the ideas which to him gave meaning to English history. Considered as history, the work is accordingly one-sided, much more a work of historical art than of historical science; it represents what historians have come to call 'the Whig interpretation of history'.

Hobbes, Thomas (1588–1679)

Philosopher. Together with the writings of ▷ Francis Bacon and ▷ René Descartes, the political and philosophical theories of Thomas Hobbes dominated thought in late 17th-century England. Yet, unlike Bacon's boundless optimism, Hobbes's philosophy appeared to be determined by an almost cynical view of human nature and society. In his great analysis of the individual and the individual's place in society. *Leviathan* (1651), Hobbes argued that human society was governed by two overwhelming individual concerns: fear (of death, other individuals, etc.) and the desire for power. For Hobbes society is organized according to these two principles, and can be rationally analysed as a 'mechanism' (an important Hobbesian concept) governed by these two concerns.

Leviathan itself emerged out of the turmoil of revolutionary upheaval in England during the ▷ Civil War, and the figure of the 'Leviathan' – the sovereign power, though not necessarily the monarch – expresses a desire for stable government. But in addition to *Leviathan* Hobbes published in various fields of philosophical and social enquiry. His interest in language and the uses of ▷ rhetoric was to be influential amongst post-Restoration thinkers. But it was his analysis of the mechanical laws (as he saw them) of production, distribution and exchange which was to be of profound importance in British economic and philosophical thought in the 18th century and later.

Hobbes's other chief works include: *The Elements of Law* (written by 1640, but published ten years later); *De Cive* (1642, translated into English in 1651); *De Corpore* (1655, translated in 1656); and *De Homine* (1658). Hobbes also undertook an analysis of the causes of the English Civil War in *Behemoth* (1682), as well as critical work – in particular his *Answer* to ▷ Sir William D'Avenant's *Preface to Gondibert* (1650).
Bib: *The English Works of Thomas Hobbes*, Molesworth, Sir W. (ed., 11 vols.); Mintz, S. I., *The Hunting of Leviathan*.

Hogarth, William (1697–1764)

Painter. He excelled in the depiction of social life, especially the heartlessness of the richer classes permeated by social arrogance and commercial greed, with the consequent neglect of the poor. He painted sequences that followed a theme, a technique which is a pictorial equivalent of a stage drama: 'I wished to compose pictures on canvas, similar to representations on the stage; . . . I have endeavoured to treat my subjects as a dramatic writer; my picture is my stage, and men and women are my players . . .' His art became extremely popular, because he made engravings of his oil paintings, and they were to be found on the walls of inns and cottages, not merely in great country houses. In his breadth of appeal and his realism, he is in strong contrast to the fashionable portrait painters of the 18th century, ▷ Joshua Reynolds and Gainsborough, and in the quality of his social indignation and his concern with unprivileged humanity he anticipates the poet-engraver ▷ William Blake. Some of his series of what he called 'pictur'd Morals' are: *A Harlot's Progress* (1731); *A Rake's Progress* (1735); *Marriage à la Mode* (1743–5); *The Four Stages of Cruelty, Beer Street* and *Gin Lane* (1751) (2.2.3) and *Election* (1754–66).

Hogarth's literary connections were close. ▷ Jonathan Swift invokes him as natural collaborator in his own kind of savage satire in his poem *The Legion Club* (1736), and his friendship with the novelists ▷ Samuel Richardson and ▷ Henry Fielding influenced the visual element which gives their novels an advantage over those of ▷ Daniel Defoe. The ordinary people who enjoyed owning and interpreting his engravings, with their satirical edge, were the foundation of the market for later cheap serial fiction, with its engraved illustrations. The importance of the visual element in serials from Charles Dickens's *Pickwick Papers* onwards owes a debt to Hogarth and his successors.
Bib: Moore, R. E., *Hogarth's Literary Relationships*.

Holcroft, Thomas (1745–1809)
Dramatist, novelist, actor, translator, largely associated with the introduction of continental melodrama to the English stage. In 1770 Holcroft obtained a post as prompter in the Dublin theatre and this was followed by a period of acting with strolling companies in England, and in 1778 an engagement at the ▷ Drury Lane Theatre, where his first play was performed. In 1780 his first novel, *Alwyn or the Gentleman Comedian* was published, drawing on his experiences as a strolling actor. His first comedy, *Duplicity*, was staged at ▷ Covent Garden in 1781. In 1784, on a visit to Paris, Holcroft was impressed by a production of Beaumarchais' *Le Mariage de Figaro* and, being unable to obtain a copy, he committed the entire play to memory. On his return, his translation was mounted at Covent Garden under the title *The Follies of the Day*. In 1792 Holcroft's most successful play, *The Road to Ruin*, was produced, again at Covent Garden.

An ardent supporter of the ▷ French Revolution, Holcroft became active on its behalf in England, and was imprisoned briefly for alleged treason. In 1799 he moved to Paris, where he lived for four years. In his absence his *A Tale of Mystery*, a translation from a play by Pixérécourt, was produced in London. He also published several translations of novels and wrote operas, afterpieces, and polemical essays.
Bib: Rosenblum, J. (ed.), *The Plays of Thomas Holcroft*.

Holy Roman Empire
Claiming to be the continuance of the Roman Empire of the West, the Holy Roman Empire lasted from the crowning of the Emperor Charlemagne by the Pope in AD 800 to its downfall in 1806 during the Napoleonic Wars. 'Holy' was added in the 12th century to emphasize that the Empire was the political counterpart of the Pope's spiritual authority over Christendom; in truth, much of European history in the 12th and 13th centuries sprang from rivalry between the two. Under Charlemagne, the

Empire covered nearly all Europe. Thereafter its frontiers shrank, but its effective core was always the German-speaking lands. The Emperor was supposed to be elected by certain German princes (hence the title of, *eg* Elector of Hanover) but from 1493 the Empire remained with the Austrian Habsburg family. Even in Germany the Emperor's authority was by no means always effective; by the 18th century the Holy Roman Empire merited ▷ Voltaire's gibe that it was neither holy, nor Roman, nor an empire.

Holy War, The (1682)
An ▷ allegory by ▷ John Bunyan. Its subject is the fall and redemption of man. The city of Mansoul has fallen into the hands of Diabolus (the Devil) and has to be recaptured by Emmanuel (Jesus Christ), who besieges it.

Homer
Ancient Greek epic poet, author of the ▷ *Iliad* and the ▷ *Odyssey*, basic works for ▷ Greek literature. Ancient traditions exist about Homer, for instance that latterly he was blind and that seven cities claimed to be his birthplace, but nothing is conclusively known about him. Archaeological investigation has disclosed that the destruction of Troy, following the siege described in the *Iliad*, took place in the 12th century BC; linguistic, historical and literary analysis of the poems show them to date as artistic wholes from perhaps the 8th century BC. That they are artistic wholes is in fact the only evidence for the existence of Homer; efforts to show that they are compilations by a number of poets have proved unconvincing, though it is clear that Homer himself was using the work of other poets between the Trojan war and his own time. The critic Matthew Arnold, in his essay *On Translating Homer* (1861), says that Homer is rapid in movement, plain in diction, simple in ideas and noble in manner; and that the translations by three eminent English poets, George Chapman (16th century), ▷ Alexander Pope and ▷ William Cowper (18th century), all fail in one or more of these qualities, however fine their verse is in other respects.

Homosexuality
Homosexuality has usually been accorded a marginal place in literary representation, but when it has been treated it has usually been hedged about with implications of the exotic, the abnormal or at least the exceptional. There are references to homosexuality in some ▷ Restoration poetry. For example, ▷ Rochester, in a 'Song' (1672–3), refers to 'a sweet, soft page [who] does the trick [sexual intercourse] worth forty wenches'.

Some lines by ▷ Aphra Behn have been interpreted as having a homosexual content, notably her 'To the Fair Clarinda, Who Made Love to Me, imagin'd more than Woman' (1688).

Horace (Quintus Horatius Flaccus), 65–8 BC)
Roman poet of the Augustan age (▷ Caesar Augustus). His work divides into three classes; his ▷ Satires, ▷ Odes and Epistles. The last includes the *Art Poetica* or *De Arte Poetica* ('Concerning the

Art of Poetry') which became an important critical document for Europe – for England particularly in the 18th century. It emphasizes the importance of cultivating art in poetry; Horace lays down the principle that if you do not understand poetry it is better to leave it alone. Art means above all the cultivation of alert judgement: expression and form must be appropriate to theme; characterization and form must be consistent with the subject and with themselves; conciseness is a virtue in didacticism; adaptation of a writer is allowed but plagiarism is not; the poet must study to be wise as a man, and he must be his own severest critic; a just critic is a severe one. The age of ▷ Alexander Pope and ▷ Samuel Johnson took these principles to heart and they also liked Horace's cultivation of balance in prosperity between wealth and poverty: he had become the friend of the rich patron of letters, Maecenas, who had provided him with a small estate in the Sabine hills. The English Augustans' concern was to cultivate proportion and balance. Criticism and satire thus became important to them as correctives of inborn human tendencies, and they cultivated the congenial spirit of Horace as Horace himself had sought to practise the virtues of the Greeks. Thus Pope entitled one of his sequences of poems ▷ *Imitations of Horace*.

Houses of Parliament
▷ Parliament.

Houyhnhnms
The horses endowed with reason in Part IV of ▷ Swift's ▷ *Gulliver's Travels*. The word imitates the whinnying of a horse. The enlightened horses are a purely reasonable aristocracy, inhabiting an island which also contains a race called ▷ Yahoos who, not endowed with reason, typify brutish and degraded behaviour. Gulliver's Houyhnhnm host recognizes that Gulliver is unlike the Yahoos in his possession of the faculty of reason, but proves to him that owing to his other qualities, which are Yahoo-like, he can only use his reason destructively.

Hudibras (1663, 1664 and 1678)
A ▷ mock-heroic satire in tetrameter ▷ couplets by ▷ Samuel Butler (1612–80). The Presbyterian Sir Hudibras, and his Independent Squire Ralpho, undergo various adventures designed to expose the hypocrisy of the Puritans, interspersed with satire on various scientific and intellectual follies. The poem's structure parodies the 16th-century epic romances of Ariosto and Spenser, and the hero takes his name from a knight in Spenser's *Faerie Queene*. In spirit it owes much to Cervantes' anti-romance satire *Don Quixote*. The poem's politics pleased ▷ Charles II who gave Butler £300 and a pension of £100 a year. Though the work fails to sustain narrative interest it establishes its own distinctive vein of rollicking farce and homespun philosophizing:

> *Honour is, like a widow, won*
> *With brisk attempt, and putting on;*
> *With ent'ring manfully and urging;*
> *Not slow approaches, like a virgin.*
> (I, ii, 911–14)

Butler's loose tetrameters with their vigorous colloquial diction and crude rhymes, became an established medium for broad satire, known as 'hudibrastics', used by, among others, ▷ Jonathan Swift, ▷ John Philips and ▷ Bernard de Mandeville.

Humanism
The word has two distinct uses: 1 the intellectually liberating movements in western Europe in the 15th and 16th centuries, associated with new attitudes to ancient Greek and Latin literature; 2 a modern movement for the advancement of humanity without reliance on supernatural religious beliefs.

1 Humanism in its first sense had its beginnings in Italy as early as the 14th century, when its pioneer was the poet and scholar Petrarch (1304–74), and reached its height (greatly stimulated by the recovery of lost manuscripts after the fall of Constantinople in 1453) throughout western Europe in the 16th century, when it first reached England. Its outstanding characteristic was a new kind of critical power. The humanists began by criticizing and evaluating the Latin and Greek authors in the light of what they believed to be Roman and Greek standards of civilization. Some of the important consequences of humanism were these: the rediscovery of many ancient Greek and Latin works; the establishment of new standards in Greek and Latin scholarship; the assumption, which was to dominate English education until the present century, that a thorough basis in at least Latin literature was indispensable to the civilized man; the beginnings of what we nowadays regard as 'scientific thinking'; the introduction of the term ▷ Middle Ages for the period between the fall of the Roman Empire of the West (5th century AD) and the ▷ Renaissance, meaning by it a period of partial and inferior civilization. In the 17th and 18th centuries, humanism hardened into neo-classicism.

2 'Humanism' is also used as a general expression for any philosophy that proposes the full development of human potentiality. In this sense, 'Christian humanism', since the 16th century, has stood for the marriage of the humanist value attached to a conception of humanity based on reason with the Christian value based on Divine Revelation. An example of a Christian humanist movement is that of the Cambridge ▷ Platonists in the 17th century. 'Liberal humanism' values the dignity of the individual and their inalienable right to justice, liberty, freedom of thought and the pursuit of happiness; its weakness lies in its concentration on the single subject and its failure to recognize the power of institutions in determining the conditions of life.

Hume, David (1711–76)
Philosopher. His first major work, *Treatise of Human Nature* (1739–40) did not arouse much interest. His *Enquiry concerning Human Understanding* (1748) and *Enquiry concerning the Principles of Morals* (1751) are revisions and developments of the first work. His theory of knowledge was distinct from those of ▷ John Locke and ▷ George Berkeley. Locke had said that ideas proceeded from sensations, *ie* from

experience received through the senses, implying that we know mind only through matter; Berkeley that on the contrary we know matter only through our mental conceptions of it and that this proves the primacy of mind. Hume said that we cannot know of the existence of mind, except as a collective term covering memories, perceptions and ideas. He further argued that there was no necessity in the law of cause and effect, except in mathematics; what we call that law is inferred but not observed, a customary association confirmed by experience but with no provable necessity in it. Thus if Locke had seemed to validate science at the expense of religion and Berkeley the reverse, Hume seemed to drive at the roots of both. The graceful lucidity with which he expounded this extreme scepticism caused a wit to summarize his philosophy in the epigram: 'No mind! – It doesn't matter. No matter! – Never mind.' In his ethics, Hume held that virtue is what makes for happiness, both in ourselves and others, and that the two kinds of happiness are in accord with each other.

Hume also wrote the first systematic history of England, beginning, at first, with the reign of ▷ James I, when, as he considered with reasonable justice, the political differences of his own day had their start. His historical view is, however, marked by his political prejudices and, since he was a Scotsman, by his suspicion of English motives towards ▷ Scotland. His *Essays Moral and Political* (1741), and later volumes, contain acute comments on contemporary society. He differed from ▷ Rousseau by arguing against the long-established hypothesis that society is based on a 'social contract'. His economic writings were a stimulus to ▷ Adam Smith.

Bib: Mossner, E. C., *The Life of Hume*; Willey, B., *The Eighteenth Century Background*; Smith, N. K., *The Philosophy of David Hume*; Pears, D. F. (ed.), *Hume: A Symposium*.

Humour

The original meaning was 'liquid'. Ancient Greek and Latin medicine passed on to the ▷ Middle Ages the theory of four liquids (humours) in the human body: phlegm, blood, yellow bile or choler, and black bile or melancholy. Individual temperaments derived their quality from the predominance of one or other 'humour'; thus we still speak of 'phlegmatic' or very calm temperaments, 'sanguine' or ardent temperaments, 'choleric' or easily angered ones, and 'melancholy' or depressive temperaments. In the later 16th century a man's humour was his characteristic disposition, whether or not related to the original four physical humours. It could also have other meanings: his mania or obsession; his caprice or whim; his passing mood.

Ben Jonson in *Every Man in His Humour* (III)., speaks of a humour as 'a monster bred in a man by self-love and affectation, and fed by folly', *ie* produced by egotism, encouraged by fashionable ostentation, and not restrained by good sense; this meaning is the origin of the principal modern use of the word. ▷ Oliver Goldsmith (*Present State of Learning*, 1759) has already gone beyond 'a humour = that which is ridiculous' to the meaning of a faculty for perceiving the ridiculous, and also the laughter-raising expression of the ridiculous, although this is not one of the definitions found in ▷ Samuel Johnson's ▷ *Dictionary of the English Language*. Goldsmith and Hazlitt (*English Comic Writers*, 1819) both distinguish this faculty from ▷ wit, though differently.

▷ Humours, Comedy of; Satire; Wit.

Humours, Comedy of

A form of drama especially associated with Ben Jonson. Starting from the traditional psychology which explained a temperament as the product of its physical constitution, Jonson treats humour as the monstrous distortion of human nature by egotism and the self-regarding appetites, notably some form of greed. Partly timeless satire on human nature, the comedy of humours is also social satire since such personal extravagances are nourished by social tendencies; new prospects of wealth let loose unbounded lusts, as with Sir Epicure Mammon (in Jonson's *The Alchemist*); the rush of speculation on often fantastic 'projects' (*ie* financial enterprises requiring investment) encourages unlimited credulity in the foolish, *eg* Fitzdottrel in *The Devil is an Ass*; the prevalence of avarice causes adventurers to overreach themselves in their contempt for their victims and in their own megalomania (Volpone and Mosca in *Volpone*). Jonson's world is a jungle of predators and victims, free from the restraint of religion, reason, or respect for tradition. But the passions which Jonson exposes in their excess arise from human energies that are themselves fine and belong to that exhilaration in the scope for human fulfilment which is characteristic of the ▷ Renaissance; Jonson's more massive characters, though they condemn themselves by the exorbitance of their language, make speeches of great poetic splendour and force. Jonson's style of characterizing protagonists according to their humours and giving them names which point these humours out, were copied by a number of later dramatists.

▷ Shadwell was a follower of Jonson and even some of ▷ Congreve's characters recall Jonson, although his plays are usually defined as ▷ comedies of Manners, or of ▷ wit rather than humour. But Jonson's vision was influential beyond the drama; its detachment, objectivity, and moral emphasis on the need to temper the passions with reason and reverence for virtue, are essentially classical and emerge again in ▷ Pope's ▷ *Essay on Man* Book II.

Humphry Clinker, The Expedition of (1771)

A ▷ picaresque novel by ▷ Tobias Smollett, written in letters. It describes a tour of England and Scotland made by Mr Matthew Bramble and his family party – his sister Tabitha, his nephew and niece Jerry and Lydia, and the maid Winifred Jenkins. Humphry Clinker is a coachman who joins the party on the way, turns out to be Mr Bramble's illegitimate son, and marries Winifred. Characterization is strongly marked but superficial, the chief object being to characterize the society of the time realistically and with an often coarse humour. This is usually held to be the most successful of Smollett's novels, and shows something of the humane sympathies of the 16th-century Spanish novelist Cervantes, whose *Don Quixote* Smollett had himself translated in 1755.

Hunting

In English, the word usually refers to the pursuit of animals on horseback and with hounds, in distinction from shooting, ▷ hawking and other forms of pursuit on foot. The pursuit of deer, for example, is called deer-stalking in the Highlands of Scotland, where it is done on foot, but stag-hunting in the south-west of England, where it is done with horse and hound.

In the ▷ Middle Ages, the wolf, the boar, the stag and the fox were the chief objects of hunting, but the first two were virtually extinct by the 16th century, and by the 18th century improved agriculture restricted the territory of deer. This has left the fox as by far the most important beast of the chase for the last 200 years.
▷ Fox-hunting.

Hutcheson, Francis (1694–1746)

Scottish philosopher, who started his own private academy of learning in Dublin, and later became professor of moral science and natural philosophy at Glasgow University. He built on ▷ Locke's distinction between sensation and reflection, and ▷ Shaftesbury's idea of 'moral sense', to argue for an innate code of conduct and ethics that has nothing to do with reason. This, he maintained, is almost as powerful as the instict for self-preservation, and ensures that the performance of virtuous action is pleasurable. He defined the greatest virtue as that most in accord with the general good, coining the phrase 'the greatest happiness for the greatest numbers', which was taken up later by ▷ Bentham and other Utilitarians (▷ Utilitarianism). He also developed a theory of aesthetics, suggesting that the appreciation of beauty, like the moral code, proceeds from an inner sense, rather than from reason or learning. His major works include *An Inquiry into the Original of Our Ideas of Beauty and Virtue* (1725), *An Essay on the Nature and Conduct of The Passions and Affections* (1726) and, his most famous, *A System of Moral Philosophy* (published posthumously in 1755). He is considered as a pioneer of the 'Scottish School' of philosophy, influencing ▷ Hume, Adam Ferguson and, in a later generation, ▷ Adam Smith, as well as the Benthamites. His ideas contributed to the growth of ▷ sensibility.
Bib: Blackstone, W. T., *Hutcheson and Contemporary Ethical Theory*; Bryson, G., *Man and Society: The Scottish Inquiry of the Eighteenth Century*; Fox, C. (ed.), *Psychology and Literature in the Eighteenth Century*.

Hutchinson, Lucy (?1620–post 1675)

English memoirist. In 1638 she married John Hutchinson, and lived near Nottingham. Hutchinson became a ▷ Parliamentary Colonel in the English ▷ Civil War (1642–1646, and 1648–1651) and signed ▷ King Charles I's death warrant, for which he was imprisoned in 1663. He died in prison in 1664, and she wrote a memoir of him, *Memoirs of the Life of Colonel Hutchinson* (not published until 1806), ostensibly for her children and 'to moderate my woe'. It is full of fascinating detail and opinions about the Civil War, and indicates the active part played by women, though written in a very self-effacing style. Of her husband's signing of the warrant she says, 'As for Mr Hutchinson, although he was very much confirmed in his judgement concerning the cause, yet herein being called to an extraordinary action, whereof many were of several minds, he addressed himself to God by prayer.' She also translated part of ▷ Virgil's ▷ *Aeneid* and ▷ Lucretius's *De rerum natura*, and wrote *On the Principles of the Christian Religion*, first published in 1816.
▷ Halkett, Ann.

Hymen (Hymeneus)

In Greek myth, the son of Dionysus, god of the vine, and ▷ Aphrodite, goddess of sexual love; as such, he was a god of fruitfulness and especially of marriage. He was sometimes said to be son of Apollo and a ▷ muse.

Hymns

The word 'hymn' is of ancient Greek origin; it meant a song of praise to the gods. Such songs have been important in all the religions that have lain behind European culture; ▷ Latin hymns were composed and sung in the Christian churches from the earliest days of Christianity, and the Jewish hymns, or ▷ Psalms, are shared by the Jewish and the Christian religions.

The English hymn began its history in the religious ▷ Reformation under ▷ Edward VI when the abandonment of the Latin form of service produced the need for hymns in English. The Psalms were the obvious resource, but they had been translated into English prose. Accordingly, in 1549, the first or 'Old Version' of metrical Psalms was published; the authors were Sternhold and Hopkins. The most famous of this collection, and the only one now generally known, is the 'Old Hundredth' (Psalm 100): 'All people that on earth do dwell'. The Old Version of the metrical Psalms was replaced by the 'New Version' (1696) by Tate and Brady. From this book, two psalms are still familiar: 'Through all the changing scenes of life' and 'As pants the hart for cooling streams'.

The majority of hymns in English, however, were not metrical Psalms, but specially composed original poems. The great period of English hymn composition was the 17th and 18th centuries. However, it is necessary to distinguish between short religious poems which have been adopted as hymns, and poems which were composed as hymns. Some of the best religious poets of the 17th century, notably ▷ Herbert and ▷ Vaughan, produced work in the first group. But the first professional hymn writer (as distinct from the composers of the metrical Psalms) was the Anglican bishop, Thomas Ken (1637–1711). His best hymns, *eg* 'Awake my soul' and 'Glory to thee, my God, this night', are distinguished poetry.

It was, however, the ▷ Dissenters – the ▷ Puritan movements excluded from the Church of

England by the ▷ Act of Uniformity (1662) – and
their ▷ Evangelical sympathizers within the Church
of England, rather than the orthodox Anglicans,
who were at first most active in hymn-writing. The
Church of England had a set form of worship in the
Book of Common Prayer; hymns (in addition to the
prose versions of the Psalms) were allowed in this
service, but no special provision was made for them.
But the Dissenting sects had no set form of worship;
hymns for this reason alone were important to them.
They were important also for three other reasons:
Dissent was strong among classes in touch with
traditions of ▷ ballad and folk-song; most forms of
Dissenting faith demanded strong participation by
the congregation in the act of worship; in the 17th
century, Dissenters underwent persecution, and
communal, militant hymn-singing encouraged their
spirit of endurance. ▷ John Bunyan included hymns
in his ▷ *Pilgrim's Progress*, written in prison; one of
these – 'Who would true valour see' – is famous.

But the greatest of the Dissenting hymn-writers
is ▷ Isaac Watts. His language combines the
homeliness of the broadside ballads of the city
streets with the dignity and musical cadence of
biblical English. ▷ Charles Wesley, the brother of
the ▷ Methodist leader ▷ John Wesley, had greater
versatility than Watts, and was very prolific; his best
hymns are impressive though without the power
of the best by Watts. Other notable 18th-century
hymn-writers were John Newton (1725–1807) and
▷ William Cowper. All these had at least some
of the force of common speech and spontaneous
emotion in their hymns. Beside them, the hymns of
the orthodox Anglican, ▷ Joseph Addison, are cold,
though dignified and sincere.

Hyperbole
▷ Figures of speech.

I

Iambic foot (Iamb, Iambus)
The classical verse foot of a short syllable followed by
a long one, which in English is an unaccented syllable
followed by an accented one. The Alexandrine, for
instance, has six such feet.

Idler, The
Essays contributed weekly by ▷ Samuel Johnson to
the *Universal Chronicle*, or *Weekly Gazette* from April
1758 to April 1760. As compared to his ▷ *Rambler*
papers, they contain more humour, and more flexible
treatment of the fictional characters such as ▷ Dick
Minim, but they have the same kind of emotional
force and moral gravity which distinguish Johnson as
a periodical essayist.

Idyll
In ancient Greek literature, it meant a short poem.
The Greek poet ▷ Theocritus called his poems
about the rural life of Sicily 'idylls'. When the
term was revived in the ▷ Renaissance, it was
consequently used for a short ▷ pastoral poem,
similar to an ▷ eclogue except that an eclogue
was more likely to be in dialogue (▷ Virgil had
drown on Theocritus' *Idylls* when writing his own
Eclogues). As pastoral verse commonly presented
happiness or virtue in pure and simplified terms,
an idyll then came to be used loosely for any piece
of writing presenting experience in such a way,
often an episode from a longer work. Poets of the
▷ Restoration period and in the 18th century turned
either to Virgil, or to Theocritus directly, for models
in the composition of pastoral.

Iliad
An ▷ epic by the ancient Greek poet ▷ Homer. Its
subject is the siege of Troy by an alliance of Greek
states; the occasion of the war is the elopement of
Helen, wife of Menelaus, king of the Greek state
of Sparta, with Paris, a son of Priam, king of Troy.
The poem is in 24 books; it begins with the Greeks
already besieging Troy. In Book I the chief Greek
hero, Achilles, quarrels with the Greek commander-
in-chief, Agamemnon, king of Argos and brother
to Menelaus. Achilles withdraws from the fighting,
and returns to it only in Book XIX after the killing
of his friend Patroclus by the chief Trojan hero,
Hector. Achilles kills Hector in XXII, and the poem
ends with Hector's funeral in Troy. Hector is the
principal hero of the epic, much of which is taken
up with his exploits, as well as with those of other
Greek and Trojan heroes and with the intervention
of the gods on either side. There is much speculation
about the date of the historical events and that of
the poem respectively. Present opinion seems to be
that the historical city of Troy fell early in the 12th
century BC and that the poem was written about 300
years later. The surviving text dates from the 2nd
century BC.

The *Iliad* has had an enormous influence on the
literature of Europe. With Homer's ▷ *Odyssey*, it
set the standard for epic poetry, which until the 19th
century was considered the noblest poetic form. Its
first successor was the ▷ *Aeneid* (1st century BC)

by the Roman poet ▷ Virgil. The poem has been
several times translated into English verse; the most
notable versions are those by George Chapman
(1611) and ▷ Alexander Pope (1720).

Imitations of Horace (1733–78)
Adaptations by ▷ Alexander Pope of the ▷ satires
and epistles of the Latin poet ▷ Horace, who had
already served as a model for satire by ▷ John
Oldham, the ▷ Earl of Rochester and ▷ Jonathan
Swift. The aim of the imitation is not merely to
translate, but to adapt the Roman model, elaborating
the parallel between Augustan Rome and modern
Britain. Sometimes the relation between original and
imitation produces ▷ mock-heroic irony as when
Pope imitates Horace's verse epistle to ▷ Caesar
Augustus. He addresses the stodgy Hanoverian
George II (who had been christened Augustus), as
though he were the great Emperor, and praises 'Your
Arms, your Actions, your Repose . . .!' More usually
Pope asserts a Horatian detachment from the vices
of the city, and praises the self-sufficient retirement
of the country gentleman: ''Tis true, no Turbots
dignify my boards,/ But gudgeons, flounders,
what my Thames affords'. The Tiber becomes the
Thames, Rome becomes London, and Horace's
estate becomes Pope's house with its five acres at
Twickenham. Despite, or perhaps because of, the
Latin parallel these poems are among Pope's most
intimate works.

Imperialism
The practice of building up an empire, that is, to
dominate politically and assimilate other countries.
It has a long history, from Rome to the present day,
although the main period of imperialism began with
the 17th-century conquests of the Americas and
reached its height in the 1880s and 90s.

Inchbald, Mrs Elizabeth (1753–1821)
Novelist, dramatist and actress. Among other plays
she translated ▷ Kotzbue's *Lovers' Vows* from the
German, and this is the play rehearsed in ▷ Jane
Austen's *Mansfield Park*. This, and some of the
other 19 plays she wrote or adapted, were popular
successes: Jane Austen assumes knowledge of it
by the reader. However, her best works are her
two novels: *A Simple Story* (1791) and *Nature and
Art* (1796).
Bib: Littlewood, S.R., *Elizabeth Inchbald and
her Circle.*

Independents
▷ Congregationalism.

Indian Queen, The (1664)
Rhymed ▷ heroic drama, the first such play to be
staged in London, by Sir Robert Howard (1626–98)
and ▷ John Dryden. The Peruvian Montezuma,
having defeated the Mexicans, is offered any object
of his desire in reward by the Inca. He asks for the
hand of Orazia, but is scornfully refused. In a rage,
he joins the Mexicans and reverses the victory.
The Mexican king's sister Zempoalla is in love

with Montezuma, but when she realizes he loves Orazia, she tries to kill her rival. Traxalla, a general who loves Orazia, and who aspires to the throne of Mexico, steps in and threatens to kill Montezuma if Orazia dies. Eventually Zempoalla gives up hope of winning Montezuma's love, and orders the seizure and execution of Montezuma and Orazia, as well as the execution of the now imprisoned Inca, as blood sacrifices on the altar of the gods. Her plan fails, however, and at the end Montezuma is revealed as the son of the Mexican queen, and hence as heir to the throne. He kills Traxalla in a fight, Zempoalla stabs herself, the Inca is appeased by Montezuma's new status, and gives Orazia to him, and the play ends with a speech on the vagaries of fate. Throughout, the heroism of Montezuma is contrasted with Zempoalla's disdain for honour.

Industrial Revolution

An industrial revolution has been defined as 'the change that transforms a people with peasant occupations and local markets into an industrial society with world-wide connections' (*Encyclopaedia Britannica*). Clearly then many countries have industrial revolutions, and more than one; for example it is currently said that Britain is undergoing a new industrial revolution in high-technology processes. However, the first great industrial revolution was the succession of changes which transformed England from a predominantly rural and agricultural country into a predominantly urban and manufacturing one in the 18th and 19th centuries, and especially between 1750 and 1850.

1 *Causes*. Although not a country of great towns, apart from London, England at the beginning of the 18th century was already a great trading nation, with much private capital ready for investment. Not only was trade free to move throughout the British Isles but there was considerable freedom of social movement between the classes, which were not rigidly defined almost into caste systems as in other European countries, *eg* France. English middle-class religion had emphasized, the individual conscience as the guide to conduct and also the moral excellence of sober, industrious employment; these values encouraged self-reliance and enterprising initiative. Although some of this middle class (the Nonconformist or ▷ Dissenting sects which rejected the Church of England) were barred from political rights and Parliament, controlled by the aristocracy, was far from truly representative, the political leaders of the country were extremely interested in commerce, which they were ready to participate in and profit from. The bent of the whole nation, from the days of ▷ Francis Bacon in the early 17th century, had been increasingly practical and the steadily growing population provided a market which invited exploitation by various methods of improved production. Once the process started, it gathered its own momentum, which was increased by the existence of large supplies of convenient fuel in the country's coalfields. Agriculture also contributed to industrial growth: the landowners were zealous farmers and their improved methods of cultivation not only freed much labour (▷ Enclosures), which

then became available for employment in the town factories, but increased the food supplies available for the towns. Finally, the 18th century (in contrast to 17th) was a time of peace and stability in Britain, undisturbed by the wars in which her armies and money were engaged across the sea.

2 *Process*. In the textile industry, already established since the 15th century as the principal industry, a number of machines were invented which increased production and reduced labour but were too large for the cottages where the processes had hitherto been carried out. They therefore had to be housed in factories and mills where large numbers of employees worked together. These machines were at first operated by water power. In the iron industry, the principal fuel used hitherto had been charcoal, the supply of which was becoming exhausted. However, improved methods of smelting using coal were discovered and ironmasters set up their blast furnaces in the neighbourhood of the coalfields in the north midlands and north of England.

Most important of all, in 1769 ▷ James Watt patented an adaptation of his steam-engine to the machines used in the textile industry; this consequently ceased to depend on water power and concentrated itself in the north of England to be near the coalfields. An important result was the immense expansion in manufacture of cotton cloth. An extensive system of canals was constructed in the 18th century for the transport of goods and fuel, and the modern methods of road and bridge building were introduced, but the decisive advance in communications was the invention of the steam rail locomotive by George Stephenson (1814); by 1850 a railway system covered the country.

3 *Consequences*. Britain was by 1850 the 'workshop of the world'; no other country was yet ready to compete with her in industrial production. The towns were the source of her wealth, though the landowners retained their social prestige and often became much richer by ownership of coalfields. The north of England, until the 18th century a backward region, was now the most advanced in Britain; its towns grew rapidly, unplanned, in ugliness and dirt. The economic motives outran the social conscience and the new urban proletariat worked and lived in evil conditions under employers who had often themselves risen from poverty and had the ruthlessness which was a consequence of the severity of their struggle. England was divided as never before; the industrial north from the agricultural south, the industrial working class from (sometimes) pitiless employers, and both from the long-established gentry, particulary of the south. Although the process of industrialization was by no means yet complete, concern about its effects was already being voiced by the middle of the 18th century. This was commonly expressed in two ways. Poets including ▷ Cowper, ▷ Goldsmith and ▷ Crabbe lamented what they saw as the demise of the traditional rural way of life, with poverty increasing, and the haemorrhage of dispossessed former labourers and small farmers to the towns in search of work. Others voiced anxiety about the towns' and cities' increasing congestion. This concern was often added to the

feelings of distaste at urban disease and corruption, which had been manifest at least since ▷ Jacobean times, shown in some of the low urban characters of ▷ Restoration comedy in the later 17th century, and in works of ▷ Defoe, ▷ Hogarth, ▷ Fielding, ▷ Lillo, and ▷ Gay in the 18th (although their works also demonstrate the city's vitality). Disquiet about the city, combined with growing sentimentality about the countryside (▷ sentiment), led to comparisons between country and town, to the detriment of the latter. An example of this happening is in these lines from one of the 'Town' or 'London' *Eclogues* by the minor poet Charles Jenner (1736–74):

> I spy no verdant glade, no gushing rill,
> No fountain gushing from the rocky hill . . .
> Where'er I cast my wand'ring eyes
> Long burning rows of fetid bricks arise,
> And nauseous dunghills swell in mould'ring
> heaps . . .

But many others celebrated the changes. Writers as diverse as ▷ Mandeville, ▷ Hume, ▷ Pope, ▷ Ferguson and ▷ Adam Smith saw in growing trade and commerce possibilities to improve the quality of life, even for the poor. Others, like the poet ▷ James Thomson, had more complicated attitudes. Simultaneously he could celebrate the achievements of the city – its commerce, its culture, and its civilized order – and condemn its crowds and corruption. ▷ Johnson's London is at once exhilarating – as in his famous 'when a man is tired of London he is tired of life' – and threatening, a place of 'Malice, Rapine, Accident', 'Rabble', and 'Ruffians', according to his imitation of ▷ Juvenal, ▷ *London*. But it was not until the turn of the 19th century that a full-blown attack was launched on the effects of industrialization, starting with ▷ Romantic poets such as ▷ Blake and ▷ Wordsworth, and reaching a climax in the novels of Charles Dickens, Benjamin Disraeli, and Elizabeth Gaskell.

Inkle and Yarico (Yariko)

Inkle was a young English trader of the 17th century who sailed from London to the West Indies. Landing on an island on the way, he and his companions were attacked by natives and all were massacred except Inkle himself, who was saved by the native girl Yarico. She hid him in a cave, cared for him, loved him, and became pregnant by him. When an English ship passed by, Inkle boarded it, taking Yarico with him. But later he sold her into slavery. These events were reported in England and their hold on people's imaginations was part of the growing appeal of the 'primitive' (▷ primitivism), which was linked to a more general criticism of established mores in society. Inkle's actions were seen by many as archetypal of the white man's perfidy towards other races, or even simply of man's betrayal of woman, while Yarico was portrayed variously as a type of ▷ noble savage or a suffering heroine. The earliest account of their story is told by the traveller Ligon in 1657. It is elaborated by ▷ Steele in *The Spectator* (13 March 1711). Thereafter the couple's history became the subject of literally dozens of poems,

plays, novels, paintings, songs, and even ballets in England and throughout Europe.
Bib: Price, L. M., *Inkle and Yarico Album*; Hazard, P., *European Thought in the Eighteenth Century*.

Inns, taverns, alehouses

These words went out of common use in the later 19th century; the modern terms are 'hotels' (formerly inns) and 'public houses' or 'pubs' (formerly taverns and alehouses). An inn was especially for travellers, who could eat, drink and sleep there; taverns existed chiefly in London and were drinking resorts; alehouses were a humbler form of tavern such as might be found in any village. From the 16th century taverns and alehouses had to receive licences for their trade from magistrates, who could withdraw these if they became places of disorder. The word 'hostelry' is equivalent to 'inn' but is still older; similarly, 'hospital' originally stood for an institution offering 'hospitality' to travellers, but by the 16th century was reserved for a refuge for the sick and aged; now, merely for the sick.

Until the 14th century travel was comparatively rare and shelter was provided chiefly by the monasteries, which continued to serve the function of inns until their dissolution in the 16th century. Already in the 14th century, however, travel was becoming more common and inns were growing up independently of monasteries; their number naturally increased after the monastic dissolution. One of the chief functions of the larger inns was to serve as 'post-houses' for mail-coaches which changed horses at them and put down travellers who were using them.

Inns were identified by the coloured signs hanging outside them, still commonly found outside pubs and some hotels today. Such signs often showed the coat of arms of the local great family and the inn would be called, *eg* 'the Neville Arms'. Still commoner as a sign was the 'crest' or symbol (often an animal) that usually surmounted a coat of arms; hence the large numbers of inns called the 'Red Lion', the 'Black Bull', the 'White Hart', etc. Sometimes the sign represented a local trade or craft (the 'Carpenters' Arms', etc.), and the habit of old soldiers turning innkeeper led to many inns and taverns being called after famous generals, particularly if they had been popular, *eg* the 'Marquis of Granby', the 'Duke of Wellington'.

Inns of Court

Institutions belonging to the legal profession, in London. There are now four, all dating from the ▷ Middle Ages: Lincoln's Inn, Gray's Inn, the Inner Temple and the Middle Temple. The buildings resemble those of Oxford and Cambridge colleges, and their function is to be responsible for the education of those students of the law who intend to become barristers, with the right to plead in the senior courts of law and – in the senior rank – the qualifications to be appointed judges. Each Inn is a separate society, governed by its senior members, called Benchers. The buildings are not exclusively occupied by barristers or their students, however; thus Furnivall's Inn (now pulled down) was for a

time the home of Charles Dickens, and one of his
characters, Pip of *Great Expectations*, had rooms in
Barnard's Inn, now part of a school.

Innuendo
▷ Figures of speech.

Inquisition, The
An organization in the Roman Catholic Church, in
the form of a judicial tribunal, whose task it was
to detect and eliminate heresy, *ie* false religious
doctrine. Officially it was known as the Holy Office,
and survives today only for the identification of
heretical literature. Its beginnings were in the 13th
century and it visited, or had branches in, the various
European countries. In England it was unpopular
even before the ▷ Reformation, but in Spain its
function of heresy hunting was not abolished until
1834. In the English Protestant mind, from the 16th
century, the Spanish Inquisition was identified with
all that was conceived to be cruel and intolerant
in the Catholic Church, and it was often confused
with the Holy Office in Rome. Nonetheless,
▷ Protestantism in Britain did not itself at first
practise tolerance. The English law of 1401 that
heretics must be burned alive was not abolished
till 1676, though the practice had long ceased; in
Scotland a young man accused of heresy was hanged
in 1696.
▷ Catholicism in Britain; Catholicism (Roman) in
English literature.

Interlude
A term of disputed origin, in use from the 13th
century at least, for dramatic performances in
general. It became the standard term for plays
performed indoors, at the feasts of rich households
or in the halls of ecclesiastical or educational
institutions.

Interregnum
The term used for the period 1649–60, between
the execution of ▷ Charles I and the accession of
his son Charles II – the ▷ Restoration. It is divided
into the period 1649–53, when England was ruled
by the House of Commons and a Council of State
(the Commonwealth), and the period 1653–8 when
▷ Oliver Cromwell and for a brief time his son
Richard were Protectors (the Protectorate).

Ireland
By 1600 Ireland was a nation of mixed English and
Celtic people, with an English-speaking aristocracy,
and firm identification with the Roman ▷ Catholic
faith. The problem as England saw it in the next two
centuries was how to subdue the country to effective
Protestant rule.

The policy of settling Protestants in Ireland was
notably successful in one of the four provinces
under ▷ James I (1603–25) when Ulster became
the Anglo-Scottish Protestant fortress which it has
remained to this day. ▷ Oliver Cromwell was savage
in subjection of Catholic Ireland to his authority,
and by extensive confiscations increased the class
of Protestant landlords. In the 18th century, penal

laws further disabled Catholic landholders, refused
political rights to Catholics, and barred them from
most professions and from education. The only Irish
university (founded by Elizabeth in 1591), Trinity
College in Dublin, was a Protestant one. However,
towards the end of the 18th century, partly owing
to the Irish patriotism of Anglo-Irish Protestants
(including ▷ Swift and ▷ Berkeley), the penal
laws were reduced in severity, and in 1782 an Irish
constitution was promulgated, by which the Irish
Protestants were given political rights and limited
powers in an Irish Parliament freed from ▷ Privy
Council control. The experiment was a failure, and
in 1801 Ireland was united politically and in all other
respects with England and Scotland, Irish Protestants
receiving for the first time representation in the
English Parliament.

Irish literature in English
Ireland – England's first and closest colony –
presents a recent history of literary movements and
concerns that is very differently paced from that of its
colonist. From 1171, the year of Ireland's conquest
by ▷ Henry II, until the latter years of the 19th
century, the history of Irish literature in English
is, largely speaking, part of the general history of
English literature.

Throughout the 18th and 19th centuries – and
into the 20th – writers from Anglo-Irish Ireland
made a rich and vigorous contribution to English
literature: ▷ Jonathan Swift, ▷ William Congreve,
▷ Oliver Goldsmith, ▷ Richard Brinsley Sheridan,
Oscar Wilde and George Bernard Shaw are
amongst the better known. Their writings were not
primarily concerned with the matter of Ireland or
their author's own Irishness. Those who did write
of Ireland, like Dion Boucicault (1820–90), who
is held by many to be the inventor of the 'stage
Irishman', and Thomas Moore (1779–1852), the
purveyor to the drawing-rooms of London of an
Ireland sugared by sentiment and exile, capitalized
on what looks with hindsight like caricature. All
these writers of the Anglo-Irish Ascendancy, coming
from their background of landed privilege, seemed
to be unaware of the still surviving Gaelic tradition of
native Irish literature, with its long ancestry and close
connections with mainland Europe.

Moreover, during this pre-Revival period only
a handful of creative writers mirrored the growing
interest that folklorists like T. Crofton Croker
(1798–1849), travellers (again, many of them from
Europe) and diarists were taking in Irish peasant life
outside the 'Pale'. ▷ Maria Edgeworth (1767–1849)
and William Carleton (1794–1869) stand almost
alone in the seriousness with which they looked at
their native land and its inhabitants. Edgeworth's
Castle Rackrent (1800) and Carleton's *Traits and
Stories of the Irish Peasantry* (1830–3) are isolated
landmarks; and Carleton, an adopted member
of Ascendancy culture who was born a Catholic
peasant, has been read in recent years with renewed
interest and recognition.

Irony
▷ Figures of speech.

Italian influence on English literature

Apart from the influence of Italian literature, Italy as a country was particularly important to England in the 16th and early 17th century. The English attitude to Italy was complicated – a mixture of admiration, envy, intense interest, and disapproval amounting to abhorrence. The Italian cities were for Englishmen the centres and summits of civilization, and such centres in most periods are supposed to represent not only what is most advanced in thought and behaviour, but also what is most extravagant and corrupt.

However, it was the independence of the best Italian minds that attracted the best English minds of the 16th and 17th centuries. The free-thinking Italian philosopher, Giordano Bruno (?1548–99), despised the stale traditions of the English universities on his visit (1583–5), but he admired Queen Elizabeth and made friends with men such as Sir Philip Sidney and Sir Walter Raleigh. The astronomer Galileo, who, like Bruno, came into conflict with the

▷ Inquisition, was studied by the poet John Donne, and received visits from the sceptical philosopher ▷ Thomas Hobbes and the Puritan ▷ John Milton. Milton's visit to Italy (1638–9) enriched him with encounters with scholars and patrons of learning, while at the same time he felt in danger from the papal police because of his religious opinions; this is another example of the complicated relationships of Englishmen with Italy.

After 1650 Italy by no means lost its fascination for the English, but it was Italy as a storehouse of the past, rather than a challenging present, that drew Englishmen. In the 18th century the English invented a sort of tourism; what was called the 'Grand Tour' formed part of the education of upper-class young men and Italy was one of its principal objectives. They were drawn to the architectural and sculptural remains of the old Roman Empire, the framework of their literary education in ▷ Latin literature.

Jacobean

Used to indicate the period of ▷ James I (1603–25) and applied especially to the literature and style of architecture of his reign. In literature, it is most commonly a way of distinguishing the style of drama under James from the style that prevailed under Elizabeth. Strictly, Elizabethan drama is experimental, expansive, sometimes ingenuous, in fairly close touch with medieval tradition but energetic with ▷ Renaissance forces. It includes the work of the University wits – Christopher Marlowe, Thomas Kyd, Robert Greene, George Peele – and also earlier ▷ Shakespeare. Jacobean drama is thought of as critical, sombre, disillusioned. It includes mature and late Shakespeare, Ben Jonson, Cyril Tourneur, John Webster, Thomas Middleton, Francis Beaumont and John Fletcher. The ▷ Caroline period is associated with such figures as Philip Massinger, John Ford and James Shirley. Courts were the centre of culture, and courts depended largely on the circumstances of monarchs; while the reign of Elizabeth was prosperous at home and (mainly) triumphant overseas, that of James saw increasing disagreement at home, and abroad was negative or even nationally humiliating. The reign of ▷ Charles I was yet more bitter in home dissensions but his court was one of distinction and refinement. The tone of the drama varied with these differences in national fortune and court conduct. However, the labelling of literary periods is always to some extent simplifying and even falsifying.

The Jacobean period was the first that was really rich in prose, with writers like ▷ Francis Bacon, John Donne and Lancelot Andrewes. Their work contrasts especially with ▷ Restoration prose, which sacrificed the poetic qualities of the Jacobean writing for the sake of grace and lucidity.

▷ 17th-century literature.

Jacobin

Originally a name given to Dominican friars in France, because their first convent was in the Rue St Jacques in Paris. The name was transferred to a political society which rented a room in the convent in the first year of the ▷ French Revolution. The society developed into a highly organized political party, led by Robespierre, who became practically dictator of France in 1793. The Jacobins were extreme in asserting the principle of equality and in their opposition to privilege. Later, when conservative reaction had set in, 'Jacobin' was used loosely for anyone with liberal political tendencies in England as well as in France. The paper *The Anti-Jacobin* was founded to combat English liberal opinion in 1797.

Jacobite

From Jacobus, the Latin form of James. ▷ James II, of the House of ▷ Stuart, was deposed in 1688 because, as a convert to ▷ Catholicism, he was considered to be conspiring against the established ▷ Protestant religion and against ▷ Parliament. His supporters were called Jacobites and this name continued for the supporters of his Catholic son and grandsons.

After the crown passed to the House of Hanover, a German Protestant family, in 1714, British Jacobites conspired to restore the House of Stuart. The Jacobite Rebellions of 1715 and 1745 were the two most formidable attempts; both had principally Scottish support, partly because the Stuarts had originally been a Scottish royal family. The ▷ 'Forty-five' rebellion quickly became a romantic legend chiefly because of the supposed gallantry and charm of its leader, Charles Edward Stuart, grandson of James II – 'Bonnie Prince Charlie' to his Scottish supporters and the 'Young Pretender' to his opponents. After the failure of the 'Forty-five' Jacobitism became increasingly a matter of sentiment which even persists to the present day, though the direct line of the Stuarts died out in 1807.

James I of England and VI of Scotland

A member of the Scottish House of ▷ Stuart, he ruled over ▷ Scotland alone (1566–1603) and then over England as well (1603–25). He was the first sovereign ever to reign over the whole of the British Isles. His accession to the throne of England was due to the death without children of his cousin Elizabeth I, last of the House of Tudor. The literature and architecture of his era is known as ▷ Jacobean, a term transferred, especially in architecture, to the greater part of the 17th century.

James II of England and VII of Scotland (1685–88)

King of Great Britain and Ireland. He was deposed because, as a ▷ Catholic, he was threatening the security of the ▷ Church of England and at the same time weakening the power of ▷ Parliament. He was succeeded by his ▷ Protestant daughter
▷ Mary II in conjunction with her Dutch husband,
▷ William III.
▷ Jacobite; Glorious Revolution.

Jane Shore, The Tragedy of (1714)

Play by ▷ Nicholas Rowe, based on a historic character, who was mistress of Edward IV, and afterwards of Thomas Grey, first Marquis of Dorset. Rowe stated on the title page that the play was 'Written in Imitation of Shakespeare's Style'. It traces Jane's descent, from wealth and influence as Edward's mistress, to ignominy and destitution. At her lowest ebb, she is rescued by her husband. The play is numbered among the so-called ▷ 'she-tragedies' of Rowe, which focus on the central figure of a suffering woman, and depend largely on pathos for their effect. Jane's story became symbolic of the reversal of fortune.

Janus

In Roman myth, the god of doorways and guardian of the city during war; he also presided over the first hour of the day, the first day of the month, and the first month of the year January is named after him.

Jeffreys, Judge

▷ Bloody Assizes; Sedgemoor, Battle of.

Jesuit

A member of the Society of Jesus, a religious order founded by Ignatius Loyola, and approved by the

Pope in 1540. The Jesuits were in the forefront in combating ▷ Protestantism. In the reign of Elizabeth I they led, or were reputed to lead, the various conspiracies against her on behalf of the ▷ Catholic claimant to the English throne, Mary Queen of Scots; they were therefore regarded as national as well as religious enemies. Their advanced training made them skilled debaters and subtle negotiators. In the 18th century, when religious conflicts had subsided, Jesuits were no longer feared in England; but their activities in Europe led to their expulsion even from Catholic lands like France and Spain, and for 41 years they were totally suppressed by the Pope.

Jevon (Jevorn), Thomas (1652–88)

Actor, dancer, singer, dramatist. Jevon started his career as a dancing master, and joined the ▷ Duke's Company, possibly before 1673. He had an irreverent sense of humour, and specialized in low comic parts. He was a favourite speaker of prologues and epilogues, and also wrote the highly successful *The Devil of a Wife* (1686), which was adapted several times in the 18th century.

Jews in England

The Jews first settled in England after the Norman Conquest and, as elsewhere, undertook the occupation of lending money on interest which in the earlier ▷ Middle Ages was forbidden to Christians. They were expelled from England by Edward I in 1290. Between 1290 and 1655, when they were readmitted by ▷ Oliver Cromwell, few Jews were admitted, and those by special licence; a number of rich Jews were living in London in the reign of Elizabeth I.

Jews returned in number to England after 1655; by the end of the 18th century there were about 20,000 living in London. Anti-semitism was relatively inconspicuous – this fact has been attributed to the assiduous Bible-reading of the English middle classes – but unless they renounced their religion they suffered restrictions on political rights and entry into certain professions (*eg* the Law) similar to those of other denominations outside the ▷ Church of England. These restrictions were not entirely removed until the middle of the 19th century, although by that time Benjamin Disraeli, a Jew who had been received into the Church of England, was already one of the country's leading statesmen.

There are numerous references to Jews in the literature of the late 17th and 18th centuries, most of them brief, and most reflecting casual or sustained prejudice. ▷ Behn, ▷ Colley Cibber, ▷ Defoe, ▷ Swift, ▷ Pope, ▷ Richardson, ▷ Fielding ▷ Sterne and ▷ Burney were all scathing in their references to Jews. The dramatist George Granville reworked ▷ Shakespeare's *The Merchant of Venice* as *The Jew of Venice* in 1701, and Jews are objects of ridicule in a number of other plays, including ▷ Richard Brinsley Sheridan's ▷ *The Duenna*. However, ▷ Smollett has both good and bad Jewish characters in his novels, and ▷ Goldsmith has several kindly references to Jews, as well as more or less neutral ones. ▷ Addison, writing in The

Spectator, speaks tolerantly of the Jews, as being necessary to commerce. By the late 18th century attitudes towards Jews were becoming generally more sympathetic for a number of reasons. These include the growing tolerance for all ethnic minorities, as part of the development of ▷ sensibility; the cult of ▷ orientalism, allowing disinterested investigation into various other cultures; the publicity accorded Lord George Gordon (1751–93), who converted to Judaism in 1787; and the admiration for the famous Spanish Jewish boxer Daniel Mendoza (1764–1836), who defeated the English champion in 1789. The Jews are championed in a number of plays and articles by ▷ Cumberland, and by a growing number of other authors in the 19th century.

John

King of England, 1199–1216. His reign was particularly disturbed; he succeeded in raising against him both his own nobles and the Church, as well as losing his father's French possessions. In 1215 the alliance of nobles and Church successfully imposed on him the ▷ Magna Carta by which he agreed not to infringe the rights of the Church or of his subjects. It was in the 17th-century quarrels between the kings and parliaments that this document became important, as seeming to justify parliamentary resistance to the Crown.
▷ Parliament.

John Bull

A personification of England, dating from a political allegory *The History of John Bull* (1712) by ▷ John Arbuthnot. The character is there described as honest but quarrelsome, his temper depending on the weather; he understands business and is fond of drinking and the society of his friends. He is intended to represent the national character.

Johnson, Samuel (1709–84)

Critic, poet, lexicographer, essayist. Born at Lichfield to elderly parents, Johnson's childhood was marred by ill health; a tubercular infection from his wetnurse affected both his sight and hearing, and his face was scarred by scrofula or the 'King's Evil'. He was educated at Lichfield Grammar School, and in 1728 went up to Pembroke College, Oxford; his studies at the university were, however, cut short by poverty, and in 1729 he returned to Lichfield, affected by melancholy depression.

After a brief period as a schoolmaster at Market Bosworth, Johnson moved to Birmingham, where he contributed articles (now lost) to the *Birmingham Journal*. In 1735 he married Elizabeth Porter a widow greatly his senior, and using her money attempted to start a school at Edial, near his home town. The school quickly failed, and in 1737 Johnson set off to London accompanied by one of his pupils, the actor ▷ David Garrick. Lack of a university degree hindered him from pursuing a profession, and he determined to make a living by writing.

Edward Cave, the founder of ▷ *The Gentleman's Magazine*, allowed him to contribute articles, and for many years Johnson lived by hack writing.

His *Parliamentary Debates* were published in this magazine, and were widely believed to be authentic. In 1738 the publication of his poem, *London*, revealed his literary abilities. But the project of compiling the ▷ *Dictionary of the English Language* which was to occupy the next nine years testifies to Johnson's concern to produce saleable material. Lacking a patron, he approached ▷ Lord Chesterfield with the plan; the resulting snub is a notorious episode in the decline of the patronage system. In 1749, the poem ▷ *The Vanity of Human Wishes* was published, and his play *Irene* staged by Garrick. In 1750 he began the twice-weekly periodical ▷ *The Rambler*, to add to his income but also as a relief from the *Dictionary* work.

The death of his wife in 1752 returned Johnson to the melancholy depression he had suffered after leaving Oxford. However, he continued to contribute to periodicals, and in 1755 the *Dictionary* was published, bringing him wide acclaim which also included, by the intervention of friends, an honorary degree from Oxford. From 1758–60 he wrote the ▷ *Idler* essays for the *Universal Chronicle*, and in 1759 ▷ *Rasselas* was published. In 1762 a crown pension relieved some of the financial pressure, and the following year he met ▷ James Boswell, who was to become his biographer.

In 1765 Johnson's spirits were much lifted as he made the acquaintance of the ▷ Thrales, and over the next few years he spent much time at their home in Streatham. In the same year, his edition of ▷ Shakespeare, for which he wrote a famous Preface, appeared.

Johnson's desire to travel was partly fulfilled by journeys made in his later years. In 1773 he and Boswell made their ▷ *Journey to the Western Islands of Scotland* (1775), and in 1774 Johnson went to Wales with the Thrale family. The following year he accompanied the Thrales to Paris, his only visit to the Continent.

In 1777 Johnson began work on ▷ *The Lives of the Poets* (1779–81), at the request of booksellers. In 1784, estranged from his friend Mrs Thrale by her remarriage, he died in his home in Bolt Court. He is buried in Westminster Abbey.
Bib: Boswell, J. (ed. Hill, G.B.; revised Powell, L.F.), *The Life of Samuel Johnson*; Bate, W.J., *Samuel Johnson*; Hardy, J.P., *Samuel Johnson: A Critical Study*.

Johnson, The Life of Samuel (1791)
▷ Boswell, James.

Jonathan Wild the Great, The Life of (1743)
A satirical romance by ▷ Henry Fielding. His purpose was to ridicule 'greatness' by telling the story of a 'great' criminal in apparently admiring terms. The subject makes clear that the admiration is ironical, but the reader is reminded that eminent statesmen and other 'respectable' men of power – all those, in fact, who are normally regarded as great – commonly pursue their aims with as little scruple. Wild was a historical character who had been executed in 1725, and made the subject of a narrative by ▷ Defoe.

In Fielding's fictional satire, Wild begins his career by being baptized by ▷ Titus Oates – also a criminal character – and takes to a career of crime in childhood. He becomes the leader of a gang of thieves, among whom he keeps discipline by threatening them with denunciation, while himself avoiding incrimination. The vilest of his crimes is the systematic ruin of his former schoolfriend, the jeweller Heartfree, whom he nearly succeeds in having executed. In the end it is Wild who is executed, but he is sent to his death with the same mock-heroic impressiveness as has characterized Fielding's treatment of him throughout.
▷ Picaresque.

Jones, Inigo (1573–1651)
Architect and stage designer. He is sometimes called 'the English ▷ Palladio' because he was strongly influenced by the Italian architect, and he was in fact the first important classical (Palladian) architect in English architecture. Outstanding buildings of his design include the Banqueting Hall in Whitehall and St Paul's church in Covent Garden, both in ▷ London. He also designed sets for ▷ masques, to which words were contributed by Ben Jonson, Samuel Daniel and other poets among his contemporaries. Scenery and music were as important in the masque as was poetry, and the fusion led to bitter rivalry between Jones and Jonson, who satirized him as In-and-In Medlay in *The Tale of a Tub*.

Joseph Andrews (1742)
A novel by ▷ Henry Fielding. It was begun as a parody of ▷ Samuel Richardson's novel ▷ *Pamela*. In Richardson's novel the heroine, Pamela Andrews, is a chaste servant girl who resists seduction by her master, Mr B, and eventually forces him to accept her in marriage. Fielding ridicules Richardson by opening his novel with an account of the resistance by Pamela's brother Joseph to seduction by his employer, the aunt of Mr B, whose name Fielding maliciously extends to Booby (= clumsy fool). Joseph is dismissed for his obstinate virtue, and sets out in search of his own sweetheart. On the journey he is befriended by his old acquaintance, a clergyman, Parson Adams. At this point Fielding seems to have changed the plan of his novel; Adams, instead of Joseph, becomes the central character on whom all the interest centres. With the change, the novel becomes something like an English *Don Quixote*, since Adams is a learned but simple-hearted, single-minded Christian whose trust in the goodness of human nature leads him into constant embarrassments.

Journal of a Tour to the Hebrides, The (1785)
▷ James Boswell's account of the tour to the Hebrides which he made with ▷ Samuel Johnson in 1773 (cf. ▷ *A Journey to the Western Islands of Scotland*). The tour gave Boswell the opportunity to encourage Johnson's consideration of many topics, and the narrative, which he showed to Johnson, records Johnson's opinions and perorations on many matters. Boswell was partly motivated in undertaking

the tour by the desire to show Johnson his homeland, but he also saw it as a good occasion to collect material for his *Life of Samuel Johnson*.

Journal of the Plague Year, A (1722)

Written by ▷ Daniel Defoe, the *Journal* purports to be the record of 'H. F.', a survivor of the plague in London of 1664–5. The initials have suggested to critics that Defoe's uncle, Henry Foe, may have provided some of the first-hand information.

The narrative tells of the spread of the plague, the suffering of the Londoners, and the attempts by the authorities to control the disease. Defoe incorporates statistical data, some of which is taken from official sources, to demonstrate the extent of the plague and its effects on the life of the capital. The 'factual' nature of the statistics stands in grim juxtaposition to the vivid recreation of death and disease, the inhabitants imprisoned in their own homes by danger and terror, and the mass burial sites and death-carts which became a familiar part of everyday existence.

Journalism

The distinction between journalism and literature is not always clear, and before the rise of the modern newspaper with its mass circulation in the second half of the 19th century, the two forms of writing were even more difficult to distinguish than they are today. The most superficial but also the most observable difference has always been that journalism puts immediacy of interest before permanency of interest, and easy readability before considered qualities of style. But of course what is written for the attention of the hour may prove to be of permanent value; a good example is William Cobbett's *Rural Rides* in his weekly *Political Register* in the early 19th century.

The ▷ pamphlets of writers such as Thomas Nashe and Thomas Dekker in the 1590s, and those on the controversial religious matters of the day such as the Marprelate pamphlets, are no doubt the earliest work with the stamp of journalism in English. However, the profession began to take shape with the wider reading public and the regular periodicals of the early 18th century. In that period we can see that it was the attitude to writing that made the difference – at least on the surface – between the journalist and the serious man of letters. ▷ Addison considered himself a serious man of letters, whereas ▷ Defoe, writing incessantly on matters of practical interest without concerning himself with subtleties and elegance of style, is more our idea of a journalist. The 18th century was inclined to disparage such writing as ▷ Grub Street, though this term included all kinds of inferior, merely imitative 'literature', that we would not accept as journalism. The trade of journalism taught Defoe the realism that went into his fiction. A good example of the combination of facts and fiction is his ▷ *A Journal of the Plague Year* (1722) which is both a fine example of journalistic reporting (from other people's accounts) and a fine achievement in imaginative realism.

Defoe in the 18th century and Cobbett in the 19th century both assumed that the main function of their writing was to *enlighten* their readers. In the 1890s, however, the 'popular press' arose in which the desire to entertain was as strong as the desire to inform, and profitability was a major concern.
▷ Newspapers; Reviews and Periodicals.

Journey to the Western Islands of Scotland, A (1775)

▷ Samuel Johnson's account of the tour which he and ▷ James Boswell made in 1773 (cf. ▷ *Journal of a Tour to the Hebrides*). The tour gave rise to Johnson's meditations on the life, culture and history of the Scottish people, as well as on the Scottish landscape. Its publication aroused the wrath of Macpherson, whose work *Ossian* (or ▷ *Oisin*) Johnson rightly regarded as inauthentic.

Junius

The pen-name of a political polemicist who published celebrated letters attacking the government of the day in the London newspaper *Public Advertiser*, 1769–72. The letters were fiercely satirical against the ministers of George III, and were notable for their unusual eloquence. The name 'Junius' was chosen from Lucius Junius Brutus, who, in legend, overthrew the Tarquin kings of Rome in the 6th century BC. The style of the letters shows the influence of ▷ Swift and of the Latin historian ▷ Tacitus. The real author has long been a mystery, but is now generally considered to have been Sir Philip Francis (1740–1818), a politician of the ▷ Whig party who supported the rights and privileges of Parliament against what they considered to be dangerous encroachments by the king and his supporters.

Jury system

The system whereby a body of citizens without legal training are summoned before a court of law and given the task, under the guidance of a judge, of deciding on the facts of a case. If the case before the court concerns a crime, the most important decision is whether the accused is guilty or not guilty. Hence it is the jury, not the judge, that tries the accused ('trial by jury') and its decision is called 'the verdict', in accordance with which the judge has to release the prisoner or decide the penalty appropriate to his offence.

The system originated in the 12th century and reached its present form by the 15th. It was often a defence against tyranny, although juries can be prejudiced (*eg* the jury in the town of Vanity Fair, in Bunyan's ▷ *Pilgrim's Progress*) or 'packed', *ie* deliberately made up from enemies or friends of the accused; or they can be intimidated.

Juries trying criminal or civil cases were technically called Petty Juries; Grand Juries (no longer in use) had the function of presenting those suspected of crime before the royal judges on their visits to the region. Small crimes have never been tried by juries but (since the early 14th century) by Justices of the Peace (Magistrates).
▷ Courts of Law; Magistrates.

Justices of the Peace

▷ Magistrates.

Juvenal (Decimus Junius Juvenalis) (AD?60–?130)
Roman satirical poet. His sixteen satires describe the
society of his time and denounce its vices. ▷ Satire
as a literary form is usually regarded as being a
Roman invention, but Juvenal was the first of the
Romans to associate it altogether with denunciation;
his predecessor ▷ Horace had used it for ironic
comment and discussion but was only intermittently
denunciatory with the moral conviction associated
with Juvenal. Like Horace, Juvenal had a strong
influence on English poetry from 1590 until 1800;
during these two centuries satire was increasingly
practised, and Horace, Juvenal, or Horace's disciple
Perseus were taken as models. Both Thomas Nashe
(1567–1601) and John Oldham (1653–83) have been
described as 'the English Juvenal', but the most
distinguished of his conscious followers is probably
▷ Samuel Johnson in his two poems ▷ *London* and
The Vanity of Human Wishes, imitations respectively
of Juvenal's third and tenth satires. It is interesting
to compare these with Pope's ▷ *Imitations of Horace*,
which Johnson was emulating. The spirit of Juvenal
is also strongly present in the satirical comedies of
Ben Jonson who used Juvenal in his satirical tragedy
Sejanus. ▷ John Dryden translated Juvenal (1692).

K

Kant, Immanuel (1724–1804)
German philosopher of Scottish descent. His
most important works include: *Critique of Pure
Reason* (1781 and 1787); *Prolegomena to every future
Metaphysic* (1783); *Foundation for the Metaphysic
of Ethic* (1785); *Critique of Practical Reason* (1788);
Critique of Judgement (1790). He counteracted
Leibnizian rationalism and the scepticism of
▷ David Hume by asserting the 'transcendence'
of the human mind over time and space (hence
'transcendental philosophy'). Time and space
are forms of our consciousness: we can know
by appearances but we cannot know 'things in
themselves'. On the other hand, it is in the nature of
our consciousness to have inherent in it an awareness
of design in nature, and of moral and aesthetic value
under a Divine moral law. His philosophy, continued
and modified by other German philosophers (Fichte,
Schelling, Hegel), profoundly influenced the poet
and philosopher ▷ Coleridge; through Coleridge,
it provided a line of thought which, in 19th-century
England, rivalled the sceptical, materialistically
inclined tradition stemming from ▷ Locke, Hume
and ▷ Bentham.
▷ German influence on English literature.

Kauffman, Angelica (1741–1807)
Swiss artist, one of the most successful women in
the history of art. Recognized as a prodigy in her
childhood, she was also an accomplished musician,
and was for a time uncertain whether to pursue a
profession in music or art. Her dilemma is reflected
in an allegorical self-portrait, painted in 1791.
She came to England in 1766 and grew rich and
famous during 15 years in this country. Kauffman
was highly versatile, working in a range of media,
including oils, mezzotint, etching, engraving, and
designing for decorative paintings. She used a variety
of subjects and styles although ▷ neo-classicism
is a recurring theme. She received commissions for
many portraits, and her work gave rise to numerous
imitations. Kauffman was married briefly in 1767
to a man who claimed to be a count, but turned out
to be a bigamous impostor, marrying her only in
order to remain in England, and then deserting her
immediately. Thereafter, she lived a single life until
1781 when she married another artist. Together
they left for the Continent, where she remained until
her death.
Bib: Roworth, W. W., *Angelica Kauffman, A
Continental Artist in Georgian England.*

Kemble, John Philip (1757–1823)
Actor, singer, manager, dramatist. Kemble was the
son of the theatrical manager Roger Kemble and
actress Sarah (née Ward). His sister became known
as the actress ▷ Sarah Siddons, and six other
siblings also went onto the stage.
 In 1777 he began acting at Liverpool, and the
following year his first play, *Belisarius; or Injured
Innocence* was staged there. He began the first of
many seasons at ▷ Drury Lane in 1783, where
his roles included Hamlet, Richard III, Shylock,
and King John. Three of his sisters acted there
during this time, and he played Othello to Sarah

Siddons' Desdemona in 1785. In 1788 he took
over management of Drury Lane, whose patent
was held by ▷ Richard Brinsley Sheridan, and
soon introduced elements of 'theatrical realism'
into his productions, such as providing what he
considered authentic Roman costumes for some of
▷ Shakespeare's Roman plays.
 After 1791 when Drury Lane was declared
unsafe, Kemble moved his company to the ▷ King's
Theatre in the Haymarket, ▷ Covent Garden and
several provincial theatres. In 1816 the advent of
Edmund Kean to the stage drew from Kemble
much of the public respect and admiration he had
enjoyed throughout his career and he retired the
following year.
 Throughout his life, Kemble was admired for
his good looks, elegance, and charm, and respected
for his forceful professional abilities as an actor
and as a manager. He had a rigorous, classical
approach to acting, excelling in parts, especially
those of Shakespeare, to which a grand manner and
style were suited. Like many of his period he had
a prodigious memory enabling him to retain many
long roles in his repertoire. He lacked the emotional
range of ▷ David Garrick, and later Edmund Kean,
and suffered from a tendency to drink to excess,
which occasionally interfered with his ability to
perform. Some 58 plays, most of them alterations,
are attributed to his authorship.
Bib: Baker, H., *John Philip Kemble*; Child, H., *The
Shakespearean Productions of John Philip Kemble*;
Donohue, J., *Dramatic Character in the English
Romantic Age*; Joseph, B., *The Tragic Actor*; Kelly, L.,
*The Kemble Era: John Philip, Sarah Siddons and the
London Stage.*

Ketch, Jack (John) (d1686)
A public executioner who made a name for himself
in popular folklore, so that later executioners bore
his name as a nickname. He was notorious for the
clumsy brutality of his executions, which took place
in public.

Killigrew, Anne (c1660–1685)
English poet and painter. She was praised for
her piety, and was greatly admired by her circle
of aristocratic contemporaries. She was Maid of
Honour to the Duchess of York. *Poems by Mrs Anne
Killigrew* were published the year after her death.
▷ Finch, Anne, Countess of Winchilsea

Killigrew, Thomas (1612–83)
Dramatist, actor, manager. Born in London to Sir
Robert Killigrew, he became a page of honour to
▷ Charles I, possibly from 1625. Killigrew wrote his
first play, *The Prisoners*, in 1635 and in the following
year he married Cecilia Crofts, a maid of honour to
Queen Henrietta Maria, by whom he had at least
one son, before she died in 1638. Killigrew remained
loyal to the king after the outbreak of the ▷ Civil
War, and was imprisoned for a time. He afterwards
travelled as an exile on the Continent during the
1640s, serving first the Duke of York, later ▷ James
II, and then Prince Charles, later ▷ Charles II. His

exploits during that period are romanticized in his play *Thomaso; Or, The Wanderer* (published 1664).

After the ▷ Restoration he was granted one of the two royal patents to form a theatre company which became known as the ▷ King's Company. In 1667 Killigrew set up a ▷ nursery to train young actors in Hatton Garden, and in 1673 he became Master of the Revels, after the death of Sir Henry Herbert (1596–1673). This made him responsible for supervising theatrical entertainment and licensing theatres and he held the post for four years before resigning in favour of his son Charles. In 1682 the King's Company, having foundered for several seasons, was effectively absorbed by the ▷ Duke's Company, but by then Killigrew had little to do with it. He was buried at ▷ Westminster Abbey, near his first wife and a sister.

Kilt

The heavily pleated skirt-like garment worn by Highland Scotsmen and reaching from the waist to the knees. Before the 17th century it was the lower part of the plaid, or large woollen cloth in which the Highlanders wrapped themselves; the kilt was the part that hung down below the belt. Plaid and kilt are now separate. The term 'kilt' is often used for the whole costume, and is regarded as the Scottish national dress. In fact, it was only worn by Highlanders of the lower classes, and was forbidden in the middle of the 18th century as part of a policy of destroying Highland ways of life by the British government. Since then, apart from its use in Highland regiments, the kilt has been revived for romantic and sentimental reasons, and is worn by Scotsmen of all classes, especially on ceremonial occasions.

▷ Highlands, The; Scotland; Tartan.

King, Henry (1592–1669)

Poet and Bishop of Chichester. King, himself the son of a bishop, was prebend of St Pauls until his appointment as Bishop of Chichester in 1642. A year later he was expelled from his bishopric by the ▷ Puritans, but was reinstated after the ▷ Restoration. The major poetic influences on King were John Donne (with whom he was friendly) and Ben Jonson. The majority of his poetry was published in 1657, when his *Poems, Elegies, Paradoxes and Sonnets* appeared. A large proportion of King's poetic output consisted of responses to public occasions, obituaries and ▷ elegies: these included two separately published elegies on ▷ Charles I (1648 and 1649).

Bib: Berman, R., *Henry King and the Seventeenth Century*.

King, William (1663–1712)

Author of satirical and ▷ burlesque works in both prose and verse, including (with Charles Boyle) *Dialogues of the Dead* (1699) and *The Art of Cookery* (1708), imitating ▷ Horace's *Art of Poetry*.

King's Company, The

Acting company formed by ▷ Sir Thomas Killigrew after the ▷ Restoration of ▷ Charles II.

It performed from November 1660 at the former Gibbons' Tennis Court in ▷ Vere Street, near Lincoln's Inn Fields, which had been converted to a theatre. In May 1663 it moved to a purpose-built theatre at Bridges Street, ▷ Drury Lane, also known as the Theatre Royal. In January 1672 that theatre was destroyed by fire and in March 1674, after a temporary sojourn at ▷ Lincoln's Inn Fields, the company moved to a new King's Theatre, or Theatre Royal, designed at Drury Lane by ▷ Sir Christopher Wren. Here it remained until its union with the ▷ Duke's Company to form the ▷ United Company in 1682.

King's Evil, The

A skin disease: scrofula. An ancient tradition maintained that kings could cure it by 'touching' the sufferer. In England the tradition goes back to King Edward the Confessor; his miraculous healing power is described by the Doctor in Shakespeare's *Macbeth* (IV. iii). The poet and critic ▷ Samuel Johnson suffered from the disease, and was 'touched' for it as a child in 1712 by Queen ▷ Anne, the last reigning sovereign to practise the rite. Her nephew Prince Charles also used it during the ▷ Jacobite Rebellion of 1745: since the power was supposed to inhere in the true royal line, the exercise of it was of propaganda value to him in his campaign for the English throne.

King's Friends

George III (1760–1820) tried to revive the power of monarchical government in England against the Whig aristocracy which, since the accession to the throne of the ▷ House of Hanover in 1714, had controlled the country through ▷ Parliament. Since the institution of Parliament was too strong for the king to ignore it, he tried to carry his purpose by securing (largely through various forms of bribery) a party to support his policies and ministers from within Parliament. These became known as the King's Friends or the New Tories.

▷ Whig and Tory.

King's Theatre

▷ Drury Lane Theatres; Haymarket Theatres.

Kingship

The British tradition of kingship has two sources: the Germanic view was that the king was the father of his people, with no particular sacredness about the authority he exercised; the Latin tradition was that the king's powers were sacred, and after Christianity became the official religion of the Roman Empire (in the 4th century AD) the Emperor represented the earthly side of the authority delegated by God to the Holy Church. The two aspects became united when the Frankish king ▷ Charlemagne was crowned Emperor of the West in 800. Medieval English kings only nominally recognized the authority of the Holy Roman Emperors who succeeded Charlemagne, but they took to themselves the same status; a king on being crowned was anointed with holy oils, and a crime against him was a crime against God. In early times kings were elected, though the elected king was traditionally of the same family as the dead king, but by degrees the nearest surviving relative assumed the crown as a matter of course and eventually by right. (In Shakespeare's *Hamlet* and *Macbeth* either young Hamlet nor Malcolm is the evitable heir to the Danish and the Scottish thrones.)

Until the 17th century, peace, law and order depended on the king's authority. In the reign of Henry II, for example, the king's judges imposed a universal 'Common Law' over the selfish interests of the competing barons, and the peace of the country was called 'the king's peace'. Everything depended on the king being universally acknowledged and respected; every kind of disaster followed when the king lost his authority like John, ceased to be respected like Richard II, was a tyrant like Richard III, was a usurper like Henry IV, or died without direct heir, leaving the succession uncertain, as seemed likely to happen after Elizabeth I.

James VI of Scotland, however, succeeded peacefully as ▷ James I of England, but almost at once his quarrels with Parliament and with the country began. James exaggerated the sacredness of kingship into the doctrine of 'the Divine Right of Kings', according to which the King was responsible to God alone; this made adjustment between royal policy and national interests difficult, and Parliament raised up Magna Carta from the reign of King John to prove the right of the people to restrain royal power. No method had yet been discovered, however, of securing stable government except through a strong king, and under James's successor, ▷ Charles I, ▷ civil war broke out, culminating in the execution of the king. It took the remainder of the 17th century and the whole of the 18th to work out the modern system of 'constitutional monarchy', in accordance with which the king or queen reigns but does not rule, and government is conducted through an elected and truly representative parliament to which, and not to the crown, the ministers are responsible. The office of kingship remained sacred, but became symbolic.

Kit-Cat Club

Founded early in the 18th century by leading Whig men of letters and politicians (▷ Whig and Tory); its members included ▷ Marlborough, ▷ Walpole, ▷ Steele, ▷ Addison, ▷ Congreve and ▷ Vanbrugh. It met at the house of a pastry-cook called Christopher Cat. Their portraits by ▷ Sir Godfrey Kneller hang in the National Portrait Gallery.
    ▷ Clubs.

Kneller, Sir Godfrey (1646–1723)

Painter, born at Lubeck, who trained at Amsterdam under a pupil of Rembrandt, and came to England in 1675. He was made court painter in 1680, serving under successive monarchs including ▷ Charles II, ▷ James II, ▷ William III, ▷ Anne and George I.

He painted hundreds of works, including portraits of nine sovereigns and many other members of the nobility, as well as leading writers, actors, actresses and politicians. His paintings are marked by a distinctive formality and grace, in a style that is easily recognizable. His best-known works are 42 portraits of members of the Whig ▷ Kit-Cat Club, known as the Kit-Cat series (1702–17). Knighted in 1692, Kneller was the first painter in England to be made a baronet, in 1715. In 1711 he founded Kneller's Academy, the first of its kind in England.

Knight, Frances Maria (fl1682–1724)

Actress whose career survived transitions of taste and her own aging, to remain on the stage for 35 years. She began as a child actress, playing the roles of young girls in plays of ▷ D'Urfey, ▷ Shadwell and ▷ Southerne, moving on to wives and mistresses in the 1690s and 1700s, and eventually to widows and at least one mother. She played heroines, coquettes and villainesses, and is said to have continued acting to the end of her life.
Bib: Howe, E., *The First English Actresses*.

Knox, Vicessimus (1752–1821)

English cleric and author, who became master of Tunbridge School in Kent. He wrote several volumes of sermons and theological and literary treatises, in a style noted for its elegance and correctness. Among them are *Moral and Literary Essays* (1777); *Liberal Education; or a Practical Treatise on the Methods of Acquiring Useful and Polite Learning* (1781); and *Elegant Extracts in Prose and Verse* (1789).

Kotzebue, August Friedrich Ferdinand von (1761–1819)

German dramatist, who directed the theatre of Vienna, and wrote some 200 plays. Several of these were translated into English, including *The Stranger*, *The Indians in England*, *Pizarro*, *Benyowski*. One of them, adapted by ▷ Elizabeth Inchbald as *Lovers' Vows*, features in ▷ Jane Austen's *Mansfield Park*. His work greatly influenced the development of ▷ melodrama on the Continent and in England.
    ▷ German influence on English literature.

Kynaston, Edward (1643–1712)

Actor. Kynaston began his theatrical career in 1660 as a boy actor in women's roles when he was considered 'a Compleat Female Stage Beauty', by the prompter, John Downes.

Kynaston soon transferred to ▷ Killigrew's ▷ King's Company, acting first at the Red Bull Playhouse, and then at the ▷ Vere Street Theatre. He began playing men's parts in addition to women's, but with the full advent of women to the stage, and his own growing maturity, he took on men's roles exclusively.

Lacy, John (?1615–81)

Actor, dancer, choreographer, manager, dramatist, Lacy came to London in 1631, probably to join the Cockpit Theatre, and became a dancer, before his career was interrupted by the ▷ Interregnum. In 1660 he joined ▷ Killigrew's ▷ King's Company, acting first at ▷ Vere Street Theatre, and soon acquired shares in the company's new building at ▷ Bridges Street, becoming a co-manager in 1663.

His first play, *Sauny the Scot* (1667), was a free adaptation of *The Taming of the Shrew*, written largely to provide a comic vehicle for himself in the part of Sauny, which became one of his major triumphs on stage. He wrote at least three other plays, all adaptations of earlier works.

His reputation was based primarily on his abilities as comedian, with a special talent for mimicry. He was the first to play Bayes in the ▷ George Villiers' ▷ *The Rehearsal*, and became a favourite of ▷ Charles II.

Lady Bountiful

A character in ▷ Farquhar's play ▷ *The Beaux' Stratagem*. She is a rich country lady who devotes her time to helping her less fortunate neighbours. She has become a proverbial figure. Farquhar portrays her satirically.

Lagado

In ▷ Swift's ▷ *Gulliver's Travels* (Part III) capital of the island of Balnibarbi and its neighbouring flying island ▷ Laputa.

Lampoon

A personal attack in the form of a verse ▷ satire, usually motivated by mere malevolence. It was common in the later 17th and 18th centuries.

Langhorne, John (1735–79)

Poet, private tutor, clergyman and Justice of the Peace. He wrote sermons, translated ▷ Plutarch and edited the poems of ▷ William Collins (1765). His own poems include exercises in the numerous genres current in the 18th century: topographical verse, animal fables, ▷ pastorals, ▷ elegies and didactic epistles. His most important work, *The Country Justice* (1774–7), in pentameter couplets (▷ metre), mixes didacticism and sentimental anecdote. Its satire on the Poor Laws imitates ▷ Oliver Goldsmith's ▷ *The Deserted Village* (1770).

Laputa

In ▷ Jonathan Swift's ▷ *Gulliver's Travels*, the flying island in the satire against the ▷ natural philosophers of Part III.

Latin literature

Rome began as a small Italian city state, and grew to an empire that surrounded the Mediterranean and extended as far north as the borderland between England and Scotland. Politically, it established the framework out of which modern Europe grew. Culturally, in part by native force and in part by its assimilation and transmission of the older and richer culture of Greece, its literature became the basis of European values, and especially those values that arise from the relationship between the individual and society.

Between 300 and 100 BC, Rome began to produce literature, and at the same time, after its conquest of the rich Greek colonies in southern Italy, to expand its imaginative and intellectual vision and to increase and refine the expressiveness of the Latin language through the study of ▷ Greek literature.

Primitive Roman literature had been of two kinds: that of the recording and examination of public life and conduct in annals of eminent men and in oratory, and that of the distinctively Roman art of ▷ satirical comedy. These centuries saw the production of the comic dramas of ▷ Plautus and of ▷ Terence. The orator and historian Cato the Censor (234–149 BC) upheld the virtues of Roman severity against Greek sophistication and luxury; the dominant figure, however, was the poet Ennius (239–169 BC) who preserved a balance between Greek and Latin values by emulating ▷ Homer in a patriotic epic in Latin idiom and Greek metre, the *Annales*.

The first half of the first century BC was the last great period of the Roman Republic. Active participation in politics was still one of the principal concerns of Roman aristocrats, and by this time Romans had studied and profited from lessons in depth and force of thinking from Greece. ▷ Cicero was the great persuasive orator of public debate; such was the power of his eloquence that the period is often known as the Ciceronian age. ▷ Julius Caesar's terse, practical account of his wars in Gaul and invasion of Britain shows a different kind of prose excellence, and the vividness of Sallust's histories of episodes in recent Roman history is different again. It was thus an age of prose, but it included one of the finest of all philosophical poems, the *De Rerum Natura* ('Concerning the Nature of Things') of ▷ Lucretius, who expounded the thought of the Greek philosopher ▷ Epicurus. It included also the passionate love poems of ▷ Catullus, who gave new vitality to Greek mythology.

Julius Caesar's great-nephew, ▷ Caesar Augustus, became the first Emperor in 27 BC, and he ruled till his death in AD 14. The Republic ended, and with it the kind of moral thought and eloquence which had made Cicero so famous. Roman literature, however, entered upon its most famous period – the ▷ Augustan Age. If the Empire had not quite reached its greatest extent, its power was nonetheless at its peak; the old traditions of austerity and energy were not yet extinct; civilization, wealth and sophistication had not yet overbalanced into decadence resulting from excessive luxury. Augustus himself was a patron of letters. In prose, the outstanding writer was the historian ▷ Livy, but it was above all an age of poetry. The most famous of Roman poets, ▷ Virgil, celebrated great traditions, looked back to by a stable society, in which active political participation had become difficult or unimportant. His contemporary ▷ Horace celebrated the values of civilized private life. Tibullus, Propertius, and above all ▷ Ovid were poets of pleasure appealing to the refined taste of an elegant society.

The last period of Roman literature lasted approximately a hundred years from the death of Augustus. The Emperors were bad, the idea of Rome was losing much of its force, society was showing symptoms of decadence. The best writers became more detached from and more critical of Roman society. In the philosophy and drama of ▷ Seneca, the heroic poetry of ▷ Lucan, the satire of Persius (34–62), the Greek philosophy of Stoicism seemed the strongest defence of human dignity against social oppression and distress. The most powerful work, however, was the savage satire of ▷ Juvenal and the sombre history of his time by ▷ Tacitus.

Literature in Latin did not of course end here, nor did it end with the Roman Empire in the 5th century AD. Latin became the language of the Roman Catholic Church, and therefore of the early medieval educated classes. It remained a living, growing language till its style was fixed by ▷ Renaissance scholars in the 16th century. Even in the 17th century, ▷ Francis Bacon wrote much of his philosophy in Latin, and ▷ Milton wrote Latin poetry. Classical Latin was read and admired in medieval England, but knowledge of it was incomplete and inaccurate; much of this knowledge was obtained from contemporary French and Italian writers whose traditions were closer to classical Latin. Virgil retained great prestige, and Terence was studied in the monasteries for the purity of his style. After 1500, the Renaissance caused English writers to study and emulate the classical writers. Writers modelled themselves on styles of classical prose; the terse manner of Seneca and Tacitus was imitated by Bacon, whereas the eloquent flow of Cicero was emulated by ▷ Edmund Burke. More important than the study of styles was the way in which English writers again and again measured themselves against their own society by placing themselves in the position of Roman writers, and then assessed their society from a Roman standpoint. So, in the late 16th century Donne modelled his elegies on those of Ovid, and a little later Ben Jonson rewrote the lyrics of Catullus; in the 17th century Milton emulated Virgil as Virgil had once emulated Homer; in the 18th century ▷ Pope took the standpoint of Horace, and ▷ Samuel Johnson adopted that of Juvenal.

▷ Classical education.

Leapor, Mary (1722–1746)

English poet. She was from the labouring classes, and worked as a kitchen maid. She was able to write poetry with the support of a patron, Bridget Fremantle, and *Poems upon Several Occassionns* (1748, 1751) was first published after Leapor died of measles. It included the ironical 'Essay on Woman', commenting 'Hymen lifts his sceptered Rod, / and strikes her glories with a fatal nod.' Her verse often uses a figure called 'Mira' to explore the familial and sexual problems of women, and she strongly associates poetry with sleep and dream. In 'The Cruel Parent: a Dream' ▷ Gothic elements interwine with labouring-class problems,

including starvation. In 'a Verse Epistle to a Lady' she describes the working woman poet who 'rolls in treasures till the breaking day: ... till the shrill clock impertinently rings,/ and the soft visions move their shining Wings'. She also wrote a blank-verse tragedy, but died while its staging was being discussed. She left a library of only sixteen or seventeen volumes, including some Pope and Dryden.

▷ Collier, Mary; Little, Janet; Yearsley, Ann.
Bib: Landry, D., *The Muses of Resistance*.

Lee, Nathaniel (?1653–92)

Dramatist. After an unsuccessful acting career Lee turned to writing plays. He became popular for his extravagant tragedies which included *Nero* (1674), *Sophonisba* (1675) and *Gloriana* (1676), and his *The Rival Queens* (1677) heralded a return to the use of blank verse for tragedy. His most serious play, ▷ *Lucius Funius Brutus*, was considered too politically dangerous and was banned after only a few performances. Towards the end of his life Lee spent five years in ▷ Bedlam and died after a drinking bout.

Lee, Sophia (1750–1824)

English novelist and dramatist, elder sister of ▷ Harriet Lee, and friend of ▷ Ann Radcliffe. Her historical fiction included *The Recess, or a Tale of Other Times* (1783–5), and she co-wrote *Canterbury Tales for the Year 1797* with her sister.

Leibniz, Gottfried Wilhelm (1646–1716)

German philosopher and mathematician, born in Leipzig, who became one of the leading representatives of the German ▷ Enlightenment. His invention of the calculus about the same time as ▷ Newton led to a dispute as to who can be called its originator. In 1676 Leibniz met ▷ Spinoza, whose work had a considerable influence on him, along with that of ▷ Descartes and ▷ Hobbes. He persuaded Frederick I to found an Academy of Sciences in Berlin in 1700, of which he himself became the first president. Leibniz developed a theory of matter, outlined in his *Theodicee* (1710) and *Monadologie* (1714), as a finite series of indivisible particles which he called 'monads', each a concentration of energy, and each representing a microcosm of the universe. They belong to a hierarchy whose highest manifestation is God, and they move according to God's laws. Leibniz argued that God, being omnipotent and perfect, could only have created the best world possible, a view propounded by ▷ Pope in his ▷ *Essay on Man* as 'One truth is clear, Whatever IS, is Right', and satirized by ▷ Voltaire in *Candide* as 'all is for the best in this best of all possible worlds'.

▷ German influence on English literature.
Bib: Hazard, P., *European Thought in the Eighteenth Century*; Sambrook, J., *The Eighteenth Century: The Intellectual and Cultural Context of English Literature 1700–1789*.

Lely, Sir Peter (1618–80)

Painter, born in Germany to Dutch parents; his name was originally Pieter van der Faes. He studied in Haarlem, and came to England in 1641. Here he began by painting landscapes and historical and religious subjects, but then turned to portrait work, painting prolifically. He was employed first by ▷ Charles I, then by ▷ Cromwell, and then as a court painter by ▷ Charles II, who knighted him in 1679. Among his best-known works are portraits of the monarchs and their families, including a double portrait of Charles I and his brother the Duke of York, which inspired ▷ Lovelace's 'See what a clouded Majesty . . .', as well as a series of *Beauties* of the court of Charles II, including one of ▷ Nell Gwynn (now kept at Hampton Court). The 13 so-called 'Greenwich Portraits', of English admirals who fought in the second Dutch war, are also highly regarded today.

Lennox, Charlotte (?1727–1804)

Charlotte Lennox was probably born in America, and grew up in New York. From an early age she is known to have been in ▷ London trying, unsuccessfully, to make a career on the stage. In 1747 she published *Poems on Several Occasions*, and in 1750, the year in which her appearance on the stage is last reported, she brought out her first novel, *The Life of Harriot Stuart*.

Lennox's literary talent was enthusiastically supported by ▷ Samuel Johnson and ▷ Henry Fielding. In 1752 *The Female Quixote* established her name as a writer. The novel tells of a naïve heroine, Arabella, whose view of the world is foolishly filtered through the romances she reads. Lennox uses this framework to satirize sexual stereotypes and the social conventions of courtship.

Johnson's help in finding publishers for Lennox was probably partly motivated by his knowledge of her circumstances as well as her literary achievements. Her husband, Alexander, was a constant drain on the family's finances, and Lennox's writing provided their only support. She worked on translations and adaptations to supplement their income, and produced three volumes of Shakespeare's sources, with Johnson's encouragement. Her final novel *Euphemia* (1790) explores the position of women in marriage, reflecting her own experience with the spendthrift husband she eventually left.

Lessing, Gotthold Ephraim (1729–81)

German author, one of the most versatile of the German ▷ Enlightenment. He wrote poetry, plays and essays, including literary criticism and philosophical and moral treatises. His play *Nathan der Weise* (Nathan the Wise, 1779), is a plea for religious tolerance, in which the eponymous Nathan, modelled on Lessing's friend the Jewish philosopher Moses Mendelssohn, answers Saladin's question, 'which is the true religion?' He relates a parable about three identical gold rings, which he compares with the varieties of religion, all equally valuable, and equally loved by God. His rationalist attacks on orthodox Christianity provoked a stream of angry responses. Other plays of his include the comedy *Minna Von Barnhelm* (1767) and a tragedy, *Emilia Galotti* (1772). His work influenced the English ▷ Romantic writers.

▷ German influence on English literature.

Letter-writing

This is clearly an important branch of literature even when the interests of the letters is essentially historical or ▷ biographical. Letters may also be, by intention or by consequence of genius, works of intrinsic literary value. The 18th century (the age of the ▷ epistolary novel) was more than any other the period when letter-writing was cultivated as an art: see, above all, the letters of ▷ Horace Walpole and those to his son by ▷ Lord Chesterfield – the former a record of events and the latter consisting of moral reflections. Earlier than the 18th century, postal services were not sufficiently organized to encourage regular letter-writing, and the art of familiar prose was inadequately cultivated; by the mid-19th century, communications had improved enough to make frequent and full letter-writing redundant.

Levellers

An important political party during the period of the ▷ Civil War and the Commonwealth. It first became prominent in 1647; the term was first found in a letter of November of that year, describing them as people who wanted to 'rayse a parity and community in the kingdom'. Mainly found among the soldiers and opposed to kingship, the Levellers feared the Parliamentary leaders were insufficiently firm. Two documents were composed by them, *The Case of the Army Truly Stated* and *The Agreement of the People*, asking for a dissolution of ▷ Parliament and change in its future constitution. They were at odds with ▷ Oliver Cromwell, who suppressed the mutinies they engineered; Parliament declared other Leveller writings by John Lilburne (1614–57) treasonable and in March 1649 their leaders were arrested. A public meeting in London in their support, and risings at Burford and Banbury, were suppressed. Associated with them were the 'True Levellers' or 'Diggers' of April 1649, who took possession of some unoccupied ground at Oatlands in Surrey and began to cultivate it. The leaders, arrested and brought before Fairfax, denounced landowners.

▷ Utopian literature.

Leviathan

▷ Hobbes, Thomas.

Lewis, Matthew Gregory ('Monk') (1775–1818)

Writer whose sensational novel *The Monk* (1796) had such success in its day that he was nicknamed after it.

▷ Gothic novels.

Licensing Act

▷ Theatres.

Lilliput

The island in Part I of ▷ Swift's ▷ *Gulliver's Travels*; the Lilliputians are diminutive in body, and their corresponding pettiness of mind is intended as satirical comment on the pettiness of contemporary English politics and society.

Lillo, George (1693–1739)

Dramatist. Lillo owned a jewellery shop in Moorgate Street, writing plays after hours, and contemporary descriptions of his character talk of him as a modest and moral man. His first piece, *Silvia, or the Country Burial*, a ballad-opera in the style of ▷ *The Beggar's Opera*, was staged at ▷ Drury Lane in 1730, and in 1731 Lillo produced *The Merchant*, afterwards renamed ▷ *The London Merchant, or the History of George Barnwell*, based on an old ballad. *The Merchant*, with its focus on a middle-class character led astray by temptation, and the depiction of his suffering, distress, and eventual penitence and execution, helped to establish the so-called domestic or bourgeois tragedy on the English stage, and was also influential in Germany and France via Lessing and Diderot. Lillo's other plays include *The Christian Hero* (1734), *Fatal Curiosity* (1736), again based on an old ballad about a murder, and *Arden of Feversham* (1736), drawing, like its Elizabethan predecessor, on an account by Holinshed.

Lincoln's Inn Fields Theatre

In March 1660 ▷ Sir William D'Avenant began conversion of Lisle's Tennis Court, built between 1656 and 1657 at Lincoln's Inn Fields, in order to house the ▷ Duke's Company under his newly confirmed patent from the king. The resulting theatre introduced the proscenium, or framed stage, to the English theatre for the first time. But increasingly the building was felt to be too small, and in 1671 the company moved to ▷ Dorset Garden. It was occupied by various companies until, in 1714, it was refurbished in grand style by Edward Shepherd, with mirrors lining the interior walls, and reopened under the auspices of the actor-manager ▷ John Rich.

Lion, (British)

The national emblem, perhaps from its representation on the coats of arms of medieval kings. The first literary mention of the British Lion is in ▷ John Dryden's poem ▷ *The Hind and the Panther*.

Lisle's Tennis Court

▷ Lincoln's Inn Fields Theatre.

Litotes

▷ Figures of speech.

Little, Janet (1759–1813)

Scottish labouring-class poet who wrote in Gaelic and English. She did not have more than a 'common education' before becoming a domestic servant to Frances Wallace Dunlop of Dunlop, the patron of Scottish poet ▷ Robert Burns (1759–1796). She later married John Richmond. She went to work in the dairy at Loudoun Castle, and her employer showed some of her poetry to Burns. In 1792 *The Poetical Works of Janet Little* was issued. Incisively aware of her own 'impudent' status as a poet, she refuses to accept received pronunciation, and threads her writing with changes in linguistic mode. She wrote, 'But what is more surprising still, / A milkmaid must tak' up her quill; / An' she will write,

shame fa' the rabble / That thinks to please with ilka bawble.' She continued to write after the publication of the book.

▷ Collier, Mary; Leapor, Mary; Yearsley, Ann.
Bib: Landry, D. *The Muses of Resistance*.

Little Theatre

▷ Lincoln's Inn Fields Theatre.

Little Theatre in the Hay

▷ Haymarket Theatres.

Lives of the Poets, The (1779–81)

By ▷ Samuel Johnson; originally entitled *Prefaces biographical and critical to the Works of the English Poets*. Johnson began work on the project at the request of a number of booksellers, who required essays on the poets which could be prefaced to editions of their works. The essays developed so successfully that it was decided to issue them in their own right. The essays are interesting both for their critical insight and because they embody their literary tastes of the time. They are idiosyncratic and prejudiced, but always lively; Johnson's bias against the ▷ metaphysical poets in particular has been challenged by changing literary tastes.

Livy (Titus Livius) (59 BC–AD 17)

Roman historian. He wrote the history of Rome in 142 books, 35 of which have survived, with summaries of most of the rest. His aims were partly to ensure that the achievements of 'the chiefest people of the world' should be remembered and partly to provide material for future political guidance.

▷ Latin literature.

Lloyd's

An association of shipowners and other business men concerned with shipping. Its activities are primarily the insurance of ships and cargoes, and the dissemination of shipping information. It arose from a ▷ coffee-house kept by an Edward Lloyd in London early in the 18th century; this was frequented by merchants and insurers of ships who eventually formed their own association.

Locke, John (1632–1704)

Philosopher. He follows ▷ Thomas Hobbes in his sceptical ▷ rationalism, but he is the direct opposite of Hobbes in his optimistic view of human nature and in the moderation and flexibility of his social and political ideas. Hobbes was born in the year of the attempted invasion by the Armada and was painfully aware of the human propensity to violence from the decade of ▷ civil wars (1642–52); Locke's sympathies were identified with the moderation of the bloodless revolution of 1688 (▷ Glorious Revolution) and the climate of reasonableness which followed it.

In his two *Treatises of Government* (1690), Locke, like Hobbes, presupposes a state of nature preceding a social contract which was the basis of political society. But whereas Hobbes saw the state of nature as a state of war, Locke saw it as a peaceful condition in which the Law of Nature and of Reason was spontaneously observed; his idea of the social contract was not, as for Hobbes, that human existence was intolerable without it, but that it merely provided additional assurance that life and property would be respected. For Hobbes sovereignty had to be single and absolute, but for Locke it was merely a public service always responsible to society, which may at any time remove it. Similarly, in his *Letters concerning Toleration* (1689, 1690, 1692 and a fourth published posthumously) Locke, unlike Hobbes, held that the state has no right to interfere in religious matters and that oppression of religion by governments caused religion to spark civil violence.

Locke's advocacy of religious toleration was consistent with his sceptical attitude to faith and knowledge. Man must first discover what he can know before he persecutes others for publishing false beliefs, and this inquiry he conducts in his ▷ *Essay concerning Human Understanding* (1690). This shows man's capacity for knowledge to be distinctly limited, but the existence of God turns out to be a necessary hypothesis discoverable by reason. Christianity therefore is inherently reasonable (*Reasonableness of Christianity*, 1695) and faith by revelation is indispensable only because the use of reason is unavailable to the majority of mankind; 'nothing that is contrary to ... reason has a right to be urged or assented to as a matter of faith' (*Human Understanding*, Bk. IV).

In his *Thoughts on Education* Locke extols reason at the expense of imagination and therefore (by implication) of the imaginative arts. When he applies his philosophy to politics or education, Locke is always guided by standards of practical utility, and in his abstract speculation he refrains from carrying his reasoning so far (as ▷ David Hume seemed to do) that the logical basis for the conduct of practical life by the light of reason was undermined. His philosophy dominated the 18th century and is at the back of such 19th-century rationalist movements as ▷ Utilitarianism.
Bib: Cranston, M., *Life*; MacLean, K., *John Locke and English Literature in the Eighteenth Century*; Willey, B., *The Seventeenth Century Background*; *English Moralists*; James, D. G., *The Life of Reason: Hobbes, Locke, Bolingbroke*.

Lombard Street

In the City of London; for centuries a centre for finance and commerce. Its name derives from the settlement of Italian merchants from Lombardy (north Italy) in the ▷ Middle Ages. To bet 'All Lombard Street to a China orange' would show great confidence.

London

The capital of Great Britain and, in particular, the capital of England. The original core of London is called 'the ▷ City'; it is the financial capital of Britain and now has only a small residential population. Its Lord Mayor is still a figure of prestige, as a kind of symbolic representative of the financial and commercial power of the country. From the early 18th century, London expanded

rapidly outwards from the City so as to absorb the surrounding villages which until 1965 retained their identity as districts within the administrative county of Greater London.

London has always had a great cultural dominance in England, partly because from the 12th century its neighbourhood was the main centre of the royal court and partly because of its great superiority in size and wealth over other English towns. In the Middle Ages the chief royal residences were the Palace of ▷ Westminster and the ▷ Tower (respectively to the west and east of the City); in the 16th century, ▷ Hampton Court; in the 17th century, ▷ Whitehall in Westminster and (at the end of the 17th century) Kensington Palace; since the middle of the 18th century, Buckingham Palace. ▷ Windsor Castle, a royal palace and stronghold since the 14th century, is not far to the west of London. London's superiority in size can be shown by the fact that in 1700 it had a population of about 600,000, whereas the cities next to it in size, Norwich and Bristol, had only about 30,000 each. A century before, in the time of ▷ Shakespeare, London's estimated population was a quarter of a million, and it was already one of the largest towns in Europe.

Districts west of the City (the 'West End') such as Westminster, Kensington, ▷ Chelsea, have always tended to be rich and fashionable; those to the east (the 'East End') the poorer areas.

The neighbourhood of the royal court was not the only cause of London's importance as the literary centre of national life. The ▷ Inns of Court – colleges of legal education originating in the 13th century – were equivalent to a university in fostering intellectual life, especially from the 15th to 17th centuries. In the later 15th century, the proximity of lawyers, courtiers, politicians, merchants and churchmen, at a time when every aspect of English society was in a critical phase of growth, gave London a peculiar vitality which expressed itself in the Elizabethan drama and in the building of the first ▷ theatres. London had virtually a monopoly of the drama until the 18th century; it was not until then that other towns began to build their own theatres. In the same century, the importance of the court as a cultural centre markedly declined. Intellectuals and men of letters met in the ▷ coffee-houses – equivalent to the cafés of 19th-century Paris – and in the town mansions of the aristocracy and richer merchants. By the 19th century the population of London had enormously enlarged, and in consequence artistic and intellectual activity tended to concentrate in certain districts of it. Thus the ▷ British Museum Library made Bloomsbury (part of Holborn) a centre of scholarship, and London University (founded 1828) has its Senate House nearby; Chelsea became a home of painters, and ▷ Fleet Street the base of journalism (▷ Newspapers).

London (1738)

A poem by ▷ Samuel Johnson in heroic ▷ couplets, written in imitation of the *Third Satire* by ▷ Juvenal. In the spirit of Juvenal, Johnson satirizes (through the character of Thales) the degenerate sophistication, the social injustice, and the crime and licence of the so-called civilization of London. The style has Johnson's typical compression and force, and the ▷ satire is more impersonal than that of his chief predecessors, ▷ Dryden and ▷ Pope who followed the more relaxed and personal style of ▷ Horace. Juvenal is not imitated slavishly but interpreted with discernment and used as a criterion for emulation.

London Bridge

The famous bridge of this name, between the ▷ City and ▷ Southwark, was completed in 1209 and until 1750 it was the only bridge across the Thames at London. It was built of stone and had 20 piers; the narrow arches caused the river to flow through them in violent and dangerous currents. The bridge was 20 feet (6.1 m) wide with a 12 ft (3.7 m) roadway between houses and shops which projected over the water on each side. Over the widest, centre arch there was a chapel dedicated to St Thomas à Becket of Canterbury. It was the approach to the ▷ City from the south and it bore two gates, on the northernmost of which the heads of traitors were exposed. The bridge was a source of civic pride, but a real inconvenience to shipping. In the second half of the 18th century two more bridges were built and the houses on London Bridge were taken down; in 1831 the bridge itself was demolished and replaced.

London Cuckolds, The (1681)

Comedy by ▷ Ravenscroft. Three old citizens, Doodle, Dashwell and Wiseacre, are married to three young women: Arabella, Eugenia, and Peggy. Each of the men believes he has made the best choice, but the play shows how the women conspire to outwit their husbands, in order to carry on liaisons with their lovers. The atmosphere is one of farcical intrigue, with scenes of concealment, duplicity, and mistaken identity. Despite contemporary attacks on its supposed indecency, the play was staged each year on the Lord Mayor's Day until 1751. It was revived in 1979 at the Royal Court Theatre, and more recently, at the Lyric Theatre, Hammersmith.

London Magazine, The

Three periodicals of this name have existed: the first ran 1732–85; the second, 1820–29; and the third, founded in 1954, still exists. The second is the most famous. It was founded as the political opponent of the right-wing *Blackwood's Magazine*, and its first editor, John Scott, was killed in a duel in consequence of the rivalry.

London Merchant, The, or The History of George Barnwell (1731)

Play by ▷ George Lillo, thought to be the first tragedy to centre on a low-born hero and the affairs of ordinary people, and to be written predominantly in prose. In the Dedication Lillo announced a specific moral purpose, 'the exciting of the passions in order to the correcting of such of them as are criminal, either in their nature, or through their excess'. The action takes place in the reign of Elizabeth I. The virtuous and inexperienced young apprentice George Barnwell is seduced and corrupted by the predatory, man-hating courtesan Millwood. She inveigles him into stealing money from his employer, Thorowgood, and then into murdering his kindly but wealthy uncle. His resulting despair causes her to fear for her own safety, so she casts him off and betrays him to the authorities. But her servants, revolted by the depths to which she has sunk, and repenting their own part in the process, in turn betray her. Millwood is condemned to death, along with her victim. In his last moments Barnwell is visited by his master's daughter, Maria, and discovers she has loved him all along.

Barnwell's descent into crime, torn by guilt and bouts of remorse, is treated with considerable sympathy and Lillo shows how hard it is for him, once he has become an outcast, to contemplate any alternative. Even Millwood is allowed some pointed comments about men's hypocrisy, the cruelty wrought by religious bigotry, and the injustices of society. But the final scenes in the prison cell of the now repentant Barnwell are laden with ▷ sentiment.

The play, with its emphasis on Barnwell's suffering and distress, helped to establish the so-called domestic or bourgeois tragedy on the English stage. *The London Merchant* is dedicated to a wealthy merchant, Sir John Eyles, and comments on the usefulness of merchants to the nation.

The original production was a family affair, with the characters of Barnwell and Maria taken by ▷ Theophilus Cibber and his wife, and the servant Lucy by Cibber's sister, ▷ Charlotte Charke. ▷ Colley Cibber later supplied a silly, comic epilogue. The villainous Millwood was played by ▷ Charlotte Butler. The play was an enormous success, and remained popular for over a century. It also influenced ▷ Diderot and ▷ Lessing, and through them, via ▷ Kotzebue, the English stage once again.

Long Parliament, The

A parliament which was summoned by ▷ Charles I in 1640 and continued until 1653, when it was dissolved by ▷ Oliver Cromwell. It was this ▷ parliament that broke with the king and started the ▷ Civil War in 1642. In 1648 those of its members who were disposed to come to terms with the king were expelled by Colonel Pride (d. 1658) ('Pride's Purge') and the remainder continued to sit under the nick-name of 'the Rump'. After dissolving it, Cromwell called parliaments of his own but after his death in 1658 it reassembled and in 1660, the year of the ▷ Restoration of the Monarchy, it dissolved itself to make way for a new parliament under the restored king, ▷ Charles II. His government did not recognize the legality of Cromwell's parliaments, so that the law in the Long Parliament was considered to have sat continuously from 1640 to 1660.

Longinus, Dionysius Cassius (1st century AD)

Greek critic. Most of his works have perished but he is the reputed author of the extremely influential treatise *On the Sublime*. This is about literary style; 'the Sublime', though the traditional rendering of the

Greek title, is usually regarded as misleading. The author is concerned with the qualities of expression that make for true impressiveness, relates them to distinction of mind in the writer and discusses faults that arise from fallacious ideas of eloquence. The French critic, ▷ Boileau, made a famous translation of the treatise in 1674, and through him it influenced 18th-century English ideas on style.
▷ Greek literature.

Lord Chancellor
The office of Lord Chancellor existed before the Norman Conquest (1066) and has always been one of the most important in the state, although its outstanding political importance diminished following the resignation of Sir Thomas More in 1532, after his disagreement with Henry VIII's religious policy. In the ▷ Middle Ages the Chancellor was the king's secretary and keeper of the seal which authorized public enactments. This closeness to the centre of power often meant that he was second only to the king himself. In the 14th century he took upon himself the task of hearing appeals from subjects who were unable to get justice through the Common Law Courts. He thus became the head of a new Court of Law, the ▷ Court of Chancery, operating a new department of law, called the Law of Equity. The Lord Chancellor also presided over meetings of the Great Council of the Barons in medieval times, and he still presides over its historical descendant, the House of Lords, *ie* the Upper House of Parliament. As the House of Lords contains judges who meet as the highest court of judicial appeal in the country, the Lord Chancellor presides over this too, and in this capacity he is the head of the English judicial system. Finally, the Lord Chancellor is *ex officio* a member of every Cabinet and the nearest equivalent in England to a Minister of Justice.

Lords, House of
Technically the Upper House of the two Houses of Parliament, the British legislature. It sits under the presidency of the ▷ Lord Chancellor, who is minister for justice and the head of the judicial system. When he sits alone with seven specially appointed judges, the Lords of Appeal in Ordinary, the House of Lords constitutes the highest court of appeal in Britain.

The House of Lords is the direct descendant of the medieval Great Council, to which the king summoned his chief landholders (the nobles or 'peers of the realm') and the leaders of the Church. The House still consists of hereditary peers in a majority, though a small number of life peers (created under the Life Peerages Act of 1958) have been added to the number of non-hereditary members, the Lords of Appeal and the Lords Spiritual (the two Archbishops and 24 other bishops of the ▷ Church of England). In theory this makes the House of Lords a very large body with about 1,060 members; in fact only those peers who are politicians normally attend, so that in practice it is a smaller body than the House of Commons.

Until 1911 the legal power of the House of Lords was about equal to that of the House of Commons, though the latter had become politically the more important as early as the 17th century. The Parliament Act of 1911 greatly reduced its powers, however, and it rarely shows opposition to the majority decisions of the Lower House. A Bill for reform of the House of Lords was dropped by the Labour government in 1968–9.
▷ Parliament.

Love for Love (1695)
A comedy by ▷ William Congreve. The plot centres on an intrigue to frustrate an uncharitable father, Sir Sampson, who wishes to disinherit his extravagant elder son, Valentine, in favour of the younger brother, Ben, a hearty but ludicrous sailor. The intrigue is managed by Angelica, a rich and spirited girl in love with Valentine. A minor plot concerns Sir Sampson's attempt to marry Ben off to an equally awkward country girl, Miss Prue, the daughter of a superstitious astrologer, Foresight. The rustic embarrassment of Ben and Prue, neither of whom wants to marry the other, nicely contrasts with the wit and grace of Valentine and Angelica. The play succeeds particularly because of its skilful and witty prose dialogue.

Love Letters Between a Nobleman and His Sister (1684–87)
▷ Epistolary fiction by ▷ Aphra Behn, based on the story of the adulterous and quasi-incestuous elopement and affair of Lady Henrietta Berkely and her brother-in-law, Forde, Lord Grey of Werke, but transposing the scene to France. The novel was originally published in three volumes from 1684 to 1687. Part one concentrates on the story of Sylvia and Philander, the second part follows Philander to Cologne, and the third part ends with the execution of the ▷ Duke of Monmouth after his attempt to depose ▷ James II.

Lovelace, Richard (1618–58)
Poet. One of the so-called 'Cavalier poets', Lovelace fought on behalf of the king during the ▷ Civil War. The majority of his poetry was written before 1649, when his collection of poems entitled *Lucasta* appeared. *Lucasta* is prefaced with a commendatory poem by ▷ Andrew Marvell, and his work might be thought of as anticipating themes expressed in Marvell's poetry – in particular the search for a form of disengagement from the world. It is not, however, with the more republican Marvell that Lovelace is associated, but with aristocratic codes of love and honour embraced by the literary and military circles in which Lovelace moved. Of special note are the series of 'bestiary poems' (*eg* 'The Snail' or 'The Grasshopper') which seem often to offer themselves as a form of disguised or encoded commentary on the political crisis of the period before the Civil War.
Bib: Wilkinson, C. H. (ed.), *The Poems of Richard Lovelace*; Weidhorn, M., *Richard Lovelace*.

Lovers' Vows (1798)
Play by ▷ Elizabeth Inchbald, adapted from *Das Kind der Liebe* by ▷ August von Kotzebue. Agatha has been seduced and abandoned by Baron

Wildenhaim, who has married another woman. Agatha has given birth to a son, Frederic, but become separated from him. He finds her sunk in deep poverty, and learns about his birth for the first time. Eventually he persuades his father, now widowed and elderly, to marry his mother, and to allow his daughter Amelia to marry the man of her choice, instead of the wealthy man her father had chosen for her. The play is featured in ▷ Austen's *Mansfield Park* (1814).

Love's Last Shift (1696)

Comedy by ▷ Colley Cibber, often said to have set the stage for 18th-century ▷ Reform Comedy. Loveless, having abandoned his wife Amanda and gone abroad, returns to England deeply in debt. She has inherited a fortune, and remained loyal to him. Amanda seduces him in disguise, then reveals her true identity. Shaken by remorse, Loveless embraces the 'chast Rapture of a Vertuous Love', and the two are reunited as a couple. The ending is said to have reduced the audience to tears, and the play was a great success. Sub-plots concern the courtships of Young Worthy and Narcissa, and of the Elder Worthy, a reformed rake and the teasing woman, Hillaria. ▷ Sir John Vanbrugh's *The Relapse* (1696) was written as a sequel and sardonic 'comment' on Cibber's play, showing that Loveless's reformation is only temporary. Cibber himself performed in both plays, as Sir Novelty Fashion, who later assumes the title of Lord Foppington.

Lucan (Marcus Annaeus Lucanus) (AD 39–65)

A Roman poet; author of the poem *Pharsalia* about the struggle for power between ▷ Julius Caesar and Pompey.

Christopher Marlowe translated the first book (1600). The translation by Rowe (1718) was greatly praised by ▷ Samuel Johnson. In ancient times Lucan was noted for his florid style, and for his gift for ▷ epigram.

Lucian (2nd century AD)

Greek satirist. He is especially known for his satirical dialogues and for his *True History*, an account of imaginary voyages which ▷ Jonathan Swift may have used as a model for his ▷ *Gulliver's Travels*.

Lucifer

A Latin name meaning 'the light-bearer'. 'Lucifer' became one of the names for Satan, the brightest of angels before his fall. He is one of the principal protagonists of ▷ Milton's ▷ *Paradise Lost*.

Lucius Junius Brutus (1680)

Tragedy by ▷ Nathaniel Lee, based on the historic overthrow of Tarquin and establishment of a republic in Rome, using ▷ Livy as a major source. It contains strong libertarian and egalitarian speeches, as when Brutus accuses Tarquin of arbitrary rule (Act II) and looks forward to a time when 'no man shall offend because he's great' (Act V). Staged at a time of high political tension in England, with the Whigs pressing the Exclusion Bill, the play was considered too dangerous and was suppressed.

Lucky Chance, The (1686)

Comedy by ▷ Aphra Behn. The title plot concerns the fortunes of Julia, Lady Fulbank, married to an old man, Sir Cautious Fulbank, but in love with the poverty-stricken Gayman. She secretly conveys money to Gayman, and then visits him disguised as an old crone. Later Sir Cautious gambles with Gayman, and stakes a night with his wife as the prize. Gayman wins, and is brought to Julia's chamber, where he makes love to her in the guise of her husband. In the secondary plot, Bellmour, having killed a man in a duel, flees to Brussels, leaving behind his fiancée Leticia. In his absence Sir Feeble Fainwou'd, an old alderman whose name describes his condition, convinces Leticia that her lover is dead, and she agrees to marry Sir Feeble, but the wedding is forestalled when Bellmour returns, and manages to thwart his rival's plans. The play ends with Lady Fulbank announcing that she is leaving her husband, and both women being united with the men of their choice. In an extended and vivid speech, Lady Fulbank defends the right of women to love where they please, even if it means cuckolding their husbands. The play was successfully staged at ▷ Drury Lane, and formed the source of ▷ Hannah Cowley's *School for Greybeards* (1786). It was revived at the Royal Court Theatre in 1984.

Lucrece (Lucretia)

A Roman lady of outstanding virtue and beauty. She was the wife of Tarquinius Collatinus but Sextus, the son of Tarquin, king of Rome, tried to seduce her and, when she resisted, raped her. She told her father and her husband of the outrage and exacted an oath of vengeance from them, after which she killed herself. In consequence, a relative of her husband, Lucius Junius Brutus, led a rebellion against the Tarquin monarchy and expelled them from the city. Lucrece was thus traditionally the occasion for the foundation of the ancient Roman Republic. The tale has been reworked many times, notably in the play ▷ *Lucius Junius Brutus*, by ▷ Nathaniel Lee, because it poses questions about guilt and innocence that are of enduring concern. **Bib:** Donaldson, I., *The Rapes of Lucrece*.

Lucretius (Titus Lucretius Carus) (1st century BC)

Roman poet; author of the great didactic poem *De Rerum Natura* ('Concerning the Nature of Things'). It outlines the philosophy of the Greek thinker ▷ Epicurus, which is based on the atomic theory of Democritus. The poet seeks to expound that all reality is material. The gods exist but they also are material, though immortal, and they are not concerned with the affairs of men; the soul exists but it, too, is material and mortal like the body, dissolving into its original atoms after death. Lucretius is not, however, a cynical poet; he testifies to the beauty of the natural world and the poem opens with an eloquent invocation to ▷ Venus. Lucretius' love of the natural world and his reverence for reason caused him to be greatly admired during the ▷ Renaissance and the succeeding two centuries; parts of the poem were finely translated

by ▷ Dryden, and also by Thomas Creech
(1659–1700).

Luggnagg
A country in Part III of ▷ Swift's ▷ *Gulliver's Travels*. It is inhabited by the Struldbrugs who have immortality, and find it a curse.

Lyric
In Ancient Greece the name given to verse sung to a lyre (from the Greek '*lurikos*' – 'for the lyre'), whether as a solo performance or by a choir. In English usage, the term has had different associations in different historical/literary periods. Elizabethan critics first used the term in England: George Puttenham (d. 1590), for example, describes a lyric poet as someone who composes 'songs or ballads of pleasure to be sung with the voice, and to the harpe'. From the illustrative quotations in the OED (*sv.* 'lyric'), it is clear that in later usage musical accompaniment was no longer considered essential to the definition of the form. In the 17th century lyric forms were widely used in poetry. Among the chief exponents were ▷ Shakespeare, Jonson, ▷ Herrick ▷ Lovelace, ▷ Marvell, ▷ Herbert, ▷ Milton and ▷ Behn. Lyric poetry was less popular in the 18th century, but is found, for example, among the works of ▷ William Collins, and ▷ Thomas Gray. ▷ Blake contributed greatly to a revival of lyric poetry, which gathered pace in the 19th century.
Bib: Lindley, D., *Lyric*.

Lyttelton, George, Lord (1709–73)
Politician and poet. Opponent of ▷ Sir Robert Walpole and for a time in 1756 Chancellor of the Exchequer. ▷ James Thomson apostrophizes him in ▷ *The Seasons* and he was a friend of ▷ Alexander Pope, ▷ Henry Fielding and ▷ William Shenstone. His own poems include *The Progress of Love* (1732), *Monody to the Memory of a Lady* (1747), and *Dialogues of The Dead* (1760–5). He also published a *History of Henry II* (1767).

M

Macaulay, Catharine (1731–1791)
English historian and Whig radical. In 1760 she
married the physician George Macaulay, and in 1763
began to publish her long 'anti-Royalist' *History of
England from the Accession of James I to that of the
Brunswick Line* (1763–1783) (compare, for example,
▷ Mary Astell's Tory history). Her husband died in
1766, and she became ill, but went to France in 1777
and visited the US in 1784, staying with President
George Washington (1732–1799). She was abused
for her second marriage to the younger William
Graham. She responded to philosopher ▷ Thomas
Hobbes and ▷ Edmund Burke, and again took issue
with Burke's ▷ *Reflections on the Revolution in France*
(1790). Her *Letters on Education* (1790) influenced
▷ Mary Wollstonecraft's ▷ *Vindication of the Rights
of Woman*. In the *Letters* (addressing 'Hortensia') she
wrote, 'The situation and education of women . . . is
precisely that which must necessarily tend to corrupt
and debilitate both the powers of mind and body.'

▷ *Essay to Revive the Antient Education of
Gentlewomen, An*; Whig and Tory.
Bib: Ferguson, M. (ed.), *First Feminists*.

Macaulay, Thomas Babington, Lord (1800–59)
Historian, ▷ essayist, politician and poet. He
was actively on the Whig side politically; that is
to say, without being a radical reformer, he had
strong faith in the virtue of British parliamentary
institutions. He was, from the publication of his
essay on ▷ Milton in 1825, a constant contributor
to the main Whig periodical, the ▷ *Edinburgh
Review*, and his *History of England* (1848 and 1855)
is strongly marked by his political convictions. He
was trained as a lawyer and became an eloquent
orator; his writing has corresponding qualities of
persuasiveness and vividness. As a historian he was
best at impressionistic reconstruction of the past, and
the same gift served him in his biographical essays
on ▷ John Bunyan, ▷ Oliver Goldsmith, ▷ Samuel
Johnson, ▷ Fanny Burney and the younger
▷ William Pitt. He represented the most optimistic
strain of feeling in mid-19th-century England – its
faith in the march of progress.

Macaulay's *Lays of Ancient Rome* (1842) were an
attempt to reconstruct legendary Roman history in
a way that might resemble the lost ▷ ballad poetry
of ancient Rome. Though not major poetry, they are
very vigorous verse with the kind of appeal that is to
be found in effective ballad poetry.

Macaulay was raised to the peerage in 1857.
▷ Histories; *History of England*.
Bib: Trevelyan, M., *Life and Letters*; Bryant, A.,
Macaulay; Firth, C., *A Commentary on Macaulay's
History of England*; Trevelyan, G. M. in *Clio: a Muse*;
Stephen, L., in *Hours in a Library*; Clive, J., *Thomas
Babington Macaulay: The Shaping of the Historian*.

**Mac Flecknoe, or a Satyr upon the True-Blew-
Protestant Poet, T. S. (1682)**
1 A ▷ mock-heroic satire by ▷ John Dryden
in ▷ pentameter ▷ couplets, written about
1678 and published in 1682. The poem attacks
▷ Thomas Shadwell, who is designated as the
successor, or 'son' of Flecknoe, a ▷ Catholic

poet previously the butt of a satire by ▷ Andrew
Marvell. Shadwell had replied to Dryden's attack
on ▷ Lord Shaftesbury in ▷ *The Medal*, with
The Medall of John Bayes, accusing the Laureate
(hence ▷ Bayes) of atheism. Dryden countered
by attacking Shadwell in ▷ *Absalom and Achitophel*,
Part II, and in this poem. It is a masterpiece of
high-spirited lampoon, in which Dryden mocks
Shadwell by making Flecknoe eulogize his 'son's'
literary ineptitude and corpulence: 'The rest to some
faint meaning make pretence,/ But Shadwell never
deviates into sense . . . Besides his goodly Fabrick
fills the eye,/ And seems design'd for thoughtless
Majesty.' Its conclusion, in which two specialists in
the new theatrical gimmicks of pantomime send 'the
yet declaiming Bard' through a trapdoor, is purely
farcical, and helps to make this one of the best comic
poems in the language.

Macheath
Central character in ▷ Gay's ▷ *The Beggar's Opera*.
Macheath is a highwayman and sexual adventurer,
who bigamously marries ▷ Polly Peachum and Lucy
Lockit, at the same time conducting a series of other
amours. Betrayed by one of his other women, he
is sentenced to be hanged. He is reprieved at the
last minute, when one of the players in the comedy
demands a happy ending, and throws in his lot
with Polly. The resolution is a satiric reversal of
the contemporary dramatic vogue for administering
poetic justice.

Macklin, Charles (1699–1797)
Actor, manager, singer, dancer, dramatist. Macklin
began employment as a scout at Trinity College
Dublin, and came to London as a waiter before
1720. Some of his early stage performances were
at ▷ Lincoln's Inn Fields, and in the next few
years, he acted at ▷ Goodman's Field Theatre, the
▷ Haymarket Theatre and ▷ Drury Lane.

In 1741 he astonished audiences with a radical
new interpretation of the role of Shylock in *The
Merchant of Venice*, hitherto played for many years
in low buffoonish style. Macklin presented him
as a harsh, stern character, dressed 'authentically'
with a red Venetian-style hat and red beard, and
a long black gown. The response was repeated
thunderous applause, such that he had to stop at
the ends of several speeches to allow it to die away.
His performance was recalled in detail by some
spectators for decades afterwards. Its naturalism
helped to render ▷ James Quin's elaborate and
stylized methods obsolete, and set a precedent
for the ultimately more successful actor, ▷ David
Garrick, whom Macklin then began to sponsor
and coach.

Subsequent years of Macklin's career were mainly
divided between Dublin and London, but in 1773 he
caused another sensation by creating a Macbeth in
'the old Caledonian habit', instead of the scarlet coat
and wig worn, for example, by Garrick in the role. By
the 1780s, Macklin's advanced age and failing health
began to interfere seriously with his performances
and he was finally forced to retire in 1789, after a
career lasting nearly 70 years.

Macklin's achievements, and his reputation, have been somewhat obscured by those of his younger, more personable and physically more attractive contemporary, David Garrick, who perfected the acting style which Macklin initiated. Macklin trained a generation of actors and actresses in his methods, and he is credited with turning acting into a 'science', a tribute to the seriousness with which he took his profession, and to his imaginative abilities. His career was constantly interrupted by squabbles with other actors and managers, fuelled by his notorious temper.

Bib: Appleton, W., *Charles Macklin an Actor's Life*; Kirkman, J. T., *Memoirs of the Life of Charles Macklin*; Congreve, F., *Authentic Memoirs of the Late Charles Macklin*.

Macpherson, James (1736–96)

The son of a farmer, educated in Aberdeen and at ▷ Edinburgh University. In 1760 he published 16 prose poems under the title *Fragments of Ancient Poetry, Collected in the Highlands of Scotland, and translated from the Gaelic or Erse Language*. He attributed them to the 3rd-century poet ▷ Ossian, an attribution which was accepted by most readers at the time, though some scholars were sceptical. After travelling in the Western Isles in 1760–61 at the expense of his supporters in Edinburgh, he published 'translations' of two complete epics by Ossian: *Fingal* (1762) and *Temora* (1763), which he claimed to have similarly 'collected'. The cloudy rhetoric and dramatic character simplification of Macpherson's prose-poetry caught the mood of the moment. ▷ Thomas Gray was enraptured by 'the infinite beauty' of the *Fragments*, ▷ William Blake was adulatory about them, and Macpherson's *Ossian* retained its popularity throughout the Romantic period, particularly on the continent. ▷ Goethe admired it; Napoleon carried a copy of Macpherson on his campaigns and took it into exile with him to St Helena. ▷ Samuel Johnson was amongst those who attacked the authenticity of Macpherson's sources, replying when asked if he believed that any modern man could have written such works: 'Yes Sir, many men, many women, and many children.' The indignant poet threatened him with physical violence. In later years Macpherson became a political journalist, wrote history with a ▷ Jacobite bias, and was elected MP for Camelford. After his death the Highland Society of Scotland undertook an inquiry into his work and in 1805 declared it to be an amalgam of freely adapted Irish ballads and original compositions by Macpherson himself.

▷ Percy, Thomas.

Magazine

Originally meaning 'storehouse', the word has also denoted, since the 18th century, a periodical containing miscellaneous material, *eg* the ▷ *Gentleman's Magazine* (founded 1731): 'a Monthly Collection to store up, as in a Magazine, the most remarkable pieces on the subjects above-mentioned' (from the introduction to the first number). In the 18th and early 19th century magazines differed from other serious periodicals only in having greater variety of content and being open to imaginative writing.

▷ Reviews and periodicals.

Magistrates

In England and Wales, magistrates (also known as Justices of the Peace or JPs) are primarily minor judges who try small offences and examine more serious charges in order to decide whether they should be taken to a senior court. Most magistrates are private citizens and the ordinary Magistrates' Court is composed of a panel of JPs, never fewer than two; they are assisted by a Clerk who is a qualified lawyer but they themselves are unpaid. Their meetings are Petty Sessions and appeal from them lies to Quarter Sessions. There are also Stipendiary Magistrates' Courts, originally set up to cover the Metropolitan Police District of London and therefore known popularly as Police Courts, a term now commonly applied to any Magistrates' Court. Stipendiary magistrates are qualified lawyers and receive a salary; they may sit alone.

In the past, however, magistrates have had much wider functions and they have played an important part in English social and political life. The office dates from the 13th century, when petty landowners were appointed as magistrates to help the sheriffs maintain order in their districts, but until the 16th century their importance was comparatively slight. The feudal lords and the abbots of the monasteries were the real powers outside London and the districts adjacent to it. But by the 16th century the feudal nobility were weakened, displaced, or overthrown and in 1536–39 Henry VIII closed the monasteries. The Tudor sovereigns relied on the magistrates to enforce governmental policy in their districts and supervised them carefully through the ▷ Privy Council. Not only did the magistrates have to execute the ▷ Poor Laws, maintain the roads and enforce law and order, but they had to carry out functions formerly exercised by the town trade guilds (now greatly weakened) such as the regulation of wages, prices, and the rules of ▷ apprenticeship. The middle class of landed gentry, from which magistrates were appointed, was the class most loyal to Tudor policies and therefore provided the most effective allies of the ruling family. These magistrates were often to some extent qualified for the legal parts of their functions by education in law at one of the ▷ Inns of Court; law was more a field for general (as distinct from professional) education than it is in modern England.

Magistrates continued to be drawn from the same class, and to have comparably wide functions, throughout the 17th, 18th and much of the 19th century, but their relationship to the Crown changed in political fact, although not in nominal allegiance. ▷ James II lost the support of the class to which they belonged by his policy of re-establishing Roman ▷ Catholicism, and the Revolution of 1688 (▷ Glorious Revolution) was carried out bloodlessly in England largely for this reason. In the 18th century they were only nominally servants of the Crown; in reality, they and their class controlled the government through ▷ Parliament. However, it was in this century that the legal authority of the amateur magistrate first met competiton from professional lawyers in the function of suppressing crime.

Magistrates were satirized at the height of their power in the 18th century by the novelists ▷ Henry Fielding and ▷ Tobias Smollett. They were often regarded as inefficient, untrained in social as well as legal experience and selfish in their interests, especially in their stern penalizing of offences against the ▷ game laws. It is clear, however, that they exercised their functions with considerable responsibility and that the magisterial function was itself valuable training in public affairs for the class which, by its preponderance of wealth; was in any case the most influential body in the country. ▷ Courts of Law.

Magna Carta

The Great Charter which King John was forced by his barons to accept in 1215. It has long been popularly regarded as the foundation of English liberties, guaranteeing such rights as freedom from arbitrary imprisonment. However, 16th-century plays on King John, *eg* ▷ Shakespeare's, omit mention of the Charter, which came to have its modern symbolic importance only in consequence of the conflicts between ▷ kings and ▷ parliaments in the 17th century.

▷ Habeas Corpus.

Makin, Bathsua (born 1600)

English poet, linguist and defender of women's education. She published poetry in languages including Greek, French, Hebrew and Spanish. She married Richard Makin in 1622, and became tutor to Charles I's daughter, Princess Elizabeth, before the outbreak of the Civil War. She corresponded with the famous scholar ▷ Anna Maria von Schurmann. At the Restoration she probably published ▷ *An Essay to Revive the Ancient Education of Gentlewomen. In Religion, Manners, Arts & Tongues* (1673), which is in part an advertisement for a school. Complaining that 'a Learned Woman is thought to be a Comet', she wrote of 'the Barbarous custom to breed Women low', and argued that in the past, gentlewomen were educated in 'the knowledge of Arts and Tongues'. Makin's argument is addressed to the upper echelons of society and her examples of feminine learning include Queen Elizabeth I, and the ▷ masque-loving Queen Christina of Sweden. She wrote, 'persons of higher quality, for want of this Education, have nothing to imploy themselves in, but are forced to Cards, Dice, Playes and frothy Romances merely to drive away the time.' Makin was one of the earliest to theorize the necessity for women's education, and to offer a school in which it could be carried out. Compare ▷ Hannah More, ▷ Mary Wollstonecraft and ▷ Sarah Fielding.

Her other publications include *Musa Virginea* (1616) and *Index Radiographer*.

▷ Astell, Mary
Bib: Myers, M., *Studies in Eighteenth-Century Culture*, 14 (1985).

Malaprop, Mrs

A character in ▷ Richard Brinsley Sheridan's comedy ▷ *The Rivals*. She is the aunt and guardian of the heroine, Lydia Languish. Her principal comic effect is her habit of misusing words; this has given rise to the term 'malapropism'.

Mallet (Malloch), David (?1705–65)

Poet. On moving from Edinburgh to London he expunged the Scotticisms from his speech and changed his name from the Scottish Malloch to the English Mallet. He is remembered for his collaboration with ▷ James Thomson on the ▷ masque *Alfred* (1740), and also for his ▷ ballad *William and Margaret* (1724), which anticipates the ▷ Gothic fashion in popular taste, and was reprinted in ▷ Thomas Percy's *Reliques* under the title *Margaret's Ghost*.

Malone, Edmund (1741–1812)

The greatest early editor of Shakespeare's works, many of whose textual emendations and editorial principles are still widely used. His greatest work remains his posthumously published edition of the complete Shakespeare (1821) and his research on the order in which Shakespeare's plays were written. He was also the first to denounce the Shakespearean forgeries of William Henry Ireland (1775–1835), one of whose fake plays, *Vortigern and Rowena*, was performed as Shakespeare's at ▷ Drury Lane.

▷ Shakespeare editions.

Malthus, Thomas Robert (1766–1834)

Economist; particularly famous for his *Essay on Population* (1798), which he reissued in an expanded and altered form in 1803. Its original title was: *An Essay on the Principle of Population as it affects the Future Improvement of Society, with Remarks on the Speculations of Mr Godwin, M. Condorcet, and other Writers*.

The essence of his view was that social progress tends to be limited by the fact that population increases more rapidly than means of subsistence, and always reaches the limits of subsistence, so that a substantial part of society is doomed to live beyond the margin of poverty. The 'natural checks' which prevent population increase from exceeding the means of subsistence are war, famine and pestilence, to which he added human misery and vice. In the second edition he added a further possible check by 'moral restraint', *ie* late marriages and sexual continence. These arguments made a strong impression on public opinion; an important practical consequence of them was the replacement of the existing haphazard methods of poor relief by the harsh but reasoned and systematic ▷ Poor Law system of 1834.

Malthus's relentless and pitiless reasoning led to political economy becoming known as the ▷ 'dismal science'. His conclusions were contested by humanitarians, and later seemed belied by factors he did not foresee, such as cheap imports of food from newly exploited colonies like Canada. Since 1918 'Malthusian' theories of the dangers of over-population have revived.

Man in Black, The

A character in the collection of essays by ▷ Oliver Goldsmith entitled *The Citizen of the World* (1762). He is prodigiously generous, but his sensibility causes him to conceal this virtue by pretending to be mean.

Mandeville, Bernard de (1670?–1733)

Of Dutch birth, Mandeville made his career in ▷ London as a doctor. His satire in Hudibrastic (▷ *Hudibras*) couplets *The Grumbling Hive, or Knaves turn'd Honest* (1705) was reissued with accompanying prose essays in 1714 as *The Fable of the Bees; or Private Vices, Public Benefits*. Mandeville followed through the economic implications of the new bourgeois individualistic ethic with enthusiastic gusto, arguing that the greatest social good was generated by allowing the individual the maximum freedom to pursue private self-interest. The hive thrives so long as this principle is respected: 'Thus every Part was full of Vice,/Yet the whole Mass a paradise'. But once the ▷ Puritan moralist camp among the bees takes control, demand for luxuries and corrupt pleasures disappears, enterprise declines and the hive is ruined. The prose ▷ essays defend public brothels, argue that without the wasteful luxury of the rich the poor would starve, and doubt the utility of Christian morality in the conduct of war. Mandeville delighted in driving uncomfortable wedges between the economic and religious components of the new bourgeois consensus, and, like a kind of conservative George Bernard Shaw he expounded unpalatable truths with unabashed vigour. His pungent intellectual honesty offended optimistic ▷ Deists and pious Puritans alike, and it proved easier for writers such as the cleric William Law (1686–1761) to attack him as a scoffing blasphemer, than to answer his impressive logic.

Manley, Delarivière (?1663–1724)

Playwright and novelist. Manley's unconventional lifestyle led to many scandalous strictures. She married her cousin John Manley at an early age, only to find he was already married, and on making this discovery left him, although she was pregnant and had no means of support. For some months she lived in the household of the Duchess of Cleveland, acting as secretary and companion, but left her patronage after rumours of an affair with the Duchess's son.

For some time she seems to have lived in the country, returning to London in 1696, when two of her plays were performed: *The Lost Lover or the Jealous Husband* and *The Royal Mischief*. At this time she became the mistress of John Tilly, the Warden of Fleet Prison.

In 1705 Manley's novel *The Secret History of Queen Zarah* appeared, and proved an enormous success. In its use of a mythical society to satirize contemporary English life, it set the pattern for her later *roman à clef*, *The New Atalantis* (1709). In 1711 Manley succeeded ▷ Jonathan Swift as editor of ▷ *The Examiner*, and in the course of her writing career produced many political pamphlets. In 1714 *The Adventures of Rivella*, apparently a fictionalized autobiography, appeared. Her final achievement

was a series of novels, *The Power of Love*, published in 1720.

Manners, Comedy of

A form in which laughter is provoked by exaggerations of fashionable behaviour, absurdities in fashion itself, or departures from what is considered to be civilized normality of behaviour. Thus a comedy of manners can only arise in a highly developed society, in which there is a leisured class which not only has standards of politeness and good sense in human relationships but tends to give such standards first importance in social life. The ▷ Comedy of Humours of Ben Jonson and his younger contemporaries dealt with fundamental human appetites, and was therefore concerned with much more than what was regarded as civilized behaviour by fashionable society, though that was often included in their purview. In the court of the French king Louis XIV in the second half of the 17th century, a highly civilized society held to a code of behaviour which was also a code of morals; the comedies of ▷ Molière were the first true examples of the Comedy of Manners, and had profundity as well as surface brilliance. His comedy influenced dramatists in England. The Comedy of Manners in England is not so much a pure variety of drama, as a framework for plays with a witty, satiric atmosphere, and social comment, which may also contain other elements, such as ▷ Spanish Intrigue, Humours, ▷ Reform, etc. The best-known comedies of this type were written after the ▷ Restoration of ▷ Charles II in 1660. Many involve a critique of marriage, and re-assessment of relations between the sexes, and of women's role in society. The plays are often sexually explicit, contributing to a growing reaction against them in the 18th and 19th centuries when, as standards of polite and rational behaviour extended through society, and audiences became more heterogeneous, drama tended to become more middle class, and to show more propriety. ▷ Goldsmith and ▷ Richard Brinsley Sheridan reacted to what they considered excessive sentimentalism in the works of some of their contemporaries, and consciously revived the spirit of Comedy of Manners in their plays, though these were never as bawdy as those of any of their predecessors.

Man of Mode, The: Or Sir Fopling Flutter (1676)

Third and last play by the ▷ Restoration dramatist, ▷ Sir George Etherege, written in the ▷ Comedy of Manners' style, and generally held to be his best. It concerns the amours of Dorimant, a rake whose character is probably based on that of the ▷ Earl of Rochester. He pursues, and then rejects, first the infatuated Mrs Loveit and then her supposed friend, the weak and stupid Belinda, who intrigues with him in secret. He ends up with the wealthy and beautiful Harriet, who has held out against his wiles until he has promised to marry her. A subplot concerns the wooing of Young Bellair and Emilia. The title derives from the foolish Sir Fopling Flutter, a minor figure who personifies slavery to fashion. Dorimant's chief charm is his acerbic wit; otherwise he is a portrait of a misogynist, who takes as much delight in hurting women as in seducing them. The play's tone is cynical rather than satirical, and the overall effect one of brilliance, but with a deeply disturbing note.

Marlborough, John Churchill, Duke of (1650–1722)

Son of Winston Churchill, a minor country gentleman. At fifteen he became a page of honour to James, Duke of York, and in 1667 he received an officer's commission in the Guards. In 1672 he showed distinction in various sieges in the Netherlands, in a campaign in which the English were allied with the French against the Dutch, and in 1685 he was made a Baron and promoted to the rank of Major General. It was largely due to his efficiency that the Monmouth rebellion, against ▷ James II (formerly the Duke of York) was defeated at the ▷ Battle of Sedgemoor. When William of Orange landed in England in 1688, however, Marlborough deserted James, and thus facilitated the bloodless Revolution by which William became ▷ King William III (▷ Glorious Revolution). Churchill was made Duke of Marlborough on the accession of Queen Anne in 1702, and his wife, Sarah, was the Queen's chief favourite. On the outbreak of the War of the ▷ Spanish Succession in the same year, Marlborough commanded the armies of the allied states against France, and won victories at ▷ Blenheim (1704), Ramillies (1706), Oudenarde (1708) and Malplaquet (1709). The country was tiring of the war, however, and the Queen was tiring of the Duchess. Marlborough was relieved of his command in 1711. In the meantime the great mansion of Blenheim Palace had been built for him in honour of his first and most remarkable victory in the war. The architect was ▷ Sir John Vanbrugh.

Marlborough, Sarah Churchill, Duchess of (1660–1744)

Essayist, letter writer and Whig politician (▷ Whig and Tory). She married John Churchill, son of Winston Churchill, in 1678. They had eight children, five of whom survived infancy. Sarah was a confidante of Princess Anne, later the queen (▷ Anne), and was able in 1702 to persuade her, despite strong opposition from the Tories, to continue the War of ▷ Spanish Succession, being conducted by Sarah's husband the Duke. Toward the end of Anne's reign, the Duke and Duchess fell out of favour, and lived abroad until they were able to regain positions with George I. The Duchess survived her husband by 22 years, during which she wrote *An Account of the Conduct of the Dowager Duchess of Marlborough* (1742), a volume of her *Opinions* (published posthumously in 1788), and a substantial correspondence. She variously befriended and antagonized many contemporary writers, including ▷ Samuel Johnson, who attacked her, and ▷ Fielding, who defended her.

Marriage

According to Laurence Stone marriage only gradually acquired its function of regulating sexual chastity in wedlock: up to the 11th century polygamy and concubinage were widespread and divorce was casual. Even after that time divorce by mutual consent followed by remarriage was still widely practised. In the 13th century, however, the Church developed its control, asserting the principles of monogamy, defining and outlawing incest, punishing fornication and adultery and ensuring the exclusion of ▷ bastards from property inheritance. In 1439 weddings in church were declared a sacrament and after 1563 in the Roman Catholic Church the presence of a priest was required to make the contract valid. In this way, what had been a private contract between two families concerning property exchange became regulated. Ecclesiastical law always recognized the formal exchange of oral promises (spousals) between the parties as a legally binding contract; as the Church got more powerful it exerted greater control over the circumstances in which those promises were made. In 1604 the hours, place and conditions of church weddings were defined and restricted; notice and publicity (the calling of the banns) were required, as a guard against bigamy and other abuses. One effect of this was to create a demand for clergymen willing to perform weddings outside the specified conditions. In 1753 ▷ Lord Hardwicke's Marriage Act was designed to close these loopholes: weddings had to be in church, duly registered and signed, verbal spousals would not be legally binding and marriages already contracted in breach of the 1604 conditions were declared invalid. No-one under 21 could marry without parental consent and there were heavy penalties for clergymen who defied these injunctions. After this, the Civil Marriage Act of 1836 was passed to regulate all marriages solemnized other than in accordance with the rites of the Church of England. Divorce, with the option of remarriage, was not available except by private Act of Parliament, which only the rich could afford: there were only 131 cases between 1670 and 1799. The poor used a ritualized wife-sale (as in Thomas Hardy's *The Mayor of Castbridge* – the last recorded example was in 1887) or desertion.

▷ Divorce; Women, Status of.

Bib: Stone, L., *The Family, Sex and Marriage in England, 1500–1800*.

Marriage à la Mode (?1671)

Play by ▷ John Dryden, sometimes described as a 'split-plot tragi-comedy', setting a serious unrhymed 'heroic' plot against a witty love plot. In the serious plot, Polydamas has usurped the throne of Sicily from the rightful prince, Leonidas, who is unaware of his rights. Leonidas is in love with Palmyra. She is courted by Argaleon, while he is loved by Argaleon's sister, Amalthea. The comic plot concerns the adulterous love between Rhodophil, a captain of the guards, and Melantha, 'an affected lady', and Rhodophil's wife Doralice and Palamede. Palamede is also a suitor to Melantha. The play's action essentially revolves round the complications arising from these situations, and has scenes of mistaken identities, including women disguised as men. A factor unifying the two plots is the theme of longing for the apparently unattainable. The play represents an attempt by Dryden to resist what he saw as the coarsening and cheapening of contemporary comedy.

In his dedication he claimed to have preserved the 'Decencies of Behaviour', but this did not prevent him from inserting a number of very bawdy songs between some serious scenes.

Marshalsea

A prison in Southwark, London. It was opened in the 13th century as a prison for the Marshalsea Court, which dealt with cases involving a member of the royal household. After the ▷ Restoration it was kept for petty debtors. Dickens' father was imprisoned there for debt, and it is described in *Little Dorrit* (1858). The prison was abolished in 1849.

Marvell, Andrew (1621–78)

Poet. He was educated at Hull Grammar School (where his father was master) and Trinity College, Cambridge. He travelled in Europe, and in 1650 became tutor to the daughter of Lord Fairfax, the ▷ Civil War Parliamentary general. In 1653 he became tutor to ▷ Cromwell's ward, and in 1657 ▷ John Milton's assistant in the foreign secretaryship. In 1659 he became Member of ▷ Parliament for Hull, which he continued to represent after the ▷ Restoration of the monarchy in 1660, apart from a period in which he was secretary to Lord Carlisle.

The main body of Marvell's ▷ lyric poetry is to be found in *Miscellaneous Poems* of 1681, which contains his best-known verse. He published, in addition to the lyric poetry for which he is famous, a number of ▷ satirical works and, in 1672–3 the curious amalgam of theological controversy and prose satire which is *The Rehearsal Transprosed* – the work for which he was most famous in the 17th century. But it is the lyric poetry that has attracted most modern critical attention. Of enduring fascination to modern criticism has been the question of the relation of Marvell's poems of the 1650s to the poet's own political sympathies. Is, for example, his celebration of the return of Cromwell from Ireland ('An Horatian Ode upon Cromwell's Return from Ireland') enlisting sympathy for Cromwell, or ▷ Charles I? Or is it, as some modern critics have argued, simply disinterested? Similarly, to what extent does his poetry represent a struggle to escape out of the turmoil of civil war? More radically, does the poetry dramatize the impossibility of any such retreat?

Together with the poetry of John Donne and ▷ George Herbert, Marvell's poetry has come to be appreciated as some of the most important to have been written in the 17th century. But modern criticism has itself not been disinterested in championing Marvell's work. For both T. S. Eliot and F. R. Leavis, Marvell became an ideological touchstone, while for Marxist literary historians Marvell's work represented a continually fascinating test-case of the relationship between literature and history.
Bib: Legouis, P. (ed.), *The Poems and Letters of Andrew Marvell*; Patterson, A., *Marvell and the Civic Crown*; Chernaik, W., *The Poet's Time*.

Mary II (1662–94)

Queen of Great Britain from 1689 to her death. She was the daughter of ▷ James II by his first wife, and was educated in Protestant doctrine, which she retained when her father became converted to Catholicism. She married William of Orange, ruler of the Netherlands, in 1677. When James was removed from the throne in the ▷ Glorious Revolution of 1688 Mary was summoned to rule the nation jointly with her husband, who assumed the throne as ▷ William III.
▷ Stuart, House of.

Masham, Damaris, Lady (1658–1708)

▷ Rationalist theological writer, born in Cambridge where her father, the well-known philosopher Ralph Cudworth, taught. She herself studied philosophy and divinity with ▷ John Locke, who described her as having one of the most learned and original minds of his day, and who moved in with her family when he became ill in 1691. She became involved in a theological discussion between Locke and the philosopher and theologian John Norris, and in 1696 published *A Discourse Concerning the Love of God*, where she argues that the development of the mind is an essential part of Christianity, rather than adjunct or even antithetical to it. She was also, along with ▷ Mary Astell, an early defender of women's education. In *Occasional Thoughts in Reference to a Vertuous or Christian Life* (1700) she urges women to learn, in spite of resistance from relatives fearful that this would alienate potential husbands. Although the path of knowledge is hard, she says, only an educated woman could teach true Christianity to her children.
▷ Women, Education of.
Bib: Reynolds, M., *The Learned Lady in England 1650–1760*; Todd, J., (ed.), *A Dictionary of British and American Writers 1660–1800*.

Masque

A form of dramatic entertainment which combines verse, music, dancing and scenic effect in about equal proportions. In England it flourished between 1580 and 1630, and was essentially an aristocratic style of entertainment, especially popular at the royal court. The performers were commonly professional actors, while the masquers themselves, who remained silent, were played by ladies and gentlemen of the court. The subject was often symbolic – a conflict between virtue and vice (as in ▷ John Milton's *Comus*) – or ceremonial, celebrating a great personage, *eg* Milton's *Arcades* in honour of the Countess of Derby. The masque was often preceded by an anti-masque, the content of which was comic and often satirical; the anti-masque was always performed by professionals.

Masques were sophisticated entertainments for carefully selected audiences. They were in keeping with many forms of imaginative expression of the age, and may be regarded as a synthesis of them. First of all, the visual sense had been highly developed by the great ▷ Renaissance schools of painting and architecture in Italy and France, and a favourite activity of artists was to translate into visual terms the allegorical vision that the Renaissance had inherited from the Middle Ages. This visual ▷ allegory influenced the poets; much of the best of ▷ Edmund Spenser's *The Faerie Queene* consists of brilliantly visualized allegorical scenes, such as the House of Busirane (Book III, canto 12). Secondly, the age attached great importance to spectacles such as pageants (*ie* ceremonial processions) which often contained symbolic, masque-like features; a famous example (which still survives) was the annual Lord Mayor's Pageant in the ▷ City of London, for which the dramatist George Peele was more than once employed as designer. Thirdly, masques appealed to the contemporary taste for imaginative extravagance, delighting in the fairytales of English folklore and in classical mythology as well as in grand pageantry. Fourthly, the fantastical styles of many Elizabethan plays – attributable partly to popular taste and partly to the explorations of humanist scholars – made them either akin to masques, or capable of including masques as part of the dramatic ingredient, *eg* ▷ Shakespeare's *Love's Labour's Lost* and *The Tempest*. Finally, it was an age of close musical and literary collaboration, and masques provided opportunities for musicians and poets to collaborate on a large scale, just as they already did on a small scale in the madrigal.

Dramatists who were eminent for their composition of masques included George Chapman, John Fletcher and James Shirley, but the greatest of them – in his own estimation and probably that of others – the composer Alfonso Ferrabosco the younger and the great architect ▷ Inigo Jones; with the latter he had bitter quarrels as to which of them had artistic control of the production. Amongst Jonson's most celebrated masques are *Masque of Blackness* (1606), *Masque of Beauty* (1608) and *Masque of Queens* (1609). The most famous of all masques, however, is Milton's *Comus*, composed for the Earl of Bridgewater, whose children acted the main parts, when he was installed as Lord President of Wales. Part of the fame of *Comus* is due to its untypical quality of containing much larger speaking parts than most masques thus Milton allowed himself more poetic scope than was usual. For this reason, some critics prefer to call *Comus* a ▷ pastoral drama, like Jonson's *The Sad Shepherd* (1637) and Fletcher's *The Faithful Shepherdess* (1610). However pastoral dramas and masques had much in common; both were spectacular and symbolic rather than dramatic.

Though designed as a form of lavish court entertainment, it is also true that, in the 1630s especially, the masque also played a significant political role in the culture of the court. It existed to legitimate, through spectacle and pageantry, the authority of the monarch and the central position of the court in the affairs of the nation. At the same time, however, the masque form is implicated in the cultural breakdown which preceded the ▷ Civil War. Not only were masques extravagantly expensive to produce (as critics of the court pointed out), but they may also have served to suggest to the monarch and those around him that a harmony pertained in the affairs of the nation, and in the court's relationship to the world outside, when no such harmony, in fact, existed.

After the ▷ Restoration, masques were sometimes used to reassert the centrality of the monarchy and to add colour and spectacle to plays. ▷ Belin uses a type of masque in *The Emperor of the Moon* (1687), and there are masques in ▷ Crowne's *Calisto* (1675) and ▷ Congreve's *The Judgment of Paris* (1701). **Bib:** Lindley, D. (ed.), *The Court Masque*.

Materialism

The philosophical theory that only physical matter is real and that all phenomena and processes can be explained by reference to it. Related to this is the doctrine that political and social change is triggered by change in the material and economic basis of society. Although now commonly associated with the philosopher Karl Marx, materialist thought has a long history, from Democritus (5th century BC) onwards, via ▷ Epicurus, ▷ Lucretius, and ▷ Hobbes. Much of the 17th-century opposition to Hobbes was a reaction to his materialism, which seemed, to contemporaries to find no place for God.

Medall, The, A Satyre against Sedition (1682)

A satire in ▷ heroic couplets by ▷ John Dryden. The ▷ Earl of Shaftesbury, leader of the Whig party which opposed the succession of the ▷ Catholic James, Duke of York, to the throne, had been acquitted on a charge of treason. Dryden found an ideal focus for his mock-heroic ridicule in the medal struck to celebrate the Whig victory, which shows Shaftesbury's head on the obverse, and on the reverse the sun rising over the Tower of London (where Shaftesbury had been imprisoned), with the legend *Laetamur* ('Let us rejoice').

Medieval, medievalism

The later 18th century saw a revival of interest in the art and literature of the ▷ Middle Ages, as part of an incipient reaction against ▷ Renaissance and ▷ neo-classical ideals of symmetry and order. It coincided to a large degree with interest in the ▷ Gothic and the ▷ primitive, and with a growing taste for the wilder forms of ▷ nature. In politics there was a harking back to the ideas of Alfred the Great, whose balanced constitution, giving equal powers to the king, lords and commons, was seen as a model; many essays and plays refer to him. ▷ Thomson's patriotic hymn 'Rule Britannia' was sung for the first time in a masque called *Alfred* (1740). Druids were idealized as early patriots in, for example, Thomson's *Liberty*, ▷ Collins' *Ode to Liberty*, and ▷ Gray's *The Bard*. The ancient British queen Boudicca, or Boadicea, was also held up as a symbol of courage and patriotism, as in ▷ Cowper's *Boadicea*. Admiration for ancient ▷ Welsh, ▷ Irish and ▷ Scottish literature is also part of the medieval revival, as is revealed in the ▷ Ossian or Oisin saga. The quest for old English as well as Celtic literature resulted in such works as ▷ Thomas Percy's *Reliques of English Poetry* (1765), which was much admired by the ▷ Romantic poets later on, and ▷ Thomas Warton's *History of English Poetry* (1774–89), which involved exploring hundreds of examples of medieval verse. The development of the ▷ Gothic novel, with its medieval associations, and a renewed interest in Spenser, ▷ Shakespeare and ▷ Milton, who were thought to have drawn their inspiration from medieval romance, formed a part of the movement. Shakespeare became admired precisely for the 'crude' elements of speech and plot structure which had alienated earlier generations, particularly immediately after the ▷ Restoration, and elements of his plays which had been excised for a hundred years or more were gradually restored to the texts performed on stage. In the 19th centry the ideas sown in the 18th developed into a full-blown and extended movement, manifest in the poetry of Keats and Tennyson, the artistic theories of Ruskin, the paintings of the pre-Raphaelites, and the theatrical productions of Edmund Kean and others.

▷ Gothic; Gothic novels; Gothic revival.

Meiosis
▷ Figures of speech.

Melodrama
The prefix 'melo-' derives from the Greek *melos*, 'music'. Originally, melodrama was a play in which there was no singing but the dialogue had a musical accompaniment; the first example is said to be ▷ Rousseau's *Pygmalion* (1775). The musical accompaniment gradually ceased; the word came to denote romantic plays of extravagantly violent action, and it is now applied to sensational action without adequate motivation, in any work of fiction.

The word has also been used to denote popular ballad operas in which spoken dialogue is used extensively. This use, however, is much less common.

Melpomene
▷ Muses.

Memoirs of a Cavalier (1724)
A work of fiction by ▷ Daniel Defoe, but it was thought that the memoirs were possibly genuine. They describe the career of a professional soldier, Colonel Andrew Newport, born in 1608. He sees military service in Europe during the Thirty Years War, and then joins the English Royalist army in the ▷ Civil War.

Menander (342–293 BC)
An Athenian comic poet whose plays were popular in the classical world and provided the characteristic matrix of ▷ New Comedy, which became the model for both ▷ Plautus and ▷ Terence. Menander is widely acknowledged by the Roman dramatists as their mentor, but it was not until the 20th century (1905) that substantial parts of manuscripts of his plays and one complete work (*Dyskolos*; 1955) were discovered. These confirmed the high regard in which Menander was held by his contemporaries.

Mercantile system
A term used by the economist ▷ Adam Smith (*Wealth of Nations*, 1776) and later writers to denote the assumptions behind the practice of commerce

from the later ▷ Middle Ages until the 18th century. In its extreme form, it identified wealth with money so that the main object of governments was to accumulate large stocks of precious metals. Smith advocated a contrary theory of free trade, which became the dominant policy by the middle of the 19th century.
Bib: Foucault, M., *The Order of Things*.

Metamorphoses
Poems in Latin by ▷ Ovid. They are a series of mythological tales whose common subject is miraculous transformation of shape, beginning with Chaos into Cosmos, ending with ▷ Julius Caesar into a star, and including such tales as Baucis and Philemon, the peasants who unawares gave hospitality to the gods, who granted them immortality as a pair of trees. They were popular in medieval Europe and afterwards, up till the 19th century, and have often been translated, in whole or in part, into English, *eg* by ▷ John Dryden in the 17th century, and ▷ Pope in the 18th.

Metaphor
▷ Figures of speech.

Metaphysical conceit
▷ Metaphysical Poets.

Metaphysical Poets
The accepted designation of a succession of 17th-century poets, of whom the following are the principal names: John Donne (1572–1631), ▷ George Herbert, Richard Crashaw (?1612–49), ▷ Andrew Marvell, ▷ Henry Vaughan, ▷ Abraham Cowley. The term came to be applied to them in a special sense; that is to say, they were not so described because their subject was the relationship of spirit to matter or the ultimate nature of reality; this is true of ▷ Lucretius, ▷ Milton and ▷ Dante, who have little else in common. It is true that some of them – Donne, Herbert, Vaughan and Crashaw especially – were metaphysical in this generally accepted sense, but the adjective is applied to them to indicate not merely subject matter, but qualities of expression in relation to subject matter.

▷ Samuel Johnson was the first so to classify these poets: 'The metaphysical poets were men of learning, and to show their learning was their whole endeavour', he wrote in his essay on Cowley in ▷ *Lives of the Poets*. The sentence shows that he is using the term disparagingly, and this disparagement had already been expressed by ▷ John Dryden: 'Donne affects the metaphysics not only in his satires but in his amorous verses . . . [he] perplexes the mind of the fair sex with nice speculations of philosophy' (*Discourse concerning the Original and Progress of Satire*, 1693). Dryden and Johnson were antagonistic to Donne and his followers because they valued above all the assurance, clarity, restraint and shapeliness of the great Augustan poets of ancient Rome. Critics and poets of the 20th century have on the contrary immensely admired Donne, Herbert and Marvell, but they still use 'Metaphysical' as the term under which to group them. H. J. C. Grierson (Introduction, *Metaphysical Poetry: Donne to Butler*) justifies it because it indicates 'the peculiar blend of passion and thought, feeling and ratiocination which is their greatest achievement.' However, they have also been labelled '*The Fantasticks*' (an anthology edited by W. S. Scott) and Professor Martz has suggested 'The poetry of meditation' (the title of his book). The first of these designations suggests resemblance between the English poets and their so-called 'baroque' contemporaries in Italy (Marino), Spain (Góngora) and France (Théophile de Viau and Saint-Amant); the second emphasizes the difference – the greater balance and control among the English poets. It may be said that Crashaw, at one extreme, belongs more to the former, and Herbert, at the other extreme, is much better described as 'meditative'.

The distinctiveness of the Metaphysicals was their use of the so-called 'metaphysical conceit' – *ie* paradoxical metaphor causing a shock to the mind by the unlikeness of the association, *eg* Donne's

> her pure and eloquent blood
> Spoke in her cheeks, and so distinctly wrought,
> That one might almost say her body
> thought.
>
> *(Second Anniversary)*

or Herbert's

> Only a sweet and virtuous soul,
> Like season'd timber, never gives;
> But through the whole turn to coal
> Then chiefly lives.
>
> *(Virtue)*

In most respects, therefore, the term is so broad, and embraces poetic styles and forms so disparate, that its use is nearly meaningless, being little more than an anthologist's convenience.

Methodism

A religious movement founded by ▷ John Wesley. The name was at first applied derisively to himself and his associates when he was a student at ▷ Oxford in 1729, referring to the strict rules that they made for themselves in order to follow a religious life; however, he early accepted the designation. From 1739, a time when the Church of England was particularly apathetic, the movement spread rapidly among the poor all over England, and it became especially strong in the industrial towns. Wesley himself had no desire to separate Methodism from the Anglican Church, but the demands on his energies forced him to ordain preachers whom the Church felt it could not accept as clergymen; consequently the Methodists developed an independent organization.

The later movement divided into a number of distinct organizations. It spread abroad, especially to the USA where the membership numbers about 13 million, as compared with rather more than half a million in Britain.

Metre

From the Greek word meaning 'measure'. In poetry, metre is the measure of the rhythm of a line of verse, when the line is rhythmically systematic, *ie* can be divided into units of 'metrical feet'. The names for these feet all derive from ancient ▷ Greek verse. The commonest feet in use in English are as follows:

Iambus *eg* the words 'again', 'revenge', 'delight'.

'Iambics march from short to long.'

Trochee *eg* the words 'never', 'happy', 'heartless'.

'Trochee trips from long to short.'

Anapest *eg* the words 'entertain', 'supersede', 'engineer'.

'With a leap and a bound the swift anapaests throng.'

Spondee *eg* the words 'maintain', 'heartbreak', 'wineglass'

'Slow spondee stalks, strong foot . . .'

Dactyl *eg* the words 'melody', 'happiness', 'sorrowful'.

'. . . yet ill able'

'Ever to come up with dactyl trisyllable.'

The illustrative lines are taken from ▷ Coleridge's mnemonic rhyme 'Metrical Feet' (the dactyl example in particular being a joke).

It is important to remember three points when analysing ('scanning') English verse:

1 Despite Coleridge's use of 'long' and 'short' for iambic and trochaic feet, these words are inappropriate to English metrical feet, which are composed of accented and unaccented syllables (two accented ones in the case of the spondee) irrespective of their length.

2 Except in the case of the iambus, it is unusual to find lines of verse composed entirely of the same foot; this is especially true of the spondee and the dactyl.

3 It is unwise to think of metre at all when reading a great deal of English verse. Old and Middle English alliterative verse was not metrical. Chaucer's is metrical, but not consistently so; his verse depends more on the natural rhythms of the English speaking voice. This is also true of Sir Thomas Wyatt in the early 16th century, of the mature dramatic verse of ▷ Shakespeare and his contemporaries, of John Donne (1572–16), of Gerard Manley Hopkins in the 19th century, and of many 20th-century poets.

Verse lines have names according to the number of feet they contain; much the commonest English line is the iambic pentameter (five feet). The hexameter has six feet, and is called an alexandrine when they are iambic. Other lengths:

monometer = one foot; dimeter = two feet; trimeter = three feet; tetrameter = four feet; heptameter = seven feet; octameter = eight feet. Some minor 16th-century poets used lines of 14 syllables known as 'fourteeners'; a couplet consisting of a fourteener and an Alexandrine, first used by Wyatt, is known as the poulter's measure.

▷ Blank verse; Free verse; Ode; Sonnet.

Middle Ages

A term used by historians to cover the period between the fall of the Roman Empire of the West (end of the 5th century) and the beginning of the ▷ Renaissance, conventionally dated from the extinction of the Roman Empire of the East (Byzantine Empire) in 1453. The expression dates from the 16th century when it is found in the Latin writings of a number of humanists – 'media aetas', 'medium aevum'. The conception in the 16th century was that civilization was renewing itself by rediscovery of the ancient civilizations of Greece and Rome; scholars considered that the centuries between the 5th and 15th were a relatively dark period of ignorance and cultural backwardness. For long after the 16th century modern history was commonly assumed to have begun with the 15th-century Renaissance. Some scholars are inclined to think this view mistaken; many of them also consider that the so-called Middle Ages had much more continuity with ▷ classical history than the men of the Renaissance supposed. The term Middle Ages is thus a misleading and erroneous one but its use has become habitual and cannot be dispensed with. Moreover the Renaissance of the 15th–16th centuries did herald an important change, however one interprets it, and it is still useful to have a term to designate the centuries which preceded it.

In English history, it is common to think of the Middle Ages as extending from the Norman Conquest of 1066 until the end of the Wars of the Roses and the accession of Henry VII (first of the House of Tudor) in 1485. The period from the 5th to the 11th century is called loosely the Old English period. The term Middle Ages was first used by John Donne in a sermon in 1621.

▷ Medieval; medievalism.

Miller, Anne (1741–1781)

English poet, patron and travel writer. She held poetry evenings in her excessively expensive villa at Bath, during which poems would be thrown into an antique vase and then each taken out and read aloud. Some were published in *Poetical Amusements at a Villa near Bath* (1775–1781), and the preface emphasizes 'the Vase, and Sprigs of Bay and Myrtle alluded to in these poems are not emblematical, but real'. When ▷ Fanny Burney visited her, she called her 'a round plump coarse-looking dame'. Miller also wrote *Letters From Italy* (1776–7).

▷ Seward, Anna

Milton, John (1608–74)

Poet and prose polemicist. Milton was born in London, the son of a scrivener and musician, and educated at St Paul's School and Christ's College Cambridge. After leaving Cambridge in 1632 Milton lived for the next five years at his father's house in Horton. During this, his early poetic career, he wrote the companion pieces *L'Allegro* and *Il Penseroso*, two ▷ masques *Arcades* and *Comus*, and the ▷ elegy *Lycidas*. From 1638 to 1639 Milton travelled abroad, chiefly in Italy. His Italian journey was to have a lasting influence on his later development, not least in the contact he established amongst Florentine intellectuals. But more than that, it re-affirmed his distaste – loathing even – for Roman Catholicism, and focused his intense opposition to the regime of William Laud in England.

Milton's continental journey was interrupted early in 1639 at Naples, where he claims to have first heard news of the political crisis in England. He was later to claim that he thought it 'base that I should travel abroad at my ease for the cultivation of my mind while my fellow citizens at home were fighting for liberty' (*Defensio secunda*). Returning to England, Milton embarked upon what has now come to be seen as the second phase of his career – that of a political prose writer, and propagandist for the anti-Royalist cause in the English ▷ Civil War. Between 1640 and 1655, Milton was to write little poetry. His energies and his sympathies were now to be engaged fully on the side of the republican forces in England – though he was not an uncritical supporter of the new experiment in government. From this period can be dated the series of great prose declarations dealing with political and religious questions – *Of Reformation* (1641), his attack on episcopacy in the *Apology for Smectymnuus* (1642), his statement on personal liberty contained in *The Doctrine and Discipline of Divorce* (1643). These works were followed by ▷ *Areopagitica* (1644), *Tenure of Kings and Magistrates* (1649), *Eikonoklastes* (1649), the two 'defences' of the English people (1651 and 1654), *A Treatise of Civil Power* (1659) and, almost at the moment when ▷ Charles II returned to England to re-establish the claims of monarchy, *A Readie and Easie Way to Establish a Free Commonwealth* (1660). The list of topics upon which Milton wrote in this period is bewildering, but running through all his prose writings is a stable belief that the English people have been chosen by God to perform a necessary political act – the establishment of a state based on principles of choice and, within certain bounds, freedom.

▷ *Paradise Lost*, Milton's great religious and political poem, was begun at some point in the mid-1650s, perhaps in the growing awareness that, though political choices had been made in England, the wrong choice had been made. The poem was not published, however, until 1667, with a second (revised) edition appearing in 1674, shortly before Milton's death in November of that year. But the period after 1660 is usually recognized as the third and final phase of Milton's career. It is the period of the publication of ▷ *Paradise Regained* and ▷ *Samson Agonistes*. Though it has long been claimed that Milton's absorption in the task of writing these works marked an end to his career of political engagement, it is probably truer to say that these works signal a renewed and possibly deeper investigation of the themes which had occupied him for most of his life – the questions of political and religious liberty, the problems associated with choice and rule, and the problematic nature of government and obedience.

Bib: Carey, J. and Fowler, A. (ed.), *The Complete Poems of John Milton*; Wolfe, D. M. (ed.), *Complete Prose Works of John Milton*; Parker, W. R., *Milton: A Biography*; Hill, C., *Milton and the English Revolution*; Nyquist, M. and Ferguson, M. (ed.), *Re-membering Milton*.

Mimesis

In ▷ Plato's *Republic* 'mimesis' is used to designate 'imitation', but in a derogatory way. The term is given a rigorous, positive meaning in ▷ Aristotle's *Poetics* where it is used to describe a process of selection and representation appropriate to tragedy: 'the imitation of an action'. Literary criticism from Sir Philip Sidney (1554–86) onwards has wrestled with the problem of the imitative function of literary texts, but after Structuralism, with its questioning of the referential function of all language, the term has taken on a new and problematic dimension. Mimesis has frequently been associated with the term ▷ 'realism', and with the capacity of language to reflect reality. At particular historical moments, *eg* the ▷ Renaissance, or the present time, when reality itself appears to be in question, then the capacity of language to represent reality is brought to the fore. The issue becomes even more complex when we realize that 'reality' may be something other than our experience of it. In the 17th and 18th centuries the concept of mimesis was central to ▷ neo-classic critical theory, and included the idea of imitating classic authors, as well as reality or nature itself. ▷ Dryden, in his *Essay of Dramatic Poesy* (1668), speaks of 'imitating the ancients well' because they have imitated nature so much better than modern authors. The principles are stated repeatedly in ▷ Pope's ▷ *Essay on Criticism*, *eg* 'Those Rules of old discovered, not devised, / Are Nature still, but Nature methodized', and 'Learn hence for ancient rules a just esteem; / To copy nature is to copy them'. In the course of the 18th century the notion of mimesis changed its meaning, and became more synonymous with 'representation' than with imitation. Bib: Abrams, M. H., *The Mirror and the Lamp*; Auerbach, E., *Mimesis*; Boyd, J. D., *The Function of Mimesis and its Decline*.

Minim, Dick

A character in ▷ Samuel Johnson's ▷ *Idler* essays for the *Weekly Gazette*. Dick Minim is a satirical representation of the kind of person who seeks a reputation for critical acumen by praising what is in fashion and sneering at what is unfamiliar.

Miss in Her Teens (1747)

A shortened (two-act) comedy by ▷ David Garrick, one of the first of its type (also known as 'petite pièce' or 'petite comédie'), adapted from D'Ancourt's *La Parisienne*, and staged as an 'afterpiece' at ▷ Covent Garden. The main plot concerns Captain Loveit's competition with his miserly father, Sir Simon Loveit, for the hand of the 16-year-old country girl and heiress, Biddy Bellair. She is also courted by two other suitors: a braggart and a fop. The Captain is assisted in his plans by the girl's own cunning and determination, and by two clever servants. A sub-plot concerns the rivalry between two of the servants for the attentions of a third. The Captain chases away the absurd rivals and confronts his father, who gives up his claim to Biddy voluntarily. The play has various patriotic elements referring to the contemporary War of the Austrian Succession: its last line, spoken by Biddy, is, 'Who fails in honour, will be false in love'. Garrick himself played the effeminate suitor, Fribble, who has some of the wittiest lines in the play; it was one of his most popular roles. The rest of the dialogue and the action are simple but very funny, and the piece was staged repeatedly.

Mnemosyne

▷ Muses.

Mock epic

A form of ▷ satire practised with most success in English by ▷ Alexander Pope. The method is to employ the dignified expression associated with epic about subjects in themselves either trivial or base. Thus ▷ *The Rape of the Lock* describes a family quarrel provoked by a young man robbing a girl of a lock of her hair; it uses a dignity of style appropriate to the Rape of Helen which gave rise to Homer's ▷ *Iliad*, and applies it to the minute detail and obviously trivial scale of emotion appropriate to the slightness of the episode. In Pope's ▷ *Dunciad* the method is rather different, because here Pope is describing what is base rather than what is petty; the contrast is not, as with *The Rape*, an ironic one between grandeur of treatment and pettiness of subject, but between the nobility of the style and the depth of meanness in the subject.

Another form of mock epic is the ▷ mock heroic poem, in which a bad man committing base deeds is described in epic style, without disguising the badness.

The mock epic is especially the product of the century 1660–1760, when admiration for Greek and Latin satire and epic was particularly high.
▷ Epic.

Mock heroic

A literary mode in which large and important events are juxtaposed with small and insignificant ones for a variety of comic, satirical or more profoundly ironic effects. In its narrow sense mock heroic is the product of the Augustan, neo-classical age. As the bourgeoisie wrested cultural hegemony from the aristocracy in the late 17th century, a new, more complex attitude to the ancient aristocratic ideals of honour and nobility developed. A new irony infused their literary expression in the classical forms of ▷ epic and ▷ tragedy. Epic retained the respect of the reading public, but it was too archaic and primitive to satisfy the modern imagination in its traditional form. ▷ John Milton's ▷ *Paradise Lost*, the only significant literary epic in English (*Beowulf* being an oral poem), has about it much of the complexity of the novel, and its more atavistic heroic elements (the war in heaven, the vision of future history) seem mechanical. In the generations following Milton the major poets, ▷ John Dryden and ▷ Alexander Pope, translated the ancient epics, but their own original work took the more complex form of mock epic.

Augustan mock heroic is a development from the conceit of the Tudor and ▷ 'metaphysical' poets, and its imaginative appeal derives similarly from far-fetched and unexpected comparisons and parallels. At its most basic it can be simply ▷ satirical. The poet contrasts a contemptible modern person or event with a respected heroic version. ▷ Samuel Butler's ▷ *Hudibras* works largely on this level, and there is a strong element of this kind of satire in Dryden's ▷ *Mac Flecknoe*. The respected touchstone need not be the classical epic, but can be any admired model from the past, or even the present. In ▷ *Absalom and Achitophel* it is the Old Testament. In parts of the ▷ *Dunciad* it is Milton and other 'classic' English poets such as ▷ Edmund Waller and ▷ Sir John Denham. In parts of the ▷ *Rape of the Lock* it is the pomp of religious ritual.

Nor need the contrast imply a moral satire on the modern world, or indeed any satire at all. At the beginning of *Absalom and Achitophel* the comparison of Charles II with King David in the Book of Kings achieves the difficult task of aggrandizing the 'merry monarch' while at the same time slyly acknowledging his libertinism. The comparison between Belinda's petticoat-hoops and Achilles' shield in *The Rape of the Lock* mocks the heroic model rather than the modern equivalent, emphasizing the delightful domestic security of Belinda's world, as against the primitive *machismo* of the ancient heroes. Often the comparison between familiar and modern on the one hand, and exotic and ancient on the other, arises from pure imaginative playfulness, as when Pope, through implied puns, compares the ceremony of preparing coffee in an English drawing-room (on 'japanned' tables), with an awesome religious ceremony in distant Japan: 'On shining Altars of *Japan* they raise/ The silver Lamp; the fiery Spirits blaze' (*Rape of the Lock*, III, II. 107–8).

Although mock heroic is most closely associated with the age of Dryden, ▷ Swift and Pope, it is found in all periods.

Modest Proposal, A (1729)

A satirical ▷ pamphlet by ▷ Jonathan Swift, written when he was Dean of St Patrick's Cathedral, Dublin. The full title is *A Modest Proposal for Preventing Children of Poor People from being a Burden to their Parents or the Country*. Indignant at the extreme misery of the Irish poor under English government, Swift, in the guise of an economic 'projector', calmly recommends that it would be more humane to breed up their children as food for the rich. The

pamphlet is an example of the controlled but extreme savagery of Swift's irony, and the fierceness of his humanitarianism.

Mohun, Michael (?1616–84)

Actor-manager. Mohun trained as a boy actor under Christopher Beeston (?1570–1638) at the Cockpit Theatre, in Drury Lane, and graduated to adult roles before the theatres closed in 1642. He joined the army on the royalist side during the ▷ Civil War, reaching the rank of major. Shortly after the theatres reopened, he became the leading actor of the newly formed ▷ King's Company under ▷ Killigrew. He created several roles in tragedy and comedy, and his Iago in *Othello* was especially admired.

Molière (pseudonym of Jean Baptiste Poquelin) (1622–73)

French dramatist. Born in the middle class, the son of an upholsterer, he became one of the most favoured playwrights at the court of Louis XIV. With one exception his plays are comedies, and a basic influence behind English comedy from 1660 to 1800. His *Les Précieuses ridicules* (1659), a satire upon an extremely fashionable, excessively sophisticated circle in contemporary Paris, marks the beginning of the ▷ Comedy of Manners tradition in which the English dramatists ▷ Etherege, ▷ Wycherley, ▷ Vanbrugh, ▷ Congreve and ▷ Sheridan all worked. He wrote over 30 plays, of which the best known are: *Sganarelle* (1660); *L'Ecole des maris* (The school for husbands, 1661); *L'Ecole des femmes* (The school for wives, 1662); *Tartuffe* (1664); *Le Festin de Pierre* (Don Juan, 1665); *Le Misanthrope* (The misanthropist, 1666); *Le Médecin malgré lui* (The reluctant physician, 1666); *L'Avare* (The miser, 1668); *Le Bourgeois Gentilhomme* (The middle-class nobleman, 1670); *Les Femmes savantes* (The learned women, 1672); *Le Malade imaginaire* (The hypochondriac, 1673). His nearest equivalent on the English stage is ▷ William Congreve, but the only achievement in English literature comparable with Molière's kind of excellence is in the Augustan ▷ satire of ▷ Dryden (▷ *Absalom and Achitophel*) and ▷ Pope, and the novels of ▷ Jane Austen.

Moll Flanders (1722)

A novel by ▷ Daniel Defoe, and his most famous, after ▷ *Robinson Crusoe* (1719). Its full title was *The Fortunes and Misfortunes of the Famous Moll Flanders*, and its substance is the adventures of an orphan girl from her early seduction through her various love affairs and her career of crime, to her transportation to Virginia and her final prosperity there. It is a realistic, episodic narrative with keen social and psychological perception in certain incidents. The book has no unifying structure, however, and none of the characters is fully established imaginatively. The conclusion is an example of Defoe's crude and superficial morality, ▷ Puritan in its tradition, but much less profound and subtle than that of his predecessor ▷ John Bunyan. The Puritanism has become simplified to commercialism, especially evident in Moll's final 'repentance'.

▷ Picaresque.

Monmouth, James Scott, Duke of (1649–85)

An illegitimate son of ▷ Charles II. Charles had no legitimate son, and the heir to the throne was consequently James, Duke of York his brother. James, however, was an open ▷ Catholic, and fear of Catholicism in England and Scotland was still very strong. Thus a movement arose in both countries to persuade Charles to exclude James from the succession, and to recognize Monmouth, who had been educated a ▷ Protestant. Exclusion Bills to secure this change were introduced into Parliament, where the Exclusionists were led by ▷ Lord Shaftesbury. Charles, however, resisted the movement, and in 1681 a reaction of opinion in the country came to the support of the King and his brother. In 1685, Charles died, and James succeeded him as ▷ James II. Some of his more fanatical Protestant opponents, such as the Scottish Duke of Argyll, persuaded Monmouth to attempt rebellion. The Monmouth Rebellion was defeated at the single ▷ Battle of Sedgemoor (1685) and Monmouth himself was executed.

▷ *Absalom and Achitophel*; Bloody Assizes.

Montagu, Elizabeth (1720–1800)

An eminent ▷ Bluestocking and famous epistolarist, Montagu's early intellectual abilities were widely remarked upon, and ▷ Samuel Johnson hailed her as 'Queen of the Blues'.

Montagu began to hold her formal receptions in the early 1750s, and she boasted to ▷ David Garrick that, whatever the social status of the guests, 'I never invite idiots'. Her patronage of young authors aided James Beattie and Richard Price.

In 1769 her *Essay on the Writings and Genius of Shakespeare*, challenging ▷ Voltaire's theories, was widely admired, though Johnson perceived its critical failings.

Montagu, Lady Mary Wortley (1689–1762)

Poet and letter-writer. In 1716–18 her husband was Ambassador to Constantinople, where she came across the practice of inoculation against smallpox, which she popularized in England. In 1716 the publisher Edmund Curll produced an unauthorized edition of her poems, from a manuscript which she had dropped in the street, under the title *Court Poems by a Lady of Quality* (the authorized edition of 1747 was entitled *Town Eclogues*). ▷ Alexander Pope took her side against Curll but they later quarrelled for some reason, and she appears in *Moral Essay II* as Sappho in her 'dirty smock'. She lived in Italy during her later years and her lively and informative *Letters* were published in 1763–7.
Bib: Halsband, R., *The Life of Lady Mary Wortley Montagu.*

Montaigne, Michel de (1533–92)

French essayist, inventor of the ▷ essay form. His life was lived partly at court, or performing the office of magistrate in the city of Bordeaux, and partly in retirement. During retirement, he wrote his *Essais*

('experiments'), the first two volumes of which were published in 1580, and the third in 1588. He was a scholar, well-read in ▷ humanist literature and in the works of the ancient Greeks and Romans. His favourite author was ▷ Plutarch.

The Essays seem to have been begun as commentaries on his reading, perhaps to assist his exceptionally bad memory. From this grew a desire to arrive at a complete image of man; as a means to this, he tried to develop a portrait of himself, since 'each man bears the complete stamp of the human condition'. The sentence shows the still-prevailing view of his time, that human beings followed general principles in the structure of their personalities – a view quite unlike the view that grew up in the 18th century and came to predominate in the 19th, that each individual is unique (see ▷ Rousseau). He recognized, however, the difficulties in arriving at conclusive ideas about human nature, and the essays are characterized by the scepticism with which he weighs contradictions and opposing views.

Montaigne was translated into English by Florio in 1603. The essays had an extensive influence upon English literature. Whether the long essay entitled *Apologie de Raimond de Sebond* had an important influence on Shakespeare's *Hamlet* is a controversial question; but Gonzalo in Shakespeare's *Tempest* quotes from Montaigne's *Des Cannibales* in II.i.143–60 ('I' th' commonwealth . . .'). More important were the emulators of Montaigne in the essay form. Montaigne's sceptical, searching, flexible mind resembles those of Robert Burton (1577–1640) and ▷ Sir Thomas Browne (▷ *Religio Medici*). These, however, were not essayists; the Montaigne tradition of essay writing was taken up later in the century by ▷ Abraham Cowley (*Essays in Verse and Prose*, 1668), ▷ Sir William Temple (*Miscellanea*, 1680, 1692, 1701) and, after the more formal period of the 18th century, Charles Lamb's *Essays of Elia* (1823).

Montesquieu, Charles de Secondat de, Baron de la Brède et de (1689–1755)

French philosopher and historian. He came to England in 1729, and studied English institutions and the ideas of English philosophers, including ▷ John Locke. He argued that human history reflects a process, influenced by many factors including geography and climate, which in turn affect such factors as religion, culture and society. He identified and discussed three sorts of government, the republican, the monarchical and the despotic, and held up the English constitution as a model of freedom. These ideas, expounded in *Considérations sur les causes de la grandeur et de la décadence des Romains* (1734) and *De l'esprit des lois* (1748), had a considerable influence on English, Scottish and Continental thinkers.

▷ French literature in England.

Moral Essays (1731–5)

Four epistles in heroic ▷ couplets by ▷ Alexander Pope, concerned with large ethical and philosophical issues. Epistle I elaborates a simplistic philosophy of 'the ruling passion' as an explanation of human psychology, and its poetic value lies in the occasional witty vignette of human folly, rather than in any profundity of thought. Epistle II, *To a Lady*, concerns the characters of women, and is addressed to Pope's close friend Martha Blount. Though the work has many memorable lines it is little more than a series of crudely sexist jibes at particular women, or at women in general: 'Nothing so true as what you once let fall, 'Most Women have no Characters at all'; 'ev'ry Woman is at heart a Rake'. Epistle III treats the right use of riches, and ends with an idealized portrait of John Kyrle, the 'Man of Ross', a celebrated philanthropist. Epistle IV, addressed to Lord Burlington, was the first to be published (1731) and is the most impressive. It again satirizes the wrong use of wealth, but focuses specifically on architecture, Burlington being an active promoter of the convenient decency of the Palladian style (▷ Andrea Palladio) as opposed to the large-scale exuberance of ▷ baroque, so much in vogue in absolutist France. Pope follows his patron also in advocating a 'natural' style of garden rather than the artificial geometricality of continental taste. The description of the discomfort of Timon's villa brilliantly satirizes such un-English grandiosity as Blenheim Palace or Castle Howard, both recently built by ▷ Sir John Vanbrugh.

More, Hannah (1745–1833)

An eminent ▷ Bluestocking, More settled in London in 1774, where she became the friend of ▷ Garrick, ▷ Johnson, ▷ Burke, ▷ Richardson, ▷ Reynolds, ▷ Percy and ▷ Montagu. She was a conservative Christian feminist who opposed ▷ Mary Wollstonecraft on women's rights. Her tragedy *Percy* was produced by Garrick in 1777, and established both her literary reputation and her social status. A tragedy, *The Fatal Falsehood*, appeared in 1779.

   ▷ Horace Walpole became her great admirer, printing *Bishop Bonner's Ghost* at the Strawberry Hill press in 1789. In 1784 her earlier poem *Bas Bleu* was published.

   More used her writing to express concern about social reform. *Village Politics* appeared in 1793, and the *Cheap Repository Tracts* of 1795–8 sold two million copies. *Thoughts on the Importance of the Manners of the Great* (1788) also ran into several editions. In 1809 More published *Coelebs in Search of a Wife*, a novel which, despite hostile reviews, proved an immense success. Her correspondence is lively and entertaining.
Bib: Jones, M. G., *Hannah More*.

Morning Chronicle, The

A London Whig ▷ newspaper founded in 1769; its contributors included ▷ Sheridan, Lamb, James Mill, John Stuart Mill, Dickens, and Thackeray. It came to an end in 1862.
   ▷ Whig and Tory.

Morning Herald, The

A London ▷ newspaper, 1780–1869. It had a large circulation, and published police cases, illustrated by the famous artist George Cruikshank (1792–1878), illustrator of Dickens' novel *Oliver Twist*.

Morning Post, The

A conservative but highly independent London newspaper, founded 1772, ceased 1936. ▷ Wordsworth, ▷ Coleridge and ▷ Southey contributed to it.

Mourning Bride, The (1697)

Congreve's only play with a tragic action, though a happy ending, set in Granada. Almeria, Princess of Granada, has secretly married Alphonso, Prince of Valentia, when she was a captive in the Valencian palace. In battle the King of Valentia, Anselmo, dies, and Alphonso disappears and is presumed dead. While mourning at his tomb, Almeria is interrupted by the prisoner Osmyn, who turns out to be Alphonso in disguise. Meanwhile the captive queen Zara has fallen in love with 'Osmyn' but, failing to win him, plots to have him killed. Belatedly she tries to save him, but unknown to her, he escapes, and the tyrant King of Granada, Manuel, is mistakenly murdered in his place. Zara, finding his headless body, believes it to be that of Osmyn, takes poison and dies. Almeria is about to do the same when Alphonso enters, and the couple are reunited. The play ends with the assurance that 'blessings ever wait on virtuous deeds'. *The Mourning Bride* was hugely successful, and survived well into the 18th century. It contains two quotations which remain famous: 'Music has charms to soothe a savage breast' and 'Heav'n has no rage, like love to hatred turn'd,/Nor Hell a fury, like a woman scorn'd'.

Muses

The nine daughters of Zeus and Mnemosyne (Memory) in Greek myth. Each presided over a separate art: Clio – history; Euterpe – lyric poetry; Thalia – comedy; Melpomene – tragedy; Terpsichore – the dance; Erato – love poetry; Polyhymnia – sacred songs; Urania – astronomy; Calliope (who ranked first) – epic poetry and eloquence. They may have originally been water deities, and various springs were associated with them – Castalia, Hippocrene, Aganippe. Water has always been associated with inspiration, and hence their later role as inspirers of the artist. They were also originally 'the mindful ones' through association with their mother, the goddess of Memory. Variations through the centuries have caused writers to attribute to them functions differing from the above list.

Mysteries of Udolpho, The (1794)

A novel by ▷ Mrs Ann Radcliffe. It achieved great fame in its own day, and is often cited as the typical ▷ Gothic novel. It is mainly set in a sombre castle in the Apennine mountains in Italy. The atmosphere is of secret plots, concealed passages, abductions, and the supernatural. ▷ Jane Austen satirized the taste for such sensational literature in *Northanger Abbey* (1818).

N

Napoleon I (Napoleon Bonaparte, originally Buonaparte) (1769–1821)

A Corsican whose unique career began in the ▷ French Revolution, when he joined the French army defending the first French Republic against European alliances. His military successes brought him to dictatorship in 1799, with the title of First Consul, and in 1804 he became Emperor. His armies dominated the greater part of Europe until 1812, when his campaign against Russia failed. His final defeat at the hands of the British and the Prussians under ▷ Wellington and Blucher at Waterloo (1815) led to his exile on the Atlantic island of St Helena, where he died.

His unprecedented success aroused contrasted feelings amongst the British. For the great majority he was a nightmare figure; mothers used his name to frighten naughty children into discipline. To a man like ▷ Wordsworth he was the tyrant who revealed the illusoriness of the ideals of universal freedom which the Revolution had seemed to express. For Byron and Shelley he was the first man in Europe to have risen to the summit of power by intrinsic merit and not at least partly through privilege; his downfall and the restoration of the traditional kinds of government that he had overthrown was for them a defeat of the new hopes for mankind. Byron described him memorably in *Childe Harold* (1812–18, Canto iii, stanzas 36–44).

▷ French literature in England.

National anthem (British)

'God Save the King', sung as a national anthem, dates back to 1745, when the throne of George II was threatened by the second ▷ Jacobite Rebellion in ▷ Scotland on behalf of the ▷ Stuart claimant. It consists of four verses of which the first only is normally sung, and the last (calling for suppression of the Scots) has been entirely forgotten. The tune has commonly been attributed to the composer John Bull (?1563–1628); alternatively, the words and the tune are said to have been the composition of the poet Henry Carey (d1743), but there is no certainty. ▷ Wales has its own separate national anthem, 'Land of my Fathers'.

National debt

The system by which a government finances itself by borrowing money from its citizens, in addition to taxing them; the lenders in effect invest money in the state as in a business enterprise. In Britain this system originated in the reign of ▷ William III and the ▷ Bank of England was founded in order to operate it.

Nationalism

The emotion or the doctrine according to which human egotism and its passions are expanded so as to become identical with the nation state. As a widespread phenomenon it is usually dated from the ▷ American War of Independence (1775–83) and from the ▷ French Revolution and the wars that followed it. This implies that it is an especially 19th- and 20th-century phenomenon, which it undoubtedly

is, but on the other hand intense national self-consciousness existed among the older European nations before, though without the fanaticism which has been characteristic of it since 1790. Thus strong national feeling arose in England and France, in consequence of the Hundred Years War in the 15th century; it arose again in the 16th and 17th centuries under the English queen Elizabeth I and the French King Louis XIV respectively. Possibly these earlier emotions should be distinguished as patriotism, but the distinction is vague.

Natural History and Antiquities of Selborne
▷ White, Gilbert.

Natural law

According to theologians (*eg* Richard Hooker), that part of the Divine Will that manifests itself in the order of the material world: distinguishable from but of a piece with human and divine law. Modern scientists define it as the principles of uniformity discernible in the behaviour of phenomena, making such behaviour predictable. For the 18th century, the existence of natural law was important as the basis for ▷ natural religion.

Natural philosophy

In the 17th and 18th centuries, the study of physics and kindred sciences. Interest in natural philosophy became organized and heightened with the establishment in 1662 of the ▷ Royal Society, which took the whole of knowledge as its province. The natural philosophers included such eminent persons as ▷ Isaac Newton, the chemist Robert Boyle (1627–91), and the naturalist John Ray (1627–1705). They were religious men and made their religion accord with their science. However, in spite of the respect accorded to some of them, especially Newton, intellectuals in the period 1660–1730 tended to react against natural philosophy with angry contempt. They were provoked not so much by the fear of the injury such thought might do to religious faith – this was much more a 19th-century reaction – as by disgust at the triviality of much scientific inquiry, the technical fruits of which were slow to appear. The most notable satire was ▷ Swift's 'Laputa' in Part III of ▷ *Gulliver's Travels*. Other examples were ▷ Samuel Butler's *Elephant in the Moon*, some of the ▷ *Spectator* essays of Addison and Steele, and the *Memoirs of Martinus Scriblerus*, published with the works of ▷ Pope in 1741, though the principal author seems to have been ▷ John Arbuthnot (▷ Scriblerus Club).

Natural religion

A belief first taught by ▷ Lord Herbert of Cherbury; according to him, belief in God and right conduct are planted in human instincts. This Christian doctrine was the basis for deistic thought (▷ deism) in the later 17th and 18th centuries, and contributed to the growth of religious toleration, though also to passivity of religious feeling and hence to indifference. Herbert's aim was to resolve the doubts arising out of the religious conflicts of his time – see *eg* Donne's *Third Satire*. For the reaction against deism, see ▷ William Blake's propositions *There is No Natural Religion* (1788).

Nature

The word is used throughout English literature with meanings that vary constantly according to period or to mode of expression, *eg* philosophical, religious or personal. The following is intended to show some of the basic approaches to the idea.

  1 *Creation and the Fall*. Fundamental to all conceptions of Nature is traditional Christian doctrine. This influences English writers even when they are using a more or less agnostic or atheistic approach. The doctrine is that Nature is God's creation, but by the fall of man, symbolized by the story of Adam's disobedience in the book of *Genesis*, earthly nature is self-willed and destructive though not to the extent that the Divine Will and Order is obliterated in it.

  2 *All-embracing Nature*. Nature is sometimes seen as the whole of reality so far as earthly experience goes. This use of the word has a different kind of significance in the 18th century when scientific reason has replaced the religious imagination as the familiar vehicle for the interpretation of reality. See 4 *Nature and Truth*.

  3 *Nature and God*. In line with traditional Christian doctrine, Natural Law is linked to Human Law and Divine Law as a manifestation of the Divine Will, in such works as Hooker's *Laws of Ecclesiastical Polity* (1597). However, from the beginning of the 17th century, there was a new interest in the function of human reason as an instrument for the acquisition of knowledge independently of religious feeling. Men like Ralegh (*History of the World*, 1614) and ▷ Bacon (*The Advancement of Learning* 1605) began to ask what, given that God was the Primary Cause of Nature, were the Secondary, or Immediate, Causes of natural phenomena. ▷ Newton's work on gravitation (*Principia Mathematica*, 1687) and ▷ Locke's ▷ *Essay Concerning Human Understanding* seemed to solve the problem, causing people to see God as the Divine Artificer whose Reason could be discerned in the government of even the smallest phenomena, as well as in the great original act of Creation.

  4 *Nature and Truth*. Nature is in the 18th century Truth scientifically considered. 'To follow Nature' (*eg* in works of imaginative literature) may mean: (i) to present things and people (*eg* an imagined character) as they really are; (ii) to reveal truths that lie beneath appearances; (iii) to follow rational principles. It was the attempt to 'follow Nature' in these ways that constituted the main discipline of the novelists ▷ Defoe, ▷ Richardson, ▷ Fielding and ▷ Smollett.

  5 *Nature as Moral Paradox*. The Christian conception of Nature as both God-created and spoilt by the fall of man led at various times to the problem that Nature is both good and evil. According to the medieval conception, maintained until the middle of the 17th century, human society was itself the outcome of the Divine Natural Order, so that it was by Natural Law that children should honour their parents, subjects their sovereigns, etc. On the other hand, the natural passions of men and beasts, unrestrained by reason, were the source of rapacity and ruin. Thus Shakespeare's King Lear begins by relying on the former conception of Nature, but he is exposed to the reality of the latter.

19th-century natural science revived the feeling that Nature was essentially destructive, and hostile or at best indifferent to men; this is the 'Nature red in tooth and claw' image of Tennyson's *In Memoriam*, set against the idea of the love of God.

  6 *Nature for Man's Use*. Implicit in Christian doctrine was the belief that Nature was created *for* man; that it was his birthright to exploit and use it. This begins with the conception of Nature as the Great Mother, originating in pre-Christian times but pervasive in medieval verse and later, *eg* in much Elizabethan ▷ pastoral poetry. It took a more active significance when the 17th- and 18th-century 'natural philosophers' from Bacon onwards sought methods by which man could increase his power over Nature; 18th-century poetry commonly shows Nature as beautiful when she is productive under the ingenuity of human exploitation.

  7 *Nature and Art*. 'Art' in earlier contexts often includes technology, *eg* in Polixenes' remarks on cultivation to Perdita in *The Winter's Tale* (IV. iii); here art is seen as itself a product of nature. But art was often set against nature in Shakespeare's time and afterwards.

  8 *Nature opposed to Court and City*. 'Art', however, was not necessarily an improvement. The city and the court, in Shakespeare's time, were the centres of new financial forces generating intrigue and 'unnatural' (*ie* inhuman) behaviour. There was also a kind of pastoral made by idealizing the life of the great country houses, *eg* Ben Jonson's *Penshurst*. In the 18th century poets like ▷ James Thomson wrote about natural surroundings for their own sake, and sometimes included wild nature as their subject, but it was ▷ Wordsworth who gave to wild nature its importance as the principal subject of what later came to be known as 'nature' poetry.

  9 *Nature in Communion with the Individual*. Wordsworth was to some extent anticipated in the 18th century by such a poet as ▷ William Cowper, and his teacher was especially ▷ Jean-Jacques Rousseau. It was Wordsworth above all, however, who gave to Nature its modern, most familiar sense – as the non-urban, preferably wild environment of man, to which the depths of his own nature always respond. Here he finds a communion which refreshes the loneliness of his spirit in a relationship which underlies and gives meaning to his human relationships.

Neo-classicism

This term can be understood for the purposes of English literary culture in two senses: 1 the broad sense, which refers to the ▷ Renaissance of Classical culture and its influence on English literature down to the end of the 18th century. This influence operated mainly by the cultivation of Latin culture, and was mediated first by Italy and later by France. 2 The narrow sense of neo-classicism refers to a European artistic movement which originated in Germany and lasted approximately from 1750 until 1830.

In the first sense, neo-classical culture affected English literature in two phases:

1 In the 16th century England developed a fine school of classical scholars, of whom the best known was Thomas More. Through travellers and scholars such as Sir Thomas Wyatt and Henry Howard, Earl of Surrey, poetry and prose received strong influences from Italian and French writers such as Petrarch and Ronsard who already belonged to the classical revival. A critic like Sidney showed the influence of Italian critics who in turn were developing 'rules' out of classical writers for dramatic construction, etc. All these influences matured in the last decade of the 16th century but their effect was uneven; the greatest of the rising dramatists, ▷ Shakespeare, ignored the neo-classical rules for dramatic construction, whereas Ben Jonson, his chief rival in the theatre by 1600, was deeply affected by classical principles and classical culture generally. ▷ Pastoral poems, deriving from Italian influences and more directly from Virgil, were numerous from Spenser's *The Shepherd's Calendar* (1579) onwards, and in the 1590s there was a widespread production of ▷ sonnets under the influence of Petrarch. Much of the classical influence was on the level of ornament, however, as it was in English architecture in the same period. Jonson was outstanding in his absorption of classical influence to a deep level, and it was deeper in his lyrical work than in his drama. He is, in fact, an important link with the next phase of English neo-classicism – that which began in 1660 and lasted throughout the 18th century.

2 The second phase was much influenced by contemporary French literature, which was marked by distinguished achievement. English culture was entering a relatively aristocratic period by reaction from the Republican decade of the 1650s; it was also undergoing an increasingly strong revulsion against religious and political passions such as produced the ▷ Civil War. The result was admiration for philosophy, reason, scepticism, ▷ wit and refinement – all qualities conducive to neo-classic culture. Significantly this was also the first important period of English criticism. Yet thoroughly neo-classic critics like ▷ Thomas Rymer were the exception. The restlessness of English society, the increasing importance of the middle class, the difficulty of making such a large exception to neo-classical principles as Shakespeare, and the hostility the English literary tradition has always shown to authoritative doctrines, all help to explain the refusal of the leading critics, ▷ Dryden and ▷ Samuel Johnson, to adopt neo-classic theory unquestioningly. Nonetheless, such a figure as the French neo-classicist ▷ Boileau was deeply respected, and the best poets and essayists (though hardly the novelists) – ▷ Addison, ▷ Swift, ▷ Pope, Johnson – all exhibited the neo-classic virtues of clarity, order, reason, wit and balance.

Neo-classicism in the narrow sense was the cultivation of Greek culture in opposition to Roman culture, and originated partly in the German movement to emancipate German culture from

France. It can be said that whereas Renaissance classicism sought to emulate the culture of Rome, this 'New Humanism' sought inspiration in the originality of the Greeks. This difference enabled the new Neo-Classicism to merge with ▷ Romanticism, whose progenitor was above all ▷ Rousseau.

▷ Classic, classics, classical; Unities; French literature in England; Italian influence in English literature.
Bib: Honour, H., *Neo-classicism*.

Neo-Platonism
▷ Platonism and neo-Platonism.

Nereid
▷ Nymph.

New Comedy
Unlike Aristophanes' Old Comedy, New Comedy as extant in the writings of ▷ Menander, ▷ Plautus and ▷ Terence does not address specific and topical issues so much as focussing on general moral and imaginative motifs. Its formulae consist of stock characters like the young rake, the wily servant (*servus dolosus*), the courtesan, the braggart soldier (*miles gloriosus*) and the irascible old man (*senex*). The plays are populated by lost children and siblings. The genre of New Comedy proved highly influential for English literature. It could more readily accommodate the neo-classical, Horatian moral stance which distinguishes much Elizabethan drama, and its generalized approach proved politically safe in a theatre where every play needed a licence for performance from the Lord Chamberlain's office.

Numerous plays of the ▷ Restoration and 18th centuries also owe a debt to New Comedy. They include ▷ Cowley's *The Cutter of Coleman Street* (1661); ▷ Dryden's *Sir Martin Mar-all* (1667) and *Amphitryon* (1690); ▷ Shadwell's ▷ *The Squire of Alsatia* (1688); ▷ Steele's ▷ *The Conscious Lovers* (1722), ▷ Fielding's *The Intriguing Chambermaid* (1733), and many more. In addition, many plays of ▷ Molière and ▷ Goldoni are either re-workings of New Comedy plays, or are strongly influenced by them. The influence has continued into modern times.
Bib: Duckworth, G. E., *The Nature of Roman Comedy*.

New Learning
Study of the Bible and the Greek ▷ classics in the original languages instead of through Latin versions. This study in the 15th–16th centuries was an important influence in the ▷ Renaissance and the ▷ Reformation.

New Model Army
Formed by Parliament in 1645 towards the end of the ▷ Civil War between itself and ▷ Charles I. The war had so far been indecisive owing to the amateurish soldiering on both sides. Parliament now secured that its own army should be highly professional. The result was the decisive victory of Naseby in June 1645. The commander was Sir Thomas Fairfax, but its most gifted general was ▷ Oliver Cromwell, who between 1646 and 1660

made the English army one of the most formidable in Europe. Cromwell's special contribution was his highly trained force of cavalry, the Ironsides.

New Science

The term 'New Science' or 'New Philosophy' is something of a catch-all phrase, but one which usually is used to suggest the revolution in scientific understanding in Europe generally in the 16th and 17th centuries. On the continent, the work of Galileo (1564–1642) in the field of astronomy and Andreas Vesalius (1514–64) in the area of human anatomy signalled a reassessment of the study of the natural world. In England the influence of ▷ Francis Bacon in the area of scientific methodology was to be of considerable importance. English science in the 16th century, however, lagged behind the work that was taking place on the continent. But, with the publication of William Harvey's discovery of the circulation of the blood (1628), an age of remarkable scientific innovation began in the British Isles.

The influence on literature of the 'New Science' of the age is a much-debated topic.

Certainly poets such as John Donne and ▷ Henry Vaughan were aware of the changes taking place in the ordering and understanding of the natural world – and this awareness is reflected in their writings. Others, such as ▷ Abraham Cowley, were enthusiastic in promulgating ideas and experimental attitudes associated with new scientific methodology. ▷ Thomas Traherne, on the other hand, found himself in the paradoxical situation of being fascinated with the products of scientific enquiry while being deeply suspicious of the anti-fideistic tendency of much of the work that was undertaken. Bib: Debus, A. G., *Man and Nature in the Renaissance*.

Newcastle, Duchess of

▷ Cavendish, Margaret, Duchess of Newcastle.

Newgate

In the ▷ Middle Ages, the principal west gate of the City of London. The gate-house was a prison from the 12th century, enlarged in the 15th century and burnt down in the ▷ Gordon Riots in 1780. Its destruction is described in Dickens' novel *Barnaby Rudge* (1841). It was rebuilt and finally demolished in 1902, when the present Central Criminal Court (Old Bailey) was built on its site.

Newspapers

Periodicals resembling newspapers began in a small way in the reign of ▷ James I; in the decades of the ▷ Civil War and the ▷ Interregnum they increased in number owing to the need of either side to engage in propaganda. From 1695 press ▷ censorship was abandoned; newspapers and weekly periodicals began to flourish.

The first English daily, the *Daily Courant*, a mere news-sheet, began in 1702, but in the earlier part of the 18th century papers more nearly resembling what we now know as the weekly reviews were of greater importance, and leading writers conducted them, *eg* ▷ Defoe's *The Review* (thrice weekly – 1704–13); ▷ Steele's ▷ *Tatler* (thrice weekly – started 1709);

Steele and ▷ Addison's ▷ *Spectator* (daily – started 1711); and the ▷ *Examiner* (started 1710), to which the chief contributor was ▷ Jonathan Swift. ▷ Samuel Johnson's ▷ *Rambler* (1750) was of the same kind. Of these men, only Defoe resembled fairly closely what we nowadays regard as a journalist as distinct from a man of letters.

Of daily papers founded in the 18th century, the ▷ *Morning Post* (started 1772) survived until 1936, and ▷ *The Times* (started 1785) is still extant, though it has a comparatively small circulation. Other important dailies with a shorter life were the ▷ *Morning Chronicle* (1769–1862), and the ▷ *Morning Herald* (1780–1869). Both reached peak circulations of about 6,000. To reach the very large circulations of today, newspapers had to await the abolition of the stamp duty – a tax on newspapers – in 1855. The Stamp Tax was started in 1712. It was a method of restricting circulations by raising the prices of newspapers. The government of the day resented criticism of its policies but did not dare revive the Licensing Act, the lapsing of which in 1695 was really the start of the British freedom of the press.

Newton, Sir Isaac (1642–1727)

Mathematician and natural philosopher. He entered Trinity College, Cambridge, in 1661, became a fellow of the college in 1667, and Professor of Mathematics in the university in 1669. He resigned the professorship in 1701; in 1703 he was made President of the ▷ Royal Society, and was re-elected annually until his death. Queen Anne knighted him in 1705.

His principal work was *Philosophiae Naturalis Principia Mathematica* (1687), written in Latin. By the application of mathematical calculation, it explained the force of gravity in its operation through the solar system. His book on *Optics* (1704) was less important, but it aroused new interest in vision and colour and influenced descriptive writing throughout the 18th century. His scientific and mathematical discoveries did not shake his religious convictions, which were very strong, and he also wrote on theology and biblical chronology. On the other hand, he did not understand and had no use for the imaginative faculty and, like ▷ Locke (whose ▷ *Essay concerning Human Understanding* was published in 1690) he dismissed poetry as an unimportant and irrelevant activity.

Despite this indifference to poetic literature, Newton's discoveries, combined as they were with his religious piety, had a great influence on 18th-century poets. He caused them to revere Reason in both Man and God, who, seen through Newton's writings, became the Divine Artist of the Universe. ▷ Pope's *Essay on Man* was a restatement of the traditional vision of the natural order newly shaped to accord with Newton's rational harmony, and it was Pope who composed for Newton the famous epitaph:

> Nature and Nature's laws lay hid in night:
> God said, 'Let Newton be!' and all was Light.

The most famous poet of the natural scene in

the 18th century, ▷ James Thomson, wrote his
▷ *Seasons* in accordance with Newtonian principles.
In the revised *Prelude* (1850) ▷ Wordsworth wrote of
the statue in Trinity College:

> *Of Newton with his prism and silent face,*
> *The marble index of a mind for ever*
> *Voyaging through strange seas of Thought, alone.*

Wordsworth thus chooses to emphasize the
mysteriousness of science, whereas Pope had
emphasized its power to clarify mystery.
Bib: Nicholson, M. H., *Newton Demands the Muse.*

Night Thoughts on Life, Death, and Immortality
▷ Young, Edward.

Noble savage
▷ Primitive, primitivism.

Nokes, James (d1696)
Actor. Nokes performed briefly at the Cockpit
in Drury Lane, largely in women's roles, before
joining the ▷ Duke's Company under ▷ William
D'Avenant in 1660 as actor and shareholder.
He usually played in low and crude comic roles,
specializing as foolish old husbands, nurses,
and fops.

Nonconformists
▷ Dissenters; Puritanism, puritans.

North Briton, The
A radical political weekly, started in 1762 by ▷ John
Wilkes and Charles Churchill. It opposed the
government of George III and his Prime Minister,
the Scotsman Lord Bute, and was aimed particularly
against Bute's journal *The Briton*, edited by the
Scottish novelist ▷ Tobias Smollett. After 45 issues
it was suppressed.

Nurseries
Training establishments for actors and actresses in
the ▷ Restoration period.

Nursery rhymes
A body of folk verse, some of it very ancient, some of
it being concealed comment on political events, some
of it apparently never having had any meaning.

Nymph
In Greek myth the nymphs were a race of minor
female deities, often attendant on the major deities
of both sexes. The word derives from the Greek for
'marriageable woman', and nymphs seem to have
been associated with fertility. They were subdivided
according to their various habitats: Naiads belonged
to rivers, springs and lakes; Oceanids or Nereids
lived in the sea; Oreads inhabited mountains and
rocky places; Dryads and Hamadryads, forests
and trees.

Oates, Titus (1649–1705)

An English conspirator. He was the son of a
▷ Puritan preacher, and himself professed to stand
for the defence of ▷ Protestantism against supposed
▷ Catholic dangers, but he was really a disreputable
adventurer who used the religious passions of
the time for his personal advantage. In 1678 he
fabricated the Popish Plot, by which he pretended
without factual basis to expose a Catholic conspiracy
against the ▷ Church of England. Popular suspicion
of ▷ Charles II, and the fact that the Queen and his
brother James were avowed Roman Catholics, caused
a national panic, and a large number of Catholics
were put to death. His evidence was eventually
proved false, and he was imprisoned. He is satirized
under the name of Corah in Dryden's ▷ *Absalom and
Achitophel*.

Observer, The

A ▷ newspaper published only on Sundays, started
in 1792. It is central in its politics, and aims to appeal
to the thoughtful, better-educated public.

Octavia

Half-sister of Octavius Caesar, who became
the first Roman Emperor, ▷ Caesar Augustus
(ruled 27 BC–AD 14) She married her brother's
rival, Mark Antony, and occurs as a character in
▷ Shakespeare's tragedy *Antony and Cleopatra* and in
Dryden's tragedy ▷ *All For Love*.

Ode

The Pindaric Ode is modelled on the works of
▷ Pindar, a Greek poet of the 5th century BC,
best known for his odes celebrating the victors at
the Olympic games. These were accompanied by
music and dance, and were disposed in a threefold
pattern corresponding to the movements of the
Greek dramatic chorus (*strophe, antistrophe, epode*).
From the 17th century onwards English poets took
Pindar as a model for lyric and declamatory verse
expressive of high-wrought emotion. ▷ Thomas
Gray's *Progress of Poesy* follows Pindar's stanza forms
with scholarly exactness, but ▷ Abraham Cowley
had earlier established the more usual 'irregular
ode', which sanctions unpredictable variations in
line-length, rhyme and ▷ metre within each stanza.
Early examples of this form are ▷ John Dryden's
Alexander's Feast and *Ode to the Memory of Anne
Killigrew*. 'Pindarics' remained popular throughout
the 18th century and became a natural vehicle for the
new ▷ 'romantick' sensibility. Gray's use of them
in ▷ *The Bard* and *The Progress of Poesy*, for all its
scholarly meticulousness, is intended to sound bold
and inspirational.

The Roman poet ▷ Horace imitated Pindar,
but his odes employ unvarying stanza forms. The
'regular' Horatian ode was imitated by ▷ Andrew
Marvell in his *Horatian Ode upon Cromwell's Return
from Ireland*, and by ▷ William Collins in *How Sleep
the Brave* and *To Simplicity*.

Odyssey

An ▷ epic by the ancient Greek poet ▷ Homer.
The hero, Odysseus King of Ithaca, is on his way
home after the Trojan war, but he is blown off
course and the return journey takes him ten years.
The principal episodes of his voyage are as follows:

1 The land of the Lotus-Eaters. Those who eat of
the lotus plant forget their homeland.

2 The land of the Cyclops. These are a race of
one-eyed giants. Odysseus puts out the eye of the
Cyclops Polyphemus, who is son of Poseidon, god
of the sea; it is to punish him for this that Poseidon
sends him wandering for ten years.

3 The Isle of Aeolus, king of the winds. Odysseus
steals from him the bag in which the winds are
contained, but his companions open it too soon, and
the winds escape.

4 Telepylus, the city of the cannibal Laestrygonians.
They destroy his fleet except one ship, in which he
escapes.

5 The Isle of Circe. She transforms his men
into swine, but with the aid of the god Hermes, he
resists her enchantments, compels her to restore
his men, and remains in the island as her lover
for a year.

6 He visits the Underworld, Hades, to learn
from the prophet Tiresias the way home. Tiresias
warns him against harming the cattle of the sun-
god, Helios.

7 He evades the enchanting songs of the Sirens,
who try to lure him on to the rocks.

8 He passes through the strait of Scylla and
Charybdis – a treacherous rock and a whirlpool.

9 He comes to the Island of Thrinacia (Sicily)
where the cattle of Helios live, which the ghost of
Tiresias has warned him not to harm, but overcome
by hunger, his companions devour them.

10 In punishment, his ship is wrecked and all his
men perish, but Odysseus reaches the island of the
goddess Calypso, who keeps him prisoner for seven
years as her lover. He eventually escapes, with the
aid of the goddess Athene, and reaches the lands
of the Phaeacians where Nausicaa and her father,
the king of the country, befriend him. The narrative
of all the above events comes to the reader through
Odysseus, who tells them to the king. The king
helps him back to Ithaca. There, with the help of his
son Telemachus, he kills the suitors who have been
pestering the chaste Penelope, his queen.

Og, king of Bashan

▷ *Absalom and Achitophel*.

Oisin

▷ Ossian.

O'Keeffe, John (1747–1833)

Actor and dramatist, who wrote many popular
comedies and comic operas in the late 18th century.
O'Keeffe was drawn to the stage by reading
▷ Farquhar and he wrote his first play, *The Gallant*,
at the age of 15. He later obtained a post as an actor.
In 1773 he took up writing seriously, and his farce,
Tony Lumpkin in Town, based on ▷ Goldsmith's
▷ *She Stoops to Conquer*, was staged in Dublin, and
afterwards at the ▷ Haymarket Theatre in London.
His *Wild Oats, or the Strolling Gentleman* (1791) was

revived by the Royal Shakespeare Company in 1976, with great success, largely because of the magnificent acting vehicle provided in the character of Rover. O'Keeffe's autobiography was published in 1826.

Old Bachelor, The (1693)

Comedy by ▷ Congreve. After being seduced and abandoned by Vainlove, Silvia sets out to marry, pretending to be sexually inexperienced. Heartwell, the aged and surly 'old bachelor' of the title, falls in love with Silvia, and marries her. He later discovers to his relief that the marriage is a sham, as the parson was only Vainlove's friend Bellmour in disguise. Afterwards Silvia traps Sir Joseph Wittol into a genuine marriage. Bellmour loves Belinda, but at first she keeps him at a distance, knowing him to be a rake: eventually they marry. In another intrigue, Bellmour is attracted to the uxorious Fondlewife's wife Laeticia, whom Vainlove has wooed, as he woos any pretty woman. In this instance Vainlove allows Bellmour to reap the fruit of his labours: Bellmour goes to Laeticia's house, disguised as a Puritan preacher, and seduces her in her husband's absence. Fondlewife returns, but the lovers convince him that she has remained chaste. Araminta, another woman whom Vainlove pursues, loves him but resists him. At last they seem near to marrying, but the ending of their plot-line remains ambiguous. The play is lively and entertaining, but cynical in tone.

Old Comedy
▷ Aristophanes.

Old English Baron, The (1778)

Historical and ▷ Gothic ▷ romance by English writer ▷ Clara Reeve, first published as *The Champion of Virtue: A Gothic Story* (1777). Sir Philip Harclay returns to England after serving Henry V, to discover that there have been strange deeds in the family of his friend, Lord Lovel, whose castle is now occupied by Lord Baron Fitz-Owen. A mystery begins to be unravelled around the well-bred but impoverished Edmund, and his banishment by an evil relative. Ultimately, the rightful claims of inheritance are asserted. In a preface, Reeve asserts that Gothic effects must 'be kept within certain limits of credibility'.

▷ *Mysteries of Udolpho, The*; Radcliffe, Ann

Old Pretender, The

James Francis Edward Stuart (1688–1766), son of ▷ King James II who had been deposed for reasons connected with his Catholicism. He was a pretender to (*ie* he claimed) the British throne on the death of his half-sister Queen Anne in 1714, but his claim was rejected because like his father he was a Catholic. Instead, George of Hanover became king as George I. In 1715, James led a rebellion on his own behalf in ▷ Scotland, but this failed. His followers were called ▷ Jacobites from the Latin 'Jacobus' = James, and he was termed the 'Old' Pretender to distinguish him from his son, Charles Edward Stuart, the Young Pretender, who attempted a similar Scottish rebellion in 1745.

▷ Stuart, House of.

Oldfield, Anne (?1683–1730)

Actress. She served in a tavern where, according to tradition, her talents as an actress were recognized by the playwright ▷ George Farquhar, who heard her reciting some lines behind the bar. She was engaged at ▷ Drury Lane from 1699 where apart from a brief sojourn at the Queen's Theatre (▷ Haymarket Theatres), she remained to the end of her career. She gradually supplanted the previous leading actress, ▷ Anne Bracegirdle.

Throughout her career Oldfield preferred comic to tragic roles, excelling in the performance of coquettes and women of fashion such as Lady Betty Modish in ▷ Colley Cibber's *The Careless Husband* (1704). Bib: Robins, E., *The Palmy Days of Nance Oldfield*; Melville, L., *Stage Favourites of the Eighteenth Century*.

Oldham, John (1653–83)

Poet. Some of his early poems were written under the influence of the ▷ Earl of Rochester, and his *Ode, Suppos'd to be spoken by a Court-Hector at Breaking of the Dial in Privy-Garden*, also known as *A Satyr against Vertue*, concerns one of Rochester's drunken exploits. His *Satyrs upon the Jesuits*, in heroic ▷ couplets (1681), ridicule Catholic superstition. He was a pioneer of the 'imitation' form, writing versions of poems by ▷ Horace, ▷ Juvenal and ▷ Boileau in urbane couplets, adapting the original to an English contemporary context. His *Poems and Translations* appeared in 1683. He died early from smallpox, and ▷ John Dryden wrote an elegy to his memory. Bib: Zigerell, J., *John Oldham*.

Olney Hymns (1779)

A collection of religious poems by the Rev. John Newton and ▷ William Cowper, so called from the village of Olney where they lived.

Omai

Tahitian, brought to England with James Cook's second voyage in 1774, and shown around as the epitome of a 'noble savage' (▷ Primitivism), one of a series of such visitors including American Indians and Eskimos. His dignified bearing and conduct, as he moved in the highest English circles, were marvelled at and seemed to bear out theories of natural virtue, compared with the corruptions of civilization. A painting by ▷ Reynolds depicts him in a turban and flowing garment, standing erect, with his right hand outstretched, in the pose of a statesman or oriental prince. His visit is mentioned by several contemporaries, including ▷ Cowper, ▷ Johnson and ▷ Burney.

Ombre

A card game introduced from Spain into England in the 17th century, and very popular throughout the 18th century. Its appeal lay in its demand on the intelligence of the players, and it was later superseded in popularity by whist and then bridge, games which make a similar demand. The name is from the Spanish for 'Man'. Ombre is the game played in Pope's famous poem ▷ *The Rape of the Lock*.

Onomatopoeia

The use of verbal sound to evoke the sound of what the word represents. Thus a cuckoo is a bird whose song resembles the two syllables of its name, which is therefore onomatopoeic.

Open-field system

That system of land use especially typical of medieval English agriculture. Land under cultivation was divided into strips, and distributed among the peasants of the village or manor. The strips were not surrounded by hedges or fences, so that good farmers suffered from the effects of the bad farming of their immediate neighbours. The system began to be replaced in the 16th century, when landowners preferred sheep-farming, and it was effectually abolished in the 18th century when, in the course of 'the agricultural revolution', the open fields were enclosed in larger arable units by the landlords.
▷ Enclosures.

Opera in England

Opera, in the sense of a staged drama in which the words and music are of equal importance, began in Italy at the end of the 16th century. It was an integral part of the ▷ Renaissance, arising out of the attempt to revive what were thought to be the performance practices of Greek drama. Subjects, therefore, were tragedies drawn from classical mythology and the words were set to a declamatory style of singing known as recitative. The first English opera was *The Siege of Rhodes*, with a libretto by ▷ William D'Avenant and music (now lost) by Matthew Locke and others. It was first produced in 1656, at a time when the ▷ Puritans had closed the theatres, and it seems to have been an attempt to circumvent the ban on plays. The convention of recitative, however, does not seem to have been to the English taste, so that, apart from Blow's *Venus and Adonis* and ▷ Purcell's *Dido and Aeneas*, the main contribution of composers in the 17th century was in the genre now known as 'dramatic' or 'semi-opera'. After the theatres reopened in 1660, many plays were given with musical interludes, ▷ Shakespeare being adapted for this purpose by ▷ D'Avenant and ▷ Dryden. Two sets of *Tempest* music exist, one by Locke, the other sometimes thought to be by Purcell. *The Fairy Queen* (1693), an adaptation of *A Midsummer Night's Dream*, is Purcell's best-known work in this field.

In the 18th century Italian opera was imported, as well as the German composer, ▷ Handel, who wrote operas in the Italian style, but the fashion for such entertainment proved to be short-lived. ▷ Addison, amongst others, ridiculed the conventions of opera in the ▷ *Spectator*. Nor, despite its popularity at the time, did ▷ Gay's ▷ *The Beggar's Opera* (1728) lead to a significant tradition of ballad opera.

Until the 20th century, London had a virtual monopoly of opera performances.

Orange, House of; Orange Free State; Orangemen

The town of Orange in southern France was originally an independent principality. Philibert of Orange (1502–30) was rewarded by the Emperor Charles V (who ruled the Netherlands amongst his other territories) with large estates in the Netherlands for his help in statesmanship and war. The Princes of Orange thus became Dutch nobles, and later William 'the Silent' of Orange established the Dutch (Netherlands) Republic by defeating the armies of the territory's former ruler, Philip II of Spain. William's leadership, and the importance of the Orange family in the Netherlands, gave the House of Orange special eminence in the Republic, and successive members of it held the high office of Stadtholder. They twice married into the ▷ Stuart family reigning in Britain: William II married Mary, daughter of ▷ Charles I, and in 1677 their son, William III, married Mary (▷ Mary II), daughter of ▷ James II. William and Mary became joint sovereigns of Britain in 1689 after the expulsion of James II. After William III's death in 1702, the family continued to be pre-eminent in Dutch politics, and were kings of Holland (the Netherlands) from 1814. In the same year the Dutch colony in South Africa was ceded to Britain; in 1836 some of the Dutch colonists, fleeing from British sovereignty, set up the Orange Free State Republic to the north of the colony.

Throughout the 17th century the House of Orange was a champion of ▷ Protestantism against the Catholic powers, first of Spain and then of France; the religious conflict was also a fight for Dutch national survival, and from 1690–1700 it was in addition one for the survival of the British system of politics. The issue was then felt most keenly in ▷ Ireland, where the northern province of Ulster was Protestant, and the southern three provinces were Catholic. Religious hostility between the north and the south continued throughout the 18th century, when it died down in most of Europe, and it is still a political issue at the present day. In 1795 'Orange Societies' were founded in Ulster, in memory of the great Protestant king William III, who had saved Ulster from being overrun by the Catholic south by defeating James II's army at the Battle of the Boyne (1690). Orangemen (*ie* members of these societies) are still an important political force in Northern Ireland, although the societies are nominally religious and not political.

Oranges and Lemons

A ▷ nursery rhyme based on the church bells of London. Each chime is given its distinctive utterance – *eg* 'Oranges and lemons say the bells of St Clement's' – culminating in 'the great bell of Bow'. The earliest record of the rhyme is 1744. It is also the basis of an old children's game.

Orders in Council

Laws or regulations made by the king or queen in conjunction with the ▷ Privy Council; in practice this means that the Prime Minister and his Cabinet advise the sovereign to issue them, and they are then accountable to ▷ Parliament for the action. Orders in Council were often used in emergency, especially in wartime.

Oriental, orientalism

The 17th and 18th centuries saw a growing fascination with the Orient, and with oriental themes. This was due in part to improvements in transport, facilitating the growth of trade and making ▷ travel accessible to an increasing number of people. It also stemmed from the discoveries of explorers, who brought back stories (▷ travel literature), and even living beings (such as ▷ Omai), from far-off lands. Narratives of the East, in verse and prose, both dramatic and non-dramatic, play a substantial part in the period. Early examples are seen in ▷ Restoration ▷ heroic tragedies, such as ▷ Dryden's *The Conquest of Granada* (1670) and ▷ *Aureng-Zebe* (1675). The English idea that despotic oriental societies might be governed by codes of honour made fitting settings for plays influenced by ▷ neo-classic theory and by the practice of dramatists such as ▷ Corneille and ▷ Racine. ▷ Nicholas Rowe, in the generation after Dryden, used an exotic venue for his *Tamerlane* (1701), a heroic play touched with pathos.

In the later 18th century the growth of ▷ Romantic ▷ sensibility, as well as political disillusionment, gave impetus to fresh appraisals of oriental societies and sympathy with their peoples. The Chinaman in ▷ Goldsmith's *A Citizen of the World* (1760–62) is an urbane and sophisticated commentator on English culture, while ▷ Samuel Johnson's *Rasselas* (▷ *Rasselas*) is also a sympathetic character, with whom the ordinary reader can identify, rather than the hero or monster of earlier works. The period also saw a growth in ▷ taste for oriental ▷ furnishings and furniture, which continued into the 19th century.

Toward the end of the 18th century, however, the democratic spirit which gave rise to the ▷ French and American revolutions led to a further reappraisal of oriental societies. Their illiberal forms of government gave them a new place in garish and exotic literature, of which ▷ Beckford's *Vathek* is a typical example.

▷ Primitive, primitivism.

'Orinda', The 'Matchless'
▷ Philips, Katherine.

Oroonoko, Or, The Royal Slave (1688)
Novel by ▷ Aphra Behn. Oroonoko is an African prince, sold into slavery and transported to Surinam. He is separated from his beloved wife, Imoinda, who undergoes a similar fate to his own: they are re-united in Surinam. The novel is in two parts: the first tells of their lives at the court of Coromantien (now Nigeria), where Oroonoko clashes with his lustful grandfather the king, who wants Imoinda for himself, before they are parted and each one is sold to slave-traders. The second part tells of their meeting in Surinam, where Oroonoko has been given the name Caesar, of the abortive slave uprising which he leads, and of their eventual deaths. The novel is part romance, part exotic travel tale, part polemic, with a wealth of critical commentary about

the hypocrisy and treachery of the white man, and his practice of Christianity, and of the corruption of colonial government – a theme Behn returned to in her play, *The Widow Ranter, Or, Bacon's Rebellion in Virginia* (1696). Oroonoko and Imoinda are 'noble savages' (▷ primitive, primitivism), whose virtue and beauty are extolled as being far superior to the qualities of the white people around them, and their sufferings are portrayed very movingly. On the other hand, the argument is not against slavery as such, but against the presumptuous and cruel treatment of the high-born by their social and moral inferiors. The novel is told by a first-person narrator, ostensibly Behn herself, who claimed to have witnessed the events in Surinam. For many years this was taken as an invention, with descriptive details about the colony being cribbed from other works. But recent scholarship accepts that Behn lived in Surinam, and based much of her narration on first-hand experience.

▷ Thomas Southerne's play *Oroonoko* (1695) is based on Behn's novel.
Bib: Duffy, M., (ed.), *Oroonoko and Other Stories*.

Osborne, Dorothy (1627–95)
Wife of ▷ Sir William Temple, statesman, diplomatist and author. Their marriage was delayed for seven years owing to the disapproval of her family, and her letters to him during a part of this time are famous social documents.

Ossian
James Macpherson (1736–96) was the author of a series of blank verse epics which he attributed to Ossian, son of Finn, and which he claimed to have translated from the Gaelic. There was considerable interest in ▷ primitivism in the 1760s, and works such as *Fingal, an Ancient Epic Poem in Six Books* (1762) and *Temora* (1763) caused a great sensation, particularly among patriotic Scots. Ossian's fame also spread to the European continent, where the poetry was read with enthusiasm by ▷ Napoleon I, and quoted by ▷ Goethe in *The Sorrows of Young Werther*. ▷ Samuel Johnson was among the earliest sceptics; when asked whether he thought that any man 'of the modern age' could have written the poems, he replied: 'Yes, Sir, many men, many women, and many children.' Following Macpherson's death, an investigating committee concluded that the poetry was a collage of edited and newly-written material. Despite this exposure, Matthew Arnold (1822–88) defended the poetry as late as 1866 for its 'vein of piercing regret and sadness'. In the ancient legends Oisin (Ossian) bridged the gap between the heroic pagan age and Irish Christianity; his longevity was due to an extended residence in Fairyland.

▷ Macpherson, James.

Otway, Thomas (1652–85)
Dramatist and poet. He made a single attempt as an actor, when ▷ Aphra Behn gave him an opportunity as the old King in her *The Forc'd Marriage* (1670). Paralysed with stage fright, he broke down, and the next night the part had to be given to another actor. Otway turned instead to writing, and had immediate

success with his tragedy, *Alcibiades* (1675), in which ▷ Elizabeth Barry made her first appearance. Otway is said to have fallen in love with her at that time, though she did not reciprocate his feelings. Otway nevertheless wrote several of his finest parts for her.

Otway followed his first play with the rhymed tragedy *Don Carlos* (1676); adaptations of a comedy by ▷ Molière as *The Cheats of Scapin* (1676) and ▷ Racine's tragedy *Titus and Berenice* (1677); and another comedy, *Friendship in Fashion* (1678). In 1678 Otway went to Flanders as a soldier, and drew on his experiences for ▷ *The Soldier's Fortune* (1681) and its sequel, ▷ *The Atheist* (1684). His best-known and most admired plays are two blank-verse tragedies, *The Orphan; Or, The Unhappy Marriage* (1680), and ▷ *Venice Preserv'd; Or A Plot Discovered* (1682). Otway also wrote prologues and epilogues, and a few poems. He died in poverty.
Bib: Taylor, A. M., *Next to Shakespeare*; Ham, R. G., *Otway and Lee*; Summers, M. (ed.), *The Complete Works of Thomas Otway*; Ghosh, J. C. (ed.), *The Complete Works of Thomas Otway*.

Ovid (Publius Ovidius Naso) (43 BC–AD 17)
Roman poet, and the last of the greatest period of Latin poetry, the ▷ Augustan Age. He wrote for the sophisticated and elegant society of the capital of the Empire, but the immorality of his *Ars Amatoria* ('Art of Love') offended the Emperor ▷ Caesar Augustus who (for this and some other more mysterious offence) exiled him to the Black Sea about AD 9. The works by which Ovid is principally known are: the *Amores*, love poems in what is called the 'elegiac' couplet; the *Ars Amatoria*; the *Remedia Amoris*, in which he tries to redeem himself for the offence he caused by the *Ars Amatoria*; the *Heroides*, in which he makes the heroines of myth give tongue to their misfortunes; the ▷ *Metamorphoses*, a collection of tales about miraculous transformation of shape; the *Fasti*, a poetic account of the Roman calendar; and the *Tristia*, verse epistles lamenting his exile.

Ovid was one of the most read and influential poets in later centuries; in England this is especially true from the 16th to 18th centuries. His most popular work was the *Metamorphoses*; this was repeatedly imitated and translated, memorably by Golding in the 16th century and by Sandys and ▷ Dryden in the 17th. As early as the 14th century Chaucer got the tales in his *Legend of Good Women*

from the *Heroides*, and these poems set a tradition in 'Heroic Epistles' which began with ▷ Drayton in the early 17th century and culminated in ▷ Pope's *Eloisa to Abelard*. Ovid's influence is traceable repeatedly in the work of ▷ Spenser and touched ▷ Milton. Thus he may be said to have affected, either in subject matter or in style, almost all the major poets from Chaucer to Pope, and his influence was equally extensive among lesser figures. The influence was not always deep, however, and it can be ascribed partly to his being the liveliest and most beguiling of the Roman poets who were regarded as the basis of a cultured understanding of literature.
▷ Elegy; Latin literature.

Oxymoron
▷ Figures of speech.

Oxford University
The oldest of the English universities. It was started by students from the still older University of Paris in the 12th century, and the colleges which give it (and Cambridge) its distinctive character began to be founded in the 13th century, as a means of housing students and keeping order among them. The colleges are not controlled by the University, but are self-governing institutions, though their members usually (always in the case of senior members) hold university appointments as well. Oxford provided the students who early in the 13th century started ▷ Cambridge University, but Oxford remained of superior importance until the 15th century, by which time it was infected by Wycliffite heresies (John Wycliffe, ?1320–84), and the major patrons (especially the Crown) began to distribute to Cambridge at least an equal share of the wealth in endowments.

Oxford produced some of the intellectual leaders of medieval Europe: in the 13th century Roger Bacon and Duns Scotus, in the 14th century Wycliffe. The New Learning of the ▷ Renaissance began in the 16th century, under the leadership of Erasmus, Thomas More, Grocyn and Colet, to oust medieval scholasticism. Since then Oxford has retained its status as one of the main channels through which persons who attain positions of power in public life receive their education.
▷ Universities.

P

Paine, Thomas (1737–1809)

Political author. The son of a small farmer, his early career in England ended in failure, and he sailed for America in 1774. In 1776 he published the republican pamphlet *Common Sense*, which set the colonists openly on the road to independence. After the start of the American War of Independence, he maintained the morale of the rebels with a series of pamphlets called *The Crisis* (1776–83). The opening sentence was 'These are the times that try men's souls'– words which became a battle-cry.

In 1787 he returned to Europe to carry on his fight for republican democracy. When ▷ Burke published his ▷ *Reflections on the Revolution in France* in 1790, Paine replied with Part I of his *Rights of Man* (1791). The Government was making the preparations for his trial for treason in 1792 when the poet ▷ William Blake got him out of the country to France, where the French revolutionary government had elected him a member of the republican Convention. In France he published his *Age of Reason* (1793) which defended a rational, abstract form of ▷ deism against orthodox Christianity. This caused him to lose his popularity in England and in America. He also lost favour with the French for his injudicious criticisms, and for a time he was imprisoned, though he was later restored to his seat in the Convention. In 1802 he returned to America to find that he had lost his influence there and he died at his farm in New Rochelle in 1809. Ten years later the English radical William Cobbett returned to England with Tom Paine's bones. For some time his works remained a text-book for English radicalism.

Pakington, Dorothy, Lady (d1679)

Moralist, considered one of the most learned ladies of her time, she remained loyal to the Church of England, and to the ▷ Stuart cause throughout her life. A number of popular conduct books (▷ conduct literature) have sometimes been attributed to her, including *The Whole Duty of Man* (1658), *The Gentleman's Calling* (1660) and *The Lady's Calling* (1673), a textbook of virtue, modesty, and duty. But nowadays doubt has been thrown on her authorship of the first two works, which are believed to be by the cleric Richard Allestree, and he may have composed the third as well. Nevertheless, her influence was considerable in her day. Lady Pakington was part of a circle of educated and devout men and women, and before the Restoration she held in her home a sort of salon for those who shared her concerns.
Bib: Reynolds, M., *The Learned Lady in England and 1650–1760*.

Palamon and Arcite

Rivals for the love of Emily in Chaucer's *Knight's Tale*, the first of the *Canterbury Tales*. ▷ Dryden paraphrased Chaucer's tale as *Palamon and Arcite*, published in his *Fables Ancient and Modern* (1699).

Palindrome

▷ Figures of speech.

Palladio, Andrea (1508–80)

Italian architect. Palladio's villas, public buildings and churches – built between 1540 and 1580, and to be found in Venice and Vicenza and the countryside around these two important ▷ Renaissance Italian cities – were to have a lasting effect on English and American architectural styles. The first great English classical architect, ▷ Inigo Jones, was strongly influenced by Palladian ideals of design. These ideals – usually manifested in symmetrical fronts and applied half-columns topped by a pediment – were themselves derived from Palladio's intense study of architectural styles to be found in the surviving antiquities of ancient Rome. Indeed, Palladio was himself the author of one of the earliest guidebooks to the city's remains when he published his *Le Antichità di Roma* in 1554. This work, together with his *Quattro Libri dell' Architettura* (1570), served to publicize the classical forms of architecture which came to dominate design in the 17th and 18th centuries.

The 'Palladian' style expresses key Renaissance aesthetic ideas. Those ideas, which encompass proportion, harmony and balance, were to become of great importance during the 18th century when Palladio's designs, and studies of his works, were much in vogue.
Bib: Wittkower, R., *Architectural Principles in the Age of Humanism*; Ackerman, J. S., *Palladio*.

Pamela (1740–1)

Subtitled 'Virtue Rewarded', *Pamela* is an ▷ epistolary novel by ▷ Samuel Richardson. The story of a young servant girl who evades her master's attempts at seduction, Richardson's novel was a great contemporary success, yet sophisticated readers were quick to see its ambiguous message. By her insistence on her country simplicity, Pamela persuades the squire to marry her; yet her self-conscious parade of 'artless' virtue suggests a level of sexual innuendo of which Richardson may or may not have been aware. ▷ Henry Fielding's ▷ *Shamela* and ▷ *Joseph Andrews* parody this element of *Pamela*.

Pamphlet

Any short treatise published separately, usually without hard covers. It is usually polemical, *ie* written to defend or attack some body of ideas, especially religious or political ones. In the 16th century and especially towards the end of the reign of Elizabeth I pamphleteering became a widespread literary industry, the beginning of ▷ journalism. In the 17th century Milton was the most famous writer of pamphlets, and his ▷ *Areopagitica* is his masterpiece. In the 18th century some of ▷ Swift's finest prose was in pamphlet form, *eg* ▷ *A Modest Proposal* (1729), and ▷ Defoe was a prolific pamphleteer. The 18th century, however, saw the rise of the weekly periodicals, which reduced the need for the pamphlet form of literature.

Panjandrum

The word first occurs in a sentence devised by the actor-playwright ▷ Samuel Foote to test the memory

of another actor-playwright ▷ Charles Macklin:
'. . . and there were present the Picninnies, and
the Joblillies, and the Garyulies, and the Grand
Panjandrum himself, with the little round button at
top.' The word came to be used for any pompous
person, or for someone of supposed power.

Pantaloon

A character in old Italian popular comedy. He
represented a Venetian, and the name derived from
the Venetian saint, San Pantaleone. He became a
popular figure in international ▷ pantomime, and
appears as a stupid old man wearing spectacles,
slippers, and clumsy trousers or pantaloons, from
which comes 'pants'. Pantaloon used also to be
a term for any feeble-minded old man, *eg* in
Shakespeare's *As You Like It*.

Pantheism

A term used to cover a variety of religious and
philosophical beliefs, which have in common that
God is present in Nature, and not separable from
it in the sense in which a cause is separable from
its effect, or a creator from his creation. Pantheism
is implicit in doctrines derived from ▷ Plato, *eg*
in some of the neo-Platonists of the 16th century,
and in some poetry inspired by the natural
environment. Amongst English poets, the most
famous example is ▷ Wordsworth in his earlier
phase (1797–1807), notably in the first two books of
his 1805 version of *The Prelude*. In his revised version
of this autobiographical poem, Wordsworth tried
to eliminate the pantheistic tendencies, since they
are not in accordance with most forms of Christian
doctrine.

Pantisocracy

The name given by ▷ Samuel Taylor Coleridge and
▷ Robert Southey to the ideal anarchistic society
which preoccupied them in 1794–5 during the first
phase of the ▷ French Revolution (from the Greek:
pan = 'all', *isos* = 'the same', *cratos* = 'power'). They
hoped to establish a community on the banks of the
River Susquehanna in the United States in which
motives of gain would be replaced by brotherly love.
They were unable to raise money, however, their
ideas changed, and they abandoned their plan.

Pantomime

Originally, in ancient Rome, a representation by
masked actors, using gestures and dance, of religious
or warlike eposodes. One actor played many parts,
male and female, with changes of mask and costume.
It was often accompanied by music. It was used
for episodes in medieval religious drama, and as
the 16th-century Italian ▷ Commedia dell'Arte
it became a form of popular drama that spread all
over Europe together with a number of traditional
characters such as Harlequin and the Clown. In the
18th century it established itself in England.

Paradise Lost (1667)

An ▷ epic poem by ▷ John Milton, first published
in ten books in 1667, but reorganized and published
in 12 books in a second edition of 1674. The

composition of *Paradise Lost* was possibly begun in
the mid-1650s, but the idea for an epic based on
scriptural sources had, in all probability, occurred to
Milton at least as early as 1640, when the four drafts
of an outline ▷ tragedy were composed. These
drafts, contained in a Trinity College, Cambridge,
manuscript, indicate that, in original conception,
Paradise Lost (or, to give the poem its draft title *Adam
Unparadized*) was to have been a sacred drama, rather
than an epic. This hint at a dramatic origin, on the
lines of classical Greek tragedy, helps to explain the
undoubtedly dramatic qualities to be found in the
poem – for example the soliloquizing habits of Satan,
and the *perepeteias*, or discoveries, where new ironies
in the narrative are allowed to unfold.

The chief source of the poem is the ▷ Bible,
but the Bible as glossed and commented upon
by the Patristic (early Christian) authorities, and
by ▷ Protestant theologians. But also important
to Milton's project were the classical writers –
▷ Homer and ▷ Virgil – from whom Milton's
conception of 'epic' was principally inherited.
▷ Edmund Spenser's *The Faerie Queene* was also
vital to Milton's handling of language and imagery.
To these principle sources can be added the
epics of Ludovico Ariosto and Torquato Tasso,
▷ Ovid's ▷ *Metamorphoses*, the *De rerum natura* of
▷ Lucretius, and the once popular, though now little
read, *La Semaine* by Guillaume de Saluste du Bartas.
Once these sources have been remarked upon,
however, the possible progenitors of Milton's poem
still remain numberless, since *Paradise Lost* draws
upon the whole field of intellectual endeavour open
to a classically trained European scholar in the 17th
century.

For all that it is a poem rooted in Milton's literary
experience, it is also a poem of, and for, its times.
The poem's chief theme is rebellion – the rebellion
of ▷ Satan and his followers against God, and the
rebellion of Adam and Eve against divine law. Within
this sacred context, Milton sets himself the task of
justifying God's creational will to his 17th-century
readers. But, in confronting questions such as choice,
obedience and forms of government, Milton also
raises the issues of freedom, social relationships
and the quality and definition of power – whether
almighty, satanic or human. We can thus understand
the poem as confronting political questions which,
in the moment of its composition and eventual
publication following the English ▷ Civil War
and the ▷ Restoration of the monarchy, were of
real urgency both to the republican Milton and
his readers. That is not to say, as some of Milton's
commentators have claimed, that the poem operates
as a veiled ▷ allegory of events in mid-17th-century
England. But the issues which the protagonists in
Paradise Lost face are also issues which were at the
heart of contemporary political debate. To entwine
matters of theology and political theory was by no
means a strange grafting to Milton's contemporaries.
Religion and politics were inseparably twinned,
and *Paradise Lost* confronts that conjunction at
every point.

The history of the poem's critical reception since
the date of its publication is itself a commentary on

the history of English literary 'taste'. For all that 18th-century writers admired Milton's grand scheme, their admiration was tinged by a certain uneasiness. Both ▷ Joseph Addison and ▷ Samuel Johnson felt that Milton's achievement was undoubtedly immense, but that it was also an achievement which could not and should not be replicated. For the poets of the ▷ Romantic period – ▷ William Blake, Percy Bysshe Shelley, John Keats, and the ▷ William Wordsworth of *The Prelude* – *Paradise Lost* was read as a significant text in the history of the individual's struggle to identify him or herself within the political and social sphere. But rather than understand the poem as a theological epic, they tended to read it as a text of human liberty, with Satan, rather than God, as the focus of the poem's meaning. In the 20th century, following the re-evaluation in poetic taste prompted by W. B. Yeats, T. S. Eliot and F. R. Leavis, *Paradise Lost* was seen, once more, as a masterpiece of questionable stature. Was it, perhaps, removed from what Eliot and Leavis in particular cared to identify as the 'English tradition'? The debate initiated by Leavis and his followers was to be answered in a series of important accounts of the poem by C. S. Lewis, William Empson and Christopher Ricks. In the 1970s and 1980s attention has been refocused, by Marxist and feminist critics especially, on what have long been unexamined aspects of the poem: its treatment of patriarchal authority and its relationship to the continuing historical debate on the intellectual culture of the revolutionary period. At the same time, Milton's themes of language and identity have rendered the poem a fruitful text for psychoanalytic criticism. We might conclude, then, that, if perhaps the greatest achievement of the English literary ▷ Renaissance, *Paradise Lost* is also a text open to continuous re-reading and revision.

Bib: Carey, J. and Fowler, A. (eds.) *The Complete Poems of John Milton.*

Paradise Regained (1671)

An ▷ epic poem by ▷ John Milton in four books, it was first published (together with ▷ *Samson Agonistes*) in 1671. Begun after the publication of ▷ *Paradise Lost* in 1667, the poem can, in some sense, be thought of as a sequel to *Paradise Lost*. In particular, the poem's treatment of Christ, his resistance to temptation, and the redeeming nature of his ministry on earth, cast him in the theologically traditional role of the 'Second Adam' – a regenerative and redeeming force in the world.

Where *Paradise Lost*, however, was conceived along lines inherited from classical epic, *Paradise Regained* is in the form of the 'brief epic' in the style of the book of *Job*. The chief subject matter of the poem is the temptation of Christ in the wilderness, described in the gospel of St Luke.

Paradox

▷ Figures of speech.

Parliament

The name of the supreme law-making body of Great Britain and Northern Ireland. It has two parts – the House of Commons, whose members are elected, and the House of ▷ Lords, the majority of whose members still sit by hereditary right. 'House' in these expressions does not refer to a building, but is equivalent to 'assembly'; the Lords and Commons meet in different chambers of the same building, officially called the Palace of ▷ Westminster but colloquially known as the Houses of Parliament.

Parliament is a direct descendant of the medieval Magnum Concilium or Great Council, composed until the end of the 13th century of the chief landowners (nobility) of the realm, together with the bishops and principal abbots. To these Edward I added representatives of the Commons, *ie* elected members from the towns and smaller landowners; his purpose was to facilitate the imposition and collection of taxes. At first the Commons assembled with the nobility or lords, but in the 14th century they began to sit as separate assemblies.

In the 16th century the great nations of western Europe became despotisms; the kings of France and Spain ceased to summon their national assemblies, which under different names were equivalent to the English Parliament. In England, Henry VIII, though no less a despot, found his Parliament useful as an instrument in asserting the independence of the ▷ Church of England, since the authority of the Pope had long been unpopular in England. The growth in wealth of the English middle class and the financial weakness of the Crown combined with religious disagreements inherited from the ▷ Reformation to make the 17th century a period of epic struggle for power between Parliament and the kings. The successive stages of this conflict – open disagreement on policy under ▷ James I, the ▷ Civil Wars under ▷ Charles I, the republican interregnum followed by the restoration of the monarchy – culminated in the complete victory for Parliament (in which the Commons were now taking the leading role) following the deposition of ▷ James II in the revolution of 1688 (▷ Glorious Revolution).

This did not mean, however, that England became a parliamentary democracy; methods of election were corrupt, and the system did not correspond to the distribution of the population, with the result that throughout the 18th century power remained in the hands of the landed aristocracy, which controlled both Houses and usually tied the hands of the kings, but retained an alliance and close connections with the middle class.

▷ Scotland had her own Parliament until the Union of Parliaments in 1707, since when she has sent representatives to Westminster; ▷ Ireland sent members from 1801, when her own parliament was abolished; ▷ Wales never had her own parliament but has sent members to Westminster since union in 1535. In 1922, Irish representation at Westminster was reduced to Ulster, or Northern Ireland, since the rest of the country became an independent republic.

Since the 17th century, the Commons has been unquestionably the more important House; since the Parliament Act (1911) the legal powers of the House of Lords have been severely reduced, by that law and by later legislation.

Parnell, Thomas (1679–1718)
Member of the ▷ Tory clique associated with
the ministry of Harley and ▷ Bolingbroke and
participant with ▷ Jonathan Swift, ▷ Alexander
Pope, ▷ John Gay and ▷ John Arbuthnot, in the
shortlived ▷ Scriblerus Club. He translated a comic
epic then attributed to ▷ Homer, *Battle of the Frogs
and Mice*, into heroic ▷ couplets (1717). He also
composed moral and allegorical ▷ fables including
The Hermit, and the drearily sexist *Hesiod: or, The
Rise of Woman*, 'A creature fond and changing, fair
and vain,/ The creature woman, rises now to reign.'
His versification has a facile elegance which was
greatly valued at the time. In *A Night-Piece on Death*,
first published in his posthumous *Poems* (1722),
the characteristic tetrameter (▷ metre) couplet
of 17th-century reflective poetry is smoothed out
and polished, transforming religious intensity into
conventional piety: 'There pass with melancholy
State,/ By all the solemn Heaps of Fate,/ And
think, as softly-sad thou tread/ Above the venerable
Dead./ Time was, like thee they Life possest,/ And
Time shall be, that you shalt Rest.' Later graveyard
musings in the 1740s and 1750s add ▷ Gothic or
sentimental elaborations to Parnell's model. Parnell's
Essay on the Different Stiles of Poetry (1713) gives
a rigid exposition of the ▷ Augustan doctrine of
literary kinds.
Bib: Woodman, R., *Thomas Parnell*.

Parody
A literary form which constitutes a comic imitation
of a serious work, or of a serious literary form.
Thus ▷ Fielding's ▷ *Joseph Andrews* is partly a
parody of ▷ Richardson's ▷ *Pamela*, and ▷ Pope's
▷ *Rape of the Lock* is a parody of grand ▷ epic in
the style of ▷ Homer and ▷ Virgil. It is difficult
to draw a line between parody and ▷ burlesque;
the latter is more obviously comic in its style of
imitation.

Parties, Political
The English political scene has been dominated by
political parties since the mid-17th century. It was
not till the 19th century that political parties became
highly organized, and though there have seldom
been more than two important ones, these have not
always been the same. Nonetheless, there has been
a continuity in the history of parties sufficient to
give a long history to political loyalties. The principal
phases of party development are summarized as
follows:

1 *1640–1660: the ▷ Civil War and ▷ Interregnum*.
▷ Parliament, especially the ▷ House of Commons,
successfully led a rebellion against the king, and
established a republic. The division was partly
religious (▷ Puritan against ▷ Anglican), and partly
economic (the commercially progressive south and
east against the more traditional north and west). A
minority of the House of Commons and a majority
of the House of Lords sided with the king against
the rest of Parliament; the supporters of the former
were known as Royalists or ▷ Cavaliers, and the
supporters of the latter as Parliament Men, or
▷ Roundheads.

2 *1660–1714: rivalry of Tories and Whigs*. The
basic opposition represented by the Civil War
continued after the ▷ Restoration. The Tories
were strong upholders of the monarchy and of the
Church of England; the Whigs, without opposing the
continuance of either as institutions, laid emphasis
on the rights of Parliament and the dangers of
a re-establishment of Roman Catholicism with
monarchical despotism. The Whigs were twice
victorious – at the bloodless ▷ Glorious Revolution
of 1688 when they succeeded in deposing ▷ James
II in consequence of his Roman Catholicism, and
in 1714 when they prevented the succession of his
son as James III, on the same grounds. (▷ Whig and
Tory – for the origin of these names.)

3 *1714–1789: the Whig Oligarchy and the Tory
Revival*. Tories virtually disappeared from the
political scene until the accession of George III in
1760. During this period Parliament dominated the
monarchy, but the Whigs divided up into a number
of family alliances and political coteries. After 1760,
George III tried to revive royal power by creating a
party in Parliament to support it; these were called
the King's Friends or New Tories. The victory of the
colonists in the ▷ American War of Independence
(1776–83) and the king's insanity destroyed his
ambitions for reviving royal power, but other issues
confirmed the Tories in power from 1783 to 1830.
Chief among these new issues dividing the nation
were: (i) the ▷ French Revolution, which influenced
the Whigs in the direction of political reform and
the Tories in the direction of resistance to change;
(ii) the English ▷ Industrial Revolution, which
was rapidly expanding an urban middle class which
lacked political rights owing to the anachronistic
parliamentary electoral system; and (iii) new social
problems arising from the growth of a large urban
proletariat.

Pascal, Blaise (1623–62)
French religious philosopher and mathematician. In
1646 he became a devout adherent of the Jansenist
movement which had its headquarters at the nunnery
of Port-Royal near Paris. Jansenism (started by
Cornelius Jansen, 1585–1638) maintained, like the
Protestant predestinarians, that salvation through
the love of God was possible only for those whom
God pleased to love, *ie* an individual was predestined
to salvation or to damnation; however it also
emphasized the necessity of belonging to the Roman
Catholic Church. The movement was strongly
attacked by the ▷ Jesuit order, and when its leading
exponent, Antoine Arnauld, was being threatened
with dismissal from his academic post, Pascal wrote
Provincial Letters (1656) in its defence. This was his
first important work, a masterpiece of lucid, ironical
controversy; in particular, Pascal advocated moral
austerity and criticized Jesuit libertinism. His *Pensées*
('Thoughts' – pub. 1670) is his more famous work;
it consists of notes for a book on religion intended
to demonstrate the necessity of the religious life.
Though fragmentary, the notes have great aphoristic
power; with an intellect as powerful and a style as
lucid as that of ▷ Descartes, Pascal criticizes the
earlier philosopher's notion of the supreme power of

human reason, and shows the limitations of reason in dealing with ultimate mysteries.

Pastoral

A form of literature originally developed by the ancient Greeks and Romans in the ▷ idylls of the former (*eg* those of ▷ Theocritus) and the ▷ eclogues of the latter (*eg* ▷ Virgil's). Ancient pastoral idealized the Greek state of Arcadia which had a rustic population of shepherds and herdsmen. The ▷ Renaissance of the 16th century, deeply interested in the literature of the Greeks and Romans, revived the pastoral mode; the earliest forms of it date back in Italian literature to the 15th century, but it was the romance *Arcadia* (1504), by the Italian poet Sannazaro, which was particularly influential throughout Europe. The appeal of the pastoral kind of literature was partly to human wishfulness – the desire to conceive of circumstances in which the complexity of human problems could be reduced to its simplest elements: the shepherds and shepherdesses of pastoral are imagined as having no worries, and they live in an ideal climate with no serious physical calamities; love and death, and making songs and music about these experiences, are their only preoccupations. Another function of pastoral, however, was as a vehicle of moral and social criticism; the shepherds and shepherdesses sought the pleasures of nature and despised or were innocent of the corrupting luxury of courts and cities. Finally, pastoral presented a means of offering, allegorically, thinly disguised tributes of praise and flattery to real people whom the poet admired or wanted to please. The satirical, moral and eulogistic functions of Renaissance pastoral all tended to make it allegorical, since it was through ▷ allegory that the poet could most safely make his criticisms felt, and could most eloquently convey his praise. Allegory also suited the neo-Platonic, idealizing cast of mind so characteristic of 16th-century writers. When we remember that the tradition of romantic love was one of the most ardently pursued inheritances from the ▷ Middle Ages, and that the circumstances of pastoral lent themselves to its expression, it is not surprising that the pastoral mode was so extensively cultivated in 16th-century Europe. To England it came late, by way of influences from France, Spain and Italy, but it lasted longer; it was especially pervasive in the last quarter of the 16th century, and continued till the mid-17th; there was a minor revival early in the 18th century.

Of the various forms of pastoral, the prose romance had the shortest life, and ended with the 16th century; the last pastoral drama was Elkanah Settle's *Pastor Fido* (1677). In non-dramatic poetry, pastoral lasted much longer. However, the most famous poems in 17th-century pastoral are Milton's: *L'Allegro* (1631) and *Il Penseroso* (1631) and his ▷ elegy *Lycidas* (1637). In the 18th century, ▷ Pope's early *Pastorals* (1709) were a small masterpiece influenced by Virgil, but his ▷ *Windsor Forest* (1713) is a more impressive work, using pastoral to extol the Peace of Utrecht (1713) which ended the long War of the ▷ Spanish Succession, and to celebrate peace, prosperity and civilization.

Classical pastoral has not been practised notably since the first half of the 18th century. However, the critic William Empson (*Some Versions of Pastoral*, 1935) sometimes uses the term more widely than classical pastoral denotes. Even so, pastoral – even of the non-classical kind – is not synonymous with 'nature poetry' or poetry of country life.

Pathetic fallacy

▷ Figures of speech.

Patronage in literature

A system by which the king or a nobleman afforded protection and livelihood to an artist, in return for which the artist paid him special honour, or returned him service in the form of entertaining his household and his guests. The great period for this system was the 16th century, but patronage continued to be an important cultural and social institution until the end of the 18th century. After the 18th century, through ▷ circulating libraries and wide circulation of periodicals, writers could rely on support from the general public; from the 16th to 18th centuries failure to secure a patron might mean oblivion, or at least starvation, as in the case of ▷ Chatterton. By the 18th century, thanks largely to the increased reading public and the growth of periodicals like Addison's ▷ *Spectator* and Jonson's ▷ *Rambler*, patronage was obsolescent, and chiefly required when a writer of slender means, such as ▷ Samuel Johnson, attempted a major task, such as his ▷ *Dictionary*. Johnson's famous letter to ▷ Lord Chesterfield is a classic example of rebuke to a neglectful patron. Political parties and leaders by this time provided extensive patronage, *eg* Harley and the Tories to ▷ Defoe. Many writers gained a livelihood through the system by which the universities and landlords inherited from the monasteries (dissolved in the 1530s) the right to appoint parish priests.

Peachum, Polly

Character in ▷ Gay's ▷ *The Beggar's Opera*. She is one of the wives of the bigamous ▷ Macheath. When, at the end, he is reprieved from hanging, he throws in his lot with her, ostensibly in preference to the others.

Penal system

As in most societies without efficient police forces, punishments were severe in England until the establishment of the Metropolitan Police by Robert Peel and his reform of the penal system between 1823 and 1827. They tended to become more severe as society became more settled and prosperous, in order to deter crime, especially robbery, by terror, so that by 1800 there were 200 offences punishable by hanging. However, the penal laws were not consistently formulated or applied. The normal form of capital punishment was by hanging, though decapitation, as more dignified, was used for the aristocracy. In the 17th century, when the colonies in America had become established, transportation was often used instead; after the loss of the colonies in 1783, Australia was substituted (▷ Botany Bay). Transportation was finally abolished in 1864.

Execution was public, and watching it a favourite amusement, until in the mid-19th century public hanging was abolished.

For minor offences, whipping was a common punishment, and it too was public until the 19th century, to increase the disgrace. Confinement in the stocks or the ▷ pillory – wooden structures with holes for the head, the legs and the arms – was used for some offences, and there were also, of course, imprisonment and fines. Ducking in a pond or river was reserved for women who had given offence by their speech.

Torture was legal to extract evidence until it was abolished in the 18th century. Mutilation – cutting out the tongue or cutting off the ears, nose or hand – was a penalty for certain offences, especially of a treasonable nature, and it survived in law until 1870, but was not used after the 17th century.
▷ Prisons.

Penkethman (Pinkethman), William (?–1725)
Actor, singer, dancer, manager. Penkethman is believed to have begun acting in 1692 with the ▷ United Company at ▷ Drury Lane where he remained for most of his career. Penkethman's forte as an actor was comedy, and he was often asked to speak prologues and epilogues. Much of his humour was conveyed through clowning and mobile facial expression, although he was accused, on numerous occasions, of over-acting, and ad-libbing to excess.

Pennington, Sarah, Lady (d1783)
Author. She married Sir Joseph Pennington, a gentleman of Yorkshire, in 1746, and separated from him in acrimonious circumstances twelve years later. Thereafter she drew on her own experiences in writing conduct-books (▷ conduct literature), letters and ▷ epistolary fiction. These include *An Unfortunate Mother's Advice to her Absent Daughters; in a Letter to Miss Pennington* (1761), her most popular and successful work, *Letters on Different Subjects* (1766), and *The Child's Conductor* (1777).
Bib: Todd, J., (ed.), *A Dictionary of British and American Women Writers 1660–1800*.

Pentameter
In English verse, usually five iambic feet, *ie* with the stress coming on every second syllable. The line has been the commonest in use since Chaucer, *eg* the *Prologue to the Canterbury Tales*:

He knew the taverns well in every town.

The commonest English uses of the iambic pentameter are in ▷ blank verse and in ▷ heroic couplets.
▷ Metre.

Pepys, Samuel (1633–1703)
Diarist. He was an industrious and highly efficient official in the Admiralty Office, and a man who had musical culture and persistent, if amateurish, scientific and literary interests. As secretary to his cousin, Edward Montagu, Earl of Sandwich, he was aboard the fleet which brought ▷ Charles II back to

England at the ▷ Restoration in 1660. His official position in the Admiralty gave him the confidence of the king's brother, James Duke of York, who was Lord High Admiral, and an opportunity for direct observation of court life. He was elected to ▷ Parliament and knew the world of politics, was a friend of a number of leading writers and musicians, and held distinguished appointments in the ▷ City of London. He was thus centrally placed to observe his age, and with all his seriousness he was pleasure-loving and witty.

His diary (kept 1660–9) is a unique document not only because he brought to it these qualities and advantages (many of which were shared by his friend the diarist ▷ John Evelyn) but because he kept it for his eye alone, and consequently wrote with unusual candour and objectivity. To prevent his servants and family from prying into it, he used a kind of shorthand cypher, which was not interpreted until 1825, when part of the diary was first published. The first more or less complete edition was in 1896. Of all diaries in English, it has the greatest appeal to the general reader, as well as having outstanding value for the historian.
▷ Diaries.
Bib: Lives by J. R. Tanner, A. Bryant, and J. H. Wilson. Letters edited by J. R. Tanner, A. Bryant, and J. H. Wilson. Marburg, C., *Mr Pepys and Mr Evelyn*; Latham, R. and Mathews, W., (eds.), *Diary*.

Percy, Thomas (1729–1811)
Clergyman and antiquarian; he became Bishop of Dromore in 1782. Along with ▷ James Macpherson, ▷ Horace Walpole and ▷ Thomas Gray, Percy was a pioneer of the literary exoticism which flourished in the later 18th century. In 1761 he published *Hau Kiou Choaan*, a translation of a Portuguese version of a Chinese romance, and in 1763 *Five Pieces of Runic Poetry*, translated from Latin versions of Old Icelandic texts. His most influential work, *Reliques of Ancient English Poetry* (1765), includes poems from a 17th-century manuscript now in the British Museum and known as 'The Percy Folio'. This manuscript contains many ballads of ancient origin which Percy edited according to 18th-century taste, adding also some modern compositions in the archaic style. Although his editorial approach was not that of a modern purist, the volume marks a significant phase in the revival of interest in early poetry, and exerted a strong influence on later poets such as ▷ Thomas Chatterton, Sir Walter Scott, ▷ William Wordsworth and ▷ Samuel Taylor Coleridge.
Bib: Davis, B. H., *Thomas Percy*.

Peregrine Pickle, The Adventures of (1751)
A novel by ▷ Tobias Smollett. The hero is an adventurer seeking his fortune in England and on the Continent. Its form is a succession of episodes without a uniting structure, depending for its interest on the vigour of depiction of the characters and incidents. It contains famous eccentric characters, especially the retired sailor and his associates, Commodore Trunnion, Lieutenant Hatchway, and Tom Pipes. The episodes give opportunity for much

social and political satire, from English village life upwards, and show an awareness of social structure like that found in the novels of ▷ Henry Fielding. Trunnion and his circle were an inspiration to ▷ Laurence Sterne's Uncle Toby in ▷ *Tristram Shandy*.

Perfectibilism

The optimistic doctrine that individuals and society are capable of achieving perfection in living. The ▷ French Revolution, with its reliance on reason for the solution of all human problems, encouraged perfectibilism, and the philosopher ▷ William Godwin was an English example.

Periodicals

▷ Reviews and periodicals.

Perrault, Charles (1628–1703)

French author, known in England chiefly for his collection of fairy tales published in 1697, *Histoires et Contes du Temps Passé* (Stories and Tales from the Past) subtitled *Contes de ma Mère l'Oie* (Tales of Mother Goose). They were translated into English by Robert Samber (1729), and have remained the best known fairy tales among English children. They were retold by Perrault from popular sources, and are as follows: *Sleeping Beauty*; *Red Riding Hood*; *Blue Beard*; *Puss in Boots*; *The Fairy*; *Cinderella*; *Riquet with the Tuft*; *Hop o' my Thumb*. Several of them provide the themes for modern Christmas ▷ pantomimes.

Personification

▷ Figures of speech.

Philemon and Baucis

A tale by the Roman poet ▷ Ovid, from the eighth book of his ▷ *Metamorphoses*. They are an aged peasant couple and very poor, but they give hospitality to the gods Zeus and Hermes, disguised as travellers. In reward, their cottage is transformed into a temple, of which they are made priest and priestess; they are also permitted to die in the same hour, and after death they are transformed into trees with intertwining boughs. ▷ Dryden's version (1693) of Ovid's poem is one of his best ▷ translations; ▷ Swift also wrote a poem on the subject (1709).

Philips, Ambrose (1675?–1749)

Poet. Associate of ▷ Joseph Addison and ▷ Richard Steele, and member of the Whig clique which frequented ▷ Button's Coffee-house. His ▷ couplet epistle, describing a snow scene addressed from Copenhagen to the ▷ Earl of Dorset, is a brilliantly evocative work, which was admired by ▷ Alexander Pope. His *Pastorals* (1709) were published in the same year as those of Pope, and the coincidence prompted a theoretical debate, which now seems quite arid, concerning the correct understanding of the form. Philips, it was felt, preserved the authentic rusticity of the ancient genre, while Pope polished it into a modern elegance. When the Buttonian ▷ Thomas Tickell pointedly praised Philip' pastorals in *The Guardian*, Pope submitted an anonymous piece *On Pastorals* to the same journal, in which with straight-faced irony he prefers Philips's poems to his own. The irony was so fine that, as ▷ Samuel Johnson relates, 'though Addison discovered it, Steele was deceived, and was afraid of displeasing Pope by publishing his paper'. Philips also edited a periodical, *The Freethinker* (1718–21), wrote several plays, Pindaric ▷ odes, and poems addressed to children, whose archness led his contemporary Henry Carey to attack him in *Namby-Pamby* (1725), from which the epithet in current use derives.

Philips, John (1676–1709)

Poet and physician. A pioneer of poetry in ▷ Miltonic ▷ blank verse. *The Splendid Shilling* (1701), described by ▷ Joseph Addison as 'the finest burlesque poem in the British language' presents a rueful self-portrait of the down-at-heel poet, without a shilling to his name. 'But I, whom griping penury surrounds,/ And Hunger, sure Attendant upon Want,/ With scanty Offals, and small acid Tiff/ (Wretched Repast!) my meagre Corps sustain:/ Then Solitary walk, or doze at home/ In Garret vile, and with a warming puff/ Regale chill'd Fingers'. The poet hides in a cupboard from a dun, then writes moody poems about disappointed love, and the work ends with an ▷ epic simile comparing the splitting of his ageing breeches to a shipwreck in the Aegean. Philips' obvious delight in self-dramatization gives the poem permanent appeal. He also wrote a serious epic, *Blenheim* (1705), but his most influential work was *Cyder* (1708), a ▷ Georgic poem in two books blending landscape description (often focused on Hereford, where he practised medicine), historical and philosophical reflection, and detailed advice on orchard-management. Its assured handling of blank verse, and its easy discursiveness of tone, were emulated and developed further by ▷ James Thomson in his *Seasons*.

Philips, Katherine (1632–1664)

Welsh poet and dramatist working during the Interregnum (1649–1660), known as 'Orinda'. Her parents were Presbyterians, and in 1647 she married James Philips, a supporter of ▷ Oliver Cromwell (1599–1658). Katherine Philips herself was a Royalist, and her poems record the difference between her own views and those of her husband. She was fluent in several languages, and a prolific writer. Thus far, 116 poems, five verse ▷ translations and translations of two plays comprise her canon. The performance of her translation of French dramatist ▷ Pierre Corneille's *Pompey* in 1663 make her the first woman to have a play staged professionally in London. In 1651, her poems began to circulate in manuscript, and they were first published in 1651, prefixed to the poems of ▷ Henry Vaughan and Thomas Cartwright. In 1664 an unauthorized edition of her poems was published, but an authorized edition appeared in 1667. Philips' 'Society of Friendship', a correspondence circle, seems to have begun in 1651 and lasted until 1666, and included Henry Vaughan, among others. Within the circle, each member was assigned a name from classical literature, and Philips was dubbed 'Matchless Orinda'. Her letters to Sir

Charles Cotterell were published as *Letters from Orinda to Poliarchus* (1705). She also corresponded with ▷ Dorothy Osborne. When she died of smallpox, her translation of *Horace* was unfinished. Philips was praised by her contemporaries as the ideal woman poet because of her modest choice of subjects (compare, for example, ▷ Aphra Behn). The majority of her poetry is written for particular occasions or persons, and in many of them she transforms the conventional language of courtship and applies it to friendships between women: 'Our hearts are mutuall victims lay'd, / While they (such power in friendship ly's) / are Altars, Priests, and off rings made, / And each heart which thus kindly dy's / Grows deathless by the sacrifise.'

▷ Polwhele, Elizabeth

Bib: Greer, G., *et al.*, Kissing the Rod; Hobby, E., *Virtue of Necessity*.

Philosophes

▷ *L'Encyclopédie*.

Picaresque

From the Spanish *picaro*, 'rogue'. The term is especially applied to a form of prose fiction originating in Spain in the 16th century, dealing with the adventures of rogues.

The first distinctive example in English is Thomas Nashe's *Unfortunate Traveller*, 1594. In the 18th century, examples include ▷ Daniel Defoe's ▷ *Moll Flanders*, ▷ Henry Fielding's ▷ *Jonathan Wild* and ▷ Tobias Smollett's *The Adventures of Ferdinand Count Fathom*. Other traditions combine with the picaresque: the mock romance in the tradition of *Don Quixote*, and the tradition of religious pilgrimage (cf. ▷ *The Pilgrim's Progress*).

Picturesque, Cult of the

A term used in the late 18th and early 19th centuries to describe a certain kind of scenery, where cultivation was employed to produce artificially 'wild' nature. Landscape gardeners incorporated 'wildernesses' into their prospects, often with fake ruins suggesting the decay of classical civilization. The writer most identified with the 'picturesque' was William Gilpin (1724–1804), who wrote a series of illustrated picturesque tours. ▷ Jane Austen in *Mansfield Park* (1814) parodies the cult.

Pierrot

A character in French ▷ pantomime plays, familiar also in English pantomimes and similar entertainments. His face and dress are always white, and the dress is loose like that of a circus clown. Originally he was a comic, playful figure, but he is often made to perform pathetic or romantic roles.

Pilgrim's Progress, The

A prose ▷ allegory by ▷ John Bunyan. *The Pilgrim's Progress from this World to that which is to come* is in two parts: Part I (1678) tells of the religious conversion of Christian, and of his religious life – conceived as a pilgrimage – in this world, until he comes to the River of Death, and the Heavenly City which lies beyond it; Part II (1684) describes the subsequent conversion of his wife Christiana and their children, and their similar journey with a group of friends.

Both parts contain episodes which symbolize real life experiences: thus, Christian, soon after the way has been pointed out to him, falls into the ▷ Slough of Despond – a bog which represents the depression which overcomes the new convert when he has passed the stage of first enthusiasm; later he has to pass through phases of spiritual despair and terror, symbolized by the ▷ Valleys of Humiliation and the Shadow of Death; he has to face the derision and anger of public opinion in the town of Vanity Fair, and so on. Christiana and the children have an easier time; perhaps Bunyan wished to show that God in his mercy shields the weaker pilgrims, or perhaps that public opinion is harsher to pioneers than to those that follow them.

The 'pioneer pilgrims' – Christian and his associates – belong to the ▷ Puritan sects, of one of which Bunyan was himself a member, who were undergoing persecution in the reign of ▷ Charles II, especially during the earlier years, when English society was in strong reaction against the previous Puritan regime of ▷ Oliver Cromwell. Yet *The Pilgrim's Progress* is much more than merely a dramatization of the Puritan spirit. By its allegorical content, it is related to the tradition of the allegorical sermon which, in village churches, survived the ▷ Reformation of the 16th century, and some of the adventures (Christian's fight with Apollyon, the Castle of Giant Despair, the character of Greatheart) are related in spirit to popular versions of medieval and 16th-century romances, surviving in the ▷ chapbooks. These aspects give it a close relation with popular traditions of culture to an extent unequalled by any other major literary work. Another element of popular culture shows in Bunyan's assimilation of the English translation of the ▷ Bible, and this reminds us that for many households the Bible was the only book constantly read, and that during the next century Bunyan's allegory took its place beside it. Still more important than these links with the past is Bunyan's anticipation of the kind of vision of human nature which in the 18th and 19th centuries was to find its scope in the novel: his allegorized characters do not, as in past allegories, merely simplify human virtues and vices, but reveal how an individual destiny can be shaped by the predominance in a personality of an outstanding quality, good or bad; the adventures of the pilgrims are conditioned by the differences of these qualities. Thus, Christian and Faithful, fellow pilgrims, have radically different temperaments and correspondingly different experiences.

▷ Celestial City; City of Destruction; Doubting Castle; Vanity Fair.

Pilkington, Laetitia (c 1708–1750)

Irish poet and memoirist, born to parents of Dutch origin in ▷ Dublin. In 1725 she married the Reverend Matthew Pilkington and met satirist ▷ Jonathan Swift and others. Swift helped Matthew Pilkington to a chaplaincy in London and when Mrs Pilkington followed she found that her husband was involved with an actress. In 1733 she returned alone to Dublin, already regarded as a woman of dubious character. In 1738 Pilkington divorced her for adultery. Pilkington did not supply much maintenance, and she and her children moved to London, where she tried to live by her writing. She began with the subject of masculine infidelity in *The Statues: Or, the Trial of Constancy* (1739) and accompanied writing with wild living. She found it hard to survive by her pen, and was imprisoned for debt, escaping to open a bookshop in St James's. She returned to Dublin in 1747, and began to publish her *Memoirs* featuring stories of Swift and ▷ Samuel Richardson, some of which settled old scores.

Her other publications include: *An Excursory View on the Present State of Things and Memoirs* (1748–1754).

Pillory and stocks

The pillory was a form of punishment in use for small offences from the early Middle Ages until its abolition in 1837. It consisted of a rectangular wooden frame raised above the ground; the pilloried man stood behind the frame, and his head and hands were thrust through holes in the horizontal bar at the top. He was often made to stand in the pillory throughout the day, and was the target for insults and missiles.

The stocks were a similar instrument. The victim was seated behind the frame, and his legs were thrust through holes in a bar along the bottom of it. Sometimes his head and his hands were also exposed through holes in another horizontal bar higher up. The stocks survived longer than the pillory; they were last used in 1865.

▷ Penal system.

Pinckney, Eliza Lucas (c1722–1793)

North American letter-writer. Born in Antigua, West Indies, and educated in England, she was the daughter of wealthy South Carolinan plantation owners. An astute and imaginative businesswoman, she managed the family plantations in the West Indies beginning in 1740. Her experiments to improve the cultivation of indigo were major contributions to that crop's importance in the West Indian and American South's economies. The *Journal and Letters of Eliza Lucas* details her life in the West Indies, her experiments with indigo, her attitudes towards marriage and her religious beliefs. After a life in which she continued her various agricultural experimentations and raised a family in South Carolina, she died in Philadelphia.

Pindar (5th century BC)

Greek poet. He is famous for his lyrical ▷ odes, *ie* poems to be sung to the accompaniment of musical instruments and dancing. The odes had a strong religious tone and were designed for solemn occasions, including sporting celebrations. The fact that their composition was influenced by their musical and dance accompaniment gives the odes an appearance of irregularity. This, and the loftiness of their emotion, made them tempting models, from the 17th to 19th centuries, for English poets when they

were writing on themes of deep emotional power and felt the need of an ample form which would allow them considerable licence in the treatment of the subject. Pindar's odes were not really as unsystematic as they seemed, however, and many English poems in 'Pindarics' have only a superficial resemblance to the kind of ode that Pindar wrote. Notable examples are ▷ Dryden's *Alexander's Feast*, and *Ode to the Memory of Anne Killigrew*.

Piozzi, Hester Thrale

▷ Thrale, Hester Lynch.

Pitt (the Elder), William, Earl of Chatham (1708–78)

English politician. He led the government during the major part of the ▷ Seven Years' War, during which the British won Canada from the French, and established themselves as the dominant political influence on the subcontinent of India. The successes of this war are usually attributed to Pitt's statesmanship.

Pitt (the Younger), William (1759–1806)

Politician. The son of ▷ William Pitt, Earl of Chatham. He led the government from 1783 to 1801, and again in the years 1804–6. He first became Prime Minister when he was only 24, at a time when George III's government had been deeply discredited by defeat in the ▷ American War of Independence, brought to an end by the Treaty of Versailles, 1783. Moreover, politics were thoroughly corrupted by various systems of bribery, and ▷ Parliament represented only the interests of various sections of the privileged classes. Pitt was as prudent a statesman as his father had been a dynamic one, and he was famous for his strict integrity. His first ministry was one of cautious reconstruction such as Britain needed for the long wars with France (War of the ▷ French Revolution, 1793–1801, and the ▷ Napoleonic War, 1803–15). Politically he was conservative 'Tory', ▷ Whig and Tory), but he was the first political leader to rely on public opinion as expressed in the electoral constituencies instead of on more or less bribed backing among Members of Parliament.

Pix, Mary (1666–1709)

Dramatist and novelist, one of the so-called 'Female Wits' satirized in a play of that name in 1696. Pix's first play, a heroic tragedy called *Ibrahim, the Thirteenth Emperor of the Turks*, was produced at ▷ Drury Lane in 1696, the same year as her novel, *The Inhuman Cardinal, Or: Innocence Betrayed*, and a comedy following ▷ Aphra Behn, *The Spanish Wives*. Another comedy, *The Innocent Mistress*, was staged at ▷ Lincoln's Inn Fields in the following year. Later plays include *The Deceiver Deceived* (1697), *The False Friend* (1699), *The Beau Defeated* (1700), *The Double Distress* (1701), and *The Conquest of Spain* (1705); Pix wrote a dozen plays in all, of which the comedies are generally considered far superior to the tragedies.
Bib: Steeves, E. L. (ed.), *The Plays of Mary Pix and Catharine Trotter*; Clark, C., *Three Augustan Women Playwrights*; Morgan, F. (ed.), *The Female Wits*.

Plague of London, The Great

A particularly severe epidemic of bubonic plague which struck London in 1664–5. Epidemics had been frequent, either of the bubonic plague or of equally deadly diseases, ever since the Black Death of the 14th century, and several times caused the compulsory closing of theatres (for fear of infection) during the lifetime of ▷ Shakespeare, but this epidemic, at its height, killed over 68,000 of London's population of 460,000 in one year. It was already declining when the ▷ Great Fire of London in 1666 helped to end it.

▷ *Journal of the Plague Year, A.*

Plain Dealer, The (1676)

Dark comedy by ▷ William Wycherley, based on ▷ Molière's *Le Misanthrope*. Manly, an 'honest' but dour sea captain, has put his trust in the duplicitous Vernish and brittle Olivia, to whom he has been betrothed. In his absence the two have secretly married, and she has appropriated the fortune that he had entrusted to her care. Manly returns from the Dutch Wars and, on learning of her marriage to an unknown man, determines to revenge himself on her by seducing her, with the help of his page. Also unknown to him, the page is a woman in disguise, Fidelia, who has loved him and gained employment with him in order to be near him. The 'youth' reluctantly agrees to address Olivia on Manly's behalf, but Olivia becomes attracted to Fidelia, and attempts to make love to her, in a scene recalling the one between Viola and Olivia in ▷ Shakespeare's *Twelfth Night*. Manly overhears Olivia acknowledge that she deceived him deliberately. Later Vernish witnesses an assignation between the women and on discovering Fidelia's sex, attempts to rape her, but is interrupted. In the final scene, Fidelia is wounded in a skirmish, defending Manly from Vernish, who is revealed as Olivia's husband. Fidelia's true identity, and status as an heiress, are also made known, and she and Manly are united. A subplot involves the litigations of the Widow Blackacre and her doltish son Jerry. The play was considered by ▷ Dryden to be Wycherley's best, and from it he derived the frequent appellation 'Manly Wycherley'. The play survived to the late 18th century, when it disappeared from the stage, but has been revived (several times) in the 20th century, including the 1988–9 production by the RSC.

Plato (?428–?348 BC)

Greek philosopher. He was a follower of the Athenian philosopher ▷ Socrates, and his dialogues represent conversations in which Socrates takes the lead. The most famous of these 'Socratic' dialogues are *Protagoras, Gorgias, Phaedo, Symposium, ▷ Republic, Phaedrus, Timaeus*. His longest work, the *Laws*, does not include Socrates as a character. His central conception is that beyond the world of transient material phenomena lies another eternal world of ideal forms which the material world represents in the form of imitations. His figure for this in the *Republic* is that men in the material world are like people watching shadows moving on the wall of a cave; they see only these shadows and not

the realities which cast the shadows. Plato is one of the two most influential philosophers in European thought, the other one being ▷ Aristotle, who was at first his pupil.

▷ Platonism and neo-Platonism.

Platonism and neo-Platonism

The term 'Platonism' is applied to the school of thought derived immediately from the Greek philosopher ▷ Plato. 'Neo-Platonism' names schools of thought which adapted his philosophy by adding to or modifying it. Two main periods of revival of Plato's thought are described as neo-Platonism: 1 that initiated by the pagan Plotinus (3rd century AD) in Rome, and at first a revival of Christianity, into which it was to some extent carried by St Augustine of Hippo (345–430) when he was converted; 2 that which Marsilio Ficino initiated by his studies of Platonic philosophy in Florence (15th century). The 17th-century group known as the ▷ Cambridge Platonists were true Platonists rather than neo-Platonists.

1 Plato had taught that beyond the world of transient phenomena that surrounds us is that of permanent and imperishable ideas, but he relied on logical reason for the development of his philosophy. Neo-Platonism added a religious aspect which depended on revelation; it derived this influence from other philosophies and from eastern religions. The elements that St Augustine transferred to Christianity remained dominant until the 13th century when Platonic influence was succeeded by that of ▷ Aristotle.

2 16th-century neo-Platonism in Italy revived the ancient neo-Platonist conception that the universe was peopled by many supernatural beings, and maintained that these existed in addition to the angels and devils allowed by Christian doctrine. It also taught that men, being essentially spirits, could, by the acquisition of wisdom and virtue, immensely increase their power and knowledge, and could control for their good and wise purposes the non-human supernatural spirits. Thus arose the idea of 'the Mage', or master of high magic; in ▷ Shakespeare's *The Tempest*, Prospero is such a neo-Platonic Mage, and Ariel is a spirit such as the neo-Platonists believed could be controlled and used.

The ordering of the universe into a hierarchical structure governed by intelligence in ▷ Milton's ▷ *Paradise Lost* is also neo-Platonic. The Platonic ideal waned in the course of the 17th and 18th centuries, although its influence is shown in the work of some poets, *eg* ▷ Collins' *Ode on the Poetical Character* (1746).

Plautus, Titus Maccius (?254–184 BC)

Roman comic dramatist. His comedies are based on situation and intrigue; they had a high reputation in his own time, but unlike the other outstanding Roman comedian, ▷ Terence, he was ignored during the Middle Ages. In the 16th century his reputation revived, and his style of comedy was emulated throughout Western Europe.

The influence of Plautus, as of Terence is pervasive in many comedies of the late 17th and 18th

centuries, *eg* plays by ▷ Dryden, ▷ Fielding and
many others.
   ▷ New Comedy.

Play on words
▷ Figures of speech.

Pleonasm
The use of unnecessary words in the expression
of a meaning, *eg* in the phrase 'a deceitful fraud',
'deceitful' is pleonastic, since a fraud is by definition
a kind of deceit.

Pliny
There were two Roman writers of this name, Pliny
the elder (1st century AD) was the author of a famous
Natural History, in which fantastic myths about
animals are mixed up with some sound early science.
His nephew, Pliny the younger, was the author of
letters which are an interesting source of information
on the ancient Roman world under the Emperor
Trajan, especially about the treatment of Christians.

Plotinus
▷ Platonism and neo-Platonism.

Plutarch (AD 46–?120)
Greek biographer and moralist. He is chiefly famous
for his 46 *Parallel Lives* in which he matches 23
famous men from Greek history with 23 famous
Romans. The *Lives* were presented in an English
version by Sir Thomas North in 1579; North did
not translate them from the original Greek but
from the French version by Jacques Amyot. North's
book was as popular and influential in England as
Amyot's was in France; Plutarch's conception of the
great and many-sided man was in harmony with the
16th-century conception of the public virtues and
personal accomplishments that should go to make
the full man and the perfect courtier. The *Lives*,
in North's version, were used as a source-book by
dramatists – notably by Shakespeare in *Julius Caesar,
Antony and Cleopatra* and *Coriolanus*. Plutarch also
wrote a number of treatises on moral and physical
subjects known as the *Moralia* – a precedent for the
essays of ▷ Bacon as well as the very different ones
of the great French essayist ▷ Montaigne.
   ▷ Translation.

Poet Laureate
The laurel, also known as the bay (*Laurus nobilis*),
was sacred to Apollo, the god most associated with
the arts. The Greeks honoured Olympic victors and
triumphant generals, by crowning them with a wreath
of laurel leaves. In the 15th century the universities
of ▷ Oxford and ▷ Cambridge gave the title
'laureate', meaning worthy of laurels, to various poets
including John Skelton, and it was later given to
court poets like Ben Jonson. In 1668 the title gained
its modern status when ▷ John Dryden was granted
a stipend as a member of the royal household
charged with writing court odes and celebrating
state occasions in verse. Since the time of Dryden
the laureateship has been awarded to a few poets of
lasting worth and to many of mediocre talent, chosen

for reasons of fashion or political acceptability. The
list is as follows: ▷ Thomas Shadwell, ▷ Nahum
Tate, ▷ Nicholas Rowe, Laurence Eusden,
▷ Colley Cibber, William Whitehead, ▷ Thomas
Warton, Henry James Pye, ▷ Robert Southey,
▷ William Wordsworth, Alfred Tennyson, Alfred
Austin, Robert Bridges, John Masefield, Cecil Day
Lewis, John Betjeman and Ted Hughes. Poets who
were offered the laureateship but declined it include
▷ Thomas Gray, Sir Walter Scott, Samuel Rogers,
William Morris and Philip Larkin.

Poetics
A treatise on poetry by the Greek philosopher
▷ Aristotle. He had already written a dialogue *On
the Poets*, which has only survived in fragments,
and a treatise on rhetoric; knowledge of both is
to some extent assumed in the *Poetics*. The *Poetics*
is considered to have been an unpublished work,
resembling notes for lectures addressed to students
rather than a full worked-up treatise for the general
public, like the *Rhetoric*. This accounts for its
fragmentary character. Thus Aristotle distinguishes
▷ tragedy, ▷ epic and ▷ comedy as the chief
kinds of poetry, but comedy is practically omitted
from fuller discussion. ▷ Lyric, though it is referred
to, is not included among the chief kinds, either
because Aristotle considered it to be part of music
or because he considered it to be taken up into
tragedy. The main part of the work is therefore
concerned with tragedy and epic – the former more
extensively than the latter. Aristotle's method is
essentially descriptive rather than prescriptive; that
is to say, he is more concerned with what had been
done by acknowledged masters such as ▷ Homer
and ▷ Sophocles, than with what ought to be done
according to so-called 'rules'.

   Nonetheless, the *Poetics* became the most
authoritatively influential of all critical works.
Its dominance in European critical thought from
the 16th to the 18th centuries was partly due
to its influence on the most widely read of the
Roman critics, ▷ Horace, and partly because it
was rediscovered at the end of the 15th century
when the ▷ Renaissance was at its height, and the
spirit of the Greek and Latin writers was felt to be
civilization itself. In England, the important critics
such as ▷ Dryden and ▷ Jonson regarded Aristotle
and neo-Aristotelianism with strong respect rather
than total reverence, but the complete submission
of minor critics such as ▷ Thomas Rymer is
exemplified by his obtuse treatment of Shakespeare's
Othello in the essay *Short View of Tragedy* (1692).

   Today the *Poetics* remains one of the most
outstanding works of European thought. Critics
still use Aristotle's terminology in classifying poetic
forms; his theory of art as imitation (different
from ▷ Plato's) is still the starting-point of much
aesthetic discussion; such terms as 'harmatia', for the
element in human nature which makes it vulnerable
to tragedy; 'peripeteia', for the reversal of fortunes
common in tragic narrative; and 'katharsis', for the
effect of tragedy on the mind of the audience, have
been useful for a long time.
   ▷ Classical unities; Mimesis; Neo-classical.

Polwhele, Elizabeth (?1651–1691)

English Restoration dramatist. Polwhele seems to have written three plays, *Elysium* (now lost) the rhymed tragedy *The Faythfull Virgins* (manuscript), and the comedy *The Frolicks*, performed at the Duke's Theatre in 1671 (▷ Dorset Garden Theatre). The play features a rake, Rightwit, who is the father of illegitimate children, and Claribell, a witty heroine. With ▷ Katherine Philips and ▷ Frances Boothby, she was one of the women writing for the stage in the early Restoration period.
Bib: Milhouse, J. and Hume R. D. (eds), *The Frolicks* (1977).

Polyhymnia
▷ Muses.

Pomfret, John (1667–1702)

Rector of Maulden in Bedfordshire and author of *Poems on Several Occasions* (1699), a collection of Pindaric ▷ odes, narrative poems, pastorals, and epistles. His most important poem, *The Choice* (1700), treats the ▷ Horatian theme of rural retirement with a bland cosiness which exactly hit the popular taste of the time. 'Near some fair Town I'd have a private Seat,/ Built uniform, not little nor too great'. He eschews aristocratic splendour in favour of comfortable amenity: 'I'd have a Clear and Competent Estate,/ That I might live Genteelly, but not Great', and advocates benevolent charity towards 'the Sons of Poverty'. *The Choice* presents an ideal of the private life to which both the aristocrat and the successful new bourgeois could subscribe, and it was immensely popular. ▷ Samuel Johnson remarked in his ▷ *Lives of the Poets* (1781): 'Perhaps no composition in our language has been oftener perused.'

Poor Laws

Laws which gave public relief to those among the poor who could not earn their own living and were not supported by others. The first great Poor Law was that of 1601, under Elizabeth I. The dissolution of monasteries and other Church institutions which had undertaken the care of the destitute, together with a number of causes of unemployment (*eg* ▷ enclosures) caused a series of poor laws to be passed in the 16th century, of which the law of 1601 was the climax. Every parish was required to appoint overseers, whose task it was to provide work for the able-bodied unemployed, and relief (through a local tax called a 'poor rate') for those who were unable to work. The law survived until the 19th century, when problems of poor relief had become too great for it to be an efficient solution. Local magistrates employed a method known as the 'Speenhamland System', from the place of its origin, by which the unemployed were given enough money to enable them to survive; the disadvantage of this system was that it demoralized those who were employed in very hard labour but unable to earn more than the unemployed who were given relief.

Pope, Alexander (1688–1744)

Poet. The son of a ▷ Catholic linen-draper in London, born significantly in the year of the 'Glorious Revolution' of 1688, which heralded the new era of optimism and national confidence reflected in much of his work. In childhood his father encouraged him to produce 'rhymes', insisting that they be perfect, and by his early teens he was already writing polished imitations of such diverse models as Chaucer, ▷ Edmund Spenser, ▷ Edmund Waller and ▷ Abraham Cowley. His *Pastorals* (1709) established his reputation, followed by the ▷ *Essay on Criticism* (1711), and ▷ *Windsor Forest* (1713). The last line of this poem is virtually identical with the first line of his *Pastorals*, indicating an ▷ Augustan parallel with Virgil, the last line of whose ▷ *Georgics* is the same as the first line of his *Eclogues*. The ▷ mock heroic ▷ *Rape of the Lock* appeared in 1712, and in an enlarged form in 1714. The characteristic miniaturizing effect of Pope's use of mock heroic can be related to the fact that he was only 4 ft 6 ins high, and suffered from curvature of the spine.

During the early years of his career he had associated with ▷ Joseph Addison, the magisterial arbiter of the new moderate bourgeois taste. But Pope's volatile temperament and Tory leanings drew him towards the more heady intellectual circle of ▷ Jonathan Swift, ▷ John Gay and ▷ John Arbuthnot, with whom in 1713 he formed the ▷ Scriblerus Club, whose object was to 'ridicule all false tastes in learning'. In 1717 Pope produced a collected volume of *Works*, in which appeared ▷ *Eloisa to Abelard* and *Elegy to the Memory of an Unfortunate Lady*, which shows a bold and unorthodox sympathy for a suicide.

Meanwhile he capitalized on his growing reputation by inviting subscriptions for a translation of ▷ Homer's ▷ *Iliad*, a new practice at the time. The work, published in instalments between 1715–20, served to make him financially secure. Several commentators remarked at the time on the failure of his brisk pentameter ▷ couplets to capture the rugged grandeur of Homer's unrhymed hexameters (▷ metre), but most were happy to have an 'English Homer', adapted to contemporary taste. He followed up his success by an advertisement 'undertaking' a translation of the ▷ *Odyssey*, which appeared in 1725–6. It leaked out, however, that much of the labour had been subcontracted to two minor poets, Elijah Fenton and William Broome, and for a time Pope was nicknamed 'the undertaker'. Unlike his original compositions, his Homer has not outlived its age. In 1725 he published an edition of the works of Shakespeare, based on textual comparisons between Quarto and Folio versions, and is thus one of the earliest editors to apply the scholarly techniques previously reserved for ancient ▷ classical literature to an English 'classic' (▷ Shakespeare editions.)

In ▷ *The Dunciad* (1728), itself a parody of a scholarly edition, Pope attacked his literary enemies, including the Shakespeare scholar Lewis Theobald, who had corrected errors in his edition. In 1733–4 he turned away from translation and editing and the squabbles in which these had involved him, and published his philosophical poem ▷ *An Essay on Man* and the four ▷ *Moral Essays* (1731–5). Between 1733 and 1737 he produced his ▷ *Imitations of Horace*, and in 1735 appeared the *Epistle to Dr Arbuthnot* which contains some of his most polished satire. In 1742 he produced the *New Dunciad*, a continuation of the earlier poem, and in 1743 this was added as Book Four to a new edition of *The Dunciad*, the hero being changed from Theobald to ▷ Colley Cibber, the ▷ Poet Laureate.

Pope's last years were spent in a rented riverside house at Twickenham, where he played out his own version of ▷ Horatian retirement. Imitating a landed gentleman, he indulged in a mock heroic, miniaturized version of landscape-gardening, designing a whimsically romantic 'grot' in a tunnel which linked the waterfront with his back garden. It was walled with shells and pieces of mirror, so as to reflect fragments of the river scene in the day, and after dark the light of a flickering lamp which was hung from the roof. Before his death he received the last sacrament, never having abandoned his Catholic religion, despite his ▷ Deist leanings and the double taxation which his recusancy incurred. He left his property to his lifelong friend Martha Blount.

All Pope's important poetry, with the exception of the Deist *Universal Prayer* (1738), is in heroic couplets, a form which he used with an idiosyncratic perfectionism, not attempted by any other poet of the period. He refined his own personal 'rules': on the exact positioning of the caesura, on the choice of diction and on perfection of rhymes (monosyllabic nouns or verbs containing long vowels are preferred). The reader's ear quickly adapts to this hyper-regularity and thus any variation in tone or rhythm, or any deliberate 'irregularity' has an explicit precision of effect virtually unknown in other poets. This characteristic is found cloying by some readers. But, particularly in his more flexible, later verse, it creates one of the most expressive and versatile literary media in the English language.

▷ Augustanism.

Bib: Johnson, S., in *Lives of the Poets*; Mack, M., *Alexander Pope: A Life*; Leavis, F. R., in *Revaluation*; Tillotson, G., *On the Poetry of Pope*; Rogers, P., *An Introduction to Pope*; Gooneratne, Y., *Alexander Pope*; Hill, H. E., and Smith, A. (eds.), *The Art of Alexander Pope*; Bateson, F. W., and Jukovsky, N. A. (eds.), *Pope* (Penguin Critical Anthology); Hunt, J. D. (ed.), *The Rape of the Lock* (Macmillan Casebook).

Popish Plot
▷ Oates, Titus.

Pornography
This is generally understood to mean representations or literature which is intended to produce sexual excitement. There is, however, a considerable degree of dispute about pornography and it has become the subject of legal cases and public campaigns.

In the 17th and 18th centuries pornographic literature circulated widely. There is an overlap between true pornography, however, and a variety of so-called 'rogue literature', which depicted the pranks and schemes of low-life characters, such as beggars, thieves, prostitutes and pimps. The characters of the whore Lucetta and her pimp Sancho in ▷ Behn's

▷ *The Rover*, for example, are in this tradition. Some of the earliest pornography in England was imported from the Continent, and some was translated. A volume called *Ragionamenti*, by the Italian Petro Aretino (1492–1557), which included illustrations of sexual activity, circulated in England from the 16th century onwards under the title *Aretin's Postures*, or simply, *Postures*. For many years the name 'Aretin' was used as a byword for matters pornographic, both humorously and otherwise. Another Italian import was *La Puttana errante*, translated as *The Wandering Whore*. A common formula for pornographic literature is the purported account of a prostitute's life, or life in a brothel, including 'advice' given by one prostitute or bawd to another. Such a one is *La Retorica delle Puttane* ('The Whore's Rhetoric') by the dissident priest Ferrante Pallavicino, who was executed in 1644, two years after its publication. This work generated various translations and adaptations; a very good one was published in 1683.

▷ Pamphlets with titles such as *The Fifteen Plagues of a Maidenhead*, *The Fifteen Comforts of Whoring*, *The Fifteen Comforts of Matrimony*, etc., were published from the early 17th century onwards. These parody a religious original from the 15th century. Interestingly, much pornographic literature in England was associated in some way with religion, particularly the ▷ Catholic faith, and this added to its *frisson*, and also provided ammunition to anti-Catholic forces. Another popular production was *Venus dans le cloître* ('Venus in the Cloister: or the Nun in Her Smock', (1724), which earned a prosecution for its publisher, Edmund Curll. Dialogues in Latin called *Satyra Sotadica*, by Nicolas Chorier, appeared in 1660 and were translated into several other languages including English.

▷ Pepys records in his diary for 13 January 1668 finding *L'Ecole des Filles* (published 1655) in a bookshop. On the 9th February he read it, 'in plain binding', because he was embarrassed to be seen with it. The book is mentioned again by Horner in Act I of ▷ Wycherley's ▷ *The Country Wife*, and in ▷ *The London Cuckolds* by ▷ Ravenscroft. But pornography also originated in Britain. A play, *Sodom*, often attributed to ▷ Rochester, circulated clandestinely in the 1680s. There are pornographic elements in a number of Rochester's poems, as well as in those of contemporaries including Wycherley and ▷ Behn.

In the 18 century pornography entered the novel. ▷ Cleland's *Fanny Hill* (1748 and 1749) was suppressed as pornography; this book was the subject of a trial after a revived edition was published in 1963. The works and activities of the ▷ Marquis de Sade attracted considerable attention, and scandal, in the later 18th and early 19th centuries.

▷ Censorship.

Positivism
▷ Comte, Auguste.

Potter, John (?–1749)
Theatre proprietor, and craftsman. Potter entered the theatre in or after 1708, probably as a carpenter and/or scene painter. He erected a playhouse known

as the French Theatre as well as the Little Theatre in the Hay, and eventually, the Haymarket Theatre (▷ Haymarket Theatres).

Precious women, *Précieuses, préciosité*
Translation of the French term *Précieuses*, applied to a group of literary women in the 17th century. The *Précieuses* were closely associated with the salon movement in the decade 1650 to 1660 and placed ever greater emphasis on refinement, or *préciosité*, in matters of social etiquette, literature and language in a bid to raise the status of women. Among the most notable were ▷ Madeleine de Scudéry and the *bourgeoises* who frequented her *Samedis* or Saturday salons. The original sense of the term was positive, reaffirming that women were 'full of value', and designating such a woman as '*celle qui raffine sur le langage, qui sait quelque chose*', ('a woman who uses refined language and knows something'). The Precious Women accordingly placed great value on women's independence from men and questioned the institution of marriage. For their *romanesque*, or romantic, ideas and linguistic excesses, they were much ridiculed by the dramatist ▷ Molière and others. In his *Dictionnaire des Précieuses* ('Dictionary of the Precious Women', 1659), Somaize (b1639) distinguished three sorts of women in French society: those with 'no knowledge and no conversation' ('*aucune connaissance, aucune conversation*'); those who were just as ignorant but engaged readily in conversation ('*aussi ignorantes, mais parlent avec promptitude*'); and those who, using their exceptional beauty to distinguish themselves from the crowd, read all the novels and verse they could in a bid to learn how to speak well. In his dictionary, Antoine Furetière (1619–88) gives the following definition: 'The epithet *Précieuse* was formerly applied to exceptionally virtuous women, who were particularly knowledgeable about society and language. The word has been devalued by the excesses and affected manners of others, who have been called false *Précieuses* or ridiculous *Précieuses*, about whom a comedy has been written.' ('*Précieuses est aussi une épithète qu'on a donné ci-devant à des filles de grande vertu, qui savoient bien le monde et la langue: mais parce que d'autres ont affecté et outré leurs manières, cela a décrié le mot, et on les a appelées fausses précieuses, ou précieuses ridicules, dont on a fait une comédie.*')
Bib: Backer, D. and Liot, A., *Precious Women*.

Predestination
A theological doctrine which holds that, since God in his eternal wisdom has foreknown the events of time since before the creation of the world, he has foreseen and chosen those individuals who are damned and those who are saved for eternal life after death. Those who are saved are called 'the elect', and those who are damned 'the reprobate'.

Presbyterianism
A doctrine of church organization maintained by an important group of ▷ Protestants. 'Presbyter' comes from a Greek word meaning 'elder', and Presbyterianism is a system of church government by councils of elders. The system was devised by

▷ Calvin; it became dominant in Scotland under the leadership of John Knox and had wide support in England from about 1570. It is still the national Church of Scotland, but in England it seceded extensively to ▷ Unitarianism during the 18th century. In 1972 the English Presbyterians joined with the Congregationalists to form the United Reformed Church.

Pretender
▷ Old Pretender, The; Jacobite.

Priestley, Joseph (1733–1804)
A nonconformist minister, scientist and teacher. He was partly educated at a nonconformist academy at Daventry; such academies existed in the 18th century to give a university education to non-conformists, who for their religious views were not admitted to the recognized universities of ▷ Oxford and ▷ Cambridge. They were commonly more advanced scientifically than the real universities; Priestley eventually became the first chemist to isolate oxygen. In 1768 he published his *Essay on the First Principles of Government*, advocating 'the happiness of the majority' as the criterion by which government must be judged. This line of thought was developed by ▷ Jeremy Bentham and his 19th-century followers, the ▷ Utilitarians. Priestley's house in Birmingham was destroyed by the mob in 1791 owing to his well-known sympathy with the ▷ French Revolution, and in 1794 he emigrated to the United States.

Prime Minister
Since the 18th century the office of greatest power in the British political system. It arose in consequence of the struggles for power between king and ▷ Parliament in the 17th century. Parliament was victorious, inasmuch as it became difficult for the king to lead the country politically without the approval of Parliament at every major step. This could be managed only by a politician who was himself a member of the parliamentary body, as the king was not; moreover George I (1714–27) and George II (1727–60), the first two kings of the House of Hanover (▷ George) had the additional disadvantage of being foreigners in the nation they were supposed to govern. Thus the 18th-century art of 'managing' parliaments grew up; the first politician to be a master of the art was ▷ Robert Walpole, whose period of power ran from 1721–42. He is usually regarded as 'the first Prime Minister' in English history, though he objected to the title. Walpole's 'management' was politically unsatisfactory, however, since it depended too much on the bribery of Members of Parliament. After his downfall, the parliamentary system went through an unsatisfactory period of about 40 years during which aristocratic coteries intrigued for power, and George III (1760–1820) made an ultimately unsuccessful attempt to recover royal political initiative. Then ▷ William Pitt the Younger took over the government with the king's approval, and retained power from 1783 to 1801. He insisted that he should have complete control; his personal integrity placed him above the suspicion of exercising it dishonestly; he based his

authority on public opinion. For these three reasons he did more even than Walpole to establish the office of prime ministership, although Parliament had to undergo the reform of 1832 before this office could achieve a strong basis in national acceptance.

Primitive, primitivism

From a literary viewpoint, the concept of primitivism revolves around the figure of the 'noble savage'. Descended from the classical notion of a ▷ Golden Age, the concept gains most popularity and intellectual resonance in the 18th century, anticipated by the figure of Man Friday in ▷ Defoe's ▷ Robinson Crusoe (1719) and ▷ Aphra Behn's novel ▷ Oroonoko, or the History of the Royal Slave ▷ (1688), successfully adapted for the stage by ▷ Thomas Southerne in 1695. Based partly on the author's experiences of Surinam, Behn's novel is one of the earliest examples of primitivism in imaginative literature, describing primitive people in 'the first state of innocence, before men knew how to sin': the whole primitivist tradition may be read as a varied series of laments for, and objections against, the myth of Genesis and the Fall of mankind. Primitivism expresses an optimistic belief in the essential goodness of human beings, corrupted and deformed by so-called civilization. The chief conduit for debate in this area was the philosopher ▷ Rousseau. His writings of the 1750s contrast the harmonious existence of primitive man in a 'state of nature' with the indolence, profligacy and selfish obsession with private property experienced by Europeans. Emile (1762) attempted to establish the principles of a new educational system, through which a child could develop rational independence of mind, while preserving a natural innocence, while the Social Contract of the same year argued for equality before the law, a more fair distribution of wealth, and a democratic subscription to the common good. While the resonance of these ideas for ▷ the French Revolution is self-evident, their influence on ▷ Romantic literature runs deep, persisting well beyond a point when the Revolution itself had been compromised by slaughter.

▷ Inkle and Yarico; Omai.

Bib: Tinker, C. B., Nature's Simple Plan, Fairchild, H. N., The Noble Savage, Whitney, L., Primitivism and the Idea of Progress, Roszak, T., Towards a Counter-Culture.

Prior, Matthew (1664–1721)

Poet and diplomat. The son of a joiner, Prior was educated under the patronage of the ▷ Earl of Dorset. While an undergraduate at ▷ Cambridge he collaborated with the Earl of Halifax on a parody of ▷ John Dryden, The Hind and the Panther transvers'd to the Story of the Country Mouse and the City Mouse (1687), and in 1700 he celebrated the arrival of William III from Holland in Carmen Saeculare. After a period as secretary to the ambassador at the Hague he allied himself to the Tory camp of Harley and Bolingbroke and was involved in secret negotiations with the French government over the Treaty of Utrecht (1713), which was nicknamed 'Matt's Peace' after him. When Queen Anne died in 1714 and the Tories fell from power he was impeached and imprisoned for two years. His Poems, published by his friends in 1718, helped to restore his fortunes. His best work is marked by an easy-going humour. Alma: or the Progress of the Mind, (1718), a long poem in loose Hudibrastics (▷ Hudibras), mocks the systematic philosophy of ▷ Aristotle and ▷ Descartes and elaborates the proposition, borrowed from ▷ Montaigne's essay 'On Drunkenness', that the mind begins in youth in the toes, and rises by degrees until it reaches the head in old age. It is in his shorter, occasional poems that Prior achieves his most satisfying poetic effects. 'Jinny the Just' (published in 1907), an elegy for his housekeeper and mistress, employs an unheroic ▷ metre of anapaestic triplets to characterize its uneducated subject, and to create a moving personal tribute:

> Tread Soft on her grave, and do right to her honour
> Lett neither rude hand nor Ill tongue light upon her
> Do all the Small favours that now can be don her.

Other poems of importance are Solomon on the Vanity of the World (1718), in heroic ▷ couplets; Henry and Emma (1707), a travesty of the old ballad The Nut-Brown Maid; and Down-Hall, a Ballad (1723). Prior was a brilliant exponent of the epigram, a memorable example being 'A True Maid':

> 'No, no; for my Virginity,
>   When I lose that, says Rose, I'll dye:
> Behind the Elmes, last Night, cry'd Dick,
>   Rose, were you not extreamly Sick?

Bib: Johnson, S., in Lives of the Poets.

Prisons

In the 11th and 12th centuries dungeons (underground cells) in castles were the prisons of those who displeased powerful barons or the king, and for long afterwards the Tower of London – fortress, palace and prison – was used for important political prisoners. In London there were the royal prisons of Newgate, the ▷ Marshalsea and the ▷ Fleet, which all lasted till Victorian times. In the 16th century houses of correction were set up for the incarceration of vagrants, who were regarded as a menace to the peace; these were modelled on the first to be established at ▷ Bridewell, London, in 1552, and were called 'Bridewells' after it. They were at first intended as 'workhouses' for the unemployed, but they became prisons in all but name. Prisoners were also kept in prison ships or 'hulks'.

Conditions in the prisons were very bad until the 19th century. Three principal reasons for this were:

1 Prisons were not considered to be the responsibility of the authorities but of the gaolers; there was thus no supervision or maintenance of even the lowest standards of decency and hygiene, or of other aspects of living conditions.

2 The gaolers were not regarded as officials, but as though they kept lodging-houses as tenants of the local or central authorities; they were paid no salaries, and drew their incomes from the prisoners who had to pay for privileges, and from whom the gaolers often extorted money by abominable treatment.

3 Public attention to the necessity of a secure but humane prison system was delayed by the practice of 'transporting' criminals convicted of the more serious crimes to the American colonies or, after 1783, to Australia; transportation only ceased in the 1840s.

John Howard in the 18th century and Elizabeth Fry in the 19th were the leaders of the movement of reform in the prison system, which only made real advances after 1850. ▷ Jeremy Bentham was also influential in making prison organization more efficient and rational.

▷ Penal system.

Pritchard, Hannah (1709–68)

Actress, singer. She joined ▷ Theophilus Cibber and other performers who seceded from the company at ▷ Drury Lane, and opened at the ▷ Haymarket Theatre in 1733, only to return to Drury Lane in the following year. By now she was frequently cast in major roles, including Phaedra in ▷ Dryden's *Amphitryon* (1690), Isabella in ▷ Sir Richard Steele's ▷ *The Conscious Lovers*, and Dol Common in Jonson's *The Alchemist*.

In 1740 Pritchard played Desdemona to ▷ James Quin's Othello, but her performance as Rosalind in *As You Like It* from the end of that year is said finally to have established her as one of the leading actresses of her generation. She appeared as Nerissa in the production of *The Merchant of Venice* in which ▷ Charles Macklin revolutionized the portrayal of Shylock, and later acted in several plays with ▷ Garrick.

In 1749 her popularity forced a change in the ending of ▷ Samuel Johnson's *Mahomet and Irene*, to the author's chagrin: she was to have been strangled on stage, but the audience would not have it, and the action was modified so that she was 'killed' away from their view instead. She was noted for the intelligence of her interpretations, her versatility, and her dedication to her profession.

Bib: Vaughan, A., *Born to Please: Hannah Pritchard, Actress*.

Privy Council

With a history going back to the king's council which in the 13th century gave the sovereign private ('privy') advice on the government of the country, this is now a body with largely formal work, mainly carried out by committees since the membership – now conferred as a special honour – is large. The former powers of the Privy Council are now exercised by the Cabinet.

▷ Orders in Council.

Protestant succession

The belief that the throne should not pass to a Roman ▷ Catholic. The arguments about the royal succession became bitter when ▷ Charles II was succeeded by his brother ▷ James II. James's Catholicism was only one reason for the ▷ Glorious Revolution of 1688 but the fear of a return of James or of later succession by other Catholics

caused further controversy and led to the ▷ Act of Settlement of 1701 and later ▷ Acts which made it impossible for a Catholic to succeed to the throne.

▷ Protestantism.

Protestantism

A term used for all varieties of Christian belief which broke away from Roman ▷ Catholicism during the ▷ Reformation in the 16th century, or for religious communities not in agreement with Roman Catholicism but originating since the Reformation. It was first used in regard to those who protested against the Emperor Charles V's condemnation of the reformers in Germany at the Diet of Spires, 1529. Protestants in Britain include Anglicans, ▷ Presbyterians, ▷ Methodists and ▷ Baptists.

Proviso scene

Scene in a play showing bargaining between lovers, typically those featured in so-called ▷ Comedies of Manners, of the Restoration, wherein they set their terms before agreeing to be married. The most famous such scene is that between Millamant and Mirabell in ▷ William Congreve's ▷ *The Way of the World* (1700), in which they guarantee one another independence within marriage, before announcing their engagement (IV, 2).

Provok'd Wife, The (1697)

Play by ▷ Sir John Vanbrugh. The drunken, boorish and misogynistic Sir John Brute, married but hating marriage, conducts a deliberate campaign to abuse and humiliate his wife and her niece Bellinda. In revenge, Lady Brute determines to cuckold him with the amorous Constant, who has been courting her for the past two years. In a parallel plot Heartfree, another misogynist, at first woos the affected Lady Fanciful, then falls in love, for the first time in his life, with Bellinda. A series of intrigues brings the pairs of lovers together in amorous assignations, although Lady Brute refrains from adultery with Constant. In the final scene Lady Fanciful attempts, but fails, to defame the reputations of both Bellinda and Heartfree, with whom she is now in love. Bellinda and Heartfree are united, while Sir John undergoes a supposed but unconvincing change of heart, and vows to be a better husband in future. The play's comedy barely sweetens its bitter comments on marriage, and especially the vulnerability of women in marriage. But it affirms the value of true love: Constant says, 'Though marriage be a lottery, in which there are wondrous many blanks, yet there is one inestimable lot in which the only heaven on earth is written'. Ironically however, he, the only admirer of women, apparently remains unmarried at the end, while the misogynists are matched.

Psalms

A book of the Old Testament composed of the sacred songs of the ancient Jewish religion. In ancient Hebrew, they were called 'praise-songs', indicating the predominant function of the collection, though other functions – lament, meditation, imprecation etc. – were included. Authorship was traditionally attributed to King David, but it is evident that the psalms either date from after the Babylonian Captivity (6th century BC) or were re-edited then; in any case they originated at different periods.

In the 16th century under the inspiration of the ▷ Protestant Reformation, the psalms were translated into English. There are two prose versions in official use in the ▷ Church of England: that of the Authorized Version of the Bible of 1611, and the older translation in the *Book of* ▷ *Common Prayer* dating from 1549. Both include some of the well-known masterpieces of English prose of the ▷ Renaissance. In addition, there are the metrical and rhymed versions especially favoured by the more extreme Protestants. The so-called 'Old Version' by Sternhold and Hopkins was published in its complete form in 1562. Another version, principally the work of Francis Rouse, came into general use in Scotland in the mid-17th century, and in 1696 Nicholas Brady and ▷ Nahum Tate produced the 'New Version'. More distinguished attempts to versify the prose psalms were made in the 16th century by Sir Philip Sidney and his sister the Countess of Pembroke; in the 17th, by George Sandys, George Wither and ▷ John Milton; in the 19th, by John Keble.

▷ Bible in England.

Public schools

In Britain these are not and have never been either schools under the state, or entirely non-feepaying schools. They are distinguished from 'private' schools in not being run for private profit by individual owners; like the colleges of Oxford and Cambridge, they were founded and endowed for the public good, often for poor scholars. Until the Education Act of 1944, they were often hard to distinguish from endowed Grammar Schools; the latter were, however, more likely to draw on the immediate locality for their pupils, whereas the public schools drew on the whole nation, with varying provision for 'poor scholars'. Until the 19th century, education was largely restricted to study of the ▷ classics – ancient Greek and Latin language and literature. They therefore tended to attract, in the ▷ Middle Ages, those who were to enter the Church and the learned professions; from the 16th century it became increasingly regarded as indispensable to 'a gentleman' that he should possess a firm classical culture, and from the 18th century, public schools began to be aristocratic educational institutions. The middle classes often had little use for the education they provided, or they were excluded as Dissenters and went to a Dissenting Academy instead, where in any case the education was wider and more practical.

Some public schools date from the 19th century, but those with most prestige are usually much older: Winchester (founded 1382); Westminster (1560); ▷ Eton (1440); ▷ Harrow (1571); Rugby (1567). The public school system is 'English' rather than 'British', since it has flourished mainly in England, and has never become characteristic of Scotland, Wales or Ireland, though distinguished public schools exist in those countries. It was at one time a predominantly masculine system, although there

are now a large number of girls' public schools and a number of boys' schools have begun to admit girls, especially into their sixth forms.

▷ Education; Schools in England.

Punch and Judy

The principal characters of a popular puppetshow. There are allusions to Punch in the diaries of ▷ Pepys and ▷ Evelyn, and the show can still be seen, especially at seaside resorts. Punch is hooknosed, humpbacked, violent and cunning; he is always represented with his wife Judy, who is not particularly grotesque, and a little dog Toby – often real. Punch kills his wife and the dog, beats the doctor who comes to visit him, hangs the hangman who is supposed to execute him, and eventually outwits the devil.

▷ Mime; Pantomime.

Purcell, Henry (1659–95)

Composer. His father and uncle held musical appointments at the Chapel Royal, and his father was also master of the choristers of Westminster Abbey. He became a chorister in the Chapel Royal as a young boy, and as a young man was made 'composer in ordinary to the king' and organist at the Abbey. He composed some instrumental pieces, but is expecially famous for his choral compositions. Some of these were church music, *eg* the *Te Deum and Jubilate* (1694), which was the first English religious work to be scored for both strings and brass. His official appointments also caused him to set choral odes written for official occasions, such as the odes to St Cecilia. In addition, he collaborated with a number of ▷ Restoration dramatists in writing for the theatre, including a musical setting for a ▷ masque in ▷ Betterton's drama *Diocletian* and musical numbers in several dramas by ▷ Dryden: *Tyrannic Love* (1687), *Amphitryon* (1690), *King Arthur* (1691). This work for the theatre included a musical version of Shakespeare's *A Midsummer Night's Dream* entitled *The Fairy Queen* (1693), and his opera *Dido and Aeneas* (1689), with a libretto by ▷ Nahum Tate.

Purcell's career concluded the period of English music which had begun in the mid-16th century. In his youth one of his principal teachers had been the English composer John Blow, but he was also a close student of French and Italian musical development. As a composer he had great freedom of imagination and strong gifts for dramatic writing.

▷ Opera in England.

Puritanism

The term is used in a narrow sense of religious practice and attitudes, and in a broad sense of an ethical outlook which is much less easy to define.

1 In its strict sense, 'Puritan' was applied to those ▷ Protestant reformers who rejected Queen Elizabeth's religious settlement of 1560. This settlement sought a middle way between Roman Catholicism and the extreme spirit of reform of Geneva. The Puritans, influenced by Geneva, Zurich and other continental centres, objected to the retention of bishops and to any appearance of what they regarded as superstition in church

worship – the wearing of vestments by the priests, and any kind of religious image. Apart from their united opposition to Roman Catholicism and their insistence on simplicity in religious forms, Puritans disagreed among themselves on questions of doctrine and church organization. The principal sects were: ▷ Presbyterians, Independents (at first called ▷ Brownists, and later ▷ Congregationalists), ▷ Baptists, and (later) ▷ Quakers. They were strong in the towns, especially in London, and in the University of ▷ Cambridge, and socially they were widespread, and included members of the aristocracy and of the working classes, as well as the middle, commercial classes where they had their chief strength. Puritanism was very strong in the first half of the 17th century and reached its peak of power after the ▷ Civil War of 1642–6 – a war which was ostensibly religious, although it was also political. Matters of church government were much involved with matters of state government, since Presbyterians and Independents, who believed in popular control of the church, were not likely to tolerate royal control of Parliament's political affairs. Puritanism was both religiously and politically supreme in the decade 1650–60, but on the ▷ Restoration of the monarchy Puritans were denied participation in the Church of England, and refused rights of free religious worship. The last was granted them by the Toleration Act of 1689, and during the 18th century both Puritanism and the official attitude to it were modified under the influence of Rationalism. Nonetheless, the ▷ Methodist movement of that century had many of the characteristics of the older Puritan sects. It was, moreover, only in 1829 that Nonconformists (as they were now called) were allowed to offer themselves as candidates for seats in Parliament, and only in 1871 did the Universities of Oxford and Cambridge cease to be the monopoly of the Church of England.

2 In the broader sense of a whole way of life, puritanism has always represented strict obedience to the dictates of conscience and strong emphasis on the virtue of self-denial. In this sense individuals can be described as 'puritan' whether or not they belong to one of the recognized Puritan sects, or even if they are atheists.

The word 'puritan' is often thought to imply hostility to the arts, but this is not necessarily true. John Milton was an ardent Puritan, but his poetry is one of the climaxes of English ▷ Renaissance art. However, it is true that the strict Puritans of the age of Shakespeare were commonly opponents of the art of the theatre; this was partly because the theatres were sometimes scenes of moral licentiousness and disorder, and partly because the strict Puritan, in his intense love of truth, was very inclined to

confuse fiction with lying. Thus in the later 17th century Bunyan was criticized by some of his Puritan comrades for writing fiction in his allegory, ▷ *Pilgrim's Progress*, and in the early 18th century ▷ Defoe had to defend his ▷ *Robinson Crusoe* against similar charges. Nonetheless, in the 18th and 19th centuries Puritanism, or attitudes derived from it, did tend to encourage 'philistinism', or contempt for culture. This was because Puritanism had always encouraged an essentially practical attitude to worldly affairs, and when religion slackened as a driving force, the practical virtues came to be regarded as the principal, if not the only ones. Art, on the other hand, encourages the contemplative virtues, which the practical man of Puritan tradition was inclined to regard as unnecessary, therefore frivolous, and so, in a puritan sense, 'sinful'. There is continuity of development from Priestley, the 18th-century scientist and preacher, through the practical philosophy of ▷ Bentham, to James Mill, the ▷ Utilitarian leader, who was an atheist.

What is called the 'Puritan conscience', on the other hand, had an important influence on one kind of art form – the novel. Puritans believed that the good life could only be lived by 'the inner light' – the voice of God in the heart – and to discern this light it was necessary to conduct the most scrupulous self-enquiry. This produced the kind of spiritual autobiography that was common in the mid-17th century, and of which the best example is Bunyan's ▷ *Grace Abounding to the Chief of Sinners*. Such self-knowledge had two important consequences: it increased interest in, and understanding of, the human heart in others as well as the self, and the first results of this are apparent in Bunyan's *Pilgrim's Progress*; but it also encouraged a sense of the loneliness of the individual – a sense that was supported by the growing economic individualism of the later 17th century. These are important constituents of the novelist's vision, and when one adds to them the preoccupation with moral values with which Puritanism is so bound up, and which are such a permanent feature of the English novel, it is possible to think that without Puritanism the novel form would never have developed indigenously in England.

▷ Reformation.

Puss in Boots

A folk tale, translated into English in 1720 from the French collection by ▷ Charles Perrault. The cat is the property of a poor man, the third son of a miller. By the animal's ingenuity, the miller's son marries the king's daughter. The story is a popular theme of Christmas ▷ pantomimes.

Q

Quadrille

1 A game of cards which replaced ▷ ombre in fashion about 1726, to be succeeded about 20 years later by whist.

2 A dance of French origin; it was first used in ballet, and then became popular in the ballroom. Introduced into England in the late 18th century.

Quakers

Originally a derisive name for the members of a religious society properly called the Society of Friends; the Friends are still known as Quakers, but the term has lost its contemptuous significance. The Society was founded by ▷ George Fox, who began his preaching career in 1647. He preached that the truth came from an inner spiritual light, and declared that no special class of men (*ie* priests) or buildings (*ie* churches) should be set apart for religious purposes. This individualism at first attracted a number of mentally disturbed followers whose ecstasies are perhaps responsible for the nickname 'Quaker', though Fox himself declared that it was first used in 1650 because he taught his followers to 'Tremble at the Word of the Lord'. They held a view, unusual among ▷ Puritans, that it was possible to gain complete victory over sin in this life. Such a doctrine, in addition to their refusal to accept those religious institutions that the other Puritans accepted, made them intensely unpopular for the first ten years of their existence. Later they became influential far beyond their numbers, which have remained comparatively few. Owing to the freedom of mind which is the essence of the movement, it is difficult to define their doctrine, which seems to vary greatly among individuals. On the other hand they are well known for a range of characteristic virtues: humanitarianism (they were amongst the first to protest against slavery, in 1688); non-resistance to violence; respect for individuals regardless of race, sex or religion; sobriety of conduct and tranquillity of mind. One of the most important of their early members was William Penn (1644–1718), the founder of the American colony of Pennsylvania. Like other Puritans, they were prominent in commerce, but took care to engage in activities that were not harmful; in consequence Quaker names are particularly well known in connection with the manufacture of chocolate. However, in the 18th century their outstanding importance was in banking: their sober-mindedness and strictness of morality counteracted the speculative manias of the time, and did much to establish secure financial foundations for the rapid expansion of British trade.

Queen's Theatre
▷ Haymarket Theatres.

Quin, James (1693–1766)
Actor, manager, singer. Born in London, Quin was the product of a bigamous union between James and Elizabeth Quin, and the grandson of a former Lord Mayor of Dublin. After 1713 he began acting at the ▷ Smock Alley Theatre in Dublin, and by early 1715 he had reached the ▷ Drury Lane Theatre in London, where he later helped to manage the company. In 1746 and 1747 Quin acted with ▷ Garrick at Covent Garden (▷ Covent Garden Theatres), and the two became friends despite their ostensible rivalry. But Garrick's light, naturalistic style made Quin's acting appear absurdly formal, pompous, and monotonous to many observers, and the older man gradually retired from the stage, to Bath.

Quin was noted for his 'strong passions', including a violent temper, but also a good humour and dignity. He was a friend of ▷ Pope and ▷ Swift, and was admired by ▷ Horace Walpole and the Prince of Wales (later George III). He held his own in parts ranging from Othello, Macbeth, Richard III, Coriolanus, Comus, Bajazet in ▷ Rowe's *Tamerlane*, and Pierre in ▷ Thomas Otway's ▷ *Venice Preserv'd*, to his most celebrated role as Falstaff. Garrick's innovations hurt his reputation more substantially, perhaps, than that of any leading actor of the period, quite suddenly making him seem outmoded. But even at the end of his career, Garrick and other colleagues continued to respect him, and he was still able to draw large crowds.
Bib: Taylor, A. M., *Life of Mr James Quin, comedian*.

Racine, Jean (1693–99)

French dramatist. His principal sources of inspiration were either classical (the larger group of his works, including *Andromaque* (1667), *Britannicus* (1669), *Bérénice* (1670), *Mithridate* (1673), *Iphigénie* (1674) and *Phèdre* (1677)) or biblical (*Athalie*, (1690)). Racine examines the nexus of passion and power, and the distorting effect these invariably have upon the heroic values which his characters inherit or purport to represent. He delineates the moral and political blindness which can all too easily sway human judgement and conduct and he highlights with particular force the destructiveness of passion from which tragedy will proceed. His dramas are tightly constructed according to classical criteria of the ▷ unities and display a virtuoso command of the 12-syllable Alexandrine line combined with a strong sense of rhyme and rhythm and a lucid, economical style. Racine was admired in England by ▷ John Dryden and ▷ Thomas Otway, whose 'heroic drama' is nevertheless no serious rival to its French counterpart.

▷ French literature in England.

Radcliffe, Ann (1764–1823)

Novelist. She was one of the most famous of the writers of ▷ Gothic novels, which sought to gain their effect through mystery and the supernatural in a setting of grand scenic description. She was immensely popular in her own day for her four novels: *The Sicilian Romance* (1790) *The Romance of the Forest* (1791) ▷ *The Mysteries of Udolpho* (1794) and *The Italian* (1797). *Udolpho* is the best remembered, owing to satirization through an account of its effect on a young girl in ▷ Jane Austen's *Northanger Abbey*.

Rambler, The

A twice-weekly periodical produced by ▷ Samuel Johnson from March 1750 to March 1752. All except five were written by Johnson himself. The papers were in the tradition of *The Tatler* and *The Spectator* essays by ▷ Addison and ▷ Steele 40 years before. The essays cover a wide variety of subjects, including eastern tales, criticism and allegories. Johnson's moral seriousness in the work is indicated by the prayer that he wrote on its commencement. *The Rambler* was pirated and copied, evidence of its great popularity, and in Johnson's lifetime ran to ten reprintings.

Ramsay, Allan (1686–1758)

Edinburgh wig-maker and father of the portrait painter of the same name. He was a prolific poet in both English and Scots, using a variety of ▷ metres, from intricate stanzas to pentameter and tetrameter couplets. His marriage of ▷ Scottish and English literary traditions, together with his earthy realism of language and dramatic flair, laid down the foundations on which ▷ Robert Fergusson and ▷ Robert Burns were later to build.

Rape of the Lock, The (1712/1714)

A ▷ mock-heroic poem in pentameter couplets by ▷ Alexander Pope. Its immediate stimulation was a quarrel between two families with whom Pope was acquainted, caused by Lord Petre cutting off a lock of Miss Arabella Fermor's hair. Pope hoped to place this act of sexual harrassment in a trivial light by his comic and burlesque treatment, which owes something to the example of ▷ Nicolas Boileau's *Le Lutrin* (*The Lectern*, 1674), a mock epic concerning an ecclesiastical quarrel over the placing of a lectern. However Pope only succeeded in giving further offence. The first published version (1712) comprised two cantos, but Pope continued to work on it after the immediate occasion had passed, and in 1714 it was issued in a much enlarged five-canto version, incorporating the epic machinery of the sylphs.

The work has been interpreted as a severe moral satire. By describing this transient quarrel in the heroic language of ▷ Homer's ▷ *Iliad*, Pope could be said to be ironically mocking the selfish vanity of fashionable society. However, the sensuous beauty of the verse and the elaborateness of the poem's imagery suggest that the young Pope was no Puritan moralist. The most vivid passages in the poem celebrate the new ease and amenity of the English middle class in its first confident phase of capitalist imperialism. The heroine's exotic cosmetics and beauty aids, brought from the farthest corners of the earth by British ships, are described with delight. The sylphs, fanciful projections of the secular drawing room, are substituted for the awesome gods of the ancient Greeks, and the primitive *machismo* of Hector and Achilles becomes the feminine 'armour' of stays and petticoats, or the elegant 'triumph' of a game of cards. Counterpointing this delight in social life is an elegiac lament over its transience, and the poem is at its most moving when it laments the imminent decay of Belinda's 'frail beauty', 'When those fair Suns shall sett, as sett they must,/ And all those Tresses shall be laid in Dust'.

Rasselas, Prince of Abyssinia, The History of (1759)

A prose work by ▷ Samuel Johnson. Tradition has it that Johnson composed the work rapidly to pay for the cost of his mother's funeral. Its theme has often been compared by critics to that of Johnson's poem *The Vanity of Human Wishes*.

The theme of *Rasselas* is 'the choice of life', a phrase which occurs repeatedly. The prince, son of the emperor of Abyssinia, is tired of the pleasant life in the 'happy valley', and in the company of his sister Nekayah, her attendant Pekuah, and the philosopher Imlac, escapes to Egypt.

Imlac's advice demonstrates to the youth the transient nature of human happiness, a state which is in any case unobtainable. Imlac also voices Johnson's views on 'the business of a poet', which is to 'examine not the individual, but the species'. The poet should aim to be 'the interpreter of nature, and the legislator of mankind', not to 'number the streaks of the tulip'. *Rasselas* often parallels ▷ Voltaire's *Candide*, published in the same year, and when Johnson later read this work he commented on the similarities.

▷ Orientalism.

Rationalism

1 In philosophy, the belief that reason, rather than sensation, is the only certain guide to knowledge.

2 In religion, the practice of seeking explanations which satisfy reason for what had been accepted as supernatural.

Ravenscroft, Edward (?1650–97)

Dramatist, popular mainly for his farces. A lawyer by training, he was a member of the Middle Temple in 1671, where he composed his first play, *Mammamouchi, or the Citizen Turn'd Gentleman*, based on ▷ Molière's play *Le Bourgeois Gentilhomme*; Ravenscroft used Molière as a source several more times. *The Careless Lovers* followed in 1673, and *The Wrangling Lovers* in 1676, again using French as well as Spanish sources. A play inspired by the ▷ Commedia dell'Arte, *Scaramouch a Philosopher, Harlequin a Schoolboy, a Bravo, Merchant and Musician*, and a play based on George Ruggle's 1615 Latin comedy, *Ignoramus, or the English Lawyer*, were produced in 1677, and *Titus Andronicus, or the Rape of Lavinia*, an alteration of the play by ▷ Shakespeare, in 1678. His most celebrated play, ▷ *The London Cuckolds*, another farce in the French manner, was staged in 1681. It became a tradition to perform this at both ▷ Drury Lane and ▷ Covent Garden on the Lord Mayor's Day (9 November) every year; the play was revived in 1782 and again by the Royal Court Theatre in 1979. Ravenscroft's great rival, Dryden, referred to his works with contempt.

Realism

A term used in various senses, both in philosophy and in literary criticism. Three principal meanings, two of them philosophical and one literary, are particularly worth distinguishing.

1 In ▷ medieval philosophy, the realists were opposed to the nominalists. Realism here means that classes of things ('universals') have reality whereas individuals have not, or at least have less: *eg* individual birds take their reality from the classification 'bird'. The nominalists considered that only the individual bird has reality, and that the classification 'bird' is only a formulation in the mind

2 Since the Middle Ages, realism has become opposed to idealism. Here realism means that reality exists apart from ideas about it in the mind, and idealism represents the view that we can know nothing that is not in our minds.

3 Literary realism is a 19th-century conception, related to 2 and coterminous with industrial capitalism. In general, it means the use of the imagination to represent things as common sense supposes they are. It does not apply only to 19th-century literature; ▷ Defoe is commonly called a realist because of his factual description and narration.

▷ Mimesis.

Reason

▷ Rationalism.

Rebellion, The Great

▷ Civil Wars.

Recruiting Officer, The (1706)

Comedy by ▷ George Farquhar. Captain Plume recruits men to the army by courting the women with whom they are in love, and his sergeant, Kite, poses as an astrologer to lure men into service. Sylvia, the daughter of Justice Ballance, loves Plume but has promised not to marry him without her father's consent. She disguises herself as a man and contrives to get herself arrested for scandalous conduct. She appears before her father, who hands her over to Plume as a recruit, and eventually the two are married. In a secondary plot, Captain Brazen seeks to marry the wealthy Melinda but is deceived into almost marrying her maid, while Melinda herself marries Mr Worthy.

The play draws on Farquhar's own experiences as a recruiting officer at Lichfield and Shrewsbury in 1705–6, and there is some amusing satire on the law in the courtroom scenes. The play captures much of the spirit of the ▷ Restoration, but its realism, rural setting (unlike the urban settings of most Restoration comedies), and broader humour, give it the hallmark of its later period.

Recusancy

A term first used under Elizabeth I for refusal, usually by Roman Catholics, to attend religious worship in the ▷ Church of England. The recusancy law continued to exist until the Toleration Act (1689) which permitted freedom of worship.

Red Riding Hood, Little

A popular fairy tale, originally derived from the French version by ▷ Perrault, translated into English in 1729. The little girl is so called because of the red hood that she wears. A wolf meets her in the forest while she is on her way to her grandmother. Having discovered the purpose of her journey, he goes on ahead and eats the grandmother and takes her place in bed; when Red Riding Hood arrives he eats her as well. In modern versions, she and her grandmother are subsequently cut out of the wolf's stomach, alive and well, by her father, a woodcutter.

Reeve, Clara (1729–1807)

Novelist, poet and critic who wrote the well-known ▷ Gothic novel ▷ *The Old English Baron* (1778). The daughter of a rector from near Ipswich, one of eight children, who started writing in the 1750s. She translated Barclay's romance, *Argenis*, as *The Phoenix* (1772), and in *The Progress of Romance* (1785) her characters comment on romance in its different historical and geographical incarnations – a process which involves a discussion of women writers, including Hortensius's opinion that the dead ▷ Aphra Behn is too risqué – 'I shall not disturb her, or her works' – but a woman speaks up for ▷ *Oroonoko*.

Other publications included *Original Poems on Several Occasions* (1769), *The Two Mentors* (1780), *The School For Widows* (1791) and *Plans of Education* (1792).

▷ Radcliffe, Ann; Haywood, Eliza.

Reflections on the Revolution in France (1790)
A political treatise by ▷ Edmund Burke. Burke
attacks the principles on which the ▷ French
Revolution was being conducted, denies that the
English ▷ Glorious Revolution of 1688 was based
on the same principles, and insists that a society is an
organic growth like a tree, requiring the same kind
of careful surgery in accordance with its principles
of growth. The book was provoked by a sermon
in praise of the French Revolution, preached by a
Nonconformist minister, Dr Price; Burke is in effect
not merely attacking the French revolutionaries,
but the reverence for abstract, rational, scientific
enlightenment which had increasingly transformed
the 17th-century Puritans into the 18th-century
rationalistic Dissenters or Nonconformists, and had
found disciples among many others of the educated
classes. The *Reflections* is a great work of conservative
political philosophy, as well as a masterpiece of
polemical prose. It represents the French Revolution
as a turning-point in history: 'The age of chivalry
is gone. That of sophisters, economists and
calculators has succeeded; and the glory of Europe is
extinguished for ever.'

Reform comedy
Comedy whose *dénouement* is dominated by a
major character repenting some wrong-doing, and
promising to reform. The type became prominent
toward the end of the 17th century, especially after
▷ Colley Cibber's ▷ *Love's Last Shift* (1696), in
which the central figure of Loveless repents, after
leading a debauched life and abandoning his wife,
leaving his debts unpaid. Attacks on the supposed
immorality and profanity of the stage by ▷ Jeremy
Collier and others encouraged the writing of more
such plays. Other early exponents, besides Cibber
include ▷ Steele, ▷ Centlivre, Wilkinson, and
▷ Pix. ▷ Farquhar also incorporates some elements
of the type in a few of his plays. Reform comedy
became more prevalent during the 18th century,
eventually overlapping with sentimental comedy, in
which didactic considerations are paramount.
Bib: Loftis, J., *Comedy and Society from Congreve to
Fielding*; Hume, R. D., *The Development of English
Drama in the Seventeenth Century*.

Reformation
An important religious movement in the 16th
century; its aim was to protest in a variety of ways
against the conduct of the Catholic Church, which
had hitherto remained undivided. The outcome
was division: the Roman ▷ Catholics remained
dominant in the countries bordering on the western
Mediterranean and in south Germany; the new
▷ Protestant churches became supreme in northern
Europe. The causes of the movement were political
(the rise of the new nation-state); moral (resentment
at the low example set by many of the clergy); and
doctrinal (disagreement, stimulated by the new
critical spirit of the ▷ Renaissance, over points of
doctrine hitherto imposed by the authority of the
Church).
  The reformation in England proceeded in three
phases.

1 Henry VIII carried out the first in merely political
terms. His desire to divorce Katharine of Aragon was
merely a pretext; he himself sought complete control
over the Church of England, and needed money; he
resented the authority of the Pope in Rome and the
internationalism of the monastic orders; he welcomed
the opportunity to increase his wealth by confiscating
their property. He declared himself Supreme Head
of the Church of England by the Act of Supremacy,
supported by Parliament and passed by it in 1533;
he dissolved the monasteries in 1536–9. On the
other hand, his Six Articles of 1539 tried to keep
the Church fully Catholic on all points except that
of papal sovereignty. As the support by Parliament
showed, he had popular opinion behind him, at
least in southern England; the English Church
had long been restive against the sovereignty of the
Pope, particularly when, in the 14th century, he had
reigned from Avignon in France, the home of the
national enemy.
  2 The second phase, under his son Edward
VI, went further and aroused more national
disagreement. The clergy were permitted to marry,
and the *Book of* ▷ *Common Prayer* included 42
articles of faith (later reduced to 39) which defined
the doctrine of the Church of England in Protestant
terms; there was extensive destruction of religious
images in churches throughout the country. Henry's
daughter Mary I undertook a complete reaction back
to Catholicism, but her persecution of the Protestants
and her subservience to her husband, Philip II of
Spain, the most fanatical of the Catholic sovereigns,
confirmed the country in a Protestant direction.
  3 Henry's remaining daughter, Elizabeth
I, contrived a religious settlement that was a
compromise between the reforms of her father
and those of her brother. The intention was to
be inclusive: Catholics were not to be driven out
of the Church of England if she could help it,
and she wanted to keep as many of her Protestant
subjects within it as possible. The result, however,
was disunion: Catholics could not subscribe
to the Church of England after the Pope had
excommunicated the Queen in 1571, and the
more extreme Protestants were constantly pressing
for further reforms, especially in the structure
of church government (they mostly wanted the
abolition of rule through bishops) and in the
conduct of worship, which they wanted in full
austerity. These ▷ Puritans, as they were called
by their enemies, eventually established their own
religious organizations, but not until after 1660.
The vagueness of the Elizabethan settlement also
gave rise to disagreement within the Church of
England, and this has lasted unil the present day:
the High Church is the section which emphasizes
the more Catholic interpretation of the settlement
(*ie* more in keeping with Henry VIII's intentions),
and the Low Church is the section which insists
that the Church of England is essentially Protestant.
This disagreement, however, has never disrupted
the organization of the Church which, under the
headship of the sovereign, is still that of the Catholic
church of medieval England.
  The reformation in Scotland proceeded side by

side with the Elizabethan phase in England, and helped to bring about a reconciliation of the two nations which had been hostile to each other for three centuries. The Scottish reformation, however, was extreme, under the leadership of John Knox, a disciple of the French reformer ▷ Calvin. The national Church of Scotland has remained Calvinist (▷ Presbyterian) to this day. Ireland remained Catholic, and in consequence suffered severe persecution by its English rulers in the 16th and 17th centuries. The only excuse for this tyranny was the real danger that Ireland might become a base for one of England's more powerful Catholic enemies – France or Spain.

Regency

In English history, the period 1811–20 when George, Prince of Wales, later George IV (1820–30), took the title of Prince Regent during the final illness of his father, George III (1760–1820). In British cultural history, the term is often applied to cover the first 20 years of the 19th century during which a certain style of taste in art and architecture prevailed. It was inspired by the taste of the first French Empire (▷ Napoleon I) which itself arose from French revolutionary cultivation of ancient Greece, especially the republic of Athens. Architecture was austerely classical (the 'Greek style'), and dress was similarly modelled on long, graceful lines suitable for men and women with slender figures.

In literature, the term covers the working life of the second generation of romantic poets (Bryon, Shelley and Keats), the work of the essayists Lamb and Hazlitt, and that of the novelists ▷ Jane Austen and Walter Scott. The best work of the essentially ▷ Augustan poet ▷ Crabbe also comes into the Regency period. The word is applied, however, more to architecture, dress and furniture than to literature, the principal architects being John Nash (1752–1835) and John Soane (1753–1837), architect of the Bank of England.

Regicides

(From Latin, meaning 'king killers'.) In English history, the group of men responsible for the execution of king ▷ Charles I. The king was tried on a charge of treason, a distinction being made between the institution of the Crown and Charles himself, who was king. 84 people, including the executioners, were said to be responsible for his trial and death. When his son was restored to the throne in 1660 as ▷ Charles II, the regicides were tried, and ten of them were executed; some of them, however, had already escaped abroad.
▷ Restoration.

Rehearsal, The (1671)

Burlesque play attributed to George Villiers, Duke of Buckingham, satirizing the heroic tragedies of the day. Bayes (a name implying that he is ▷ Poet Laureate) takes two friends, Johnson and Smith, to see a rehearsal of his latest play, which concerns the struggle for the Kingdom of Brentford. Most of the action consists of scenes from the absurd play

within a play, punctuated by the two spectators' incredulous, sardonic or contemptuous questions and comments, and Bayes's ridiculous explanations to them and instructions to the players. Finally, the two observers, and then the actors themselves, steal off before the play is finished, and the piece ends with Bayes vowing to revenge himself on 'the Town' for its ill-use of him and his plays. ▷ D'Avenant and ▷ Dryden are thought to have been the main targets of the satire; the figure of Drawcansir has been viewed as a parody of Almanzor in ▷ Dryden's *The Conquest of Granada*. His name became symbolic of blustering, bragging characters.

Relapse, The; Or, Virtue in Danger (1696)

Play by ▷ Sir John Vanbrugh, written as a sequel to, and gentle satire on, ▷ Colley Cibber's ▷ *Love's Last Shift* (1696), in which the central character stages a repentance which Vanbrugh found unbelievable. This did not prevent Cibber himself from acting the part of Lord Foppington in *The Relapse* with relish and to great acclaim. Loveless is now living quietly in the country with his faithful and virtuous wife Amanda, whom he had abandoned and then rejoined in *Love's Last Shift*. They return to the town for the winter season, whereupon he falls in love with Amanda's gayer cousin, Berinthia. Meanwhile, Worthy, an old flame of Amanda's, begins a new pursuit of her. Berinthia becomes an accomplice in his plan to seduce Amanda, so as to clear the path for her affair with Loveless. The affair is consummated, but Amanda summons her resources to resist Worthy's advances. A separate plot involves the impoverished Young Fashion's scheme to impersonate his older brother Lord Foppington, so as to marry the wealthy and lustful country girl, Miss Hoyden. At the end Worthy is shown unfulfilled and now in love with Amanda, while she achieves another uncertain reunion with her husband. The play's humour resides more in comic action than in witty dialogue, and there is a good deal of crude farce. Amanda's sobre virtue is somewhat at odds with the rest of the play, while the consequences of Loveless' intrigue with Berinthia are left unclear.

Religio Laici (1682)

A poem in heroic ▷ couplets by ▷ John Dryden, defending the tenets of the Church of England against the extremes of ▷ Deism and Roman Catholicism. It is frequently compared with ▷ *The Hind and the Panther* which Dryden published five years later after becoming a ▷ Catholic.

Religio Medici (1635)

(*The Religion of a Physician*). A work of spiritual and autobiographical reflection by ▷ Sir Thomas Browne. It was written around 1635, and seems not to have been intended for publication but for circulation among the author's friends. After its publication without Browne's permission in 1642, however, an authorized text was issued in 1643 which was subsequently translated into Dutch, German, Latin and French. As a form of ▷ autobiography, the work presents the image of a relaxed, sceptical, philosophic and endlessly self-intrigued author. Informed by a desire to reconcile religious belief with the kind of scepticism associated with the ▷ New Science of the mid-17th century, Browne's work became something of a best-seller. Stylistically, in its engaging enjoyment of digressive, curious and highly intellectualized speculation, the work can be compared to the poetry of John Donne or, later, ▷ Henry Vaughan. But it also forms part of the trend towards sceptical enquiry which was to be fostered by ▷ Thomas Hobbes and ▷ John Locke.

Reliques
▷ Percy, Thomas.

Renaissance in England, The
'Renaissance' (or 'Renascence') derives from Latin *renascentia* = 'rebirth'. The word was first used by Italian scholars in the mid-16th century to express the rediscovery of ancient Roman and Greek culture, which was now studied for its own sake and not used merely to enhance the authority of the Church. Modern scholars are more inclined to use the term to express a great variety of interdependent changes which Europe underwent politically, economically and culturally between 1450 (although the starting points were much earlier) and 1600. The religious outcome of these changes is expressed through the terms Reformation and Counter-Reformation, a sequence of events which were closely bound up with the Renaissance.

In England, the Renaissance is usually thought of as beginning with the accession of the House of Tudor to the throne in 1485. Politically, this marks the end of the period of civil war amongst the old feudal aristocracy (the Wars of the Roses) in the mid-15th century, and the establishment of something like a modern, efficient, centralized state; technically, the date is close to that of the introduction of printing into England – an invention whithout which the great cultural changes of the Renaissance could not have occurred. Culturally, the first important period in England was the reign of the second Tudor monarch, Henry VIII. This was the period of the English humanist Thomas More. (1478–1535) and the poet Sir Thomas Wyatt (1503–42).

Several distinctive features characterize the English Renaissance. The first is the lateness of its impact; Italian, French, German, Dutch and Spanish scholars had already worked on the ancient Greek and Latin writers, and had produced works of their own inspired by the classics; in consequence, English culture was revitalized not so much directly by the classics as by contemporary Europeans under the influence of the classics. Castiglione's *The Courtier* (1528), Machiavelli's *The Prince* (1513), Ariosto's *Orlando* (1532), were as important in the English Renaissance as the works of ▷ classical authors such as ▷ Virgil's ▷ *Aeneid*, or the plays of ▷ Seneca, and it was characteristic that North's 1579 translation of ▷ Plutarch's *Lives* was not from the original Greek but from a French version. A further characteristic of English Renaissance literature is that it is primarily artistic, rather than philosophical

and scholarly, and another is ▷ the coinciding of the Renaissance and the ▷ Reformation in England, in contrast to the rest of the Europe where the Reformation (or, in countries that remained Roman ▷ Catholic, the Counter-Reformation) succeeded the Renaissance.

The English Renaissance was largely literary, and achieved its finest expression in the so-called Elizabethan drama which began to excel only in the last decade of the 16th century and reached its height in the first 15 years of the 17th; its finest exponents were Christopher Marlowe (1564–93), Ben Jonson (1572–1637) and ▷ William Shakespeare. Non-dramatic poetry was also extremely rich, and reached its peak in the same period in the work of ▷ Edmund Spenser, Philip Sidney (1554–86), Shakespeare and John Donne (1572–1631), but it is typical of the lateness of the Renaissance in England that its most ambitious product, ▷ John Milton's epic ▷ *Paradise Lost*, was publised as late as 1667. Native English prose shaped itself more slowly than poetry; Thomas More wrote his *Utopia* in Latin, which was the vehicle of some other writers including ▷ Francis Bacon in much of his work owing to its advantages (for international circulation) over English, at a time when the latter was little learned in other countries. Nonetheless English prose developed with vigour in native English writers such as Roger Ascham (1515–68), Thomas North (1535–1601), Richard Hooker (1553–1600) in the English works of Francis Bacon, and in the translators of the ▷ Bible.

Republic, The
A philosophical dialogue by the Greek philosopher ▷ Plato. ▷ Socrates discusses with his friends the nature of justice, and the conversation leads to an outline of the ideal state. Public life must exhibit the highest virtues of private life, and justice is achieved if the classes work together to contribute to society the virtues in which each excels. Democracy (the rule of the people), oligarchy (the rule of a small powerful group), and timocracy (the rule of men of property) are in turn rejected, in favour of aristocracy – the rule of the best, trained by an exacting system of education. The aristocrat will seek wisdom, whereas the man of action seeks honour, and the merchant gratifies his appetites. Wisdom is a direct apprehension of the good conceived as a system of ideal forms; Book VII contains the famous parable of men sitting with their backs to these forms (the only substantial reality) watching the shadows on the wall of the cavern – *ie* phenomena apprehended by the senses – and supposing these shadows to be the only reality. Book X contains Plato's notorious rejection of poetry: poets must be expelled, though with honour, because they frustrate the pursuit of true wisdom by extolling the illusory phenomena of this world, and weaken the mind by stimulating wasteful sympathy with the misfortunes of men.

Restoration
The word is used in two senses: the re-establishment of the Stuart monarchy in the person of ▷ King Charles II after the republican experiment of 1649–60; and as a period designation, often to cover

the last 40 years of the 17th century, *ie* not only the reign of ▷ Charles II but that of his brother ▷ James II, and that of ▷ William III and ▷ Mary II. This period was marked by special cultural characteristics which were promoted by the political fact of the restoration of the monarchy. In this sense the term is most commonly used to identify three principal literary products: **1** Restoration prose; **2** Restoration drama (especially comedy); **3** Restoration poetry.

1 Restoration prose is marked by a very conscious determination by leading writers to use prose as a vehicle of reason. It had of course already been used in this way by, for instance, ▷ Francis Bacon, but even Bacon did not distinguish the virtues of prose for such a vehicle. It was one of the aims of the new ▷ Royal Society to cultivate these virtues, which were described by Thomas Sprat in his *History of the Royal Society* (1667): 'a close, naked, natural way of speaking; positive expressions; clear senses; a native easiness; bringing all things as near the Mathematical plainness, as they can: and preferring the language of Artisans, Countrymen, and Merchants before that of Wits, or Scholars'. Sprat thus describes what have been considered the normal qualities of good prose ever since, and the Restoration period is indeed the first age of modern English prose writing. Its master was the poet ▷ John Dryden in his prose criticism, for instance his *Essay on Dramatic Poesy* (1668).

2 Restoration drama. This period is sometimes described as the 'silver' age of English drama, by comparison with the 'golden' age of Shakespeare. Owing to the hostility of the ▷ Puritans to drama, the art had practically ceased to be practised in the period of their power, 1642–60 when the public theatres were closed; it was then continued with ardour, but in less promising circumstances than in the 'golden' age. The decline had indeed already been evident before the close of the ▷ theatres in 1642, and a dramatist such as ▷ James Shirley, writing in the 1630s, exhibits many of the characteristic virtues and weaknesses of the Restoration. The audience had already ceased to be drawn from all classes, and was restricted to people of fashion and refinement; wit, elegance of speech and skilful stage technique were the qualities which were sought after, and they implied a drama different from that of Shakespeare and his contemporaries, which had been intended to please alike the learned and the simple, the profound and the frivolous. After 1660, the French drama of ▷ Molière in comedy and of ▷ Corneille and ▷ Racine in tragedy were the dominating influences of the English stage, but English society was not so constructed as to be able to emulate the French 'golden' age. English 'heroic' tragedy, with the exception of a few plays by Dryden and ▷ Otway, lacked the conviction of French tragedy in a comparable style, and the comedy of ▷ Etherege, ▷ Wycherley, ▷ Vanbrugh, ▷ Farquhar, and of ▷ Congreve, is slight and superficial by comparison with that of Molière. However, Restoration comedy is in prose, unlike most of the tragedy, and the virtues of Restoration dramatists are especially in the wit, grace and poise of their prose dialogue; the comedies are still

successful and even popular on the English stage, whereas few of the tragedies are ever performed.

3 Restoration (non-dramatic) poetry. This, especially the poetry of Dryden, is really the beginning of ▷ Augustan poetry. The virtues admired in the prose of the time reigned also over the poetry, so that a 'close, naked, natural way of speaking' is as evident in the verse as in the prose of Dryden. Besides him, ▷ Samuel Butler and the ▷ Earl of Rochester are the principal names classifiable as 'Restoration poets', but the foremost poet of the reign of Charles II, ▷ John Milton, cannot be so classified. The Restoration poets excelled in satire whereas Milton, in his epics and his one tragedy in so different a style from the neo-classic French tragedies, is a late product of the English ▷ Renaissance, profoundly modified by Puritanism.

Review, The

Periodical written by ▷ Daniel Defoe and published three times weekly from 1704 to 1713. Politically impartial; it expressed Defoe's opinion on current political events, and also on literature and manners. Defoe has been called the inventor of the leading article, a feature of modern newspapers.

Reviews and periodicals

The English periodical press arose gradually from the controversial religious and political pamphleteering of the late 16th and 17th centuries. It became established as a recognized institution early in the 18th century, and it was also in the 18th century that the review, which expresses opinion, became distinguished from the newspaper, which gives priority to information on current events ▷ Journalism.

Revolution of 1688
▷ Glorious Revolution.

Reynolds, Sir Joshua (b1723–92)

One of the leading portrait painters of the 18th century, the great age of English portrait painting. He was the first President of the ▷ Royal Academy, and the author of *Discourses, ie* lectures, delivered to its students between 1760 and 1790, on the principles of art. The friend of ▷ Samuel Johnson, he was a founder-member of the Literary Club of which Johnson was the centre. Reynolds was strongly representative of 18th-century aristocratic taste, and in the opinion of ▷ William Blake, writing about 1808, 'This man was Hired to Depress Art'. However, his *Discourses* were admired by the greatest 19th-century English art critic, John Ruskin.

Rich, Christopher (1657–1714)

Theatre manager. Rich assumed full control of the ▷ United Company in 1693, but his mismanagement contributed to the defection of the leading actors, including ▷ Thomas Betterton, ▷ Elizabeth Barry, and ▷ Anne Bracegirdle, in 1695. Even so, he succeeded in building up an able company in their place, including the young ▷ Colley Cibber, William Bullock, Joe Haines, ▷ John and ▷ Susannah

Verbruggen, ▷ Anne Oldfield and ▷ William Penkethman, as well as bringing in foreign performers as attractions.

In 1701 Rich weathered an attempt to oust him from control of ▷ Drury Lane, but he continued to invite conflict with both actors and dramatists, and in 1709 he was forced to close Drury Lane on an order from the Lord Chamberlain, after his attempt to deny his actors their full profits from benefit performances. Rich was not allowed to form a new company until 1714, but he died just six weeks before the scheduled opening.

Bib: Highfill, P. H. Jr., Burnim, K. A. and Langhans, E. A. (eds.), *A Biographical Dictionary of Actors, Actresses, Musicians, Dancers, Managers, and Other Stage Personnel in London 1660–1800.*

Rich, John (1692–1761)

Actor, manager, dancer, dramatist, son of ▷ Christopher Rich. John inherited the largest share of the theatrical patent owned by his father, and took over the refurbished ▷ Lincoln's Inn Fields Theatre opened by his father before his death in 1714. He soon began acting and dancing at the theatre, and built up its repertory of dance, variety, and pantomime programmes, for whose growing popularity he was largely responsible.

During the following years he gained a mixed reputation for, on the one hand, allegedly degrading the stage, and on the other hand, providing popular entertainment by talented performers in settings of great magnificence. He was also complimented for reviving the best of the old plays, and encouraging new authors. It was under his auspices that ▷ John Gay's ▷ *The Beggar's Opera* was first staged in 1728, making (according to a well-known quotation) 'Gay rich and Rich gay'. The profits from *The Beggar's Opera* helped finance a new theatre in Covent Garden on the site of the present Royal Opera House (▷ Covent Garden Theatres), which opened in 1732 with a cast headed by ▷ James Quin. A fierce rivalry developed between Covent Garden and ▷ Drury Lane under ▷ Garrick's management, highlighted in 1750–51, when the theatres staged *Romeo and Juliet* simultaneously. For decades after his death, theatres continued to honour Rich in tributes on stage, or by borrowing devices from his shows.

Bib: Highfill, P. H. Jr., Burnim, K. A. and Langhans, E. A. (eds.), *A Biographical Dictionary of Actors, Actresses, Musicians, Dancers, Managers, and Other Stage Personnel in London 1660–1800.*

Richardson, Samuel (1689–1761)

Novelist. Richardson was the son of a furniture-maker, born near Derby, though most of his childhood was spent in London as the family returned to live there. Little is known of his education, though by the age of 13 he is known to have written love letters on behalf of his friends, an activity relevant for his later choice of the epistolary genre.

In 1706 Richardson was apprenticed to a printer, and in 1715 became a freeman of the Stationers' Company. In 1721 he began his own business, which proved successful for the rest of his life. In the same year he married the daughter of his former master. His wife died ten years later, and in the early 1730s he suffered the deaths of all the six children born to the marriage.

In 1733 he remarried, again to the daughter of a colleague, and four of their daughters survived. In the same year he published *The Apprentice's Vade Mecum*, a conduct guide to moral behaviour. In 1739 his own, deliberately moral, version of *Aesop's Fables* appeared.

The moral intention of his early works is evident in his fiction, though the creations of his imagination frequently escape any strict schemata. ▷ *Pamela*, begun in the same year as *Aesop's Fables* appeared, started as a series of conduct guides or 'Familiar Letters', which his friends encouraged him to write. Richardson's professional life, meanwhile, was proving rewarding. In 1723 he had begun to print *The True Briton*, an influential Tory journal, and in 1733 the House of Commons was using his presses. In 1742 he gained a lucrative contract as printer of the Parliamentary Journals.

His social life was proving equally enjoyable. He particularly relished the company of young women, whom he referred to as his 'honorary daughters', and while writing ▷ *Clarissa* (probably begun in 1744) he frequently asked them for their comments and teased them with speculations about the fate of his heroine. The first two volumes appeared in 1747 and were widely acclaimed; five more followed in 1748. The novel was praised, but readers were uneasy about its sexual elements, and its popularity proved less than that of *Pamela*.

About 1750 Richardson embarked on a new project, which was to be centred on the 'good man'. In 1752 ▷ Samuel Johnson read the draft manuscript of the work, ▷ *The History of Sir Charles Grandison*, and the novel appeared in seven volumes in 1753–4. Again, there was some doubt about the morality of the book, an ironic fate for a writer with Richardson's intentions.

In 1755 Richardson published a volume of selections from his three novels, in a form which he considered contained the essence of his writing; he was constantly concerned about the length of his fictions, and continually worked on revisions. His novels develop the ▷ epistolary style to a great degree of psychological subtlety, and he has long been regarded as one of the chief founders of the English novel.

Bib: Eaves, T. C. D. and Kimpel, B. D., *Samuel Richardson*; Kinkead-Weekes, M., *Samuel Richardson, Dramatic Novels*; Flynn, C. H., *Samuel Richardson, A Man of Letters.*

Ridotto

A kind of public social gathering, with dancing and music, introduced into England in 1722, and very popular in the 18th century.

Rights of Man

▷ Paine, Thomas.

Rivals, The (1775)

A prose comedy by ▷ Richard Brinsley Sheridan.
It is set in the fashionable city of Bath, and the plot
concerns parents and guardians at cross purposes with
their children. The central situation is that the young
and sentimental Lydia Languish, a great novel reader,
prefers the idea of marrying a young, penniless officer
to the possibility of a rich young heir as a husband.
Captain Absolute is such an heir and genuinely in
love with her, but to win her affections he disguises
himself as the penniless Ensign Beverley. His father,
Sir Anthony Absolute, a rich baronet, is determined to
make an unromantic marriage of convenience between
his son and Lydia, but the Captain dare not disclose
his disguise and so seems to be disobeying his father's
wishes. Mrs Malaprop, Lydia's guardian, is equally
anxious for the worldly match and disapproves of
Beverley, but at the same time she is making love by
letter to the aggressive Irishman, Sir Lucius O'Trigger,
who supposes that the letters come from Lydia, and is
one of her suitors. An additional complication is that
the so-called Beverley and Sir Lucius have as another
rival an absurd young country squire, Bob Acres. A
sub-plot is another love affair between Julia Melville
and the morbidly jealous Faulkland.

Sheridan's comedies – of which *The Rivals* is
the first – are, like those of ▷ Goldsmith at about
the same time, above all a reaction against the
sentimental tradition, and recall the wit and theatrical
deftness of ▷ Restoration drama without its sexual
explicitness.

Robinson Crusoe, The Life and Strange
 Surprising Adventures of (1719)

A novel by ▷ Daniel Defoe. The first part was
based on the experiences of a sailor, ▷ Alexander
Selkirk, who went ashore on the uninhabited island
of Juan Fernandez in 1704, and remained there until
he was rescued in 1709. Crusoe runs away to sea (as
Selkirk had done) and after a number of adventures
is wrecked on an uninhabited island, where he
remains for 20 years. Defoe describes the industrious
and methodical way in which he builds up a life for
himself, how he is endangered by the periodic visits
of a race of cannibals, how he tames one of them
into an ideal servant, Man Friday. The island is
eventually visited by a ship in the hands of mutinous
sailors; he subdues the mutineers and rescues the
officers, who take him back to England, leaving the
repentant mutineers behind as a colony, together
with some Spaniards whom he had previously
rescued from the cannibals.

In *The Farther Adventures of Robinson Crusoe*,
published in the same year, Crusoe revisits the
colony and relates its fortunes; he also travels
elsewhere, visits China, and returns to England
across Siberia and Russia. The third part, *The Serious
Reflections of Robinson Crusoe* (1720), consists of moral
essays in which Defoe represents the book as an
▷ allegory of his own life. This was partly a defence
against the disapproval of his fellow ▷ Puritans
who regarded fiction as hardly distinguishable from
lies; on the other hand, Defoe's tale is certainly an
image of the loneliness and arduousness of the life of
individual economic enterprise which was becoming

increasingly typical of society; Crusoe is made to
say that he has been more lonely since his return to
London than he ever was on his island.

Modern critics have noticed how Crusoe sees
human beings merely in terms of their economic
virtues. The book has always been praised for its
detailed verisimilitude, which caused it to be received
at first as an authentic account; the descriptions
are almost entirely in terms of what the philosopher
▷ John Locke had distinguished as the objectively
discernible 'primary qualities' (▷ *Essay concerning
human understanding*) as opposed to the subjectively
experienced 'secondary qualities' (colour, beauty,
etc.) which it is difficult to verify. The style of
the writing is extremely plain, in keeping with the
principles that Thomas Sprat had laid down for
the ▷ Royal Society in 1667 (*History of the Royal
Society*): 'the language of Artisans, Countrymen, and
Merchants'. That Crusoe appears much less religious
than Defoe intends is also often remarked; on the
other hand, if there is a principle of unity in the long,
episodic narrative, it is the function of God as the
basic Providence, subjecting chaos so that man may
use his constructive virtues for the building of an
orderly world.

Robinson, Mary (1758–1800)

Novelist, poet and actress. Although Mary Robinson
is now known for her ▷ Gothic novels, during her
lifetime she was infamous for her affair with the
Prince of Wales. He saw her in the role of Perdita
in 1779–80 and became enamoured of her. The
relationship lasted just over a year, leaving Robinson
the butt of crude satire and with the lasting nickname
'Perdita'. In 1783 she became paralysed from the
waist down after a miscarriage and from then on she
was forced to earn her living by writing. Her poetry
was never very original, picking up populist sentiment
in relation to current events, such as the storming
of the Bastille, and when her collection *Lyrical Tales*
in 1800 was published ▷ Wordsworth considered
changing the title of his own work. In comparison
her novels are sharp and witty, tinged with liberal
sentiment; they include, *Vacenza* (1792), *Angelina*
(1795) and *Hubert de Sevrac* (1796).
Bib: Bass, P., *The Green Dragon*; Rodgers, K.,
Feminism in Eighteenth-century England.

Rochester, John Wilmot, Second Earl of
 (1647–80)

Poet and libertine. His father had been ennobled by
Charles II for his support during his exile and he
enjoyed a privileged position at the ▷ Restoration
court, being more than once banished (and later
pardoned) for his unruly behaviour and verses.
His reputation among his contemporaries can be
gauged from the portrait of the elegant and witty
Dorimant in ▷ Sir George Etherege's ▷ *The
Man of Mode* (1676) which is based on the poet.
He showed conspicuous courage in battle during
sea-engagements with the Dutch. Later, however,
he was suspected of acting less honourably in having
▷ John Dryden set upon in an alley, believing him
to be the author of an anonymous satire in a poem by
the Earl of Mulgrave. Rochester's motive for refusing

to fight a duel with Mulgrave is unclear. It is unlikely to have been the simple lack of courage which his enemies attributed to him at the time, though he did recommend cowardice in his poetry.

Rochester's combination of aristocracy and rigorous intellectual honesty set him at odds with the emergent bourgeois ethos of the time. He followed ▷ Hobbes and the ancient philosophers ▷ Lucretius and ▷ Seneca in consistent philosophical materialism. He was a ▷ Deist who believed that God, if He existed, could take no interest in petty human affairs, that there was no life after death and that the soul was merely a function of matter. His translation of lines from Seneca's *Troades* dismisses Hell and the afterlife as 'senselesse Storyes, idle Tales/Dreames, Whimseys, and noe more.'

Also he wrote freely about sexual intimacy, both in its pleasurable and disgusting aspects, flouting bourgeois prudery and linguistic censorship. There is sometimes a trivial, unpleasant tone to his writing in this vein, for example in *Signior Dildo* and the Chloris lyrics. But his obscenity is more often psychologically profound and philosophically disturbing, as in *A Ramble in St James's Park* and *The Imperfect Enjoyment*. Moreover, as an aristocrat, he was contemptuous of the proprietorial sexism of the new bourgeoisie. His friend Gilbert Burnet, later bishop of Salisbury, showed the orthodox attitude when he argued that Rochester's libertinism amounted to 'theft' by one man from another: 'men have a property in their wives and daughters, so that to defile the one, or corrupt the other, is an unjust and injurious thing'. In contrast, though Rochester could scarcely be called feminist, his ambiguous satire on the Earl of Mulgrave, *A Very Heroical Epistle in Answer to Ephelia*, shows an insight into what we would now call male chauvinism, which is most unusual for the period.

Rochester's Puritan mother and his friend Burnet refused access to his libertine friends as he lay dying of syphilis, and apparently persuaded him to turn to orthodox religion. After the poet's death Burnet published *Some Passages of the Life and Death of the Earl of Rochester* (1680), and over the next two-and-a-half centuries Rochester's poetry (much of it suppressed) was overshadowed by the edifying legend of the atheist's death-bed repentance. The argument over whether he 'really' repented as he lay in his syphilitic delirium is, however, irrelevant to his poetry, all of which is consistently materialist and libertine. The pious poems attributed to his last days are not by him and lack the quality of his genuine work.

His poetry is diverse, reflecting the social and cultural transitions of his time. He wrote some exquisite lyrics in the 'cavalier' tradition, including the movingly philosophical *carpe diem* poem 'All my past life is mine noe more' (sometimes called *Love and Life*). Much of his best work, however, is in the new medium of heroic ▷ couplets, a form which he uses, in such poems as *A Satyr against Reason and Mankind*, *Timon*, and *Tunbridge Wells*, with a conversational ease and freedom much admired and imitated by later ▷ Augustans. His *An Allusion to Horace, the Tenth Satyr of the First Book* is the first

example of the characteristically Augustan genre of the 'imitation', also adopted about this time by ▷ John Oldham.

Bib: Johnson, S., in *Lives of the Poets*; Pinto, V. de S., *Enthusiast in Wit*; Adlard, J., *The Debt to Pleasure*; Treglown, J., *Spirit of Wit: Reconsiderations of Rochester*; Farley-Hills, D., *Rochester's Poetry*.

Roderick Random, The Adventures of (1748)

A novel by ▷ Tobias Smollett. It is based on Smollett's own experience as a naval doctor at the siege of Cartagena in 1741; it is episodic in form, and vivid but somewhat brutal in manner. In the Preface, the author pays tribute to the comic genius of Cervantes, author of *Don Quixote*.

Rogers, Samuel (1763–1855)

Poet. The wealthy son of a banker from Stoke Newington, he wrote an *Ode to Superstition* (1786) and the popular reflective poem, *The Pleasures of Memory* (1792). *Columbus*, a fragment of an epic, appeared in 1810, and a narrative poem, *Jacqueline*, was published together with Lord Byron's *Lara* in 1814. He was offered the ▷ Poet Laureateship on the death of ▷ William Wordsworth in 1850, but declined. He has been referred to as 'the last Augustan'.

Romanticism

Two phases in the development of this concept need to be distinguished:

1 *'Romantick' taste* (c1650–c1789) The adjective 'romantic' came into use in the mid-17th century, at the point when the romance form, which had dominated secular literature during the Middle Ages and the ▷ Renaissance, fell from prominence. As ▷ Enlightenment philosophy and neo-classical taste developed, the romance form was subjected to self-conscious analysis and criticism. In its early stages the word took various forms: 'romancy', 'romancical', 'romantique', 'romantick'. Its meaning, 'like a romance', carried a number of different connotations, related to the various features of romance: the archaic rituals of chivalry, magic, superstition, improbable adventures, idealistic love, and wild scenery. ▷ Samuel Pepys used the word in 1667: 'These things are almost romantique, and yet true'. And the *Oxford English Dictionary* cites a 1659 reference to 'An old house in a romancey place'.

During the 18th century romantic wildness was disapproved of by the more puritanical, rational and enlightened reader. Some thinkers, however, such as the third ▷ Earl of Shaftesbury, self-consciously boasted of their emotional idealism and enthusiasm for wild scenery. Also most readers enjoyed the 'romantick' alternatives to neo-classicism indulged in at times by the poets and prose writers. Sometimes poets employed imitations of ornamental, medieval or ▷ Gothic forms, such as the ▷ Spenserian stanza and the ▷ ballad, though romantic sensibility could also be expressed in the heroic ▷ couplet. ▷ Alexander Pope's ▷ *Eloisa to Abelard* and *Elegy to the Memory of an Unfortunate Lady*, ▷ James Thomson's ▷ *Castle of Indolence*, ▷ Thomas Gray's translations of Norse and Welsh ballads and his ode

▷ *The Bard*, and ▷ James Macpherson's ▷ *Ossian*, illustrate the range of romantic taste in the 18th century. The subjects of these works: passionate love, religious enthusiasm, laziness, medieval history, suicide, lie outside the mainstream of Augustanism, and they all share (with different degrees of seriousness) a sense of daring literary excess.

2 *The Romantic Movement* (1789–1824) The six great poets of what is now generally called the Romantic Movement, are in many ways extremely diverse. ▷ William Blake, the pioneer of the group, was broadly speaking a fundamentalist Christian, who felt that ▷ William Wordsworth's ▷ pantheistic 'natural piety' made him 'a Heathen Philosopher at Enmity against all true Poetry'. Lord Byron (1788–1824) emulated the wit and urbanity of Alexander Pope, whereas John Keats (1795–1821) was contemptuous of neo-classical couplet writers who 'sway'd about upon a rocking horse,/ And thought it Pegasus'. Percy Bysshe Shelley (1792–1822) was an atheist, ▷ Samuel Taylor Coleridge became an apologist for the Church of England. However, despite their differences, these poets show essential similarities in their response to the same historical situation, and do form a coherent group. It will be best to begin by describing their characteristics, leaving the label, 'Romanticism', to be explained afterwards. Fundamental to romanticism is a new attitude towards the role of man in nature. The writers of the Enlightenment period, ▷ the Earl of Rochester, ▷ John Dryden and Pope had shared with the ancients a certainty as to what nature was, and a confidence about their place in it. For them *human* nature was an integral part, even the greatest glory, of 'Nature', and (like gravity) obeyed 'Nature's laws'. In the early stages of Enlightenment it seemed easy to reconcile the new exploitative science and technology with a traditional piety about God's creation. But by the end of the century a crisis had developed. Enlightenment had finally robbed nature of its authentic, primitive awesomeness. More practically its manipulative exploitation by man seemed in danger of destroying nature itself. ▷ William Cowper expressed this new mood of diffidence and alienation in his aphorism: 'God made the country, and man made the town', while Shelley declared more boldly that 'man, having enslaved the elements, remains himself a slave'. ▷ Newton's light had reduced nature to a manipulable material system. It had become either a useful recreational facility (Wordsworth wrote a guidebook to the picturesque Lakes), or – in atavistic reaction – a mystical substitute for religion. Shelley's proposed answer to the crisis of Enlightenment, like that of all the Romantic poets, was to cultivate the 'imagination' and 'the poetical faculty'.

Nature thus ceases to be an objective intellectual concept for the Romantics, and becomes instead an elusive metaphor. The brisk clarity of Pope's: 'First follow *Nature* . . . which is still the same', is replaced by the anxious emotive rhetoric of Wordsworth's: 'And I have felt/A sense sublime/ Of something far more deeply interfused'. Romanticism thus stands as an emotional reaction against the rational classicism

of 18th-century Augustanism. It is important to remember that all these terms embody large simplifications. If they are used without a sense of the historical complexities which lie behind them, they can distort the literature to which they refer, rather than illuminating it.

Bib: Abrams, M. H., *The Mirror and the Lamp*; Praz, M., *The Romantic Agony*; Ford, B. (ed.), *New Pelican Guide to English Literature, Vol. 5: From Blake to Byron*; Bloom, H., *The Visionary Company*; Watson, J. R., *English Poetry of the Romantic Period: 1789–1830*; Butler, M., *Rebels and Reactionaries: English Literature and its Background: 1760–1830*; McGann, J., *The Romantic Ideology*; Mellor, A. K., *Romanticism and Feminism*.

Roscommon, Wentworth Dillon, Fourth Earl of (?1633–85)

Critic and ▷ Restoration courtier. His translation of ▷ Horace's *Art of Poetry* (1680) in blank verse, and his *Essay on Translated Verse* (1684), in heroic couplets, were greatly admired at the time, and his versification was praised by ▷ Alexander Pope.

Rosicrucianism

A system of philosophical and mystical beliefs professed by an organization known as the Ancient Mystic Order of Rosa Crucis (the 'red cross'). Its origins are obscure; it is first mentioned in 1614. Part of its doctrine has consisted in the belief that the universe contains a hierarchy of spirits governing the various elements. Pope, in his second version of ▷ *The Rape of the Lock*, used this system for satirical purposes; he needed for his ▷ mock epic a supernatural system comparable to the ancient Greek gods and goddesses of ▷ Homer's ▷ *Iliad*, but adapted, as they would not be, to the pettiness of his theme. He used the Rosicrucian system because it provided spirits of all degrees of importance.

Roundheads

A name for ▷ Puritan supporters of the ▷ Parliamentary party in the ▷ Civil Wars of 1642–51. They were so called because they habitually cut their hair close to their heads, whereas the Royalists (▷ Cavaliers) wore their hair ornamentally long. This Cavalier habit was regarded by the Puritans as a symptom of worldliness. The word has been traced back to 1641, when a Cavalier officer was quoted as declaring that he would 'cut the throats of those round-headed dogs that bawled against bishops'. Earlier than this, a pamphlet against long hair was published under the title of 'The unloveliness of lovelocks'.

Rousseau, Jean-Jacques (1712–78)

French-Swiss thinker. His chief works were: *Discourse on the Influence of Learning and Art* (1750), which he argues that progress in these areas has not improved human morals; *Discourse on Inequality* (1754), in which society is considered to have spoilt the liberty and virtue natural to primitive peoples; a novel, *The New Héloise* (1761), in which the return to primitive nature is considered in relation to the relationships of the sexes and the family; ▷ *The*

Social Contract (1761), a political treatise with the theme that the basis of society is artificial, not binding on individuals when society ceases to serve their interests; *Emile* (1762), advocating education through the evocation of the natural impulses and interests of the child, and the *Confessions*, an autobiography which was self-revealing without precedent, published after his death.

Rousseau was immensely influential, not only in France but throughout Europe. His praise of nature and protests against society were significant contributions to the creation of a revolutionary state of mind, culminating in the ▷ French Revolution of 1789. Education from nature, his conception of nature as a life-giving force, was of great importance in the background of ▷ Wordsworth, and through Wordsworth, of much of English 19th-century imaginative thinking, and linked with his devotion to nature was his equally influential reverence for childhood. As an autobiographer (▷ autobiography), Rousseau was one of the first to base the importance of individual experience on its uniqueness, not on its moral excellence or intellectual attainment. This was quite contrary to the characteristic 18th-century view, expressed in works like Samuel Johnson's ▷ *Rasselas*, in which the valuable experience was conceived to be only that which was true of and for humanity at large.

Rover, The (1679)

Comedy by ▷ Aphra Behn, reworked from ▷ Thomas Killigrew's play *Thomaso* (1663–4). The play concerns four cavaliers, exiled in the cause of the future Charles II, and the women whom they meet during a sojourn in Naples. Penniless Willmore (the Rover) is accompanied by the English Colonel Belville, his friend Frederick, and an English country gentleman called Blunt. Hellena, a 'gay young woman design'd for a Nun', is determined to avoid her fate and find a husband, while her sister Florinda is equally determined to avoid marrying the man intended for her by her brother. She has fallen in love with Belville, while Hellena, attending a carnival in disguise with her sister and two other women, falls in love with Willmore. He, however, is attracted to the wealthy and beautiful courtesan Angelica Bianca, and determines to gain her services without payment. Hellena pursues him, at one time disguised as a boy, while he woos Angelica Bianca, whom he eventually manages to bed. No sooner has this happened than he loses interest in her, while she is now painfully in love with him. She plans to kill him, but at the last moment is interrupted, and then finds herself unable to pull the trigger. Willmore marries the wealthy and virtuous Hellena, while Florinda, after a series of incidents, is united with Belville. Frederick marries Florinda's and Hellena's kinswoman Valeria, and the foolish Blunt, after being deceived and robbed by the prostitute Lucetta, remains unattached. The play takes place at carnival time, and there are colourful scenes of dancing and singing, wit and clowning. But the anguished character of Angelica Bianca adds a solemn note to the action, which also contains some ugly episodes, as when the enraged Blunt attempts to revenge himself for Lucetta's perfidy by raping

Florinda. The other men join him, and only the appearance of Valeria saves her. The play achieved great success, and remained popular until late in the 18th century. It generated a sequel, *The Rover, Part II*, and some imitations, including ▷ John Kemble's *Love in Many Masks* (1760).

Rowe, Elizabeth (Singer) (1674–1737)

English poet and journalist from Somerset – where her father had settled after being imprisoned for religious Nonconformity. Of ▷ Dissenting religious principles, she began to publish, and the Thynnes became her patrons (▷ Frances Seymour, Countess of Hertford). Her *Poems on Several Occasions* (1696) contains several different kinds of poetry. In her preface she writes that male writers have the traditions of writing, and try to 'Monopolize Sence too' so that not 'so much as Wit should be allowed us'. She sees such assertion as 'Violations of the liberties of Free-born English women' – language which recalls the radical political associations of Nonconformist religion with the English ▷ Civil War (1642–6) and (1648–51). She married the writer Thomas Rowe (1710), and after his death in 1715 she lived in Frome, Somerset, working as a teacher. Religion became her topic in the *Friendship in Death* (1728) – letters from the dead to the living. More letters followed, *Letters Moral and Entertaining* (1729–33) and the verse *History of Joseph* (1736).

▷ Scott, Mary (Taylor)

Rowe, Nicholas (1674–1718)

Poet and dramatist, known today chiefly for his so-called ▷ 'she-tragedies', in which the distresses of female victims are displayed, and for his edition of Shakespeare (▷ Shakespeare, editions). Rowe was initially a barrister in the Middle Temple, but gave this up for the theatre when his father died leaving him an inheritance, in 1692. He became in due course a friend to ▷ Pope and ▷ Addison. Rowe's ▷ blank-verse tragedy *The Ambitious Stepmother* was staged successfully at ▷ Lincoln's Inn Fields in 1700, with ▷ Betterton, ▷ Barry and ▷ Bracegirdle in the cast. His *Tamerlane* (1702), a tragedy whose figures of Tamerlane and Bajazet were modelled on those of ▷ William III and Louis XIV, became a stock play. *The Fair Penitent* (1703), based on Massinger's *The Fatal Dowry* followed, to great acclaim. The heroine Calista, abandoned by the 'gallant, gay Lothario', and eventually committing suicide, drew enormous sympathy from audiences; she was played first by Elizabeth Barry and later by ▷ Sarah Siddons. The characters formed part of ▷ Richardson's inspiration in his writing of ▷ *Clarissa* (1747–8). Rowe's edition of Shakespeare (1709; reissued in 1714) is often considered the first attempt to edit Shakespeare in the modern sense, dividing the plays into acts and scenes according to fixed principles, marking actors' entrances and exits, clarifying the texts, and supplying lists of characters. ▷ *The Tragedy of Jane Shore* (1714), was written 'in Imitation of Shakespeare's Style', although as Odell and others have pointed out, many would barely discover Shakespeare among the lines. Both this and *The Tragedy of Lady Jane Grey* (1715), continued

Rowe's tradition of suffering heroines. The former, like *Tamerlane* and *The Fair Penitent*, lasted into the 19th century, and all three became well-known in translation, in France. In 1715 Rowe became ▷ Poet Laureate.

Bib: Canfield, J. D., *Nicholas Rowe and Christian Tragedy*.

Rowson, Susanna Haswell (1762–1824)

British/North American novelist, dramatist, poet and essayist. Born in Portsmouth, England, she was brought to North America at the age of five. Although she returned to England periodically thereafter, because of political persecution or economic need, she became one of North America's earliest and most popular novelists. Extraordinarily diverse in her literary talents, she published ten novels, including ▷ *Victoria* (1786), *Charlotte, a Tale of Truth* (1791), *Mentoria* (1791), *Rebecca* (1792) and *Lucy Temple: a Sequel to Charlotte Temple*; a dozen plays, most notably *Slaves in Algiers* (1794); several collections of poetry, including *A Trip to Parnassas* (1788); and numerous other miscellanies, including textbooks and historical accounts of famous women. Her novels combined traditional didactic seduction plots with a more 'feminist' treatment of women's situation. Acknowledging the power of sexuality and the dangers of women's economic dependency (especially dependency on those who prove unreliable), Rowson's fiction shows links with the later 19th-century woman's novel formula.

She pursued various other careers during her life, including actress and songwriter; but, in addition to her literary career, her role as head of the Young Ladies' Academy was her most influential position. Intellectually demanding and yet warm and caring, she is cited in numerous private journals of the era as an excellent teacher. Although her life was one of constant financial hardship, it was also notable for her extraordinary literary productivity and attention to women's lives.

Roxana, or the Fortunate Mistress (1724)

A novel by ▷ Daniel Defoe presented as a fictional autobiography. 'Roxana', the daughter of French Protestant refugees, is deserted and left destitute by her first husband, and, with a taste for the finer things in life, sees prostitution as her only lucrative profession. A second marriage to a Dutch merchant leaves her widowed, but she climbs to a state of social importance by a series of increasingly grand affairs, one of which is hinted to be with the king. As in ▷ Defoe's ▷ *Moll Flanders*, the whore repents; but the penitence of Roxana is also ambiguous, and her thoughts are haunted by the illegitimate daughter whose death is on her conscience.

Royal Academy of Arts

Founded with the approval of King George III in 1768 'for the purpose of cultivating and improving the arts of painting, sculpture and architecture'. The first President (PRA) was the portrait painter ▷ Sir Joshua Reynolds. ▷ Angelica Kauffmann was a founding member, although women were not permitted to study in the life classes. An elected

council of 40 Royal Academicians are entitled to place 'RA' after their names, and a further number of Associates bear the letters ARA.

Royal Martyr, The

▷ Charles I, so called by his supporters in consequence of his trial and execution by the revolutionary ▷ Parliament of 1649. Charles was devout, and the ▷ Civil Wars broke out for reasons which were partly and ostensibly religious; the victory of Parliament was also that of the ▷ Puritans, and entailed the temporary overthrow of the ▷ Church of England. Charles was consequently not only regarded as a martyr for the Anglican Church, but even by some as a saint, and a few churches exist dedicated to King Charles the Martyr.

The Royal Martyr is also the subtitle of a play otherwise called *Tyrannic Love* (1669) by ▷ John Dryden.

Royal Society

Founded with the authority of ▷ Charles II in 1662; its full name was 'The Royal Society of London for Promoting Natural Knowledge'. It grew out of a philosophical society started in 1645 and was composed of 'divers worthy persons, inquisitive into natural philosophy and other parts of human learning, and particularly of what hath been called the New Philosophy or Experimental Philosophy', in other words, of men whose minds were moving in the way opened up by ▷ Francis Bacon. The Society took the whole field of knowledge for exploration; one of its aims was to encourage the virtue of intellectual lucidity in the writing of prose, and Thomas Sprat, writing the *History of the Royal Society* in 1667 defined the standards which writers were to emulate (▷ Restoration, 1). The Royal Society was thus central in the culture of its time; it was promoted not only by scientists such as the chemist Boyle, but by poets – ▷ Cowley, ▷ Dryden, ▷ Waller – the biographer ▷ Aubrey, and the diarists ▷ Evelyn and ▷ Pepys. Since its foundation, the Society has become increasingly scientific; the title 'Fellow of the Royal Society' (FRS) is today much esteemed by scientists. Part of its function is to advise the government on problems which require scientific elucidations. Its original meeting place was Gresham College, which since its foundation by Sir Thomas Gresham in 1597 had always served more practical branches of knowledge than the universities of Oxford and Cambridge; since 1857 it has been situated at Burlington House, premises which it shares with the ▷ Royal Academy.

Rule Britannia (1740)

A patriotic poem by ▷ James Thomson, occurring in the ▷ masque *Alfred* (1740) by Thomson and ▷ David Mallet. The universally known musical setting is by Thomas Arne (1710–78).

Rupert, Prince (Count Palatine of the Rhine, and Duke of Bavaria) (1619–82)

Son of Frederick of the Palatinate and ▷ James I's daughter Elizabeth. Rupert was an able cavalry commander on the Royalist side in the ▷ Civil

Wars, and after the ▷ Restoration, an enthusiastic supporter of the ▷ Royal Society.

Russell, Lady Rachel (1636–1723)

Letter-writer. Married at 17 to Lord Vaughan she was widowed in 1665 and left rich by the death of her father, the Earl of Southampton, in 1667. In 1669 she married William Russell, a man three years younger, in a passionate love match which became a deeply happy marriage. But Russell, a zealous Protestant (▷ Protestantism) and Whig (▷ Whig and Tory), got involved with a group of people who discussed rising up against the king, ▷ Charles II, and replacing him with his illegitimate son, the Duke of ▷ Monmouth, in a conspiracy known as the ▷ Rye House Plot. Arrested and convicted on flimsy evidence of treason, Russell was beheaded in 1683. Throughout his arraignment and trial Lady Russell supported him, collecting evidence to defend him, standing next to him in the courtroom, and appealing to the king for clemency. After her husband's death she focused her attention on restoring his reputation (a task achieved when his attainder was reversed in 1689), and seeing to her children's marriages. She remained inconsolable for her husband's death, and achieved heroic stature among her contemporaries for her fidelity and fortitude. Her letters, describing her life in detail, were published in 1773 and 1817. Bib: Fraser, A., *The Weaker Vessel*.

Rye House Plot (1683)

A plot led by the ▷ 1st Earl of Shaftesbury, the leader of the Whig Party, to kidnap ▷ Charles II and force him to summon a parliament. The plot was discovered, and the consequent discredit of the Whigs, together with Charles II's popularity, caused a public reaction against them, and enabled ▷ James II to succeed peacefully in 1685, in spite of his open Roman Catholicism.
▷ Whig and Tory.

Rymer, Thomas (1641–1713)

A rigidly neo-classical critic, chiefly known for his obtuse though witty and amusing *Short View of Tragedy* (1692) in which he condemned ▷ Shakespeare's tragedy *Othello* for a barbaric failure to observe the ▷ classical unities.

S

Sackville, Charles
▷ Dorset, Sixth Earl of.

Sade, Donatien Alphonse, Marquis de (1740–1814)
French novelist and poet. His belief that his
destructive impulses were part of his nature,
and yet uncontrollable, counterbalanced the
doctrine of ▷ Rousseau, according to whom man
undistorted by social forces was naturally good.
Sade's ideas profoundly influenced the dark side of
▷ romanticism.

Sadler's Wells
Originally a health resort in north London, on
account of its mineral spring. A theatre was built
there in the 18th century, and in the 19th century
this became – like the Old Vic in south London –
famous for its productions of Shakespeare.

St James's Palace
One of the royal palaces in London, built in the
16th century by Henry VIII. In the 18th century
it superseded ▷ Whitehall as the official royal
residence; hence foreign ambassadors have ever since
been officially accredited to 'the Court of St James',
a metonym for Great Britain, although in the reign
of Victoria it was in turn superseded by Buckingham
Palace close by.

St Paul's Cathedral
The cathedral of the City of London, and its
principal church. The old cathedral was burnt
down in the ▷ Great Fire of London (1666) and
the present one was built according to the design
of ▷ Sir Christopher Wren. Until the 18th century
not only the churchyard but the building itself was
a public meeting-place for much besides Christian
worship; news was exchanged there, servants were
hired, and business was conducted. The central aisle
was called Paul's Walk, and a Paul's Man was a term
for one of its frequenters.

Sally Lunn
A kind of sweet bun, apparently called after a young
woman who sold them in Bath in the late 18th
century.

Samson Agonistes (1671)
A ▷ tragedy in ▷ blank verse by ▷ John Milton,
published (with ▷ *Paradise Regained*) in 1671. It is
an example of Milton's blended ▷ Puritan-biblical
and ▷ Renaissance-classical inspiration: the subject
is drawn from the Old Testament (*Judges* 16)
and the form from the ancient Greek tragedies of
▷ Aeschylus and ▷ Sophocles.

Samson, the Jewish hero, has been betrayed
by his Philistine wife, Dalila (spelt Delilah in the
Authorized Version of the ▷ Bible, where she is
not his wife), to her people, who are the foes of the
Jews. His hair, on which depended his exceptional,
God-given strength, has been cut off; he has been
blinded, and cast into prison in Gaza; here his hair
is allowed to recover its former length and he is
subjected to slavery by his enemies. The play opens
while he is resting from his enormous labours and he
is approached by a chorus of lamenting Jews. In his
mood of extreme despair, he is visited by his father
Manoa, who hopes to negotiate his release from the
Philistines; Samson, however has the moral strength
to refuse Manoa's suggestions, on the grounds that
his lot is a consequence of his own moral weakness
in betraying the secret of his strength to his wife.
His next visitor is Dalila herself, who seeks his
forgiveness in return for alleviation of his sufferings;
he replies, however, that if he cannot pardon himself,
her crime is still more unpardonable. This double
moral victory heartens him enough to enable him
to frighten away his third visitor, the Philistine giant
Harapha, who comes to mock him. Next a messenger
arrives with an order that he is to come before the
Philistine lords in order to entertain them with feats
of his strength. To the dismay of the chorus, he
accepts the order, but we learn from a messenger
that it is only to destroy the entire assembly
(including himself) by rooting up the two pillars
which support the roof of the building. The chorus is
left to chant praise of the hero and of the wisdom of
God, who sustains his people.

It has long been assumed that *Samson Agonistes*
was written after Milton had finished *Paradise
Lost* (ie between 1667 and 1671). This traditional
dating reinforces the connection between the blind
and defeated hero of the work, and the blind and
(ideologically) defeated figure of Milton after the
▷ Restoration. However, strong reasons have now
been advanced for dating Milton's drama to a much
earlier period of his career, between 1647 and 1653.
The two principle themes of modern criticism of
the work have centred on the question of 'structure'
(▷ Samuel Johnson initiated the debate by claiming
that the play has a beginning, an end, but no middle),
and the question of whether the guiding spirit of
the play is 'Hellenic', 'Hebraic' or 'Christian'. In
essence, both of these questions address a problem
that *Samson Agonistes* has long posed to readers –
that interpretation of the work rests on locating it in
relation to other texts (Greek ▷ tragedy or the Old
Testament, for example) and to a specific historical
moment.

Sansculottes
The name for recruits from the poorer classes to the
▷ French Revolutionary army. The word means
'without breeches' – kneebreeches being then the
wear of all but the poorest. The sansculottes wore
loose trousers or 'pantalon'.

Sappho (Psappho) (7th–6th century BC)
Greek poet from Lesbos. Daughter of
Scamandronymus and Cleis, and sister of three
brothers. At some time she visited Sicily. The many
anecdotes about Sappho's life, drawn from her works
and from comic dramas written about her, make
accurate biography impossible. She may have had a
daughter, Cleis, although Sappho refers to her with
a word that may simply be a term of affection. The
stories that she committed suicide for love of Phaon
probably come from 4th-century BC comic drama.

Her work is the largest corpus written by an

ancient Greek woman, although very fragmentary. It shows, in a variety of metres, Sappho as leader of a band of young girls in worship of the goddess of love ▷ Aphrodite. The *Hymn to Aphrodite*, in a metre called 'sapphic', after her, is an address to the goddess to aid her seduction of a young girl whom Sappho loves. It neatly employs traditional hymnic commonplaces to describe a female object of desire. A second fragment was preserved which evocatively describes the symptoms of one in love, as she watches the woman she loves beside her bridegroom. Sappho wrote many marriage songs and was famous for them in antiquity.

Other fragments include a description of the beauty of the woman Anactoria, a poem to her 'daughter' Cleis, good wishes to her brother as he sets out on a voyage, a narrative poem on the marriage of Hector and Andromache (▷ epic characters) and a poem for a girl, Lydia, who is compared to the moon outshining the stars.

Sappho occasionally used epic metaphors and images of war to describe love, and thus played an important part in the development of the theme of 'love as war' in later Latin elegiac poetry. This literary transference of male war imagery to female love poetry is one further sign of her literary ability. Another is the variety of metres employed in her lyric poetry. Her poetry was translated into Latin and imitated by Roman poets such as ▷ Catullus and ▷ Horace in the 1st century BC. Antipater of Thescalonica (2nd century BC) includes her in his list of nine women poets, and another Greek ▷ epigram styles her 'the tenth Muse' (▷ Muses). In the 17th and 18th centuries, a woman poet was somtimes referred to as 'Sappho'. A notable Sappho was ▷ Katherine Philips. Another was ▷ Madeleine de Scudéry.
Bid: (text & trans.) Campbell, D. A., *Greek Lyric*; de Jean, J., *Fictions of Sappho* 1546–1937.

Satan

A Hebrew word meaning 'adversary'; in the Christian tradition, one of the habitual names for the Devil. In *Job* (Old Testament), an older tradition is evident in I:6–12 and II:1–6. Satan is a servant of God, and his special function is to test the virtue of men by trials and suffering.

Satan is a central character in ▷ Milton's ▷ *Paradise Lost*, and some commentators have seen his presence there as even more important that that of Adam or Eve.
▷ Lucifer

Satire

A form of attack through mockery; it may exist in any literary medium, but is often regarded as a medium in itself. The origins of the word help to explain the manifestations of satire. It derives from the Latin *satura* = a vessel filled with the earliest agricultural produce of the year, used in seasonal festivals to celebrate harvest; a secondary meaning is 'miscellany of entertainment', implying merry-making at such festivals, probably including verbal warfare. This primitive humour gave rise to a highly cultivated form of literary attack in the poetry of ▷ Horace,

Persius (1st century AD) and ▷ Juvenal. Thus from ancient Roman culture two ideas of satire have come down to us: the first expresses a basic instinct for comedy through mockery in human beings, and was not invented by the Romans; the second is a self-conscious medium, implying standards of civilized and moral rightness in the mind of the poet and hence a desire on his or her part to instruct readers so as to reform their moral failings and absurdities. The two kinds of satire are inter-related, so that it is not possible to distinguish them sharply. Moreover, it is not easy to distinguish strict satire in either of its original forms from other kinds of comedy.

1 Strict satire, *ie* satire emulating the Roman poets. The great age of the strict satire was the 18th century, notably in the work of ▷ Pope who emulated the relatively genial satire of Horace, and ▷ Samuel Johnson, who emulated the sombre style of Juvenal. Satire of this sort makes its object of attack the social forms and corruptions of the time, and its distinctive medium is the 10-syllable rhyme ▷ couplet, perfected by Pope and used with different force by Johnson.

2 ▷ Comedy of Humours and ▷ Comedy of Manners. These are the most easily distinguishable forms of dramatic satire. The former is associated chiefly with Ben Jonson (1572–1637), and has its roots in the older Morality drama, which was only intermittently satirical. The 'humours' in Jonson's conception are the obsessions and manias to which the nature of human beings invites them to abandon themselves; they have a close relation to the medieval ▷ Seven Deadly Sins, such as lust, avarice and gluttony. The Comedy of Manners belongs to the period 1660–1800, and especially to the first 40 years of it. Its most notable exponents are ▷ Congreve at the end of the 17th century and ▷ Sheridan at the end of the 18th. This comedy is less concerned with basic human dispositions and more with transient social ones; rational social behaviour is the standard in the mind of the dramatist. Both these forms of satire were taken over by novelists; the 18th-century novelist ▷ Fielding began as a writer of dramatic comedies of manners, but Dickens in the 19th century writes more distinctly in the tradition of the comedy of humours, with a strong addition of social stagnation.

3 Satire of ▷ parody and irony. This includes the most skilful and powerful satire in the language; its most productive period is between 1660 and 1750. Parody at its most powerful implies the writer's complete respect for the serious form which he is using in a comic way; thus in this period (which included the very serious ▷ epic ▷ *Paradise Lost*) the prestige of the epic form was still high, and ▷ Dryden (▷ *Absalom and Achitophel*) and ▷ Pope (▷ *The Rape of the Lock* and ▷ *The Dunciad*) used their appreciation of epic to make ironic contrast between the grandeur of its style and the pettiness, meanness and destructiveness of their chosen subject. Similarly ▷ Samuel Butler used the mode of romantic epic to attack the ▷ Puritans in ▷ *Hudibras*.

Irony does not necessarily use parody, but even when it does not, it operates in a similar way, by addressing the reader in terms which he has learnt to receive as acceptable at their face value, and then shocking him into recognition that something quite unacceptable is the real subject.

5 Novelistic satire. Much satire in novels from the 18th to the 20th century cannot be summed up under comedy of manners. The novels of Peacock, for example, establish a tradition of comic discussions mocking at contemporary trends of though. Another variant is the 'anti-utopia', using an imaginary country to satirize actual tendencies in contemporary Britain. A notable example of this is *Erewhon* by Samuel Butler and ▷ Swift's ▷ *Gulliver's Travels*. It is difficult in fact to find a novelist who does not use satire, at least intermittently, usually as a social comment. ▷ Henry Fielding and ▷ Jane Austen are two eminent examples.

Savage, Richard (?1697–1743)

Poet. Savage claimed to be the illegitimate son of the Countess of Macclesfield, and spent his life in petulant complaint against her, and in cultivating wealthy patrons. He was accused of being ▷ Alexander Pope's spy at the time of the composition of ▷ *The Dunciad*, and after his death was the subject of an intimate biography by ▷ Samuel Johnson. His monologue in heroic ▷ couplets, *The Bastard* (1728) dramatizes his situation following the death sentence passed on him after he had killed a man in a brawl. It contains some vigorous lines:

> *Blest be the Bastard's birth!* . . .
> *No sickly fruit of faint compliance he;*
> *He! stampt in nature's mint of extasy!*
> *He lives to build, not boast, a gen'rous race:*
> *No tenth transmitter of a foolish face.*

On the intervention of his friends he was pardoned and a long poem, *The Wanderer*, appeared in 1729. Savage also wrote satirical poems in couplets, including *The Progress of a Divine* (1735).

School for Scandal, The

A comedy by ▷ Richard Brinsley Sheridan, first produced in 1777. Two of the central characters are brothers: Charles Surface, whose character is open-hearted but reckless and extravagant, and Joseph Surface, a meanhearted hypocrite. The principal women are Lady Teazle, the young, gay wife of the elderly Sir Peter Teazle, and Maria, his ward, with whom Charles is in love and whom Joseph is trying to marry for her money, while he also makes love to Lady Teazle. Sir Oliver Surface, rich uncle to the two brothers, returns from India in disguise in order to spy on his nephews, thereby to discover their true characters. In the background, a group of scandal-lovers (Lady Sneerwell, Mrs Candour, Sir Benjamin Backbite) do their worst to damage as many reputations as possible. Sir Oliver satisfies himself, in scenes of extremely successful theatrical comedy, about which of his nephews truly deserves his affection: Charles marries Maria, and the deceitfulness of Joseph is exposed.

The comedy is Sheridan's masterpiece, and the

last notable play in the tradition of the English ▷ Comedy of Manners until Oscar Wilde at the end of the 19th century.

Schools in England

The following is an alphabetical list of most kinds of school mentioned in English literature.

Almonry schools. One of the forms of grammar school (see below) in the ▷ Middle Ages; they were usually attached to monasteries, and the boys followed the rules of monastic life.

Board schools. These got their name from the School Boards, ie committees responsible for education in a neighbourhood, set up by the Education Act of 1870, which provided for universal elementary education to the age of 11. The boards were abolished by the Education Act of 1902 and were replaced by the usual local authorities (County Councils, etc.)

Boarding schools. Schools where the pupils live during their terms of study, as opposed to Day schools from which they return each evening. Most boarding schools are either private or public (see below).

Charity schools. Set up in the 18th century for children (of both sexes) of the very poor. The schools were endowed or maintained by the churches, and gave only elementary education. They were widespread but their distribution was uneven, so that many villages were without one.

Comprehensive schools. A large school giving secondary education of all types in one complex of buildings so that in theory there is equality of educational opportunity given to all pupils, there being no selection (as by an examination at the age of 11 or later) for grammar school, modern school, etc. (see below). The most popular form of state education at the present time.

Dame schools. Characteristic of the 18th and early 19th centuries, and so called because they were commonly owned and run by poor, single women to make a small income. Only reading and writing and the beginnings of arithmetic were taught.

Dissenters' schools and academies. In the 18th century, Protestants who did not belong to the ▷ Church of England (ie ▷ Dissenters or Nonconformists) were not allowed to attend its schools. They could enter Scottish but not English universities. They therefore set up their own educational institutions which provided efficient education, often more up-to-date than that in the schools attended by ▷ Anglicans.

Elementary schools. This is either a general term for schools of any period which taught nothing more than reading, writing and arithmetic, or for the state schools established by the the Act of 1870 providing for education up to the age of 11. The term 'Elementary' was abandoned by the Education Act of 1944, and 'Primary' was substituted.

Finishing schools. Schools for girls, fairly common in the 19th and early 20th centuries. They cater for the richer classes and take adolescents. Emphasis is commonly laid on behaviour and artistic accomplishments, though the education is sometimes more thorough. They are often situated in France, Germany, Switzerland or Italy, to facilitate the learning of a foreign language.

Girls' schools. Until the dissolution of the monasteries in the 1530s, many convents of nuns ran schools for girls. In the 16th and 17th centuries girls' schools for the wealthier classes were rather rare, and such girls received their education at home from private teachers, *ie* governesses. This was still usual in the 18th century, though private boarding schools for girls were increasing number.

Grammar schools. In the Middle Ages the various kinds of monastery school for older children had Latin grammar as their principal subject. This continued to be true when such schools were taken out of the hands of the Church between 1530 and 1560 and endowed by public funds or placed in the hands of town councils etc. An example is the Grammar School at Stratford-on-Avon, probably attended by the young Shakespeare. As time went on, the educational curriculum changed, but the term 'grammar school' remained for all schools providing an academic education up to university entrance standard, unless they were called 'public schools' – which were usually richer and drew their pupils from a wider area. Now largely merged with other secondary schools in the Comprehensive system.

High schools. Until 1944, equivalent to grammar schools, but usually for girls. Nowadays the term is merely a survival.

Modern schools. Set up in 1944 to provide for education of children who were not attending a grammar school, attendance at one or other type of secondary school being then made compulsory till the age of 15.

National schools. Schools founded in the 19th century by the Church of England 'National Society for Promoting the Education of the Poor in the Principles of the Established Church'.

Preparatory schools. In the 19th and 20th centuries, schools which prepared the sons of the wealthier classes for public schools. They were and are nearly all privately owned. Boys pass from them to public schools at the age of 13.

Private schools. Used either for schools under private ownership (*ie* not endowed, and not run by public subscription or by the state), or as an alternative term for 'preparatory schools'.

▷ **Public schools.** Here, it is relevant to point out that they are schools neither run by the state nor under private ownership.

State schools. Applicable to all schools, since 1870, run under the authority of the state but the term is used to distinguish those which do not make a direct charge to parents and are most closely regulated by the state.

Secondary schools. Applicable to state schools providing education over the age of 11.

Sunday schools. Started in 1780 for the education of poor children on the one day in the week on which they were likely to be free from employment. They are now wholly religious in their instruction.

Technical schools. In the second half of the 19th century, places for training youth in industrial and craft skills; schools called 'polytechnics' and

technical colleges became common. Since 1944, while polytechnics and technical colleges continued and increased, the term 'technical school' has been restricted to alternatives to grammar schools and modern schools, providing a more technical education than either. Technical colleges receive only students over the age at which compulsory education ceases.

Voluntary schools. A term applicable to all schools supported by voluntary contributions.

Schuurman (Schurman), Anna Maria van (1607–1678)

Prose writer and poet from the northern Netherlands. The daughter of a nobleman from Antwerp who settled with his family in Utrecht in 1615, she received an excellent education. In an era when the Renaissance adoration of women came into vogue, van Schuurman, with her considerable knowledge of languages and her artistry, attracted the attention of many people, including Queen Christina of Sweden, and ▷ René Descartes. She completed her theology studies in Utrecht, attending lectures in a small room adjacent to the classroom of the male students. Her *Amica dissertatio inter Annam Mariam Schurmanniam et Andr. Rivetum de capacitate ingenii muliebris ad scientias* (1638) (A Friendly Discourse Between Anna Maria Schurmann and A. Rivetus Concerning the Capacity of Women for Scholarly Pursuits) is a learned dialogue on the question of whether women are capable of studying the sciences and the arts. *A Learned Maid*, written in 1641, was translated into English by Clement Barksdale. She devoted herself to ▷ Calvinism, and later to Labadism. On her life and theological views she composed in Latin *Eucleria* (1684, Dutch translation *Eucleria of uitkiezing van het beste deel*, 1684) (Eucleria or Selection of the Best Part). Apart from poems and letters, she wrote *Paelsteen van den tijt onzes levens* (1639) (Boundary Stone of Our Lifetime), and a festive song on the occasion of the inauguration of the University of Utrecht.

Scotland

The northern kingdom of Great Britain. Geographically, racially, linguistically and culturally, it has two parts.

The northern and north-western half, known as the ▷ Highlands and the Islands, is Celtic in race, with a Norse admixture. The native language was originally the Celtic one called Gaelic, but this is now spoken only by a small minority. Until the middle of the 18th century its social structure was of the semi-tribal clan system under hereditary chieftains. Its culture was chiefly oral and Gaelic-speaking, and much of it has been lost. The so-called Scottish national dress, of the ▷ kilt woven into chequered designs known as ▷ tartans, was peculiar to this region; it was forbidden after the second ▷ Jacobite Rebellion of 1745, when the British government started its policy of colonizing the Highlands, but it was revived in the 19th century as a sentimental fashion for the upper classes and is now an extremely profitable export item. This region of Scotland, though extremely beautiful, has had a torn history; centuries of clan warfare were followed by a century and a half of economic neglect and depopulation, during which the small farms or 'crofts' were steadily replaced by 'grouse moors', preserved by rich landlords for hunting and shooting.

The southern and eastern half of the country is called the Lowlands, and contains all the important cities including the capital, ▷ Edinburgh, and the largest, Glassgow. These two cities are respectively at the east and west ends of the narrowest part of the country, and the plain between them is a rich coal-mining area. The Lowlands are geographically hilly, in spite of their name. Racially, the population is as Germanic in origin as that of most of England, and with small exceptions it has always been English-speaking. It has never been subjected to the clan system of the Highlands, although the great families along the border with England had, until the 17th century, an influence comparable to that of the clan chieftains of the Celtic north. Economically and politically, the Lowlands have always been the richer and more important part of the country. When we speak of Scottish culture, we are nearly always thinking of the literature of the Lowlands; this has had its distinctive tradition, but it has become increasingly absorbed into English culture since the 16th century.

Scott, Mary (Taylor) (1752–1793)

English poet. She lived in the same house as ▷ Elizabeth Rowe in Somerset, and who knew ▷ Anna Seward. She wrote in favour of women's education. In *The Female Advocate* (designed as a sequel to John Duncombe's *Feminiad*) she praises past and contemporary women writers, saying of ▷ Sarah Fielding, "Twas *Fielding's* talent, with ingenious Art, / To trace the secret mazes of the Heart', and of ▷ Anne Killigrew, 'in thee ... we find / The Poet's and the Painter's arts combin'd'. In the same text she reserves a special place for ▷ Lady Mary Chudleigh, who had the courage to assert that women were naturally equal to men and to 'plead thy hapless injured sex's cause'. She married John Scott in 1788, when her mother died. In the same year she published *The Messiah*, and she also wrote hymns. Her son founded the Manchester *Guardian*.

▷ Astell, Mary; Williams, Helen Maria

Scott, Sarah (Robinson) (1732–1795)

English novelist, writer of utopias and historian. She was the sister and correspondent of ▷ Elizabeth Montagu, the ▷ Bluestocking. She wrote for money after leaving her husband (whom she had married in 1751) and moved with Barbara Montagu to launch a female community at Bath Easton, where they taught poor children. They lived here from 1754 to 1756. Scott wrote six novels, but her well-known *Description of Millenium Hall* (1762) uses this idea of a woman's community. This secular separatist community based around rational virtues provided at least one answer to the unstable social and economic place of the unmarried or – particularly – separated woman. The novel opens with a man whose coach has broken down in Cornwall impressed by the rational yet pleasurable employments of the women. He first sees

them engaged in their rational pursuits: 'in the bow [window] sat two ladies reading, with pen, ink and paper on a table before them, at which was a young girl translating out of the French.'

Other publications: *The History of Cornelia* (1750); *A Journey Through Every Stage in Life* (1754); *Agreeable Ugliness, or the Triumph of the Graces* (1754); *Sir George Ellison* (1766), and *The Test of Filial Duty* (1772).

Scottish literature in English

This belongs above all to the Lowlands (▷ Scotland); it is a distinctive branch of literature in the English language, the Lowland Scottish form of which had originally a close resemblance to that spoken in the north of England. Racially, linguistically and culturally, Lowland Scottish ties with England were close, despite the constant wars between the two countries between the late 13th and mid-16th centuries. In contrast, until the 18th-century destruction of Highland culture, the Lowlanders had little more than the political bond of a common sovereign with their Gaelic-speaking fellow-countrymen of the north. While it is not true to say that Scottish literature is a branch of English literature, the two literatures have been closely related.

In Scotland, the 15th century saw the beginning of a golden age, covering the careers of Robert Henryson (1425–?1500), William Dunbar (?1460–?1520) Gavin Douglas (?1475–1522) and David Lindsay. The climax of this period was the reign of the exceptionally able King James IV (1488–1531), who produced an unusual state of order and civilization in the country.

The flowering of high Scottish poetry was halted by the Scottish religious ▷ Reformation, and all the political troubles attendant on it from 1550 till 1700. In the 18th century a revival took place, the first noteworthy example being Allan Ramsay's *The Gentle Shepherd* (1725). ▷ Robert Burns is perhaps the first famous Scottish poet since the 16th century. By now, however, the tide of English influence had moved strongly in Scotland; Walter Scott (1771–1832) collected Scottish ▷ ballads, and produced a few fine examples in the ballad tradition, but his longer poems belong to the history of English verse narrative, though their subject was often Scottish history and legend.

Gaelic literature of the Highlands had what is said to be a 'golden age' in the later 18th century, just at the time when Gaelic culture was being destroyed by the English and the Lowland Scots for political reasons. The work in it (*eg* that of Alexander Macdonald, Dugald Buchanan) is little known outside the comparatively small number of Gaelic speakers in the Highlands, and does not belong to English literature. For the alleged translations of the Ossianic poems by ▷ James Macpherson (1736–96) see under Oisin.

Scottish prose literary tradition may be seen in medieval philosophers such as Duns Scotus and ▷Renaissance humanists such as George Buchanan (16th century) who wrote principally in Latin. Thereafter the great Scottish writers (especially from the 18th century) were mainly anglicized in their prose expression; ▷ David Hume and ▷ Adam Smith in the 18th century, Walter Scott and Thomas Carlyle in the 19th.

Scriblerus Club

Formed in 1713 by ▷ Alexander Pope, ▷ Jonathan Swift, ▷ John Gay, ▷ Thomas Parnell, ▷ John Arbuthnot, and the Tory politician, Lord Oxford. The aim was to satirize 'false tastes' through the fictional memoirs of a conceited and arrogant 'modern' writer, Martinus Scriblerus. The club's members were scattered when the Tories fell from power after Queen ▷ Anne's death in 1714. Only the first volume of the memoirs was completed, and this was published in Pope's works in 1741. However, the ideas initiated at this time saw fruit in various later works, in particular Pope's ▷ *Dunciad*, many of the notes of which are signed 'Scriblerus', and in the satire on science and learning in the third book of Swift's ▷ *Gulliver's Travels*.

Scudéry, Madeleine de (1607–1701)

French writer of epic novels, *nouvelles* (short fiction), letters and occasional verse, and a notable *précieuse* (▷ Precious Women). In her youth, she frequented the *Chambre bleue*, the salon of the Marquise de Rambouillet (1588–1665), with her brother, the dramatist and Academician Georges de Scudéry (1601–67). Madeleine lived with her brother in Paris and Marseille until his marriage to Marie-Madeleine du Moncel de Martinval in 1654, writing a series of *romans-à-clef*, set in exotic locations; the characters, though in disguise, could easily be identified from among their friends and acquaintances. Although mercilessly mocked by the writers Charles Sorel (c 1600–1674), Jacques-Bénigne Bossuet (1627–1704) and others, these novels were of great importance for raising the status of women and fiction.

Ibrahim, ou l'illustre Bassa (1641) contains one of the few theoretical prefaces to be written by a novelist in the 17th century. It seeks to give fiction ▷ classical antecedents, by aligning the novel with the ▷ epic poem and identifying history as the mainstay of *vraisemblance* (verisimilitude) in the novel. The success of this four-volume novel encouraged Madeleine de Scudéry to use wider canvases for her next two novel, *Artamène, ou le Grand Cyrus* (1649–1653, translated as *Artamenes, or The Grand Cyrus*, 1653–5), which contained a *mise en abyme* of the Hôtel de Rambouillet and her own *samedis* (Saturday *salons*) at the rue de Beauce in Paris, and *Clélie, histoire romaine* (1654–60, translated as *Clelia: An excellent new romance*, 1661). Both these novels also appeared under Georges de Scudéry's name, though there is a marked change of tone after their separation at the end of volume 2 of *Clélie*, which is the most 'feminist' of Madeleine de Scudéry's writings and includes the celebrated 'Carte de Tendre', an allegorical map of love. Known as the 'incomparable ▷ Sappho', Madeleine de Scudéry was noted for her intellect and learning even among the most respected scholars of her day, though her lack of Latin and Greek meant that she could not consult the many classical historians on whom she

loosely based her fiction in the original. Despite the innumerable anachronisms in her novels, she may be regarded as the 'mother of the historical novel in France'. She also wrote *Les Femmes illustres, ou les Harangues héroïques* (The Illustrious Women, or The Heroic Speeches), *Célinte, nouvelle première* (1661), *Mathilde d'Aguilar* (1667) and *Célanire* (1669), which includes *La Promenade de Versailles*.

In 1657, Mademoiselle de Scudéry received a pension from the superintedent of finances, Nicolas Fouquet (1615–80), to whom she remained a loyal friend. Among her other benefactors were the First Minister, Mazarin (1602–61), Queen Christina of Sweden (1626–89) and Louis XIV (1638–1715), though she always had difficulty making ends meet. Madeleine de Scudéry was elected to the Academy of the Ricovrati in 1684 and is said to have been the first woman to have been considered for election to the French Academy. Her ugliness was frequently remarked upon. She admits to having received three proposals of marriage, but, in keeping with the theory of *amitié tendre* (loving friendship) developed in her novels, she refused even to marry the Academician Paul Pellisson (1624–93), who was devoted to her. A series of influential selections from the dialogues in her novels was published during the 1680s.
Bib: Tallemant des Réaux, *Historiettes*: Aronson, N., *Mademoiselle de Scudéry*.

Scudéry, Marie-Madeleine du Moncel de Martinval (1627–1711)

French correspondent and co-author of a novel. She helped her husband, the dramatic poet Georges de Scudéry (1601–67), to write the novel *Almahide, ou l'esclave reine* (Almahida, or The Slave Queen, 1661–3) and is noted for her cultivated correspondence with, among others, the exiled writer Roger de Bussy–Rabutin (1618–93). The main theme of her letters is the value of friendship. She appears in Somaize's *Dictionnaire des Précieuses* (Dictionary of the Precious Women, 1659) under the pseudonym Sarraïde, as '[I]' *une des plus grandes précieuses du royaume*, ('one of the greatest *précieuses* of the realm') (▷ Precious Women). The memoir-writer Tallemant des Réaux (1619–1692) portrays her as a romantic woman yearning to work on a novel, and who married late in life under the mistaken illusion that Georges de Scudéry had written the great novels published under his name. Of her relationship with her husband, Tallemant writes: 'their marriage was made in their writings rather than in the normal way, for their mutual inclination was a question of the similarities in their style of writing which came before their wedding.' It was generally felt that her prose was better than his verse, and her letters have recently been reappraised.
▷ Scudéry, Madeleine de
Bib: Tallemant des Réaux, *Historiettes*; Mesnard, J., 'Mme de Scudéry', *Actes de Caen* (1980).

Seasons, The (1726–30)

Four ▷ blank-verse poems by ▷ James Thomson. *Winter* was published in 1726, followed by *Summer* (1727), and *Spring* (1728). *Autumn* first appeared in the collected *Seasons* in 1730, which also contained a concluding *Hymn on the Seasons*. The work blends numerous strands: the classical spirit of ▷ Virgil's *Pastorals* and ▷ *Georgics*, a self-conscious sublimity which comes from ▷ John Milton, and the topographical genre popularized by ▷ Sir John Denham's ▷ *Cooper's Hill* (1642) and ▷ Alexander Pope's ▷ *Windsor Forest* (1713). Thomson's blank verse is an extremely flexible and capacious medium, though always affecting a somewhat mechanical Miltonic dignity. On the one hand there are charming descriptions of the natural scene, such as the famous snow scenes in *Winter*, the nest-building passage in *Spring*, and the *Summer* thunderstorm. There are discussions of philosophy and morality, such as the condemnation of blood-sports in *Autumn*, and the expression of ▷ 'natural religion' in the concluding hymn. There are celebrations of British history, industry and commerce in *Summer* and *Autumn*, and sentimental vignettes of rural life, such as the man dying in the snow in *Winter* and Amelia struck by lightning as she is embraced by her astonished lover in *Summer*.

An important element is Thomson's scientific and practical approach to nature. In *Summer* he describes the beginning of the Newtonian universe, as the 'unwieldy planets' are 'launched along/ The illimitable void'. In *Autumn* he speculates on the migration of birds, and throughout the poems he is concerned to use a kind of poetic version of Linnaean taxonomy, stressing the generic qualities of animals and plants: 'plumy people' (birds) 'the finny drove' (fish) and 'woolly people' (sheep). Typically nature is seen as providing a livelihood to man. Despite their influence on later more romantic 'nature poets', such as ▷ Mark Akenside, ▷ William Collins, ▷ William Cowper, ▷ Thomas Gray and ▷ William Wordsworth, the *Seasons* in themselves are peculiarly smug and inert in their Augustan optimism. Thomson's is a world in which, without a qualm, 'Man superior walks/ Amid the glad creation', where farm labourers are picturesque adjuncts of the landscape, and where British industry and commerce subject the world. Its ideal for living smacks of bourgeois self-congratulation:

> *An elegant sufficency, content,*
> *Retirement, rural quiet, friendship, books,*
> *Ease and alternate labour, useful life,*
> *Progressive virtue, and approving Heaven!*

Sedan chair

A portable covered chair, carried on two poles by chairmen, and with a trap in the roof so that the passenger could stand. It was introduced into England in 1634, and was much used as a way of getting about towns in the 18th century.

Sedgemoor, Battle of (1685)

The culmination of a rising of west-of-England ▷ Puritans against Charles II's openly ▷ Catholic brother ▷ James II. It was led by Charles's illegitimate son, the Duke of Monmouth. The battle was won by the government troops, and was followed by the ferocious punishment of the rebels by Judge Jeffreys in his notorious ▷ Bloody Assizes. Sedgemoor was the last battle fought on English (as distinct from British) soil.

Selborne, Natural History and Antiquities of
▷ White, Gilbert

Selkirk, Alexander (1676–1721)

A sailor, whose experiences on the uninhabited island of Juan Fernandez, where he was landed at his own request and remained from 1704 to 1709, are the basis of the desert island part of ▷ Daniel Defoe's ▷ *Robinson Crusoe*.

Seneca, Lucius Annaeus (?4 BC–AD 65)

Roman philosopher and dramatist. He belonged to the Stoic school of philosophy, which taught that men should seek virtue, not happiness, and that they should be superior to the influences of pleasure and pain. As an orator, he was famous for the weight and terseness of his expression – the 'Senecan style'. He was tutor to the emperor Nero during the latter's boyhood, but later was suspected of being involved in a conspiracy against him; Nero accordingly ordered him to end his life, which he did with true stoical dignity. His nine tragedies were modelled on those of ▷ Aeschylus, ▷ Sophocles and ▷ Euripides, but there is much doubt whether they were ever intended to be performed in a theatre; they seem to be designed for declamation to small circles. They contain no action, though the subjects are of blood-thirsty revenge. Their titles: *Hercules Furens; Thyestes; Phoenissae; Phaedra (Hippolytus); Oedipus; Troades (Hecuba); Medea; Agamemnon; Hercules Oetaeus*. A tenth, *Octavia*, has proved to be by another author.

Neither as a philosopher nor as a dramatist was Seneca one of the most important figures of the ancient Mediterranean world, but he had great importance for the 16th-century ▷ Renaissance in Europe, and particularly for English poetic drama between 1560 and 1620. This influence was of three kinds: 1 Seneca's dramas provided inspiration for Elizabethan revenge tragedy or 'tragedy of blood'; 2 at a time of English literature when there was keen interest in modes of expression but no settled standards about them, Senecan style was one of the favourite modes, both inside and outside the drama; 3 at a time when inherited ideas about the ordering of society and the ethical systems that should control it were undergoing alarming transformations, Senecan stoicism had an appeal for thoughtful men that harmonized with ▷ Protestant strictness and individualism of conduct. The influence of Seneca is seen indirectly, in some of the bloody ▷ heroic dramas of the late 17th century.

Sensibility

The term 'sensibility', indicating the tendency to be easily and strongly affected by emotion, came into general use in the early 18th century. At this time writers and thinkers, such as the third ▷ Earl of Shaftesbury, in reaction against the practical, materialist philosophy of ▷ Hobbes, began to promote an idealistic, spiritual alternative, based on personal feeling. ▷ Joseph Addison in 1711 defined modesty as 'an exquisite Sensibility', 'a kind of quick and delicate Feeling in the Soul'. By the middle of the 18th century the word 'sensibility' had grown in stature, indicating the capacity for compassion or altruism, and also the possession of good ▷ taste in the arts. ▷ Joseph Warton in 1756 declines to explain a subtle point since 'any reader of sensibility' will already have taken it. ▷ Laurence Sterne in his ▷ *Sentimental Journey* (1768) eulogizes 'Dear Sensibility! source unexhausted of all that's precious in our joys or costly in our sorrows!' The word remained fashionable in this sense in the early 19th century when ▷ Jane Austen used it in the title of her novel *Sense and Sensibility* (1811).

Recently some critics have begun to refer to the period from about the time of the death of ▷ Alexander Pope in 1744 until the publication of *Lyrical Ballads* in 1798 as the 'Age of Sensibility'. This label is preferred to 'late Augustanism' or 'pre-Romanticism', since it stresses the distinctive characteristics of the period rather than relating it by negative contrast to a different one. The poets of this time, ▷ Thomas Gray, ▷ William Collins and ▷ William Cowper, share a distinctive emphasis on feeling as an end in itself, rather than as part of some larger philosophical scheme. This can be seen both in the resonant truisms of Gray's ▷ *Elegy* and *Eton College Ode*, and in the descriptive delicacy of Collins's *To Evening* or Cowper's *The Poplar-Field*. Even the conservative neo-classicist ▷ Samuel Johnson shows something of this sensibility in the emotional intensity of his Christian stoicism.

However, the cultivation of sensibility also led to experiment and restlessness in poetic form. Emotional novelty was sought in exoticism and medievalism. The oral ▷ ballad was given respectability by ▷ Thomas Percy's *Reliques*, while ▷ James Macpherson, ▷ Thomas Chatterton, and ▷ Thomas Warton all adopted various medieval, ▷ 'Gothic' tastes or literary forms. These developments in poetry were paralleled in the 'Gothic story', ▷ *The Castle of Otranto* (1765) by ▷ Horace Walpole. The new intensity of feeling took a less exotic form in the profuse sentiment of ▷ Samuel Richardson's novels, and also in the cult of sentimentalism promoted by Sterne's *A Sentimental Journey* and Henry Mackenzie's ▷ *The Man of Feeling* (1771).
Bib: Todd, J., *Sensibility*; Hilles, F. W. and Bloom, H. (eds.), *From Sensibility to Romanticism*; Frye, N., *Towards Defining an Age of Sensibility*.

Sentiment, sentimental

False, exaggerated or superficial feeling, where the focus is on the feeling itself or on the person experiencing the feeling, rather than on any object or person supposedly stimulating the feeling. In literature this often results in formulaic expressions of grief, sympathy or remorse. Examples in the 17th and 18th centuries are in some of the poems of ▷ Cowper and ▷ Gray, the novels of ▷ Richardson, especially ▷ *Pamela*, and in the plays of ▷ Cibber, ▷ Steele, and ▷ Cumberland.
▷ Sensibility; Reform Comedy; Bathos.

Sentimental Journey through France and Italy, A (1768)

A narrative, part novel and part travel book, by ▷ Laurence Sterne (under the pseudonym of 'Mr Yorick' – the same of a character in Sterne's ▷ *Tristram Shandy*), based on his stay in France, 1762–4. It was intended to be longer, but Sterne died after the publication of the first two volumes in 1768.

Serious Proposal to the Ladies for the Advancement of Their True and Greatest Interest, A (1694)

Polemical essay by ▷ Mary Astell, arguing the case for women's education, in a developing tradition of serious writing by and for women. A second part of the *Serious Proposal* was published in 1697. Astell prescribes learning to raise women's understanding, develop their self-esteem and give them what we would now call confidence in their own judgement, the better to live a Christian life. 'There is a sort of bravery and greatness of soul', she says, 'which does more truly ennoble us than the highest title, and it consists in living up to the dignity of our natures, scorning to do a mean, unbecoming thing ...'. Astell proposes to set up a seminary or retreat for women, which she calls a 'religious retirement', for contemplation and study. Thus, she says, women would be equipped to 'see through and scorn those silly artifices which are used to ensnare and deceive them ... (then) She would know, that not what others *say*, but what she herself *does*, is the true commendation and the only thing that exalts her'. The book was criticized by some who, like ▷ Bishop Burnet, interpreted it as merely advocating a type of convent. But it encouraged and influenced numerous women contemporaries, such as ▷ Lady Mary Chudleigh, ▷ Lady Damaris Masham and ▷ Lady Mary Wortley Montagu, and contributed to a flood of treatises in women's defence.
Bib: Perry, R., *The Celebrated Mary Astell, An Early English Feminist*; Rogers, K. M., and McCarthy, W. (eds.), *Meridian Anthology of Early Women Writers: British Literary Women from Aphra Behn to Maria Edgworth 1660–1800*.

Sermons

The word 'sermon' is used in English to denote a speech from a church pulpit for the edification of the audience, always in this context called a 'congregation'. The sermon considered as a means of communication had a central importance in English life until the 19th century, when universal literacy and the rise of the mass-circulation newspaper tended to eclipse it. Three famous preachers of the golden age of Anglicanism in the first half of the 17th century have left sermons addressed to the Court or to other highly educated audiences. The best known of these is the poet John Donne, who became Dean of St Paul's in 1621. Lancelot Andrews (1555–1626) was a subtle and elaborate analyst in language, and appealed more exclusively to the intellect, and ▷ Jeremy Taylor was described by ▷ Coleridge as the 'Spenser of prose' because of his command of musical cadence and linguistic flow.

A change came over English in the middle of the 17th century which emphasized flexibility, control, and lucidity at the expense of poetic emotive power. It is heralded by John Wilkins's book on preaching, *Ecclesiastes* (1646), which teaches the virtue of strict method in organizing a sermon. The main Anglican preachers of the next hundred years, were Robert South (1634–1716), notable for his succinctness and ▷ satire, Isaac Barrow (1630–77), whom ▷ Charles II called 'the best scholar in England', John Tillotson (1630–94), famous for the elegance of his prose, and Joseph Butler (1692–1752), an acute thinker. The virtues of this kind of sermon, and the vices that it sought to combat, are tersely expressed by ▷ Swift (whose own sermons are exemplars of the ideal) in his *Letter to a Young Gentleman entered into Holy Orders* (1721). The best of the ▷ Puritan preachers followed a similar course in a more popular idiom, for instance the Presbyterian Richard Baxter (1615–91) who declared 'The Plainest words are the profitablest oratory in the weightiest matters', and this is a criterion which ▷ Bunyan exemplifies at its noblest.

During the 18th century there was a tendency for sermons to lose touch with the common people. The sermons of William Paley (1743–1805) owed their fame to his talents as a teacher, but they show mediocrity of thought and tepidity of feeling. Those of the novelist ▷ Laurence Sterne (*Sermons of Mr Yorick*, 1760) and of the poet ▷ George Crabbe have merit (especially Sterne's) as literary essays in ethics, but that is what they are, rather than spiritual discourses. It was left to those outside the Anglican tradition, ▷ John Wesley, the founder of ▷ Methodism, and George Whitefield (1714–70) to address themselves to the less educated.
Bib: Henson, H. (ed.), *Selected English Sermons* (World's Classics); Sampson, A. (ed.), *Famous English Sermons*.

Settlement, Act of
▷ Act of Settlement.

Seven Years' War (1756–63)
Frederick the Great of Prussia, in alliance with Great Britain and Hanover, fought an alliance of France, Austria and Russia. Frederick kept his dominions by the Treaty of Hubertusberg. The importance of the war for Britain was that it left her predominant in North America and in India (Treaty of Paris, 1763). An indirect consequence of this was that the American colonists, no longer afraid of conquest by the French, now felt free to resist the British policy of taxing them without allowing them representation in ▷ Parliament; this led to the ▷ American War of Independence (1775–83) and the establishment of the United States.

The Seven Years' War produced three war-leaders: in India, Robert Clive, victor of the battle of Plassey, 1757; in America, James Wolfe, captor of Quebec, 1759; and ▷ William Pitt the Elder, Earl of Chatham, the minister who controlled the strategy of the Franco-British struggle.

17th-century literature
The 17th century was one of the richest periods in the history of English literature, both for achievement and for variety. It also saw a revolution in the human mind, not only in Britain but elsewhere in Europe – a revolution which constitutes the birth of the modern outlook. The century begins with writers like ▷ William Shakespeare and John Donne (1572–1631) whose language fused thought and feeling in both poetry and prose; it ends with ▷ John Dryden and ▷ John Locke, writers whose language was shaped by a new ideal of prose, who opposed 'judgement' to 'wit' – that is to say, the analytic to the synthetic powers of the mind. Another way of putting it is to say that the century opens with one of the most exciting periods of poetic drama in the whole history of Europe, and it closes with the most influential period of English ▷ satire, and the prose of fact which in the next century was to find its most ample form of expression in the novel.

We are in the habit of using the term 'Elizabethan drama' for this period of the English theatre, but in fact it was in the reign of ▷ James I, the ▷ Jacobean period, that this type of drama came to fruition. By 1600, Shakespeare was only approaching his best work and Ben Jonson (1572–1637) was just beginning his career. The finest of this drama was the result of a precarious balance, which kept the long medieval past in mind together with the social and intellectual changes of the present, and communicated with the populace as well as with the court. Already by 1610, this balance was being upset; the elegant but superficial taste of the younger dramatists, Francis Beaumont (1584–1616) and John Fletcher (1579–1625), was turning a national drama into an upper- and middle-class London theatre, which has remained dominant to the present day. By the time of the Caroline drama of the reign of ▷ Charles I, this transformation was nearing completeness in the plays of Philip Massinger (1583–1640) and John Ford (1586–1640). But in the meantime, the peculiar genius of the best dramatists, especially Shakespeare, had helped to produce among the lyric poets the school now so much admired under the name of the ▷ Metaphysicals. The great Metaphysical poets (notably John Donne, ▷ George Herbert, and Andrew Marvell, 1621–78) owe their name to the possession of a quality which is central to Shakespeare's genius: the capacity to unite oppositions of thought and of feeling under the control of a flexible, open, but poised intelligence; their poetry, like Shakespeare's work, thus expresses a peculiarly rich body of experience, united from different levels of the mind.

But the Metaphysicals were not the only fertile school of poets in the first half of the century, nor was Shakespearean drama the only kind from which poets could learn. Shakespeare's rival Ben Jonson was, as a dramatist, in isolated opposition to the Shakespearean drama. The difference lay partly in conceptions of form. Jonson imposed his form upon his matter; the confusion and violence of experience is shaped by a selective process which is a disciplining of the mind as well as a critical analysis of the subject. In his lyric poetry as well as in his dramas, this discipline shows itself in irony, proportion, and a union of strength with elegance. Jonson's example influenced the later Metaphysicals, notably Marvell, but it also led to a different school, not always to be sharply distinguished, which we know as the Cavalier Poets, such as Thomas Carew (1594–1640) and Robert Herrick (1591–1674). Above all, Jonson's criteria anticipated the 'classicists' of the later part of the century, especially Dryden.

But yet another poet left an important legacy to the 17th century. This was Edmund ▷ Spenser (1552–99) who had perfected those qualities of musical cadence and sensuous imagery which many readers think of as essentially 'poetic'. He had his followers in the first 30 years of the 17th century, though none of note, but it is to him that ▷ John Milton owes most among his predecessors. In Milton, we have two very different 17th-century outlooks uneasily united: the love of all that is implied by the ▷ Renaissance, that is to say the revaluation of classical literature and the discovery of the glories of earthly civilization as opposed to those of a heavenly destiny, and devotion to ▷ Puritanism, implying the extreme Protestant belief that not only is all truth God's truth, but that the sole ultimate source of it is the Bible. This uneasy union produced in Milton the determination to impose on his society a Judaic-Christian conception of human destiny so grand that it compelled acceptance, and to use as his medium what was considered to be the grandest of all the ancient artistic forms, the ▷ epic.

▷ *Paradise Lost* (1667) was so impressive as an attempt to realize this impossible ambition, and so imposing in its union of the classical form and the biblical subject, that it has retained its power through three centuries. But Milton's sonorous eloquence, like Spenser's sensuous music, was a kind of magic that subdued the intellect rather than persuaded it. The unfortunate consequence was the common belief among 18th- and 19th-century poets that 'sublime' poetry should elevate the emotions while passing the intellect by. This Miltonic influence no doubt encouraged the exponents of reason like Locke (*An Essay concerning human understanding*, 1690) to believe that poetry belongs to an immature stage of mental development, before the mind has acquired reason and respect for facts, the best medium for which is prose.

From the beginning of the century, prose writers showed signs of seeing their function as clarifying the reason as opposed to enlarging the imagination. This turning away from the imagination went naturally with a gradual relegation of religion. ▷ Francis Bacon, in his *Advancement of Learning* (1605), treats religion with respect and then ignores it, and he ends his few remarks on poetry with the sentence: 'But it is not good to stay too long in the theatre.' Shelley (in his *Defence of Poetry*, 1821) was nonetheless to consider Bacon himself to be a poet, but the vivid imagery which strikes out of his terse style is more functional than that of earlier prose writers. Bacon's main theme is the inductive method of acquiring knowledge through experiment, and all his prose, including his *Essays*, is essentially practical. Although the imaginative connotations

are preserved, the dominant tendency in the first half of the century is to use prose descriptively and analytically. ▷ Thomas Browne's ▷ *Religio Medici* (1642–3) is written, like his other works, in the most sonorous prose in the English language, but Browne is defending his religious faith just because it exceeds his reason, and his poetic style (in contrast to that of the great sermon writers like John Donne) is partly a conscious contrivance. (In the ▷ Romantic period, it would have had some influence on Thomas De Quincey).

In the middle of the century, ▷ Thomas Hobbes published his treatise on political philosophy ▷ *Leviathan* (1651) ▷ in which, with pungent ruthlessness, he forced his readers to face the 'facts' of human nature in their grimmest interpretation. After the ▷ Restoration of the Monarchy (1660), the historian of the ▷ Royal Society, Bishop Sprat, laid down the new standards that were to guide the prose writer: 'a close, naked, natural way of speaking; positive expressions; clear senses; a native easiness'. This is the prose we find in the dialogue of Restoration comedy, in the literary criticism of Dryden, and above all in the sceptical, reasonable philosophy of Locke. However, the spiritual life of the middle and lower classes was not yet permeated by this rationalism. The spirit of Puritanism, still biblical and poetic, is expressed in the spiritual autobiographies of the Puritan leaders, such as the Quaker ▷ George Fox (*Journal*, 1694), and, at its most impressive, that imaginative work ▷ *The Pilgrim's Progress* (1678), by the Baptist tinsmith, ▷ John Bunyan. In this work, the old ▷ allegories of the ▷ Middle Ages reach forward into the field of the novel, the new form which was to come into being in the 18th century.

▷ Dissociation of Sensibility Manners, Comedy of; Restoratio

Seward, Anna (1742–1809)

English poet. Known as 'the Swan of Lichfield', she was born and brought up in the historic village of Eyam in Derbyshire, where her father was rector. In 1754 he became Canon of Lichfield, and Anna looked after him there in his old age. She began to write in her mid-thirties, attending ▷ Anne Miller's poetry evenings. Her elegies on ▷ David Garrick and ▷ Captain Cook brought her to public notice. Her novel *Louisa* was published in 1784, and she continued to publish verse, letters and poems in periodicals, including ▷ *The Gentlemans Magazine*. She was very well known in the 1780s, and a formidable (if ridiculed) figure throughout this and the next decade. Her *Poems* was published in 1810. She knew ▷ Helen Maria Williams, the Ladies of Llangollen, and ▷ Hester Lynch Thrale.
▷ Scott, Mary

Bib: Lonsdale, R., *Eighteenth Century Women Poets*.

Seymour, Frances, Countess of Hertford (1669–1754)

English poet, aristocratic patron and correspondent and editor of ▷ Elizabeth Singer Rowe. After her first marriage in 1715 to Algernon Seymour, she moved in court circles, and in 1723 became Lady

of the Bedchamber to the Princess of Wales. In 1748 she became the Duchess of Somerset on her marriage to the Duke of Somerset. Her poems were published in anthologies. She was related to ▷ Ann Finch.
Bib: Hull, T. (ed.), *Selected Letters*.

Shadwell, Thomas (?1642–92)
Dramatist and poet. Born in Norfolk. Shadwell was educated at Bury St Edmunds and at Cambridge and entered the Middle Temple in 1658. However, he decided on a literary career instead of the law. He travelled on the Continent, and married Ann Gibbs, an actress in the ▷ Duke's Company. Shadwell was a disciple of Ben Jonson and admirer of ▷ Molière, on whose play *Les Facheux* he based *The Sullen Lovers* (1668). Shadwell wrote 17 plays, of which the best known are *Epsom Wells* (1672), ▷ *The Virtuoso* (1676), an engaging satire on the Royal Society, and *The Squire of Alsatia* (1688) (the latter refers to Whitefriars, a London district where those liable to arrest took sanctuary, and the play makes free use of the cant language of thieves and their associates).

A convinced Whig, unlike most of his leading contemporaries in the theatre, Shadwell incurred the fierce enmity of the Tory ▷ John Dryden. At first the two men were on good terms, but they took opposite sides when ▷ Lord Shaftesbury clashed with ▷ Charles II on the issue of the Protestant succession to the throne. Dryden attacked Shaftesbury in ▷ *Absalom and Achitophel* and *The Medal*; Shadwell retorted with *The Medal of John Bayes: A Satire Against Folly and Knavery* (1682). Dryden then stigmatized Shadwell in *Mac Flecknoe, Or A Satire on the True Blue Protestant Poet, T.S.* (1682) as one who 'never deviates into sense', and as Og in the second part of *Absalom and Achitophel*. Shadwell attempted counter-attack in an adaptation of ▷ Juvenal's tenth satire, but Dryden's proved the more lasting reputation, and Shadwell has retained an unfair image as a dull author. However, he had some revenge by superseding Dryden as ▷ Poet Laureate after the Protestant triumph in the Glorious Revolution of 1688. A regular user of opium, Shadwell died suddenly, supposedly after an overdose. His daughter Anne became an actress, the celebrated ▷ Anne Oldfield, and a son, Charles, became a dramatist.
Bib: Dobrec, B., *Restoration Comedy*; Summers, M. (ed.), *Works*; Borgman, A.S., *Thomas Shadwell: His Life and Comedies*.

Shaftesbury, Lord (Anthony Ashley Cooper, 1st Earl of Shaftesbury, 1621–83)
Politician. He first took the side of the king in the ▷ Civil War of 1642–46, but changed sides because he considered that Royalist policy threatened the ▷ Protestant religion. He later became a parliamentary opponent of ▷ Cromwell, however, and after the ▷ Restoration he became one of ▷ Charles II's chief ministers. Charles II, however, was ▷ Catholic in sympathy, and Shaftesbury again went into opposition in 1673. By the Exclusion Bill, he tried to exclude Charles's openly Catholic brother, James, Duke of York, from succession to the

throne, advancing the claims of Charles's illegitimate son, the ▷ Duke of Monmouth, in James's place. The alliance of Shaftesbury and Monmouth is satirized in Dryden's ▷ *Absalom and Achitophel*, one of the best-known satirical poems in the English language. Charles II's statesmanship outwitted Shaftesbury, who fled to Holland and died in exile.

Shaftesbury, Lord (Anthony Ashley Cooper, 3rd Earl of Shaftesbury, 1671–1713)
A moral philosopher, with great influence in the first half of the 18th century. His main beliefs are contained in his *Characteristics of Men, Manners, Opinions, Times* (1711; revised edition, 1713). He was a Deist (▷ Deism), a Churchman, and a Platonic idealist. His optimistic philosophy was in direct opposition to that of ▷ Thomas Hobbes, author of ▷ *Leviathan*. He believed that men have 'natural affections' which are capable of going beyond self-interest. The cultivation of disinterested affection for others will produce virtue and the true social morality. His concept of these 'natural affections' seemed to make the supernatural elements of Christian doctrine unnecessary to the acquirement of true religion. On this ground he was opposed by Bishop Butler in his *Analogy of True Religion* (1736). On a purely theoretical level, Shaftesbury anticipated the beliefs about Nature of the poet ▷ William Wordsworth, and he encouraged the growing emphasis on sentiment and sensibility in criticism and poetry in the 18th century.
Bib: Willey, B., *in Eighteenth-century Background and The English Moralists*; Brett, R. L., *The Third Earl of Shaftesbury: a Study in Eighteenth-century Literary Theory*.

Shakespeare, William (1564–1616)
Dramatist and poet. He was baptized on 26 April 1564; his birth is commemorated on 23 April, which happens also to be St George's Day, the festival of the patron saint of England. His father, John Shakespeare, was a Stratford-on-Avon merchant who dealt in gloves and probably other goods; his grandfather, Richard Shakespeare, was a yeoman, and his mother, Mary Arden, was the daughter of a local farmer who belonged to the local noble family of Arden, after whom the forest to the north of Stratford was named. John Shakespeare's affairs prospered at first, and in 1568 he was appointed to the highest office in the town – High Bailiff, equivalent to Mayor. A grammar school existed in Stratford, and since it was free to the sons of burgesses, it is generally assumed that William attended it. If he did, he probably received a good education in the Latin language; there is evidence that the sons of Stratford merchants were, or could be, well read and well educated. He married Anne Hathaway in 1582, and they had three children: Suzanna, born 1583, and the twin son and daughter, Hamnet and Judith, born 1585.

Thereafter Shakespeare's life is a blank, until we meet a reference to him in *A Groatsworth of Wit* (1592), an autobiographical pamphlet by the London playwright Robert Greene, who accuses him of plagiarism. By 1592, therefore, Shakespeare was already successfully embarked as a dramatist in London, but there is no clear evidence of when he went there. From 1592 to 1594, the London theatres were closed owing to epidemics of plague, and Shakespeare seems to have used the opportunity to make a reputation for himself as a narrative poet: his *Venus and Adonis* was published in 1593, and *The Rape of Lucrece* a year later. Both were dedicated to Henry Wriothesley, Earl of Southampton. He continued to prosper as a dramatist, and in the winter of 1594 was a leading member of the Lord Chamberlain's Men with whom he remained for the rest of his career. In 1596 his father acquired a coat of arms – the sign of a Gentleman – and in 1597 William bought New Place, the largest house in Stratford. There he probably established his father, who had been in financial difficulties since 1577. In 1592, John Shakespeare had been registered as a recusant; this might mean that he was a Catholic, but is more likely to show that he was trying to escape arrest for debt.

In 1598, Francis Meres, in his literary commentary *Palladis Tamia, Wit's Treasury*, mentions Shakespeare as one of the leading writers of the time, lists 12 of his plays, and mentions his sonnets as circulating privately; they were published in 1609. The Lord Chamberlain's Men opened the Globe Theatre in 1598, and Shakespeare became a shareholder in it. After the accession of James I the company came under royal patronage, and were called the King's Men; this gave Shakespeare a status in the royal household. He is known to have been an actor as well as a playwright, but tradition associates him with small parts: Adam in *As You Like It*, and the Ghost in *Hamlet*. He may have retired to New Place in Stratford in 1610, but he continued his connections with London, and purchased a house in Blackfriars in 1613. In the same year, the Globe theatre was burnt down during a performance of the last play with which Shakespeare's name is associated, *Henry VIII*. His will is dated less than a month from his death. The fact that he left his 'second-best bed' to his wife is no evidence that he was on bad terms with her; the best one would naturally go with his main property to his elder daughter, who had married John Hall; his younger daughter, who had married Thomas Quiney, was also provided for, but his son, Hamnet, had died in childhood. His last direct descendant, Lady Barnard, died in 1670.

Owing to the fact that the subject-matter of ▷ biography was restricted until the mid-17th century to princes, statesmen and great soldiers, the documentary evidence of Shakespeare's life is, apart from the above facts, slight. His contemporaries, Christopher Marlowe and Ben Jonson are in some respects better documented because they involved themselves more with political events. Many legends and traditions have grown up about Shakespeare since near his own day, but they are untrustworthy. He was certainly one of the most successful English writers of his time; his income has been estimated at about £200 a year, considerable earnings for those days. After the death of Marlowe in 1593, his greatest rival was Ben Jonson, who criticized his want of art (in *Discoveries*, 1640), admired his character,

and paid a noble tribute to him in the prefatory poem to the First Folio collection of his plays (1623).
Bib: Chambers, E. K., *William Shakespeare: A Study of Facts and Problems*, 2 vols.; Schoenbaum, S., *Shakespeare's Lives*; *William Shakespeare: A Documentary Life*.

Shakespeare criticism

As with any author of the first greatness, different ages have appreciated different aspects of Shakespeare. In his own day, popular taste, according to Ben Jonson, particularly enjoyed *Titus Andronicus*, now regarded as one of the least interesting of his plays. ▷ John Dryden (▷ *Essay on Dramatic Poesy*) picked out *Richard II*; ▷ Samuel Johnson (*Preface to Shakespeare*, 1765) admired the comedies. It is possible to understand these preferences: *Titus* is the most bloodthirsty of all the plays, and suited the more vulgar tastes of an age in which executions were popular spectacles. Dryden and Johnson both belonged to ▷ neo-classical periods. Johnson, like Dryden, was troubled by the differences in Shakespeare's tragedies from the formalism of ancient Greek and 17th-century tragedy which the spirit of their period encouraged them to admire, and Johnson's warm humanity caused him to respond to the plays which displayed wide human appeal while their mode permitted some licence of form. Both Johnson and Dryden rose superior to the limitations of their period in according Shakespeare such greatness. The inheritor of ▷ Johnson's mantle as the most perceptive critic of Shakespeare in the 19th century is ▷ Coleridge, whose seminal lectures on Shakespeare were inspired by German Romanticism. In his letters John Keats offers some of the most enduringly valuable comments on Shakespeare's works before A. C. Bradley published *Shakespearean Tragedy* in 1904, which was to prove the most influential text on Shakespeare for two generations.

If the 20th century has not produced a Johnson, or Coleridge or Bradley in Shakespeare studies, G. Wilson Knight (*The Imperial Theme, The Crown of Life*), Harley Granville-Barker (*Preface to Shakespeare*) and others such as D. A. Traversi (*An Approach to Shakespeare*) and H. C. Goddard (*The Meaning of Shakespeare*) have all contributed to our deeper understanding of the plays and poetry. Shakespeare's education has been closely scrutinized by T. W. Baldwin in two volumes, *Shakespeare's Smalle Latin and Lesse Greeke*, and Geoffrey Bullough's eight volumes on Shakespeare's sources, *Narrative and Dramatic Sources of Shakespeare*, are indispensable to Shakespearean critics. Increasingly the critical debate has been conducted in a number of specialized journals, particularly the long-established *Shakespeare Jahrbuch, Shakespeare Survey, Shakespeare Studies*, and *Shakespeare Quarterly*. A few books are outstanding in their focus on particular aspects of Shakespeare, such as C. L. Barber's influential essay on Shakespearean comedy and the rituals of English folklore and country customs, *Shakespeare's Festive Comedy*, and Northrop Frye's archetypal study of comedy and romance, *A Natural Perspective*. Howard Felperin's distinguished book on Shakespeare's last plays, *Shakespearean Romance* and Janet Adelman's thought-provoking study of *Antony and Cleopatra* and its mythopoeic imagery in *The Common Liar*, both reflect the influence of Frye in their sober and formally predicated approaches.

Of a more radical bent is Jan Kott's famous essay on *King Lear* in *'King Lear, or Endgame'* (1964) which argued the case for Shakespeare as our contemporary, with his finger imaginatively on the pulse of a dark, modern human predicament. On the same lines Peter Brook's famous production of *A Midsummer Night's Dream* in 1970 emancipated the play from its putative operatic and conformist frame and irretrievably altered our perception of it. By thus indicating the extent to which the theatre can influence interpretation of plays, Brook materially contributed to redirecting critical attention back to the stage.

Modern social and critical movements have made their impact felt in the field of Shakespeare studies: deconstruction, in the guise of a creative disintegration of the texts' organic status, and feminism provide the impetus for some of the most controversial writing on Shakespeare in the 1980s, as do 'cultural materialism' and particularly 'New Historicism'. The latter in particular seems set to command a wide audience in the works of Stephen Greenblatt and Louis Montrose, whose work combines the scholarly scruples of the older tradition with an acute sceptical and self-critical awareness of the historical and epistemological contexts of literary criticism in society.

Bib: Bradley, A. C., *Shakespearean Tragedy*; Barber, C. L., *Shakespeare's Festive Comedy*; Coleridge, S. T., *Shakespearean Criticism*; Dollimore, J., *Radical Tragedy*; Dryden, J., *Essays*; Frye, N., *A Natural Perspective*; Greenblatt, S., *Renaissance Self-Fashioning*; Jardine, L., *Still Harping on Daughters*; Johnson, S., *On Shakespeare*.

Shakespeare editions

Apart from a scene sometimes ascribed to Shakespeare in the play *Sir Thomas More* (1596), none of Shakespeare's work has survived in manuscript. In his own lifetime, 18 of his plays were published in separate volumes (the Quartos), but this was probably without the author's permission, and therefore without his revisions and textual corrections. His non-dramatic poems, including the ▷ sonnets, were also published during his lifetime. After his death, his fellow-actors, Heming and Condell, published his collected plays (except *Pericles*) in the large, single volume known as the First Folio, and this was succeeded by the Second Folio (1632), and the Third (two editions) and Fourth in 1663, 1664 and 1685. The Second Folio regularized the division of the plays into Acts and Scenes, and the second issue of the Third added *Pericles*, as well as other plays which are certainly not by Shakespeare. In several important respects the Folio editions were unsatisfactory:

1 The texts of some (though not all) of the smaller quarto volumes of the plays published during the poet's lifetime differed materially from the text of even the First Folio, which in turn differed from the later folios.

2 The First Folio arranged the plays according to their kinds (Comedies, Histories, or Tragedies) and gave no indication of the order in which the plays were written.

3 There was no evidence that even the first editors had had access to the best manuscript texts, and there were evident errors in some passages, the fault of either the editors or their printers, and editors of the later Folios made alterations of their own. Consequently, there was plenty of work during the next two centuries for scholars to re-establish, as nearly as possible, Shakespeare's original text. Work also had to be done on the chronological order of the plays, discovery of the sources of their plots, philological investigations of linguistic peculiarities, and research into the conditions in which the plays were originally acted.

Two of the most eminent 18th-century writers published editions of the plays; these were
▷ Alexander Pope (in 1725 and 1728), and
▷ Samuel Johnson (in 1765). Neither, however, was a sound scholarly edition, though Johnson's was important for its critical Preface and annotations. Lewis Theobald (1688–1744) attacked Pope's poor scholarship in his *Shakespeare Restored* (1726), and published his own edition in 1734. He was the first enlightened editor, and did permanently useful work both in removing post-Shakespearean additions and alterations and in suggesting emendations of corrupt passages. After him came Steevens and Capell, who compared the original Quarto texts with the Folio ones, and ▷ Edmond Malone (1741–1812), the most eminent of the 18th-century Shakespeare scholars. In 1778 he made the first serious attempt to establish the chronological order of the plays, and in 1790 he brought out the best edition of them yet established.

Shakespearean scholarship in the 18th century was more the work of individuals than a collaborative enterprise. They saw many of the problems involved in estimating the relative values of the early texts, the possibilities of scholarly emendation of corrupt passages, and the necessity of eliminating the errors of unscholarly 17th- and 18th-century editors. This work culminated in the publication of 'Variorum' editions of the plays, 1803–21. But the establishment of a really sound text required the study of wider subject-matter: Shakespeare's work had to be estimated as a whole so that its development could be understood; philological study of the state of the language in his time was needed; historical events had to be examined for their possible relevance; many sources for the plots remained to be discovered; theatrical conditions and the relationship of Shakespeare to dramatists contemporary with him needed exploration; even handwriting was important, for the detection of possible misprinting. All this was the work of the collaborative scholarship of the 19th century. It was carried out by German scholars, by the English Shakespeare Societies led by Halliwell and Furnivall, and by the universities.

In the later 18th century Shakespeare became an inspiration to the movement in Germany for the emancipation of German culture from its long subjection to French culture, represented by the very different genius of ▷ Racine. A. W. Schlegel's remarkable translations (1797–1810) were fine enough to enable Germans to adopt Shakespeare as something like a national poet. German scholars such as Tieck, Ulrici, Gervinus and Franz adopted Shakespearean studies with thoroughness and enthusiasm. They stimulated the foundation of Shakespeare Societies in England, and in 1863–6 the Cambridge University Press was able to publish an edition of Shakespeare's works, which, in its revised form (1891–93), is substantially the text now generally in use.

There has been considerable editorial activity in the 20th century, and it was to be expected that the 'New Bibliography', spearheaded by A. W. Pollard, R. B. McKerrow and W. W. Greg would produce a major reconsideration of the Shakespearean test. In the end the fruit of their research, and particularly of McKerrow's brilliant *Prolegomena for the Oxford Shakespeare* (1939), needed to wait for nearly 40 years before they were put to use by the editors of the *Oxford Shakespeare*, Gary Taylor and Stanley Wells. In the meantime Charlton Hinman produced two seminal volumes on the collations of the extant Folios in *The Printing and Proof-Reading of the First Folio* and incorporated his findings in *The Norton Facsimile: The First Folio of Shakespeare*, which remains a standard work of reference. All the major university and other presses turned their attention to re-editing Shakespeare in the late 1960s and early 1970s. At a time when Oxford University Press was printing two complete one-volume Shakespeares (one old spelling and another modern spelling) as well as a huge textual companion and the entire works in separate editions for the Oxford English Texts, Cambridge University Press published the first volume of Peter Blayney's exhaustive survey of the 'origins' of the First Quarto of *King Lear; The Texts of 'King Lear' and their Origins*. Cambridge, Methuen (New Arden), Macmillan and Longman have pursued similar goals: updating and editing afresh Shakespeare's works, each bringing to the canon a different approach. Whereas most of the editions have followed basically conservative principles, most have embraced to a greater or lesser degree the Oxford view of the plays as primarily works for the theatre. Increasingly Oxford's view of Shakespeare as a dramatist who regularly reshaped his plays in line with theatrical and aesthetic demands is gaining ground. The particular focus for this hypothesis has become the two-text (Quarto and Folio) *King Lear* which most editors now agree reflects two different versions of the play. The same editorial principles are being applied to other texts which reflects similar source situations such as *Richard III*, *Hamlet* and *Othello*. Among Oxford's most radical proposals are the printing of two versions of *King Lear*, the calling of Falstaff 'Oldcastle' in *Henry IV*, *Part I*, as well as boldly recreating the text of *Pericles*.

The history of Shakespeare editing in Britain towards the end of the 20th century is ultimately one of the creative disintegration of the shibboleths of traditional editorial policy, even if all the changes proposed by contemporary scholars do not find favour with posterity.

Bib: Bowers, F., *On Editing Shakespeare*; Greg. W. W., *The Shakespeare First Folio: Its Bibliographical and Textual History*; Honigmann, E. A. J., *The Stability of Shakespeare's Text*; McKerrow, R. B., *Prolegomena for the Oxford Shakespeare*.

Shakespeare's plays

Earliest publications. The first collected edition was the volume known as the First Folio (1623). This included all the plays now acknowledged to be by Shakespeare, with the exception of *Pericles*. It also includes *Henry VIII*. Stationers (the profession then combining bookselling and publishing) were glad to bring out individual plays in quarto editions in his lifetime, however, and since there was no law of copyright these were often 'pirated', *ie* published without the permission of the author. On the whole, Shakespeare's company (the Lord Chamberlain's Men) did not want such publication, since printed editions enabled other acting companies to perform the plays in competition. 18 of Shakespeare's plays were published in this way, sometimes in more than one edition, and occasionally in editions that varied considerably. Since none of the plays has survived in the original manuscript, the task of modern editors is often to reconcile different quartos (where they exist) with each other, and any quartos that exist with corresponding versions in the First Folio. The following is a list of the separate editions of the plays, published while Shakespeare was alive or soon after his death, with dates of different editions where they substantially disagree with one another:

Titus Andronicus (1594)
Henry VI, Part II (1594)
Henry VI, Part III (1595)
Richard II (1597, 1608)
Richard III (1597)
Romeo and Juliet (1597, 1599)
Love's Labour's Lost (1598)
Henry IV, (Part I) (1598)
Henry IV, (Part II) (1600)
Henry V (1600)
A Midsummer Night's Dream (1600)
The Merchant of Venice (1600)
Much Ado About Nothing (1600)
The Merry Wives of Windsor (1602)
Hamlet (1603, 1604)
King Lear (1608)
Troilus and Cressida (1609)
Pericles (1609)
Othello (1622)

Order of composition. The First Folio does not print the plays in the order in which they were written. Scholars have had to work out their chronological order, on three main kinds of evidence: 1 external evidence (*eg* records of production, publication); 2 internal evidence (*eg* allusions to contemporary events); 3 stylistic evidence. The following is an approximate chronological arrangement, though in some instances there is no certainty:

1590–91 Henry VI, Parts II and III
1591–92 Henry V, Part I

1592–93 Richard III
   The Comedy of Errors
1593–94 Titus Andronicus
   The Taming of the Shrew
   Two Gentlemen of Verona
1594–95 Love's Labour's Lost
   Romeo and Juliet
1595–96 Richard II
   A Midsummer Night's Dream
1596–97 King John
   The Merchant of Venice
1597–98 Henry IV, Parts I and II
1598–99 Much Ado about Nothing
   Henry V
1599–1600 Julius Caesar
   The Merry Wives of Windsor
   As You Like It
   Twelfth Night
1600–1 Hamlet
   Measure for Measure
1601–2 Troilus and Cressida
1602–3 All's Well that Ends Well
1604–5 Othello
   King Lear
1605–6 Macbeth
1606–7 Antony and Cleopatra
1607–8 Coriolanus
   Timon of Athens
1608–9 Pericles
1609–10 Cymbeline
1610–11 The Winter's Tale
1611–12 The Tempest
Shakespeare is now believed to have written all of
Henry VIII and to have collaborated with Fletcher on
Two Noble Kinsmen.

Shakespeare's sonnets
First published in 1609, but there is no clear
evidence for when they were written. They are
commonly thought to date from 1595–9; Francis
Meres in *Palladis Tamia* (1598) mentions that
Shakespeare wrote sonnets. There are 154 sonnets;
numbers 1–126 are addressed to a man (126 is
in fact not a sonnet but a 12-line poem) and the
remainder are addressed to a woman – the so-called
'dark lady of the sonnets', since it is made clear
that she is dark in hair and complexion. There has
been much speculation about the dedication: 'To
the only begetter of these ensuing sonnets Mr W.
H. all happiness and that eternity promised by our
everliving poet Wisheth the well-wishing adventurer
in setting forth T. T.' 'T. T.' stands for Thomas
Thorpe, the stationer (*ie* bookseller and publisher of
the sonnets); speculation centres on what is meant
by 'begetter' and who is meant by 'W. H.' W. H.
may stand for the man (William Hughes?) who
procured the manuscript of the sonnets for Thorpe,
if that is what 'begetter' means. But if 'begetter'
means 'inspirer', it has been conjectured that W. H.
may be the inverted initials of Henry Wriothesley,
3rd Earl of Southampton, to whom Shakespeare
had dedicated his *Venus and Adonis* and *The Rape of
Lucrece*, or they may stand for William Herbert, Earl
of Pembroke, or for someone else. Guesses have also
been made as to the identity of the 'dark lady', who

has been thought by some to be Mary Fitton, a Maid
of Honour at Court who was a mistress of William
Herbert. There is too little evidence for profitable
conjecture on either subject.

Critics and scholars disagree about the extent
to which the sonnets are autobiographical (and if
so what they express) or whether they are 'literary
exercises' without a personal theme. A middle view
is that they are exploratory of personal relations
in friendship and in love, and that some of them
rehearse themes later dramatized in the plays –
for instance Sonnet 94 suggests the character of
Angelo in *Measure for Measure*, and the recurrent
concern with the destructiveness of time seems to
look forward to *Troilus and Cressida* and the great
tragedies. Since it is unknown whether the edition
of 1609 is a reliable version, there is also some
doubt whether the order of the sonnets in it is that
intended by Shakespeare; most scholars see little
reason to question it.

One of the most valuable recent editions of the
Sonnets is Stephen Booth's which uses the 1609
text, rightly accepting its ordering of the poetry as
binding. Booth's edition compares the modern text
with the Quarto versions at each stage. But if his
extensive notes are instructive, they also tend to be
too comprehensive in their suggestions of infinite
and ultimately meaningless ambiguities in the text.
John Kerrigan's edition of *The Sonnets and A Lover's
Complaint* provides a sensitive text, informative notes
and does justice to the often neglected *A Lover's
Complaint*. Kerrigan authoritatively attributes the
poem to Shakespeare and offers the best commentary
on it to date.
Bib: Leishman, J. B., *Themes and Variations in
Shakespeare's Sonnets*; Schaar, C., *Elizabethan Sonnet
Themes and the dating of Shakespeare's Sonnets*; Smith,
H., *The Tension of the Lyre: Poetry in Shakespeare's
Sonnets*.

Shamela (1741)
An Apology for the life of Mrs Shamela Andrews,
published pseudonymously by ▷ Henry Fielding,
parodies ▷ Samuel Richardson's ▷ *Pamela* of
the preceding year. The plot and characters are
taken from Richardson's novel, yet the tone reveals
what Fielding saw as Richardson's hypocritical
morality, where virtue is rewarded by worldly wealth
and status.

She Stoops to Conquer
A comedy by ▷ Oliver Goldsmith, first acted in
1773. The basic comedy is that of a morbidly shy
man misled into a situation in which he behaves in
a way such as to horrify him when he awakes to
the true circumstances. The young man is Marlow,
sent by his father to court in marriage the daughter
of his friend Hardcastle. Marlow loses his way, and
is deceived into supposing the Hardcastle house
to be an inn. In a gentleman's house he is horribly
embarrassed, but in an inn he is at ease; he proceeds
to behave off-handedly to old Hardcastle as to a
landlord, and to make love to his daughter, as to
a waiting maid. The arrival of his father clears up
the situation, and the mistake turns out to Marlow's

advantage. The play is one of Goldsmith's best works, and an example of the brief revival of the Comedy of ▷ Manners in the 1770s.

She-tragedy

Type of pathetic ▷ tragedy, related to ▷ heroic tragedy, and popular in the last decade of the 17th century and in the early 18th, focusing on the distresses of exalted women characters. Women's sufferings form an important element in plays such as ▷ Cibber's ▷ *Love's Last Shift*, Vanbrugh's ▷ *The Provok'd Wife*, and ▷ Southerne's ▷ *The Wives Excuse*. But the women in these plays are more ordinary than those in true she-tragedies. The form is exemplified in plays including ▷ Banks' *Virtue Betrayed* (1682), on Anne Boleyn, and *The Island Queens* (1684), on the execution of Mary Queen of Scots, performed under the title *Albion's Queen* in 1704, ▷ Mary Pix's *Queen Catharine: or The Ruines of Love* (1698), Motteux's *Beauty in Distress* (1698), and ▷ Nicholas Rowe's *The Fair Penitent* (1703), ▷ *The Tragedy of Jane Shore* (1714), and *The Tragedy of Lady Jane Grey* (1715).

She Wou'd If She Cou'd **(1668)**

Play by ▷ Sir George Etherege, with a cynical and bawdy atmosphere. Two gallants, Courtall and Freeman, are out to seduce and ruin women, but fall in love with Gatty and Ariana in spite of themselves, and are united with them after several scenes of bantering flirtation. The character referred to in the title is Lady Cockwood who, being badly treated by her despicable husband, longs to cuckold him. Courtall and Freeman make sport with her, openly leading her on, but privately mocking and insulting her. The play is derogatory of marriage, despite its endings in espousal, and heavy with race-course imagery, with women seen as horses for men to ride.

Shenstone, William (1714–63)

Poet and landscape gardening enthusiast. He wrote *The Schoolmistress* (revised version 1742), a ▷ Spenserian ▷ burlesque, celebrating Sarah Lloyd, the schoolmistress of a village near Shenstone's family estate. The condescending ▷ sentimentalism of this poem, and the facile lyricism of such works as *A Pastoral Ballad*, in anapaestic quatrains (*Poems on Various Occasions*, 1737), make Shenstone an important representative of the new post-Augustan ▷ sensibility of the time. ▷ Thomas Percy consulted him in the preparation of his *Reliques*, and he wrote several ▷ essays on landscape gardening. His estate at Leasowes near Halesowen, Staffordshire, because famous for its ingenious 'natural' effects.

Sheraton, Thomas (1751–1806)

Next to ▷ Chippendale the most famous English furniture designer. His reputation, which began about 1790, was built up on his severe and graceful style; later, under the influence of French Empire furniture, his designs became much more elaborate. He had many imitators, and the name 'Sheraton' is usually associated with a general style rather than with the works of the original master.

Sheridan, Frances (1724–66)

Novelist and dramatist, born in Dublin. Forbidden by her father to study, Sheridan was taught in secret by her brothers, and clandestinely went with them to the theatre. In 1746 she published a ▷ pamphlet supporting the actor-manager ▷ Thomas Sheridan, in a dispute over his Dublin Playhouse, and they married in the following year. They had four children, one of whom was the future dramatist ▷ Richard Brinsley Sheridan. They moved to London in 1754. Frances Sheridan's best-known work was the novel *The Memoirs of Miss Sidney Biddulph*, published anonymously in 1761, in three volumes. A two-volume sequel, *Conclusion of the Memoirs of Miss Sidney Biddulph*, followed in 1767. These were very well received, and were translated into French, by the Abbé de Prevost (author of *Manon Lescaut*). Incidents from the novel feature in Richard Brinsley Sheridan's ▷ *The School for Scandal*. In 1763 Garrick staged, very successfully, Mrs Sheridan's comedy *The Discovery*, with himself and Thomas Sheridan in the cast. The draft of another comedy, *A Journey to Bath*, was rejected by Garrick, but eventually published in 1902. Her last work, *The History of Nourjahad* (published posthumously in 1767), a didactic story with an ▷ oriental setting, was another success, translated into several languages, and staged as a musical play in 1813.

Bib: Hogan, R., and Beasley, J. C. (eds.), *The Plays of Frances Sheridan*; Todd, J. (ed.), *A Dictionary of British and American Women Writers 1660–1800*.

Sheridan, Richard Brinsley (1751–1816)

Dramatist and politician. Like many dramatists of note writing in English during the 18th and 19th centuries, he was of Irish extraction, born in Dublin. His courtship of his future wife, Elizabeth Linley, began with his carrying her off to a French nunnery to save her from the attentions of a suitor to whom she objected; he returned to fight two duels with his rival; in 1773 his secret marriage to her in France was publicly recognized. In 1776 he became principal director and, a little later, sole proprietor of the ▷ Drury Lane Theatre in London; it was twice burnt down and rebuilt during his proprietorship. He entered Parliament in 1780 and was famous for his oratory there; his opposition to the ▷ American War of Independence caused the American Congress to offer him £20,000, which he refused. His most famous oratorical exploit was his impeachment of Warren Hastings in 1787. During the ▷ French Revolution he supported the ▷ Whig leader, Fox, in opposing military intervention against France. Later he held an independent position politically, but he was influential, partly owing to his friendship with the Prince Regent (later George IV). He ended his life deeply in debt.

His memorable plays are ▷ *The Rivals* (1775), ▷ *The School for Scandal* (1777), and ▷ *The Critic* (1779); they show a reaction against the sentimental comedy which had dominated the English theatre for much of the 18th century, and the first two belong to a revival of the Comedy of ▷ Manners which had been dominant at the beginning of it. They are still

appreciated for the freshness of their dialogue and the ingenuity of their comic situations. Other plays: *St Patrick's Day* (1775); *The Duenna* (a comic opera, 1775); *A Trip to Scarborough* (1777), an adaptation of ▷ Vanbrugh's ▷ *Relapse* (1696), and the tragedy *Pizarro* (1799).
Bib: Sichel, W., *Life*; Nicoll, A., *A History of Late Eighteenth-century Drama*; Sadleir, T. H., *The Political Career of Sheridan*; Danziger, M. K., *Oliver Goldsmith and Richard Brinsley Sheridan*.

Sheridan, Thomas (1719–88)

Actor-manager, teacher and author, born in Dublin. He was a godson of ▷ Swift, husband of ▷ Frances Sheridan, and father of ▷ Richard Brinsley Sheridan. His parents intended him to be a schoolmaster, but his preference for the stage was confirmed in 1743, with the success of his performance of *Richard III*. He became manager of the Theatre Royal in Dublin, to which he returned after a period acting at ▷ Covent Garden in London. By then a theatre opened in Dublin by his rival, ▷ Spranger Barry, reduced his audiences, and he moved to England with his family for good. He began a new career as a teacher and lecturer on elocution, travelling around the country to speak. His house became a gathering-point for literary figures, including ▷ Samuel Johnson. But the two men quarrelled, and Johnson later described Sheridan as 'dull, naturally dull'. Sheridan wrote extensively on grammar and language in general, as well as education and elocution. He published the *Works of Swift, with Life* in 18 volumes in 1784.

Ship Money

An ancient tax for providing ships to defend the country in time of war. ▷ Charles I revived it in 1634 in time of peace and without the consent of ▷ Parliament. His action caused great resentment, but 12 judges gave their verdict that it was legal. Nonetheless, repeated revivals of the tax aroused positive resistance, notably from John Hampden, and it was one of the contributory causes of the ▷ Civil War that broke out in 1642. In 1641 Parliament passed a law declaring Ship Money an illegal tax.

Shirley, James (1596–1666)

Dramatist. He was one of the last dramatists of the great Elizabethan-Jacobean-Caroline period of English drama, a period which lasted from 1580 to 1640 and included the career of ▷ Shakespeare. Shirley wrote fluent, graceful ▷ blank verse and is at his best in social comedy; in many ways he anticipated the ▷ Restoration writers of Comedies of ▷ Manners after 1660. His audience, as in Restoration comedy, was that of the elegant, refined court; it was not drawn from all social classes like the audiences for Shakespeare and Ben Jonson, so that his plays have a comparatively narrow, though sophisticated, range of interests. He wrote over 40 plays, which the best known are the tragedies *The Traitor* (1631); and the *Cardinal* (1641); and the comedies *The Lady of Pleasure* (1631) and *Hyde Park* (1632).

Siddons, Sarah (1755–1831)

Actress. The most celebrated woman on the stage in the 18th century. She was the eldest child of the actor-manager Roger Kemble and Sarah (née Ward), and was born into what became an important acting dynasty. Siddons began acting as a child, including the part of Ariel in a performance of the ▷ Dryden/▷ D'Avenant version of *The Tempest* (1667), in which her future husband, William Siddons (1744–1808), played Hyppolito. She fought her parents' disapproval in order to marry him in 1773, and the couple continued acting in the provinces. ▷ Garrick engaged her for a season at ▷ Drury Lane, 1775–6, but her first appearances there were poorly received. Her fortunes turned during a visit to Manchester, and her reputation as an actress was consolidated at Bristol and at Bath. In 1782 she appeared again at Drury Lane, playing Isabella in Garrick's version of ▷ Thomas Southerne's *The Fatal Marriage*. Her triumph was immediate, and she went on to play a succession of major roles with the company, including Belvidera in ▷ Otway's ▷ *Venice Preserv'd*. It is said that people breakfasted near the theatre, so as to be first in the queue for tickets to see her, some coming from as far away as Newcastle, and prices rose to as much as a hundred guineas. Contemporaries commented on her beauty, stately dignity, and expressiveness, as well as her articulacy, so that not a word was lost. Her capacity to convey passion and grief was legendary. But she was sometimes criticized for her lack of variety, was poor in comic roles, and although she had many friends in high places, she had a reputation for being difficult to work with, and mean with money.

In 1785 Siddons played her most famous part, Lady Macbeth, for the first time, later performing it on occasion by royal command. She added to her repertoire Cordelia, Cleopatra, Desdemona, Rosalind in *As You Like It*, other major Shakespearian roles and many other roles, some written especially for her. Her career was interrupted only for brief intervals by the births of her seven children. In 1803 she followed her brother ▷ John Philip Kemble to Covent Garden. In old age she became fat and had to be helped out of a chair, the fact disguised by other actresses being similarly treated. Widowed in 1805, Siddons retired in 1812, afterwards appearing only at special benefits.
Bib: Boaden, J., *Memoirs of Mrs Siddons* (2 vols); Campbell, T., *Life of Mrs Siddons*; Manvell, R., *Sarah Siddons*; Kelly, L., *The Kemble Era: John Philip and the London*

Siege of Rhodes, The (1656, revised in 1661)

Opera-cum-heroic drama by ▷ Sir William D'Avenant, thought to have been written, originally as a play, with music added later in order to circumvent the Commonwealth law against purely dramatic entertainment, and gain the Government's permission to mount it at Rutland House. The performance helped pave the way for the re-opening of the theatres, and for D'Avenant's own receipt of one of the monopoly patents as theatre manager. The action concerns the siege of Rhodes by

Soleyman the Magnificent, and Duke Alphonso's unreasonable jealousy of his wife, the virtuous Ianthe, who eventually saves her husband and the island. D'Avenant said he wrote it partly to illustrate 'the Characters of Vertue in the shapes of Valor and Conjugal Love'. The staging as with the earlier court ▷ masque was accompanied by lavish spectacle.

Simon Pure

Character in ▷ *A Bold Stroke for a Wife* (1718), the comedy by ▷ Susannah Centlivre, who is described in the list of *Dramatis Personae* as 'a Quaking Preacher'. He is impersonated by Colonel Fainwell, as part of the latter's plot to impress the guardians of Mrs Lovely, and gain their permission to marry her. The scene in which this occurs is interrupted by the arrival of Simon Pure himself, giving rise to the expression, 'the real Simon Pure', meaning the real, genuine, or authentic person or thing.

Sir Charles Grandison, The History of (1753–4)

The last of the three novels presented through letters by ▷ Samuel Richardson. It is an attempt to present the type of the perfect gentleman, just as its predecessor, ▷ *Clarissa* had represented the perfect woman. It prescribes the kind of behaviour which ▷ Addison had preached in his periodical ▷ *The Spectator*. However, it suffers much more than does *Clarissa* from the excessive idealization of its central character. The theme is right conduct in acute sentimental and ethical dilemma; Grandison is in love with Harriet Byron (whom he rescues from the vicious Sir Hargrave Pollexfen), but has obligations to Clementina Porretta, member of a noble Italian family. Among other lessons, Sir Charles shows how a gentleman can avoid fighting a duel without losing his honour. The book has some good minor characters, and is an interesting study in manners, though Richardson did not understand the Italian aristocracy of his period. As a psychological study, it is much inferior to *Clarissa* but it influenced the work of ▷ Jane Austen.

Sir Patrick Spens

An old Scottish ▷ ballad describing the loss at sea of a Scottish ship, its commander Sir Patrick and all the crew. It exists in several versions; in the shortest, the ship puts to sea in bad weather at the order of the king and Sir Patrick foresees the disaster – brought about, apparently, by royal vanity. In the longest version, the ship goes to Norway to bring back a princess, who may be based on the Maid of Norway who died at sea in 1290, or may be the Scandinavian queen of James VI (16th century); the Norwegian lords complain about the behaviour of the Scottish nobility, who leave suddenly, in bad weather, having taken offence. Both versions are fine examples of the art of the ballad, but the shortest exhibits that form at its most economical and dramatic. The first printed version is in ▷ Percy *Reliques*. The best-known version is probably Walter Scott's.

Slavery

Slavery grew during the 17th century, and people of colour entered England through the ports, especially Bristol, which was the centre of the slave trade.

African slaves were taken to English colonies in the West Indies, where the slaves and the colonized native population might not share a language, so the new forms of English from these regions did not emerge as written discourses until after the 18th century. Writers from ▷ Aphra Behn to ▷ Hannah More wrote about slavery, and abolitionist activity began towards the end of the 18th century, by which time there was an active oral culture among slaves using song in African and English languages (see Sir Hans Sloane, *A Voyage to the Islands Madera, Barbados, Nieves, S. Christophers and Jamaica*, 1707). Women writers in the 17th and 18th centuries also had a keen awareness of slavery as a ▷ feminist issue. Many identified the condition of women in society, and particularly in ▷ marriage, as one of slavery; *eg* ▷ Sarah Fyge's, 'From the first dawn of life into the grave, / Poor Woman kind's in every state a slave'.

▷ Wilberforce, William; Feminism, Augustan.
Bib: Pratt, M. L., *Imperial Eyes*.

Sleeping Beauty, The

A famous fairy story in the collection made by ▷ Charles Perrault, translated into English in 1729. A baby princess is doomed by a wicked fairy to prick herself on the finger and die, but a good fairy changes death into a hundred years' sleep, from which the princess is awakened by the kiss of a prince.

Slough of Despond

A boggy place in ▷ John Bunyan's allegory ▷ *Pilgrim's Progress*. Christian sinks into it immediately after taking flight from the ▷ City of Destruction. It signifies the period of depression into which a convert is liable to fall after the first enthusiasm of his conversion.

Smart, Christopher (1722–71)

Poet. He showed early poetic gifts, and received support from the aristocratic Vane family, on whose estates his father was a steward. He made a precarious living through his early poems, which followed the fashions of the time. His *Poems on Several Occasions* (1752) include *The Hop-Garden*, a blank-verse ▷ Georgic in the manner of ▷ John Philips's *Cyder*, and a satirical poem, *The Hilliad* appeared in 1753. In the 1750s he developed a religious mania which drove him to continuous prayer, and he was for a time locked up in an asylum where he developed the original poetic style for which he is now best known. After his release he published *A Song to David* (1763), an ecstatic poem in praise of David as author of the ▷ *Psalms*. It is written in six-line stanzas rhyming *aabccb*, and owes something to the biblically inspired poetry and hymns of such writers as ▷ Isaac Watts and ▷ Charles Wesley. Smart's work was ignored at the time and much of it, including *Jubilate Agno, A Song from Bedlam*, was not published until 1939.
Bib: Ainsworth, E. G., and Noyes, C. E., *Life*.

Smectymnuus

A name under which five ▷ Presbyterian writers wrote against episcopacy – rule of the Church by bishops – in the 17th century. The name was suggested by the initial letters of the names of the writers: Stephen Marshall, Edward Calamy, Thomas Young, Matthew Newcomen, and William Spurstow. Their ▷ pamphlet was attacked by Bishop Joseph Hall, and was defended in two pamphets by ▷ John Milton in 1641 and 1642. ▷ Samuel Butler, in his poetic satire ▷ *Hudibras*, written against the ▷ Puritans, calls the Presbyterians the 'Legion of Smec'.

Smith, Adam (1723–90)

Political economist. His important work was *An Enquiry into the Nature and Causes of the Wealth of Nations* – always referred to as *The Wealth of Nations* – published in 1776, at the outbreak of the rebellion of the colonists in America which he predicted, 'will be one of the foremost nations of the world'. The especial influence of this book comes from his discussion of the function of the state in the degree and kind of control it should exercise over the activities of society, and in particular, of trade. He concluded that the traditional ▷ mercantile system (nowadays called 'protection') was based on a misunderstanding of the nature of wealth, and that nations prospered to the extent that governments allowed trade to remain freely competitive, unrestrained by taxes intended to protect the economy of a nation from competition from other nations. His opinions became increasingly influential and eventually dominant in British economics during the first half of the 19th century; his opposition to *unnecessary* interference by the government in trade and society became harmful in that it was interpreted by later governments as an excuse not to remedy social abuses arising from industrialism.

▷ Free trade.

Smith, Charlotte (1749–1806)

Poet, novelist and translator, born in London. She began writing for the *Lady's Magazine* when she was only 14. Married in 1764 or 1765 she had two pregnanicies before she was 17. Her *Elegiac Sonnets* (1784) was moderately successful, her first novel, *Emmeline* (1788), much more so, and this was followed by another nine novels, including *Ethelinde* (1789), *Celestina* (1791), *The Old Manor House* and *The Wanderings of Warwick* (both 1794), *Montalbert* (1795), *Marchmont* (1796), *The Banished Man* and *The Young Philosopher* (1798). The novels contain elements of ▷ satire, ▷ sentiment and the ▷ Gothic, and were compared favourably with those of ▷ Fanny Burney, and ▷ Anne Radcliffe, whom she influenced. Smith was also sympathetic to the ▷ French Revolution and ▷ American War of Independence, and comments on these in several of her works. She wrote a number of children's books, and made translations from the French.

Smith, William (d 1696)

Actor. Smith joined the ▷ Duke's Company under ▷ Sir William D'Avenant in 1662, where he became one of its leading actors, and created many prestigious roles of the period, including Sir Fopling Flutter in ▷ Sir George Etherege's

The Man of Mode, Pierre in ▷ Thomas Otway's ▷ *Venice Preserv'd*, a part written for him, and Willmore in ▷ Aphra Behn's ▷ *The Rover* (*Parts I and II*). Tall and handsome, Smith was viewed by his contemporaries as a gentleman, of high moral reputation. He is said to have acted in both comedy and tragedy with dignity and flair.

Smock Alley Theatre, Dublin

This was important not only in its own right, but also to the London theatre as a venue for preview performances. In addition, many of the great names in the English theatre began their careers in Dublin, including ▷ Spranger Barry, ▷ Kitty Clive, Thomas Doggett (c1670–1721), ▷ George Farquhar, ▷ Charles Macklin, ▷ James Quin, ▷ Richard Brinsley Sheridan (whose father ▷ Thomas acted at Smock Alley for many years), ▷ Robert Wilks, and ▷ Peg Woffington. Others like ▷ David Garrick and ▷ Barton Booth acted in Dublin on various occasions.

Smollett, Tobias (George) (1721–71)

Born near Dumbarton, the son of a Scots laird, Smollett studied at Glasgow University and was then apprenticed to a surgeon. In 1739 he moved to London, trying to stage his play *The Regicide*, but the attempt was unsuccessful, and he joined the navy as a surgeon's mate, sailing for the West Indies.

In 1744 Smollett returned to London and set up a medical practice in Downing Street, though he never made a living out of medicine. His first publication, a poem entitled *The Tears of Scotland*, appeared in 1746, and later that year he published a satire on London life, *Advice*. In 1747 a further satire, *Reproof*, appeared, and he wrote the novel *The Adventures of ▷ Roderick Random*, published to great acclaim in 1748. Further novels, which draw on his experiences in the navy and his continental travel, include *The Adventures of ▷ Peregrine Pickle* (1751) and *The Adventures of Ferdinand Count Fathom* (1753).

Smollett, now married and a father, struggled to support his family by editorial work, working on *The Critical Review* (1756–63) and publishing his translation of *Don Quixote* in 1755. Finally, his *Complete History of England* proved a commercial success, and was followed by *Continuation* volumes. In 1760 Smollett began *The British Magazine*, where *The Life and Adventures of Sir Lancelot Greaves* was run as a serial; in the same year he was fined and imprisoned for a libellous article in the *Critical Review*.

Smollett had been suffering from ill health for several years, and in 1753 he began to show symptoms of consumption. In 1763 his daughter died, and he abandoned literary work to travel with his wife in Italy and France. On their return in 1765 he wrote the epistolary work *Travels through France and Italy*, which drew from ▷ Sterne the nickname 'Smelfungus'. His final major work was *The Expedition of ▷ Humphry Clinker*, published shortly before his death in 1771.

Bib: Knapp, L. M., *Tobias Smollett: Doctor of Men and Manners*; Boucé, P. G., *The Novels of Tobias Smollett*.

Social contract

A doctrine about the origins of society especially associated with the English thinkers ▷ Thomas Hobbes and ▷ John Locke, and the French thinker ▷ Jean-Jacques Rousseau. Hobbes (in ▷ *Leviathan*) argued that people were naturally violent and rapacious, and that they contracted to put themselves under strong government in order to make the continuance of life and property possible. Locke (*Treatise on Government*) thought the social contract was a convenience rather than a necessity, arguing that private property could have existed in pre-social humanity, but that people contracted to accept government to make themselves secure. Humanity for Locke was not necessarily violent, and government should be tolerant and humane. Rousseau (*Social Contract*) argued that primitive peoples were above all timid, and that they contracted to form governments which rested on the consent of the people, who should overthrow them if they were inefficient or tyrannical. Rousseau's view supported the action of the French revolutionaries and encouraged the growth of democratic ideas in the 19th century. All three opposed the beliefs maintained until the mid-17th century everywhere, that rulers owed their authority to the will of God.

Society for Promoting Christian Knowledge (S.P.C.K.)

Founded in 1698; it was then an unusual collaboration of all the ▷ Protestant sects to help in the education of the poor by founding 'charity schools', and to extend religious education by the circulation of inexpensive Bibles and other religious literature. A subsidiary was the missionary Society for the Propagation of the Gospel in Foreign Parts, in the 19th century a channel for the movement against slavery and the slave trade.

▷ Schools in England.

Socinianism

A theological doctrine associated with two 16th-century Italian theologians, Lelio and Fausto Sozzini (latinized to Socinus). They regarded Jesus Christ as wholly human (*ie* not a member of the Holy Trinity) but as divinely inspired. They were thus ▷ representative of that side of the ▷ Protestant Reformation that sought to simplify and rationalize Christian doctrine; in Britain in the 17th century 'Socinians' were substantially what in the 18th century became known as ▷ Unitarians.

Socrates (?470–399 BC)

Greek philosopher. He taught entirely by word of mouth, the so-called 'Socratic method' being the discovery of the truth by putting appropriate questions. Because he wrote nothing, all information about him depends on the writings of two contemporaries – the historian Xenophon (*Memorabilia*) and the philosopher ▷ Plato, who was personally taught by Socrates. Plato puts his own ideas into the mouth of Socrates in his philosophical dialogues, and it is of course difficult to know just how much and in what ways he expanded the Socratic philosophy. This was the idea that the true end of philosophy is not to discover the nature of the world but the nature of goodness and how to lead the good life; related to this is the doctrine of Forms, according to which reality is seen as fundamentally spiritual, and the real in a person is their soul.

Socrates is said to have had a beautiful soul in an ugly body; he was married to a woman called Xanthippe. He fell out of favour with the ruling party of Athens, his native city, because he befriended enemies of the party; he was accordingly made to put himself to death by drinking hemlock.

Soldier's Fortune, The (1681)

Comedy by ▷ Thomas Otway. Beaugard and Lady Dunce have loved one another for seven years, but during his absence in France, she has been prevailed on by her family to marry Sir Davy Dunce. Aided by the unpleasant pander, Sir Jolly Jumble, the former lovers plot to cuckold Dunce, duping him into carrying their messages and even facilitating their adulterous liaison unwittingly. This intrigue is offset against the witty courtship of Sir Jolly's adopted daughter Sylvia and the impoverished Courtine. She quite literally snares him in a noose, in order to win him. In a comical ▷ proviso scene, full of *double entendre*, he undertakes to farm her lands and keep other tenants away, unless he finds the property 'too common' already. The play is fast-moving, but rather episodic in structure. It is expressly royalist, but there are elements of social comment, as in the references to the poverty of the king's loyal soldiers and servants (▷ Charles II was notoriously bad at paying his debts to those whom he employed). A sequel, ▷ *The Atheist*, appeared in 1684.

Some Reflections on Marriage (1700)

Polemic by ▷ Mary Astell, attacking the contemporary conditions of marriage; it was occasioned by reading about the forced marriage of the Duchess of Mazarin to a man she disliked, which led to the marriage's breakdown, and a series of extra-marital affairs, including one with ▷ Charles II. Astell analyses the causes of the many unhappy unions in her day, identifying the unequal power relations between men and women, and men's contempt of women, as the major factors. These, she says, deprive women of a proper choice before marriage, and keep them as slaves or prisoners within it. Astell argues that too often the man's motive in marrying is to gain possession of a woman's estate, rather than love, and that tyranny in marriage ought not to be tolerated any more than despotism in a state. And echoing her own arguments in ▷ *A Serious Proposal to the Ladies* Astell advocates education to strengthen women's capacity for judgment, and men's respect. She herself resolved the problem, however, by remaining single.
Bib: Perry, R., *The Celebrated Mary Astell. An Early English Feminist*; Rogers, K. M., and McCarthy, W. (eds.), *The Meridian Anthology of Early Women Writers: British Literary Women from Aphra Behn to Maria Edgworth 1660–1800*.

Somerset House

A building on the north bank of the Thames, which was used to house state departments concerned with records of births, deaths, wills, marriages and income tax. The General Register Office for births, marriages and deaths, formerly at Somerset House, became part of the Office of Population Censuses and Surveys in 1970 and moved to St Catherine's House on the Strand. The present building dates from the 18th century; its name derives from a 16th-century palace on the same site, belonging to the Duke of Somerset.

Somerville, William (1675-1742)

Author of *The Chace* (1735), a poem in Miltonic ▷ blank verse celebrating the various branches of hunting. He followed this in 1740 with *Hobbinol*, a ▷ mock heroic piece set in rural Gloucestershire and a poem on hawking, *Field Sports* (1742).

Songs of Innocence and Experience (1789-1794)

Two collections of lyric poems by ▷ William Blake, engraved and illuminated by hand. The *Songs of Innocence* were completed in 1789, and the *Songs of Experience* were added in an enlarged edition in 1794. They were intended to be read by children, and although frequently profound and complex, are perfectly lucid and easy to comprehend. They present 'the Two Contrary States of the Human Soul', and are thus complementary, since in Blake's dialectical view 'Without Contraries is no progression'. The world of Innocence is without morality, repression or fear, and in Blake's dynamic interpretation of Christian mythology, 'unfallen'. Inevitably some of the *Innocence* poems, such as 'The Lamb' and 'A Cradle Song' seem sentimental and oversweet to the adult, 'fallen' reader, and others, such as 'Holy Thursday' and 'The Chimney Sweeper' can seem highly ironic in their trusting attitude towards corrupt parental and political authority. But irony is no part of Innocence, and the Experience counterparts to these poems are in no sense a debunking of the *Innocence* versions. However it must be admitted that the bitter social criticism and moral indignation of *Experience* produce more memorable verse (though again perhaps this is more the case for the adult reader than the child). 'The Tyger', 'The Clod and the Pebbles', and 'The Sick Rose' are the most concentrated symbolic poems in the language, remarkable for their combination of emotional complexity and intellectual clarity. It is characteristic of Blake's dialectical approach that the later poem 'To Tizrah', added to *Experience* in the 1801 edition, flatly contradicts the sexual libertarianism of the other poems in the *Experience* collection, depicting the freeing of the soul from its physical bonds.

Sonnet

A short poem of 14 lines, and a rhyme scheme restricted by one or other of a variety of principles. The most famous pattern is called the 'Petrarchan sonnet', from its masterly use by the ▷ Italian poet Petrarch. This divides naturally into an eight-line stanza (octave) rhyming *abba abba*, and a six-line stanza in which two or three rhymes may occur, the two stanzas provide also for contrast in attitude to the theme. The origin of the sonnet is unknown, but

its earliest examples date from the 13th century in Europe, although it did not reach England until the 16th century. The immense popularity of the form perhaps derives from its combination of discipline, musicality and amplitude. The subject-matter is commonly love, but after the 16th century it becomes, at least in England, much more varied.

The first writers of sonnets in England were Sir Thomas Wyatt (1503-42) and Henry Howard Surrey (?1517-47); the popular anthology *Tottel's Miscellany* (1559) made their experiments widely known. The first really fine sonnet sequence was Sir Philip Sidney's (1554-86) *Astrophil and Stella*. Its publication in 1591 set an eagerly followed fashion for its distinctively English form. This consisted of a single stanza of 14 lines concluding in a ▷ couplet; it is thought that the comparative scarcity of rhyming words in the English language may be the explanation of the greater number of rhymes and freedom in the rhyming scheme in contrast to the Petrarchan form. The greatest of the succeeding sequences was undoubtedly ▷ Shakespeare's.

The sonnet form continued to be used after 1600, notably by ▷ John Milton, but much less for amorous themes and more for religious ones for expressions of other forms of personal experience (*eg* Milton's 'On his Blindness' for political declamation. Milton used the Petrarchan rhyme scheme, but he kept the English form of using a single stanza. From the mid-17th to mid-18th century the different style of thought and feeling suggested by the heroic couplet kept the sonnet out of use; the cult of sentiment by poets such as ▷ Thomas Gray and ▷ William Cooper then brought it back, but a real revival had to wait for the first 30 years of the 19th century in the work of the ▷ Romantics.

Sophia (fl1739-41)

English writer. Sophia was the name attached to two out of three essays on the relative merits of the sexes. *Woman not Inferior to Man* (1739) and *Woman's Superior Excellence over Man* (1740) are adaptations of publications by the French ex-Catholic cleric, François Poulain de la Barre, first translated into English in 1677. She wrote, 'surely the *Women* were created by Heaven for some better end than to labour in vain their whole life long.' The whole exchange took the same shape as the French when a reply to the first tract appeared, purporting to be by a man. Sophia refers to her attacker in *Man Superior to Woman* (1740) as 'one of those amphibious things between both, which I think they call a Wit'.

▷ Astell, Mary; Chudleigh, Lady Mary; Feminism; Feminism, Augustan.

Bib: Ferguson, M (ed.), *First Feminists*; Seidel, M, *Journal of the History of Ideas* 35, 3 (1974), pp. 499–508.

Sophocles (495-406 BC)

One of the three foremost ancient Greek dramatists, the other two being ▷ Aeschylus and ▷ Euripides. He wrote about 100 dramas, of which only seven survive: *Oedipus the King; Oedipus at Colonus; Antigone; Electra; Trachiniae; Ajax; Philoctetes*. His poetic language shows more flexibility than that

of Aeschylus – their relationship in this respect
has been compared to that of ▷ Shakespeare and
Marlowe (1564–93) – and he used three actors
on the stage instead of only two (not counting the
Chorus). In his relationship to Euripides, he is
quoted by ▷ Aristotle as saying that he depicted
men as they ought to be whereas Euripides depicted
them as they were.

Sophy
Originally the surname of the ruling family of Persia
(16th–18th centuries) and later adopted as a title of
the ruler.

South Sea Bubble
The name given to a series of extensive speculations
in 1720 involving the South Sea Company, founded
in 1711. In 1720 individuals who had lent money
to the government through the Bank of England
were invited to exchange their claims for shares in
the Company, which had a monopoly of trade with
Spanish America and was very prosperous. This
project led to irresponsible financial speculation in
a number of dishonest companies, financial scandals
in which ministers of the Crown were involved, and
a major financial collapse in which thousands were
ruined. The South Sea Company survived until the
19th century. Its headquarters, South Sea House,
was for a time the place of employment of the
essayist ▷ Charles Lamb, and is the subject of one
of his essays.

Southcott, Joanna (1750–1814)
A religious fanatic who attracted a following of about
100,000 early in the 19th century. She is particularly
known for her sealed box, which she declared should
be opened in the presence of the assembled bishops
at a time of national crisis. It was opened in 1927,
in the presence of only one bishop but was found to
contain unimportant objects.

Southerne, Thomas (1659–1746)
Dramatist. A Tory, Southerne wrote his first play,
The Loyal Brother; Or, the Persian Prince (1682), to
honour the Duke of York, later ▷ James II, and
satirize ▷ Shaftesbury and the Whigs. Southerne
found his path to an intended military career blocked
because of his political sympathies, and he turned
more seriously to writing plays. He became a friend
of ▷ Dryden, whose tragedy, Cleomenes, he was
asked to complete in 1692, and of ▷ Aphra Behn,
whose work he used repeatedly for source material.
His The Fatal Marriage; Or, the Innocent Adultery
(1694) and Oroonoko (1695) are based on two of her
novels, with added material from one of her plays,
and several other works drew on plays attributed to
her, or sources used by her. Southerne is identified
with a wave of so-called 'marital discord comedies'
of the 1690s (other writers include ▷ Vanbrugh
and ▷ Farquhar) which focused on the problems
of marriage, as much as on courtship. Southerne
had a capacity for seeing difficulties from a woman's
point of view; for example, his ▷ The Wives Excuse:
Or Cuckolds Make Themselves (1691) presents the
dilemma of the woman trapped in an unhappy

marriage to a shamelessly unfaithful husband, while
she restrains herself from accepting the advances of
another man.
▷ Whig and Tory.
Bib: Root, R. L., Jr., Thomas Southerne.

Southey, Robert (1774–1843)
Poet and historian. He was a friend of ▷ Samuel
Taylor Coleridge (they married sisters) and also
of ▷ William Wordsworth. Southey shared their
revolutionary ardour in the 1790s, but his opinions,
like theirs, became conservative at about the turn of
the century, and when the Tory ▷ Quarterly Review
was founded in 1809 he became one of its leading
contributors. He was made ▷ Poet Laureate in
1813. Southey wrote long heroic ▷ epics (Thalaba,
1801; Madoc, 1805; Roderick, 1814) which at the
time were much admired. The best known of his
shorter poems is The Battle of Blenheim. He wrote
several historical works in prose, including The Life
of Nelson (1813) and A History of the Peninsular War
(1823–32). His change in political opinion, and in
particular his position as Poet Laureate, drew the fire
of the second generation of Romantic poets, and he
lacked the poetic originality which partially redeemed
Wordsworth and Coleridge in their eyes. In 1821 his
poem A Vision of Judgement, describing the admission
of George III into heaven, provoked Byron's The
Vision of Judgement, with its brilliant caricature of
Southey as servile turncoat and bumbling hack:
'He had written much blank verse, and blanker
prose,/ And more of both than anybody knows.' He
also features as Mr Feathernest in Thomas Love
Peacock's satirical novel Melincourt (1817).
▷ Pantisocracy.
Bib: Curry, K., Southey; Madden, L. (ed.), Robert
Southey: The Critical Heritage.

Spanish influence on English literature
The earliest translation of a Spanish masterpiece
into any language was that of Cervantes' Don Quixote
(1605–15) by Thomas Shelton in 1612 (Part I) and
1620 (Part II). Of all Spanish texts, Don Quixote was
to have the most profound influence on English
literature: in the 17th century Francis Beaumont's
The Knight of the Burning Pestle (1607) and ▷ Samuel
Butler's ▷ Hudibras (1663) utilized the comic
elements of the novel, while Philip Massinger's
The Renegado (1624) combined material from Don
Quixote together with Cervantes' play, Los Baños de
Argel (1615). In the 18th century ▷ Henry Fielding's
Don Quixote in England (1734) and ▷ Laurence
Sterne's ▷ Tristram Shandy (1760–67), and in
the 19th century the novels of Walter Scott and
Charles Dickens perpetuate English indebtedness to
Cervantes.

The 16th and 17th centuries in Spain are known
as the Golden Age, which paralleled in quality,
but greatly exceeded in abundance of texts, the
creativity of the Elizabethan and Jacobean ages in
England. The plays of Pedro Calderón de la Barca
(1600–81) have often been compared to those of
▷ Shakespeare, for example by Shelley, who learned
Spanish in order to read Calderón's dramas and who
partially translated into English Calderón's famous

religious drama, *El mágico prodigioso* ('The Wonder-Working Magician', 1637). Shelley also admired *La cisma de Inglaterra* ('The Schism of England', perf. 1627), a play dealing with the same subject as Shakespeare's *Henry VIII*. Spanish Golden Age influence on contemporary English drama can be seen in James Shirley's *The Young Admiral* (1633) and *The Opportunity* (1634), as well as in Beaumont and Fletcher's *Love's Cure* (1629) (▷ Spanish intrigue comedy).

The 17th-century translations by James Mabbe further facilitated Spanish literary influence in England; works translated by Mabbe include Cervantes' *Novelas ejemplares* (1613; 'Exemplary Novels', trans. 1640); the late medieval novelesque play *La Celestina* (c1499) by Fernando de Rojas (c1465–1541); and Mateo Alemán's (1547–?1614) ▷ picaresque novel, *Guzmán de Alfarache* (trans. 1622). The latter text, with *Don Quixote*, formed part of the broader, generic development of the picaresque novel in Spain, England and elsewhere in Europe, while *La Celestina* was one of the earliest medieval texts to be translated into English. The tradition of translating Iberian masterpieces into English continues through to the 20th century: Joan Martorell's novel, *Tirant lo Blanc* (1490), was translated in 1984 by D. H. Rosenthal.

Translation has inevitably played an important role in the interrelationship between Spanish and English literatures, but occasionally the two cultures actually converge, as in the English poetry of the Spanish romantic poet and intellectual, Joseph Blanco White (1775–1841) whose sonnet 'To Night' appears in *The Oxford Book of English Verse 1250–1918* (ed. A. Quiller-Couch).

Spanish intrigue comedy

English comedy influenced by, or using as its source, a type of Spanish play known as the 'comedia de capa y espada' (comedy of cape and sword). The originals include works by Pedro Calderón de la Barca (1600–81), Lope de Vega (1562–1635), and Tirso de Molina (1571–1648). The plays frequently turn on conflicts of love and honour and are dominated by busy intrigue plots involving problems of mistaken identity, duelling, and concealment. One of the first of this variety was Sir Samuel Tuke's *The Adventures of Five Hours* (1663), based on a play by Calderón, and commissioned by ▷ Charles II. Other elements of the type include rigid fathers, brothers and uncles attempting to force young relatives into unwelcome marriages, and high-spirited women active in determining their own fates. This helped to make the form popular with women dramatists, including ▷ Aphra Behn, ▷ Susannah Centlivre, and ▷ Mary Pix.

▷ Spanish influence on English literature.
Bib: Loftis, J., *The Spanish Plays of Neoclassical England*.

Spanish Succession, The War of (1702–13)

A war fought to determine the succession of the Spanish throne, and ultimately the balance of power in Europe, after the death of Charles II of Spain. The French king ▷ Louis XIV supported the candidacy of his grandson Philip of Anjou. England, whose interests had changed since the accession of the ▷ Protestant ▷ William III in 1689, and which feared the expansion of French power, supported instead the claim of the Archduke Charles, son of the Holy Roman Emperor (▷ Holy Roman Empire) Leopold I. A third claimant was the Bavarian Prince Joseph Ferdinand. England formed the Grand Alliance with the Holy Roman Empire and the Netherlands, while Bavaria joined with France, Spain, Savoy and Portugal. The last two, however, quickly changed sides. England achieved a series of successes under the ▷ Duke of Marlborough. England's involvement in the war ended with the Treaty of Utrecht in 1713–14. Philip's accession as Philip V was confirmed, but major transfers of territory in Canada, from France to Britain, were also part of the settlement.

Spectator, The

The name of two periodicals, the first appearing daily (1711–12 and 1714), and the second a weekly founded in 1828 and still continuing. The earlier is the more famous of the two, owing to the contributions of its famous editors, ▷ Addison and ▷ Steele; it had an important influence on the manners and culture of the time. The later *Spectator* has also had a distinguished history, however; it began as a radical journal, but is now the leading intellectual weekly periodical of the right.

▷ Reviews and periodicals.

Spens, Sir Patrick
▷ Sir Patrick Spens.

Spenser, Edmund (?1552–90)

Poet. Spenser's poetry, and in particular *The Faerie Queen*, was possibly the single most influential body of writing to appear in the ▷ Renaissance period in England. Throughout the 17th century his influence was immense, not least on ▷ John Milton. In the 20th century, however, his reputation began to decline – readers preferring the so-called ▷ metaphysical school of writing represented by John Donne. Yet, in recent years, there has been a revival of interest in Spenser, particularly among 'New Historicist' critics for whom *The Faerie Queen* has become an endlessly fascinating text.

Spenser was born in London, but lived for most of his adult life in ▷ Ireland. He first visited Ireland in 1577, becoming in 1580 private secretary to Lord Grey, the newly appointed lord deputy of Ireland. From 1580 onwards Spenser's fortunes were connected with his progress through the ranks of the colonial administration of Ireland, and by 1588 Spenser had occupied the forfeited estate of the Earl of Desmond. The estate, at Kilcolman in County Cork, Spenser developed as a small 'colony' of six English householders and their families. Kilcolman was to be Spenser's home until 1598 when, in October of that year, the castle of Kilcolman was destroyed in the course of 'Tyrone's Rebellion'. Following the upheaval, Spenser returned to London for the last time, where he died, according to Ben Jonson 'for lack of bread' in 1599.

Spenser's first published works were anonymous translations from Petrarch and the French poet du Bellay which appeared in a violently anti-Catholic collection in 1569. It was not, however, until the publication of *The Shepherd's Calender* (1579, with five editions by 1597) that Spenser's poetic reputation became established. In 1580 he published a correspondence with Gabriel Harvey, an old friend from his Cambridge days, which set out his views on ▷ metre and prosody. The correspondence is not, perhaps, of startling critical force. Further collections of poetry appeared in 1591, followed by his sonnet sequence *Amoretti*, together with *Epithalamion* in a single volume in 1595. The autobiographical *Colin Clout's Come Home Again* (1594) was followed by the Platonic *Fowre Hymnes* of 1596 and his celebration of the marriage of the daughters of the Earl of Worcester, *Prothalamion*, also in 1596. Spenser's major poetic work, *The Faerie Queene*, begun prior to 1579, appeared first in 1590 when the first three books of the poem were published. The second edition of Books I–III appeared together with Books IV–VI in 1596, and the final version (as we have it) of the poem after Spenser's death when a folio edition including the 'Mutabilitie Cantos' was published in 1609.

In the late 16th century, Spenser was the dominating literary intellect of the period, and his reputation was sustained throughout the 18th century, reaching an apotheosis amongst the ▷ romantic poets. To the modern reader he presents a complex set of problems and responses. As a 'source' for wide areas of Renaissance intellectual culture he has been continuously explicated and re-explicated, his texts being examined for their Platonist, numerological, Lucretian (▷ Lucretius) and ▷ Calvinist elements. But he is also a writer whose engagement with the creation of a national myth of identity was part of a vital Elizabethan project.

Bib: Greenlaw E. *et al.* (eds), *Works of Edmund Spenser*, 10 vol.; Nohrnberg, J., *The Analogy of 'The Faerie Queene'*; Sale, R., *Reading Spenser*; Goldberg, J., *Endlesse Worke: Spenser and the Structures of Discourse.*

Spenserian stanza

A verse form devised by ▷ Edmund Spenser for his poem. *The Faerie Queen*. It consists of eight ten-syllable lines, plus a ninth line of 12 syllables (Alexandrine), an iambic rhythm and a rhyme scheme as follows: *a b a b b c b c c*. Example from *The Faerie Queene*:

And as she looked about, she did behold,
How over that same door was likewise writ,
'Be bold, be bold,' and everywhere 'Be bold',
That much she mused, yet could not construe it
By any riddling skill, or common wit.
At last she spied at that room's upper end,
Another iron door, on which writ,
'Be not too bold'; whereto though she did bend
Her earnest mind, yet wist not what it might
intend.

(Book III, Canto xi, 54)

The stanza was used by Spenser's poetic disciples, ▷ Giles and ▷ Phineas Fletcher, early in the 17th century. It was revived in the 18th century by reflective poets such as ▷ James Thomson (▷ *The Castle of Indolence*), ▷ Mark Akenside (*Virtuoso*, 1737), ▷ William Shenstone (*Schoolmistress*, 1742), ▷ James Beattie (*Minstrel*, 1771).

Spinoza, Baruch (1632–77)

Philosopher, theologian and mathematician, born in Amsterdam of a Portuguese Jewish family. He was excommunicated from the Jewish community because of his unorthodox beliefs and became a Christian. After an attempt was made to assassinate him, he left his home and earned a living grinding lenses for microscopes and telescopes. At the same time he became the leader of a philosophical circle. Building on the rationalism of ▷ Hobbes and ▷ Descartes, Spinoza speculated that matter is eternal, and the universe is God. His pantheistic belief that minds and bodies are both aspects of God resolves the Cartesian dualism of mind and matter as inhabiting separate systems, the spiritual one ordered by God, the material one by secondary causes. Spinoza also suggested that everything happens according to a 'logical necessity' determined by God, which restricts the possibility of free will, except insofar as acting according to the will of God makes man free. Among his most famous works are the *Tractatus Theologico-Politicus* (1670) and *Tractatus Politicus* (1677).

Spleen, The

1 Title of a Pindaric poem by ▷ Anne Finch, Countess of Winchilsea, published in 1713. She uses the term variously, sometimes to mean melancholy, and sometimes anger or ill-humour. In the poem she examines its place in history, then describes her personal struggle with recurring bouts of it, and finally discusses its manifestations in marriage, and in religious practice, which can result in religious melancholia.

2 Poem by ▷ Matthew Green, which uses a ▷ pastoral framework to celebrate rustic simplicity.

Spondee

▷ Metre.

Sporus

A homosexual favourite of the Emperor Nero. His name was used by ▷ Alexander Pope for the sexually ambiguous ▷ John Hervey, politician and adviser to the Queen, in *Epistle to Dr Arbuthnot* (ll. 305–333).

Stationers

In modern English, sellers of writing materials. In the ▷ Middle Ages and until the mid-17th century, however, they were booksellers, and were so called from their practice of taking up stalls or 'stations' at suitable places in cathedral towns (*ie* against the walls of St Paul's Cathedral in London) and universities. In the 16th and early 17th centuries they not only sold books, but printed and published them as well. The absence of a law of ▷ copyright (until 1709) made it lawful for stationers to publish author's manuscripts whenever and however they could procure them, without the authors' permission. This kind of unauthorized publishing is now called 'pirating'. 18 of Shakespeare's plays were possibly pirated before the publication of the first collected edition of his plays in the First Folio of 1623, and the fact has caused some difficulties to scholars (▷ Shakespeare editions); there is no assurance that their publication was authorized by the poet, that he had revised the plays for publication, or even that the stationer had procured a reliable version.

The Stationers' Company was formed in 1557 by royal charter; by this charter, no one not a member was entitled to publish a book except by special privilege, and all stationers had to record the titles of books they published; the Company's record of books is thus an important source of information for the literary historian, and particularly valuable evidence in dating many Elizabethan plays. The Company gradually lost its publishing monopoly in the 17th century.

The modern institution, Her Majesty's Stationery Office, publishes official government documents.
▷ Stationers' Register.

Stationers' Register

An important source of bibliographical information for the 16th and 17th centuries. In 1557, Mary I granted the Worshipful Company of ▷ Stationers and Papermakers of London the monopoly of printing. Under the charter granted to the company, all printers were enjoined to record the titles of any works intended for publication for the first time in a register. Once a title had been recorded, no other member of the company was allowed to publish the book. The Stationers' Register thus *should* include the titles of all books intended for publication between 1554 and 1709. In practice, however, the record is incomplete. First, records for the years 1571–6 have been lost. Secondly, titles were sometimes entered but the book never published. Thirdly, on occasion a book was published without being entered. Finally, though titles were usually entered shortly before the actual publication of a book, there are cases where a period of years elapsed between the entering of a title and the final publication of a work. Nevertheless, the Stationers' Register is an important record of the English book trade in the period. Not least, it provides a valuable indication of what works were being considered for publication at a particular moment.
Bib: Arber, E. (ed.), *A Transcript of the Register of the Company of Stationers of London, 1554–1640*, 5 vols.; Eyre, G. E. B. (ed.), *A Transcript of the Register of the Worshipful Company of Stationers from 1640 to 1709*, 3 vols.

Steele, Sir Richard (1672–1729)

Essayist and journalist. He was educated (with ▷ Addison) at Charterhouse School and at ▷ Oxford University. On graduation he entered the army. His prose treatise *The Christian Hero* (1701) attracted the favour of the king, ▷ William III, but caused Steele the inconvenience of finding that he was expected to live up to his own precepts. This his pleasure-loving nature did not find convenient, and he redressed the balance by his comedy *The Funeral* (1701). He wrote other comedies: *The Lying Lover* (1703); *The Tender Husband* (1705), an imitation of ▷ Molière's *Sicilienne*; and *The Conscious Lovers* (1722). It is not, however, for his comedies that he is now read, but for a new kind of periodical ▷ essay of which he was practically the inventor, and which he published in ▷ *The Tatler*, started in 1709, and appearing three times weekly. Although since the lapsing of the Licensing Act in 1695 there was no active ▷ censorship of political opinion, Steele found it safer to avoid politics, at least after the Tory party came to power in 1710, since he was a consistent Whig (▷ Whig and Tory). His essays treated daily life, manners and behaviour, in a way calculated to educate middle-class readers and win the approval of people of virtue, and yet always to entertain them. These motives, and the kind of interest that his essays inspired, anticipate the character of later 18th-century novels, especially those of ▷ Samuel Richardson. *The Tatler* was already a success when ▷ Joseph Addison started to collaborate with Steele, but they closed it down in 1711, and started the still more famous ▷ *Spectator* (1711–12). The crisis of succession to the throne grew intense in 1713–14: the Whigs favoured the Protestant House of ▷ Hanover and a powerful Tory faction was ready to support ▷ Anne's half-brother James if he would turn Protestant, though other Tories remained loyal to the ▷ Act of 1701 in favour of Hanover. Steele was consequently attacked by the Tory journalist ▷ Jonathan Swift, both for his conduct of his next paper, *The Guardian* (1713), and for his ▷ pamphlet in favour of the ▷ Protestant succession, *The Crisis* (1714). In 1714 the Whigs returned to power and Steele's political fortunes revived; he was knighted in 1715, and received various official posts. In 1714 he produced his autobiographical *Apology for Himself and his Writings*; he also edited a number of other periodicals, all of them short-lived, and none with the fame of *The Tatler* and *The Spectator*: *The Englishman, The Reader, Town Talk, Tea-Table, Chit Chat, Plebeian*. The last, a political paper, led to a quarrel with Addison in 1718.
▷ Coverley, Sir Roger de.
Bib: Aitken, G. A., *Life*; Hazlitt, W., *The English Comic Writers*; Dobree, B., *Variety of Ways*; Bateson, F. W., *English Comic Drama, 1700–50*.

Stella

1   The name used by Sir Philip Sidney for Penelope Devereux in his ▷ sonnet sequence *Astrophil and Stella* ('Star-lover and star') published in 1591; she married Lord Rich.
2   The name used by ▷ Jonathan Swift for Esther Johnson in his *Journal to Stella*, published in 1768.

Sterne, Laurence (1713–68)

Sterne was born at Clonmel in Ireland, the son of an improvident army officer. After leaving ▷ Cambridge University he became an Anglican priest near York, where his great-grandfather had been Archbishop. His celebrated novel ▷ *The Life and Opinions of Tristram Shandy* appeared in successive volumes from 1760 until 1767. Opinions have always been divided about the qualities of this book, although Sterne's reputation rests principally upon it. ▷ Samuel Johnson found it eccentric and shallow, declaring, 'Nothing odd will do long. *Tristram Shandy* did not last'; but in the 20th century the critic Viktor Schlovsky has argued that '*Tristram Shandy* is the most typical novel of world literature.' ▷ *A Sentimental Journey through France and Italy*, which demonstrates many of the same stylistic idiosyncracies, appeared in 1768, the last year of Sterne's life. His *Journal to Eliza*, published posthumously, is a curious, quasi-autobiographical work that hovers uneasily between fact and fiction, tragedy and farce. The same blend of seriousness and whimsicality is evident in Sterne's sermons, he published under the name of one of the characters from *Tristram Shandy* as *The Sermons of Mr Yorick*. A contemporary review took offence at this jesting allusion. 'We have read of a Yorick likewise in an obscene romance,' it thundered. 'But are the solemn dictates of religion fit to be conveyed from the mouths of buffoons and ludicrous romancers?'

Sterne's characteristic blending of sentimentality and farce, although distinctive in style, is not without precedent. His main literary influences can be found in Rabelais (1495–1553), Cervantes (1547–16), and ▷ Montaigne, although there are also debts to Burton's *Anatomy of Melancholy* (1621–51), Locke's *Essay on Human Understanding*, and ▷ Swift's ▷ *Tale of a Tub*. From Rabelais Sterne derived not only his bawdy humour, but also his fascination with exuberant word-play, his love of lists and puns, his delight in the sonorous malleability of words and his absurd parodies of learned debates. From Locke he borrowed and parodied the theory of the association of ideas, a theory which allows him to present each of his characters trapped in a private world of allusions. Thackeray objected to the self-indulgence of Sterne's wit; 'He is always looking on my face, watching his effect, uncertain whether I think him an impostor or not; posture-making, coaxing and imploring me.' Yet it is precisely this fictional virtuosity that has recommended Sterne as a model to later writers keen to assert not only that all art is artifice, but that history and biography too are merely varieties of elaborate fiction.
Bib: Cash, A. H., *Laurence Sterne*; New, M., *Laurence Sterne as Satirist*.

Stock Exchange
An institution in London for the purchase and sale of investments in the form of shares, stocks and bonds. London stockbrokers once met at the Royal Exchange and elsewhere for the transaction of their business, but in 1802 they formed themselves into a society and built their own premises on a site between Throgmorton Street and Old Broad Street.

Strawberry Hill
▷ Walpole, Horace.

Strophe
A Greek word meaning 'turn'. It is used as a term in Greek versification, for example, the Pindaric ▷ ode, for a passage which is sung and danced (or 'turned') by a chorus. When another passage succeeds it, to be danced and sung by another part of the chorus, this second passage is known as an 'antistrophe'.

Stuart (Stewart), House of
The family from which came the sovereigns of Scotland between 1371 and 1603, and the sovereigns of Scotland, England and Ireland between 1603 and 1714. The family originated in Brittany from where they migrated to England in the 11th century and to Scotland in the 12th, where they acquired the surname 'Stuart' (variously spelt) by serving the kings of Scotland as Stewards. They came to the Scottish throne by intermarriage with the Bruce family, and the reigns until 1603 were as follows: Robert II (1371–90); Robert III (1390–1406); James II (1406–37); James II (1437–60); James III (1460–88); James IV (1488–1513); James V (1513–42); Mary (1542, deposed 1567); James VI (1567–1603). In 1603 Elizabeth I of England died childless, and James VI inherited the crown of England by virtue of his descent from Elizabeth's aunt Margaret, who had married James IV. James VI thus became also ▷ James I of England, and ruled over the two countries until 1625. The succession continued as follows: ▷ Charles I (1625–49), after whom there was an ▷ interregnum until 1660 when the monarchy was restored in his son, ▷ Charles II (1660–85); ▷ James II (1685–88) was deposed in the ▷ Glorious Revolution of 1688 and was succeeded by his daughter ▷ Mary and her husband ▷ William III reigning jointly. After the death without surviving children of ▷ Anne (1702–14), the ▷ Protestant line of the Stuarts died out, and ▷ Parliament established the Protestant and German House of ▷ Hanover (descended from a daughter of James VI and I) on the throne of the United Kingdom. James II had left a Catholic descendant behind him, however, and the Catholic Stuarts twice attempted to regain the throne in the ▷ Jacobite Rebellions of 1715 and 1745. The direct line of the House of Stuart died out in 1808.

Supernatural, supernaturalism
Use of the supernatural, in the form of ▷ ghosts, ▷ witches, and other apparitions has a long history in English literature, stretching back to the Old English *Beowulf* and the medieval *Sir Gawain and the Green Knight*. Such phenomena are employed by ▷ Spenser in *The Faerie Queen*, and in a number of Shakespeare's plays, including *Hamlet* and *Macbeth*. ▷ Perrault's fairy tales, which became popular in England, also contain many manifestations of the supernatural. The 18th century saw a growing fascination with the supernatural, especially as used in ▷ Gothic plays and novels, including ▷ Walpole's ▷ *The Castle of Otranto*, ▷ Anne Radcliffe's ▷ *The Mysteries of Udolpho*, and ▷ Lewis's *The Monk* (1796) and *The Castle Spectre* (1796).

Swedenborg, Emanuel (1688–1722)

Swedish scientist, philosopher and theologian. The
earlier part of his life was dedicated to the natural
sciences, and his theories anticipate important
discoveries in geology, cosmology, and especially
in the physiology of the brain. Later he devoted
himself to religion and had mystical experiences:
his religious beliefs led to the founding of the New
Jerusalem Church and the English Theosophical
Society. According to Swedenborg's beliefs, God is
Divine Man, whose essence is infinite love; there
are correspondences between spiritual nature and
material nature, but the former is alive and the
latter is dead; both in God, and in man and nature
there are three degrees, those of love, wisdom and
use, or end, cause and effect; by a love of each
degree man comes into relation with them, and his
end is to become the image of his Creator, God.
Swedenborg's *Heaven and Hell* and *True Christian
Religion* were translated into English in 1778 and
1781, and amongst his followers were the father of
the poet ▷ William Blake, and Blake's friend, the
sculptor John Flaxman. Swedenborg's doctrines
are the starting point of much of Blake's thinking.
But Blake, who wrote comments on Swedenborg's
doctrines, came to disagree with the philosopher in
important respects.

Swift, Jonathan (1667–1745)

Satirist. He was of an old English family, but his
grandfather seems to have lost his fortune on the
Cavalier side in the ▷ Civil Wars of the mid-17th
century. The poet ▷ Dryden was his cousin. Swift
was educated in Ireland, where he had the future
playwright ▷ Congreve as a schoolfellow, and took
his degree at Trinity College, Dublin. He began
his working life as secretary to the statesman and
writer ▷ Sir William Temple in 1689, left him to
take orders as a priest in the Church of England
in 1694 (receiving a small ecclesiastical office in
Ireland), and returned to remain in Temple's
service until Temple's death in 1699. Throughout
the reign of Queen ▷ Anne (1702–14) he played
a large part in the literary and the political life of
London, though he was dividing his time between
England and Ireland. He contributed some numbers
to ▷ Addison's and ▷ Steele's journals ▷ *The
Tatler* and ▷ *The Spectator*, and together with
▷ Pope and Arbuthnot founded the ▷ Scriblerus
Club. Politically he at first served the Whig party,
but in 1710 he changed over to the Tories, led by
Edward Harley, Earl of Oxford, and the brilliant but
unreliable ▷ Bolingbroke (▷ Whig and Tory). He
served the Tories by his ▷ pamphlet *The Conduct of
the Allies* (1711) advocating peace in the War of the
▷ Spanish Succession, and by his conduct of the
journal *The Examiner* (1710–11). His assistance was
invaluable to the Tory party, who held power from
1711 until the death of the Queen; in 1713 Swift
was rewarded by being made Dean of St Patrick's
Cathedral, Dublin, an office which he at first held
as an absentee. By this time, however, the Queen
was dying, and Harley and Bolingbroke, divided
over the succession to the throne, were opponents:
Bolingbroke offered Swift great rewards for his

support, but Swift preferred to remain with Harley,
who had lost power and for a time was even in
danger of losing his life. In 1714 the Queen died,
the Whigs returned to power, Bolingbroke fled, and
George I came over from Germany as king. Swift
left England for his Deanery in Ireland. At first
he had few friends there, but between 1720 and
1730 he wrote a number of eloquent pamphlets in
the interests of the oppressed Irish, and ended by
achieving great popularity. The same decade saw the
crisis of his relationships with the two women who
loved him: Esther Johnson, the 'Stella' of his *Journal
to Stella*, compiled 1710–13, and Esther Vanhomrigh,
whom he called 'Vanessa'. The relationship with
the latter was tragically concluded with her death
in 1723; Stella died in 1728. Swift lived as a
conscientious and efficient Dean almost to the end
of his life, unselfishly disposing of most of his wealth
for the poor, but he went out of his mind in 1742.

Swift wrote a great deal of prose, chiefly in the
form of pamphlets, and not all of it is satire; *The
Conduct of the Allies* is not, for instance, nor are his
▷ sermons. However his great reputation rests
principally on his prose satire, and he is especially
admired for the very subtle and powerful form of
his irony. The surface of his prose is limpidly clear
and beguilingly placid, but his use of it is to enforce
by close logic an impossible and often very shocking
proposition, which is driven home with distinct and
startling imagery. His position was that of a sincere
Christian who advocates reason; he despised alike
the emptiness of the ▷ Deists and the emotionalism
of ▷ Puritans. He was at the same time a strong
humanitarian, revolted by injustices leading to so
much suffering, but despairing of the capacity of the
human race to rid itself of its tendency to bestiality
and heartlessness. Though a believer in reason, he
despised the pedantry of so many scholars, and the
irrelevances of the 'natural philosophers' in their
pursuit of science. He has been censured on two
grounds: first, the minor but undoubted one that his
disgust at some aspects of human existence derived
from his own morbidity, and secondly, the much
more controversial one that his vision is in the end
negative and destructive. His most famous works
are as follows: ▷ *The Battle of the Books* (written
1697, published 1704), a contribution to the dispute
between the relative merits of the ancients and the
moderns in literature; ▷ *A Tale of a Tub* (1704), a
satire on 'corruption in religion and learning' and
one of his masterpieces; *Argument against Abolishing
Christianity* (1708), a satire on the irreligion of
the time; ▷ *Drapier's Letters* (1724), against the
monopoly granted by the English government to
William Wood to provide the Irish with a copper
coinage; ▷ *Gulliver's Travels* (1726); and ▷ *A
Modest Proposal* (1729), a most forceful exposure of
the conditions of the Irish poor. Swift's poetry has
only recently received the critical attention that it
deserves. His most admired poem is *Verses on the
Death of Dr Swift* (1731), a partly satirical piece in
which he imagines public reaction to the news of his
death, and then gives his own deliberately deceptive
assessment of his life and achievements. *Cadenus
and Vanessa* is an equally deceptive poem which

purports to give an account of his love affair with
Esther Vanhomrigh. It was published, at her request,
after her death in 1723. ('Cadenus' is an anagram of
'Decanus' = Dean.)

Bib: Ehrenpreis, I., *Swift, The Man, His Works and
The Age*; Nokes, D., *Jonathan Swift, A Hypocrite
Reversed*.

Syrinx
In Greek myth, a maiden pursued by the god ▷ Pan;
she threw herself into the river Ladon, where she
was changed into a reed, from which Pan made his
pipe. Her legend is retold by ▷ Pope in his pastoral
poem ▷ *Windsor Forest* (1713).

T

Tacitus, Cornelius (AD ?55–?120)

Roman historian. He was eminent in Roman political and social life, and the son-in-law of Gnaeus Julius Agricola, the governor of Britain who effectively transformed the island into an orderly Roman province. His surviving works are the *Dialogue on Orators*, consisting of conversations about the decay of Roman education; the *Life of Agricola*, including an account of Britain under the rule of his father-in-law; *Germany*, an account of the characteristics of the land and its people, contrasting their freedom and simplicity with the degeneracy of Rome; the *Histories*, a fragment of an account of the Roman Empire during the last 30 years of the 1st century, and the *Annals*, a fragment of a history of the Empire in the first half of the century.

Tacitus was a contemporary of the satirical poet ▷ Juvenal; together they represent the last significant phase of classical ▷ Latin literature; both have a strong ethical concern with the condition of Roman civilization, and Tacitus reveres the austere virtues of the pre-imperial republic, though he accepts the Empire as a political necessity. His style is distinguished for its brevity, and his works were an outstanding constituent of English education from the 16th to 19th centuries.

▷ Classical education.

Talbot, Catherine (1721–70)

Poet, essayist and letter-writer, admired by contemporaries for her learning. Almost all her works were published posthumously, by her close friend ▷ Elizabeth Carter, including her collection of essays *Reflections on the Seven Days of the Week* (1770), and by Carter's nephew Montagu Pennington, who brought out the *Series of Letters between Mrs Elizabeth Carter and Miss Catherine Talbot* and Talbot's *Works*, both in 1809.

Tale of a Tub, A (1704)

A prose satire by ▷ Jonathan Swift. The title is the same as that of one of the last and least interesting comedies by Ben Jonson, but Swift ironically explains it in his Preface as derived from the practice of sailors of tossing a tub to a whale in order to divert it from attacking the ship. The ship, Swift explains, is an image of the state, and the whale is ▷ *Leviathan*, ▷ Hobbes's political treatise, from which the wits of the age drew their dangerous armament of scepticism and satire; he pretends that he has been employed to divert these attacks by his engaging nonsense. For the next edition (1710), Swift added *An Apology*, in which he discloses his true aim – to satirize 'the numerous and gross corruptions in Religion and Learning'. The real meaning of the title is that Swift is beguiling readers so as to expose them the more effectively to the ferocity of irony. The central fable of the *Tale* is the story of three brothers, Martin, Peter and Jack, who inherit three simple coats from their father, whose will enjoins that the coats must in no way be altered. Under the leadership of Peter, however, the brothers find it convenient to alter the coats beyond recognition to comply with fashion. Peter's authority eventually becomes so insanely domineering that Martin and Jack revolt against him;

Martin tears off the ornaments on his coat, but stops before he altogether disfigures it; Jack, however, reduces his to a squalid rag. The fable is an allegory of the ▷ Reformation: Peter represents the Church of Rome, Martin the Church of England, in which Swift was a priest, and Jack the extremer Protestants, or ▷ Dissenters; the coat is the Word of God as expressed in the New Testament. Swift's main object of attack is Jack, since he regarded the Dissenters, with their claim to receipt of divine inspiration and their resistance to authority, as the principal threat to the rule of right reason, true religion, and fine civilization in his time. The fable is interspersed with digressions, satirizing the arrogance of those who set up their private intellects or privileged inspiration as guides to their fellow-men; by Section XI the digressions come together with the fable, and Jack is declared to be the leader of the ▷ Acolists, who expound their doctrines through 'wind', from Aeolus, Greek god of the winds. The satire is essentially an attack on the 'windiness' that Swift discerned in the more pretentious philosophical and religious teaching of his time.

Tartan

Cloth woven into chequered designs; this cloth was formerly the regional dress or 'plaid' in the Scottish ▷ Highlands. The plaid was draped about the body and hung down below the belt as a skirt or ▷ kilt. It is commonly believed that each Highland clan has always had its own tartan of distinctive colour and weave. The evidence that this was true before the prohibition of Highland national dress (which followed the ▷ Jacobite Rebellion of 1745 and lasted until 1782) is uncertain. Undoubtedly many existing tartans ascribed to clans are the invention of 19th-century romanticism (especially stimulated by Sir Walter Scott) and the tourist industry. However, tartan weaves certainly varied from region to region of the Scottish Highlands, and to this extent there must have been some degree of distinction among the clans.

Task, The (1785)

A long ▷ blank-verse poem by ▷ William Cowper, combining ▷ mock heroic with ▷ Georgic and ▷ sentimental elements. It begins in heavily Miltonic vein with an account of the history of Cowper's own sofa. Later passages concern the joys of rural retirement, gardening, the peculiarities of various local characters, and the moral and religious corruptions of the day, which are condemned at great length. The poem manages to achieve a distinctive and engaging tone, despite the miscellaneousness of its literary elements, and its simplicity of diction foreshadows that of ▷ William Wordsworth in *Lyrical Ballads*.

Taste

The 18th century saw the development of 'taste' as an ideal, accompanying the growth and spread of wealth among the middle and upper classes. Among the *nouveaux-riches* especially, good taste seemed to demonstrate good breeding, creating a distance between the person of good taste, and the class from which he or she might have come. Thus, by expressing taste, they could appear to overcome any deficiencies of birth.

Discussions of taste grew partly out of a philosophical concern to identify universal aesthetic criteria. Thinkers including ▷ Hutcheson and ▷ Hume believed in ideal standards of taste, although they did not agree about what these were. Addison, in ▷ *The Spectator* in 1712, likened 'mental taste' to taste of the palate. He also defined taste as 'that faculty of the soul which discerns the beauties of an author with pleasure, and the imperfections with dislike', implying that beauties and imperfections existed in and of themselves, and taste was only a matter of being able to recognize them for what they were. Later in the century, however, more subjective criteria were applied, as when a reviewer in the ▷ *Gentleman's Magazine* in 1767 commented that 'in questions of taste . . . everyone must determine for himself'.

Yardsticks of taste could be applied to almost any sphere of life that lends itself to consumption, including art and literature as well as goods. But a persistent view of 18th-century taste strongly associates it with new appetites for consumer durables, including fashionable houses, furniture, household effects, paintings, sculptures, clothes, jewellery and other possessions. A growing breed of professional designers, such as ▷ Robert Adam, ▷ Thomas Sheraton and ▷ Josiah Wedgwood, catered to such demands. Taste is also associated with codes of behaviour, such as gentility and displays of ▷ sensibility in order to demonstrate fine feeling. Good taste was thought by many to be a guide to character, so that fine taste in fashion and moral refinement went hand in hand.
Bib: Lynes, R., *The Tastemakers*; Williams, R., *Keywords: A Vocabulary of Culture and Society*; Campbell, C., *The Romantic Ethic and the Spirit of Modern Consumerism*.

Tate, Nahum (1652–1715)

Educated in Dublin. He assisted ▷ John Dryden with the second part of ▷ *Absalom and Achitophel*, and wrote the libretto of ▷ Purcell's opera *Dido and Aeneas* (performed 1689). His metrical version of the psalms, written with Nicholas Brady, appeared in 1696, and his revised version of *King Lear*, with a happy ending, was that performed through most of the succeeding century. His *Panacaea – a Poem on Tea* appeared in 1700.

Tatler, The

A periodical published three times a week, between 1709 and 1711, by the Whig author and editor ▷ Richard Steele. It contained essays and reviews on topical issues, including politics, entertainment, and fashionable gossip, at first supposedly emanating from the popular chocolate and ▷ coffee-houses of the day. Most of these were written by Steele himself, others by ▷ Joseph Addison. Steele borrowed from ▷ Swift the name 'Isaac Bickerstaffe' as his editorial pseudonym, and became for a time the chronicler and even arbiter of ▷ taste.

Increasingly moral issues, such as the evils of drinking and of duelling, were discussed. In 1711 the *Tatler* was succeeded by ▷ The Spectator.
▷ Reviews and periodicals.

Taylor, Jeremy (1613–67)

Clergyman and religious writer. He was one of the representatives of Anglicanism in its most flourishing period, and his career shows the vicissitudes of the ▷ Church of England in the 17th century. The son of a barber, he was educated at a Cambridge grammar school and in the University of Cambridge. His talent for preaching attracted the favour of Archbishop Laud, to whom and to king ▷ Charles I he became chaplain. In 1645 he was captured by Parliamentary troops, and until 1660, while the Church of England was in abeyance, he was private chaplain to the Earl of Carbery. It was during this period that he wrote much of his best work. Later, he was made Bishop of Dromore in Ireland, where, contrary to his inclination, he was obliged to discipline clergy who were hostile to the Anglican establishment. He thus stands in contrast to his former patron, the authoritarian Archbishop Laud, and the change marks not merely a difference in personalities but the growth in the spirit of Anglican tolerance in the later 17th century. His *A Discourse of the Liberty of Prophesying* (1646) was a plea for religious toleration; his other outstanding works were his *The Rule and Exercises of Holy Living* (1650) and *The Rule and Exercises of Holy Dying* (1651).
▷ Sermons.
Bib: Stranks, C. J., *Jeremy Taylor*; Gosse, E., *Jeremy Taylor*; Smith, L. P., *The Golden Grove: Selected Passages from Jeremy Taylor*.

Temple, Dorothy

▷ Osborne, Dorothy; Temple, Sir William.

Temple, Sir William (1628–99)

Statesman, diplomatist, essayist. In English literature Temple is especially known as the patron of ▷ Jonathan Swift, who lived at his house (Moor Park) as his secretary from 1689 to 1694, and again from 1696 till Temple's death. Temple's most famous ▷ essay was his contribution to the controversy about the relative merits of ancient (*ie* Greek and Latin) and modern literature. Entitled *Of Ancient and Modern Learning*, it praised the *Letters of Phalaris* as a notable example of ancient work. Unfortunately the great scholar ▷ Bentley exposed the Letters as a forgery. Temple's embarrassment provoked Swift to come to his aid with his first notable essay, ▷ *The Battle of the Books*. Temple was a model of the cultivated aristocracy of his time, and his essays (chiefly on political matters) were regarded as setting standards for correctness and elegance of expression. His wife was ▷ Dorothy Osborne and her letters to him before their marriage (in 1655) were first published in 1888; her position resembled that of ▷ Samuel Richardson's heroine in his novel ▷ *Clarissa*, inasmuch as her parents were opposed to the marriage. Temple's memoirs were published by Swift in 1709.
Bib: Lives by C. Marburg and H. E. Woodbridge.

Temple Bar
Originally a gateway between the City of London
and the City of Westminster, now marked by the
effigy of a griffin on a pedestal, situated opposite the
Law Courts, at the junction of Fleet Street and the
Strand, near the Temple Church. A stone gateway
was designed and erected by ▷ Sir Christopher
Wren in 1672; this was removed in 1878 and later
re-erected at Theobald's Park, Hertfordshire. The
heads of executed traitors used to be displayed on
spikes on Temple Bar.

Terence (Publius Terentius Afer, ?190–?159 BC)
Latin dramatist. His six comedies are adaptations
of older Greek comedies, especially those of
▷ Menander. They have been praised for the purity
of their Latin and criticized for their deficiency of
comic power. They were known, read and imitated
throughout the Middle Ages and afterwards, *eg* his
Heautontimorumenos (163) was adapted by Chapman
into *All Fools* (1605), and his *Andria* (166) was
adapted by ▷ Steele into ▷ *The Conscious Lovers*
(1722). Other dramatists such as Ben Jonson used
some of his themes and his comic devices such as the
role of the crafty slave (*eg* in *Volpone*).
   ▷ New Comedy; Plautus.

Terpsichore
▷ Muses.

Theatres
No special buildings were erected in England for
dramatic performances until late in the 16th century.
The earliest form of regular drama in England was
the Mystery Plays, which began as interpolations in
religious ritual in the churches. By the 15th century
these plays were being performed at religious
festivals in towns on movable stages or pageants,
conveyed from point to point on wagons. In country
districts at seasonal festivals such as May Day,
primitive dramas of pagan origin – jigs, May games,
Morris dances – were performed in the open air. The
absence of theatres did not indicate scarcity of
drama, but its wide pervasion of ordinary life.
   Secular dramas of entertainment, such as we
know today, grew up in the 16th century; they were
performed in the courtyards of inns and in the great
halls of country mansions, royal palaces, Oxford and
Cambridge colleges, and the ▷ inns of court of
London. The performers were professional actors
who were usually incorporated in companies attached
to noble or royal households, but by degrees this
attachment became increasingly nominal, and actors
required places where they could work independently
and permanently. Hence the first playhouse, known
as The Theatre, was erected by James Burbage in
Shoreditch, outside the City of London, in 1576–7.
It was followed by many others, including the
Globe (1598) which is the most famous owing to
its association with ▷ Shakespeare. None of these
theatres survived the middle of the 17th century, but
a contemporary sketch of one of them (the Swan)
exists, and there is a detailed description in the
contract for Fortune (1600).

It was only after the ▷ Restoration of the
Monarchy in 1660 that the theatre began to assume
its modern shape, with a proscenium arch dividing
the audience from the stage, thus providing greater
scope for scenery and illusion. One of the earliest
English theatres of this style was ▷ Drury Lane,
which had already been a theatre in the reign of
James I and was rebuilt in 1662. From this time
the theatre became the special entertainment for
the middle and upper classes, largely cut off from
the mass of the people, and it has, on the whole,
remained that way. It was still, however, a place
of influence, and in 1737 the government found it
convenient to pass a Licensing Act which had the
effect of restricting the theatres in London to three
– the Haymarket opera house, Drury Lane, and
Covent Garden – until the act was repealed in 1843,
though licences were issued for a few theatres in the
provinces, at Bath, Bristol and Liverpool. The law
greatly hindered the development of a creative drama
in 18th-century England, though it was a period of
great actors and actresses.

Theocritus (3rd-century BC)
Greek poet. Little is known about him, but his
importance is that he originated ▷ pastoral poetry
in his ▷ 'idylls' – short poems about shepherds
and shepherdesses living in primitive simplicity
in the rural parts of Sicily. He may have written
these in the Egyptian city of Alexandria for urban
readers; one of the characteristics of pastoral
has been that it has expressed the town-dwellers'
fantasy of the beauty of country surroundings, the
simplicity of country living and the purity of country
air. Theocritus was emulated by the Roman poet
▷ Virgil, and both Theocritus and Virgil were
taken as models by the 16th-century ▷ Renaissance
poets in Western Europe, of whom the most notable
English example is ▷ Edmund Spenser and by poets
in the 17th and 18th centuries including ▷ Behn,
▷ Pope and ▷ Thomson

Thomson, James (1700–48)
Poet. Born in the Scottish border country, the son
of a minister. He studied divinity at Edinburgh
University, but in 1725 sought his fortune in
London, where he became tutor in an aristocratic
family. His poem *Winter* was published in 1726 and
its success encouraged him to write poems on the
other three seasons during the following years, the
▷ *Seasons* being completed in 1730. Thomson's
artificially dignified Miltonic ▷ blank verse, and the
miscellaneousness of his subject matter, struck the
new bourgeois taste exactly, and the *Seasons* were
extremely popular. He possesses a facility, almost
amounting to genius, for holding together in loose,
artificial suspension all the characteristic elements of
the popular culture of his day: Augustan patriotism,
▷ Classicism in diction and tone, ▷ Gothic excess,
▷ sentimentalism. His most original passages
elaborate ▷ Virgilian pastoral into a pleasantly
self-indulgent enthusiasm for the natural scene.
Rhetorical patriotism, of which he is the period's
most unembarrassed exponent, features also in his
next large-scale poem, *Liberty* (1735–6), and also

in the ▷ masque *Alfred*, written and produced with ▷ David Mallet in 1740 , which contains the song ▷ *Rule Britannia*. Thomson also wrote tragedies, which were very successful at the time, but are now forgotten (*Sophonisba*, 1730; *Agamemnon*, 1738; *Edward and Eleanora*, 1739; *Tancred and Sigismunda*, 1745; *Coriolanus*, 1749). His Spenserian imitation, ▷ The Castle of Indolence (1748) is far more successful, eclectically combining ▷ mock-heroic ▷ burlesque, sensuous description, whimsical self-mockery, patriotism and didactic moralizing. **Bib:** Johnson, S., in *Lives of the Poets*; Grant, D., *Thomson, Poets of the Seasons*; Cohen, R., *The Art of Discrimination*; Cohen, R., *The Unfolding of the Seasons*.

Thoughts on the Education of Daughters (1787)

English writer ▷ Mary Wollstonecraft's earlier publication on education. She advocates the education of women both for material reasons – to enable them to obtain such work as is permitted to women, if they have need – and for spiritual and intellectual comfort.

▷ *Vindication of the Rights of Women.*

Thrale, Hester Lynch (1741–1821) (later Hester Thrale Piozzi)

Born Hester Salusbury, she married Henry Thrale in 1763. Thrale was a wealthy brewer with political ambitions, and when in the following year they made the acquaintance of ▷ Samuel Johnson, Johnson assisted Thrale by writing election addresses. The friendship between Johnson and Hester Thrale became very close, and at various times Johnson lived with the family in their home at Streatham. When Thrale died in 1781, Hester Thrale remarried. Gabriel Piozzi, her second husband, was an Italian musician, and her friends and family vociferously disapproved. The marriage ended the friendship with Johnson, who sent her an anguished letter on the subject.

Hester Thrale's biography of Johnson, *Anecdotes of the late Samuel Johnson*, was strongly contested by ▷ Boswell when it appeared in 1786; his motives in challenging her account probably stem from literary rivalry. Hester Thrale was also an energetic letter writer, and ▷ *Thraliana*, a selection of anecdotes, poems, jests and journal entries, covers the period 1776–1809.

Bib: Clifford, J. L., *Hester Lynch Piozzi.*

Thraliana

Journal of ▷ Hester Lynch Thrale, covering the years 1776–1809, and including many of her poems. They began as a set of six blank books presented to her by her husband Henry Thrale as an anniversary gift. The journal contains vivid and often humorous portraits and anecdotes concerning her many friends and acquaintances, including ▷ Samuel Johnson and her two husbands, as well as accounts of contemporary life and customs. Passages from it read like extracts from novels or plays. Johnson's other biographer ▷ Boswell admired but also disparaged her as a rival whom he feared.

Threadneedle Street, The Old Lady of

A familiar term, dating from the 18th century, for the ▷ Bank of England, which stands in a street of that name. The name of the street seems to derive from its original occupation by tailors.

Three Hours After Marriage (1717)

Burlesque comedy by ▷ Pope, ▷ Gay, and ▷ Arbuthnot, satirizing several contemporary literary figures, including John Dennis (Sir Tremendous), ▷ Colley Cibber (Plotwell), and the Countess of Winchilsea (▷ Anne Finch) (Phoebe Clinket). The play was at first a success, but its production occasioned a furious hostility between Gay and Cibber, and it was not revived for another 20 years.

Thucydides (5th–4th centuries BC)

Greek historian of the Peloponnesian war. His is one of the earliest historical works in European literature in its distinct care for accuracy. Nearly a quarter of the book however, is devoted to political speeches, including the great Funeral Oration by Pericles; these give an important insight into Greek attitudes to politics. Thucydides has been a principal text for English ▷ classical education.

Tickell, Thomas (1686–1740)

Member of the clique which frequented ▷ Button's Coffee-house and whose leader was ▷ Joseph Addison. He contributed to *The Guardian* and ▷ *The Spectator*. ▷ Alexander Pope suspected that Addison had attempted to spoil his success by inciting Tickell to publish his translation of the first book of ▷ *The Iliad* just before the appearance of Pope's translation of the first two books (1715). Tickell edited Addison's works after his death, his edition being prefaced by a moving ▷ elegy in heroic ▷ couplets (1721).

Times, The

British newspaper. It was founded in 1785 as *The Daily Universal Register*, and took its present name in 1788. In the 19th century it took the lead in contriving new methods of collecting news (notably through the employment of foreign correspondents), and its succession of distinguished editors and contributors gave it an outstanding status among British newspapers. Though always in private ownership, it has always claimed to be an independent newspaper rather than a party one.

▷ Newspapers.

Timon (5th century BC)

A rich citizen of Athens (5th century BTC) he was celebrated for his hatred of mankind. He is referred to by a number of ancient Greek writers including Aristophanes, and notably by ▷ Plutarch, in his life of Mark Antony, and by ▷ Lucian in his dialogue *Misanthropos*. Shakespeare (*Timon of Athens*) makes him a rich, ostentatious philanthropist who becomes a misanthropist through disillusionment at men's ingratitude. Pope, in his ▷ *Moral Essays* (iv–1734) described a rich Timon of his own day – perhaps the Duke of Chandos – laying emphasis on tasteless ostentation and indifference to people rather than hatred of them.

Tithes

A system for the maintenance of the parish clergy of the ▷ Church of England, consisting, originally, of one-tenth of the produce of the parish farmers. It was replaced during the 18th century by an annual rent and was abolished altogether by Parliament in 1936

Toleration, Act of (1689)

Act of Parliament which granted freedom of worship to ▷ Dissenters, one of the first Acts passed by the ▷ Protestant monarchs ▷ William III and ▷ Mary II after their accession. It went some way to eliminating the discrimination against non-conformists of the years preceding, and the resentment this caused. Dissenters were still not allowed to hold official positions, but many of them succeeded in doing so without retribution. ▷ Catholics continued to be forbidden to vote or to hold office.
▷ Puritanism.

Tom Jones, a Foundling (1749)

A novel by ▷ Henry Fielding. The central character begins life as a baby of unknown parentage (ie 'a foundling') who is discovered in the mansion of the enlightened landowner, Squire Allworthy. Allworthy adopts him, and he grows up a handsome and generous-hearted youth, whose weakness is his excess of animal spirits and inclination to fleshly lusts. He falls in love with Sophia Western, daughter of a neighbouring landowner, Squire Western, who is as gross, ignorant and self-willed as Allworthy is refined and enlightened. Western intends Sophia for Blifil, Allworthy's nephew, a mean and treacherouly hypocritical character, who is supported against Tom by two members of Allworthy's household, the pedantic chaplain Thwackum and the pretentious philosopher, Square, who counterbalance each other. They succeed in disgracing Tom, whom Allworthy is persuaded to disown. The central part of the novel describes his travels and amorous adventures in the company of a comic follower, Partridge. Sophia also leaves home, to escape from Blifil, and nearly falls victim to a plot by Lady Bellaston, with whom Tom has become amorously entangled, to place her in the power of Lord Fellamar. Tom is eventually identified as the son of Allworthy's sister; the plots against him are brought to light; he is received again by Allworthy, and marries Sophia.

The novel, like its predecessor by Fielding, ▷ *Joseph Andrews*, is a 'comic epic', offering a wide range of social types of the age, all of whom are presented as permanent human types rather than as unique individuals, as 19th-century novelists would show them. Fielding's method is expository; he does not attempt to create illusions of characters with interior lives of their own, but expounds behaviour, with the aid of prefatory essays to his chapters, always light-heartedly, but always with a view to exhibiting basic human motives as they have always existed, rather in the manner of the 17th-century Comedies of ▷ Humours and of ▷ Manners. He owes much to ▷ Cervantes' comic romance ▷ *Don Quixote* and to the studies of contemporary morals and manners by the painter ▷ William Hogarth. To some extent the book was written in rivalry to ▷ Samuel Richardson's ▷ *Clarissa*, a novel written in a tragic spirit and in a strenuous and idealistic moral tone. It was Fielding's tendency to 'correct' Richardson's idealism and partly self-deceiving moral rigour by reducing events to more usual human experience and interpreting this in the light of tolerant comedy instead of grand tragedy; for instance, Lovelace, in *Clarissa* is a human fiend (though also an interesting psychological study) where Tom is merely a healthy young man whose licentiousness is bound up with his virtue of outgoing sympathy and generosity. Thus, *Tom Jones* is both one of the first important English novels, a new kind of imaginative work, and one that embodies highly traditional values.

Tom Thumb the Great (1730)

▷ Burlesque play by ▷ Fielding, expanded and performed as *The Tragedy of Tragedies, or, The Life and Death of Tom Thumb the Great* in 1731. The piece satirizes heroic tragedy, somewhat in the manner of ▷ *The Rehearsal*, but in ▷ blank verse rather than ▷ heroic couplets. In addition, the satire works entirely through the absurdity of the lines, and the device of having the tiny Tom Thumb as 'hero', without the benefit of commentary from sources outside the 'tragic' action. Fielding acknowledged his debt to ▷ Pope's *The Art of Sinking in Poetry* by attributing the play to 'Scriblerus Secundus'.

Tory

▷ Whig and Tory.

Tower of London

A medieval fortress, the central part of which – the White Tower – was built after the Norman Conquest by William I to subdue the City of London; it stands by the Thames at the south-east corner of the old City, and counterbalances the ▷ Palace of Westminster (now the Houses of ▷ Parliament), also on the river, at the western end of the City. The Tower was extended later in the ▷ Middle Ages, and incorporated a royal palace, which was pulled down in the 1650s by the order of ▷ Oliver Cromwell. The frequent mention of the Tower in English history and literature is due to the imprisonment there (and often execution there or on the adjacent Tower Hill) of numerous eminent men and women. For instance Edward V and his brother were imprisoned in it by Richard III and probably murdered there; other victims include two of the queens of Henry VIII, Anne Boleyn and Catherine Howard, Sir Thomas More (beheaded in 1535), Sir Walter Raleigh (1618), and Charles II's illegitimate son, the Duke of ▷ Monmouth (1685). The Tower continued to be used as a prison until the 19th century.

Tract

An ▷ essay or treatise, usually short but published singly and usually on a religious subject. Tracts proliferated during the ▷ Civil War, and were used periodically thereafter, often by revivalist or minority religious movements including ▷ Methodism in the 18th century, and the Oxford Movement in the 19th.

Tragedy

Tragedy as it is understood in Western Europe has its origins in the Greek dramas by the Athenian dramatists ▷ Aeschylus, ▷ Sophocles and ▷ Euripides, in the 6th–5th centuries BC. Essentially the spirit of this writing was that inevitable suffering overwhelms the characters, and yet the characters maintain their dignity in the face of this suffering, and prove their greatness (and the capacity of human beings for greatness) by doing so. Greek tragedy arose out of their religious interpretation of the nature of human destiny. When Christianity prevailed over Western Europe, a much more hopeful interpretation of human destiny dominated and the thought of writers, and tragedy, in the Greek sense, became difficult to imagine and unnatural: if good men suffer in this world, they are rewarded in Heaven, and this is not tragic; wicked men who happen to suffer in this world may be damned in the next, but this is also not tragic because they are wicked. Hence medieval tragedy was on the whole reduced to the conception of the Wheel of Fortune – that chance in this world is apt to take men from prosperity to misfortune, whatever their spiritual merits.

In the late 16th century the tragic vision of human experience was rediscovered by some English dramatists, notably by Marlowe and ▷ Shakespeare. Insofar as it had a literary ancestry, this was not the tragedy of the ancient Greeks, which was scarcely known, but the comparatively debased imitation of it by the Roman poet ▷ Seneca, which helped to give rise to Elizabethan Revenge Tragedy or 'Tragedy of Blood'.

Among Shakespeare's later contemporaries and his successors, several dramatists wrote distinguished plays in the tragic style, eg Middleton's *The Changeling* (1622) and Webster's *The Duchess of Malfi* (1613) and *The White Devil* (1608). Numerous attempts were made to write tragedy in the Greek style, or in the neo-classical French style of ▷ Corneille and ▷ Racine, after 1660, but they lacked conviction; perhaps the best is ▷ Dryden's *All for Love*. Various attempts were made by 19th-century poets to revive the Shakespearean mode of tragedy.

Tragicomedy

Drama in which the elements of both ▷ tragedy and comedy are present. Examples are ▷ Behn's *The Forced Marriage* (1670), ▷ Dryden: ▷ *Marriage à la Mode* (1671) and ▷ Southerne's *Oroonoko* (1696).

Many of the ▷ reform and ▷ sentimental comedies of the 18th century have elements of tragicomedy, and show their descent from the tragicomedies of the period after the ▷ Restoration.

Traherne, Thomas (c1638–74)

Poet and religious writer. In the 17th century, the only works published by Traherne were three religious pieces, all of them in prose. In 1896,

however, the editor A. B. Grosart discovered a collection of manuscripts in a London bookshop which he believed to be by ▷ Henry Vaughan. The manuscripts were identified as being those of Traherne, and comprised religious poems and the remarkable mystical prose work *Centuries of Meditation*. This latter constitutes a spiritual autobiography, tracing the author's progress towards 'felicity' (a key term for Traherne). Criticism of Traherne's poetry has in the 20th century, concentrated on his affinity with ▷ George Herbert, and on his visionary delineation of childlike experience. Understood as a mystic, and as an intellectual conservative in comparison to the rationalism of 17th-century science, Traherne has been closely linked with the ▷ Cambridge Platonists – almost as though he were the poetic 'voice' of that group. Yet, for all Traherne's concern with 'the inward eye', in fact his approach to language, his undoubted fascination with the possibilities of rational science (particularly as it had unfolded a new perspective in which to understand the human body) and his experimental verse forms make him one of the most remarkable of later 17th-century writers. Bib: Margoliouth, H. M. (ed.), *Traherne's Centuries, Poems and Thanksgivings*; Clements, A. L., *The Mystical Poetry of Thomas Traherne*.

Translation

The life of English literature has always issued from a combination of strong insular traditions and participation in wider European traditions. Translation has always been the principal means of assimilating European literatures into the English idiom, and it was particularly important before the 18th century, when the main streams of European cultural life were flowing through other languages. The aim of translators was then less to make an accurate rendering than to make the substance of foreign work thoroughly intelligible to the English spirit; the character of the translation thus proceeded as much from the mind of the translator as from the mind of the original writer. If the translator had a strong personality, the translation often became a distinguished work of English literature in its own right. Translators with less individuality often produced work of historical importance because of its contemporary influence on English writing.

Translations from contemporary European languages were numerous in the 16th and early 17th centuries, and indicate the constant interest of English writers in foreign literatures. Sir John Harington translated Ariosto's *Orlando Furioso* in 1591; Tasso's *Jerusalem Delivered* was translated as *Godfrey of Bulloigne* or *The Recovery of Jerusalem* (1600); Castiglione's very influential *Il Cortegiano* was translated by Sir Thomas Hoby (1561). The best known of all these contemporary works is John Florio's rendering of the ▷ *Essays* of ▷ Montaigne, published in 1603. Part I of Cervantes' *Don Quixote* was translated in 1612 before Part II was written; the whole work was three times translated in the 18th century, by Motteux (1712), Jarvis (1742) and ▷ Smollett (1755). The first three books of Rabelais' *Gargantua and Pantagruel* were translated notably by

Thomas Urquhart; two were published in 1653, and the third in 1694. The fourth and fifth books were added by Motteux in 1708.

Many of the translations made before 1660, especially those in prose, were marked by a super-abundance of words, characteristic of much English writing in the 16th and 17th centuries; the originals tended to be amplified rather than closely rendered. After the ▷ Restoration in 1660, writers attached importance to discipline and control, and to emulating these virtues as they were exemplified in the old Latin poets and in contemporary French writers of verse and prose. In consequence, ▷ John Dryden accomplished some of his best work in translating Latin poetry, especially Ovid (eg ▷ *Philemon and Baucis*) and the ▷ *Aeneid* of Virgil, whose works he translated entire, completing them in 1697. ▷ Pope's translations of Homer's *Iliad* and *Odyssey*, which appeared in 1720 and 1726, greatly enhanced his reputation, but despite the skill of the versification, they are obviously much further from the spirit of Homer than Dryden's renderings are from the Latin poets; the British Augustans were much closer in feeling to the Roman Augustans than they were to the ancient Greeks. As the century went on, writers became restless under Augustan restraints, and became interested in literatures that had hitherto been ignored or despised; ▷ Thomas Gray imitated Icelandic and Celtic verse. Macpherson's versions of Gaelic legends, which he alleged to be by the legendary poet ▷ Ossian, were more inventions and adaptations than translations, but they probably had a wider influence in other countries than any other English work going under the name of translation, with the exception of the English ▷ Bible. Sir William Jones (1746–94), the first important British Oriental scholar, published in 1783 a version in English of the ancient Arabic poems called *Moallakat*, as well as other work from Persian and from Sanskrit.

Travel and transport

Until the 18th century, hard roads were seldom constructed, apart from a few causeways which merchants sometimes arranged for over marshy places. There were not only the problems of impassability in bad weather, but also the dangers of highway robbery.

The badness of roads made water transport preferable; rivers were used whenever they were navigable. Heavy goods were transported by sea; hence the expression 'sea coal' for coal brought from Newcastle to London.

By later standards, trade was necessarily much restricted, but many traders would risk one journey a year for the sake of gain; hence the importance of the annual fairs. From the 14th to the 19th century, there were numerous fairs throughout England, and many survive today, although their purpose is now often entertainment rather than trade. The size of the region from which fairs drew traders varied greatly; it might consist of a few neighbouring villages, or – like the Stourbridge Fair at Cambridge – it might draw traders from the extremities of the country and even from foreign lands.

The Protestant ▷ Reformation in the 16th century put an end to pilgrimage; it forbade the reverence hitherto paid to the bones of the saints, and Rome was no longer the capital of Christendom for Britain. But the pilgrims were replaced by students and writers seeking enlightenment at the sources of ▷ Renaissance culture, especially in Italy. The idea of travel as a means of education became normal among the educated classes of the 17th century, and in the 18th century it became an enthusiasm, until in 1785 40,000 Englishmen were said to be doing the 'Grand Tour'. Besides travel for education, there was the constantly increasing travel for trade. By far the most important technical advance in the 16th century was the adoption of a new structure of sail enabling ships to voyage much farther: this made possible the great voyages of discovery which, in the last 30 years of the century, enormously expanded trade.

Overland transport, however, was difficult. The increasing movement of goods about the country in huge carrier's wagons drawn by teams of six or more horses caused the bad roads to deteriorate still further. In the 16th century the care of the roads was in the charge of the country parishes under the supervision of the magistrates, but the work was neglected, since it was not the countrymen who were the chief users of the roads. In the second half of the 17th century, the 'turnpike system' was introduced, to transfer the cost of road repairs on to the road users. The turnpikes were barriers across the roads at suitable places, where travellers were compelled to pay tolls before they were allowed to proceed. The system worked with uncertain success, and extended to remote regions only slowly, but in the 18th century it improved. In the second half of the 18th century roads were immensely improved by the great engineers Macadam, who invented the method of building road surfaces from broken stone, and Telford, who was also a great bridge-builder. By the end of the century, foreign observers acknowledged English roads to be the best in Europe.

The improvement naturally affected ways of travel and styles of vehicle. A system of post-horses for royal messengers already existed in the 16th century: relays of horses were established about the country to expedite their journeys. As early as 1660 stage coaches which changed horses at fixed stages, were available; a century later the improvement of the roads made this the usual way of travelling on long journeys. The system of 'post-horses' was by then at the disposal of people who could afford to travel in privately owned or hired post-chaises; these light vehicles made it possible to accomplish in a day journeys of a hundred miles which had taken three days at the beginning of the century. By the beginning of the 19th century, various styles of vehicle existed.

For heavy transport, water was still more convenient than land, and in the 16th and 17th centuries, rivers were deepened, locks were built and the first canals were dug. But it was again the second half of the 18th century that was the great period for the improvement of water transport. By his wealth and political influence, the Duke of Bridgewater was largely responsible for the construction of a system of canals throughout England. His enterprise was very important in advancing the ▷ Industrial Revolution, since it not only facilitated the distribution of heavy manufactures but enabled large supplies of corn and other foodstuffs to be brought to the new population centres.

Travel literature

This large branch of English literature may be conveniently divided into three headings: 1 fantasy purporting to be fact; 2 factual accounts; 3 travel experiences regarded as material for art. The first group is largely confined to pre-Renaissance writers. This developed into the second group as extensive travel became more widespread. Indeed, the steady growth of English overseas trade kept alive a taste for accounts of great voyages throughout the 17th and 18th centuries. At the end of the 17th century Captain William Dampier published three books which included the imaginations of ▷ Aphra Behn, ▷ Daniel Defoe and ▷ Jonathan Swift: *New Voyage Round the World* (1697), *Voyages and Descriptions* (1699), and *Voyage to New Holland* (1703). Dampier was an excellently direct and clear writer of his own books, but Lord George Anson's voyage round the world (1740–44) was written up from his journals by his chaplain, R. Waters, and depends on the singularly dramatic events for its force of interest. The last of these outstanding accounts of great voyages were the three undertaken by Captain James Cook, *A Voyage Round Cape Horn and the Cape of Good Hope* (1773), *A Voyage Towards the South Pole and Round the World* (1777) and *A Voyage to the Pacific Ocean* (1784). With the discovery of the coastlines of Australia and New Zealand, the main outlines of world geography became known, and the interest of both explorers and their readers passed to the mysteries of the great undiscovered interiors of the continents. With this change in subject matter, a change also came over the style of travel literature.

The third group may be characterized by Sir Richard Burton's (1821–90) book about India, *Scinde or the Unhappy Valley* (1851), and his later books about his exploration of East and Central Africa (*First Footsteps in East Africa*, 1856; *The Lake Region of Central Africa* (1860) bear more of the stamp of the author's personal feelings and reactions.

Treatise of Human Nature, A
▷ Hume, David.

Treatises of Government
▷ Locke, John.

Triplet
In verse, three lines rhyming together, occasionally used among ▷ couplets to introduce variety.

Tristram Shandy, The Life and Opinions of (1760–7)
A novel by ▷ Laurence Sterne, published in successive volumes, 1 to IX from 1760 to 1767. Any attempt to paraphrase the 'plot' of this eccentric masterpiece would be doomed, like trying to net the wind. Sterne deliberately flaunts his freedom to tease and surprise the reader with his interruptions and digressions. 'If I thought you was able to form the least judgement or probable conjecture to yourself, of what was to come in the next page,' he writes, 'I would tear it out of my book.' Tristram, the nominal hero, plays little part in the action of the book, though as the authorial voice of the narrative his random associations determine its form. As a character he is not born until volume IV, and never gets beyond infancy. The bulk of the novel is taken up with the theories and hobby-horses of Tristram's father, Walter Shandy, and his uncle Toby; these two brothers appear like comic caricatures of ▷ Locke's theory of the association of ideas. Each of them is trapped in his own private world of associations; for Walter these centre on his obsessions with noses and names; for Toby they are based on military science and his quest to determine the circumstances of the wound in the groin which he suffered at the siege of Namur. The other characters, Dr Slop, Corporal Trim, parson Yorick, Mrs Shandy and the Widow Wadman are swept up in the general associations – many of them sexual – of noses and wounds, breeches and ballistics.

'Shandy' is an old Yorkshire dialect word meaning crackbrained, odd or unconventional, and it suits this book perfectly. With its black and marbled pages, its flash-backs and interpolations, its asterisks, blanks and dashes, this novel defies any attempts to unscramble a straightforward narrative theme. The effect on the reader is to suggest that the conventional notion of a biographical narrative, with a distinct beginning, sequence of events and ending, is untrue to human experience which finds that beginnings do not really exist, and orderly sequences are frustrated by every kind of distraction. Tristram Shandy has been called 'the greatest shaggy-dog story in the language' and a satiric essay on human misunderstanding. It is a joyous, exuberant cock-and-bull story, in which the juggler Sterne shamelessly leads the reader by the nose on an endless quest for the elusive copula that links cause and effect, intention and achievement.

Trochee
▷ Metre.

Trotter (Cockburn), Catherine (1679–1749)
English dramatist and, after her marriage to the Reverend Patrick Cockburn in 1708, writer of theological works. Until 1707 she was a Roman ▷ Catholic. She began publication very young with the ▷ epistolary novel *Olinda's Adventures or, The Amours of a Young Lady* (1793), and her verse dramatization of ▷ Aphra Behn's story *Agnes de Castro* was acted at Drury Lane in 1695. *The Fatal Friendship* (1698) was her most admired play. She contributed to *The Nine Muses* (1700). In 'To Mrs Manley' on ▷ Delarivière Manley's play *The Royal Mischief* (1696) she wrote 'Th' Attempt was brave, how happy your success, / The Men with Shame our Sex with Pride confess.'

Her other publications include: *The Unhappy Penitent* (1701).
▷ Pix, Mary

Bib: Greer, G. *et al.*, *Kissing The Rod*.

Turpin, Dick (Richard) (1706–39)

A famous English highwayman and thief, hanged at York for horse-stealing. He was greatly romanticized by the novelist Harrison Ainsworth in his novel *Rookwood* (1834), in which Turpin's famous ride from London to York on his mare, Black Bess, is described. The ride, like other romantic episodes told about him, is fictional.

Tyburn

The site of public executions by hanging until 1783. The gallows stood near the modern Marble Arch, at the end of Oxford Street and on the edge of Hyde Park, about three miles north-west of the old ▷ City of London.

Underhill, Cave (1634–?1710)
Actor. Underhill joined John Rhodes's company before the ▷ Restoration, and afterwards became a member of the ▷ Duke's Company under Sir William D'Avenant, specializing in comic roles, including the eponymous Cutter, in ▷ Abraham Cowley's *Cutter of Coleman Street*, the first Gravedigger in *Hamlet*, and the Clown in *Twelfth Night*. Tall, with a large face, flat nose, and 'unwandering eye', coupled with an apparently stolid, stupid, or lugubrious manner, he is said to have inclined people to laugh, merely by looking at him.

Uniformity, Acts of
Laws passed by Parliament during and after the ▷ Reformation to secure religious union in England. The first was that of 1549 (under Edward VI) and the second and more important in 1559, under Elizabeth I. Both required the common use in church worship of the ▷ Book of Common Prayer. In 1662, under ▷ Charles II, another Act of Uniformity insisted on its use by all clergy and schoolmasters, and marks the beginning of the ▷ dissenting sects as formally separate religious bodies, distinct from the ▷ Church of England.

Union, Act of (1707)
Government Act by which Scotland was united with England, and given representation at Westminster. The Act was imposed on Scotland as an English reaction, during a period of war with France (▷ Spanish Succession, War of), to continuing Scottish efforts to achieve greater independence from England, and to restore to the throne the deposed ▷ James II then his descendants. The aim was to pacify Scotland, and prevent any possibility of an alliance between that partly ▷ Catholic nation and France. Under the legislation, the Scots were allowed to vote on all issues in both the House of Commons and the House of Lords, and in return they had to agree to the Hanoverian succession. Much bitterness was created by the loss of Scottish autonomy which the Act entailed.

Unitarianism
A doctrine of religion that rejects the usual Christian doctrine of the Trinity, or three Persons in one God (the Father, the Son, and the Holy Ghost), in favour of a belief in the single person of God the Father. It originated in Britain in the 18th century and was in accord with the rationalistic approach to religion of that century. The first Unitarian church opened in London in 1774; many English ▷ Presbyterians (in the 16th and 17th centuries one of the largest sects outside the Church of England) became Unitarians.

United Company, The
Acting company formed by the union of the ▷ King's Company with the ▷ Duke's Company in 1682. In effect the stronger Duke's Company absorbed what had been its rival for 21 years, because of the latter's ailing state. The United Company lasted until 1695, when its leading players, including ▷ Thomas Betterton, ▷ Elizabeth Barry, and ▷ Anne Bracegirdle, defected, because of a dispute with the theatre management, and moved to the remodelled ▷ Lincoln's Inn Fields Theatre. Until that time the United Company occupied both the Theatre Royal at ▷ Drury Lane and the ▷ Dorset Garden Theatre, using the Theatre Royal mainly for plays and Dorset Garden for the larger spectacles and musical performances.

Unities, Classical
▷ Classical Unities.

Universities
Until 1828, England possessed only two universities, those of ▷ Oxford, founded from Paris in the 12th century, and of ▷ Cambridge, founded largely by an emigration from Oxford in the early 13th century. Scotland's first university was St Andrew's (1411), followed by Glasgow (1451), Aberdeen (two – 1494 and 1593) and Edinburgh (1582). That of Dublin (Trinity College) was opened in 1582. Medieval universities were in the hands of the clergy, which mattered little when the Church was undivided and Christian belief was almost universal. After the ▷ Reformation in the mid-16th century, Catholics were excluded, and from 1660 (the ▷ Restoration) all Protestants who were not members of the ▷ Church of England were excluded from the English universities, though not from the Scottish ones, since the Anglican Church was not established there.

▷ Dissenters established their own academies in the 18th century, and in the early 19th century a movement was started among prominent Dissenters to establish the University of London, which opened in 1828.

Urn Burial, or Hydriotaphia (1658)
A treatise by ▷ Sir Thomas Browne, published in 1658. Its starting point is the discovery of ancient burial urns in Norfolk; this leads to an account of various ways of disposing of the dead, and meditations on death itself.

Utilitarianism
A 19th-century political, economic and social doctrine which based all values on utility, *ie* the usefulness of anything, measured by the extent to which it promotes the material happiness of the greatest number of people. It is especially associated with ▷ Jeremy Bentham, at first a jurist concerned with legal reform and later a social philosopher. Followers of the movement are thus often called 'Benthamites' but Bentham's disciple John Stuart Mill used the term 'Utilitarians'. Owing to their habit of criticizing social concepts and institutions on strictly rational tests, the leaders of the movement were also known as Philosophical Radicals.

Utilitarianism dominated 19th-century social thinking, but it had all its roots in various forms of 18th-century ▷ rationalism. In moral philosophy, ▷ David Hume had a strong influence on Bentham by his assumption that the supreme human virtue is benevolence, *ie* the disposition to increase the happiness of others. Psychologically, Bentham's principle that humans are governed by the impulses to seek pleasure and avoid pain derives from the associationism of ▷ David Hartley. But Bentham and his associates believed that the virtue of benevolence, and human impulses towards pleasure, operate within social and economic laws which are scientifically demonstrable. Bentham accepted ▷ Adam Smith's reasoning in *The Wealth of Nations* (1776) that material prosperity is governed by economic laws of supply and demand, the beneficial operation of which is only hindered by governmental interference. ▷ Malthus, in his *Essay on the Principle of Population* (1798), maintained that it is mathematically demonstrable that population always tends to increase beyond the means of subsistence, and Ricardo, a friend of Bentham's, applied Malthus's principle to wages, arguing that as the population increases wages will necessarily get lower, since the increase is more rapid than that of the wealth available to support the workers. Smith, Malthus and Ricardo were masters of what was called the science of Political Economy, and the inhuman fatalism with which they endowed it caused it to be known as the ▷ dismal science. However, it was not dismal for the industrial middle class of employers, whose interests it suited; they were already 'utilitarians' by self-interest and thus willing converts to the theory.

Utopian literature

Thomas More's *Utopia* (1516) introduced into the English language the word 'utopian' = 'imaginary and ideal', and started a succession of 'utopias' in English literature. The idea of inventing an imaginary country to be used as a 'model' by which to judge earthly societies did not, however, originate with More, but with the Greek philosopher ▷ Plato, who did the same in his dialogues *Timaeus* and *Republic*. *Utopia*'s most notable successors in the 17th century were ▷ Bacon's unfinished *New Atlantis* (1626), in which science is offered as the solution for humanity, and James Harington's *Oceana* (1656), which put forward political ideas that were to have a powerful influence in America.

However, from the 18th century, much utopian literature has been satirical, intended to give warning of vicious tendencies of society rather than to exemplify ideals. An example of this is Bernard de Mandeville's (1670–1733) *Fable of the Bees* (1714), about the downfall of an ideal society through the viciousness of its inhabitants; and Swift's ▷ *Gulliver's Travels* (1726) can be put in the same class.

Utrecht, Treaty of
▷ Spanish Succession, War of.

Valley of Humiliation; Valley of the Shadow of Death

Two places of trial through which pilgrims had to pass in ▷ John Bunyan's ▷ *Pilgrim's Progress*. The Valley of the Shadow of Death is a reference to Psalm 23 in the ▷ Bible (Authorized Version).

Vanbrugh, Sir John (1664–1726)

Architect and dramatist, who designed Blenheim Palace for the Duke of ▷ Marlborough, the Queen's Theatre in the ▷ Haymarket, and (with Nicholas Hawksmoor) Castle Howard in Yorkshire. He also wrote several plays of distinction. The son of a London tradesman whose father was a Protestant refugee from Ghent, Vanbrugh became a captain under Marlborough, and was imprisoned from 1690 to 1692 in the Bastille, where he wrote parts of his play, ▷ *The Provok'd Wife*, eventually staged in 1697. His first performed play was ▷ *The Relapse: Or Virtue in Danger* (1696), a satiric response to ▷ Colley Cibber's ▷ Reform comedy, ▷ *Love's Last Shift*. He wrote several other lively comedies, mostly adaptations from the French, including *The False Friend* (1701), *The Country House* (1703), *Squire Trelooby* (1704), and *The Confederacy* (1705), performed by Thomas Betterton's company at the newly opened Queen's Theatre, which Vanbrugh managed for a time with ▷ William Congreve.

Vanbrugh was one of the dramatists singled out for attack by ▷ Jeremy Collier in his *A Short View of the Immorality and Profaneness of the English Stage* (1698), to which he responded vigorously in *A Short Vindication of the 'Relapse' and 'The Provok'd Wife' from Immorality and Profaneness* in 1698. He was knighted and became Clarencieux king-of-arms in 1705, and was made comptroller of royal works in 1714. His last play, *A Journey to London*, was left unfinished at his death, and was completed by Cibber as *The Provok'd Husband* (1728). ▷ Richard Brinsley Sheridan reworked *The Relapse* as *A Trip to Scarborough* (1777). The original version was revived in 1947 and again by the ▷ Royal Shakespeare Company in 1967.

Bib: Whistler, L., *Sir John Vanbrugh, Architect and Dramatist*; Berkowitz, G. M., *Sir John Vanbrugh and the End of Restoration Comedy*; Beard, G., *The Work of John Vanburgh*; Downes, K., *Sir John Vanburgh: A Biography*.

Vanessa

▷ Jonathan Swift's name for Esther Vanhomrigh who was in love with him between the years 1708 and 1723.

Vanity Fair

A town through which the pilgrims pass in ▷ John Bunyan's ▷ *Pilgrim's Progress*. It is a vivid representation of the pleasure-loving worldliness of society in the reign of ▷ Charles II, seen from a ▷ Puritan point of view. 'Vanity' in the biblical sense is equivalent to triviality and worthlessness, and it includes all the good things of this world, when compared to the values of the heavenly world of the spirit: 'Vanity of vanities, saith the Preacher, vanity of vanities; all is vanity.' (*Ecclesiastes* 1:2). The town is a great market (fair) for these vanities; the townsmen are not only trivial but heartless, and also bitterly resentful when the pilgrims despise their vanities. Faithful is martyred there, but in Part II he has left disciples behind him and they are to some extent tolerated. Perhaps this is Bunyan's way of acknowledging that the spirit of his age was becoming more tolerant of the Puritans.

Vanity of Human Wishes, The (1749)

An imitation of ▷ Juvenal's Tenth Satire in heroic ▷ couplets by ▷ Samuel Johnson. Where the tone of the imitations of ▷ Horace by other poets is detached and urbane, Johnson's poem affects the moral earnestness and ruggedness of Juvenal. The poet reflects upon the vanity of ambition as illustrated by the lives of various historical figures, including Cardinal Wolsey the statesman, a number of famous scholars, and the 'warrior' Charles XII of Sweden. The poem is remarkable for its sonorous authority of tone, exemplified by the famous first lines: 'Let observation with extensive view, / Survey mankind, from China to Peru'. It is packed with memorable generalizations, expressing a kind of Christian stoicism. All human activity ends in disappointment and all life ends in death: 'From Marlb'rough's eyes the streams of dotage flow. / And Swift expires a driv'ler and a show.' The universality of the poem can descend to mere platitude, and its unremittingly emphatic gloom risks lugubriousness. It has consequently been felt to embody a decadent, mechanically inauthentic Augustanism. In fact, it shows a morally hypersensitive poet taking refuge from despair in satisfyingly rhetorical pessimism and pious abjection: hence its surprisingly moving, personal intensity. It is as much a product of the age of ▷ sensibility as a 'late Augustan' work.

Vaughan, Henry (1622–95)

Poet. Henry Vaughan, together with his brother, Thomas Vaughan (1622–66), the alchemist and poet was born at Newton-by-Usk in Wales. Vaughan's Welsh roots were to feature prominently in his writing. He termed himself 'The Silurist' after a local Welsh tribe termed the Silures by ▷ Tacitus, and his third published collection of poems was entitled *Olor Iscanus* (1651), which can be translated as 'The Swan of Usk'. In addition to *Olor Iscanus*, three collections of Vaughan's poetry appeared in his lifetime: *Poems with the Tenth Satire of Juvenal Englished* (1646), *Silex Scintillans* (1650, revised ed. 1655), and *Thalia Rediviva* (1678).

Silex Scintillans perhaps provides a clue as to Vaughan's intellectual identity. The title means 'The Flashing Flint' – an image which was given emblematic significance on the title-page of the collection where a hand, issuing from a cloud, is shown striking fire from a flintstone, fashioned in the shape of a heart. The image, which signifies a 'stony' heart surrendering flames of divine love when struck by God's spiritual force, suggests ▷ George Herbert's influence on Vaughan. But the image, with its conjunction of stone and fire suggestive of a religious awakening (a theme explored in the

collection of poems as a whole), also alerts us to another side of Vaughan's writing. In 1655 Vaughan published a translation of an 'Hermetic' work entitled *Hermetical Physick* and in 1657 appeared his *The Chymists Key*. Hermeticism – the linking of alchemy, magic and science – might also be thought of as represented in the physical image of the flint flashing with fire. These two elements in Vaughan's intellectual life combine in his poetry in a way which is reminiscent of ▷ Thomas Traherne's concern for expressing the physical and spiritual worlds.
Bib: Martin, L. C. (ed.), *Works*; Hutchinson, F. E., *Henry Vaughan: A Life and Interpretation*; Post, J., *Henry Vaughan: The Unfolding Vision*.

Vehicles

Travelling overland in the ▷ Middle Ages was chiefly on foot (for the poor) or on horseback. The sick and aged would be carried by a portable bed known as a 'litter', suspended between horizontal poles; heavy goods went by ox- or horse-drawn wagons, of a design similar to the farmers' wagons still in use in the first half of the 20th century, and light goods went by packhorse. Travel by barge along the rivers was common.

The first coach in England was built in 1555, and in the next century and a half coaches came more and more into use among the nobility; in the 17th century hackney coaches (*ie* coaches for hire) were already beginning to put the Thames watermen out of business. By the 18th century the stage-coach was in use for general travel; it was so called because horses were changed at fixed 'stages' on the journey. More rapid travel was undertaken by privately hired post-chaises. Movement about towns was by sedan-chair, resembling a light litter except that the traveller was seated. The great improvement in roads towards the end of the 18th century led to a great increase in light private carriages of various designs; gigs and curricles were the lightest, favoured by young men.

Venice Preserv'd: or, A Plot Discovered (1682)

▷ Tragedy by ▷ Thomas Otway, his sixth and last, set in Venice, and based on an original work by Cesar Vischard, Abbé de Saint Real. Jaffeir, married to Belvidera, pleads with her father Priuli, a wealthy Venetian senator, to make peace with him. Priuli adamantly refuses; he is outraged because Jaffeir, having been made welcome in Priuli's house after saving Belvidera's life, 'stole' her from him, and married her secretly. Jaffeir's friend Pierre enters, and privately they commiserate over the tyranny of the Senate. Pierre's beloved Aquilina has been taken from him by the rich, elderly senator Antonio, and Pierre tells Jaffeir his property is being confiscated by Priuli, leaving him and his wife destitute. The two plot rebellion and revenge, but the conspiracy fails, and Jaffeir betrays Pierre, who is taken and condemned to death. But at the end Jaffeir repents, stabs Pierre to preserve him from a shameful death, then stabs himself. Belvidera is driven mad and dies. The tragedy was topical: the character of Antonio is a satire on the ▷ Earl of Shaftesbury, and the 'plot' referred to in the sub-title was related by many to the ▷ 'Popish plot' to murder ▷ Charles II and reinstate ▷ Catholicism, in which Shaftesbury played a large part. The play has been seen as transitional in the move toward the domestic tragedy of the 18th century.

Venus

▷ Aphrodite.

Verbruggen, John (dc 1707)

Actor, singer, dancer, manager, dramatist. He joined the ▷ United Company in 1688, acting at first under the name of Alexander.

A handsome man, Verbruggen was often in trouble because of his fiery temperament: on one occasion he got into a brawl with the Duke of St Albans behind the scenes at ▷ Drury Lane, and afterwards apologized publicly for hitting and insulting the Duke. He created many important roles, including Loveless in ▷ Colley Cibber's ▷ *Love's Last Shift* and ▷ Sir John Vanbrugh's ▷ *The Relapse*; Constant in Vanbrugh's ▷ *The Provok'd Wife*; the King of Granada in ▷ William Congreve's ▷ *The Mourning Bride*, and Mirabel in his ▷ *The Way of the World*.

His wife was the actress ▷ Susanna Verbruggen.

Verbruggen, Susanna (?1667–1703)

Actress. Susanna Verbruggen (née Percival) acted at the Theatre Royal, and later at ▷ Dorset Garden, with the ▷ United Company, and in 1686 married the popular actor and dramatist William Mountfort (1664–92). By 1690 she was recorded as being one of the leading actresses of the company. Two years after Mountfort's death, she married the actor ▷ John Verbruggen, and died in childbirth.

Susanna Verbruggen excelled in comedy, was a superb mimic, and according to ▷ Cibber 'gave many heightening touches to Characters but coldly written, and often made an Author vain of his Work, that in it self had little merit.' She was famous for her special talents in men's parts, playing Bayes in ▷ George Villiers' ▷ *The Rehearsal* to great acclaim, and in the roles of hoydens and female fops. Cibber described her performance as Melantha in ▷ Dryden's ▷ *Marriage à la Mode* as '(containing) the most compleat System of Female Foppery, that could possibly be crowded into the tortur'd Form of a Fine Lady'.

Vere Street Theatre

One of the first venues used for stage performances after the ▷ Restoration, before the construction of purpose-built theatres, and, like ▷ Lincoln's Inn Fields, it involved conversion of a former tennis court.

Vers de société

A kind of poetry originating in France in the 17th century, distinguished by its content, and the treatment of it: light, graceful, witty comment on current manners. In England it was particularly characteristic of early 18th century – much of the work of ▷ Prior, ▷ Gray and ▷ Swift. An example is Swift's *A Soldier and a Scholar* (1732).

Versailles

A town near Paris where Louis XIV of France (1638–1715) built the most splendid of all the European royal palaces. It was also the scene of two important treaties: the Peace of Versailles (1783) which ended the American War of Independence, and the Treaty of Versailles (1919), concluding World War I.

Vicar of Bray, The

The title of an anonymous 18th-century song in which a parish priest boasts of having changed his views to fit every political and religious regime from the time of ▷ Charles I to that of ▷ George I. The figure may be based on Simon Aleyn, who actually belongs to an earlier period. He was vicar of Bray in Berkshire from about 1540 to 1588, and changed his religion several times to suit the policies of Henry VIII, Edward VI, Mary I, and Elizabeth I. 'Vicar of Bray' has become a byword for a time-server.

Vicar of Wakefield, The (1761–2)

A novel by ▷ Oliver Goldsmith written 1761–2 but not published until 1766. Dr Primrose, a good-natured and innocent vicar, lives in comfortable circumstances with his wife and six children. Then their life is overturned by a series of disasters, reducing them to poverty and disgrace; the vicar endures his troubles with sweetness and stoicism. Eventually, they are restored to prosperity by the friendship of a benefactor, Mr Burchill, who turns out to be Sir William Thornhill, whose nephew had originally caused their misfortunes. The novel has conventionally been interpreted as a simplistic moral fable, the chief virtue of which is its sentimentality. Recent critics however suggest an element of satiric irony, drawing parallels with Goldsmith's complex creations in other genres.

Village, the English

Before the Norman Conquest of 1066, the Anglo-Saxon rural communities were the 'vils'; these became more or less identified with the Norman manor, the basic social and economic unit of the ▷ Middle Ages. Each manor usually had a 'lord of the manor', or principal landowner, but it was common for one lord to hold several manors and his authority in the village was then exercised (through the manor court or 'court leet') by his 'reeve' or steward. Most of the peasants were 'serfs'; that is to say, in return for their lord's protection, they were compelled to work on his land, owed him certain gifts on such occasions as the marriage of a daughter or the death of the head of a family, and were not allowed to leave their settlements. Their own land consisted of large open fields which were divided into strips for cultivation, each husbandman being awarded particular strips in the manor court. This is known as the ▷ open-field system of agriculture. Beyond the arable fields was another area of pasture for grazing the peasants' cattle; this was held in common by all the villagers and was known as 'common land'.

The status of 'serf' could be 'commuted', if the lord agreed, by the payment of a sum of money in consequence of which the serf might become a landless labourer, free to work for wages, or a tenant farmer, paying rent. There were many degrees and kinds of serfdom, but in no case was the serf a mere slave; he owed his services to the lord, but the lord had no rights over his person. The lord could not usually impose his own will over the manor court which decided the domestic affairs of the village; its law was 'customary', *ie* decided by tradition and precedent, much as the ▷ Common Law of England was. There were even cases when the lord was fined by the manorial court, like any of his serfs, for infringing the customary law. In addition to the lord and his steward or reeve, an important person in each village was the priest or parson (such as Chaucer describes in the *Canterbury Tales*), supported by 'tithes' or tenths of the agricultural produce of the villagers.

The first important change in this system came as a result of the devastations of the Black Death epidemic of about 1348–9, which greatly reduced the population of serfs and the available labour on the manors. Lords found it convenient to hire labour, and by the 16th century serfdom, with a few exceptions, had gone from England. The peasants were now tenant farmers paying rents to the lord of the manor, who farmed his own land by hired labourers. The next important change was the enclosure of land by the landlords in the 16th century. The profitability of sheep-farming was such as to make it worth the lord's while to deprive the peasants of their holdings in order to turn arable land over to grazing. Enclosures of land continued until the 19th century for different motives, with the consequence that the small farmer ('yeoman' or 'smallholder') ceased, at least from the mid-18th century, to be typical of English rural society in the sense that he is typical, for instance, of French society.

Villiers, George, 2nd Duke of Buckingham (1627–87)

Courtier and dramatist, son of the statesman, the 1st Duke of Buckingham, who had been a favourite of ▷ James I, and who was assassinated in 1628. Villiers, the 2nd Duke, accompanied ▷ Charles I to Scotland during the ▷ Civil War, and again into exile later. In 1657 he returned secretly to England, and married the daughter of Lord Fairfax, the parliamentary general who had charge of his confiscated estates. These were returned to him after the ▷ Restoration. He became one of Charles II's 'cabal' of intimates, and wrote a number of plays, of which the ▷ burlesque ▷ *The Rehearsal* is the best known. He was parodied by ▷ Dryden as Zimri in ▷ *Absalom and Achitophel*.

Vindication of the Rights of Woman (1792)

Tract by English writer ▷ Mary Wollstonecraft. It follows her *Vindication of the Rights of Man* (1790). She returns to the question of women's education (which she had addressed in ▷ *Thoughts on the Education of Daughters*, 1787) to argue that uneducated girls are often 'cruelly left by their parents without any provision, and, of course, are dependent on not only the reason but the bounty of their brothers'. She speaks of such women as 'unable to work, and ashamed to beg'. Thus in Wollstonecraft's polemic, work and the ability to work is increasingly seen as important in terms of a woman's self-definition and survival in the world. This shifts the debate from the terrain of provision to one of rights, but it is coupled with a spiritual and psychological polemic – she wants women to 'acquire strength of mind and body' to combat their situation physically, but also to resist psychologically the categories constructed for them. She asks, 'Why are girls to be told that they resemble angels; but to sink them below women?' In the same work, Wollstonecraft expresses radical views on ▷ marriage, including the view that seduction should be regarded as marriage (she was writing after Hardwicke's 1753 Marriage Act made it harder for women to sue for breach of promise) and that 'the man should be legally obliged to maintain the woman and her children, unless adultery, a natural divorcement, abrogated the law.'

Virgil (Publius Vergilius Maro) (70–19 BC)

Roman poet. He was born on a farm not far from Mantua in northern Italy, and is often referred to as 'the Mantuan'. He greatly esteemed the farming section of society to which he belonged, and valued the farming way of life. He was not, from the place of his origin, of Roman descent, but belonged to the first generation of Italians who felt a consciousness of nationhood, with Rome as their capital. By 40 BC he was in Rome, under the patronage of the wealthy Roman patrician (nobleman), Maecenas. He wrote the first work for which he is famous, the ▷ Eclogues or Bucolics (▷ eclogue), between 42 and 37 BC; their intention is merely means 'short, selected pieces', but his intention is to praise the Italian countryside as the Greek poet, ▷ Theocritus had praised the countryside of Sicily. The ▷ Georgics (37–30 BC), written at the instigation of Maecenas to encourage a sense of the value of a stable and productive society, is devoted to the praise of the farming way of life. The ▷ Aeneid written during the remainder of his life, is an ▷ epic about the travels of Aeneas the Trojan, and emulates Homer's ▷ Odyssey. Its purpose is not merely this, but to relate the Romans to the great civilization of the Greeks, on which their own civilization was so much based, by making Aeneas the ancestor of the Roman nation. The Aeneid, with the epics of Homer, is one of the basic poems in the culture of Europe and is taken as a standard for what was, perhaps until the 19th century, regarded as the noblest form of literature.

Not even Homer exceeds Virgil in the extent of his influence and prestige in the 20 centuries of European culture. He did not, like all the Greek poets and many of the Roman ones, have to wait for the ▷ Renaissance to 'discover' him, for he was esteemed in the ▷ Middle Ages, when, indeed, he became a legend. This was partly owing to his Fourth Eclogue which celebrated the birth of a child who was to restore the Golden Age (▷ Ages, Golden, Silver), a poem which in the Christian centuries was supposed to be a prophetic vision of the birth of Christ. He was thus regarded as more than merely a pagan poet, and Dante chose him as his guide through Hell and Purgatory in his 13th-century Christian epic, the Divine Comedy. In direct literary influence, he was, even more than Theocritus, the pattern for ▷ pastoral poetry, and even more than Homer, for the epic, although he was himself a student of both.

▷ Caesar Augustus; Augustanism; classics; neo-classicism.

Virtuoso, The (1676)

▷ Comedy by ▷ Shadwell, which satirizes contemporary scientific endeavour, and the efforts of the ▷ Royal Society in particular. The virtuoso of the title, Sir Nicholas Gimcrack, conducts absurd experiments on respiration, for example, which mock researches carried out by the physicists Robert Boyle, Robert Hooke and other members of the Royal Society. In the same famous scene, Gimcrack demonstrates swimming upon a table, without the use of water, which he abhors and considers unnecessary to the purpose. The episode ridicules excessive reliance on scientific theory. There is also some serious romantic action involving two pairs of lovers: Longvil and Clarinda, and Bruce and Miranda, as well as scenes which involve the aged Lady Gimcrack's attempts to flirt with the young lovers. An historically interesting element is the besieging of Sir Nicholas's house by weavers, enraged by his purported invention of a mechanical loom.

Voltaire (pseudonym of François Marie Arouet, 1694–1778)

French writer. He wrote prolifically, and in his own day was regarded as above all a poet and a philosopher, but his international fame rests more on his prose work – satirical essays and the ironical romance, Candide (1759). He is even better known as the pattern of humane intellectuals: he was the determined opponent of beliefs and institutions sanctified by tradition but really disguising the selfishness and inhumanity of privileged classes of society. His dictum 'Ecrasez l' Infâme' (Crush the Evil) is not, as it has often been thought to be, a slogan against religion as such, but against intolerance, superstition and unjustified privileges supported by religious institutions. He gained immense prestige all over Europe, and corresponded with Frederick II of Prussia and Catherine II of Russia. Candide was published at almost the same time as ▷ Rasselas by ▷ Samuel Johnson, and Johnson himself remarked on the extraordinary similarity of their themes, although there was no direct exchange of ideas between the two men. In general, Voltaire had strong sympathies with English trends of thought, and his long visit to England (1726–9) was an important episode in his development. In his Lettres sur les Anglais he used his English experiences as a basis for his attack on the French establishment. Correspondingly, Voltaire was admired in England and his influence is pervasive in English 18th-century writing.

▷ L'Encyclopedie.

Wales

A mountainous country to the west of England; it
has been united to England politically since 1536,
but it has preserved national individuality and its
native Celtic language, though this is now spoken
by only about 20% of its 2.8 million population.
The geography of the country has always been
a hindrance to its unity, and before the English
conquest it tended to divide into separate northern
and southern regions. Just before the Norman
Conquest of England (1066), however, Gruffudd
ap Llywelyn, a Welsh prince, succeeded in briefly
uniting the country, and Wales in consequence
seemed formidable enough for the first Norman
king of England, William I, to establish three strong
earldoms for the defence of England along the
Welsh frontier. These earldoms correspond to the
former English counties of Hereford, Shropshire and
Cheshire, long known as the Marches.

After his conquest of Wales, Edward I in 1301
gave his eldest son the title of Prince of Wales, a
custom which has been followed by many English
monarchs since then. However, until the 16th
century, they did very little else to govern Wales.

The ▷ Reformation made slower headway
in Wales than in England, but it was effectively
established by the end of the 16th century. In the
18th and 19th centuries, ▷ Methodism became
very strong in Wales, to the extent that the Church
of England was disestablished (ie it ceased to
be the state Church) by a law passed in 1914.
The Welsh Nonconformist churches are thus not
'nonconforming' in the English sense; the country is
divided among a number of religious denominations
(of which Anglicanism is only one), none of which
have any official pre-eminence over the others.
The Methodist churches in particular have done
much to keep the Welsh language alive and vital.
Education is conducted in the Welsh language mainly
in state schools in those regions where families
are predominantly Welsh-speaking: one or more
subjects are taught in the medium of Welsh in 20%
of primary and 16% of secondary schools, whereas
Welsh is taught as a language in 80% of primary and
88% of secondary schools (these statistics relate only
to the state system throughout Wales).

Whereas, since 1350, the principal output of
literature in Scotland and Ireland has been in
English, though with Scottish and Irish national
colouring, Welsh literature has chiefly been in the
native Welsh language. It is thus scarcely possible
to say that English literature has been distinctively
modified by the literature of Wales, as can be said of
the literatures of Scotland and Ireland.

Waller, Edmund (1606–87)

Poet. As with so many of his contemporaries,
Waller's career reflects the vicissitudes of public
life in the revolutionary period of the mid-17th
century. As a Member of ▷ Parliament prior to the
▷ Civil War, he opposed the bishops, but, on the
outbreak of hostilities, he was on the Royalist side.
In 1643 he was found guilty of plotting to surrender
London to the Royalist armies, and was banished.
In exile in Paris he became friendly with ▷ Thomas

Hobbes, before returning to England (having secured
permission) in 1651. On his return he wrote a
'Panegyric to my Lord Protector' (1655), addressed
to ▷ Oliver Cromwell, but with the ▷ Restoration
in 1660 Waller was fully restored to the king's favour,
and proceeded to write a second panegyric, this time
to ▷ Charles II.

Waller's chief verse collections were his *Poems* of
1645 (a second part being published in 1690) and
his collection of religious verse *Divine Poems* (1685).
After 1660 he produced numerous occasional verses,
including *To the King, Upon His Majesty's Happy
Return* (1660) and *To the Queen, Upon Her Majesty's
Birthday* (1663). But it is as a transitional figure that
he has attracted critical comment. Waller's poetry
can be seen as marking the transition from the 'witty'
▷ conceits of poets such as John Donne to the
smoother ▷ neo-classicism of 18th-century poetry.
Indeed, ▷ John Dryden, ignoring figures such as
Robert Herrick and Ben Jonson, claimed that, if
Waller had not written, 'none of us could write'.
Bib: Thorn-Drury, G. (ed.), *Poems*, 2 vols.;
Chernaik, W. L., *The Poetry of Limitation: A Study
of Waller*.

Walpole, Horace (1717–97)

Letter-writer, antiquarian, connoisseur. He was
son of the powerful statesman ▷ Robert Walpole,
and for a short time followed a political career, but
he abandoned it, though he continued his interest
in politics. His father's influence procured for him
three sinecures (ie posts under the government
which carried salaries though they required very
little work) and these enabled him to pass his life
as an assiduous spectator and man of pleasure. He
developed a strong taste for the Gothic style in all
its forms, converting his house (Strawberry Hill,
Twickenham, where he settled in 1747) into what he
called 'a little Gothic castle', and writing the first of
the ▷ Gothic novels, ▷ *The Castle of Otranto* (1764).
He is chiefly famous for his letters, however, and is
regarded as one of the best correspondents in the
best period of ▷ letter-writing. Their main quality is
their liveliness, humour, and vividness of observation.
Bib: Lives by Ketton-Cremer and Lewis, W. S.;
Stephen, L., in *Hours in a Library*.

Walpole, Sir Robert (1676–1745)

Statesman. He is sometimes called 'the first
▷ Prime Minister', meaning that he was the first
statesman to hold chief power in the state and at the
same time to base this power on the ▷ House of
Commons. His practice of consulting his ministers
in a private office or 'cabinet' and of insisting that
they should comply with his policies or resign their
posts has also caused him to be credited with the
invention of the cabinet system of government. In
both, he is a figure of importance in the history
of the development of the British constitution. He
held power continuously from 1721 to 1742, and
was enabled to do so partly by his financial ability
(he came to office at the time of the ▷ South Sea
Bubble crisis), and partly by the incapacity of the
German-born kings, George I (1714–27) and George
II (1727–60), to manage English politics.

Walsh, William (1663–1708)

Minor poet, called by ▷ John Dryden the best critic in the language. The youthful ▷ Alexander Pope was encouraged by his advice that 'though we had several great poets, we never had any one great poet that was correct; and he desired me to make that my study and aim'.

Walton, Izaac (1593–1683)

Biographer. Izaac Walton's popular reputation has rested on his *The Compleat Angler* (1653, with revised editions in 1658 and 1661) – ostensibly a fishing manual. The comprehensive nature of the work is, however, hinted at in its subtitle: *The Contemplative Man's Recreation* – an evocation of an idyllic, reflective, ▷ pastoral nostalgia. As a biographer Walton was the author of a series of important 'lives' of 17th-century poets and divines. His *Life of John Donne* was published in 1658, and was followed by lives of Richard Hooker (1665), ▷ George Herbert (1670) and Robert Sanderson (1678). *The Life of Sir Henry Wotton* first appeared appended to a posthumous edition of Wotton's poetry in 1640 and was published separately in 1651. The biographies of Donne and Herbert are the most renowned. Walton is concerned with recording his subjects' piously Anglican Christian virtue, but they are, nevertheless, important statements concerning the contemporary perception of these major writers and instances of a 17th-century art of hagiographic ▷ biography.
Bib: Keynes, G. L. (ed.), *The Compleat Walton*; Novarr, D., *The Making of Walton's Lives*.

Ward, Edward ('Ned') (1667–1731)

Tavern-keeper and ▷ Grub Street writer, specializing in doggerel verses and humorous sketches of London life. His prose work *The London Spy* (1698–1709) takes us on a tour of the sights of London, and is full of humorous anecdotes and eccentric characters. His *Hudibras Redivivus* was published 1705–7 (▷ *Hudibras*).

Warton, Joseph (1722–1800)

Critic and poet; headmaster of Winchester School and the brother of ▷ Thomas Warton. His *Essay on the Genius and Writings of Pope* (vol. I, 1756; vol. II, 1782) distinguishes the 'true poet' from the mere 'man of wit' and is often seen as a 'pre-Romantic' document, though Warton himself admired ▷ Alexander Pope and edited his works (1797).

Warton, Thomas (1728–90)

Professor of Poetry at Oxford (1757–67) and later (1785–90) ▷ Poet Laureate. His *Poems* (1777) include several ▷ sonnets, a form neglected in previous decades. His *The Suicide: An Ode* and *Verses on Sir Joshua Reynolds' Painted Window*, toy with 'romantick' excess and ▷ Gothic medievalism, without ever having the courage of their convictions, and his comic verse is perhaps more successful. He edited the humorous miscellany, *The Oxford Sausage* (1764). It is in his criticism, with its scholarly approach to early literature that his real importance lies. His *Observations on the Fairie Queene of Spenser*

(1754) shows a sensitive historical perspective, and his *History of English Poetry* (1774–81), conveys his fascination with the 'Gothic' Middle Ages more convincingly than the dilettantism of his poems. Breaking off at the death of Elizabeth I, it complemented ▷ Samuel Johnson's ▷ *Lives of the Poets*, and despite their aesthetic differences the two men were on friendly terms. In 1785 he published an edition of ▷ John Milton's early poems.
▷ Romanticism.
Bib: Pittock, J., *The Ascendancy of Taste: The Achievement of Joseph and Thomas Warton*; Rinacker, C., *Thomas Warton: A Biographical and Critical Study*.

Washington, George (1732–99)

Leader of the rebel forces in the ▷ American War of Independence (1775–83); president of the American convention, 1787; first President of the United States, 1789. He served in the British forces during the wars against the French and Indians in the 1750s and was a rich and efficient tobacco planter, but he did not play a leading part in American politics until relationships with Britain became critical in the 1770s. He was however noted as 'a young man of an extraordinary and exalted character'. Washington's great-grandfather had emigrated from Britain in 1657.

Watt, James (1736–1819)

Scottish engineer, inventor, and scientist. His outstanding achievement was the improvement of the steam engine, the principles of which (apart from ancient Greek experiments) had been discovered in the 17th century. Newcomen's improvements on existing models in 1705 enabled it to be put to practical use, but it was Watt in 1763 who made it commercially successful and one of the main instruments for the ▷ Industrial Revolution, the beginnings of which are sometimes dated from his time. Watt's engine made deep mining for coal possible when it was applied to pumping; it could be used for driving machines in factories, and it led in the 1820s to the invention of railway locomotives.

Watts, Isaac (1674–1748)

Poet and ▷ hymn writer. He was minister of an Independent church in London until in 1712 ill health forced him into an early retirement in the household of the Whig merchant Sir Thomas Abney in Hertfordshire. His verse appeared in *Horae Lyricae* (1706), *Hymns* (1707), *Divine Songs for Children* (1715), *Psalms of David* (1719). Later in life he turned to prose tracts on theology. Much of his work is charged with a ▷ Puritan dogmatism, but sometimes more literary instincts prevail. Watts experimented with classical ▷ metres, and wrote bold Pindaric ▷ odes and distinctive ▷ blank verse. Some of his hymns, for instance 'O God, our help in ages past' and 'When I survey the wondrous cross' are famous. His songs for children became a part of popular British culture, and form the basis of some of ▷ William Blake's ▷ *Songs of Innocence and Experience*.

Way of the World, The (1700)
A comedy by ▷ William Congreve, produced
in 1700. The plot is a complicated succession of
intrigues which surround the love affair between
the sparkling young rake, Mirabell (a hero in the
tradition of ▷ Etherege's Dorimant in ▷ *The
Man of Mode*), and the urbane and witty heroine,
Millamant. Mirabell's aim is to trick or persuade
Millamant's aunt, Lady Wishfort, into consenting to
their marriage; and his efforts include pretending to
make love to Lady Wishfort herself. This intrigue
is frustrated by Mrs Marwood, embittered against
Mirabell because he has previously rejected her.
Mirabell then attempts further intrigue, and this
leads to counter-intrigues by Mrs Marwood in
alliance with Mirabell's treacherous friend Fainall,
who combines them with conspiracies against his
wife, a former mistress of Mirabell's, and blackmail
of Lady Wishfort. Mirabell finally succeeds in
defeating his enemies and saving Lady Wishfort from
the threats against her; in gratitude, she consents to
his marriage to Millamant. The intrigues serve as
a framework for theatrically very successful comic
scenes and imaginatively witty dialogue. Millamant
and Mirabell set out the conditions on which they
agree to relinquish their freedom and submit to
marriage, in a famous ▷ Proviso scene (IV, vi).
Millamant's charm and independence have made her
role a star part for great actresses, and supply a main
reason for the play's lasting reputation.
  ▷ Manners, Comedy of.

Weak ending
In ▷ blank verse an unstressed syllable in the place
of the normally stressed one at the end of a line;
also, a word such as a conjunction or preposition
which may bear metrical stress but cannot bear
speech stress.

Wealth of Nations, The
▷ Smith, Adam.

Wedgwood
The name of a firm of distinguished manufacturers
of china. The founder of the firm, Josiah Wedgwood
(1730–95), was the son of a potter of Burslem.
He perfected an English style of pottery called
cream ware, and later Queen's ware. He then
developed a new style of classical designs, inspired
by contemporary interest in ancient Greek pottery
and by the discovery of the Roman city of Pompeii in
southern Italy. The most famous of the Wedgwood
designers in this style was the friend of the poet
▷ William Blake, John Flaxman. The Wedgwood
factory near Hanley is called Etruria; the firm
continues in production at the present day. Josiah's
son, Thomas Wedgwood (1771–1805), was a
generous patron to the poet ▷ Coleridge.

**Wellington, Arthur Wellesley, 1st Duke of
(1769–1852)**
General and statesman. By origin, of Anglo–Irish
aristocracy. He joined the army in 1787, and between
1796 and 1805 he had a distinguished military career
in India, where his eldest brother was Governor-
General. Arthur Wellesley then returned to Britain.

Between 1808 and 1814 he gained fame for his
resistance to the French armies of ▷ Napoleon I
on the Spanish Peninsula. He was created Duke in
1814. In 1815, with the Prussian general Blücher, he
inflicted the final defeat on Napoleon at Waterloo.
  He took part in the Congress of Vienna, which
made the peace treaty with France, and his influence
did much to prevent the partition of the country.
Thereafter, his career was in British politics, where
he was one of the principal leaders of the Tory
(Conservative) party. He gave way, however, over one
issue, that of ▷ Catholic Emancipation (*ie* granting
Catholics full political rights) because he understood
its political inevitability; he was less clear-sighted
about Parliamentary reform, and was forced to resign
in 1830. He again held ministerial posts, though
not that of Prime Minister, in 1834, and 1841–6,
under the leadership of Robert Peel. After his death,
Tennyson commemorated him with one of his best
poems, his *Ode on the Death of the Duke of Wellington*.
He was popularly known as 'the Iron Duke', and
used proudly to call his London mansion at Hyde
Park Corner, 'Number One, London'.

Welsh literature in English
Before the ▷ Romantic period, Welsh literature was
virtually unknown in English, since it had not been
translated from the Welsh language. However, Celtic
material generally benefited from the antiquarian
excavations of the Augustan period, and the later
Romantic interest in myth, the ▷ Gothic and
the search for literary origins (▷ Macpherson;
▷ Ossian). The first major translation of Welsh
poetry, *Some Specimens of the Poetry of the Ancient
Welsh Bards* (ed. Ieuan Brydydd Hir; 1764) had an
important influence, on, for example, ▷ Thomas
Gray's ▷ *The Bard* (1757) and 'The Triumph of
Owen' (1768). Such was the demand for similar
works that Iolo Morganwg successfully passed off his
own work as supposed early Welsh 'bards'. The early
Arthurian tales were translated first by Dr Owen
Pughe in *Relicks of the Welsh Bards* (1795–1829), and
later by the English author, Lady Charlotte Guest,
who gave them their, somewhat incorrect, title *The
Mabinogion* (1838–49).
Bib: Stephens, M., *Oxford Companion to the Literature
of Wales*.

Wesley, Charles (1707–88)
▷ Hymn writer. Brother of the evangelist, ▷ John
Wesley, he was the poet of the ▷ Methodist
movement. He wrote about 6,500 hymns of unequal
merit. Some of them, such as 'Hark the Herald
Angels Sing', 'Jesu, lover of my soul', and 'Love
divine all Love's excelling' show genuine poetic
feeling, and are well known.

Wesley, John (1703–91)
Evangelist and founder of the ▷ Methodist
religious movement. At Oxford, with his brother
▷ Charles, he became the centre of a society
which regulated the lives of its members; this led
to their being described as 'Methodists'. He was
at first a strict Anglican, conforming rigidly to
▷ Church of England liturgies and doctrines, but

on a voyage to America in 1735 he became deeply
impressed by the purity and undogmatic spirit of
fellow-passengers belonging to the German sect
known as the Moravians. On his return to England,
Wesley preached up and down Britain. Both the
Church of England and the ▷ Dissenters who were
heirs of the 17th-century ▷ Puritans had by now
relatively little to offer to the minds of the simple
people; reaction against the violent conflicts of
the previous century had caused the clergy of all
denominations to obscure the sense of religion as
a power in individual lives. Wesley taught both that
every man was naturally a sinner, and that the power
of God was available to all for spiritual salvation. In
this he followed the Arminian tradition of religious
belief, instead of the belief in ▷ Predestination more
prevalent among the 17th-century Puritans. Wesley's
direct challenge to the hearts and the wills of his
hearers caused deep psychological disturbances,
and the Methodists were despised by many for
the hysteria and emotionalism of their meetings.
Nonetheless, the influence of Wesley was extensive
and profound, and bore fruit in other religious
revivals in the 19th century. He was courteous and
had a pleasant wit. When confronted by an arrogant
opponent in a narrow street who declared 'I never
make way for fools!', Wesley stood aside politely,
replying: 'I always do.'
▷ Sermons.

West Indian, The (1771)

Comedy by ▷ Richard Cumberland. Belcour has
been brought up in the West Indies; he is honest
but unsophisticated. Arriving in London, he falls in
love with Louisa, the daughter of the impoverished
Captain Dudley, but is deceived into thinking her
the mistress of Charles, who is in fact her brother.
He makes advances to her as if she were a whore
and she repels him with the classic phrase, 'Unhand
me, sir!' Meanwhile, Charles loves his wealthy
cousin Charlotte, but will not acknowledge the fact
because of his own poverty. Belcour comes to the
aid of Captain Dudley. Eventually Charles and
Louisa are revealed as heirs, Belcour and Louisa
become reconciled and are married, and Charles
marries Charlotte. The play contains references
to the workings of Providence in refusing to allow
'innocence to be oppressed', or cruelty and cunning
to prosper; it has often been cited as an archetypal
example of ▷ sentimentality in the drama of
the period.

Westminster, Palace of

Though it still officially bears this title, the
building is more familiarly known as the Houses
of ▷ Parliament. It already existed as a palace
under Edward the Confessor. As such, it was the
meeting-place of the House of Lords and the House
of Commons in the ▷ Middle Ages. In 1512, the
palace was damaged by fire and it has not been a
royal residence since. In 1834, it was further and
more seriously damaged, and all that now remains of
the medieval palace is the great Hall built by William
II in 1097 and reroofed by Richard II in 1399, and
the crypt to the chapel of St Stephen's, under the

present House of Commons. The rest of the present
building dates 1840–67; it contains the two chambers
of the House of Lords and the House of Commons.
The latter was destroyed by a bomb during
World War II, but it was afterwards reconstructed
identically in every detail.

Westminster Hall has been the scene of many
famous state trials including those of the Scottish
patriot William Wallace; the kings Richard II and
▷ Charles I; the Catholic martyrs Sir Thomas More
and Edmund Campion; George IV's queen Caroline
(1820), and the Governor-General of India, Warren
Hastings (1788–95).

Westminster Abbey

Originally an abbey of monks on the bank of the
Thames and to the west of the City of London. The
abbey was dissolved by Henry VIII in 1539, and the
present building is the old abbey church. It was built
by King Edward the Confessor in 1065 and rebuilt
by Henry III, whose structure still stands. It has long
been the state church of England; since William I
the sovereigns have been crowned in it, and many
have been buried there. To be buried in Westminster
Abbey is a national honour, and the church is in
consequence lined with monuments. The Poets'
Corner contains monuments to eminent writers, not
all of whom are buried in the Abbey; they include
Chaucer, ▷ Spenser, ▷ Shakespeare, Ben Jonson
and ▷ Milton.

Wharton, Anne (1659–1685)

English dramatist and poet, niece of John Wilmot,
▷ Earl of Rochester. In 1673 she was married to
Thomas Wharton, later Whig politican, who ignored
her. Some of her letters to him survive. When
Rochester died, she became close to ▷ Bishop
Gilbert Burnet, who was critical of her poetry. Her
tragedy, *Love's Martyr, or Witt Above Crowns* was
not acted, but is a political allegory of the Exclusion
Crisis (1679–80). Her poetry circulated during her
lifetime, but it only began to appear in print after
her death. She paraphrased the letter from Penelope
to Ulysses in Ovid's *Heroides*: 'Would Troy were
glorious still, so I had you.'

Her other publications include: *Poems by Several
Hands* (ed. ▷ Nahum Tate 1685); *Idea of Christian
Love* (1688); *A Collection of Poems* (1693), and
Whartonia (1727).
Bib: Greer, G. *et al.*, *Kissing the Rod.*

Wheatley, Phillis (?1753–1784)

The first black poet in English. As a child she was
sold as a slave to the Wheatley family in Boston, who
treated her well and encouraged her inclination to
write. Her *Poems on Various Subjects, Religious and
Moral*, published in London in 1773, comprises
derivative and conventional verses on didactic
themes: 'Remember, *Christians, Negroes*, black as
Cain,/ May be refin'd, and join the angelic train.'

Whig and Tory

Political terms distinguishing the two parties
which were the forebears of the present ▷ Liberal
and Conservative parties respectively. They were

originally terms of abuse, provoked by the attempt of ▷ Lord Shaftesbury in 1679 to exclude James Duke of York (later ▷ James II) from succession to the throne because he was a ▷ Catholic. Shaftesbury and his party were called Whigs because their preference for the ▷ Protestant religion over the law of hereditary succession caused their opponents to liken them to the Scottish ▷ Presbyterian rebels of the time – called derisively 'whigs' from the nickname given to Scottish drovers. They retaliated by calling the supporters of James, 'tories', from the Irish term for robbers, implying that they no more cared about safeguarding the Protestant religion than did the Irish Catholic rebels. The Exclusion question was settled in favour of James, but not for long, since the Tories did in fact care greatly about the maintenance of the ▷ Church of England, and when James II was clearly seen to be acting in Catholic interests, the Tories united with the Whigs in deposing him in 1688. The political terms remained because, though not very consistently, the parties remained; and the parties survived because they represented distinct social interests in the country, though also not very consistently. The Whigs were especially the party of the landed aristocracy, who cared less for the institutions of the Crown and the Church of England than for their own power; since this was allied to the commercial interests of the country, they tended to gain support from the merchants of the towns, many of whom were ▷ Dissenters opposed to the Church of England. The principal Tory support came from the smaller landed gentry, or squirearchy, whose interests were conservative, and whose fortunes seemed best protected by introducing as little change in the established institutions, whether of Church or of State, as possible. In the major crises the Tories were generally defeated, but they had extraordinary survival capacity by virtue of their willingness to accept changes once they had become inevitable. Their first major defeat was in 1714 when the Tory party was split between ▷ Bolingbroke's anti-Hanoverian faction and those loyal to the 1701 ▷ Act of Settlement by which the throne went to the House of ▷ Hanover and not to Anne's Catholic half-brother.

Whigs were then supreme for 40 years (though they disintegrated into rival groups), until after the accession of George III in 1760. George tried then to revive the power of the throne by securing supporters for his politics in Parliament; these supporters were known as 'the King's Friends' or 'New Tories'. This policy was also defeated, however, by their loss of prestige as a result of the victory of the American rebels in the ▷ American War of Independence (1775–83). The country was not then in a mood to see the return of the restless and corrupt Whigs, and Tory governments continued in power until 1832.

About 1830 the names Liberal and Conservative began to replace Whig and Tory in popular use, and these terms were officially adopted some 30 years later. 'Tory' survives, to some extent, as interchangeable with Conservative (it is shorter for newspaper headlines), but 'Whig' has been altogether superseded.

White, Gilbert (1720–93)

Writer on natural history. He was born at Selborne, a village in Hampshire. After spending some years as a Fellow of Oriel College, Oxford, he became a country curate, and spent the last nine years of his life in the village of his birth. His *Natural History of Selborne* (1789) is a record of the plant, animal and bird life there, inspired by genuine scientific curiosity and showing great delicacy and charm of expression. The book has been described as the first to raise natural history to the level of literature, and is the fruit of the development of 17th- and 18th-century natural science, partly initiated by the greatest of English naturalists, John Ray (1627–1705), author of *The Wisdom of God Manifested in the Works of his Creation* (1691), a scientist who shared ▷ Newton's intellectual curiosity and his religious awe at the spectacle of divine organization in the universe. Another tradition leading to White was the newly awakened sensibility for natural surroundings in the poetry of ▷ William Collins, ▷ Oliver Goldsmith and ▷ William Cowper. The poetic movement culminated in the 19th century in the work of ▷ Wordsworth and Clare.

Bib: Holt-White, R., *Life and Letters*.

Whitehall

A street in London that runs between Trafalgar Square and Parliament Square. It is mainly occupied by the buildings of government ministries, so that 'Whitehall' is often used as a term for the state bureaucracy. The name derives from the royal palace that formerly stood there, of which only ▷ Inigo Jones's Banqueting Hall (erected under ▷ James I) now remains. Until the fall of Cardinal Wolsey (1530) it was called York Place, since he built the palace when he was Archbishop of York:

1ST GENTLEMAN: *Sir,*
> *You must no more call it York-place, that's past;*
> *For, since the cardinal fell, that title's lost:*
> *'Tis now the king's, and call'd Whitehall.*
>
>   (*Henry VIII* IV. i.94)

It was outside the Banqueting Hall that ▷ Charles I was executed in 1649.

Wilberforce, William (1759–1833)

Philanthropist and politician. He devoted much of his life to the campaign to abolish the slave trade and ▷ slavery in overseas British territories. In 1807, the slave trade was made illegal, and so was slavery itself in the year of his death. He was leader of the ▷ Evangelical Movement, particularly of a group known as the Clapham Sect because it met in his house at Clapham.

Wild Gallant, The (1663)

Play by ▷ John Dryden, which has been seen by some as the first ▷ Restoration Comedy of ▷ Manners. Constance, a rich heiress, is in love with the charming but penniless Loveby. She steals money from her father in order to supply her lover secretly; he, however, thinks it is a gift from the devil. He expresses his appreciation of the devil in a number of lines bordering on blasphemy. Eventually, by pretending to be pregnant Constance gains leave to wed the man of her choice, and marries Loveby. In a separate but linked plot Isabella, a witty and charming relative of Constance's, wants to marry a man with money and chooses the wealthy Timorous, to whom she is somewhat attracted, although she does not love him. She wins him by means of various intrigues and disguises, including passing herself off as Constance. The play has some farcical comic business: in one sequence Constance persuades the men in the play that they too are pregnant. There is also some feminist comment, as when Constance complains that 'Women are tied to hard unequal laws: the passion is the same in us, and yet we are barred the freedom to express it'.

Wilkes, John (1727–97)

Journalist and politician. He was dissolute, and notorious for his membership of the scandalous Hell-Fire Club at Medmenham Abbey, with its motto 'Fay ce que voudras' = 'Do as you will'. Politically he was radical and courageous, and a popular hero. In 1762 he attacked George III's administration under Lord Bute in *The North Briton*, a periodical which countered *The Briton* edited by the novelist, ▷ Tobias Smollett. As an MP, he was twice expelled from the House of Commons for libel, and in 1769 he was three times elected to Parliament by the county of Middlesex, the election each time being annulled. He was allowed to sit in 1774, in which year he was Lord Mayor of London. His character was such as to win the respect of ▷ Dr Johnson, a man of opposite moral and political principles: 'Jack has great variety of talk, Jack is a scholar, Jack has the manners of a gentleman.' (Quoted in ▷ Boswell's *Life of Johnson*.)

Wilks, Robert (?1665–1732)

Actor, manager. Wilks made his first public appearance, as Othello, at the ▷ Smock Alley Theatre in Dublin in 1691, and in the following year he was employed as an actor by ▷ Christopher Rich in London. He became noted for his gentlemanly style of acting, and was the original Sir Harry Wildair, in his friend, ▷ George Farquhar's ▷ *The Constant Couple*.

Wilks became co-manager first of the ▷ Haymarket, and then, from 1709, of ▷ Drury Lane, in combination with several others including, at various times, Owen Swiney (1675–1754), ▷ Colley Cibber, Thomas Doggett (c1670–1721), Richard Estcourt (1668–1712), ▷ Sir Richard Steele, ▷ Barton Booth, and ▷ Anne Oldfield. He shared control for the rest of his career, while at the same time continuing to strengthen and build up his repertoire as a leading actor, succeeding more in comedies than in tragedies.

Throughout his life Wilks maintained a reputation for sobriety and conscientiousness. Cibber also speaks of his superb memory which, coupled with his diligence, meant that he was almost invariably word-perfect, in an age when ad-libbing on stage was common. However, he could be unduly exacting of others and at times quarrelsome. Wilks is generally credited with a large share of responsibility for Drury Lane's prosperity during the 1710s and 1720s.

William III (1689–1702)

King of Britain, reigning jointly with his wife ▷ Mary II until her death in 1694. As William of Orange, Stadtholder of Holland, he was leader of the European opposition to the power of Louis XIV, which also menaced Britain. His wife was the daughter of ▷ James II, deposed for his ▷ Catholicism and his threat to the liberty of ▷ Parliament. His reign was largely taken up with war against France. The political power of Parliament was further increased by his foreign preoccupations, and by the fact that, as a foreigner, he lacked experience of English political affairs.

Williams, Helen Maria (1762–1827)

English poet, novelist and correspondent. Brought up in Berwick-on-Tweed, she first published the verse romance *Edwin and Eltruda*, and *Peru* (1784) and sonnets in 1786. Her *Poem on the Slave Trade* (1788) was commented on by ▷ Mary Scott. After she settled in France she reworked ▷ Jean Jacques Rousseau's *Julie: ou, la nouvelle Héloïse* (1761) in *Julia* (1790). Her radical letters from France describing the Revolution (▷ French Revolution) were published in 1790. In France she lived with the divorced John Hurford Stone. She translated the popular bestseller *Paul et Virginie* – the text chosen for its apolitical status in case of raids. She writes, 'no danger could be more imminent than that of living under the very tyranny which I had the perilous honour of having been one of the first to deprecate and to proclaim.' She was lucky enough to get a passport to Switzerland, which resulted in *A Tour in Switzerland* (1798).
Bib: Scheffler, J., *The Wordsworth Circle*, No. 19 (1988).

Will's Coffee-house

Named after its owner William Unwin, it was the haunt of such authors as ▷ John Dryden, ▷ William Wycherley, ▷ Joseph Addison and ▷ Alexander Pope. It became dominated by the older, mainly Tory set in the early years of the 18th century and ▷ Button's Coffee-house was set up as a fashionable rival, with a more Whiggish clientele.

Wilmot, John

▷ Rochester, John Wilmot, Second Earl of.

Winchilsea, Countess of

▷ Finch, Anne, Countess of Winchilsea.

Windsor, House of

Since 1917, the official designation of the British royal family, which, previously, had been known as the House of ▷ Hanover. The change was made by George V, in deference to British hostility to Germany during World War I.
▷ George.

Windsor Castle

The principal residence of the English royal family since the 11th century. Its most conspicuous feature is the huge round tower at the summit of the hill on which the castle is built; it was constructed by Edward III on the site where, according to the contemporary French chronicler Froissart, King Arthur had sat surrounded by his Knights of the Round Table; Edward, who had founded the knightly Order of the Garter, still the most distinguished order of knighthood, built the tower as a meeting-place for it, in emulation of Arthur.

Windsor Forest (1713)

A poem by ▷ Alexander Pope in heroic ▷ couplets describing the landscape around his home, and reflecting on its history and economic importance. It blends ▷ Georgic, ▷ pastoral and topographical elements in an engaging expression of Augustan optimism.

Wine

This was previously a rich man's drink in England, though in the 17th and 18th centuries, because beer and ale were considered low class, it was more frequently and widely drunk. Home-grown British wines existed at least until the 18th century, but as early as the 14th century ships were sent in convoy to Bordeaux in south-west France to import claret. Spanish wines such as sherry and canary were drunk in the 16th and 17th centuries; French burgundy is mentioned in 1672 in a play by ▷ Wycherley; champagne is first mentioned in 1700, and the sweet Portuguese wine, port, in 1711. For 150 years the last was above all the gentleman's drink, taken among the men as they sat round the table after dinner when the ladies had departed to the 'withdrawing room'. Rhenish wines from Germany were popular from the 16th century. Until the 18th century, wine was not allowed to mature, nor, until the mid 17th century, were glass bottles used, and wine glasses were often imported from Venice. By the 19th century, taste was much more sophisticated; gentlemen 'laid down' bottles to be drunk by their sons, and such a legacy was much prized.

   ▷ Drinks.

Wit

This word has a number of distinct, though related, meanings.

1 The oldest meaning is identical with 'mind', as in Wycliffe's 14th-century translation of the ▷ Bible: 'Who knew the wit of the Lord?' (*Romans* II: 34). This use of 'wit' rarely occurs in the literature of the last hundred years.

2 Another long-established meaning is 'a faculty of the mind'. This is still in use today, as when we speak of someone having 'lost his wits', *ie* lost the use of his mental faculties.

3 A common meaning in the 17th and 18th centuries was the capacity to relate unlike ideas, as in ▷ Locke's definition: 'Wit lying in the assemblage of ideas, and putting these together with quickness and variety wherein can be found any resemblance or congruity, thereby to make up pleasant pictures in the fancy' (▷ *Essay concerning Human Understanding*, 1690). ▷ Cowley, in his poem *Of Wit* (1656) wrote

'In a true piece of wit all things must be./Yet all things there agree'. ▷ Samuel Johnson, in his *Life of Cowley* (1779), wrote: 'It was about the time of Cowley that Wit, which had been till then used for Intellection, in contradistinction to Will, took the meaning, whatever it be, which it now bears.' Johnson here refers to the original meaning of wit as 'mind' or 'understanding', and points to the complex and important suggestiveness of the word in his own day.

4 During the same period, but chiefly in the 'Age of Reason' (about 1660–1800), wit was also thought of as meaning fine and clear expression: ▷ Dryden's 'propriety of thoughts and words elegantly adapted to the subject' (*Heroic Poetry and Poetic Licence*, 1677), and ▷ Pope's 'what oft was thought but ne'er so well expressed' (▷ *Essay on Criticism*). Johnson went some way to reconciling interpretations 3 and 4 in his own definition: 'that which is at once natural and new, and that which though not obvious is upon its first production acknowledged to be just . . . that which he that never found it wondered how he missed it'.

5 Definition 3 points to the element of surprise in wit; this often induces laughter. Thus wit has also been considered, since 1600, to be one of the principal sources of comedy, and it is in this sense that it is chiefly used in 20th-century English.

6 In the personal sense, in the later 17th and 18th centuries a wit was a man with clear insight into many aspects of life and manners, capable of summarizing and relating these aspects lucidly and forcefully. The term is often used disparagingly, however, for pretentious young people who try to achieve reputations for themselves by their superficial but fashionably clever talk. Nowadays, a wit is often seen as a person capable of expressing him- or herself in concise and memorably amusing language.

Witches

People supposed to be in league with the devil, who gives them supernatural powers. The name 'witch' was sometimes used for both sexes, though those accused of being witches were usually women. They commonly had 'familiars' in the form of spirits disguised as animals of bad or sinister reputation – toads or cats of certain colours. To work their magic, witches uttered 'spells' of specially devised words, or they used objects ('charms') supposed to have magical properties; witches used to gather in small communities known as 'covens', and they assembled on one day of the year (a 'witches' Sabbath') to worship the Devil.

The common explanation of witchcraft is that, in Europe at least, it represents the long survival of pre-Christian pagan religions in which the gods were the embodiments of the powers of nature, usually in the forms of animals, often a goat, but in Britain commonly the bull, the dog, or the cat. More recently witchcraft, or the accusation of witchcraft, has been regarded as a 17th-century mechanism of social control, used to discourage women from living alone outside the authority of a male-dominated household.

The first law making witchcraft an offence

punishable by death in England was passed in 1603 (though causing death by witchcraft had been so punishable since 1563) and it was not repeated until 1736. ▷ Sir Thomas Browne declares his firm belief in it in *Religio Medici* (1643); the last learned defence of the belief was *Saducismus Triumphatus* (1681) by the scholar and clergyman Joseph Glanville. The belief seems to have been particularly strong among ▷ Puritans and in Puritan countries, for instance in ▷ Scotland, 17th-century New England, and England under the ▷ Long Parliament. Rare survivals of it have been found in 20th-century England. It has been suggested that the prevalence of the belief in the 17th century and among Puritans is that their superstitious impulses were no longer satisfied by the ▷ Catholic system of mysteries (miracles, lives of the saints, etc.) which they had expelled from their faith by its 'purification'.
Bib: McFarlane, A., *Witchcraft in Tudor and Stuart England*; Thomas, K., *Religion and the Decline of Magic*.

Wither, George (1558–1667)

Poet. Between 1612, when Wither's first publication appeared, and the poet's death in 1667, there were very few years which were not marked by the publication of at least one volume of verse or prose from this prolific author. Wither was possibly the most imprisoned writer in the history of English literature. In 1613 his ▷ satiric work *Abuses Stripped and Whipped* earned him a period of imprisonment, a punishment which he earned once more, in 1621, when *Wither's Motto* appeared, and which was to befall him again in 1646 (on publication of his ▷ pamphlet *Fustiarius Fustificatus*) and in 1660 (appearance of unpublished satire: *Vox Vulgi: A Poem in Censure of Parliament*). His later works were written in the belief that he was God's prophet. Of note, however, are several volumes of earlier verse, and his collection of emblems which appeared in four volumes in 1635.

Wives Excuse, The: Or Cuckolds Make Themselves (1691)

Play by ▷ Thomas Southerne, identified with a wave of so-called 'marital discord comedies' of the 1690s by writers including ▷ Vanbrugh and ▷ Farquhar, which focused on the problems of marriage, as much as on those of courtship. Southerne concentrated on showing up the sexual double standard and its effects on women. *The Wives Excuse* bleakly presents the dilemma of the woman trapped in an unhappy marriage to a man whose shameless infidelity goes unpunished, while she stands to lose her dignity, reputation, and remaining peace of mind if she succumbs to the advances of her would-be lover. Mrs Friendall wrestles with temptation in the form of the attractive but unscrupulous Lovemore, while Mr Friendall pursues an affair with Mrs Wittwoud. At the end, the couple agree to separate. Southerne implies that Mrs Friendall will eventually give in to Lovemore, only to be abandoned when he tires of her. The play was unsuccessful, but is now considered one of the great plays of the period, its polish and sophistication serving only to point

up the hypocrisy underlying the situation which it portrays.

Woffington, Peg (Margaret) (?1714–60)

Actress. At the ▷ Smock Alley Theatre, Dublin, in 1740, she played the first of many performances as Sir Harry Wildair in ▷ George Farquhar's ▷ *The Constant Couple*. She repeated the role at ▷ Covent Garden and at ▷ Drury Lane, and became so celebrated in it that even ▷ Garrick could not equal her when he took on the same part.

The rest of her career from 1741 was spent largely at Drury Lane, but with further appearances at Covent Garden and in Dublin. She became the mistress of Garrick, and a theatrical rival of ▷ Kitty Clive, and ▷ George Anne Bellamy, whom she literally stabbed during a performance of Nathanial Lee's (c1653–92) *The Rival Queens*, just as ▷ Elizabeth Barry had done to ▷ Elizabeth Bowtell more than half a century before.

Peg Woffington was described as the most beautiful woman to have appeared on the stage in her own day. She was said to be full of vitality, elegance, and wit. During a career lasting over 30 years, she took on major roles in well over a hundred plays, sometimes acting different parts in the same play, at different periods in her life. She was especially famous for her talent in men's roles.
Bib: Daly, A., *Life of Peg Woffington*; Molloy, J. F., *The Life and Adventures of Peg Woffington*.

Wolcot, John (1738–1819)

Poet. After a career as a doctor in Jamaica and Cornwall, Wolcot accompanied the painter Opie to London, intent on a career in literature. His poems, published under the pseudonym Peter Pindar are crude if vigorous ▷ satires on respectable public figures and institutions: *Lyric Odes to the Royal Academicians* (1782–5), *The Lousiad* (1785), *Instructions to a Celebrated Laureat* (1787). His *Bozzy and Piozzi* (1786) is a whimsical poem in which ▷ James Boswell and ▷ Hester Lynch Thrale are shown reminiscing about ▷ Samuel Johnson, who had died two years earlier.

Wolley (Woolley), Hannah (?1621–?1676)

English writer on household management and ▷ conduct, who was a servant and then married a headmaster (and others), and published a sequence of books on cooking, medicine and the household. She writes in *The Cook's Guide* (1664) that she has 'sent forth this book, to testifie to the scandalous world that I do not altogether spend my time idly'.

Her other publications include: *The Ladies Directory* (1661); *The Queen-Like Closet* (1670), and *The Ladies Delight* (1672).

Wollstonecraft, Mary (1759–97)

Pamphleteer and novelist. Wollstonecraft is notable for her outspoken views on the role of women in society, and on the part played by education in woman's oppression. After running a school in London with her sister, she set out her ideas in the early pamphlet *Thoughts on the Education of Daughters* (1787). The following year her novel *Mary* developed this theme, together with a satirical perspective on the manners of the aristocracy, possibly based on her own experiences as governess with the family of Lord Kingsborough in Ireland.

Wollstonecraft's most famous work, ▷ *A Vindication of the Rights of Woman* (1792) now stands as one of the major documents in the history of women's writing. Attacking the 'mistaken notions of female excellence' which she recognized in contemporary attitudes to 'femininity' and the cult of the ▷ sentimental, Wollstonecraft argued that women were not naturally submissive, but taught to be so, confined to 'smiling under the lash at which [they] dare not snarl'. Although widely caricatured by critics for her own 'immoral' life – an affair with Gilbert Imlay, and subsequent marriage with ▷ William Godwin – Wollstonecraft's ideas are closely related to the moralist tradition of writing addressed to young women. Arguing that the true basis of marriage must be not love but friendship, she continues the rational proposals outlined by the 17th-century pamphleteer ▷ Mary Astell in such works as *A Serious Proposal to the Ladies*. The most radical of her thoughts concern the treatment by society of unmarried mothers, whom she believed were worthy of the respect and support of their families and lovers. Her novel *Maria: or, The Wrongs of Woman* (1798) remained unfinished and was published posthumously, but develops the ideas of *A Vindication* in a more complex and experimental context. The philosophical tradition behind her writings is evident in *A Vindication of the Rights of Man* (1790), a reply to ▷ Burke, and in the dedication of *Rights of Woman* to Talleyrand.
Bib: Tomalin, C., *The Life and Death of Mary Wollstonecraft*.

Women, Education of

In medieval convents, nuns often learned and received the same education as monks. Thereafter, women's intellectual education was not widely provided for until the later 19th century, though much would depend on their social rank, their parents, or their husbands. Thomas More in *Utopia* advocated equal education for both sexes; ▷ Swift in the 'Land of the Houyhnhnms' (▷ *Gulliver's Travels*) causes his enlightened horse to scorn the human habit of educating only half mankind, and yet allowing the other half (*ie* women) to bring up the children. On the other hand, in the 16th century the enthusiasm for education caused some highly born women to be very highly educated; this is true of the two queens, Mary I and Elizabeth I, of the 'ten-days queen', Lady Jane Grey (whose education is described in Ascham's *Schoolmaster*, 1570), and of the Countess of Pembroke, Sidney's sister. In the 17th century we see from ▷ Pepys's Diary how he tried to educate his French wife, and ▷ Evelyn, the other well-known diarist, describes his highly educated daughter. Rich women were expected to have some social and some artistic accomplishments, but Pepys for example did not expect his wife to share his scientific interests.

It is often difficult to interpret the evidence from the past as it is sometimes based on assumptions or fears about women's education that enlightened people do not now share.

Boarding schools for girls came into existence in the 17th century and became more numerous in the 18th, but either they were empty of real educational value or they were absurdly pretentious, like Miss Pinkerton's Academy described in Thackeray's *Vanity Fair* (1848); ▷ Mrs Malaprop in ▷ Richard Brinsley Sheridan's comedy ▷ *The Rivals* (1775) is a satire on the half-educated upper class women. Upper-class girls had governesses for general education, music masters, dancing masters, and teachers of 'deportment', *ie* in the bearing of the body; lower-class women were illiterate, unless they learned to read and write at 'charity schools'. On the other hand they had a much wider range of domestic skills than is usual with modern women, and among the poor, a rich store of folklore. However, in the 18th century there was already a shift in values. Swift, in his letter to a young lady about to enter marriage, points out that the way to keep a husband's affections was to grow in maturity of mind, and the ▷ bluestocking women of the middle of the century were entertainers of the intellectual elite of their society.

▷ School in England.

Women, Status of

Unmarried women had few prospects in Britain until the second half of the 19th century. In the ▷ Middle Ages they could enter convents and become nuns, but when in 1536–9 Henry VIII closed the convents and the monasteries, no alternative opened to them. Widows like Chaucer's Wife of Bath in *The Canterbury Tales* might inherit a business (in her case that of a clothier) and run it efficiently or like Mistress Quickly in Shakespeare's *Henry IV, Part II* they might run inns. The profession of acting was opened to women from the ▷ Restoration of the Monarchy in 1660, and writing began to be a possible means of making money from the time of ▷ Aphra Behn. Later the increase of interest in education for girls led to extensive employment of governesses to teach the children in private families; such a position might be peaceful and pleasant, like Mrs Weston's experience in the Woodhouse family in ▷ Jane Austen's *Emma*, but it was at least as likely to be unpleasant, underpaid, and despised, as the novelist Charlotte Brontë found. Nursing was also open to women, but nurses had no training and were commonly a low class of women like Betsey Prig and Mrs Gamp in Dickens' *Martin Chuzzlewit* until Florence Nightingale reformed the profession.

Wives and their property were entirely in the power of their husbands according to the law, though in practice they might take the management of both into their own hands, like the Wife of Bath. A Dutch observer (1575) stated that England was called the 'Paradise of married women' because they took their lives more easily than continental wives. Nonetheless, a middle-class wife worked hard, as her husband's assistant (probably his accountant) in his business, and as a mistress of baking, brewing, household management and amateur medicine.

▷ Feminism, Augustan literature.

Women's movement

The women's movement – under many names – is dedicated to the campaign for political and legal rights for women. It wishes to prevent discrimination on the grounds of gender and is, generally, a movement for social change.

There is no single source, although the history of women's quest for equality is a long one. The *Querelle des Femmes* in the medieval period, ▷ Ahpra Behn and ▷ Mary Astell in the 17th century, and ▷ Mary Wollstonecraft in the Romantic Age ▷ all furthered women's rights. In the Victorian period feminism became linked with other social movements such as anti-slavery campaigners, evangelical groups and ▷ Quakers. The suffragette movement (1860–1930) united women and this solidarity was to re-emerge in the radicalizaton of the 1960s.

▷ Feminism in Augustan literature; Women, Status of.

Bib: Mitchell, J. and Oakley, A. (eds.), *What is Feminism?*; Eisenstein, H., *Contemporary Feminist Thought*.

Wonder, A Woman Keeps a Secret, The **(1714)**
Comedy by ▷ Susannah Centlivre, partly based on ▷ Ravenscroft's *The Wrangling Lovers* (1677), and often considered her best play. It is set in Lisbon, where Don Felix, son of a Portuguese grandee, Don Lopez, wounds Antonio in a duel, after refusing to marry Antonio's sister. He goes into hiding, but secretly visits Donna Violante, a young woman intended for a nun, with whom he is in love, and who loves him. In the secondary plot, Don Lopez wants his daughter, Isabella, to marry the wealthy but foolish Don Guzman, and locks her into a room to await her suitor. She escapes into the arms of Colonel Britton, a Scotsman on his way back to England. He takes her to another house, which turns out to be Violante's, and asks for her to be cared for. Violante recognizes her and agrees to hide her and keep the secret. In fact she conceals not only Isabella, but Felix as well, and, further, hides Isabella from Felix. All the lovers are united at the end. The title is gently ironic for in the play's final triplet Felix remarks that Violante's steadfastness has shown 'That Man has no Advantage but the Name'. *The Wonder* was first produced at ▷ Drury Lane with ▷ Robert Wilks as Don Felix and ▷ Anne Oldfield as Violante, to whom Centlivre paid tribute as being largely responsible for its success. But it was revived numerous times during the 18th and 19th centuries, notably with ▷ Garrick as Felix, from 1756 onwards, and ▷ John Philip Kemble in the part afterwards. Garrick chose the play to end his theatrical career in 1776. It survived to 1897.

Wordsworth, William (1770–1850)

Poet. He was born in Cumberland, the son of a law-agent. His mother died when he was only eight, and when his father died five years later, he was sent to school at Hawkshead, where he led a life of solitary freedom among the fells. In 1787 he went to Cambridge, but more inspiring in their influence were his two visits to revolutionary France: the first in 1790, and the second lasting a year, from November 1791. During the second visit his love affair with a surgeon's daughter, Annette Vallon, resulted in her pregnancy, and she bore him a daughter. Forced to leave Annette behind on his return Wordsworth underwent a period of turmoil intensified when England went to war with France in 1793. The emotional trauma of this period in his life seems to have been displaced into the searching anxiety which underlies much of his early poetry. The love affair is not mentioned explicitly in his work but is recounted at one remove in the story of *Vaudracour and Julia* (written c1804; published 1820.

Wordsworth's relatives intended him for the Church, but his religious views at this time tended towards an unorthodox ▷ pantheism, evolved during his strangely lonely but happy childhood. Moreover, the writings of the extreme rationalist philosopher ▷ William Godwin influenced him still further against the possibility of a career in the Church of England. Fortunately in 1795 a friend left him a legacy sufficient to keep him independent, and he settled down in Somerset with his sister Dorothy, one of the most sustaining personal influences of his life. By 1797 he had made the friendship of ▷ Samuel Taylor Coleridge, who came to live nearby, and in 1798 the two poets collaborated in producing *Lyrical Ballads*. In 1799 William and Dorothy moved to Dove Cottage, Grasmere, and in 1802 Wordsworth married Mary Hutchinson. By this time, he was disillusioned with France, now under dictatorship, had abandoned Godwinism, and was beginning to turn back to orthodox religion. He also became more conservative in politics, to the disgust of younger men such as Byron and Shelley. The great decade of his poetry ran from 1797 to 1807. Thereafter it declined in quality while his reputation slowly grew. By 1830 his achievement was generally acknowledged, and in 1843 he was made ▷ Poet Laureate.

Wordsworth's first volumes (*Descriptive Sketches, An Evening Walk*, 1793) show the characteristic tone and diction of 18th-century topographical and nature poetry. They were followed by a tragedy, *The Borderers* (not published until 1842). The *Lyrical Ballads* collection marks a new departure however, in the uncompromising simplicity of much of its language, its concern with the poor and outcast, and its fusion of natural description with inward states of mind. These qualities have caused the volume to be viewed as the starting point of the ▷ Romantic Movement. The *Preface* to the 1800 edition of *Lyrical Ballads* also contained Wordsworth's attack on the 'gaudiness and inane phraseology' which he felt encumbered contemporary verse. With the encouragement of Coleridge, he planned a long philosophical poem to be called *The Recluse*, and in preparation for it wrote *The Prelude*. This was completed by 1805, but not published until 1850, and then in a revised form. In 1807 Wordsworth published *Poems in Three Volumes* and in 1814, *The Excursion*, the only part of *The Recluse* to be completed besides *The Prelude*. These were followed by *The White Doe of Rylstone (1815)*; *Peter Bell (1819)*; *The River Duddon (1820)*; *Ecclesiastical Sketches (1822)*; *Sonnets (1838)*.

Wordsworth's greatness lies in his impressive, even stubborn authenticity of tone. Sometimes this is achieved through the use of primitive or simplistic literary form as in such lyrical ballads as 'We are Seven' and 'The Thorn', and also the Lucy poems. Sometimes Wordsworth develops the discursive ▷ blank-verse manner of the 18th-century ▷ Georgic into an original, profoundly introspective vehicle for what John Keats called his 'egotistical sublime', as in *The Prelude, The Ruined Cottage* and *Tintern Abbey*. Frequently he succeeds in convincing the reader that subject matter which in other poets would be merely banal or even comic, is in fact of mysterious portentousness. This technique is particularly impressive in poems which treat the poor, the mad, the senile, members of humanity generally disregarded in earlier poetry. In these works his diction and tone brush aside the class-based doctrine of kinds, and the related conceptions of 'high' and 'low'

Workhouses

Institutions to accommodate the destitute at public expense, and to provide them with work to ensure that they were socially useful. They were first established under the ▷ Poor Law of 1576; they increased in number, but by the 18th century the administration of them, the responsibility of the parish, had become seriously inefficient, and ▷ magistrates were more inclined to administer financial relief to the paupers in their homes. This 'outdoor relief' – the 'Speenhamland System', so called from the parish in which it was first used – tended to be demoralizing to the working poor, who earned very little more than the workless paupers. The whole system was remodelled by the New Poor Law of 1834, by which workhouses were established regionally and administered by Boards of Guardians. The philosophy behind the Poor Law was that most destitution was due to laziness and vice, so that workhouses ought to be practically penal institutions. Consequently, though they ceased to be places of brutality and vice as they had been in the 18th century, they became coldly inhuman, providing only the barest necessities of existence.

Wren, Sir Christopher (1632–1723)

Architect. He was also a distinguished mathematician and astronomer, a member of the circle which in 1662 became the ▷ Royal Society. He was in fact a representative of his age, which regarded the great cultural tradition of Europe as descending from ancient Rome and Greece and immensely valued the scope and power of the human reason. His masterpiece is ▷ St Paul's Cathedral in London; even before the old Cathedral was burnt down in

1666, he proposed to remodel it 'after a good Roman manner' not following 'the ▷ Gothic rudeness of the old design'. Wren's cathedral is an example of an English version of the classical style known as Baroque elsewhere in contemporary Europe. He also proposed a replanning of the City of London, in an arrangement of wide streets radiating from a central space, but difficulties in agreeing about property valuations with the existing landowners prevented this. He did, however, rebuild 52 London churches after the ▷ Great Fire of 1666, giving them towers and spires of ingeniously varied and graceful designs in white stone that stood out against the black dome of the cathedral – an effect now entirely ruined by the alteration of the skyline by commercial buildings. Wren also contributed fine buildings to Oxford and Cambridge.

Wycherley, William (1640–1716)

Dramatist of the ▷ Restoration period. Born at Clive near Shrewsbury, the son of a lawyer, and educated first in France, where he became a ▷ Catholic, and then at Oxford. He studied law at the Inner Temple, but preferred to write for the stage, and to mix in courtly literary circles, associating with such individuals as the ▷ Earl of Rochester, ▷ Sir George Etherege, and Sir Charles Sedley (1639–1701). His first play, *Love in a Wood; Or St James's Park* (1671), is dedicated to one of ▷ Charles II's mistresses, the Duchess of Cleveland, who later became his mistress as well. After this he served for a time in the fleet, and was present at a sea-battle. His second play, ▷ *The Gentleman Dancing Master* (1672) is an adaptation of a play by Calderón, and written in the ▷ Spanish intrigue style.

It is for his last two plays that Wycherley is now best remembered: ▷ *The Country Wife* (1675) and ▷ *The Plain Dealer* (1676), in which his deep cynicism lends savagery to his wit. ▷ Dryden praised the 'satire, strength and wit of Manly Wycherley', punning on the name of Manly, the chief character in *The Plain Dealer*, and Wycherley was often referred to in this way thereafter. In 1676 he stopped writing for the stage, and in 1679 married the Countess of Drogheda, a wealthy widow. She died in 1681, leaving him her fortune, but the bequest involved him in litigation, and he was reduced to poverty and imprisoned for debt for four years (1682–6). During this period he wrote *Epistles to the King and Duke* (1683), expressing his need. James II secured his release from prison, paid his debts, and awarded him a pension.

Bib: Nicoll, A., *Restoration Comedy*; Dobree, B., *Restoration Comedy*; McCarthy, E. B., *William Wycherley: A Biography*; Thompson, J., *Language in Wycherley's Plays: Seventeenth Century Language Theory and Drama.*

Y

Yahoos

Primitive and filthy creatures with the bodies of humans but base and simple minds, whose barbarism is contrasted, in ▷ Swift's ▷ *Gulliver's Travels*, with the civilized behaviour of the ▷ Houyhnhnms, a race of gentle and intelligent horses. The Yahoos are used by Swift to satirize the human race in general. The term became synonymous with a boor or brute.

Yearsley, Ann (1752–1806)

English poet, novelist and dramatist. Originally a milkwoman, she was taught to read and write by her brother. She married John Yearsley in 1774, and in 1784, when her family were living in terrible conditions, she showed her verses to ▷ Hannah More, who arranged for the publication by subscription of *Poems on Several Occasions* (1785). However, More kept control of Yearsley's access to the proceeds, and in a later edition she complains of this. More's attitude seems to have been very patronizing – *Poems on Several Occasions* carries a letter from her to Mrs Montagu, in which she discusses Yearsley's 'wild wood notes', and goes out of her way to mention that Yearsley's husband was 'honest and sober'. Eventually, Yearsley's rejected More's attempts at intellectual control. She published *Poems on Various Subjects* (1787), including a poem (like More) on the ▷ slave trade. Her play *Earl Goodwin* was acted and published, she wrote a novel, *The Royal Captives* (1795), and she ran a ▷ circulating library. Her final publication was *The Rural Lyre*.

▷ Collier, Mary; Leapor, Mary; Little, Janet
Bib: Landry, D., *The Muses of Resistance*.

Yorick

1 In Shakespeare's *Hamlet*, the former king's jester whose skull the gravedigger turns up in V. i, giving Hamlet a subject for meditation.

2 In ▷ Sterne's novel ▷ *Tristram Shandy* the witty parson who, Sterne suggests, is probably a descendant of Shakespeare's Yorick. Sterne also used Yorick as the pen-name under which he published his ▷ sermons, and as his pen-name in his ▷ *Sentimental Journey*.

Young, Edward (1683–1765)

Royal chaplain and later Rector of Welwyn in Hertfordshire. He wrote three tragedies which were successfully acted in Drury Lane, and a series of didactic satires: *The Force of Religion* (1714) in ▷ couplets, and *The Love of Fame* (1725/18), *The Vindication of Providence* (1728) and *Resignation* (1762), all in Miltonic ▷ blank verse. His most important work, the melancholy and reflective poem *The Complaint or* ▷ *Night Thoughts on Life, Death and Immortality* (1742–5), consisting of 10,000 lines of blank verse, was considered by ▷ Samuel Johnson to display 'the magnificence of vast extent and endless diversity', and became immensely popular both in Britain and on the continent. As their titles suggest, Young's poems are marked by a crushing orthodoxy of religious sentiment, and their turgid rhetorical dogmatism makes them very difficult to read today. Young's influential prose essay *Conjectures on Original Composition* (1759) focuses on the nature of artistic 'genius' and marks an important stage in the development of pre-romantic literary theory.
Bib: Wicker, C. V., *Edward Young and the Fear of Death*.

Zeugma
▷ Figures of speech.

Zimri
▷ *Absalom and Achitophel.*